ON COMMON GROUND

Forthcoming Common Ground Monographs

Land Tenure Insecurity in Latin America and the Caribbean:
Preventing Displacement through Community Control of Land
(Spanish)

Why Community Land Trusts?
The Philosophy Behind an Unconventional Form of Tenure
(Spanish and English)

Community Land Trust Applications in Urban Neighborhoods
(Spanish and English)

The Growth of Community Land Trusts in England and Europe
(English)

Impactful Development and Community Empowerment:
Balancing the Dual Goals of a Global CLT Movement
(Spanish and English)

Community Land Trusts and Informal Settlements in the Global South
(English)

ON COMMON GROUND

International Perspectives on
the Community Land Trust

John Emmeus Davis
Line Algoed
María E. Hernández-Torrales

EDITORS

TERRA NOSTRA PRESS
Madison, Wisconsin, USA

TERRA NOSTRA PRESS

Center for Community Land Trust Innovation
3146 Buena Vista Street
Madison, Wisconsin, USA 53704

Publisher's Cataloging-in-Publication Data

Names: Davis, John Emmeus, editor. | Algoed, Line, editor. | Hernández-Torrales, María E., editor.
Title: On common ground : international perspectives on the community land trust /
John Emmeus Davis ; Line Algoed ; María E. Hernández-Torrales, editors.
Description: Includes bibliographical references and index. | Madison, WI: Terra Nostra Press, 2020.
Identifiers: Library of Congress Control Number: 2020902607 | ISBN 978-1-7344030-0-8 (hardcover) |
ISBN 978-1-7344030-2-2 (paperback) | ISBN 978-1-7344030-1-5 (ebook)
Subjects: LCSH Land trusts. | Land tenure. | Land use. | Land use, Urban. | Nature conservation. |
Landscape protection. | Sustainable development. | Sustainable development—Developing countries. |
Economic development—Environmental aspects. | City planning—Environmental aspects. |
Community development. | Urban ecology (Sociology) | BISAC POLITICAL SCIENCE /
Public Policy / City Planning & Urban Development | LAW / Housing & Urban Development |
BUSINESS & ECONOMICS / Development / Sustainable Development |
SOCIAL SCIENCE / Sociology / Urban
Classification: LCC KF736.L3 O6 2020 | DDC 333.2—dc23

We abuse land because we regard it as a commodity belonging to us.
When we see land as a community to which we belong,
we may begin to use it with love and respect.

— Aldo Leopold, *A Sand County Almanac,* 1949

Our present property arrangements are not working well enough.
It makes sense to look for alternative approaches that are based on
respect for the legitimate interests of both individuals and communities
and that provide an effective means of balancing these interests.
The community land trust is one such approach.

— *The Community Land Trust Handbook,* 1982

Esta tierra es nuestra, y nadie nos la quitará.

— Caño Martin Peña CLT, 2020

CONTENTS

PART TWO. NATIONAL NETWORKS
Examining the Proliferation and Cross-Pollination of CLTs in the Global North

PART THREE. REGIONAL SEEDBEDS
Exploring the Potential for CLT Growth in the Global South

PART FOUR. URBAN APPLICATIONS
Measuring the Progress of High-Performing CLTs in Selected Cities   281

PART FIVE. CRITICAL PERSPECTIVES
Meeting the Challenges of a Changing Environment

FIGURES

ON COMMON GROUND

Foreword

Jerry Maldonado
FORD FOUNDATION

As a social justice foundation committed to the advancement of human dignity, the Ford Foundation has prioritized the reduction of inequality as a central, unifying goal across its diverse program areas. While most debates on inequality focus narrowly on the ways in which income and wealth disparities have dramatically increased over the past few decades, less attention is typically paid to the ways in which inequality is often hardwired into the built environment.

In cities and regions across the globe, housing, land use and infrastructure decisions have often accelerated, reinforced and sustained the physical, economic and social disparities that divide communities. Discriminatory land use, housing and urban development policies have perpetuated racial and economic segregation. In the United States, the country's massive racial wealth gap was built on the back of racially exclusive housing and land use practices that systematically restricted the ability of African-Americans, Latinos, and other communities of color to build assets through the ownership of land and housing. Urban renewal, redlining and the construction of the country's federal highway system targeted low-income communities of color, stripping them of their assets, and laying the foundation for today's highly segregated physical and social landscape.

Structural racism, segregation and market fundamentalism are a toxic mix. Together, they have produced one of the most radically unequal global economies of our time, concentrating economic and political power in fewer and fewer private hands at enormous cost to our fragile planet and our shared humanity. Today, millions of people across the globe—from New York to Puerto Rico, from Johannesburg to Rio de Janeiro—have been systematically deprived of their basic human rights to decent housing, work and other essential services, while corporate profits have soared. Sadly, our rapidly escalating global housing and displacement crisis represents just the latest incarnation of a broader boom-bust, predatory real estate investment and development cycle that continues to actively marginalize countless communities. These growing economic and physical divides are neither morally nor politically sustainable.

But inequality is not inevitable. It is the result of conscious decisions, policies and politics that perpetuate a culture of scarcity and competition. It's fueled by extractive economic development policies that too often exploit workers, land and communities in pursuit of short-term profits. As such, the contestation over land, development and housing can be viewed as part of a broader struggle over power and the future of our democracies. Who decides and who benefits from development? Who belongs and who is excluded? Whose history and culture is valued and whose is rendered invisible? The choices we make around land use and housing reflect our collective answers to these questions. As such, they are fundamentally moral decisions—reflections on which communities are "valued" and which are deemed "expendable."

In this moment of extreme global polarization, it is more urgent than ever that we find a new, COMMON GROUND that recalibrates and rebalances the relationship between the market, government and civil society. Over the last several decades, community-based organizations across the globe—a number of which are featured in this book—have not only challenged exclusionary housing and development practices, but have also demonstrated that another way is possible. From the Champlain Housing

> The CLT movement is unique in the way that it centers housing and land as part of a broader movement for community self-determination.

Trust (Vermont), to the Dudley Street Neighborhood Initiative (Boston), to the Fideicomiso de La Tierra in El Caño Martín Peña (Puerto Rico), organized leaders and communities have pioneered innovative models of inclusive development that have helped revitalize distressed communities, prevent forced evictions, and promote land security and stability. The community land trust movement is unique in the way that it centers housing and land as part of a broader movement for community self-determination. At their best, community land trusts not only function as tools for preventing displacement and preserving long-term affordability, but also as vehicles for collective deliberation, action and accountability that help to bend the arc of development toward justice.

The visionary leaders, communities and organizations featured in this book are at the forefront of a broader national and global movement attempting to recalibrate the relationship between governments and markets in housing and development policy. Significantly, many of the case studies in this book highlight the critical role that the public sector can and must play in order to significantly scale up these community-led interventions. National, state and local governments all have an important role to play in creating the right land use, housing and investment policies that not only constrain some of the market's worst excesses, but also harness development in a way that preserves public resources and assets in perpetuity for the common good.

Helen Keller once famously argued that "the heresy of one age becomes the orthodoxy of the next." It is our hope that the lessons, insights, struggles and victories captured in this book challenge and inspire policymakers, advocates and community leaders around the globe to reimagine the relationship between people, communities and land in a way that centers human dignity, shared prosperity and the long-term stewardship of our natural assets.

—

David Ireland
WORLD HABITAT

What makes good housing? Read the adverts in glossy magazines and you might be led to think that people aspire to glassy high-rise apartments with swanky roof terraces and all the latest designer gadgetry. Speak to ordinary people and the answer is very different.

This is a book that proposes an answer to that question. It describes the growth and global spread of one of the most important ideas of the last century—the community land trust. It describes how communities in very different contexts have adapted and are using the community land trust model to change the way land is owned, create new homes and protect their community. Ultimately it allows ordinary people to lead happier lives.

The World Happiness Report is a global annual survey measuring people's general happiness. It identifies several factors that make people most happy about where they live. It cites family support and security, personal health, the freedom to make choices, people's generosity, and a perception of fairness and the absence of corruption.

Most people spend around half of their lives in and around their home. Good housing is perhaps the single most important factor in ensuring people lead happy, healthy and fulfilled lives. Housing is the backdrop to our lives. It's where our family life takes place, where we come home to after being at school or work. It's where we become part of a community. It becomes part of our identity. It's where we're from. It's where we call home.

Yet for an increasing number of people around the world, the very factors that make housing good are under threat. Global capital has moved into rented housing with devastating consequences for the people who live there. Leilani Farha, the UN Special Rapporteur on Housing Rights, calls it the "financialization of housing." From mass forced evictions to make way for luxury developments, to nameless corporations buying up real estate, to empty homes and people being pushed out of their communities because they simply cannot afford to live there, the repercussions are being felt across the globe.

Across most of the developed world, government-funded social or public housing was once available as a right for people who could not afford the cost of market housing. But austerity and a shift in political philosophy have caused much of this government-funded housing to be sold off and, for much that is left, its security has been watered down. In many countries, the poorest are left to fend for themselves at the bottom end of the private market. Forced into overcrowded and often insanitary accommodation, some are driven into homelessness.

The Climate Emergency is harming the places that many people live. Rising temperatures, droughts, wildfires, hurricanes, and floods are making the places many poorer communities live more dangerous and unhealthy. The future for some communities is bleak as they watch their homeland become uninhabitable.

If people's legal rights are weakened, if the private market is more hostile, and if nature itself is so damaged that it reacts against us, who can we turn to; who will protect us and our homes? The answer is our community.

The community land trust, along with other forms of community-led housing, is a powerful response, based on the simple principle that people are stronger when they work together. Their strength is magnified when they collectively control the land on which their housing is built. Community-owned land and community-led development go hand-in-hand in the community land trust, providing the legal muscle to resist threats from predatory land developers and the financial strength to insulate people

> Communities are given the strength to shape their own destiny; individuals are given the freedom to lead their own lives.

from the affordability jeopardy caused by financialization. It also gives communities the strength to commission and design better homes that meet people's needs and that are capable of withstanding the dangers wreaked by an increasingly unpredictable climate.

The community land trust movement has taken those principles and enshrined them in a set of simple rules for structuring an organization and for structuring the tenure of land and housing. These rules give communities the legal and financial strength to shape their own destiny, while allowing individual households the freedom to lead their own lives. The community land trust relies on a democratic model that gives people a voice and a stake in their community. It's a compelling idea that provides an answer to an increasingly dysfunctional housing system and a less benign world.

Although community land trusts can trace their origins back many decades, it is almost as if they were invented just yesterday as a specific response to the problems of the modern world. It should be no surprise that the community land trust movement is growing and spreading. Its forms of organization and tenure are being recognised in law and the model itself is being adapted to different circumstances and cultures.

My own organisation has recognised and championed this growth and global spread. In 2008 we presented the World Habitat Award to the Champlain Housing Trust in Vermont, an early pioneer in a movement dedicated to creating homes that are affordable in perpetuity in real estate markets that are squeezing out lower- and middle-income earners. The Award helped the CLT concept to transfer across the Atlantic and inspired the first community land trust in Europe—founded in Brussels. We have continued to recognise the growth of the movement with Communauté Milton-Parc in Montreal, Canada, Tanzania-Bondeni in Kenya, Habitat para la Mujer in Bolivia, and Grandby Four Streets in Liverpool, UK. All of them receiving recognition in the World Habitat Awards.

I am particularly excited by the Fideicomiso de la Tierra del Caño Martín Peña in Puerto Rico which received the World Habitat Award in 2015. It has adapted the community land trust model to an informal settlement for the first time. Informal settlements are home to over a billion of the poorest people around the world. In the Caño Martín Peña, the community land trust has helped protect the community against the twin threats of predatory land speculation and flooding from a local watercourse. This innovation has the potential to pave the way for community land trusts to be adopted in other countries as a way of regularizing tenure and improving conditions in informal settlements, improving the lives of millions of people living in the most insecure and unsafe housing. The movement is spreading through Europe too, providing new options for communities in Eastern Europe where the mass privatization of state housing in the late 1980s left a distorted and inflexible housing market.

My own experience of visiting community land trusts around the world leaves me with many memories, but one overriding emotion: happiness. Every resident involved in creating a community land trust or lucky enough to live in a community land trust home has talked of how the land trust has improved their lives. Where they live, makes them happy. It's an unarguable endorsement of this form of housing and the best evidence of what good housing really is.

Introduction
On Common Ground

John Emmeus Davis, Line Algoed,
and María E. Hernández-Torrales

Fifty years after the appearance of the first community land trust (CLT) in the United States, an invention forged in the crucible of the Civil Rights Movement, CLTs have multiplied. In its country of origin, over 260 CLTs are operating in cities, suburbs, islands, and towns. Nearly every state has at least one, as does the District of Columbia. Beyond the United States, over 300 CLTs are up and running in the United Kingdom. Others have been established in Australia, Belgium, Canada, and France. Interest has been rising in Germany, Ireland, Italy, the Netherlands, Portugal, Scotland, and Spain.

To date, most of the growth in what is becoming a worldwide CLT movement has occurred in the Global North. But that is changing, due in part to the example and impact of the Caño Martín Peña CLT in Puerto Rico. This community-led initiative for regularizing tenure and for securing the homes of families residing in informal settlements has made steady progress despite natural disasters and the island's ongoing economic distress, attracting the attention of people living in similar situations in Latin America and the Caribbean. Community activists in Africa and South Asia have taken note of the CLT as well, exploring whether some version of this strategy might be used to promote equitable and sustainable development in rural and urban areas within their own countries.

Community land trusts have been noticed too by the United Nations. At the 2016 Conference on Housing and Sustainable Urban Development in Quito, Ecuador, community land trusts were included among the "policies, tools, mechanisms, and financing models" named in the UN's *New Urban Agenda* for promoting access to housing and making cities more inclusive. CLTs were touted as one of several "cooperative solutions" for addressing, in the *Agenda's* words, "the evolving needs of persons and communities, in order to improve the supply of housing, especially for low-income groups, prevent segregation, and [prevent] arbitrary forced evictions and displacements . . . with special attention to programmes for upgrading slums and informal settlements."

CLTs acquire, manage, and develop land for a variety of purposes, but most of them do have a programmatic focus on promoting and preserving access to housing, "especially for low-income groups." Many CLTs pay special attention, moreover, to addressing the needs of people at risk of being displaced, either because they are residing on lands for which they do not hold formal title or because they are being priced out of areas where land values and housing costs are rapidly rising.

This puts the emerging CLT movement at the intersection of two world-wide movements for social change. The first is occurring in places where people who are land-insecure are struggling to gain recognition, registration, and legal protection for collective property, acreage that is occupied under some form of informal landholding system. Depending on the country, such property is termed communal, collective, customary, native, indigenous, or community land. Secondly, CLTs are part of an increasingly powerful housing rights movement that is surfacing in cities around the world. The issues being championed by this amorphous movement include a "right to the city," rent control, community-led development, and housing that remains permanently affordable.

Rising international interest in the community land trust, spurred in part by the alignment of CLTs with these other global movements, is what prompted us to produce the present volume. Our purpose in commissioning the original essays contained herein was four-fold. We wanted to fill a gap in current research which has largely overlooked the appearance of a world-wide CLT movement and the existence of cross-national connections and influences. We wanted to raise the profile of exemplary CLTs having particular relevance for equitable development in communities facing similar challenges, including those in which most residents are living without security of tenure. We wanted to provoke greater peer-to-peer learning across national borders, fostering the spread of innovative strategies and best practices. Finally, as unapologetic advocates for this particular approach to community-led development on community-owned land, we wanted to spur the formation of new CLTs in communities and countries that are currently without one. By sharing the stories of practitioners and projects in places where CLTs have had success in providing homes (and other community assets) that remain permanently affordable, we hope to encourage community organizers, public officials, and nongovernmental organizations to give the CLT a try.

WHAT'S IN A NAME?

Community land trusts are not all alike. Among the hundreds of CLTs that already exist or are presently being planned, there are numerous variations in how these organizations are structured, how their lands are utilized, how development is done, and how the stewardship of housing is operationalized. What is called a "community land trust" can vary greatly from one country to another, even from one community to another within the same country.

The basic features of the modern-day CLT were originally outlined in a popular book published in 1972. The design for this "new model for land tenure in America" was drawn mostly from New Communities Inc., a rural settlement founded three years earlier by African-American activists who sought to combine community ownership of land, individual ownership of multi-family and single-family housing, and the cooperative organization of agricultural production. The book's authors drew, too, on a number of historical precedents, including the collectively owned lands of indigenous peoples, the town commons of colonial New England, the *moshav ovdim* of Israel, the *ejidos* of Mexico, the *Ujamaa Vijijini* of Tanzania, and the *Gramdan* villages of India.

The model described in 1972 also bore a close resemblance to the mixed-ownership scheme that Ebenezer Howard had proposed in 1898 for the Garden Cities of England. The houses, stores, orchards, and factories in the new towns he wanted to establish on the outskirts of major cities would be privately owned by individuals, cooperatives, or for-profit businesses, but the underlying land would be owned forever by a nongovernmental organization, created expressly for that purpose. These scattered parcels of land, despite their removal from the speculative market, would be made available for planned development and productive use through long-term ground leases, executed between the non-profit landowner and myriad individuals who owned buildings or operated enterprises on the leaseholds. Land was to be held and managed on behalf of *all* residents — rich and poor, present and future — enabling a community to direct its own development, to determine its own fate, and to capture for the common good a majority of the gains in land value that society as a whole had helped to create.

To the mixed-ownership model pioneered in England, India, and elsewhere, the visionaries who created New Communities, Inc. — and the reflective practitioners who followed in their wake — added organizational and operational features of their own, turning the model into something different, something new. Community-owned land remained the foundation on which a CLT was to be established, with a private, nonprofit corporation holding and managing scattered parcels of land for the benefit of residents of a particular locale, especially low-income families in need of housing. What got *added* were mechanisms for ensuring that the development done by a CLT would be guided by the community, as would the organization itself. This was not development from above, dictated by a governmental body, a charitable investor, or a benevolent provider of social housing. It was development from below, directed by residents of the community a CLT had been organized to serve. Ownership and empowerment were to go hand-in-hand. Added, too, was an operational commitment to the stewardship of any lands entrusted to the CLT and of any buildings erected on its lands, most of which would be owned by somebody else. Projects pursued by a CLT were designed to ensure that housing, nonresidential

> The development done by a CLT would be guided by the community, as would the organization itself.

COMMUNITY
(Organization)

LAND
(Ownership)

TRUST
(Operation)

buildings, and other land uses would remain continuously affordable, long after development was done.

These distinctive features of ownership, organization, and operation, overlapping and interacting in a dynamic model of place-based development, became known as the "classic" CLT. Almost as soon as nearly everyone came to agree on this particular conception and configuration of the community land trust, however, the model began to be modified in countless ways. Variations arose in every feature of the "classic" CLT as practitioners in different places adapted it to fit conditions, needs, and priorities in their own communities or to fit customs and laws in their own countries.

This continuing process of innovation and adaptation has helped the CLT to spread across a disparate international landscape and to thrive in a range of settings. At the same time, the diversity of meanings attached to the model and the variety of ways in which CLTs are structured have introduced a degree of difficulty to the task of explaining exactly what a CLT might be. Today, there is ambiguity — even a dose of controversy — to be found in the description and implementation of every component.

Community. Throughout the world, most organizations that call themselves a CLT are committed to involving a place-based population in their activities, incorporating a participatory ethos into their organization's purposes, practices, and structure. People who live on the CLT's lands and those who live nearby are encouraged to become voting members of the organization. They are recruited to serve on its governing board.[1] They are invited to participate in shaping the uses and projects proposed by the CLT. Development is "community-led," along with the organization that initiates and oversees that development.

Ambiguity enters the picture because of the varying arrangements that CLTs employ in striving to engage and to empower their community. Controversy arises because some CLTs have dispensed with community altogether, causing critics to question whether they should even be considered a "real" CLT. The traditional model's distinctive features of ownership and operation might be present, but residents who are served by the organization neither govern nor guide it; that is, "community" is missing from the make-up of the entity doing development. Variations like these create perennial challenges for CLT advocates whenever they try to reach a consensus as to what deserves to be deemed a "community land trust."[2]

Land. The typical CLT is a nonprofit organization that removes land permanently from the marketplace, managing it on behalf of a place-based community while making it available for long-term use by individuals and organizations. Title to the buildings on a CLTs land, either those existing when the CLT acquired the land or those constructed later on, is held individually by any number of parties — homeowners, cooperatives, businesses, gardeners, farmers, etc. The underlying land is leased from the CLT by the buildings' owners.

> This is ownership for the common good, balanced between individual property and collective property.

This mixed-ownership arrangement blurs the legal and conceptual boundary between conventional categories of tenure, where real property is presumed to be one thing or the other. A community land trust messes up this tidy picture, for it is balanced half-way between the two extremes of *individual property*, owned and operated primarily for the purpose of promoting private interests; and *collective property*, owned and operated to promote a common interest. The CLT tilts toward the former in its treatment of buildings. It tilts toward the latter in its treatment of land, making the CLT a first cousin to cooperatives, co-housing, and various forms of communal, collective, and tribal land.

Although a CLT's lands are frequently and fairly characterized as "community-owned" or, in the parlance of the present volume, as "common ground," these landholdings are neither collectively nor cooperatively owned by the people living on them or around them. Title is held exclusively by the CLT. A community land trust is ownership for the common good, not ownership in common.[3]

There are places, however, where the separation of ownership is made difficult (or impossible) by quirks in the property laws of a particular country or by the quibbles of prospective funders.[4] CLTs have sometimes been compelled, therefore, to retain ownership of buildings as well as the land or to relinquish ownership of both, while imposing long-lasting restrictions on the use and affordability of these properties. Another variation has been developed in Puerto Rico, where the Caño Martín Peña CLT holds the underlying land but uses a durable surface rights deed, rather than a ground lease, to provide security of tenure for people who own and occupy houses on the CLT's land. Some of them are living on sites their families have occupied for nearly a hundred years.

Trust. Although "trust" is part of their given name, CLTs have rarely been established as real estate trusts.[5] Most are NGOs — private, nonprofit corporations with a charitable purpose of meeting the needs of populations who are regularly underserved by both the market and the state. "Trust" refers not to how a CLT is organized, but to how it is operated. "Trust" is what a CLT *does* in overseeing the lands and buildings under its care and in performing the duties of stewardship. Foremost among these duties is the preservation of affordability, ensuring long-term access to land and housing for people of modest means and preventing their displacement due to gentrification and other pressures. Stewardship also includes such responsibilities as preventing deferred maintenance in housing and other buildings on the CLT's land and intervening, if necessary, to protect occupants against predatory lending, arbitrary eviction, mortgage foreclosure, and other threats to security of tenure.

Some CLTs are focused less on the provision of housing, however, than on the preservation of watersheds, woodlands, or agricultural lands, either in rural or urban areas. The stewardship responsibilities of a CLT entrusted with managing such lands can look very different than the stewardship needed when affordable housing is a CLT's operational focus.

Model. In 1972, the first book to describe the community land trust called it a "new model of land tenure." It has been called a "model" ever since. A number of practitioners and researchers have grown uncomfortable with the term, however. Some object because "model," from their perspective, carries a negative connotation of something experimental, unfinished, unreliable. They point to fifty years of success, saying that the CLT is no longer a working prototype, but a road-tested, high-performing vehicle that has gone the distance and proven its effectiveness under challenging conditions.

Others object because "model" seems to imply there is only one proper way of structuring a CLT, when the reality unfolding around the world is the emergence of many structures and strategies. Each country and community is composing its own variation on the theme of CLT classic. "Model" tends to be especially problematic for organizers in the Global South, for whom the term is tainted with a whiff of Yankee arrogance, as if there exists some sort of universal blueprint for building a CLT, indelibly stamped with "Made in America." Most organizers outside of the Global North tend to avoid the term, therefore, preferring to describe the CLT as a mechanism, instrument, or tool.

On the other hand, there are still many practitioners and researchers for whom "model" remains their term of choice. It holds for them a positive, prescriptive message of a design, pattern, or practice that is exemplary and worthy of consideration by anyone involved with affordable housing or community development. They are unconcerned that "model" may also suggest that the CLT is still being fine-tuned, still in a state of flux. After all, a restless search for better ways of configuring and combining ownership, organization, and operation is part of the reason why CLTs have been able to thrive in so many political and economic environments, some of which were initially hostile to their germination.

A majority of our book's contributors have in fact continued the custom of referring to the CLT as a "model," but we have not discouraged contributors who have preferred to call it something else. Even authors who regularly refer to the CLT as a "model" also describe it, on occasion, as a strategy, platform, mechanism, vehicle, construct, or tool — sometimes within the same essay. These terms are used interchangeably throughout the book.

WHAT'S IN THE BOOK?

The volume is divided into five sections, each containing a collection of chapters addressing a similar topic:

- *I. Bright Ideas:* five essays provide an overview of strategies, structures, definitions, and justifications for doing community-led development on community-owned land, surveying the diverse landscape of the community land trust.

- *II. National Networks:* the proliferation of CLTs in the Global North is examined in four essays focused on the development of robust CLT movements in the United States, England, Canada, and Europe.

- *III. Regional Seedbeds:* six essays explore the potential for future CLT growth in the Global South, viewed through the lens of a seminal CLT in Puerto Rico and other noteworthy initiatives in Latin America, Africa, and Asia.

- *IV. Urban Applications:* case studies of CLTs in London, in Brussels, and in three cities in the United States — Boston, Burlington, and Denver — demonstrate the model's success in providing affordable housing, promoting commercial development, and spurring neighborhood revitalization. Another essay is devoted to the acquisition and stewardship of land for urban agriculture, showing that CLTs are not only about housing.

- *V. Critical Perspectives:* a handful of shorter essays reflect on the changing environment to which CLTs must adapt in the years ahead and the emerging opportunities for CLTs to "go to scale." Several contributors call attention to the need for CLT practitioners to make their organizations more inclusive and responsive to the communities they serve if CLTs are to succeed in reclaiming the commons and transforming property and power in the place of residence.

Production of this book was made possible by the Center for CLT Innovation and by the generous financial support of World Habitat, the Urban Land Conservancy, Solidus Inc., and Sustainable Housing for Inclusive and Cohesive Cities, a cross-national initiative funded by the European Union. Translation and production of the Spanish edition was made possible by a substantial grant from the Ford Foundation, arranged by Jerry Maldonado. Artwork was donated by Bonnie Acker. The book was designed by Sara DeHaan.

We must also express our gratitude, of course, for the forty-two authors from a dozen different countries who donated their time and talents to this project. When recruiting this remarkable parliament of scholars and practitioners, we recognized that perspectives on the CLT were bound to differ. As an initial prompt, we proposed a working definition of the CLT: *community-led development of permanently affordable housing on community-owned land*. But we anticipated — correctly, as it turned out — that some authors would choose to shrink the boundaries of that broad definition, while others would want to expand it. We welcomed both. We tried to respect, as well, the distinctive voices that contributors brought to the task of reporting their findings and telling their stories. Some chapters are conventionally academic in style, therefore, while others are more anecdotal, written by practitioners talking candidly about their personal experience in working with CLTs in their own communities.

> We proposed a working definition of the CLT: community-led development of permanently affordable housing on community-owned land.

Although neither conceptual nor stylistic uniformity is to be found in the current collection of essays, there are commonalities nonetheless. What unites a global community of CLT practitioners and scholars is more important than what separates us. Woven throughout the book's twenty-six chapters are recurring themes that provide something of a *lingua franca* for understanding what it means for an organization to be a CLT and to behave like one. There is a shared commitment to reinventing and repurposing real estate for the common good. There is a shared conviction that community-owned land, in particular, is likely to do a better job of promoting equitable and sustainable development than land that is commodified and owned individually, especially in places populated by groups that have long been disadvantaged and disempowered.

Another trait that is shared by most CLT scholars and practitioners, another theme that is threaded through the present volume, is a conviction that the whole of a CLT is greater than the sum of its parts. Across the diverse landscape of CLTs, ownership, organization, and operation are not configured exactly the same in every town and country. Wherever this strategy has been adopted, however, there is a general recognition that it takes more than a single component to make a CLT; it takes more than the reinvention of any one of them to bend the arc of development toward a fairer distribution of property and power. Community-owned land, by itself, is not enough. Community-led development is not enough. Permanently affordable housing is not enough. It is their *combination* that gives a CLT its distinctive identity and transformative potential.[6]

To be sure, there are places in the world where CLTs have been effective without adopting every feature of the "classic" CLT. That model is no longer a template, but it remains a touchstone. It is where most people start, when striving to adapt this complex form of tenure to their own situations. It is where most people hope a CLT will lead, when envisioning a better outcome from their arduous, virtuous labors, whether providing affordable housing, rebuilding residential neighborhoods, regularizing tenure in informal settlements, or preserving productive lands and local enterprises at risk of being lost to market pressures.

When land is owned for the common good of a place-based community, present and future; when development is done by an organization that is a creature of that community, rooted in it, accountable to it, and guided by it; when stewardship is deliberate, diligent, and durable . . . justice is more likely to be achieved. And more likely to last. That is the moral impetus and lofty promise of common ground.

Notes

1. Organizationally, the model promoted by the Institute for Community Economics during the 1980s had an open membership and a three-part board, representing the interests of the people who live on the CLT's land, people who live within the CLT's service area, and institutions that serve that geography, including government, churches, banks, businesses, and other NGOs. See Institute for Community Economics, *The Community Land Trust Handbook* (Rodale Press, 1982).

2. To a certain degree, we have sidestepped this definitional debate in the present volume by featuring a number of organizations that *self-identify* as a community land trust, even if they do not exhibit every feature of what is known in the USA as the "classic" CLT. Our ecumenical embrace had limits, however. We admitted to the company of CLTs only organizations that are committed to removing land permanently from the stream of commerce, placing it under the ownership or control of a designated community and stewarding that land for the common good.

3. This echoes the earliest description of the CLT (International Independence Institute, *The Community Land Trust: A Guide to a New Model for Land Tenure in America,* Cambridge MA: Center for Community Economic Development, 1972: 1): "The community land trust is not primarily concerned with common ownership. Rather, its concern is ownership for the common good, which may or may not be combined with common ownership." Although the people living on a CLT's land do not hold title to the underlying land, the resale formula used by some CLTs does provide for a modest increase in the homeowner's equity if the land has appreciated in value during the homeowner's tenure.

4. North Carolina and Ohio are two examples of states in the USA where laws have posed difficulties for the separation of ownership. CLTs in England and Australia have faced a similar hurdle, requiring them to find legal work-arounds.

5. Trusts are established by individuals to control the distribution of their property, either during the individuals' lifetimes or after death. Property is often real estate, but it can also be stocks, bonds, or other assets. The person who creates the trust is the "settlor." The person who manages the property on another's behalf is the "trustee." The latter takes title to the property (although, under a "revocable trust," the settlor may later reclaim ownership). Proceeds from the trust are distributed by the trustee to a list of

beneficiaries named by the settlor when the trust was created. This is definitely not how the typical CLT is established, structured, or operated.

6. The synergy that comes from combining the components of a CLT is explored in greater detail in Chapter 26 of the present volume: "Better Together: The Challenging, Transformative Complexity of Community, Land, and Trust."

PART ONE
BRIGHT IDEAS

Surveying the Diverse
Landscape of Common Ground:
Structures, Strategies, and
Justifications

1.

In Land We Trust

Key Features and Common Variations
of Community Land Trusts in the USA

John Emmeus Davis

The Community Land Trust: A Guide to a New Model for Land Tenure in America was published in 1972. It was written by Robert Swann, Shimon Gottschalk, Erick Hansch, and Edward Webster of the International Independence Institute, a nonprofit organization founded five years earlier by Ralph Borsodi. The successor to that organization, the Institute for Community Economics, published *The Community Land Trust Handbook* in 1982, adding organizational and operational refinements to the model that Swann and his colleagues had introduced a decade before.

These two books provided the conceptual framework for what eventually became known in the United States as the "classic" CLT. Years later, this framework was given solidity and durability when a federal definition of the community land trust was inserted into the Housing and Community Development Act of 1992 by then-Congressman Bernie Sanders.

By the start of the New Millennium, therefore, a standard definition of the CLT had gained wide currency among community activists and public officials. There could be found in most community land trusts in the United States the same features of organization, ownership, and operation that characterized the "classic" CLT. But that was not true in every case. As practitioners adapted the model to fit the preferences, politics, and needs of their own communities, they modified some features of the classic CLT, while retaining others. This has created a CLT landscape of enormous diversity.[1]

I. ORGANIZATION: HOW IS A CLT STRUCTURED?

Nonprofit, Charitable Corporation

CLT classic: Organizationally, a community land trust is a private, not-for-profit corporation that is chartered under the laws of the state in which it is located. (Legally, a CLT is not a "trust," but an entity that is called in many other countries an NGO: a "nongovern-mental organization.") Most CLTs in the United States target their activities and resources toward charitable activities like providing housing for low-income people, combating neighborhood deterioration, or what federal law describes as "lessening the burdens of government." Most CLTs qualify, accordingly, for a charitable designation from the U.S. government that exempts them from paying federal income taxes and that gives private citizens a tax deduction when donating money or property to a CLT.[2]

CLT variations: Although most CLTs are autonomous organizations created "from scratch," some have been established as a corporate subsidiary or internal program of an older nonprofit organization. In a few cases, a local government or a municipal cor-poration like a redevelopment authority or a public housing authority has developed resale-restricted, owner-occupied housing on leased land, administering a program that resembles a CLT.

When a new CLT is established within the corporate shell of a pre-existing organiza-tion, the CLT usually becomes a permanent part of that organization's on-going opera-tions. This arrangement can be temporary, however, with the CLT eventually spun off as a separate entity when it has the capacity, constituency, and funding to thrive by itself. Another variation has occurred among a handful of CLTs that have chosen not to seek a tax exemption from the federal government in order to serve households earning more than the median or to pursue other activities that do not qualify as "charitable."

Place-Based Membership

CLT classic: The CLT operates within the physical, geographic boundaries of a targeted locale. It is guided by — and accountable to — the people who call that locality their home. Any adult who resides on the CLT's land and any adult who resides within its geo-graphically defined "community" is eligible to become a voting member of the CLT. The duties and powers granted to this corporate membership are spelled out in the organiza-tion's bylaws. Members typically nominate and elect a majority of the governing board. Members also approve proposed amendments to the bylaws, including any changes to the resale formula setting the future price of CLT homes.

CLT variations: Most CLTs are membership organizations, drawing their members from a community that is geographically defined. Within the diverse world of CLTs, however, there is considerable variation in the size of that "community." Two decades ago, the area served by most CLTs was a single inner-city neighborhood or a small rural town. That has changed. Many CLTs formed in more recent years have staked out a wider service area, encompassing multiple neighborhoods, an entire city, an entire county, or, in a few cases, a multi-county region.

There are also many variations in the composition of a CLT's membership. Some CLT's have opened their membership to individuals who reside *outside* of the CLT's target area. Other CLT's have expanded their membership beyond individuals to allow nonprofit corporations, local governments, or private institutions like hospitals, churches, or businesses to become voting members of the CLT. There are also some CLTs without a membership and a few where the entire board is appointed by a municipal government, by a community foundation, or by some other corporate sponsor.

Tripartite Governance

CLT classic: The board of directors of the "classic" CLT is composed of three parts, each containing an equal number of seats. One third of the board represents the interests of people who lease land from the CLT ("leaseholder representatives"). One third of the board represents the interests of residents from the surrounding "community" who neither lease land from the CLT nor live in CLT housing ("general representatives"). One third is made up of public officials, local funders, nonprofit providers of housing or social services, and other individuals who are deemed to speak for the public interest ("public representatives"). Control of the CLT's board is diffused and balanced to ensure that all interests are heard but that no interest is predominant.

CLT variations: Although the governing board of nearly every CLT is distinguished by a diversity of interests and by a balance of interests, the exact make-up of this board can vary greatly from one CLT to another. Many start-up CLTs, moreover, have interim boards that are quite different in their composition from the broadly representative, member-elected, tripartite board that will ultimately govern the CLT.

Every CLT has a board or advisory committee with leaseholder representatives, but some CLTs subdivide this leaseholder category among directors who represent the interests of leaseholders occupying single-family homes and those occupying co-op units or commercial buildings. CLTs that are managing rental housing may reserve leaseholder seats for tenants. All CLTs have "public representatives," but some CLTs fill these seats exclusively with representatives from local or state government, while others include within this "public" category representatives of local churches, foundations, banks, social service agencies, tenant rights organizations, or community development corporations.

II. OWNERSHIP: WHO HOLDS THE REAL ESTATE?

Dual Ownership

CLT classic: A nonprofit corporation (the CLT) acquires multiple parcels of land throughout its targeted geographic area with the intention of retaining ownership of these parcels forever. Any buildings already located on these lands or later constructed on these lands are eventually sold off to other parties. A building's owner may be an individual family, a limited equity housing cooperative, a limited liability company, a cohousing community, a small business, or any other entity or combination of entities.

CLT variations: Although dual ownership is a characteristic of nearly every organization that calls itself a community land trust, buildings that are renter-occupied are sometimes treated differently than buildings that are owner-occupied. Some CLTs, when dealing with multi-unit rentals, for example, whether residential or commercial, retain ownership of the buildings as well as the land. The reverse sometimes happens in the case of multi-unit condominiums when a CLT does not own the underlying land. The CLT possesses, instead, a covenant attached to individual condominiums, granting the CLT a durable right to repurchase these condominiums for an affordable, formula-determined price when an owner later decides to sell. This has occurred most frequently in cities where a CLT has been assigned responsibility for monitoring and enforcing affordability controls over inclusionary housing units extracted from for-profit developers by a municipality.

Leased Land

CLT classic: Although CLTs plan never to resell their land, they provide for the exclusive occupancy and use of land by the owners of any buildings located thereon. Parcels of land are conveyed to homeowners (or to the owners of other types of residential or commercial structures) through ground leases that typically run for 99 years. This two-party contract gives the lessee an exclusive right to occupy the CLT's land, while giving the lessor (i.e., the CLT) a durable right to control how the land is used and how any buildings on its land are priced, financed, repaired, and resold.

CLT variations: The ground lease employed by most CLTs in the United States for the conveyance of land is based on a "model CLT ground lease" that has been refined by CLT practitioners over the past 50 years. The exact terms and conditions in this two-party contract can vary greatly from one CLT to another, however, especially with regard to restrictions on subletting, improving, and reselling the buildings. Another variation has been pioneered in Puerto Rico, where the Caño Martín Peña CLT uses a surface rights deed, rather than a ground lease, to give homeowners security of tenure on land that continues to be owned by the CLT.

Diverse Development

CLT classic: The CLT is a tool of enormous flexibility, accommodating a variety of land uses, property tenures, and building types. CLTs across the United States have made land available for the construction — or for the acquisition, rehabilitation, and resale — of housing of many kinds, including single-family homes, duplexes, condominiums, cooperatives, multi-unit rental housing, homeless shelters, and mobile home parks. CLTs have helped to create nonresidential facilities for neighborhood businesses, recreation, education, job training, and the arts. CLTs have also made their lands available for uses where there are few (if any) buildings, providing sites for community gardens, urban farms, and neighborhood parks or, in more rural areas, providing extensive acreage for farming, forestry, and conservation. Community-owned land is the common ingredient, underlying all of these buildings and uses.

CLT variations: Some CLTs focus on a single type and tenure of housing, like detached, owner-occupied houses. Some focus on a single use of their land, like urban agriculture or rural farming. Other CLTs assemble a diverse portfolio of lands and buildings, taking full advantage of the model's flexibility. The same CLT, therefore, may be the landholder and long-term steward for a mix of owner-occupied housing and renter-occupied housing or for a wide range of residential and commercial buildings.

III. OPERATION: WHAT DOES A CLT DO?

Mission-Driven Growth

CLT classic: By virtue of their charitable status and social mission, CLTs dedicate most of their resources to serving people who are economically precarious — an operational priority that is sometimes characterized as a "preferential option for the poor." Spurred by the needs of people and places they serve, CLTs pursue a strategy of active acquisition, aimed at steadily expanding the number of acres, homes, and buildings brought into the CLT's protected domain of non-market ownership and permanent affordability.

CLT variations: The scale and pace of acquisition can vary widely from one CLT to another; so can the households a CLT will serve and the roles it will play in expanding its portfolio. Some CLTs grow slowly, each year purchasing only a few parcels of land on which are constructed (or rehabilitated) a handful of single-family houses. Other CLTs grow rapidly, benefiting from private donations or public largess that allow them to acquire larger parcels of land and to develop many units of housing. Some CLTs target their activities to the very poor, while others serve households above median income.

Finally, some CLTs do development that is initiated and supervised by their own staff; others leave development to nonprofit, for-profit, or governmental partners, confining their efforts to assembling land, leasing land, and preserving the affordability of any housing entrusted to the CLT's stewardship. Between these two extremes of the CLT-as-developer and the CLT-as-steward, there are various roles that different CLTs have embraced in expanding their holdings.

Perpetual Affordability

CLT classic: The CLT retains a preemptive option to repurchase any residential (or commercial) structures located upon its land, whenever the owners of these buildings decide to sell. The resale price is determined by a formula contained in the ground lease.

This limited-equity formula is designed to give present homeowners a fair return on their investment, while giving future homebuyers fair access to housing at an affordable price. By design and by intent, the CLT is committed to preserving the affordability of housing (and other structures) forever — one owner after another, one generation after another.

CLT variations: While permanent affordability is a commitment of every CLT, the formula that defines and enforces affordability can vary greatly from one CLT to another. That is due, in part, to the different methods that CLTs adopt in calculating the resale price for any housing located upon their land. Different formulas may also result from different goals that particular CLTs are trying to achieve or from different populations they are trying to serve. Furthermore, while the vast majority of CLTs adopt a *single* resale formula, covering all types and tenures of housing within their portfolio — and covering every neighborhood in which they work — a few CLTs have fine-tuned their resale formulas to allow some variation among different components of their housing stock (distinguishing, for example, among detached, single-family houses, condominiums, and cooperatives). A few other CLTs have tailored their resale formula to account for varying conditions between hot and cold sub-markets within their service area.

Perpetual Responsibility

CLT classic: The CLT does not disappear once a building is sold to a homeowner, a cooperative, or some other entity. As the owner of lands beneath any number of buildings and as the owner of an option to re-purchase these buildings for a formula-determined price, the CLT has a continuing interest in what happens to the structures — and to the people who occupy them. The ground lease requires responsible use of the premises. Should a building become a hazard, the ground lease gives the CLT the right to step in and to force repairs. Similarly, should a homeowner get behind in making mortgage payments, the ground lease gives the CLT the right to step in and to cure the default, forestalling foreclosure. The CLT remains a party to the deal, safeguarding the structural integrity of buildings and the residential security of the people who occupy them.

CLT variations: Some CLTs provide a full menu of pre-purchase and post-purchase services. They go to great lengths to prepare people for the responsibilities of homeownership and to support their homeowners, in good times and bad. Other CLTs do little more than monitor and enforce the occupancy, eligibility, and affordability controls embedded in the ground lease, intervening only to prevent the loss of a building faced with foreclosure. The intensity of a CLT's post-purchase involvement in the lives of its leaseholders depends mostly on a CLT's capacity. It is also affected, however, by the CLT's own preferences, as each CLT tries to find an acceptable, sustainable balance between supporting the success of newly minted homeowners, while leaving them alone to enjoy the privacy and independence that homeownership is supposed to provide.

Fig. 1.1

The "Classic" Community Land Trust (USA)

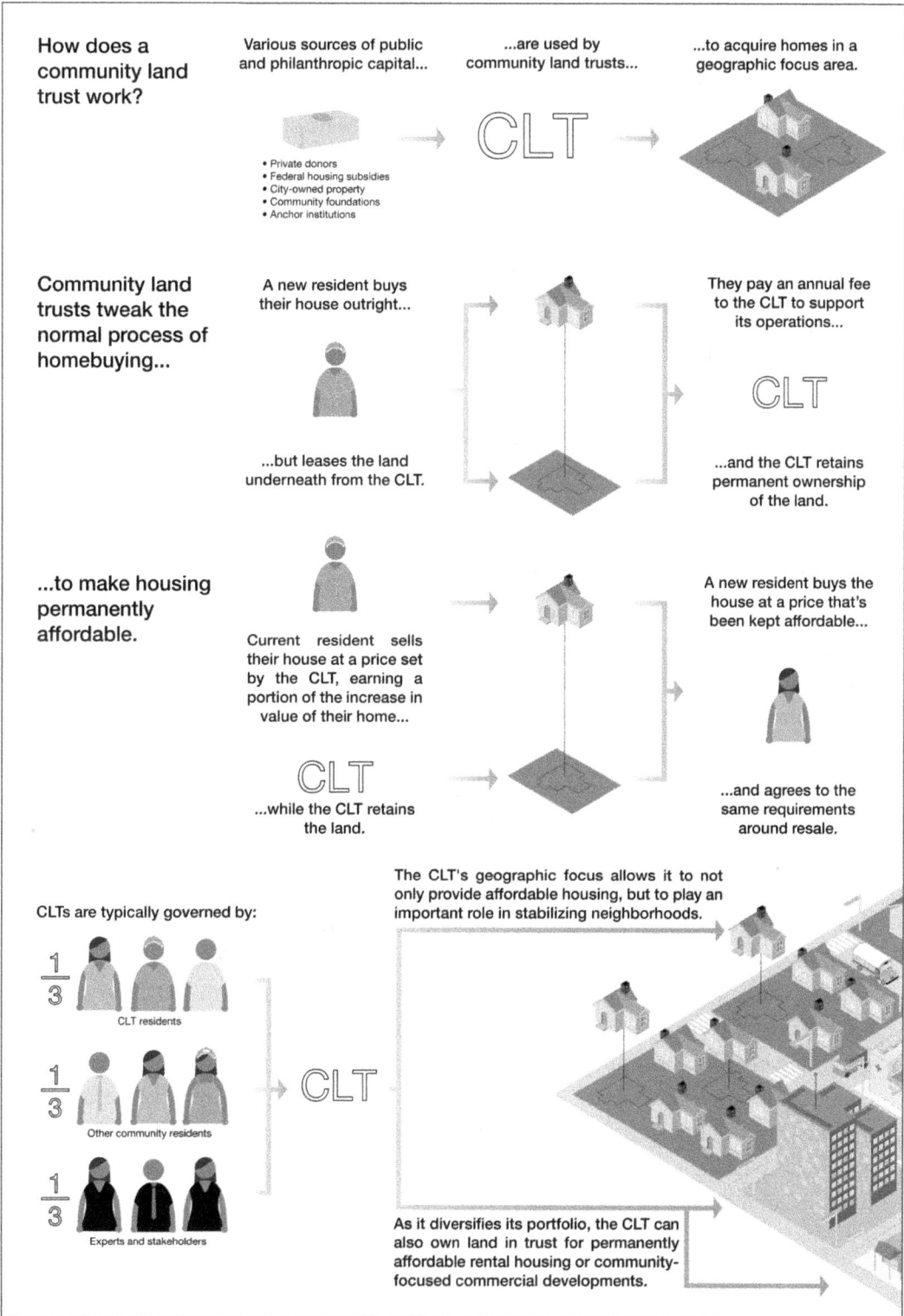

How does a community land trust work?

Various sources of public and philanthropic capital...

• Private donors
• Federal housing subsidies
• City-owned property
• Community foundations
• Anchor institutions

...are used by community land trusts...

CLT

...to acquire homes in a geographic focus area.

Community land trusts tweak the normal process of homebuying...

A new resident buys their house outright...

...but leases the land underneath from the CLT.

They pay an annual fee to the CLT to support its operations...

CLT

...and the CLT retains permanent ownership of the land.

...to make housing permanently affordable.

Current resident sells their house at a price set by the CLT, earning a portion of the increase in value of their home...

CLT

...while the CLT retains the land.

A new resident buys the house at a price that's been kept affordable...

...and agrees to the same requirements around resale.

CLTs are typically governed by:

$\frac{1}{3}$ CLT residents

$\frac{1}{3}$ Other community residents

$\frac{1}{3}$ Experts and stakeholders

CLT

The CLT's geographic focus allows it to not only provide affordable housing, but to play an important role in stabilizing neighborhoods.

As it diversifies its portfolio, the CLT can also own land in trust for permanently affordable rental housing or community-focused commercial developments.

BENZAMIN YI, DEMOCRACY COLLABORATIVE

IV. CAUSES OF CONTINUING VARIATION

A standard definition of the "classic" community land trust was crafted during a forma-tive, twenty-year period between 1972 and 1992. This conception of what it meant to be a CLT and to behave like one became the foundation on which early CLT practitioners in the United States built their organizations, projects, messaging, and "brand."

The CLT did not stand still, however. Practitioners were soon hard at work tailor-ing the model's features to meet local circumstances. Some of these variations occurred within the framework of the model's basic structure and did little to alter the "classic" CLT. Others went much further, changing the CLT's "classic" structure into something quite different. Even when that occurred, however, most organizations calling themselves a CLT retained the model's core commitments to land stewardship, perpetual affordabil-ity, perpetual responsibility, and organizational accountability to residents of the places they serve.

There have been many causes behind the continuing process of experimentation and variation among CLTs in the United States. The most influential of these factors, causing the most significant modifications in standard features of the "classic" model, have been the following:

- *Density of the organizational landscape.* In localities where a number of nonprofit housing development organizations already exist, it has occasionally been prudent and practical to establish a CLT under the sponsorship — or inside the corporate shell — of another nonprofit, instead of starting a new corporation from scratch. At other times, in other places, independently incorporated CLTs have sought a special niche within a densely populated organizational landscape by focusing on functions or roles that are not only different than those of existing nonprofits but also different than those which a "classic" CLT has traditionally embraced.

- *Density of residential development.* In communities where buildable land is expen-sive, the development of new housing is more economical when it takes the form of multi-unit condominiums, cooperatives, rentals, or manufactured housing. Multi-unit housing works well with a CLT, but often requires modifications in the CLT's ground lease. It may also engender modifications in the structure of a CLT's membership and governing board. That is not to suggest that the "classic" CLT is to be found only in communities where detached, single-family houses on separate parcels of land are the primary form of housing production. It is to say that the experience of developing multi-unit housing has often been a spur to innovation, causing several variations in the "classic" model.

- *Requirements of funders.* Changes in the model are sometimes provoked by the demands of public agencies and private lenders on which a CLT must depend for the funding and financing that make its projects possible. Innovation may also occur when a municipality looks to a CLT to serve as the long-term steward for affordability controls mandated by the municipality — either for publicly-subsidized housing on a CLT's land or for inclusionary housing units that are scattered throughout a larger residential project.

- *Marketing an unfamiliar model.* The CLT is sometimes modified to make an unfamiliar model of homeownership look and feel more like the "deal" that is typically offered to more affluent households when buying a home on the open market. By tinkering with the bundle of rights and responsibilities that are provided to a CLT leaseholder/homeowner, especially those affecting the use, improvement, and resale of a CLT home, practitioners attempt to develop and to market a form of housing that is different enough from traditional homeownership to protect the long-term interests of the community, but close enough to traditional homeownership to attract investment and support from prospective homebuyers.

- *Development versus organizing.* It is difficult for any community-based housing organization to wear two hats. As a *developer,* a CLT is accountable to a constellation of funders, contractors, deadlines, and demands that drive the business of getting affordable housing constructed and occupied. As an *organizer,* the CLT is accountable to a constellation of interested parties who lease its land, reside within its community, make up its membership, and serve on its board. While the "classic" CLT strives to serve both sets of interests, this balancing act is not to the liking of everyone. For CLTs that favor development over organizing, especially where a CLT program has been grafted onto the structures and programs of an existing community development corporation or where a CLT has been initiated by a municipal government, there has sometimes been a tendency to modify, dilute, or even abandon membership features or board features that make a CLT directly accountable to a local constituency of lower-income residents. Conversely, for CLTs that favor organizing over development, there has sometimes been a tendency to spend more time on building and sustaining the organization than on building and managing an expanding stock of affordable housing. The most successful CLTs have found a sustainable balance between these extremes of the CLT-as-developer and the CLT-as-organizer.

Because of factors such as these, the CLT landscape in the United States has become increasingly diverse over the years. The model has continued to evolve. These variations have helped the model to spread into new areas and to be applied in new ways. Much of the growth in the CLT movement can, in fact, be attributed to the model's adaptability and plasticity.

Something is lost whenever fundamental features of the "classic" CLT are altered, however, since there are sound philosophical and practical reasons for every one of them. On the other hand, something of value is sometimes gained. Over time, some of these variations will be discarded, while others will prove so beneficial and so effective that they eventually become a permanent part of what the "classic" CLT is thought to be.

Notes

1. Adapted from "The Diverse World of Community Land Trusts," Chapter One of a manual authored by John Emmeus Davis in 2001 and revised in 2006. The full manual, entitled *Development without Displacement: Organizational and Operational Choices in Starting a Community Land Trust,* is available on-line at: *burlingtonassociates.com*

2. This tax exemption is granted to nonprofit organizations that are organized and operated to serve "charitable purposes," as defined under Section 501(c)(3) of the Internal Revenue Code.

2.

The Once and Future Garden City

Yves Cabannes and Philip Ross

Over 100 years ago, Ebenezer Howard set out on an intellectual journey to define what would make a Garden City. The result, in 1898, was his book *Garden Cities of To-Morrow —A Peaceful Path to Real Reform*. It was written in an age when the memory of the Paris Commune was still fresh, when Marxism was still being formulated, when imperial Europe was at its zenith, and when a young Lenin was still in a reflective mood. It was written in the shadow of the co-operative movement which showed that people were capable of coming together to build their own institutions. In the late 1800s, there were around 27,000 registered mutual societies.

The book led to the founding of Letchworth Garden City, the world's first Garden City. Howard had been reflecting on the industrialisation process that was still underway in Britain at the time. He aimed to bring the best of town and country together in the ideal town. In Howard's vision, the citizen would be King and the ills of the time — landlords, squalor, pollution and poverty — would be tackled and beaten.

Printed word became reality when funding was found to purchase a large parcel of land on which to build this new town. As Letchworth took shape, inspiring architecture was a key component and the layout of the town was planned with simple rules that reflected common sense. For example, factories were placed in the east so the smoke didn't blow over the town. The architects were inspired by the Arts and Crafts Movement and driven by a belief in green spaces, a healthy environment, and a sympathetic layout.[1] These were the watchwords guiding this new utopia.

However, Howard and his supporters knew that there was more to a good community and a vibrant town than a carefully designed site plan and attractive architecture. The social aspects would be of equal importance, with ownership and citizenship the key ingredients. A Garden City was designed to be just and fair for the people who would live there. At its heart was the radical proposition of the common ownership of land. This was

Fig. 2.1. Letchworth today, still alive and beautiful. YVES CABANNES

important because the Garden City needed to be more than a well-meaning attempt to build affordable homes. Although Howard may have articulated it differently, the Garden City needed to be sustainable in the longer term. It needed to be economically sustainable in its own right, which is why the capture of rising land values was crucial. Community-owned land was needed if the Garden City was to be socially sustainable and to maintain a balance of affordability as land values rose. The Garden City also needed to be ecologically sustainable in terms of its impact on the environment. Planning played a part here, as did local food production, which was built into the heart of the model. But underlying it all was the notion that the Garden City should own itself.

Letchworth's socialist architects, Barry Parker and Raymond Unwin, were soon helping to design the Hampstead Garden suburb and other areas in the UK, including Welwyn Garden City in England, built on a grander scale than Letchworth. The Garden City Movement quickly crossed the English Channel and inspired Cités Jardins in the Coal Mining Region of Northern France as early as 1905, and new towns around Brussels just after the First World War. Garden Cities appeared around Paris, as well as in Germany, Switzerland, Portugal, and The Netherlands. There were also a number established around Moscow, a result of Howard's book having been translated into Russian as early as 1912, inspiring Russian city planners before and after the 1917 Bolshevik Revolution.

Garden Cities and Garden Neighbourhoods soon expanded beyond the European borders. They appeared in Cairo, Buenos Aires, and Santiago to name a few. Brazil deserves a special mention since Barry Parker, one of the principal planners of Letchworth, advised the City of São Paulo in establishing the Jardim America development between 1917 and 1919. This was the starting point for a significant number of Garden Neighbourhoods and Garden Cities throughout Brazil — more than 45 of them. The concept of Garden Cities also influenced planning in North America. Three Greenbelt towns built during the 1930s — Greendale, Wisconsin; Greenhills, Ohio; and Green-belt, Maryland — are among the most iconic examples.[2]

It is now more than 110 years since the founding of the first Garden City. With all this history and experience of town design, community development, and various applications of the Garden City model, it is time to ask what lessons can be learned. What should the principles of a 21st Century Garden City be? We believe that many of Howard's original instincts were correct, but how can his vision for the Garden City be delivered in a modern setting?

GUIDING PRINCIPLES OF A GARDEN CITY

The place to start is with a declaration that a Garden City is a fair, just, and harmonious community. It should be a place that is economically, socially and ecologically sustainable. It is not restricted to new cities or towns, even to those that were built following traditional Garden City town planning, architectural, or design principles. A Garden City is about community, not merely about architecture and urban design. It is about building a harmonious community, balancing and combining the best of town and country to create a community where the measure of success is ultimately the happiness of the people who live in it.

As described in a "manifesto" we published in 2014, there are twelve principles that we believe underlie a Garden City in the 21st Century.[3] They are inspired by Howard's ideas, by the legacy of Letchworth, and by successful international practice. We declare that any town or city or neighbourhood can be considered a Garden City if it embraces the following principles:

- Residents are citizens.

- The Garden City owns itself.

- The Garden City is energy efficient and carbon neutral.

- The Garden City provides access to land for living and working to all.

- Fair Trade principles are practised.

- Prosperity is shared.

- All citizens are equal, all citizens are different.

- There is fair representation and direct democracy.

- Garden Cities are produced through participatory planning and design methods.

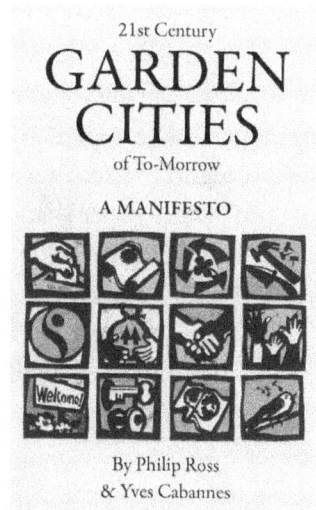

21st Century

GARDEN CITIES

of To-Morrow

A MANIFESTO

By Philip Ross
& Yves Cabannes

Fig. 2.2. Cover of the 2014 "Manifesto." Earlier editions appeared in 2012 and 2013.

- A City of Rights builds and defends the Right to the City.

- Knowledge is held in common, shared and enhanced.

- Wealth and harmony are measured by happiness.

These principles represent multiple doorways into the Garden City. You can enter using any of them, but deny or contradict any one of them and they become exits. Let's concentrate, however, on the principle that is most relevant to community land trusts: "the Garden City owns itself." That doesn't mean that CLTs do not also strive to put the other principles into practice. But land that is owned and managed for the common good is the main intersection between the Garden City and the CLT.

THE GARDEN CITY OWNS ITSELF

The Garden City is ultimately owned by its local community and not by a series of landlords. This ownership and governance is derived from the people who live and work in the city and who are its citizens acting for the common good. If the Garden City is its own landlord, then it is answerable to and controlled by its citizens, ideally as a community land trust managed by democratic structures that make it both inclusive and accountable.

This principle is the most powerful of all because it is a tangible realisation of citizenship. It is about the real and tangible ownership of the Garden City. It is about common and collective forms of tenure of the city and citizen control of the assets within it. Ownership itself isn't enough, however. There must also be participation: active citizens who are capable of holding the landowner to account. Otherwise the Garden City will not work.

We believe that if people who live in a city have a stake in its prosperity, that will help to engender the idea of citizenship. This is what Ebenezer Howard understood when he envisaged the first Garden City. The Garden City was not to be a charity or something held benignly in trust; it was to have common ownership. Nor was it about people holding just passive paper-shares in the city, speculating on its success, but instead participating in it, building it, making it an "oeuvre d'art"— making it a masterpiece, sharing in its success, and shouldering its responsibilities as well.

The owner of the city's landed assets — or the owner of land underlying a neighborhood — isn't a distant landlord, nor is it the local city council or central government. Nominally, the assets might be placed under the control of the "local council," but in the UK at least, people wouldn't have confidence that the council would defend or protect those assets. For instance, many people believe that if the assets in Letchworth had been placed under control of the district council, they would have been sold off piecemeal over the years to fund lower taxes and to gain political favour with voters. Instead, by locking the assets inside of a trust, Letchworth's lands have been kept together for the long-term benefit of the community —"in perpetuity," as community land trust slogans usually say.

Garden Cities are more than just housing, however. Howard's focus — and ours — encompasses the whole town, not just the housing stock. Agriculture, shops, offices, and other commercial spaces, even industry — anything can be located on land that is owned and operated for the common good.

How can this be done? How can people hold the land in common? There are many ways that residents can be their own landlords. This can be done through a co-operative model, a co-operative land bank, or a community land trust.

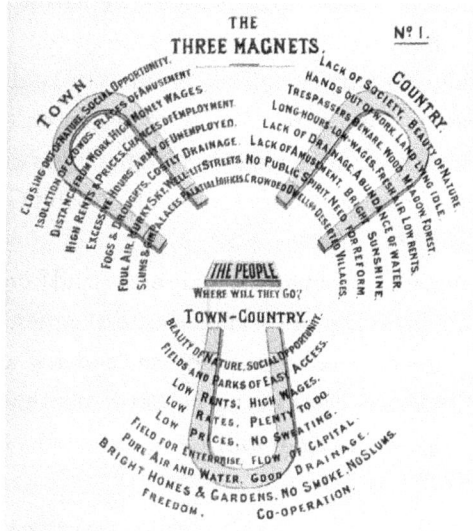

Fig. 2.3. Garden Cities were envisioned to combine the best of town and country, depicted by Howard in his famous image of the "Three Magnets" (right). Letchworth did just that, making land available not only for housing, but for manufacturing (left) and gardening (bottom) as well.
YVES CABANNES

COMMUNITY LAND OWNERSHIP

One of the most successful models of common land ownership is the community land trust (CLT), originated in the United States by Ralph Borsodi and Robert Swann. The prototype for the modern-day community land trust in the USA was formed in 1969 near Albany, Georgia by leaders of the Southern Civil Rights Movement. These CLT pioneers drew upon earlier examples of planned communities on leased land including Howard's Garden Cities, single tax communities in the USA, and Gramdan Villages in India, where wealthy landowners voluntarily gave a percentage of their land, which was then held in trust for lower castes by the entire village.

Basically, a CLT separates the ownership of land from that of any structures that are built on that land. The community land trust retains ownership of the land, whereas houses, commercial buildings, restaurants, etc. sited on that land are sold off, rented out, or owned and managed as cooperatives or for-profit small businesses. We especially like the definition from Diacon, Clarke, and Guimarães on how a CLT works:

> A CLT separates the value of the land from the buildings that stand on it and can be used in a wide range of circumstances to preserve the value of any public and private invest-ment, as well as planning gain and land appreciation for community benefit. Crucially, local residents and businesses are actively involved in planning and delivering affordable local housing, workspace or community facility.[4]

THE UNEARNED INCREMENT

Why bother with this complicated form of ownership? The answer has to do with land values and the fact that they continue to rise. When writing about the revenue of the Gar-den City and how it might be obtained, Ebenezer Howard said the following:

> Thus, while in some parts of London the rent is equal to £30,000 an acre, £4 an acre is an extremely high rent for agricultural land. This enormous difference of rental value is, of course, almost entirely due to the presence in the one case and the absence in the other of a large population; and, as it cannot be attributed to the action of any particular individuals, it is frequently spoken of as the "unearned increment," i.e. unearned by the landlord, though a more correct term would be "collectively earned increment."
>
> The presence of a considerable population thus giving a greatly additional value to the soil, it is obvious that a migration of population on any considerable scale to any par-ticular area will be certainly attended with a corresponding rise in the value of the land to settled upon, and it is also obvious that such increment of value may, with some foresight and pre-arrangement, become the property of the migrating people.
>
> Such foresight and pre-arrangement, never before exercised in an effective manner,

are displayed conspicuously in the case of Garden City, where the land, as we have seen, is vested in trustees, who hold it in trust (after payment of the debentures) for the whole community, so that the entire increment of value gradually created becomes the property of the city, with the effect that though rents may rise, and even rise considerably, such rise in rent will not become the property of private individuals.[5]

Cost and value of land tend to rise, while wages typically increase at a lesser rate, or remain stagnant. Sometimes this land value rises when the taxpayer invests money in improving the local infrastructure, yet it is property owners (and not tenants or lease-holders) who gain the most benefit. The real winners are those who hold a deed to land.[6]

THE CLT AS A VEHICLE FOR CREATING A GARDEN CITY

Despite the prominence given to community-owned land in Howard's vision of the Garden City, as well as in that vision's early implementation at Letchworth and Welwyn, this guiding principle got diluted over time. In many places that called themselves a Garden City, it disappeared altogether. Sadly it was the architectural and design principles that would be copied and celebrated, as architects tried again and again to build the perfect city or town through bricks and mortar alone. Garden Cities became the acceptable face of town and city planning. Its more radical elements, like the common ownership of land, were often left behind.

Community land trusts are a means of restoring community-owned land to the conception and implementation of the Garden City, as well as a means of revitalizing citizenship, another of our twelve principles for creating a Garden City. CLTs are also a way to remove the biggest obstacle to making Garden Cities a reality today. The Garden City envisioned by Howard had a particularly daunting requirement. A group of trustees had to locate and to acquire 6000 acres of vacant land on which to construct a new town accommodating 32,000 residents. That might have been possible in the early half of 20th Century, as dozens of towns, suburbs, and neighbourhoods were being planned and built, incorporating design features that Parker and Unwin had pioneered at Letchworth. That is less likely to be a real possibility today, especially in settled areas of the Global North.

> CLTs insist on the essential conjunction between ownership and citizenship.

We would argue, however, that any town or city or neighbourhood can become a Garden City by embracing the twelve principles we identified earlier, including that a "Garden City owns itself." How does that happen, however, if the likelihood of acquiring thousands of acres of vacant land is remote?

Community land trusts provide a partial answer. They are a vehicle for gradually assembling land and putting Garden City principles into practice — now not later. There

Fig. 2.4. Knowledge sharing, a guiding principle of Garden Cities in the 21st Century. Students visiting Letchworth on a rainy day in 2012. YVES CABANNES

is no reason to wait until thousands of acres are purchased. And land doesn't have to be vacant. Even land with buildings already on it can be brought into a CLT, allowing existing neighbourhoods to be transformed over time into something resembling a Garden City. As John Emmeus Davis wrote in the Postscript to our 2014 Manifesto:

> The promise of the CLT was that Garden City principles could be put into practice right away. Something resembling a Garden City could be created incrementally. It could start small and steadily expand. It could construct new buildings or be woven as a bright thread of rehabilitation and renewal into the gray fabric of a built environment already in place.[7]

Not only do community land trusts allow Garden City activists to get started right away. CLTs also insist on the essential conjunction between ownership and citizenship, as do we. While we extol the virtues of community-owned land, this form of ownership can only be effective if it is accountable. It is by being accountable to the community it serves that a CLT can share its prosperity fairly. Yet this accountability only works if residents are empowered enough to realize that individually and collectively they have the power to question, to scrutinize, and to hold to account those who are operating the CLT.

A community land trust is, by its very nature, accountable to the people who inhabit and surround its lands. It is of the upmost importance, therefore, that the governance and management of the CLT be fair and equitable; otherwise, it can quite easily move from being a socially engaged organization to becoming, at best, a paternalistic one; or become, at worst, a neo-feudal one that exercises control, but is not accountable to its community. A CLT without democratic governance and scrutiny could become the worst of all landlords. A CLT that is dominated by a small group has failed; it is no longer the owner of land of the people, by the people, and for the people.

A community land trust that is economically aware and empowered, one that is socially responsible and driven by those principles, and one that is committed to ecologically sustainable practices is a settlement that is truly ready to pick up the torch for Garden Cities in the 21st Century.

For Howard, it may have been a leap of faith to create a Garden City, but today we know that all the principles of the Garden City have been proven in practice. They have been implemented in settlements across the globe. Individually, each makes a positive impact. But the more of them that we can establish and connect, the greater their impact will be.

The Garden City isn't simply a utopian or idealist vision, but a practical one. It works. It can create a community that is socially, economically and ecologically sustainable. There may be different reasons for choosing a model based on these principles, but at the top of the list is the realization that it will deliver a successful and sustainable community for the long term. To those considering adopting such a model, take courage; you do not stand alone. History, common sense, and a whole movement is ready to stand with you.

Notes

1. The Arts and Crafts Movement began in Britain around 1880 and quickly spread to America, Europe, and Japan. Inspired by the ideas of John Ruskin and William Morris, it advocated a revival of traditional handicrafts, a return to a simpler way of life, and an improvement in the design of ordinary domestic objects.

2. Despite its swift expansion, the worldwide Garden Cities movement became disarrayed with the emergence of the modernist movement and the Athens Charter, signed in the mid-1930s. See: Y. Cabannes and P. Ross, "Food Planning in Garden Cities: The Letchworth Legacy," RUAF Working Papers (Leyden: RUAF Foundation International Network of Resource Centres on Urban Agriculture and Food Security, 2018).

3. Philip Ross and Yves Cabannes, *21st Century Garden Cities of To-Morrow: A Manifesto* (2014).

4. D. Diacon, R. Clarke, and S. Guimarães, S. (eds), *Redefining the Commons: Locking in Value through Community Land Trusts,* Joseph Rowntree Foundation (Coalville: Building and Social Housing Foundation, 2005).

5. Ebenezer Howard, *Garden Cities of To-Morrow* (Available at: *https://www.sacred-texts.com/utopia/gcot/index.htm*).

6. In Letchworth, for example, it is the Trust that owns the land and captures the land's rising value. In 2017, the Trust's tangible assets, made up mostly of lands underlying Letchworth, were reported to have a net asset value of £146 million — which was £12 million more than in 2016 (LGC Heritage Foundation, 2018).

7. J.E. Davis, "A Community Land Trust Perspective on Building the Next Generation of Garden Cities." Pp. 187–197 in Philip Ross and Yves Cabannes, op. cit.

3.

Common Ground

Community-Owned Land as a Platform for Equitable and Sustainable Development[1]

John Emmeus Davis

Land, labor, and capital have long been considered the primary factors of production, regardless of whether one is planning for the fabrication of durable goods in an industrial plant or for the revitalization of dilapidated homes in a residential neighborhood. Every analysis of a project's feasibility begins here. Much creative thought is devoted to these essential inputs, weighing how best to tweak their design, to reduce their cost, and to increase their effectiveness. Creativity of this sort is especially important in community development, where the production of goods and services for people of limited means must be heavily subsidized out of public coffers and private contributions. Every dollar must be inventively stretched and cleverly invested for maximum effect.

Land has been the glaring exception to this predilection for innovation. Experimentation has been the norm in community development when it comes to finding new ways to improve infrastructure, to incubate enterprises, to finance homeownership, or to train low-skilled workers. Far less ingenuity has gone into designing new ways of owning, controlling, and utilizing land to make distressed places more livable or to make prosperous places more inclusive.

This pattern has persisted despite the presence of an innovative model of community-led development on community-owned land that has spread steadily across the United States and is now becoming rooted in other countries as well. Known as the community land trust (CLT), this unconventional approach to place-based development has three distinguishing features: (1) a private, nonprofit organization, acting on behalf of a geographically defined community, acquires and retains scattered parcels of land that are put to a variety of uses through long-term ground leasing; (2) residential or nonresidential buildings located on these leaseholds are sold off to individual owners — families, cooperatives, farmers, small businesses, etc. — whose ownership interest is encumbered by long-lasting affordability controls over each building's use and resale; and (3) the non-profit landowner is guided in the development and stewardship of lands and buildings under its care by people who use its land, occupy its housing, or reside within the surrounding community.

A shorthand description of this strategy, pursued by CLTs and other nongovernmental organizations operating in a similar fashion, is *community-led development of permanently affordable housing (and other assets) on community-owned land.* Or, shorter still, *common ground.*

Any sort of building can be raised on a foundation of community-owned land, although CLTs have devoted most of their resources to date to the production and preservation of housing. On leased land, CLTs have developed many types and tenures of renter-occupied and owner-occupied housing, all priced within the financial reach of persons of limited means. The particular forte of community land trusts is not development, however, but *stewardship:* taking care of this housing long after it is created. CLTs have been effective in preventing the disappearance of affordability when real estate markets are hot and have been equally effective in preventing the erosion of owner equity, the neglect of necessary repairs, and the loss of homes to foreclosure when markets turn cold.

Despite the documented success of CLTs in making such "counter-cyclical stewardship" a reality, many nonprofit organizations in the United States have been slow to incorporate common ground into their programs.[2] The simplest explanation for their hesitancy is that doing development on community-owned land is hard work, especially when a community's residents are given a say in deciding how land should be used and developed. Most nonprofit housing developers choose an easier path. They sell off local lands. They shut out local voices. They roll out affordably priced housing that looks familiar to public funders and private lenders, while minimizing their own responsibility for preserving the affordability, quality, and security of those homes after they are built.

This essay argues that common ground is worth the extra effort. It is a strategy for redistribution, putting property and power into the hands of people deprived of both. It is also a bulwark against loss, protecting hard-won gains in ownership and empowerment from leaking away over time. For *impoverished* neighborhoods needing revitalization, CLTs allow investment to occur and development to proceed without the wholesale displacement of lower-income households, low-profit enterprises, and beloved spaces that populated an area before it began to improve. For *prosperous* neighborhoods lacking economic and racial diversity, CLTs allow housing to be produced for lower-income people that will remain affordable forever. On the platform of common ground, equitable development and sustainable development become two sides of the same coin. Places are made more just. Justice is made to last.

I. REDISTRIBUTION:
THE PURSUIT OF EQUITABLE DEVELOPMENT

Every investigation into whether place-based development is *equitable* begins with a question that city planners ask less frequently than they should: *Cui bono,* who benefits? Equally relevant is the converse: Who's harmed? When new investment is brought into a neighborhood, when new housing is built, when social conditions improve and land values rise, the lion's share of the benefits will go either to people in need or to people who already possess an abundance of property and power. Similarly, the burdens of development will either be apportioned fairly or fall disproportionately upon the shoulders of people who are least able to bear them.

> Common ground tips the scales in favor of people who have been excluded from the benefits of land-based wealth and who have lacked the power to shape development.

Strategies and outcomes of place-based development are always to be found somewhere along the contested continuum between these poles. Either they tilt toward *redistribution,* challenging the existing landscape of inequality, or they tilt toward *reinforcement,* etching patterns of privilege more deeply into the social structure of place. Common ground does the former. It tips the scales in favor of people who have been excluded from the benefits of land-based wealth and who have lacked the power to shape development within their own neighborhoods, be those places urban, suburban, or rural.

A. Street Level Land Reform:
The Economic Case for Common Ground

The community land trust is a hybrid of three strategies used around the world to redistribute landed resources to achieve a more equitable allocation of income and wealth. In their commitment to community-owned land, CLTs are part of a *collective tradition* of land reform in which private estates or public lands are transferred intact to collectives, cooperatives, or village trusts.[3] In their commitment to expanding individual access to lands and buildings, CLTs are inheritors of a *distributionist tradition* in which concentrated landholdings are broken into smaller homesteads and put into the hands of families, farmers, and entrepreneurs. In its commitment to the fair allocation of appreciating real estate values, CLTs are part of a long tradition of *value recapture* that can be traced from the "social increment" of John Stuart Mill, through the Single Tax crusade of Henry George, to the Garden Cities of Ebenezer Howard.[4]

CLTs are unique not only in combining these three traditions of land reform, but in doing so at a different *level* than attempted in the past. Most land reform schemes have been targeted to an entire country. By contrast, community land trusts are tailored to fit the geography and circumstances of place-based communities as small as a single neighborhood, city, or county. Even when a CLT carves out a much larger geography, the economic benefits of common ground are realized at the micro-level of neighborhood and household.

Common ground is a versatile foundation on which any type of building can be constructed and on which any use of land can be secured. Although most CLT activity has centered on expanding access to affordable housing, the lands owned by CLTs have also been used in the development of community centers, day care centers, office space for other NGOs, and commercial buildings for neighborhood retail. Community-owned land has been leased out for community gardens, greenhouses, and commercial farming. In more rural areas, CLTs have been used to preserve access to productive lands for small farmers.

Although some CLTs are heavily involved in developing rental housing, homeownership has been the priority of most community land trusts in the United States. By boosting lower-income people into homeownership, either in houses, townhouses, condominiums, or cooperatives, CLTs put these households on a path toward stabilizing their finances and, over time, toward increasing their personal wealth.

CLTs are hardly alone in using public subsidies and private donations to make homeownership more widely available. There are two significant advantages, however, that community-owned land and long-term ground leasing bring to the whole business of building economic prosperity for low-income people when helping them to buy a home.

First, common ground is an effective shield against financial shocks that can strip low-income people of the prosperity they thought was theirs when purchasing a home. A painful lesson of the Great Recession was that personal wealth, when embedded in residential real estate, is less secure than commonly assumed. Homeowners only build wealth if they can hang onto their homes, which many could not when the Recession hit and the mortgage market collapsed. Between 2007 and 2012, 12.5 million market-rate, owner-occupied homes went into foreclosure in the United States. Communities of color bore the brunt of it, due in large measure to the higher incidence of homes that had been mortgaged using high-priced, variable-rate subprime loans.[5]

The owners of resale-restricted homes developed by CLTs fared much better, experiencing rates of default and foreclosure during the worst of the Great Recession that were a tenth of the rate experienced by the owners of market-rate homes.[6] What the former had that the latter did not was a partner that stood protectively between them and their lenders. At the front end of the lending process, the CLT was by their side, reviewing and approving proposed mortgages and preventing predatory lending. Later on, the CLT was prepared to act on their behalf, should the owners of resale-restricted homes get behind in their payments, intervening to halt foreclosure and to prevent the loss of household wealth. The CLT's stewardship regime was not only effective in preserving affordability for the *next* generation of homebuyers, therefore; it also proved effective in preserving the equity invested and earned by the *current* generation of homeowners.

Community land trusts have also shown themselves to be unusually effective at capturing and distributing land-based wealth inter-generationally. They do so by preventing the removal of public and private subsidies invested in the privately-owned housing on their lands. Subsidies that are retained in CLT homes (along with much of a home's appreciation) reduce the price for subsequent buyers, in effect sharing land-based wealth between one generation of homeowners and another. This feat of redistribution, achieved through a pricing formula and preemptive option embedded in the ground lease, puts the CLT squarely within the land reform tradition of value recapture pioneered by Henry George and Ebenezer Howard, while adding a street-level focus contemplated by neither.

B. Empowerment of Community:
The Political Case for Common Ground

A particular strength of community-owned land is the opportunity provided to a place-based community to impose its will on *what* is developed and *how* development is done, making collective decisions about the common good. As Harry Smith has said about the CLT created by the Dudley Street Neighborhood Initiative in Boston, "The land trust doesn't exist just to acquire and manage land. It's really about engaging community to decide together what they want on their land."[7]

Land that is *community-owned* provides a foundation for development that is *community-led*. This is more than simply opening up a developer's planning process to community participation, inviting residents to voice opinions about the kind of improvements needed to make their neighborhood nicer, safer, or more affordable. A nonprofit organization that owns and manages leaseholds has a head start on creating a place-based constituency that is capable of defending and advancing the interests of everyone who calls that neighborhood their home.

1. Sharing Power

Among the myriad NGOs doing community development in the United States, there has been a notable decline in the number that incorporate participatory strategies and structures into their organizations and operations. Too many have drifted away from what used to be an article of faith among nonprofits dedicated to housing low-income people or to revitalizing low-income neighborhoods; namely, a core belief that the beneficiaries of an organization's projects and services should have a voice in planning those activities and in guiding and governing the organization that carries them out.

A philosophical commitment to democratic governance may help to arrest that slide, although that is hardly unique to CLTs. What *is* unique to a CLT is the practical necessity of anticipating and managing the risk of leaseholder discontent. Landowner-leaseholder relations are not always smooth. Indeed, they can become downright bumpy, an ever-present possibility in the dual-ownership intricacies and intimacies of ground leasing. A desire to reduce the severity of these clashes and to protect its own reputation in the larger community can be strong incentives for a nonprofit landowner to create a structure and culture for leaseholder engagement. The easiest way for a nonprofit organization to ensure that its beneficiaries are cheerleaders rather than critics is to make them partners in guiding and governing the organization itself.

Cost is a factor in this calculation. The least expensive stewardship regime is one in which compliance is routine and enforcement is unnecessary, one in which the occupants of price-restricted buildings police themselves, voluntarily abiding by the contractual conditions that encumber their homes. Compliance with these restrictions is more likely when the people whose homes are encumbered are given a voice in directing the activities of the organization that is managing the land beneath their feet and overseeing the buildings in which they live.

2. Building Power

A nonprofit that is holding land on behalf of a place-based community and doing ground leasing cannot confine its activities to being a developer; it must be an educator and organizer as well. That is not only because its leaseholders may sometimes insist on their "landlord" entering the fray on their behalf, but also because the difficulties that accompany this unconventional form of tenure make it necessary for a nonprofit lessor to build awareness and acceptance at the same time it is building housing. The very things that make ground leasing harder to implement and to manage tend to force any nonprofit doing ground leasing to behave (at times) like a community organizer and to use (on occasion) whatever power it has accumulated to defend the interests of its leaseholders, its community, and itself.

> Land that is community-owned provides a foundation for development that is community-led.

Building power for a CLT begins with the "captive audience" of the organization's own leaseholders. As Jesse Myerson has observed, "Land removed from the private market, decommodified and placed under the ownership and management of the people who live there, is land that creates and renews its own political constituency."[8] This constituency is helped to grow by the versatility of ground leasing, where anything can be developed on community-owned land. When a nonprofit organization takes full advantage of this versatility, shopkeepers, service providers, and community gardeners are added to the ranks of residential leaseholders, broadening the base of a CLT's support.

C. Development with Justice:
The Preservationist Case for Common Ground

Most place-based development is aimed at aggressively rebuilding impoverished localities in which an absence of investment has caused conditions inimical to surviving and thriving for all residents. But place-based development may also be aimed at *prosperous* localities, where an abundance of investment (combined, perhaps, with a pernicious dose of discriminatory zoning) has elevated land values and left little room for housing that is affordable, effectively excluding the poor and people of color. Equitable development is not only about lifting up the worst places; it is also about opening up the best places.

In both situations, the special dilemma for practitioners committed to producing equitable outcomes is how to protect redistributive gains that are achieved in the present against their steady erosion by market forces in the future; even more, how to avoid inadvertently accelerating that process by a practitioner's own success in turning a neighborhood around. The preservationist case for common ground addresses this dilemma head-on, arguing that common ground can provide a foundation for equitable development *and* sustainable development, enabling the implementation of both.

1. Do No Harm

Public agencies, private foundations, and community development organizations of every stripe too rarely *plan for success* when endeavoring to improve distressed neighborhoods. They seem unable to imagine a day when their own efforts might cause property values to rise and market pressures to mount, threatening the wellbeing of the disadvantaged population they set out to help. Focused so intently on doing something good for places urgently in need, these well-meaning interventionists provide no protection against the possibility of something bad happening down the road.

Planning for success when *equitable* development is the goal begins by honestly acknowledging the pain that place-based development often inflicts on economically precarious people and accepting responsibility for doing something to prevent it. By that light, any funder or practitioner who intervenes in a low-income neighborhood with the intention of bettering the lives of those residing there should approach such places with a caution and humility akin to that embodied in the Hippocratic Oath: "Take care that they suffer no hurt or damage."

One of the surest ways of "taking care" is for a community to "Take a Stand, Own the Land," as the organizing slogan of the Dudley Street Neighborhood Initiative (DSNI) once put it. In the 1970s, residents of the Boston neighborhood of Roxbury welcomed the prospect that transit-oriented development might attract investment into an area that had experienced decades of redlining, abandonment, and arson for profit. But they also worried that rising rents and prices might follow in its wake, displacing families with limited incomes. The solution championed by DSNI was to begin acquiring a significant percentage of the neighborhood's land *before* it was caught up in market forces that the government's investment in infrastructure would unleash. A community land trust subsidiary named Dudley Neighbors Inc. (DNI) was established by DSNI in 1988 to hold that land, while also preserving the affordability of any rental housing, cooperative housing, and owner-occupied houses, duplexes, and triplexes constructed on its land.[9]

A similar strategy has been pursued in the Tenderloin neighborhood of San Francisco, where a long-standing partnership between municipal agencies and nonprofit providers of affordable housing has resulted in a steady stream of land being moved into social ownership over the span of many years:

> Starting in the 1970s and continuing uninterrupted over the decades since, Tenderloin activists, working with city government and a set of strong nonprofit partners, bought or otherwise obtained control over a significant share of the area's real estate. . . . It's a 'win-win' strategy that could be dismissed as wishful thinking in any other contested neighborhood. But in the Tenderloin, community control of land makes it possible for community leaders to risk improving the neighborhood without worrying that new investment will push out all the low income people. . . . In fact, this strategy of steady land acquisition and permanent affordability controls is probably the only approach to combating gentrification that can actually win.[10]

Community-owned land cannot prevent market forces from buffeting a neighborhood, any more than an umbrella can stop the rain. It cannot prevent affluent people from moving into a low-income area that is newly attractive to homebuyers and entrepreneurs who, sensing a change in the area's fortunes, are now willing to settle their families or businesses there. What community-owned land *can* do is to keep the poor from getting drowned in the deluge. It is a bulwark against displacement, protecting clusters of affordably priced housing that funders and practitioners have worked so hard to create; preventing endangered islands of security and opportunity from being washed away.

Affordable housing is not the only "lower" land use that is threatened when neighborhoods improve. The same is true for many nonresidential land uses that serve and employ people of modest means. Here, too, common ground can be a bulwark against displacement. A community-based organization that holds land under a variety of buildings and leases out land for a variety of purposes can prevent the loss of small manufacturers, retail establishments, artist spaces, community facilities, and open lands that are put under pressure whenever real estate values rapidly rise. It can also preserve cooperatively owned enterprises that may be tempted to "demutualize" when the enterprise thrives.[11]

Especially vulnerable in neighborhoods undergoing rapid improvement are the sites that Ray Oldenburg has called "third places."[12] These are informal, celebratory spaces in which neighboring occurs and community happens. Often, the most endangered of these spaces in neighborhoods having large concentrations of lower-income people are community gardens. When a neighborhood is economically depressed, the supply of land for community gardens is often cheap and plentiful. When the neighborhood rebounds and land values rise, sometimes as a result of public investment or as a result of residents cleaning up vacant lots and planting verdant gardens, third spaces devoted to urban agriculture are among the first to go.[13]

> In places where the economic tide has turned, common ground can bend the arc of prosperity toward justice.

In sum, common ground can serve as a durable protection for people, uses, and spaces that were tenaciously there long before a disadvantaged place began to improve. It can help to ensure that the *benefits* of development do not accrue primarily to the few who had the foresight and fortune to buy up a neighborhood's real estate when prices were depressed. It can help to ensure that the *burdens* of development do not fall disproportionately on individuals who are the least able to bear them. In places where the economic tide has turned, often as a direct or indirect result of the intervention of public funders, private foundations, and nonprofit developers, common ground can bend the arc of prosperity toward justice.

2. Make It Last

Conditions of surviving and thriving for persons of limited means are not only lacking in places of poverty, they are also lacking in many places of prosperity. The usual culprit in the latter is the scarcity of affordable housing. Low-income people may work in affluent neighborhoods, suburbs, and towns. They may shop there. But they often cannot live there, excluded by rents and prices far beyond their reach.[14]

Opening up privileged enclaves from which low-income families and people of color are regularly barred has been as much a focus of community land trusts in the United States as improving distressed neighborhoods in which underprivileged populations are concentrated. At present, there are even more CLTs working in areas where housing prices are robust than in places where housing prices are depressed. Despite the differences between strong-market cities and weak-market cities, there is often a similar lack of attention that is paid by policymakers to protecting whatever success they have had in improving conditions for people of limited means. Similar, too, is the preservationist role that CLTs have been asked to play.

Most affordably priced homes produced in affluent areas would not exist without the investment of public dollars from a federal, state, or city agency, without the imposition of municipal mandates like inclusionary zoning, or without the beneficence of density bonuses, parking waivers, tax abatements, land donations, infrastructure extensions, and other incentives. Governmental intervention and governmental largess are essential to making newly constructed housing "affordable," allowing homes to rent or to sell for below-market prices that are within the financial reach of people on the lower half of the income ladder.

In too many places, however, this heavily subsidized affordability is not designed to last very long. Restrictions (if any) are imposed on rents and resales that are allowed to lapse after five, fifteen, or thirty years. Prices may then rapidly rise to meet the market. Public subsidies get stuffed into private pockets. Low-income people get displaced. This

programmed loss of publicly assisted, privately owned housing has been a dominant feature of most housing policy in the United States, at all levels of government, for decades.[15]

Calm acceptance of the planned attrition of subsidized housing was shaken by the
affordability crisis of the 1980s and 1990s and by the foreclosure crisis of the Great
Recession in 2007–2009. These disruptions caused a grudging shift in the tectonic plates
of American housing policy. At the municipal level, in particular, increased attention
began to be paid to preventing the loss of publicly subsidized housing, whether to market pricing, deferred maintenance, or foreclosure.[16] That was especially true in stronger
markets where regulatory measures like inclusionary zoning were being used to bring
this housing into being. The disappointing performance of many of the earliest cities that
adopted inclusionary housing programs, where thousands of affordably priced homes
were lost to the market because of short-term affordability controls, provided a corrective
lesson for later adopters. Municipal officials began paying closer attention to preserving
the affordability of inclusionary housing for a much longer period of time.[17] Stewardship
rose higher on the public agenda.

That has created an opportunity for CLTs to show they can do what conventional tenures and programs do not, since stewardship is what community land trusts do best. They
stay in the picture long after affordably priced housing has been produced, making sure
that it lasts. CLTs, in this regard, are the ultimate preservationists: acting to ensure the
lasting affordability and continuing upkeep of privately owned homes, while helping to
ensure the ongoing success of the homeowners or renters who occupy them. As Connie
Chavez, the former executive director of the Sawmill Community Land Trust in Albuquerque, New Mexico was fond of saying, "We are the developer that doesn't go away."

II. RESILIENCY:
THE PURSUIT OF SUSTAINABLE DEVELOPMENT

Community land trusts are not the only way to preserve the affordable housing that a
local government or a private charity has helped to create. Other models and mechanisms
are often tapped to play this stewardship role by government officials and housing professionals, who consider them equivalent to the CLT. From their perspective, it "doesn't
matter" which method is used as long as subsidies are retained, affordability is perpetuated, and homeowners (and renters) are helped to hang onto their homes.[18]

The assumption of equivalency may actually be true, as long as nothing goes wrong.
But stability can be hard to come by. The fortunes of low-income people, low-income
neighborhoods, and the nonprofit organizations that serve them are constantly in flux
and unavoidably precarious. Among the private developers of subsidized housing, for
example, there may be shenanigans in trying to bypass affordability and eligibility restrictions that encumber their properties. Among the owners of resale-restricted homes,
there may be delays in doing repairs or delinquencies in paying their mortgages. Among

> Place-based development is equitable only if it can be sustained. It is worth sustaining only if it is equitable.

organizations charged with stewardship, there may be lapses in intervening when housing is at risk. There may be flaws in the organizations themselves, moreover, leading to a failure to thrive — or a failure to fulfill their stewardship responsibilities.

If affordable housing is to be preserved, the contractual and organizational system put in place to make it last must be able to withstand such challenges. It must be able to cope with occasions when people and organizations do not behave as they should. It must not only plan for success; it must also plan for failure. In a word, that system of stewardship must be *resilient*.

Just as equitable development revolves around the question of "who benefits," sustainable development hinges on the question of "how long" — with *forever* being the end to which practitioners aspire. These are overlapping concerns: making it fair and making it last go hand in hand. Place-based development is equitable only if it can be sustained. It is *worth* sustaining only if it is equitable.

Sustainability, for purposes of the present discussion, is couched narrowly in terms of preserving affordable housing and other facilities, spaces, and activities made available for people of limited means, rather than in terms of conserving the natural resources of a limited planet — the more familiar meaning of "sustainable development."[19] Narrowing the discussion further still, our focus is on the preservation of resale-restricted, owner-occupied homes on land belonging to a CLT. This provides something of a test case, showing how the model can perform in challenging circumstances. If the affordability, quality, and security of *owner-occupied* homes are likely to last when homes are sited on a CLT's land, then *other* types and tenures of housing should be sustainable as well.

My argument is this: When it comes to sustainability, preserving affordably priced homeownership in the face of market pressures and changing conditions, common ground is not "equivalent" to other models and mechanisms. It is better. There are advantages to be found in the long-term leasing of community-owned land that cannot be matched by other approaches to stewardship. These advantages allow a CLT to continue doing good even when things go bad.

A. Dependable Intervention:
The Operational Case for Common Ground

Operationally, CLTs are in a league of their own when assigned responsibility for watching over homes entrusted into their care. By owning the land beneath resale-restricted housing, CLTs are more likely to know when their homeowners are having problems. CLTs are more likely to prevail in negotiations with private lenders to prevent these problems from leading to the loss of lands and buildings from the organization's portfolio. CLTs are more likely to intervene when problems arise.

1. Intelligence

One of the keys to effective stewardship is learning about difficulties long before they become too serious to solve and too costly to fix. A particular advantage of community-owned land is that ground leasing contains a formal and informal "early warning system" that other programs for boosting low-income households into homeownership do not.

The *formal* components of this system are: (1) the collection of ground lease fees from homeowners; and (2) the notification from lenders of any mortgage delinquencies. The revenues raised from lease fees are useful in covering a portion of the steward's operating costs, but they serve another function as well. They give the CLT's staff a regular glimpse into how the organization's leaseholders are faring. The first thing the owners of buildings on leased land tend to stop paying, when experiencing financial distress, are the lease fees owed to the benevolent owner of the land beneath their feet. A pattern of late fee payments or mounting arrearages is usually an indication of more serious problems, alerting a CLT of the need to intervene.

Most CLTs selling homes on leased land have a second tripwire built into their system. They become a party to the mortgages on houses or condominiums. Lenders agree to notify the landowner if any homeowners become seriously delinquent in their payments. A lender may do the same when receiving an application to refinance a home on leased land. Such notifications alert the CLT to changes in a leaseholder's financial circumstances that may jeopardize the homeowner's ability to hang onto his or her home.

The *informal* components of a lessor's early warning system are: (1) the continuing relationship between lessor and lessee; and (2) the continuing visibility of the landowner in the eyes of neighbors and city officials. The very structure of ground leasing requires the landowner and homeowners to stay in touch and, to some degree, to get along. If this relationship is a good one, homeowners are more likely to volunteer information about disruptions in their financial situations, giving the CLT an opportunity to help. This marriage of convenience is forged early in the process of preparing prospective homebuyers for life on the steward's land. "During every community land trust homebuyer education class," says Devika Goetschius, director of the CLT in Petaluma, California, "I've looked each person in the eye and told them, 'When your financial circumstances change — good or bad — you call me.'" With admirable regularity, they do.[20]

Admittedly, any organization that serves as the steward for resale-restricted, owner-occupied housing can establish a trusting relationship with those who are buying the organization's homes. My argument is that such a bond is more likely to exist in programs where the steward owns the underlying land. That is partly a consequence of the landowner and homeowner being materially and psychologically tied together, but it is also a function of the CLT being constantly reminded of this relationship by parties looking on from outside. Neighbors are likely to complain to the landowner when homes are not kept in good repair or when lots become cluttered with junk cars. City officials are likely to notify the landowner when there are violations of building or zoning codes, or when homeowners fail to pay special assessments or property taxes. Such pesky calls provide a CLT's staff with valuable on-the-ground intelligence of any looming problems in the CLT's portfolio of resale-restricted housing.

2. Leverage

Owning the underlying land gives a CLT a wider range of options in dealing with a home-owner who is not complying with provisions in her ground lease; for example, not occu-pying the home as her primary residence or not keeping the home in good repair. The landowner's ultimate leverage in compelling compliance is the threat of eviction from the leasehold, but ground leases also contain a graduated series of less-drastic warnings, penalties, arbitration, and opportunities for injunctive relief. Nearly all violations are cor-rected long before reaching the dire straits of a CLT acting to remove a homeowner from the land.

Equally important, ownership of the underlying land gives a community land trust greater leverage in negotiating with a private lender or public funder who holds a mort-gage on a troubled home. What is mortgaged in most ground leasing programs — and what a lender is allowed to seize if a loan goes bad — is the building, *not* the land. This strengthens the CLT's hand, multiplying the possibilities for dealing with mortgage defaults and foreclosures. The lender may enlist the CLT's cooperation in negotiating a workout with the homeowner, keeping the mortgage in place while putting the home-owner on a schedule to resolve the delinquency. Or the CLT may accept a deed-in-lieu-of-foreclosure from the homeowner. Or the CLT may decide to buy back the house from the lender, following foreclosure.

In short, even when a home (or other building) slides toward foreclosure, and even should a foreclosure actually occur, the community land trust stays stubbornly in the pic-ture.[21] The landowner's presence, interests, and powers cannot be ignored.

3. Intervention

Any NGO that has agreed to serve as the long-term steward of resale-restricted housing is likely to reserve the right to intervene in order to preserve the homeownership oppor-tunities it has worked so hard to create, regardless of whether such authority is granted through a ground lease, a deed covenant, or some other mechanism. But having the *right* to intervene is not the same as having the *will* to do so. In this regard, the long-term leas-ing of community-owned land comes out ahead.

It is not that the people who run CLTs are more virtuous or energetic than the lead-ers of other NGOs; rather, their *incentive* to intervene is greater when problems arise. When the homes for which the steward is responsible are located on land that the steward owns, it is harder for that organization to ignore its stewardship responsibilities. To put it bluntly, the steward is "stuck." Those buildings that are not being maintained? They are

Stewardship is more certain when the organization assigned
responsibility for stewardship is not only vigilant but vested,
ensnarled in a benevolent web of its own making.

on the steward's land. Those homes with taxes or mortgages in arrears? They are on the steward's land. And everybody knows it, especially any governmental agencies that may have granted or loaned money to the CLT to develop that housing.

In the face of the many *dis*incentives to intervention, including the time required, the money involved, and the risk of antagonizing homeowners who would rather be left alone, stewards using mechanisms other than a ground lease are more likely to decide that the cost is simply too high to go to the extra trouble of rescuing a distressed property. Owning the land tends to nudge this calculation in the opposite direction, creating an incentive to act that outweighs the disinclination to do so. Ground leasing, in this regard, is what behavioral economists call a *commitment device*.[22] It locks a CLT into living up to its own promises, raising the reputational cost of not intervening to protect the buildings upon its land. Stewardship is more certain when the organization assigned responsibility for stewardship is not only vigilant but vested, ensnarled in a benevolent web of its own making, compelled to do the right thing even when tempted to look the other way.

B. Graceful Failure:
The Organizational Case for Common Ground

An under-appreciated function of common ground is that it tends to make organizational failure less likely and, should a CLT begin to founder, to render its distress or demise less disastrous. Common ground builds greater resiliency into a stewardship regime.

It might seem self-defeating to mention failure while extolling the virtues of community-owned land and long-term ground leasing, but the emphasis here is on what is known as "graceful failure." This is a fault-tolerant principle lifted from the world of engineering and computer programming, where complex systems are designed to continue operating properly even when there is a failure in one of the components. Engineers do not set themselves the impossible goal of building a transportation network, an electrical grid, or a computer program that will never fail. They strive, instead, to create systems that are robust and resilient. Such a system, when subjected to extreme conditions, may bend, but it does not break. Should it crash, it does so with enough warning and backup so as to protect its most valuable components.

Graceful failure is designed into a housing delivery system whenever stewardship is added as a backup for low-cost homes and low-income households assisted with public or private dollars. A stewardship regime makes failure less likely. It also helps to ensure that when failures do occur, which cannot be entirely avoided when dealing with economically vulnerable people, structurally vulnerable assets, and a hopelessly convoluted system for regulating, financing, and subsidizing affordable housing, these failures will not be catastrophic. When stewardship accompanies the deal, homes are more likely to last.

Earlier, it was argued that the *operational* effectiveness of a stewardship regime is enhanced by a steward's ownership of the land beneath residential buildings for which it is responsible. But what of the *organizational* effectiveness of the steward itself? If it is true that some organization must stay watchfully in the picture for many years for affordability, quality, and security to be preserved, then stewardship must necessarily depend on the viability of that organization. It must have the capacity to do the job and the ability to survive. The steward, too, must be designed to last.

One of the best ways to ensure that a CLT will be around for the long haul is to build a diverse portfolio of revenue-generating assets, thereby reducing the organization's dependency on outside funders. Ground leasing, in this regard, can contribute significantly to a steward's bottom line, depending on the magnitude of the organization's holdings. Ground lease fees collected from the owners of buildings on the steward's land can be used to cover a growing portion of the landowner's operating costs, especially those incurred in meeting its stewardship responsibilities. Furthermore, when that portfolio includes multi-unit rental housing on leased land, and perhaps commercial buildings as well, the operational revenue from lease fees can become substantial.

But many CLT's will never develop a sizable and diverse portfolio. Smaller CLTs will sometimes (not always) find it harder to survive. Even CLTs with substantial portfolios may be put in jeopardy by a failed project or by a loss in governmental support, caused by a sudden change in the political winds. What matters the most in these situations, whenever a CLT finds itself on shaky ground, is saving the affordable housing into which low-income people have poured their savings and dreams. In a time of crisis, a nonprofit landowner with a charitable mission must think first of the wellbeing of the homeowners (and renters) who live on its land. Its primary obligation is to them. The governing board of a shaky CLT must do whatever is necessary to protect its leaseholders, including perhaps the prudent decision to lease out some of its land for a "higher" use than housing — or even the painful decision to sell some of its land.

The board may be led in more extreme cases of organizational distress to look for a suitor; that is, another nonprofit organization that is willing to absorb the CLT through a corporate merger or one that is willing to accept the CLT's assets upon the latter's dissolution. A steward with land on its books, along with a guaranteed stream of revenue from future lease fees, brings a lucrative dowry to the search for a partner or successor. This can increase the odds of attracting and negotiating an attractive organizational match that will protect the homes on the CLT's land and perpetuate the stewardship regime surrounding them.

The key point, in these cases, is not only that landownership and ground leasing give the board of a faltering organization more options, but also more motivation to pursue them. Similar to a CLT's commitment to oversight and intervention, a lessor and its lessees are married to one another in a mixed-ownership arrangement that is not easy to unwind. The difficulty of doing so can be a good thing in a time of crisis, forcing everyone to slow down, dig in, and work harder to solve the organization's problems. When there is more at stake, as there is when low-income households live on land that is owned by a CLT, the governing board will do almost anything to make things right, even to the point of sacrificing the organization itself through a merger or dissolution if that means saving its leaseholders' homes.

III. JUST PLACES: THE TRANSFORMATIVE POTENTIAL OF COMMON GROUND

Long ago, Andre Gorz, a social philosopher living in France, drew a distinction between ameliorative measures that buttress existing relations of property and power versus those that open tiny cracks in the structure of inequality, slowly accumulating over time to offer an ideological and political challenge to the status quo. He called the first "reformist reform" and the second "non-reformist reform."[23]

Gorz's categories were later revived and provocatively applied by James Meehan in his examination of community land trusts in the United States, using the Dudley Street Neighborhood Initiative in Boston as his principal case. He concluded:

> It is clear that CLTs, in their diverse character and situations, walk the fine dividing line between the two tendencies of reformist and non-reformist. In many cases, the CLT legal model has been used as a gimmick to keep low-income housing costs low (thus taking pressure off the state and the private sector). In others, they play a role in raising consciousness to the realities of power in regard to land, questioning speculative owner-ship of land, and enabling some degree of community control over the local land base.[24]

Meehan captures well the tension between the pedestrian, day-to-day practice of CLTs and the loftier, transformative possibilities that may result from their work. CLTs are, in fact, an effective scheme for lowering housing costs, preserving affordability, promoting upkeep, and preventing foreclosures. This full-cycle commitment to cost reduction at the front end and dependable stewardship at the back end is a marked improvement over the build-and-bolt mentality embodied in most other programs for boosting low-income people into homeownership.

At the same time, a community land trust, like every other organization working to improve conditions and to expand opportunities for disadvantaged people, inadvertently reinforces the hold of dominant institutions. When CLTs expand access to mortgage cap-ital for populations and places that have experienced redlining in the past, they contrib-ute to the legitimization of a system of private finance that has been a source of woe for low-income communities, especially communities of color. When CLTs expand access to homeownership for people who have been excluded from the private market, they affirm the individualization of property that has been a flashpoint in the politics of place, where interests of property drive a contentious wedge between owners and renters, and between haves and have-nots. Community land trusts, from this perspective, can be seen as a reformist tool for propping up the status quo, softening the edges of a harmful system that is left unchallenged and unchanged.

There is another way of looking at it, however, for the cumulative effect of community-led development on community-owned land may be to transform that system into something else. An ideology of possessive individualism, used by landlords and homeowners alike to justify their capture of all gains in value accruing to real property, is challenged by a CLT's dogged pursuit of a more equitable balance between the legitimate interests of individual residents and the legitimate interests of the community around them, secured through common ground.[25] The power of private lenders is moderated by the CLT's front-end right to approve all mortgages for buildings sited on its land, screening against predatory lending; it is also blunted by the CLT's back-end right to intervene in cases of mortgage default, preventing most foreclosures. The politics of place are modified by a nonprofit landowner that is drawn into sharing and wielding power on behalf of residents living on and around its land.

Admittedly this happens within the geographic confines of a rather limited territory, encompassing a service area as small as a single neighborhood for some CLTs. It also happens within the functional confines of a limited circle of institutions that determine how land-based wealth is distributed and how real estate is owned, regulated, and financed. Community-owned land may be a creative vehicle for non-reformist reform, but its territorial and institutional reach may not extend very far.[26]

It may be argued, on the other hand, that any institution that offers a counter-narrative to practices and meanings that buttress inequality carries a seed of possibility for influencing a wider circle of places, institutions, and policies. When one community prudently plans for success by improving conditions in a particular place without displacing its most vulnerable residents, it raises the question of why *equitable* development isn't a priority of every neighborhood improvement plan. When community-led development on community-owned land creates a stock of housing that is permanently affordable in the face of market forces that pose a credible threat to all affordably priced housing, most of which would not exist without governmental funds or inclusionary mandates, it raises the question of why *sustainable* development is not a requisite of all housing policy.

A community land trust, from this perspective, represents what Ulrich Beck has called a "creative construction," a social innovation that not only transforms relations within its particular sphere of influence but brings pressure to bear on the intellectual and political systems that surround it, "besieging what exists with a provocative alternative."[27] In a similar vein, Erik Olin Wright has pointed to "community-controlled land trusts" as one of several strategies for achieving what he calls "interstitial transformations." These are alternative institutions that "seek to build new forms of social empowerment in the niches and margins of capitalist society, often where they do not seem to pose any immediate threat to dominant classes and elites."[28]

It cannot be said that most people who are drawn to a CLT, whether as practitioners or beneficiaries, are motivated by the prospect of mounting some sort of ideological, institutional, or political challenge to the status quo. Most have little interest in "besieging" anything. They may be blissfully unaware of the transformative potential of community-owned land beyond its immediate utility in helping low-income people to obtain and retain a home. Even those who passionately embrace the CLT as a vehicle for moving toward a more just society may speak only in whispers about the radical proposition at the heart of the model they employ. As the sweet old lady confided to a colleague of mine several years ago, while talking proudly about the success of her own CLT in doing both urban agriculture and affordable housing on community-owned land, "What we are really about is land reform, but we hide behind the tomatoes."

> "What we are really about is land reform, but we hide behind the tomatoes."

Such reticence is understandable. A community land trust must think twice about calling too much attention to unconventional (and sometimes controversial) elements in its make-up when its leaders must continually beg for grants from public funders, apply for loans from private lenders, and anticipate attacks from reactionary neighbors opposed to anything being built near their own backyards.

Stealth has a price, however. When an innovation like common ground is cautiously kept out the limelight, it is simultaneously kept off the stage, waiting forever in the wings. To move from the periphery to the mainstream, CLTs must be prepared to strut their stuff and prove their worth, confidently proclaiming that *their* way of doing community development is preferable to the way it is normally done. Hiding behind the tomatoes may help a fledgling CLT to get established or may enable a beleaguered CLT to survive, but it does little to demonstrate the comparative advantage of common ground. It hides the fact that community-led development on community-owned land is not "just as good" as more conventional strategies of place-based development. It is better.

It is better because community land trusts are, at heart, more than simply another gimmick for lowering the cost of housing and cultivating a new crop of homeowners. What they are "really about" is equitably and sustainably replanting the contested ground at the intersection of property, power, and place. That may not be something to which all CLT practitioners aspire. That may not be something of which all CLT practitioners speak. But whenever land is controlled by a community within the participatory framework of a CLT, the transformative potential is present to nudge the places where people reside toward greater security and opportunity for all. Common ground provides a versatile platform for promoting development with justice—and justice that lasts.

Notes

1. This chapter is an abbreviated version of an essay published by the *University of San Francisco Law Review* v. 15, no. 1 (2017).

2. An argument for strategies and policies that preserve affordable housing in good economic times and bad can be found in John Emmeus Davis, "Homes that Last: The Case for Counter-Cyclical Stewardship," *Shelterforce* (Winter 2008). Reprinted in J.E. Davis (ed.), *The Community Land Trust Reader* (Cambridge MA: The Lincoln Institute of Land Policy, 2010).

3. While this tradition inevitably invokes images of state confiscation of the estates of a purged aristocracy, there are less draconian examples. The Gramdan Movement in India relied on voluntary donations of land from wealthy landlords in the 1950s. The contemporary land reform movement in Scotland relies on state funds, raised largely through the national lottery, and a 2003 law enacted by the Parliament in Edinburgh that gave communities a first option to purchase the feudal estates on which those communities are sited.

4. An earlier attempt to situate the CLT within the context of different approaches to land reform can be found in John Emmeus Davis, "Reallocating Equity: A Land Trust Model of Land Reform," Pp. 209–232 in *Land Reform, American Style* (Totowa NJ: Rowman & Allanheld, 1984). Reprinted in J.E. Davis (ed.), *The Community Land Trust Reader* (Cambridge MA: The Lincoln Institute of Land Policy, 2010).

5. Evidence for the disparate impact of the mortgage crisis on communities of color can be found in Jacob S. Rugh & Douglas S. Massey, "Racial Segregation and the American Foreclosure Crisis," *American Sociological Review* 75, 2016: 629, 633; and Debbie Gruenstein Bocian, Wei Li, Carolina Reid, & Roberto G. Quercia, *Lost Ground: Disparities in Mortgage Lending and Foreclosures* (Center for Responsible Lending, 2011).

6. Emily Thaden, "Stable Homeownership in a Turbulent Economy: Delinquencies and Foreclosures Remain Low in Community Land Trusts," Working Paper (Cambridge MA: Lincoln Institute of Land Policy, 2011). See also John Emmeus Davis & Alice Stokes, *Lands in Trust, Homes That Last: A Performance Evaluation of the Champlain Housing Trust* (Burlington VT: Champlain Housing Trust, 2009).

7. Penn Loh, "How One Boston Neighborhood Stopped Gentrification in Its Tracks," *YES! Magazine* (January 28, 2015).

8. Jesse A. Myerson, "How to Get Rid of Your Landlord and Socialize American Housing, in Three Easy Steps," *The Nation* (December 8, 2015).

9. The story of DSNI is told by Peter Medoff and Holly Sklar, *Streets of Hope: The Fall and Rise of an Urban Neighborhood* (Boston MA: South End Press, 1994).

10. Rick Jacobus, "The Gentrification Vaccine," *Rooflines* (August 13, 2015).

11. A rise in the value and profitability of a cooperatively-owned enterprise can tempt the firm's shareholders to sell out to an outside buyer, removing the cooperative structure and reaping personal gains, a process known as "demutualization." Just as the leased land beneath a limited-equity housing cooperative can prevent its conversion to a market-rate cooperative or condominiums, a ground lease beneath a worker cooperative or consumer cooperative can give a CLT the ability to prevent demutualization.

12. Ray Oldenburg, *The Great Good Place* (Paragon House, 1989). Quoted at p. 14.

13. Jeffrey Yuen and Greg Rosenberg, "Hanging on to the Land," *Shelterforce* (February 11, 2013). Available at: *http://www.shelterforce.org/article/3068/hanging_on_to_the_land/*

14. To focus on the cost of housing, as I am doing here, is not to ignore the presence of other barriers to geographic mobility, past and present, including discriminatory lending and exclusionary zoning.

15. Jake Blumgart, "Have We Been Wasting Affordable Housing Money?" *Rooflines* (December 3, 2015). Available at: *http://www.shelterforce.org/article/4322/have_we_been_wasting_affordable_housing_money/*. See also: John Emmeus Davis, "Plugging the Leaky Bucket: It's About Time," *Rooflines* (January 27, 2015). Available at: *https://shelterforce.org/2015/01/23/plugging-the-leaky-bucket-its-about-time/*

16. John Emmeus Davis and Rick Jacobus, *The City-CLT Partnership: Municipal Support for Community Land Trusts* (Cambridge MA: Lincoln Institute of Land Policy, 2008).

17. "The overwhelming trend has been for inclusionary housing programs to adopt very long-term affordability periods." Rick Jacobus, *Inclusionary Housing: Creating and Maintaining Equitable Communities* (Cambridge MA: Lincoln Institute of Land Policy, 2015, p. 35).

18. Overviews of these models and mechanisms can be found in John Emmeus Davis, *Shared Equity Homeownership: The Changing Landscape of Resale-Restricted, Owner-Occupied Housing* (Montclair NJ: National Housing Institute, 2006); and Jarrid Green, *Community Control of Land and Housing* (Washington DC: Democracy Collaborative, 2018).

19. That is not to say CLTs ignore the more typical concerns of "sustainable development." Just the opposite. The longer time horizon of the "developer that doesn't go away" makes CLTs more receptive to environmental issues and more attentive to installing durable materials and energy efficient systems than developers who build and bolt.

20. Quote by Devika Goetschius, Executive Director of the Housing Land Trust of Sonoma County, in Emily Thaden and John Emmeus Davis, "Stewardship Works," *Shelterforce* (December 24, 2010). Available at: *https://shelterforce.org/2010/12/24/stewardship_works/*

21. If the home does go into foreclosure and the lender sells to a buyer that is not a low-income or moderate-income household, the CLT has the option (via the ground lease) of charging that upper-income homebuyer a market-rate ground rent.

22. See, for example, Gharad Bryan, Dean Karlan, & Scott Nelson, "Commitment Devices," *2 Annual Review of Economics 2* (2010); and Colin Camerer, Samuel Issacharoff, George Loewenstein, Ted O'Donoghue, & Matthew Rabin, "Regulation for Conservatives: Behavioral Economics and the Case for 'Asymmetric Paternalism'" *University of Pennsylvania Law Review 151* (2003).

23. Andre Gorz, *Strategy for Labor: A Radical Proposal* (Boston MA: Beacon Press, 1964).

24. James Meehan, "Reinventing Real Estate: The Community Land Trust as a Social Invention in Affordable Housing," *Journal of Applied Social Science 20* (2013, p. 113).

25. From the earliest days of the CLT, its advocates have wrestled with the question of exactly what these "legitimate" interests might be. A seminal discussion of this issue can be found in Institute for Community Economics, *The Community Land Trust Handbook* (Emmaus PA: Rodale Press, 1982). Many other thinkers have wrestled with the same philosophical question. See: R.H. Tawney, *The Acquisitive Society* (New York: Harcourt, Brace and World, 1920); and Reinhold Niebuhr, *The Children of Light and Darkness* (New York: Charles Scribner and Sons, 1944).

26. James DeFilippis, for one, has expressed doubts about CLTs producing society-wide change. While conceding that CLTs "provide a framework for ownership that is both equitable and viable," he notes their lack of an oppositional politics and their limited institutional reach. James DeFilippis, *Unmaking Goliath: Community Control in the Face of Global Capital* (New York: Routledge, 2004). Quote at p. 148.

27. Ulrich Beck, *Individualization: Institutionalized Individualism and Its Social and Political Consequences* (Mike Featherstone ed., 2005). Quote at pp. 190–191.

28. Erik Olin Wright, *Envisioning Real Utopias* (London: Verso, 2010).

4.

Making a Case for
CLTs in All Markets,
Even Cold Ones

Steve King

The Community Land Trust is a proven tool
for change. When shall we dare use it?[1]
— *Susan Witt and Robert Swann*

Over the past several decades in the United States, there has been a resurgent interest in a certain quality of life afforded by dense urban living, particularly among well-
educated, high-income earners. This has precipitated a re-segregation of the population
in hot-market metropolitan areas like the one surrounding San Francisco, where housing
production has failed to keep pace with economic growth. The persistent, racialized disinvestment and neglect that for decades targeted sections of the Bay Area, including East
and West Oakland, Bayview Hunters Point, East Palo Alto, and Richmond, has nearly
vanished, as real estate speculators have found opportunities to buy up land and buildings
in proximity to downtown San Francisco and Silicon Valley. Long-time working-class
residents have been steadily pushed to far-flung exurbs in search of affordability, at the
expense of social networks, increased commute times, and diminished cultural connection. Many who remain in the inner Bay Area have been subjected to adverse housing-
related by-products of the booming economy, including skyrocketing rents, involuntary
displacement, no-fault evictions, tent encampments, and a near paralysis among public
officials over how to ameliorate the resulting harm.

This predicament is not unique to the Bay Area, and it is also not shared uniformly
across the United States. At the other end of the economic spectrum, many older industrial towns, cities, and regions have experienced a seemingly irreversible downward spiral
marked by a long decline of the manufacturing sector, a shrinking middle class, white
flight and suburbanization, and the recent foreclosure crisis. Many places that once flour-
ished around specific industries are struggling to survive in the absence of the economic

We are still lacking a broader argument for why CLTs might be effective in places that are plagued by disinvestment, not reinvestment.

engines that once powered them. Abandonment, high vacancy rates, plummeting home values, municipal fiscal crises, and extreme poverty are but a few of the challenges left in the wake of economic decline. For people living in such cold-market neighborhoods or cities, the prospect of gentrification seems remote, a distant threat that is unlikely ever to materialize.

Urban growth and decline are both uneven and cyclical. If there is one constant about cities in an advanced capitalist economy, it is that they change over time. Indeed, these antipodal cases mask the middling nuances of urban development in post-Industrial American cities. As the urban planner Alan Mallach has noted, even in shrinking, "divided" cities like Detroit, Cleveland, and St. Louis, the investment in high-end, amenity-rich housing is an emergent phenomenon; just a few blocks away from new, upscale development there remains relentless neighborhood decline and poverty.[2]

In hot-market coastal cities and in cold-market metro areas alike, therefore, economic opportunity is not equitably distributed. The benefits of development overwhelmingly accrue to the wealthy, while the burdens disproportionately impact the poor. A similar pattern is found in housing and land use. History is replete with examples of how both public policies and private actions have been divisive, exclusionary, predatory, and destructive, especially for African-American neighborhoods and other communities of color.

Fig. 4.1. Weak-market neighborhood, Old North St. Louis, Missouri, 2014.

A premise and promise of the community land trust model is that it aims straight for the heart of a major cause of these persistent inequities: the ownership and control of land. The fundamental desires for freedom, self-determination, and rootedness *in place* were core motivations for the creation of the first modern CLT in Albany, Georgia nearly fifty years ago. And they remain so today, which is a reason why CLTs are increasingly utilized in neighborhoods and cities with ascending real estate markets. Community activists — and some public officials — see in the CLT a strategic tool to counter the negative externalities of market-driven development that are inflicted disproportionately on low-income households and communities of color. A forceful rhetorical case has been made — and some empirical evidence is beginning to appear — demonstrating that community control of land via a CLT can be an effective hedge against market forces that otherwise displace precariously housed people in disempowered neighborhoods.[3] The development of CLTs in cities like Seattle, Portland, San Francisco, Los Angeles, Denver, Austin, Houston, Washington, DC, Boston, and New York City attests to the allure and applicability of CLTs in ascending markets.

In contrast — and strangely so — a compelling case has never been made for CLTs in cold-market locales, despite the fact that a number of CLTs have succeeded in places where real estate markets are weak.[4] John Emmeus Davis has offered a cogent argument that "counter-cyclical stewardship," the particular forte of CLTs, can be a stabilizing force amidst market fluctuations.[5] We also have some evidence of CLTs bearing out this promise of stability in market troughs, as happened during the foreclosure crisis of 2008–2012 when CLT homeowners did not lose their homes.[6] Nevertheless, we are still lacking a broader argument for why CLTs might be effective in places that are plagued by disinvestment, not reinvestment; that is, places where affordability is not the most pressing issue and where market-instigated displacement is not an imminent threat. This essay is an initial attempt to fill this void, offering a rationale and a provisional menu of strategic options for community control of land via a CLT in cold-market areas.

CHALLENGES AND OPPORTUNITES FOR CLT DEVELOPMENT IN COLD MARKETS

There is a widespread belief amongst practitioners, funders, and institutions in the broader community development and affordable housing fields that the CLT model is neither needed nor workable in cold real estate markets. This reductive conclusion belies an unfortunate misunderstanding of the goals and values of many emerging (and established) CLTs. It is a potentially destructive preconception that can stifle support of new CLT initiatives and thwart important community-driven work before it is given a chance to thrive. Before delving squarely into the qualities of cold-market places and the potential for CLTs in those areas, therefore, it is necessary to consider briefly the question of the relationship between the "strength" of a local real estate market (hot/strong vs. lukewarm/moderate vs. cold/weak) and the prospects for creating a viable CLT.

CLTs operate in a manner that works to correct for defects in both the private market and the broader political system, producing equitable and sustainable outcomes that would not otherwise emerge from either. This ameliorative impact can occur in *any* market. In this respect, the market itself is a precondition for a CLT. If a more just and democratic system was in place that equitably distributed land, housing, and economic opportunity, a CLT might not be needed. In the absence of such a system, however, there is a redistributive and reparative role for CLTs to play, regardless of the relative strength of the local economy and local real estate market.

The feasibility and viability of a CLT in any market — including cold ones — will depend on a complex array of local conditions and factors, including: the type of activities a community is hoping a CLT will undertake; who is invited to (or excluded from) a CLT's decision-making table; and, perhaps most importantly, the presence (or absence) of residents who have organized to improve their neighborhood and to secure a more just allocation of resources. Each of these contingencies offers a window into why a CLT might be the ideal vehicle for equitable development in a cold market.

Cold-market challenges. What are some of the conditions and challenges for doing community development in cold-market areas? By its very nature, a cold-market city or neighborhood suffers from a lack of investment and has relatively little economic activity. Within these geographies, economic opportunity for low-income residents is typically scarce and may lead to declining or unstable populations. The relative lack of private economic activity is often matched, moreover, by limited public investment in services and infrastructure.

> Just because property values have declined in a cold market does not mean that housing tenure is secure.

Spillover effects of a depressed economy are reflected in the built environment. Elevated vacancy levels are a common attribute of cold markets, including both unoccupied or abandoned buildings and vacant or undeveloped land. When vacancy levels climb, the condition and value of the overall building stock begins to deteriorate. Declining property values attract unscrupulous speculators looking to drain the remaining value at the further expense of the building stock and to the detriment of existing residents. This speculative activity is frequently carried out by absentee owners — investors with no connection to the community and no qualms about extracting wealth from struggling residents and their neighborhoods. These conditions invariably put a strain on local government, as property tax revenues wither and the requisite finances for public services begin to evaporate. Public education, infrastructure, public works, parks, and other public facilities — the basic building blocks of civic life — can languish as a result of diminished municipal revenues. Thus begins a vicious, self-reinforcing web of disinvestment and deterioration that is difficult to arrest.

Just because property values have declined in a cold market does not mean that housing tenure is secure. Nor does it mean that housing quality is safe and healthy or that rents are affordable relative to wages. Evictions occur across the entire strong-market/weak-market continuum in the United States, with especially high concentrations in many cold-market areas of the American South, and disproportionate impacts for low-income, African-American, and female-headed households.[7]

While low-income renters are the most vulnerable in this regard, market-rate homeownership is not necessarily more secure. One indication is the ten million home foreclosures that occurred during the Great Recession, beginning in 2008. Another indication is the enormous number of "severely cost-burdened" homeowners in the United States who earn below the median income for their area and pay more than half their income for housing. In cold-market areas, homeownership might be relatively more affordable for households of modest means, compared to hot-market cities, but it may still be out of reach because wages have stagnated amidst a distressed economy. Moreover, for households who do manage to buy a home in cold-market places, the quality of that housing may be low, especially at the bottom end of the market. And for cost-burdened homeowners, there is usually little money left after paying their monthly housing bills to keep up with necessary repairs.

For residents living in areas where these types of conditions exist, there can be deep physical and psychological trauma, as well as other health-negating influences, including a lack of access to essential services and healthy food options, limited opportunities for sufficient and meaningful work, fractured networks of social capital, poor housing conditions, and overall neighborhood distress. All are fundamental determinants of health and well-being. All tend to deteriorate in a cold-market city or neighborhood where opportunity is restricted.

Cold-market assets. Despite the compounding negative conditions facing residents of cold-market cities and neighborhoods, these places are also replete with many positive and potentially productive assets. The challenge is how to utilize and to leverage those assets in a context of scarcity. Conditions will vary from one place to another, but there are four key assets that may form the basis for CLT development in cold-market areas.

First, land may be plentiful and relatively inexpensive. This is typically one of the most significant barriers to CLT expansion in hot-market areas. By contrast, in cold markets, land that is undeveloped, underutilized, or vacant is often more plentiful — and potentially less costly.

Second, the market demand for buildings (along with land) of any type (residential, commercial, industrial, etc.) is likely suppressed, which may be accompanied by deteriorated physical conditions, tax delinquency, or functional obsolescence. These are not insignificant challenges in terms of liability and the resources needed for acquisition,

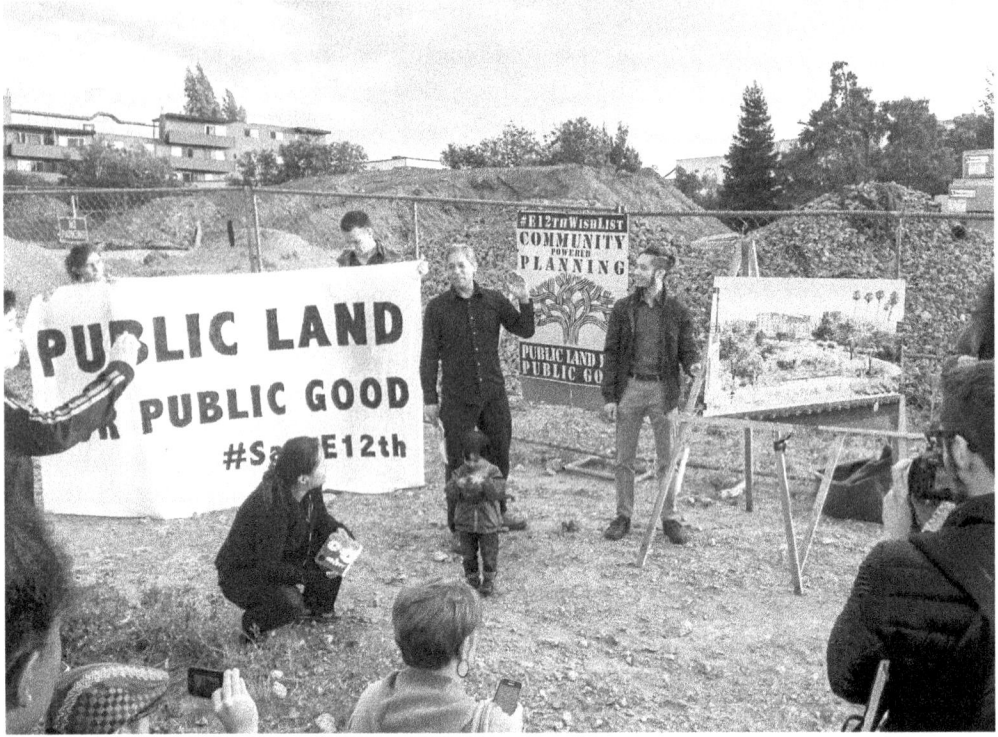

Fig. 4.2. Resident leaders of the East 12th Street Coalition, Oakland, California, demanding community involvement in planning for the redevelopment of land.

rehabilitation, or even demolition, yet a building stock with limited demand and a low cost may still provide an opportunity for CLT development.

Third, people with roots in any place-based community are its most valuable asset. Long-time residents, newcomers, children, families, elders, the displaced, and the house-less — all form the potential base of people-power, waiting to be engaged, to lead, and to craft new solutions to old problems.[8]

Finally, most cold-market places already have a set of community development enti-ties, nonprofit organizations, and faith-based institutions working in and among the com-munity, providing social services and tackling many of the problems noted above. These groups can be sources of financial, technical, and political support for a new CLT. In some cases, a preexisting organization may even take the lead in initiating a CLT or choose to house a fledgling CLT under its corporate umbrella.[9]

These place-based assets provide the opportunity to think expansively about the value and possibilities of the CLT model in areas where the economic rationale around perma-nent affordability — the most frequently touted benefit of CLTs — is less than compel-ling due to prevailing market conditions. If the looming loss of housing affordability as a market feature is not a pressing issue, however, then why else might a community want to consider creation of a CLT? Some strategic possibilities are considered below.

BEYOND HOMEOWNERSHIP: EXPLORING THE MYRIAD OPTIONS FOR COMMUNITY-OWNED LAND IN COLD MARKETS

One of the most powerful attributes of the CLT model is its versatility; it is deployable across a range of land uses and societal needs, as identified by its community. Yet, this broad applicability has been underutilized as CLTs have grown in popularity for a primary use: affordable housing in general, and owner-occupied housing in particular.

> Community-led development on community-owned land is the essence of a CLT.

The scant attention paid to CLT development in cold-market areas, therefore, may derive in part from the manner in which the field has advanced over the past several decades. CLTs have become largely synonymous with the production and stewardship of *permanently affordable homeownership*. This is undoubtedly an important and laudable achievement. But narrowing the model's focus to a single purpose has resulted in minimizing the importance of a more fundamental building block: community-owned and community-governed land. Indeed, it can be argued that community-led development on community-owned land is the essence of a CLT, rather than the permanent affordability of owner-occupied housing. The former is *the* feature that connects the CLT of today to the founders of New Communities, Inc. and their struggle for justice, liberation, and self-determination.[10]

The framework of community-led development on community-owned land forms the basis for considering the strategic potential of CLTs in cold-market areas. It provides an opening to explore nascent possibilities for project development and collective action that are currently under-examined and undervalued in the burgeoning CLT field, at least in the United States. Beyond permanently affordable homeownership, the range of opportunity for CLTs is extensive. Many housing-oriented CLTs have, in fact, already expanded their purviews to include projects with non-residential land uses, with affiliated or mission-supporting lines of business. A cursory look at some of these expansive uses and creative possibilities will help to demonstrate the potential for community-owned land in cold-market areas.

Community Gardens, Sustainable Agriculture, and Open Space

One of the most common non-residential uses of CLT land has been for food production. This option may be particularly relevant in low-income, cold-market neighborhoods where access to fresh and healthy food is often limited. There are plentiful examples of existing CLTs that steward land for growing food and food-related businesses.[11] These range from small infill community gardens to multi-acre farms and large-scale open space and agricultural land conservation. In cold-market areas where vacant land may be relatively accessible (either via fee simple ownership or long-term leasing arrangements managed by a CLT), small-scale urban agriculture or community gardening can serve as a catalytic starting point for new organizations that may not yet have the capacity or resources to undertake larger or costlier real estate projects. Additionally, the activation of an underutilized or problematic parcel with neighborhood residents and partners can serve as a powerful community-building and organizing vehicle to develop goodwill, awareness, and support for additional activities on community-owned land.

As one example, the first property acquired by the Parkdale Neighbourhood Land Trust (PNLT) in Toronto, Canada was a site for gardening, and has served as a successful precursor to other CLT acquisitions. In 2017, PNLT acquired the 7,000 square-foot Milky Way Garden parcel to be permanently preserved as a community-controlled asset. The site plays a particularly vital role for newcomers from Tibet to build community and to grow culturally-appropriate produce. The campaign to acquire the lot also played a galvanizing role to raise funds from community residents and to bolster awareness of the mission of the CLT. PNLT owns the lot and is active in facilitating the community vision for the parcel, leasing the land to a partner organization to manage on a day-to-day basis.

On a much larger scale, the Athens Land Trust (ALT) in Athens, Georgia has established an impressive program of land conservation and community agriculture in addition to their affordable housing work. As of 2017, the Athens Land Trust had protected 16,485 acres of land in 36 Georgia counties via both conservation easements and ownership. These holdings included "natural habitats and river frontage, working agricultural land and land of historical significance, and land for public recreation."[12] Additionally, ALT's vibrant community agricultural program provides much-needed access to land — as well as programmatic support — for growing food and food-related businesses. As a steward of land across a diverse range of uses, ALT utilizes these assets to create programs

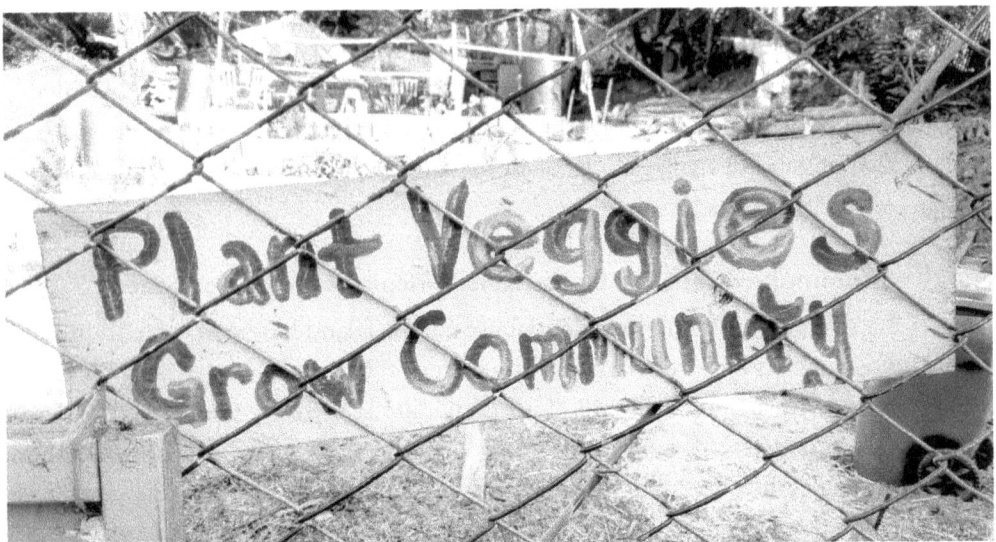

Fig. 4.3. Community garden, Oakland, California.

offering paid career development and training opportunities for young people in the construction trades, urban farming, and land conservation—all with an eye toward nurturing future generations of local leadership around land-based justice and opportunity.

Commercial Land Uses

Commercial uses for community-owned land span an incredibly diverse mix of options and scales. The possibilities are endless, limited only by what a community can envision and by what a municipality will permit according to its zoning and building codes. In the commercial context, as with other CLT land tenure arrangements, a CLT can play the foundational role of acquiring land and leasing it out to support community-prioritized economic development, or the CLT can own and manage both the land and the improvements.[13] Existing commercial CLT uses include not only stewarding land and buildings for mission-aligned nonprofit and community-serving organizations, but also for more unusual uses such as a gas station in a rural California coastal community (the Bolinas CLT's Bo-Gas) and a mobile meat-processing facility in rural Washington State (Lopez CLT).

In cold-market areas, a CLT might play a particularly valuable role in supporting non-residential strategies that produce targeted economic benefits and job opportunities for residents who have been harmed by disinvestment. To cite an example from another country, the Homebaked CLT in Liverpool, England got started in 2012 as a reaction to a top-down, government-initiated urban renewal plan to demolish a swath of historic buildings in the neighborhood of Anfield.[14] In response, residents coalesced around a vision to save a cherished neighborhood bakery, turning it into a cooperatively owned business. The Homebaked CLT was established to acquire the bakery building and to implement a community-led vision for redeveloping the neighborhood's commercial district. Saving the bakery served as the catalyzing project by: initiating the CLT; preserving a visible anchor business; and laying the groundwork for a more expansive agenda for community-owned land in the neighborhood.

Back in the USA, the Lopez CLT in Washington State serves as the steward for a number of commercial storefronts that provide incubator space for small, local businesses. All twelve of the businesses that utilize these spaces are owned by homeowner-leaseholders of the Lopez CLT. Connecting economic and housing security, these commercial spaces offer CLT residents an opportunity to build individual assets in ways that do not put their homes at risk, while generating local economic benefits that circulate within the community.

Subsidiary, Affiliated, and Mutually-Supporting Businesses

Across the national landscape, there are more and more cases of CLTs creating affiliated entities or businesses that either bolster the work of the CLT or create aligned opportunities for CLT residents and members. For instance, both Proud Ground, a CLT in

Portland, Oregon, and the Northern California Land Trust in Berkeley, California have established real estate brokerages to support in-house property transactions and to generate revenue for the CLT through non-CLT transactions. One Roof Community Housing, a CLT in Duluth, Minnesota has set up a subsidiary firm to do construction and home rehabilitation for the parent organization. In Berkeley and Oakland, California, three CLTs have come together to explore the creation of a worker-owned property management cooperative to support the needs of resident-operated CLT properties, housing cooperatives, worker cooperatives, and other aligned organizations. It is envisioned that the property management cooperative will leverage the skills of existing CLT residents and co-op worker-owners to provide basic property management services as well as capacity building among a broad network of allied organizations.

CLT as Steward and Supporter of Community Health and Stability

As John Emmeus Davis has reminded us, the stewardship function of a CLT is not just about maintaining affordability — it also includes the preservation of housing *quality* and *security*.[15] Even in markets where affordability may not be a pressing concern, there are important roles a CLT can play in supporting residents with maintenance, repair, and overall housing quality, as well as intervening to cure defaults, advocating for better public policies and services with and for CLT homeowners and tenants, and preventing displacement via foreclosure or eviction.

Some of these services may also be offered to non-CLT residents, particularly in areas where such services are lacking. Many existing CLTs, for example, already provide pre- and post-purchase homeowner education, credit counseling, and income and asset development coaching for anyone living within their service area, regardless of whether they are CLT homeowners. Depending upon what is needed in a community, a CLT might offer home repair and maintenance support, small business coaching and loans, tenant legal services, and various forms of renter, homebuyer, homeowner, and homelessness assistance.[16]

BEYOND DEVELOPMENT:
PLANNING, ORGANIZING, AND BUILDING POWER

In cold-market areas where housing affordability is not a priority issue, there may still be significant barriers to engagement, democratic participation, and decision-making related to intersecting economic, political, and ecological issues that disproportionately impact low-income residents and people of color. For these reasons, the resident-centered governance structure of a CLT can serve as a hub to meaningfully assess, analyze, and advance the needs of those struggling most severely in a cold market. Further, a CLT can be a potent vehicle for leadership development, resident organizing, and base-building as a precursor to actually pursuing community-led real estate activities.[17] Community organizing and base-building can, in turn, help to nurture the conditions in which a CLT emerges, grows, and thrives. An organized cohort of resident leaders and CLT members can hold elected officials accountable, exert political pressure when needed, and wield the people-power required to evidence a demand for community-led development on community-owned land.

The Dudley Street Neighborhood Initiative (DSNI) — and its affiliated CLT, Dudley Neighbors, Inc. (DNI) — in the Roxbury section of Boston provide instructive examples of community organizing and base-building in what was once a cold-market neighborhood. DNI is frequently touted as one of the most successful community land trusts in the United States, although few other CLTs have taken up their intentional model of broad-based resident empowerment and community-led planning and development. That approach to community development remains as audacious today as it was in 1984 when DSNI was founded.[18]

From the outset, DSNI was strategically oriented to support two core activities: place-based organizing of neighborhood residents and resident-led visioning and planning. When combined with the organization's affiliated community land trust, these activities comprised the productive inputs for enacting a community-building strategy on community-owned and community-controlled land.[19] This approach remains particularly vital because it puts the leadership of existing residents at the center of a strategy that builds

Fig. 4.4. Alliance of Californians for Community Empowerment. Oakland CLT homeowners, Shekinah Samaya-Thomas and Chris Thomas, join Vanessa Bulnes (with megaphone), advocating for resident-controlled housing on community-owned land.

upon both individual and community capacities and assets. In cities and neighborhoods where low-income residents and communities of color have been systematically disempowered and traumatized by market activity and public policy, this is a fundamental first step toward a restorative, just, and equitable redistribution of power. As Gus Newport, DSNI's former executive director, has observed:

> To successfully redevelop neighborhoods which have become blighted through years of neglect due to bank "redlining," failed government programs and poor planning, the only way that these areas can be turned around is with the will and involvement of concerned neighbors. A true foundation which will assure long term participation and neighborhood stabilization only happens when people can see and feel that their involvement and control (empowerment) is real. Anything short of this will result in additional failure, which is what we have in the majority of inner cities across the United States.[20]

BEYOND THE COLD-MARKET PRESENT: PLANNING FOR A JUST AND EQUITABLE FUTURE

Market Conditions Change: Safeguarding the Future

For people affiliated with CLTs in warm-market or hot-market areas, it is common to wistfully ponder an alternate reality in which the CLT might have emerged a decade or two earlier, when land and housing cost a fraction of current prices. By contrast, in cold-market areas, few people can imagine a future reality when costs will soar and a wave of investment and high-end development will threaten to displace low-income and moderate-income residents who are presently there. How can these two disparate perspectives be reconciled?

Equitable development is possible, but it must be coaxed into existence with political pressure and inclusive, democratic participation.

History serves as a guide on a specific point related to the failure of markets to provide for those most in need and the inability of political institutions to anticipate or to pre-emptively set the stage for truly equitable outcomes from development. Disinvestment has often been a precursor to new waves of private investment in stagnant real estate markets. The priority of government officials in such situations is often to incentivize *any* investment in housing or commercial development, rather than risk scaring investors away by requiring the benefits of development to be shared with residents who are most in need.

Equitable development is possible, but it must be coaxed into existence with political pressure and inclusive, democratic participation. This provides a basic rationale for building the infrastructure of a CLT in the absence of an imminent threat of displacement. Quite simply, local residents, who are often excluded from participating in development decisions, deserve a seat at the table. In many communities, the only way to assert this right is to organize, to build community power, to demand accountability, and to take control of development under the collective formation of a CLT.

There is also a need for a more nuanced understanding of the profound temporal balancing act in which CLTs are engaged. CLTs hold land for community benefit for a very long time. While CLTs and their members enact programs that address immediate resident-identified needs, CLTs must simultaneously uphold an extraordinary long-term vision for land reform and social justice. This delicate balance of community priorities across different timelines is a rarely acknowledged and woefully underappreciated hallmark of the CLT. In a cold market, the organizational container to hold land and to promote equitable development across a longer arc of time may reveal new avenues for pursuing community resilience and sustainability.

Markets Are the Problem: Planning for a Future We Actually Want

Given the legacy and persistence of racial discrimination in housing and urban development and the disparate impact of development on specific populations, it is practical for a historically deprived and disempowered community to demand more control over the ownership, use, and development of land. In cold-market areas, in particular, it is both logical and strategic to pursue alternative solutions rather than the same top-down, market-reliant approaches that have harmed, disenfranchised, and marginalized communities in the past.

There is a growing cohort of community development organizers and practitioners who view the common stewardship of land as part of a fundamental bridge to an emancipatory future that will supplant the current market-based system. These explicitly visionary, transformational, and political efforts are ambitious roadmaps for a *just transition* to a more equitable, healthy, and sustainable future.[21]

Cooperation Jackson in Jackson, Mississippi provides an especially compelling example of a comprehensive project for sustainable, resident-led development, economic democracy, and community ownership. Jackson is a city that exhibits many features of a cold market. The organizers of Cooperation Jackson understand, however, that should the local economy eventually improve through market-based approaches, the needs of Jackson's black and brown residents are unlikely to be met.

Kali Akuno of Cooperation Jackson sees a strategic opportunity in the fact that Jackson's economy is presently depressed. It creates "breathing room" on the margins to envision and to enact a grand plan for a better, more just future. In his words:

> We harness this breathing room by exploiting the fact that there is minimal competition in the area to serve as a distraction or dilution of our focus, a tremendous degree of pent-up social demand waiting to be fulfilled and a deep reservoir of unrealized human potential waiting to be tapped.[22]

Along with a solidarity network of democratically-run, worker-owned cooperative enterprises, Cooperation Jackson has developed the Fannie Lou Hamer Community Land Trust as a core element of its long-term vision for developing and sustaining a new economic base for local residents. The importance of bringing more land into the CLT is one of long-term survival in the face of ongoing racial discrimination and economic austerity. As Akuno has said: "If the land shifts, the power shifts."[23]

Restoring Indigenous Land Stewardship

For those who come to the CLT in search of a model for land-based justice, many believe that the only way to achieve a truly just and equitable future will be to acknowledge and to repair the centuries of harm that have been inflicted upon indigenous peoples through colonial systems of enclosure, exclusion, and expropriation of tribal lands.

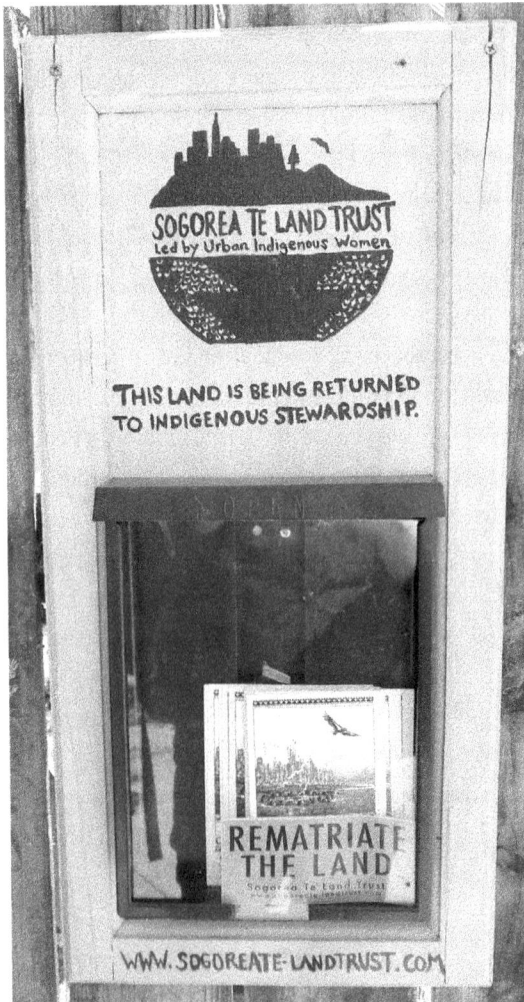

Fig. 4.5. Rammay Garden, Sogorea Te Land Trust, West Oakland, California, 2019.

Indigenous women leaders of the Sogorea Te Land Trust in Northern California provide one example. They are developing a new pathway to return ancestral Chochenyo and Karkin Ohlone lands to indigenous steward-ship. Their vision is to restore sacred Ohlone land to a state that precedes and transcends the market-based system of private property. The leaders of the Sogorea Te Land Trust are seed-ing a transformative conversation that invites all residents of the Bay Area to reevaluate their relationship to the land they inhabit and to acknowledge that indigenous people co-inhabit their ancestral homelands alongside non-native residents, despite a con-tested history.

CLTs everywhere have an import-ant role to play as allies in support of indigenous land struggles. In the particular context of cold markets, one potential avenue for advocacy resides in the re-conveyance of land that has been cheapened in terms of market logic, but may hold deep religious or cultural value for indigenous peoples.

In some cold-market neighborhoods, cities, and regions, a depressed economy with devalued real estate may present a unique opportunity, where a restorative conversation around returning land to indigenous stewardship could take root.

⏤

CONCLUSION

Even in stable markets with established CLTs, private and public support for community-led development on community-owned land often remains tenuous. The model has yet to gain the broad-based acceptance it deserves, despite the stellar performance of CLTs to date.[24] Given that many CLTs work exclusively in communities of color and that most CLT housing is developed for low-income households, the inequitable distribution of resources to support the development and expansion of affordable housing on CLT land must necessarily be viewed as a racial and economic justice issue. This is a reality affecting hot, cold, and lukewarm markets alike.

> The lack of resources being made available for the expansion of CLTs in the USA is due less to what a CLT is, than to who it benefits.

The lack of resources being made available for the expansion of CLTs in the USA is due less to what a CLT *is,* than to *who* it benefits. It is a reflection of how deeply entrenched the current system of housing delivery remains; how little room there is for models of tenure that push beyond the reductive dichotomy of renting versus owning; and how little political will there is to reform that system to allow more just forms of landownership to flourish in all markets.

CLTs continue to be criticized by skeptics for "not getting to scale," measured solely in terms of the number of housing units in a CLT's portfolio. A rejoinder to this narrow conception of scale has been offered by Zachary Murray of the Oakland CLT, who points out that many grassroots CLTs are seeking to elevate something far more fundamental: community control of land in places where, for generations, residents have been denied any sort of collective control over how land has been used or developed. It can also be said that scale should be measured *horizontally,* counting the number of communities that have adopted strategies that put land use decision-making and long-term control in the hands of residents who have been systematically and historically cut out of the frame.

To date, cold-market cities and neighborhoods have been an overlooked part of the horizontal potential and performance of CLTs. As the CLT model continues the long journey towards acceptance and professionalization, however, there exists an opportunity to apply the model in places and ways that go beyond its current hot-market focus on preserving the affordability of owner-occupied housing. In this context, cold markets are prime areas for CLT invention and exploration. They provide opportunities for community-led development on community-owned land that include more than housing;

opportunities to build resilient models of democratic participation and governance through which residents can influence current and *future* development; and opportunities to restore land justice in communities that have been harmed by government policy, market activity, and white supremacy. The road may be rockier in cold markets, but the long-term growth, vitality, and acceptance of the CLT movement demands a model that is inclusive and deployable in any market.

Notes

1. Susan Witt and Robert Swann, "Land: Challenge and Opportunity," Schumacher Center for a New Economics, May 1995. (*https://centerforneweconomics.org/publications/land-challenge-and-opportunity/*).

2. Alan Mallach, T*he Divided City: Poverty and Prosperity in Urban America* (Washington, DC: Island Press, 2018).

3. Myungshik Choi, Shannon Van Zandt, and David Matarrita-Cascante, "Can community land trusts slow gentrification?" *Journal of Urban Affairs,* 40:3, 394-411 (2018).

4. Various terms are used throughout this essay to refer to cold-market areas, including struggling, declining, weak, divided, declining, or shrinking — mainly echoing the range of descriptors used in the voluminous literature on urban decline. Admittedly, these terms are imprecise and not necessarily synonyms. Note, too, that this essay does not take a position on geographic scale, recognizing that weak-market dynamics are relative and can play out at the neighborhood, city, and/or regional level.

5. John Emmeus Davis, "Homes That Last," *Shelterforce,* National Housing Institute, December 2008 (*https://shelterforce.org/2008/12/22/homes_that_last/*).

6. Emily Thaden, "Stable Home Ownership in a Turbulent Economy: Delinquencies and Foreclosures Remain Low in Community Land Trusts," Lincoln Institute of Land Policy, Working Paper WP11ET1, July 2011.

7. Max Blau, "Black Southerners Are Bearing the Brunt of America's Eviction Epidemic," Stateline [online], January 18, 2019 (*https://www.pewtrusts.org/en/research-and-analysis/blogs/stateline/2019/01/18/black-southerners-are-bearing-the-brunt-of-americas-eviction-epidemic*). T. Cookson, et. al., *Losing Home: The Human Cost of Eviction in Seattle,* A Report by the Seattle Women's Commission and the Housing Justice Project of the King County Bar Association, September 2018 (*https://www.kcba.org/Portals/0/pbs/pdf/Losing%20Home%202018.pdf*). Matthew Desmond, "Poor Black Women Are Evicted at Alarming Rates, Setting Off a Chain of Hardship," MacArthur Foundation Policy Research Brief, March 2014 (*https://www.macfound.org/media/files/HHM_Research_Brief_-_Poor_Black_Women_Are_Evicted_at_Alarming_Rates.pdf*).

8. The "displaced" are included here because there are many instances of people maintaining connections to neighborhoods from which they've been displaced. Folks who have been forced to move away from a neighborhood in which their families may have lived for several generations, frequently make the trek back to attend church, to shop, or to see family and friends. Many would welcome the chance to return — and a CLT might be a vehicle to facilitate their return. A handful of cities have adopted "right to return" policies or given housing preferences for displaced residents.

9. Existing groups can also be gatekeepers to accessing essential resources and knowledge or can be dismissive of innovative ideas and approaches — both common reactions to new CLT efforts in areas where the model is unfamiliar.

10. "Community-led development on community-owned land" aka "common ground" is John Davis' phrasing. John Emmeus Davis, "Common Ground: Community-Owned Land as a Platform for Equitable and Sustainable Development," *University of San Francisco Law Review,* Vol 51, No. 1, 2014.

11. Greg Rosenberg and Jeffrey Yuen have surveyed the field and compiled a useful compendium of both agricultural and commercial CLT projects. See Greg Rosenberg and Jeffrey Yuen, "Beyond Housing: Urban Agriculture and Commercial Development by Community Land Trusts," Lincoln Institute of Land Policy, Working Paper WP13GR1, 2012.

12. Athens Land Trust, "2017 Annual Report." (*https://athenslandtrust.org/wp-content/uploads/2019/01/2017-Annual-Report-1.2.19-1.pdf*).

13. For a discussion of opportunities and challenges for commercial CLT applications, see: Elizabeth Sorce, "The Role of Community Land Trusts in Preserving and Creating Commercial Assets: A Dual Case Study of Rondo CLT in St. Paul, Minnesota and Crescent City CLT in New Orleans, Louisiana" (2012). University of New Orleans Theses and Dissertations. Paper 1501 (*http://scholarworks.uno.edu/td/1501*).

14. See the Homebaked CLT website for more information: (*http://homebaked.org.uk/about/we_are_homebaked/*).

15. John Emmeus Davis, "Homes That Last," op. cit.

16. Services that are offered to residents who do not live in CLT housing may enable a CLT to diversify its revenues, gaining access to new sources funding.

17. Many CLTs adopt strong community organizing and political strategies in advance of — or alongside — actual real estate development work. For instance, TRUST South LA has a vibrant resident-centered transportation and mobility justice program that advocates for healthy, walkable, and "bikeable" streets — a major quality-of-life issue for residents of this Los Angeles neighborhood. In New Orleans, the Jane Place

Neighborhood Sustainability Initiative has advanced a robust advocacy agenda around the impacts of short-term rentals (such as AirBnB) on the growing affordability crisis, as a separate yet related component of their CLT work.

18. For a history of the early years of DSNI, see Peter Medoff and Holly Sklar, *Streets of Hope: The Fall and Rise of an Urban Neighborhood* (Boston, MA: South End Press, 1999) and *Holding Ground: The Rebirth of Dudley Street* [Video], directed by Mark Lipman and Leah Mahan, Holding Ground Productions, 1997.

19. Dudley Street Neighborhood Initiative, *From the Bottom Up: The Dudley Street Neighborhood Initiative Strategy for Sustainable Economic Development,* Unpublished Draft Manuscript, November 1997.

20. Eugene "Gus" Newport, *The Dudley Street Neighborhood Initiative, Roxbury, Massachusetts: History and Observations,* Unpublished Manuscript, July 1991.

21. On the concept of "just transition," see Movement Generation Justice and Ecology Project, *From Banks and Tanks to Cooperation and Caring: A Strategic Framework for a Just Transition.* (*https://movementgeneration.org/wp-content/uploads/2016/11/JT_booklet_Eng_printspreads.pdf*).

22. Kali Akuno, "Build and Fight: The Program and Strategy of Cooperation Jackson," in Cooperation Jackson (Kali Akuno, Sacajawea Hall, and Brandon King) and Ajamu Nangwaya (eds.), *Jackson Rising: The Struggle for Economic Democracy and Black Self-Determination in Jackson, Mississippi,* Daraja Press, 2017.

23. Hazel Sheffield, "Cooperation Jackson on How to Build an Alternative Economy for People of Colour," The Independent UK, May 31, 2019 (*https://www.independent.co.uk/news/business/indyventure/cooperation-jackson-solidarity-economy-neoliberalism-alternatives-a8936801.html*).

24. This has been correctly characterized as a new form of redlining — a systemic bias in both the government and finance sectors that are connected to real estate, housing, and social programs. See: John Emmeus Davis, "A New Kind of Redlining: Punishing Success," *Shelterforce,* May 6, 2013 (*https://shelterforce.org/2013/05/06/a_new_kind_of_redlining_punishing_success/*).

5.

Challenges for the New Kid
on the Block—Collective Property

Liz Alden Wily

A study was published in July 2018 by the World Resources Institute, examining the quest of private companies to secure formal title to land, compared to communities looking to do the same (Notes et al., 2018). Companies found titling to be easy and fast, while communities struggled with complex and costly procedures. This was hardly surprising given the heated climate of globalized demand for land in which "ease of doing business" has become a benchmark. More interesting was that the driving question was no longer "is it possible for communities to register as owners?" The study simply presumed the answer to be "yes."

This reflects changing times for the nearly three billion land dependents who acquire and hold lands through customary, neo-customary, or more recently, state-established community-based tenure systems. At six to seven billion hectares, the global community's land area is half or more of the world's lands (LandMark, 2019). Less than one-fifth of this is formally registered, and public maps of these lands cover less than fifteen percent (15 percent) of these. Nevertheless, it is now possible for communities in *most* countries to secure lands as their formal property, as indicated in state-compiled land registers. While a great deal is involved in reaching the point of registration for communities, this possibility contrasts starkly with the situation 50 years past.

In fact, the strength of legal change affecting collective landholding suggests that this may feature prominently in the land registers of the world by the end of the current century. By hectares, community property may eventually account for the largest sector of state-recognized landholdings.

If this is so, it will be no mean achievement in context of the (very) long *dureé*, considering that Aristotle and Plato feistily debated the relative merits of individual and communal tenure two-and-a-half millennia ago (Pipes, 1999). The matter was put to bed by Rome a millennium later (509 BC–AD 395) as the city state expanded into an empire, turning thousands of captured hectares into *ager publicus* (public land) for disposal by the Emperor to (privileged) individuals. The next millennium saw these Roman norms profoundly shape European property law and, thence, the statutory laws of effectively all 195 modern states today. The odd exception aside (Mexico in the 1930s stands out), it has only been during the last half century that states have come to recognize communally held lands as something more than permissive occupation on unowned or government lands.

> Collective lands are, at one and the same time, material property and an inseparable regime of community-based land governance.

Before this new development is explored, questions arise. First, *what exactly is the identity of this exciting and perhaps excitable new kid on the property block?* Depending on the country and framework, collective property is termed communal, collective, customary, native, indigenous, or community land. These properties are variously vested directly in the community or held in trust for them by a cooperative, shareholding, or non-shareholding and nonprofit body like a community land trust, the subject of the present volume.

The most common feature across the species is that the landholding has a socio-spatial basis involving residents who have an identifiable social identity as communities or groups. These are not corporations comprising remote or disparate individuals, acting for disparate shareholders unknown to each other. It is also usual for the social group to hold lawful decision-making rights. Collective lands are, at one and the same time, material property and an inseparable regime of community-based land governance.

A second question might be: as land is a finite resource, with little of it beyond the polar regions that is deemed unowned today, *where is this supposed cornucopia of collective holdings coming from?*

The answer is that these collective holdings derive almost entirely from *ager publicus,* which modern governments define as their own property under government, state, national, public or similar categories. Thousands of rural communities live therein, their traditional right-holding arrangements overlaid by such classifications, reducing them in law to tenants at will. This has made them easy to evict for greater ambitions of the state, including the plethora of large-scale allocations to foreign and local investors. It is the belated transformation of ownerless occupancy into legally protected property interests that principally anchors contemporary tenure reforms. And, as elaborated later, it is anxiety by governments around the consequent decline in the scale of the state-controlled *ager publicus* that poses the greatest constraint to the delivery of acknowledged community property, beyond legal declamations that this exists or can be entrenched through formalization.

A third question is: *Why would modern communities prefer to secure lands collectively rather than through individual entitlement?* To generalize, settled farming communities in particular *do* seek private rights to well-established house plots and farms within community domains. However, while permanent farmland will expand from its present 11–15 percent of global land area (FAO, 2015), the larger resource of most communities is comprised of naturally collective forests, rangelands, swamps, steep areas, and arid lands. These landscapes are neither easily nor productively divisible into individual parcels and, where shifting cultivation is practiced, not all areas are distinct from farms. The importance of shared off-farm land resources to livelihood and socio-culture is such that communities are loathe to lose them.

The habit of Twentieth Century farm titling programmes of co-opting all but permanent farms as government property has also left a legacy which communities do not want to see extended in de facto compulsory individualization, where this remains the only means to gain state recognition of rights. Communities are equally wary of losing the accessible, adaptable, and cost-free decision-making and dispute resolution that governs community-based tenure. Millions of rural communities have seen these powers transferred to remote government offices, not easy or free to access or to hold to account (Bruce *et al.*, 2013). State trusteeship of customary lands has been a particularly ripe arrangement for abuse. Sustaining the right to *govern* local landholding has become a core element of community land claims today.

> Sustaining the right to govern local landholding has become a core element of community land claims today.

The same concerns can be found among communities in fertile zones whose domains are almost entirely comprised of family properties, such as in Fiji, Gabon, or family lands across the Caribbean. Even without substantial collective assets to protect, community jurisdiction over rural lands continues to provide social assurance of rights, continuity in social norms (such as around land inheritance), protection from elite land-capturing interests, and solidarity for decision-making where single voices against external threats do not prevail. These concerns are echoed in urban areas, as noted in other essays in the present volume, examining community land trusts.

This helps to answer a fourth pair of questions: *Is collective property only relevant to the rural domain, and is not the rural domain declining with urbanization?*

To address the second of the pair first, this presumption needs modification. While cities and towns indisputably dominate in terms of population, they absorb surprisingly little land, from one to three percent globally, not expected to exceed eight to ten percent by the century's end (Mertes *et al.*, 2015). It is true that rural population growth is not expected to keep growing, other than in Africa and Asia where absolute numbers will rise (UN, 2018). A high proportion of community lands are in these regions. In

> There exists a massively untapped potential for the adoption of collective property norms in urban areas.

addition, rural communities already face soaring demand for a share of their lands by urban dwellers with origins in those villages (Jayne *et al.* 2016). Classical distinctions between rural and urban domains is becoming more, not less, blurred in agrarian economies, supporting findings that many urban dwellers want to see home rural communities and their lands survive. And while, ideally, farms will expand and intensify to help feed 11 billion people by 2100, even if this has tripled by that year, the major land resource will remain neither urban nor farmed, but exist in billions of hectares which are by character naturally communal — forests, pastures, waterlands, mountains, etc. Not surprisingly, communities are their logical guardians. As failures in resource conservation rise and threats of climate change mount, the formal empowerment of communities as forest and rangeland owners has risen as an advocated strategy, with most implementation thus far in the natural forest sector (RRI, 2018).

Meantime, there exists a massively untapped potential for the adoption of collective property norms in urban areas, especially in city slums where 2.5 billion will live by 2050, the majority of them in Asia and Africa. This is because the poorest live in fragile shelters on parcels too small to render individual titling a practical path for regularization of occupancy. These are also areas where community (neighborhood) governance evolves as a matter of necessity to provide services and to protect human rights. Even when slum dwellers have the opportunity to convert compressed shacks into a high-rise apartment block, inclusion requires cooperation and solidarity. It is partly in light of this urban potential that it was suggested earlier that collective tenure, despite roadblocks, could become the major form of property in time.

How realistic is this? This is a hard call, because another reality is that a legal framework for collective property may widely exist on paper, but is complex to achieve in practice. The rest of this essay looks at what exists in law, and the constraints confronting this reform.

LEGAL PROVISION FOR COLLECTIVE PROPERTY

A global comparison of 100 national land laws in 2018 found that 73 of these laws provide for communities to secure lands as collective owners (Alden Wily, 2018). In addition, two-thirds stipulate that collective properties enjoy legal force and effect on a par with registered individual and corporate properties.

Such provisions have historically been most prevalent in Latin America and Oceania and, more recently, in Africa. They are least available in the Middle East. In Europe, some countries have never extinguished communal landholding (e.g. Switzerland, Austria, Ireland, Norway, Sweden) and there has been a recent revival in countries like Spain and

Portugal, as the logical route to protect fire-threatened forests and pastures. There has also been resuscitation of suppressed community ownership of forests and pastures in some former Soviet Union states and satellites, since the Soviet Union's collapse in 1989. Examples are Romania, where communities now lawfully own and govern 800 communal forests and pastures, and Armenia, where the most local level of state cooperatives that existed under Soviet rule have been converted into some 400 community-owned and administered areas.

Types of socially-collective property vary. At one extreme are modern state-defined collectives, such as provided in one million rural communities in China, which together cover 49 percent of China, albeit with community control that is sometimes frustrated by the number of Communist Party directives. At the other extreme are parliaments which have seen to fit to simply declare, either in national constitutions or land laws, that customarily held lands are now deemed to be property, whether owned by individuals, families, or communities, thus covering all types of estates. This is now the case in around fifteen African countries, from Kenya to Mozambique to Liberia. Other laws are less fulsome in the support they provide, such as not fully liberating communities from root title held by chiefs or governments; or they fail to provide easy and cheap routes through which communities can double-lock their rights in entitlements. In between these extremes are tenures like the community land trust, where lands are held by a community-controlled NGO, which acquires, holds, and manages real property on behalf of a place-based community.

> Thousands of communities are already titled owners.

Thousands of communities are already titled owners. Examples include: the case of China above; indigenous communities in Australia and Canada, who respectively hold title to 30 and 44 percent of the acreage in those countries; 32,000 indigenous and farming communities, who own 52 percent of Mexico; 7,200 indigenous and farming communities in Peru; and an estimated 20 percent of the Philippines that is subject to Certificates of Ancestral Title of Domain. There are other examples, including Fiji, Vanuatu, Papua New Guinea, Tanzania, Mozambique, Malawi, Mali, and Uganda, where titling is not compulsory. On paper, customary ownership is unaffected, although case-by-case titling is underway. Arrangements differ. In Tanzania, 12,450 elected village councils legally govern tenure within their recorded domains. Although individual and family rights may be recorded in village land registers and certificates of title issued, the community must first record the shared lands to protect these from encroachment.

While many other cases of legally secure community-based tenures exist, the majority of community lands globally are not yet acknowledged and secured as property, nor have these lands been designated exclusively for community-based tenure and governance (RRI, 2015).

The 2018 study of national land laws found a significant difference between the 44 percent of countries in the study's sample that acknowledge community property as already

> Legal provision for community property has been slowly rising.

existing and protect these rights in principle, and the 55 percent of national laws that guarantee recognition and protection only where community property is formally adjudicated, surveyed, and registered. This opens the door for reluctant governmental administrations to delay titling.

Requirements to establish legal entities in which to vest title have also handicapped delivery of title to community property in several countries, including Peru and Australia. The Ivory Coast is notorious in this regard, where the titling procedure has proved so expensive and bureaucratic that not a single community has been successful since 1998. The law was amended in 2013 to ease this.

Legal provision for community property, however, has been slowly rising since 1980, especially since 2000 (49 percent of first-time legal provision). At least two new laws have been enacted since the study was published in mid-2018 (Liberia and Tunisia). At least ten more countries currently have bills in parliament (e.g. South Africa) or in circulated draft (e.g. Ghana), or under draft (e.g. Nepal, Myanmar, Sierra Leone, Indonesia). Demand remains high. Coverage is also expanding from indigenous peoples to populations of all types, recently including former slave communities in parts of Latin America. In fact, two-thirds of the laws examined by the World Resources Institute in 2018 did not specify the populations to which these laws applied. This trend is represented at the international level in the UN's *Declaration on the Rights of Peasants and Other People Working in Rural Areas* (2018), designed to cover all rural communities and requires, *inter alia*, individual and collective land rights to be upheld.

Legal content is also maturing. The newest laws strongly require inclusive decision-making within communities, including provisions for enabling members who have moved to cities for education or for work to be permitted to vote on matters specified as most important. Added to some of these laws is a requirement that lands be zoned or re-zoned to ensure that communal areas are not randomly encroached upon. Stipulations are also appearing requiring communities to record parcels under accepted exclusive family or individual usufruct, defined as inheritable and disposable interests in accordance with community rules.

These measures lessen the pressure to privatize all lands for the purpose of securing rights. Nevertheless, the desire to secure houses and farms as absolutely private property is quite likely to remain, ultimately subtracting such settlements from the overall community domain, focusing collective tenure on shared lands.

Meanwhile, it is more common today for new laws to define a place-based community as a juridical person, alleviating any need for the formation of a corporate entity in which to vest title. Some define community in such a manner that an urban community could adopt the same construct, which is already the case in Vietnam, Laos and China. Newest enactments, where some or all of the above are apparent, include countries as far apart as East Timor, Kenya, Liberia, Malawi, Mali, Vietnam, Tunisia and Vanuatu.

THE LIMITS OF LEGAL PROVISION

Of course, what the law says and how it is applied are different matters. Push-back can begin early, as in countries where governments fail to enact essential application decrees or regulations, even a decade after a law is enacted (e.g. Argentina and Angola). Quite a number of governments have taken years to budget for supporting institutional and survey services. Even where laws for titling community property have been enacted and applied, some governments have eventually found a reason to turn back the clock, enacting inhibiting regulations (e.g. Peru), halting new allocations (e.g. Brazil), or even doing away with the relevant law altogether (e.g., Antigua and Barbuda). Court rulings can also take their toll. In India, for example, the Supreme Court in February 2019 ordered that forest peoples be evicted in 21 states, potentially affecting 8 million of the poorest land-dependents, despite being guaranteed ownership under a Forest Rights Act of 2006. On appeal, a "stay" of the eviction was temporarily granted, returning the case to the Supreme Court.

> Orthodoxies die hard, including beliefs that collective landholding is archaic.

More subtle means of curtailing collective land rights occur through natural resource and investment laws, through which watersheds, traditionally-mined surface minerals, sites of cultural importance, and even public service areas which communities themselves have instituted on their lands, are redefined by the government as public, not community property. Declaration of investment zones and infrastructural corridors have the same effect. Public interest is often expanded to cover commercial investments and investment zones. Security zones requiring the eviction of all inhabitants also occurs. Another tactic being deployed is the accelerated official declaration ("gazettement") of state-owned protected areas. This removes yet more forest, wildlife-rich rangelands and waterlands from communities, all essential to local economies. In short, push-back from governments has been substantial.

Reasons for this are quite similar across regions. Orthodoxies die hard, including beliefs that collective landholding is archaic; that wealth creation and capital surplus for investment can only be triggered through individual or corporate accumulation; and that land markets only work with individual, fungible rights. The fact that communist regimes in the Twentieth Century co-opted and reconstructed collective tenure as state-owned production units also undermined the case for community-based collective property as a viable basis for economic growth. Insufficient progress has yet been made in demonstrating the contrary; namely, that growth and development can be achieved through strategic investment in community-owned land and co-owned investor-community enterprises, in which a place-based community is the lessor.

Instead, orthodoxies are being revitalized by the fast globalizing land market, feeding commercial and government capture of large lands in what has commonly been referred to as a "global land rush." A decade after the 2008 financial crisis, this land rush is no longer a temporary surge, but a fixture in bilateral trade relations. Untitled community lands are an obvious and easy target, encouraging governments to "adjust" the definitions of public, government, and community lands. Thousands of communities have been involuntarily displaced by their governments to make way for such land-based invest-ments and their supporting infrastructure.

Compulsory land acquisition laws are not being reformed as quickly as needed to make assistance for resettlement obligatory, nor to compensate takings at levels that come anywhere near to replacement costs. Governments are hardly proactive on these matters with the notable exception of India, due to landmark legislation in 2013. Laws in other countries may even limit rather than expand the grounds on which compensation is required in cases of compulsory acquisition and may value communal lands at levels far below their livelihood and social values.

Yet the greater source of governmental reluctance to move forward swiftly to help com-munities to double-lock their land domains in formal titles stems from a belated recogni-tion by governments that, by acknowledging community ownership in the first instance, they risk depriving themselves of millions of hectares that a government has come to assume as their own, under a previous designation as public or government lands. The increasing value of natural resources adds grist to governmental reluctance to reduce the public estate. This is the case from Afghanistan to Brazil, from Uganda to Cambodia, and from Timor Leste to Madagascar.

Yet, once out of the box, Pandora, in the form of accumulating recognition of mil-lions of rights under the aegis of community tenure, is not easily returned to its sup-pressed condition. Modern communities are increasingly well-versed in constitutional rights. They communicate among themselves. They are loath to surrender strengthening paths to land security. They are more demanding of international support. Recourse to the courts is becoming common on all continents, although hardly swift or necessarily incorruptible. Protests against land takings are on the rise, sometimes with fatal results for the land defenders. It seems inevitable that this thread of social transformation will continue, but not without difficulty. In truth, brave optimism aside, it is still too early to predict where the balance will lie half-a-century hence.

Bibliography

Alden Wily, Liz, "Collective Land Ownership in the 21st Century: Overview of Global Trends, *Land*, 7, 68 (2018).

Bruce, John, Tidiane Ngaido, Robin Nielsen, and Kelsey Jones-Casey, *Land Administration to Nurture Development (Land), Protection of Pastoralists' Land Rights: Lessons from Interna-tional Experience*, USAID (2013).

FAO (UN Food and Agriculture Organization) "World Agriculture: Towards 2015–2030: A FAO Perspective", FAO (2015).

Jayne, Tom, Jordan Chamberlain, Lulama Traub, Nicholas Sitko, Milu Muyanga, Felix Yeboah, Ward Anseeuw, Antony Chapoto, "Africa's changing farm size distribution patterns: the rise of medium-scale farms," *Agricultural Economics* 47 (2016): 197–214.

LandMark, Global Platform of Indigenous and Community Lands (www.landmarkmap.org).

Mertes, C., M. Schneider, D. Sulla-Menashe, A. Tatem, B. Tan "Detecting change in urban areas at continental scales with MODIS data," *Remote Sensing of Environment* 158 (2015): 331–347.

Notes, Laura, Peter Veit, Iliana Monterroso, Andiko, Emmanuel Sulle, Anne Larson, Anne-Sophie Gindroz, Julia Quaedvlieg, Andrew Williams, World Resources Institute (WRI), *The Scramble for Land Rights Reducing Inequity between Communities and Companies* (Washington: World Resources Institute, 2018).

Pipes, Richard, *Property and Freedom* (New York: Alfred A. Knopf, 1999).

Rights and Resources, Woods Hole Research Center, LandMark, "Towards a Global Baseline of Carbon Storage in Collective Lands, An Updated Analysis of Indigenous Peoples' and Local Communities' Contribution to Climate Change Mitigation" (2016).

Rights and Resources Initiative (RRI), *Who Owns the World's Land? Global baseline of formally recognized indigenous & community land rights* (Washington: RRI, 2015).

Rights and Resources Initiative (RRI), *At a Crossroads Consequential Trends in Recognition of Community-Based Forest Tenure from 2002–2017* (Washington: RRI 2018).

United Nations, *World Urbanization Prospects: The 2018 Revision.* (New York: UN Economic and Social Affairs 2018).

PART TWO
NATIONAL NETWORKS

Examining the Proliferation
and Cross-Pollination of CLTs
in the Global North

6.

From Model to Movement
The Growth of Community Land Trusts
in the United States

John Emmeus Davis

Countries that have experienced robust growth in the number of community land trusts have followed different trajectories in seeding and cultivating this unusual form of tenure. Just as the model itself has often been adjusted to accommodate a country's politics, customs, and laws, so too have the strategies for promoting the model been tailored to fit whatever opportunities for political acceptance and financial support may present themselves. No country can serve as a precise template for another, therefore, in saying how to turn this unique approach to affordable housing and community development into a national movement. Nevertheless, by telling our stories about what worked well (and what did not) in our own countries, we add to the pool of strategic ideas from which everyone may draw. When it comes to movement building, nationally and internationally, CLT practitioners are doing what we have always done: learning together and learning as we go. We are all walking each other home.

In the United States, it all started with New Communities Inc. There were many precursors, both in the USA and in other countries, but this organization is generally credited with having been the "first" community land trust. An outgrowth of the southern Civil Rights Movement, New Communities was established in 1969 by African-American activists who had led the struggle for voting rights and racial equality in Albany, Georgia. They had come to believe that one of the keys to securing political and economic independence for their people was for them to own land. But individual ownership was out of reach for most African-Americans in the Deep South and too easily lost if they managed to acquire a farm, a plot of land, or a house in town. By contrast, the ownership of land by a not-for-profit, nongovernmental organization seemed a more secure form of tenure. This community-owned land could be combined with individual ownership of newly built houses, offering low-income people an opportunity to become homeowners. Community-owned land could also provide a platform for the cooperative organization of farming and other enterprises, offering low-income people a shot at economic prosperity. "Community land trust" was the name given to this ingenious hybrid, which contemplated a mix of tenures occurring under the guidance and stewardship of a nonprofit landowner, acting on behalf of its chosen community.[1]

The story of New Communities was featured in the first two books to describe the unique combination of ownership, organization, and operation that made up a CLT.[2] These seminal texts, published in 1972 and 1982, inspired a new crop of rural and urban CLTs that sprang up in the 1970s and 1980s. The model then started spreading across the United States. By the mid-1990s, there were over a hundred CLTs. Ten years later, there were nearly two hundred. Today, the number is approaching three hundred nongovernmental organizations in forty-seven states, Puerto Rico, and the District of Columbia that either call themselves a community land trust or contain enough organizational and operational features of a CLT to be considered one.[3]

The Community Land Trust Handbook, which appeared in 1982, had spoken grandly of a "CLT movement." In truth, less than a dozen CLTs existed at the time. And only a few closely resembled the "classic" model described in that book. What was wishful thinking in the early 1980s, however, was on its way to becoming a reality by the turn of the century. How did that happen? How did a hothouse flower with an unusual mix of characteristics become firmly rooted and widely dispersed across the American landscape? There were numerous causes. Some were serendipitous, a matter of robust seeds falling upon fertile ground at an opportune time. Others were intentional, the result of dedicated practitioners working separately and cooperatively to prepare the ground and to nourish the growth of these seedlings. Among the many causes of the model's proliferation in the USA, five had the most impact:

1. A standardized message was developed and disseminated that defined what it meant to *be* a CLT and to *behave* like one;

2. A cadre of pioneering practitioners championed CLTs in their own communities, while sharing what they had learned with their peers in other parts of the country;

3. A handful of high-performing CLTs showed that stewardship works, providing a proof of concept for the model as a whole in both delivering and sustaining homeownership for the missing middle;

4. The policy environment for permanently affordable housing changed for the better, especially at the municipal level, making money available for projects and operations of local CLTs; and

5. The model itself was repeatedly reinvented and reinvigorated, "keeping the edges hot."

These factors and actors were instrumental in taking a fragile hybrid that had been pioneered on a remote farm in southwest Georgia and turning it into a hardy, field-tested perennial with an urban and suburban appeal far beyond its original habitat. They helped the number of CLTs to grow and the size of their holdings to expand. They provided the impetus and foundation for a model to become a movement.

MESSAGE: DEVELOPING A COMMON CONCEPTION OF THE CLT

The early growth of community land trusts was a consequence, in part, of an intentional strategy of developing a coherent and consistent narrative about how a CLT was structured, who it served, and what it could do. The principal architect behind this effort to create a common understanding of the CLT was the Institute for Community Economics (ICE).[4] Although other organizations eventually eclipsed ICE, for several decades the Institute played the leading role in refining and publicizing the CLT. In 1972, the Institute's small staff authored *The Community Land Trust: A Guide to a New Model for Land Tenure in America* and, in 1982, the Institute assembled the twelve-person team who produced *The Community Land Trust Handbook.* Three years later, the Institute introduced the CLT to a wider audience through *Common Ground,* a narrated slideshow featuring the Community Land Cooperative of Cincinnati, the first urban CLT. In 1998, ICE commissioned a video entitled *Homes and Hands: Community Land Trusts in Action,* profiling CLTs in Durham, North Carolina; Albuquerque, New Mexico; and Burlington, Vermont.

Pitched to a general audience, the descriptions, images, and stories presented in these publications and productions had a purpose that was simultaneously educational and rhetorical. They instructed people in the distinctive way that property was owned by a CLT, the distinctive way that a CLT was organized, and the distinctive way that a CLT was operated to preserve the affordability, quality, and security of housing and other buildings, a cluster of features that became known as the "classic" CLT. This standardized description of the model's unique treatment of ownership, organization, and operation helped to differentiate *community* land trusts from the *conservation* land trusts that had begun to proliferate in the 1980s. It also helped to distinguish the CLT from older models of

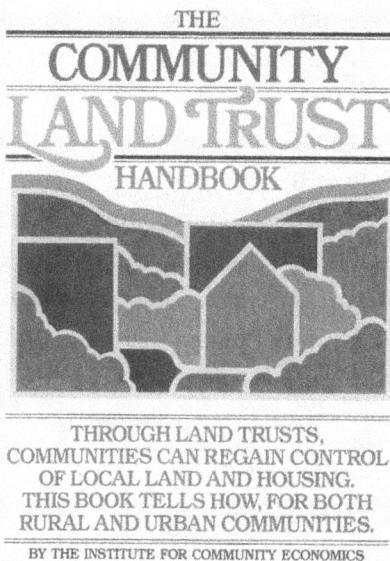

THE **COMMUNITY LAND TRUST** HANDBOOK

THROUGH LAND TRUSTS, COMMUNITIES CAN REGAIN CONTROL OF LOCAL LAND AND HOUSING. THIS BOOK TELLS HOW, FOR BOTH RURAL AND URBAN COMMUNITIES.

BY THE INSTITUTE FOR COMMUNITY ECONOMICS

Fig. 6.1. Cover of the 1982 Handbook, published by Rodale Press.

private, nonmarket housing like limited equity cooperatives. Intended to persuade as much as to inform, these materials were designed to convince an audience of the model's practicality and worth and to encourage activists to give this "new model of land tenure" a try.

Equally essential to the creation of a clear, consistent — and persuasive — conception of the CLT were the efforts made by ICE to produce technical materials for groups of professionals that CLTs would need if they were to gain a foothold in the American landscape: *lawyers* who would help to create a framework for incorporating CLTs, for leasing out a CLT's land, and for restricting the use and resale of CLT homes; *bankers* who would be asked to finance CLT homes; and *public officials* who would be asked to subsidize a CLT's projects. Teams of professionals and practitioners were periodically recruited by ICE to produce "model" documents and technical guides for establishing a CLT. These materials were collected in *The Community Land Trust Legal Manual*, published in 1991. A second edition was published in 2002. A third edition, entitled *The Community Land Trust Technical Manual*, made numerous revisions to the "model" ground lease and added half-a-dozen chapters pertaining to the operation of CLTs. It was published in 2011.

Another factor that proved pivotal in developing a common conception of the model was a definition of "community land trusts" that was added to national legislation in 1992. CLT practitioners pushed for this addition in order to gain access to federal funding, but they also wanted to ensure that the way in which their model was defined in federal law was consistent with the way that CLTs had been defining themselves. They asked then-Congressman Bernie Sanders, whose mayoral administration had seeded the Burlington Community Land Trust when he earlier led Vermont's largest city, to insert their hand-crafted definition of a community land trust into the Housing and Community Development Act of 1992. Sanders shepherded this amendment through Congress, seeing it signed into law without modification.[5]

None of these efforts made every CLT look and act alike. But activists, professionals, public officials, and private lenders inside and outside of the fledgling movement were steadily provided with a sharper picture of how a CLT was structured, how it differed from other models of tenure, and how its projects might best be funded and financed. Just as importantly, they were given a common vocabulary for exchanging information about a relatively unfamiliar model of housing and community development that was still very much a work-in-progress.

CHAMPIONS: CULTIVATING AND CONNECTING CLT PRACTITIONERS

The second factor spurring the growth of community land trusts in the United States was the rise of a scattered cadre of fervent advocates in the 1980s and 1990s who stepped forward to promote, to plan, and to establish CLTs in their own communities. The pioneers who started dozens of CLTs in the 1980s and 1990s were, in many respects, making it up as they went along. They designed resale formulas, arranged mortgages, sold homes, and adopted policies and procedures for a form of tenure with virtually no track record. They were supported in their efforts by the Institute for Community Economics, whose itinerant lecturers and trainers planted the seeds for new CLTs and whose publications provided essential tools.[6] But the Institute's most important contribution during this period of early growth was to create opportunities for local CLT practitioners to share

> They learned by doing. And they learned from one another.

their stories about what worked well — and what did not. They learned by doing. And they learned from one another.

Some of their communication was indirect. CLT activists gleaned information about each other's programs and procedures by reading *Community Economics*, a newsletter published and distributed by ICE from 1983 to 1996. In an average year, two or three issues were mailed out to hundreds (and later thousands) of people across the United States, many of whom were at an early stage of planning, organizing, or operating a CLT. The stated purpose of this publication was to "strengthen the connections between the theory and practice of community economics." More importantly, the publication strengthened the connections among far-flung CLTs, helping local practitioners to learn from the successes and mistakes of their peers.

Peer-to-peer learning among CLT practitioners happened directly at national conferences convened every year or two by ICE.[7] The first conference was held in 1987 in an African-American church in Atlanta, a fitting venue since the country's first CLT had been organized in Georgia by veterans of the Civil Rights Movement.[8] One of those veterans, John Lewis, who had attended one of the first planning sessions for New Communities Inc. in 1968, was the keynote speaker. He reminded participants at the Atlanta conference of the CLT's roots, while applauding how far the model had come.

The main business of that conference, like all that followed, was the exchange of stories, ideas, and technical information among people who were trying to get organizations and projects off the ground. Everyone had something essential to learn and, because the model was so new, anyone with more than a year of CLT experience had something valuable to teach. Nobody was an "expert," so everybody was. Eventually, a pool of professional CLT consultants arose, but they were never a substitute for CLT practitioners on the ground, swapping information with one another. The real experts remained those who were governing or running CLTs day to day. Keeping them connected was an essential ingredient in the movement's growth.

PERFORMANCE: REINVENTING HOMEOWNERSHIP FOR THE "MISSING MIDDLE"

As CLTs began to spread in the 1980s from lightly populated areas that were primarily rural in character to more densely settled cities, suburbs, and towns, the organizers of

Fig. 6.2. John Lewis, National CLT Conference, Atlanta, Georgia, 1987.

new CLTs frequently found themselves in a crowded organizational landscape. The organizations they were hoping to establish had to vie with existing NGOs for governmental funding, private donations, and local members. In a competitive environment, advocates for a new CLT were forced to address such existential questions as: How are you different? What population will you serve that is not already being served by another NGO? What can a CLT do better than anybody else?

The most common answer from CLTs during the 30-year growth spurt between 1970 and 2000 was homeownership; more specifically, homeownership for families who earned *too little* to buy a house or condominium, but *too much* to qualify for publicly subsidized rental housing. This was a population that became known in some policy circles as the "missing middle."

CLTs promised to serve the missing middle in a way that other developers did not. CLTs provided newly built or newly rehabilitated housing that low-income and moderate-income families could afford to buy, similar to what was being done through many other first-time homeownership programs supported with public subsidies and operated by nonprofit organizations. Unlike the majority of these other programs, however, community land trusts stood behind their owner-occupied homes — and their newly minted homeowners — long *after* the housing was developed and sold. Committed to the sustainability of the homeownership opportunities they had worked so hard to create, CLTs used their ownership of the underlying land and a long-term ground lease to preserve the housing's affordability, to keep the housing in good repair, and to intervene, if necessary, to prevent foreclosures. This trio of responsibilities came to be known among CLTs as the "three faces of stewardship."

A specialized niche of *sustainable* homeownership allowed CLTs to differentiate themselves from other nonprofit housing developers in a dense urban ecology. It was a political gauntlet that CLTs threw at the feet of public officials and other NGOs, who celebrated ribbon cuttings for new homeowners, but cared little about whether those homes *remained* affordable and whether new homeowners *remained* in their homes many years down the road. CLTs challenged this short-sighted approach. As ICE's executive director, Chuck Matthei, declared at the first National CLT Conference in Atlanta in 1987:

> No program, public or private, is a true or adequate response to the housing crisis if it does not address the issue of long-term affordability. It's time to draw the line politically. This is a practical challenge that confronts policy makers; it's the practical challenge that confronts community activists; and, happily, it is a practical challenge that the community land trust model has an ability to meet.

The key question, of course, was *does it work?* Local practitioners who were selling CLT homes echoed the claims of national advocates, who had been saying for years that the model functioned in a counter-cyclical fashion; that is, CLTs were effective in preserving affordability when markets were hot and were equally effective in preventing deferred maintenance and reducing foreclosures when markets turned cold.[9] There was anecdotal evidence giving credence to both, but quantitative data was needed if skeptics were to be persuaded that CLTs could actually do what they promised to do.

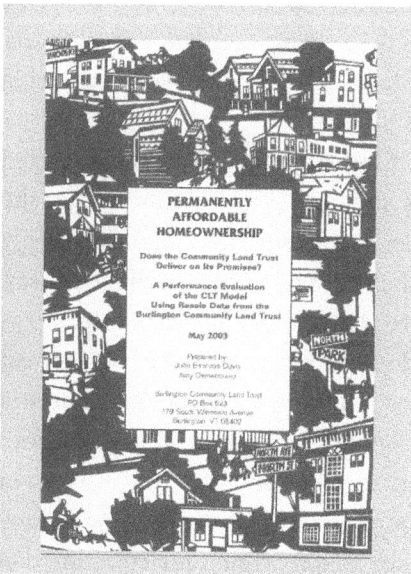

Fig. 6.3. First quantitative, longitudinal evaluation of a CLT's performance, 2003.

Beginning in 2003, a series of data-based evaluations began to appear that closely examined the performance of the resale-restricted, owner-occupied housing held by CLTs.[10] They looked at whether the stewardship regime at the center of this unfamiliar form of tenure actually delivered better outcomes for the people being boosted into homeownership. The most pressing concerns were the following:

- Do community land trusts *preserve affordability* for lower-income households who are hoping to buy CLT homes in the future, while also allowing households who later choose to sell their CLT homes an opportunity to *build wealth*; and

- Do CLTs *enhance the security* of lower-income homeowners, reducing the incidence of mortgage foreclosure, while *allowing mobility* for any homeowners who may choose eventually to leave the CLT?

These studies answered in the affirmative, providing hard evidence that a CLT's specialized focus on the post-purchase stewardship of owner-occupied housing did, in fact, enable CLTs to deliver on their promises. That was true when hot markets threatened affordability. It was also true when cold markets threatened security of tenure. Even during the mortgage meltdown of the Great Recession beginning in 2008, CLT home-owners experienced fewer defaults and fewer foreclosures, by a wide margin, when compared to the dismal performance of conventional, market-rate homes. The success of CLTs in sustaining homeownership for the missing middle, during good economic times and bad, helped the model's visibility and popularity to rise.

POLICY: MUNICIPAL SUPPORT FOR PERMANENTLY AFFORDABLE HOUSING

Despite mounting evidence of the model's counter-cyclical success, most public officials were slow to amend policies and programs that had long allowed subsidized homes to leak into the market on a regular basis. Only in cities where local officials actually *cared* about the lasting affordability, quality, and security of the housing they had helped to create were CLTs able to gain access to the governmental resources they needed to assemble a sizable portfolio of resale-restricted housing.

These were not priority concerns in most cities. Most housing policy in the United States, then and now, had been to use public dollars and public powers to subsidize the *production* of affordably priced housing, with little regard for its *preservation*. This deeply entrenched public policy began slowly to change in the 1980s, with cities leading the way. The election to the presidency of Ronald Reagan forced municipal officials to step up as federal officials stepped back. Under Reagan, the federal government beat a hasty retreat from the field of affordable housing, repudiating a commitment to a "decent home and suitable living environment for every American family" that had been endorsed by both national parties since the Housing Act of 1949. Cutbacks in federal funding resulted in less affordably priced housing getting constructed or subsidized. Older housing in low-er-income areas deteriorated, as government grants for neighborhood revitalization disappeared and as private capital for mortgages and home improvements were withheld from areas that had long been redlined by private lenders. Homelessness, largely invisible since the Great Depression, reappeared with a vengeance. At the same time, short-term affordability controls began expiring on thousands of units of publicly subsidized, privately owned rental housing that had been built decades before under a variety of federal programs.

This was also a period when the price of owner-occupied housing began a steep and sustained thirty-year climb, even as household incomes stagnated for the bottom three quintiles of the population and as mortgage interest rates rose to historic heights. A new phrase entered the lexicon of housing policy in the 1980s, the "affordability gap." This referred to the widening chasm between housing prices and household incomes.

With the federal government doing less for affordable housing, cities were forced to

> Permanent affordability began to look less like a radical proposition and more like a prudent course of action.

do more. Attempting to replace some of the federal monies they had lost, many cities raised new funds from local sources, depositing them into dedicated accounts called "housing trust funds." They made wider use of regulatory measures like inclusionary zoning and density bonuses, forcing private developers to set aside affordably priced units within larger, market-rate residential projects. They also exerted greater control over the disbursement of the federal monies that remained, a consequence of the Reagan Administration's policy of "devolving" authority to lower levels of government. Because of devolution, many of these federal funds now flowed through the hands of municipal officials.[11]

As municipalities began expending more of their own financial and political capital to subsidize affordable housing for lower-income renters and homeowners, the preservation of that investment became a higher priority. Permanent affordability began to look less like a radical proposition and more like a prudent course of action; a policy more fiscally responsible and politically defensible than continuing to allow public subsidies and private affordability to leak away. Municipal officials became increasingly receptive to the arguments being made by CLT practitioners, among others, that the public's investment should not be lost, nor should the affordably priced homes resulting from that investment. Particularly in cities with hot real estate markets, where rents and house prices were soaring, the demonstrated success of CLTs in preserving affordability was the kind of fiscally prudent program that even a conservative mayor or city councilor could support.

This precipitated a slow, seismic shift in municipal policy. Instead of allowing homeownership subsidies to be pocketed by homeowners when reselling their assisted homes, some municipalities began looking for ways to lock those subsidies in place. Instead of allowing the affordability of publicly assisted homes to lapse, these municipalities began looking for ways to make affordability last. As municipal officials sought to plug holes in the leaky bucket created by previous policies and programs, CLTs found an increasingly receptive audience and, on occasion, they became a favored recipient of municipal largess.[12]

HYBRID VIGOR: KEEPING THE EDGES HOT

A coherent message; a widening cadre of inter-connected champions; a record of success in delivering and sustaining homeownership for the "missing middle;" and an improving policy environment, prioritizing permanent affordability: all were critical to the growth of community land trusts in the United States during the period between the seeding of New Communities Inc. and the early years of the New Millennium. The number of CLTs rose higher. The size of CLT portfolios got bigger.

One additional factor figured prominently in the growth of CLTs: the creativity of practitioners in *mixing* the model with other forms of tenure and *applying* the model in novel ways. By doing so, practitioners expanded the boundaries of the CLT, enhancing its productivity and adaptability. This process of restless reinvention is what a colleague once dubbed "keeping the edges hot."

It might also be called "hybrid vigor." What is widely known in the United States as the "classic CLT" was created by selecting favorable characteristics of ownership, organization, and operation from different strands of social change and combining them to form a new breed of land tenure. This is analogous to what is regularly done in horticulture when two or more species with different characteristics are combined to create a new plant variety that is more productive and resilient, across a wider range of habitats and conditions — a desirable result that plant breeders call "hybrid vigor."

In the case of the CLT, hybridization produced a versatile model that could thrive not only in rural areas and small towns where it was first introduced, but also in inner-city neighborhoods and suburban enclaves. The "classic" model that gained a foothold in a number of American cities in the 1980s was hardly an end to hybridization, however. The process has continued to the present day: blending the CLT with other tenures; grafting the CLT onto other organizational structures; and applying the CLT in new ways. The salubrious result has been an increase in the model's productivity and adaptability.

For example, although many CLTs in the United States still focus on expanding and sustaining homeownership opportunities for the missing middle, the populations they serve have become more diverse. So have their real estate portfolios. The types and tenures of housing that are today being developed on community-owned land are more varied than the detached, owner-occupied houses that were once a CLT's main line of business. CLTs are now engaged in the development and stewardship of limited-equity condominiums and cooperatives, multi-unit rental housing, manufactured housing in resident-managed mobile home parks, and transitional housing and temporary shelters for the homeless. CLT landholdings are being increasingly used for non-residential projects as well, including community gardens, commercial greenhouses, urban farms, neighborhood parks, social enterprises, social service facilities, and multi-story, mixed-use buildings with retail or office space on the ground floor and residential space in the stories above. In rural areas, some CLTs have expanded their focus beyond the development of affordable housing to include the preservation of farmland, forests, wetlands, and open space.[13]

Not only is there more mixing of tenures and uses, there is more mixing of organizations as well. Although many CLTs in the United States are still being started from scratch, forming a brand new nonprofit corporation, the path to organizing a CLT has become more diverse. In localities that already possess an established nonprofit infrastructure for the development of affordable housing, it has become increasingly common for key features of the "classic CLT" to be grafted onto an existing community development corporation, Habitat for Humanity affiliate, or even an agency or department of local government. In these instances, community-owned land, long-term ground leasing, and permanent controls over the affordability of residential and commercial buildings are operationalized as an internal program or corporate subsidiary of another entity that was doing business long before the idea of creating a CLT came along.

> *Mixing the CLT with other tenures and other organizations has sometimes deleted or diluted characteristics that make the model unique.*

When CLTs are combined with other models of tenure or when a CLT program is grafted onto an existing nonprofit, adjustments are often made to the democratically elected, three-part board of the "classic" CLT. In some cases, the composition of a CLT's membership or governance has been reconfigured to allow local governments or other nonprofits to appoint their own representatives, serving alongside the residents representing a place-based community. Some CLTs have dispensed with a membership altogether. Notably, in cases where a municipal government has taken the lead in establishing a CLT — or in cities where the main function of the CLT is serving as the steward of affordable housing created through a municipal mandate or municipal money — city officials have sometimes been reluctant to relinquish control over the organization. This can result in a CLT board where leaseholders and their neighbors are no longer a majority.

Hybridization has added vigor. It has brought more lands and buildings into CLT portfolios. It has garnered more support for CLTs. It has helped the model to spread into places and spaces where CLTs were previously unknown. But hybridization has also brought challenges. The process of mixing the CLT with other tenures and other organizations has sometimes deleted or diluted characteristics that make the model unique, changing what it essentially means to be a CLT and to behave like one. Three challenges loom the largest in this regard:

- *Keeping the "C" in CLT:* Will there still be a place for community in the organizational structure of the CLT? Or will the heightened influence of municipal governments and the increasing number of CLT programs that are placed under the corporate umbrella of other NGOs reduce the active voice of local residents in guiding and governing the CLT?

- *Keeping the "L" in CLT:* Will land still matter? Or will a narrowing focus on affordable housing, in general, and owner-occupied housing, in particular, cause CLTs to ignore other uses of land or to abandon ground leasing altogether in favor of selling their land and employing mechanisms like deed covenants to preserve affordability?[14]

- *Keeping the "T" in CLT:* Will the CLT still hold real estate in trust for disadvantaged populations, preserving a "preferential option for the poor" in making lands available, keeping homes affordable, and protecting security of tenure for low-income families and individuals — or will the Gandhian legacy of "trusteeship" be lost in a scramble to broaden the model's middle-class appeal?[15]

Beyond the challenge of keeping each of these components intact, there is the stiffer challenge of keeping *community*, *land*, and *trust* together. Each component of the "classic" CLT is a worthy innovation in its own right, representing a marked improvement over the way that land is typically owned, used, and conveyed; a marked improvement over the way that nonprofit organizations are typically structured; and a marked improvement over the way that housing and other land-based assets are typically operated. But the capacity of a CLT to transform a place of residence comes less from the *reinvention* of ownership, organization, and operation and more from the synergy created by their *combination*. Will these components continue to work in concert, each enhancing the effectiveness of the others? Or will CLT practitioners yield to the temptation to remove key components in the name of simplification, hoping to make the model easier to "sell" to public funders, private bankers, or reluctant homebuyers?[16]

BACK TO THE FUTURE:
REAFFIRMING VALUES, RENEWING VOWS

A contest for the soul of the community land trust is contained within these clusters of questions. How they are answered will determine whether the CLT of tomorrow continues to resemble the model that arose in the United States nearly fifty years ago. It could go either way. It is not predestined that CLTs of the future will be dramatically different than today. People who have spent a lifetime advocating for community-led development on community-owned land are a stubborn lot. They will not be easily persuaded to abandon features that have grounded and energized the model in the past. Plus, not all of the changes and challenges currently swirling around the CLT compel it away from what it has been. Some coax it back, returning the model to its roots.

The recent revival of interest in the CLT among grassroots organizers working in communities of color is a case in point, especially in neighborhoods where lower-income households predominate. These are places that are the most susceptible to gentrification and displacement. Their vulnerability is particularly high when these neighborhoods are proximate to an expanding downtown or situated beside a river, lake, or ocean. During good economic times, people of color get pushed aside as lands rise in value and become coveted by investors (and politicians) for conversion to a "higher use." These areas also get hit the hardest when economic times are bad and foreclosures rise or when natural disasters like wildfires or hurricanes depopulate large swaths of land for luxury redevelopment.[17]

The boom-and-bust depredations inflicted upon communities of color have created a broadening constituency for a model of tenure that has proven its effectiveness in sustaining homeownership opportunities for lower-income households of all races. Stewardship works, at both ends of the business cycle. That makes the CLT a prime candidate for consideration by community leaders who are looking for a bulwark against displacement, protecting against market forces and public policies that threaten the loss of minority-owned lands and the removal of people, spaces, and enterprises that have historically defined a neighborhood's racial or ethnic identity.

Ironically, at the same time as interest in the model was increasing within communities of color, harkening back to earlier era of the struggle for racial justice, there was a rising generation of practitioners who were mostly unaware of the CLT's origins. They certainly understood how a CLT's approach to homeownership differed from more conventional forms of housing. They were just as dedicated as their predecessors had been to using the CLT to improve the lives of lower-income families and, in many respects, they were more skillful in doing so. But these younger practitioners were many years removed from the Civil Rights Movement that had spawned the modern-day CLT. They were less likely to see themselves as part of a larger movement for social change, even where a majority of people in the places they served were members of a racial or ethnic minority.

This was symptomatic of a larger problem. The model was on its way to becoming a movement by the first decade of the New Millennium, but the values and vows that had provided the underpinnings of the CLT were beginning to wobble. An increasing number of organizers, practitioners, and public officials understood *how* to deliver a CLT's services, but the *why* had begun to fade from memory. Fewer people were familiar with the original rationale for reinventing and combining ownership, organization, and operation in precisely this way.

The CLT movement, in this regard, was no different than any other. Social movements of every stripe, if they are to endure, must stay rooted in the bedrock principles on which they were founded, giving motivation and momentum to the people who are drawn to them. Simultaneously, a movement must stay open to new recruits and new ideas, taking wing on an influx of fresh energy. The early growth of CLTs was grounded and buoyed by both. Drawing on social innovations and experiments in land reform from other countries and inspired by the Civil Rights Movement in the United States, the CLT had sturdy roots. It soon found its wings as well, when a feisty generation of community activists seized upon a model pioneered in rural America and applied it in novel ways in urban and suburban neighborhoods throughout the country.

But values are precarious and easily lost as a movement's origins become more distant. Likewise, edges become less permeable as a newly created organization consolidates its niche in a competitive environment and seeks to institutionalize practices that brought it earlier success. Instead of the open borders of a movement, barriers to entry gradually

CLT leaders were not spared this movement-versus-industry dilemma, but they tried to thread the needle, embracing the best attributes of both.

arise, becoming higher over time. Instead of the hydra-headed energy of a movement, where thought leaders and inventive practitioners appear unpredictably on the periphery or arise unexpectedly within the ranks, there develops a leadership cadre that becomes increasingly stable, hierarchical, and self-perpetuating over time.[18]

Whenever that occurs in the natural life cycle of a social movement, its leaders are faced with a difficult choice. They must decide whether to dampen the passions and trappings of a movement, adopting standards and structures that make their organizations and networks behave more like an industry, or act intentionally to preserve the precarious values and permeable edges that gave birth to their movement and infused it with the vitality of youth.

CLT leaders in the United States were not spared this movement-versus-industry dilemma, but they tried to thread the needle, embracing the best attributes of both. They believed it was possible for members of their national network to incorporate characteristics and standards of a more formal organization without losing the aspirational, inclusive vitality that had made CLTs a movement. Conversely, they believed it was possible for local CLTs — and for the movement as a whole — to preserve the precious, precarious values at the heart of the CLT, while keeping the edges of their organizations permeable to new ideas and new entrants.

The National CLT Network embarked on a series of key interventions that sought to walk this tightrope. The first was the National CLT Academy, established in 2006. The Academy was concerned with the nuts and bolts of making CLTs work better by documenting and teaching "best practices" in the organization and operation of CLTs. Through the courses it developed and the documents it published,[19] the Academy promoted the sort of standardization and professionalization characteristic of an "industry." At the same time, the Academy attempted to inculcate the values of a "movement," articulating a clear rationale for the CLT and playing a role of messaging similar to the role once played by the Institute for Community Economics. Through its courses and publications, the Academy tried to remind practitioners of where the model had come from and why it was configured in such an unconventional way.[20]

Two years after launching the Academy, the National CLT Network established the Heritage Lands Initiative, a program dedicated to supporting CLT development in communities of color.[21] Here too there was a focus on improving the standard of practice, accompanied by an emphasis on familiarizing present-day practitioners with values and pioneers from the CLT's past. Out of this Initiative came two film projects: *Streets of Dreams: Development without Displacement in Communities of Color*; and *Arc of Justice: The Rise, Fall, and Rebirth of a Beloved Community*.[22] Both documentaries were graphic

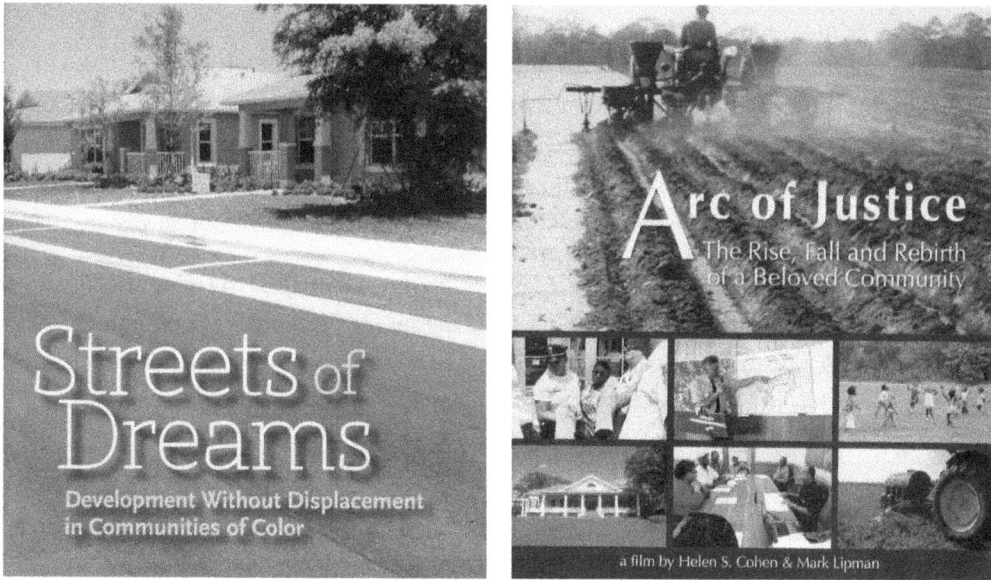

Fig. 6.4. Two films from Open Studio Productions, exploring origins and applications of the CLT in communities of color.

reminders that the model's origins were not to be found in the lofty theories of academics, but in the moral struggle of African-Americans for social justice.

There was a virtuous cycle here. Mounting interest in CLTs among communities of color spurred the Network and its members to do more to address their concerns. Conversely, the trainings, publications, and films produced by the National CLT Academy and the Heritage Lands Initiative helped to legitimize the CLT in the eyes of activists, organizers, and prospective homebuyers who were living and working within these minority communities.

It is too soon to predict how this dynamic might affect the ways in which CLTs are being structured, accepted, and applied — or what its effect might be on meeting the latest challenges to the model's integrity. What can be said, at this point, is that the growing interest in the model among communities of color — and the increasing commitment by many of the movement's leaders to an agenda of diversity, equity, and inclusion — is showing signs of reinvigorating values that gave rise to the first CLT fifty years ago. It is opening up the present-day CLT movement in the United States to new people and new possibilities.

In sum, at the same time that internal changes and external pressures are pushing the CLT toward becoming something different than it once was, there are old constituencies and new energies that are pulling it back toward the vision and values of the model's pioneers. The CLT, as both a model and a movement, remains a work in progress. Experimentation helped it to grow. Adaptation helped it to spread. It continues to evolve. A long time coming, the CLT still has a long way to go.

Notes

1. More information on ideas and experiments that gave rise to the CLT can be found in "Origins and Evolution of the Community Land Trust in the United States." Pp. 3–47 in J.E. Davis (ed.) *The Community Land Trust Reader* (Cambridge MA: Lincoln Institute of Land Policy, 2010); and in "Les Philosophes de Terrain et Les Pionniers." Pp. 19–44 in *Manuel d'antispeculation immobiliere* (Montreal, Quebec: Les Editions Ecosociete, 2014).

2. International Independence Institute, *The Community Land Trust: A Guide to a New Model for Land Tenure in America* (Cambridge MA: Center for Community Economic Development, 1972). Institute for Community Economics, *The Community Land Trust Handbook* (Emmaus PA: Rodale Press, 1982).

3. A directory and interactive map of all CLTs in the United States is maintained by the Center for CLT Innovation (*www.cltweb.org*).

4. Founded by Ralph Borsodi in 1967 as the International Independence Institute, the organization changed its name to the Institute for Community Economics soon after publication of the 1972 book.

5. Early in 1992, Congressman Sanders invited the first director of the Burlington Community Land Trust, Tim McKenzie, to testify before a congressional subcommittee. McKenzie's well-received testimony caused Sanders to see that an opening might exist for federal legislation supportive of the CLT model. Asked by Sanders for suggestions, McKenzie brought John Davis into the conversation. McKenzie and Davis urged Sanders to propose a statutory definition of the CLT that would make it easier for CLTs to receive federal funding. Sanders agreed. A one-page definition of the "community land trust" was drafted by McKenzie and Davis and sent off to Sanders' office. Their definition was inserted by Sanders into the Housing and Community Development Act of 1992.

6. The first generation of peripatetic proselytizers were Ralph Borsodi, Mildred Loomis, and Arthur Morgan. They were advocates for leased-land communities long before the founding of New Communities Inc. and remained active into the 1960s. But Morgan was 92 by the time New Communities was up and running; Borsodi was 84; Loomis was 70. Their days of hitting the road to talk about land trusts were coming to an end. Plus, the message and model had evolved. The CLT that emerged from the crucible of the southern Civil Rights Movement and from a redesign engineered by ICE was different than the land trusts of previous years. In the 1970s, the Institute fielded a new generation of lecturers and trainers: Bob Swann, Erick Hansch, Shimon Gottshalk, and Terry Molnar. During the 1980s, Chuck Matthei was ICE's best known and most widely travelled advocate for the CLT.

7. The first national conferences were convened by ICE. In 2006, the National CLT Network took over responsibility for organizing them and continued to do so after merging with the Cornerstone Partnership in 2016 and changing its name to Grounded Solutions Network.

8. An earlier conference had been hosted by ICE at Voluntown, Connecticut in 1983, but it was hardly a "national" CLT conference since only a few CLTs existed at the time. This was more a gathering of community organizers and housing professionals who were interested in starting a CLT. The 1987 conference in Atlanta was always considered by ICE to have been the "first" national CLT conference.

9. J.E. Davis, "Homes That Last: The Case for Counter-Cyclical Stewardship." Pp. 562–570 in *The Community Land Trust Reader* (Cambridge MA: Lincoln Institute of Land Policy, 2010).

10. John Emmeus Davis and Amy Demetrowitz, *Permanently Affordable Homeownership: Does the Community Land Trust Deliver on Its Promises?* (Burlington VT: Burlington Community Land Trust, 2003); John Emmeus Davis and Alice Stokes, *Lands in Trust, Homes That Last* (Burlington VT: Champlain Housing Trust, 2010); Emily Thaden, *Outperforming the Market: Making Sense of the Low Rates of Delinquencies and Foreclosures in Community Land Trusts* (Portland OR: National CLT Network, 2010); Kenneth Temkin, Brett Theodos, and David Price, *Balancing Affordability and Opportunity: An Evaluation of Affordable Homeownership Programs with Long-term Affordability Controls* (Washington DC: The Urban Institute, 2010); and Emily Thaden, *Stable Homeownership in a Turbulent Economy: Delinquencies and Foreclosures Remain Low in Community Land Trusts* (Cambridge MA: Lincoln Institute of Land Policy, 2011). See, more recently, Ruoniu Wang, Claire Cahen, Arthur Acolin, and Rebecca J. Walter, *Tracking Growth and Evaluating Performance of Shared Equity Homeownership Programs During Housing Market Fluctuations* (Cambridge MA: Lincoln Institute of Land Policy, April 2019).

11. John Emmeus Davis, "Between Devolution and the Deep Blue Sea: What's a City or State to Do?" Pp. 364–398 in Rachel G. Bratt, Michael E. Stone, and Chester Hartman (eds.), *A Right to Housing* (Philadelphia PA: Temple University Press, 2006).

12. A more detailed discussion of this policy shift toward the preservation of publicly subsidized housing, at least at the local level, can be found in John Emmeus Davis and Rick Jacobus, *The City-CLT Partnership: Municipal Support for Community Land Trusts* (Cambridge MA: Lincoln Institute of Land Policy, 2008).

13. See Kirby White, *Preserving Farms for Farmers* (Turners Falls, MA: Equity Trust, 2009). A few CLTs like the one in Athens, Georgia straddle the line between urban and rural, developing affordable housing in the city and conserving farmland, forests, and open space in the countryside. The Athens Land Trust also operates a weekly farmers market (*https://athenslandtrust.org*).

14. This was one of Bob Swann's abiding concerns: "Creating perpetually affordable housing is a good idea. The only thing is that there is a danger of losing track of the land itself." See the interview with Bob Swann conducted by Kirby White in *Community Economics* (Number 25, 1992), Pp. 3–5. Reprinted in J.E. Davis (ed.), *The Community Land Trust Reader* (Cambridge MA: Lincoln Institute of Land Policy, 2010).

15. The "preferential option for the poor" was a principle of Catholic social teaching articulated in liberation theology and championed by many Christian democratic parties in Latin America at the end of the 20th Century. That principle, combined with Gandhi's concept of "trusteeship," influenced the thinking, teaching, and practice of many CLT advocates during the 1970s and 1980s.

16. A detailed argument against the model's dismemberment can be found in J.E. Davis, "Better Together: The Challenging, Transformative Complexity of Community, Land and Trust," Chapter 26 in the current volume. A less temperate commentary, berating the tendency to remove components of the model that seem "too difficult," can be found in: J.E. Davis, "Ground Leasing Without Tears," *Shelterforce Weekly* (February 4, 2014).

17. When the mortgage crisis rolled across the USA during the Great Recession, the brunt of that economic disaster was borne by African–Americans and Latinos. They lost their homes to foreclosure in disproportionate numbers relative to the rest of the population. When hurricanes ripped through New Orleans, Houston, and Puerto Rico, a new breed of "disaster capitalists" saw opportunities to buy up valuable land at bargain prices.

18. Previous commentaries on this dilemma can be found in J.E. Davis, "Precarious Values and Permeable Edges in Community Development," *Shelterforce Weekly* (January 10, 2013); and in "Is Community Development an Industry — or a Movement?" *Shelterforce Weekly* (September 17, 2014).

19. *The Community Land Trust Technical Manual,* commissioned, researched, and published by the Academy in 2011, is the best example of these publications.

20. Outside of the classroom, two other spin-offs from the National CLT Academy further extolled the CLT's history. In 2010, the Lincoln Institute of Land Policy published *The Community Land Trust Reader.* That volume included an introductory essay laying out the origins and evolution the CLT in the United States, along with essays, interviews, and speeches documenting the theory and values behand the CLT. A few years later, two of the Academy's founders, Greg Rosenberg and John Emmeus Davis, created *Roots & Branches,* a digital archive of CLT history (*http://www.cltroots.org*).

21. The CLT Academy and the Heritage Lands Initiative were chartered programs of the National CLT Network, each with its own advisory board. They were absorbed into the committee structure of the Network in 2012. Two years later, the CLT Network merged with the Cornerstone Partnership and changed its name to Grounded Solutions Network.

22. *Streets of Dreams* was produced by Helen Cohen and Mark Lipman (New Day Films, 2010). *Arc of Justice* was produced by Helen Cohen, Mark Lipman, and John Emmeus Davis (New Day Films, 2016). For the latter film, a website was also created to provide additional information about events, people, and organizations featured in this documentary (*http://www.arcofjusticefilm.com*).

7.

Origins and Evolution of Urban Community Land Trusts in Canada

Susannah Bunce and Joshua Barndt

The development of community land trusts in Canada offers an interesting study of the often individualized and ad hoc processes involved in CLT creation. While certainly not as numerous as CLTs in the USA and England, CLTs in Canada have burgeoned over the past several decades. They have been on the forefront of addressing affordable housing shortages and offered new ways to consider community land stewardship in Canada. The earliest CLTs were primarily located in Canadian cities, established as independent land trust initiatives through cooperative housing organizations, and as responses to affordable housing challenges in cities such as Montreal, Toronto, Winnipeg, and Vancouver. More recently, there has been an increasingly robust and more formalized network of CLTs emerging across Canada in response to on-going affordable housing shortages, gentrification processes, and a renewed interest in community-led practices that extend beyond affordable housing provision. Our chapter explores the historical appearance of CLTs in Canadian cities and why they continue to be an important community-led, non-governmental organizational model in a nation where government has traditionally played the leading role in the provision of affordable housing and social services.

Despite Canada's social democratic roots, different levels of government have been actively dismantling social programs over the last several decades, including a withdrawal from the funding and delivery of social housing programs starting in the early 1990s (Hulchanski 2001, 2007; Leone and Carole, 2010; Moore and Skaburskis, 2004; Wolfe, 1998).[1] Increasing governmental reliance on the private, for-profit sector for the delivery of housing and fiscal cutbacks to social services have had a detrimental impact on both housing affordability and the presence of social and community-based programs.[2]

Community-led CLT organizations have emerged within the context of these broader political-economic transformations in Canada, which have shaped the organizational structure, community actions, and programming of CLTs over time.

We identify two "generations" of community land trust organizations in Canada — the first being a small group of CLTs, arising in the l980s to around 2012, that were largely focused on the acquisition of land for affordable housing provision. These CLT organizations, inspired by the CLT model in the United States, differed from land trust organizing in Canada that had traditionally focused on the conservation of wilderness and agricultural areas. The emergence of this new form of land trust in Canadian cities occurred within the context of a lack of public policy and legislative support for the creation of CLTs. As a result, they were primarily formed by cooperative housing federations, nonprofit developers, and activist groups, often in partnership with specific governmental affordable housing programs.

A "second generation" of CLTs has emerged since 2012, both as a response to increasing gentrification pressures in urban areas and as a result of renewed interest in affordable housing development. New CLTs have emerged in cities such as Toronto and Vancouver, for example, cities that have experienced a steady rise in single-family homeownership and property speculation over the past decade, along with quickly rising housing prices and increased constraints on already tight affordable rental housing markets (Gee, 2017; King, 2016; McClearn, 2017). These second-generation CLTs have forged connections with existing and new CLT organizations across Canada and have interacted with an emergent international CLT movement. Locally, the activism of these CLT organizations has often extended beyond the land trust model itself, responding to broader urban issues such as the impact of rapid gentrification and displacement, decreases in affordable housing supply, advocacy for urban food security, and solidarity with racialized and culturally diverse communities, including building allyship with Indigenous peoples. These second-generation CLT organizations are distinguished by new approaches to the development and provision of communal and shared equity housing, by varied forms of neighbourhood and city-wide activism, and by a community land trust network being built across Canada.

> Canadian CLT development has been eclectic, sometimes incorporating features of the American model and sometimes not.

Our chapter traces the evolution of Canadian CLTs and underlines the importance of their self-identification as CLTs in structuring their own organizations and operations. More often than not, Canadian CLT organizations view themselves as being a community land trust regardless of whether they exhibit all the characteristics of the traditional or "classic" CLT, as that model has been defined and implemented in the United States. The American "classic" model was premised on: a two-party ownership structure, whereby the CLT acts as the owner and long-term lessor for multiple parcels of land underneath buildings that are separately owned by individuals, cooperatives, or other nonprofit or for-profit entities; an organizational structure with a tripartite board and a place-based membership that emphasizes the participation of CLT residents, local community members, and members of the public; and an operational commitment to the permanent affordability of any housing located on the CLT's land, along with other stewardship duties designed to protect the condition of the structures and the security of tenure for the occupants (Davis, 2007; 2010). By comparison, Canadian CLT development has been more ad hoc and eclectic, sometimes incorporating these "classic" features and sometimes not, depending on their individual contexts and familiarity with the American CLT model. As such, Canadian CLTs have forged "home-grown" CLT characteristics that are primarily constituted by the very localized circumstances of their formation.

We trace the evolution of CLT development in Canada in a chronological way, through a narrative of the organizational objectives and projects of first- and second-generation CLTs. The CLTs that are discussed are organizations with which we are familiar, as CLT researchers and practitioners, and which offer certain insights into the origins and evolution of CLTs in the Canadian context. We conclude by suggesting that a steady increase in the presence of CLTs in Canada has necessitated the creation of formalized networks of knowledge transfer and information sharing in order to build solidarity and connections among CLT organizations and communities across Canada. An example of this is the recent emergence of the Canadian CLT Network that is fostering regular communication among CLT organizations across the country.

THE FIRST GENERATION OF CANADIAN CLTs
1980s–2012

A defining characteristic of this first cluster of largely sector-based CLTs,[3] which emerged from the 1980s to 2012, was the primary focus on the provision of cooperative and other forms of affordable housing through land ownership by the CLT organization. The emphasis on co-op housing provision derived from the strong Canadian cooperative housing movement that started in the 1930s (Hulchanski, 1988) and became a dominant affordable housing model in cities in the 1970s, with the development of well-regarded co-op housing projects such as St. Lawrence in Toronto and with the support of housing activists and municipal, provincial, and federal governments for this form of housing.

The CLT model, adopted through informal activist knowledge of the American CLT movement, became a conduit through which affordable housing, primarily co-op housing, was produced at a localized scale. We also observe a notable difference in the size and scope of CLTs during this period. Some CLTs, such as Colandco in Toronto and the Vernon District Community Land Trust in Vernon, British Columbia, adopted a sector-based and city-wide organizational approach with little community-led direction over the CLT organization itself. Conversely, other CLTs such as the West Broadway CLT embraced a more community-led, neighbourhood-based approach in the provision of affordable housing.

Colandco (Toronto)

The first two CLTs in Canada, both formed in the 1980s, focused on the provision of cooperative housing: Colandco in Toronto and Milton-Parc in Montreal. Colandco (initially called Inner City) was established in 1986 as a land holding and sector-based development company by the Co-operative Housing Federation of Toronto. Colandco purchased existing rental apartment buildings as well as parcels of land for the purpose of developing new multi-unit residential projects. Colandco retained ownership of the land and the buildings, while executing a 49-year lease with each cooperative for both. This arrangement provided the co-ops with use of the properties for the term of the lease. By retaining long-term ownership and control of the land and buildings, Colandco could ensure that the housing would remain affordable in perpetuity (Communitas Inc. 1985; Hulchanski, 1983; Interview with Tom Clement, February 18, 2019).

Colandco successfully leveraged its initial $2 million (CAD) of seed funding to develop an initial project,[4] the City Park Co-op, that secured 770 cooperative housing units through the acquisition of a privately owned rental project that was in receivership. Using the revolving fund as a deposit to secure the site, Colandco was subsequently able to mobilize funding and financing from the provincial government to complete the $63 million purchase. By the early 1990s, Colandco had assembled land ownership on a large scale for the development of fourteen housing cooperatives, containing a total of 2,350 housing units scattered across central Toronto, Scarborough, and Oshawa (Canada Mortgage and Housing Corporation, 2005; Co-operative Housing Federation of Toronto, 2019).

Colandco's program of land expansion and residential development started to face challenges in 1994, however, as a result of a global financial recession that began in the early 1990s and was significantly felt for several years in the province of Ontario. The withdrawal of governmental support for social housing and other affordable housing programs during the same period also impacted Colandco's projects. These pressures caused Colandco to downsize its housing development activities and to focus increasingly on retaining land ownership through a land trust arrangement with individual co-operatives (Canada Mortgage and Housing Corporation, 2005; Hulchanski 1983). Colandco entered into contractual agreements with individual nonprofit housing cooperatives to operate housing on its land, an approach that has had significant success and longevity in Toronto.

In 2017, Colandco and the Co-operative Housing Federation of Toronto took the lead in forming the Co-op Housing Land Trusts, consisting of four different land trusts: Colandco; the Bathurst Quay Co-op; Colandco's City Park Co-op; the Naismith Non-Profit Land Trust; and the Tenants Non-Profit Redevelopment Foundation (TNRC). These land trusts operate as a group. With the exception of the Bathurst Quay Co-op, each land trust has the same Board of Directors. Importantly, each land trust owns the land that is occupied by its cooperatives. As the leasee, each co-op is responsible for the management of its buildings. At the end of the land lease, the buildings will be transferred to the land trust unless the lease is renewed.

As a whole, the cooperatives that constitute the Co-op Housing Land Trusts are made up of thirty-two buildings, containing a total of 4,196 apartments or houses that are occupied by approximately 10,000 residents (Correspondence with Tom Clement, 2019). It is important to note that co-op residents are not organizational members of the Co-op Housing Land Trusts, but remain members of their individual cooperatives. This arrangement points to an innovative utilization of the community land trust model, where particular aspects of the CLT, such as land ownership and ground lease agreements, are combined with the autonomy of the co-op buildings. Resident members govern their individual cooperatives, but they may or may not have any involvement with the entity that owns the underlying land.

Communaute Milton-Parc (Montreal)

The Milton-Parc community, located in the downtown core of Montreal, has had similar success and longevity in the production of cooperative housing, while putting a creative, homegrown spin on the traditional CLT model. The idea for Communaute Milton-Parc (CMP) emerged from a lengthy resident-led and community-based struggle to save the neighbourhood from urban renewal plans proposed by a consortium of Montreal-based property developers. The activism of the Milton Parc Citizens Committee in the late 1960s and 1970s, which included street sit-ins and the occupation of buildings slated for demolition, succeeded in halting the renewal plans. The activists then formed multiple cooperative housing communities to purchase and to renovate the buildings, preserving this housing for low-income and middle-income residents (Kowaluk and Piche-Burton, 2012; Roussopoulos and Hawley, 2018).[5]

A growing concern about gentrification and displacement in the 1980s then led to the creation of the Communaute Milton-Parc in 1986. Approved by Quebec's provincial government, the CMP was viewed by the individual cooperatives as a way to protect housing affordability by protecting and stewarding the neighbourhood's land. Land titles in Milton-Parc are collectively owned by a syndicate of fifteen individual cooperatives and six nonprofit housing corporations through a Declaration of Co-Ownership. The CMP is governed by a general assembly constituted by the syndicate of co-owners. CMP acts as a governing and community decision-making body that regulates and sets guiding policy for cooperative ownership and community responsibility. CMP also owns and maintains the land beneath the common areas and enforces non-speculative restrictions on land uses and any land sales that might be contemplated by an individual cooperative (Ibid.).

Fig. 7.1. The Milton Parc neighbourhood, Montreal. OLIVIA WILLIAMS

CMP is an innovative take on the traditional structure of the CLT model. In the latter, the use of land and the affordability of housing are regulated through a ground lease for land that is owned by the CLT. Communaute Milton-Parc, by contrast, does not own the land beneath the housing itself but works as an overarching governance body for the Milton Parc neighbourhood that presently includes 148 buildings, 616 affordable units, and 1500 residents (Milton Parc, 2013). As a governance and decision-making body, the CMP arrangement offers a uniquely localized arrangement in which land is utilized and regulated in a way that best suits the preferences and circumstances of a particular neighbourhood. The organization has, over time, put in place a fulsome governance structure with a sophisticated assemblage of decision-making protocols and community engagement practices that connect the individual cooperatives and the overarching CMP body. This is combined with a focus on stopping residential displacement and supporting the longevity of affordable cooperative housing.

Milton Parc is the single largest cooperative housing neighbourhood in North America. Its size and success made Communaute Milton-Parc a finalist in the UN World Habitat Awards in 2013 (CMHC, 2005; World Habitat, 2017). Today, Milton Parc's residents remain active in public discussions about gentrification, displacement, and the need for affordable housing in Montreal. Importantly, they self-identify and publicly characterize their unique combination of fifteen cooperative housing communities, a single landholding syndicate, and an overarching structure of governance as being a community land trust.

CLT Formation in Central and Western Canada

In Colandco, the Co-op Housing Land Trusts, and Communaute Milton-Parc, we observe an emphasis on and support for long-term retention of affordable housing, whereby land trust arrangements serve as an innovative platform for producing and preserving housing that is cooperatively owned and managed. There was a similar focus on affordable housing provision among the community land trust organizations that arose in central and western Canada from the mid-1990s to mid-2000s. Without the existence of a formalized CLT network and, in most cases, without the existence of government legislation that would have legitimized or supported the existence of CLTs, such development tended to be ad hoc and localized.[6]

These CLTs were initiated by community activists who were searching for alternative, practical methods by which to attain affordable housing. They focused on individual homeownership, rather than cooperative housing, while working in partnership with private, for-profit developers and philanthropic affordable housing developers such as Habitat for Humanity. There is also evidence of informal knowledge sharing among these Canadian CLT organizers, who sometimes drew on personal information gathered about the implementation of the CLT model in the United States (Bunce, Khimani, *et al,* 2013).

West Broadway Community Land Trust (WBCLT) was the earliest example. It was established in 1999 as a subsidiary of the West Broadway Community Development Corporation (CMHC, 2005), located in the West Broadway neighbourhood of downtown Winnipeg, Manitoba. The community development corporation was a particularly innovative community development organization that focused on affordable housing and other social initiatives such as a community credit union, and was guided by concerns over local poverty issues caused by public disinvestment and encroaching gentrification/rising residential prices (Beaubien and Ring, 2006).

The intention of the WBCLT was to provide more diverse affordable housing tenure options in the form of rent-to-own homeownership, individual homeownership, cooperative homeownership, and affordable rental units (CMHC, 2005). A 2006 study of the WBCLT noted, however, that the primary focus of WBCLT was rent-to-own homeownership, addressing the needs of low-income households who were unable to move directly into homeownership but who might become homeowners over time with assistance (Beaubien and Ring, 2006). WBCLT assembled neighbourhood land parcels and purchased existing housing stock over a five-year period, offering a rent-to-own plan that was secured through a ground lease agreement between WBCLT and the tenant (who was also the potential owner).

This arrangement entailed the oversight of extensive renovations and the management of a complex array of funding from different governmental housing programs (Ibid., p. 3). Ultimately, WBCLT was unable to sustain the organizational and funding capacity that was needed both to undertake these renovations and to maintain the units through the duration of the rent-to-own period. This resulted in the eventual closure of the WBCLT as an arm of the West Broadway Community Development Corporation and the sale of some of its housing at market rate. Despite this failure, as Beaubien and Ring (Ibid.) noted, WBCLT played an important role in galvanizing community engagement and increasing public debate about land tenure as a component of community development, having a positive and lasting significance for the West Broadway community.

Other first-generation CLTs in central and western Canada faced similar challenges. The *Vernon and District Community Land Trust Society* (VDCLT) was formed in the province of British Columbia in 2008 to accrue public and philanthropic donations of lands and buildings for the development and management of affordable housing (Vernon and District Community Land Trust Society, 2012). The VDCLT's first project was a joint initiative with the City of Vernon, whereby the local government purchased land near the downtown core that was leased to the VDCLT through a long-term contractual arrangement and a small lease payment. The VDCLT, with Habitat for Humanity as a development partner, subsequently constructed rental units for low-income families and people with disabilities on this site. Since this initial project, the VDCLT has focused its efforts on accruing title to other lands and attaining public and philanthropic funding for additional affordable housing projects. It remains engaged with local communities in advocating for affordable housing in Vernon.

Also appearing in western Canada during this period was the *Calgary Community Land Trust* (CCLT). The CCLT was formed by the Calgary Homeless Foundation and was incorporated as a nonprofit organization in 2003 (Canada Mortgage and Housing Corporation, 2005). The CCLT focused on the assembly of land and building stock, as well as obtaining funds for the development and operation of affordable housing (Calgary Community Land Trust, 2012). CCLT received a donation of surplus federal government land, the result of a land swap between the federal government and the municipal government of Calgary, acquired for the purpose of building affordable housing on the land. The CCLT's first affordable housing project was the Sun Court development, completed in 2007, consisting of 27 units of owner-occupied family housing built by Habitat for Humanity Calgary (Calgary Homeless Foundation, 2012). The CCLT then went dormant for several years, as the work of the Calgary Homeless Foundation shifted towards more immediate and front-line initiatives to address homelessness in Calgary. It is now functioning as a CLT again, as we will discuss in the next section, reporting on more recent Canadian CLTs.

The *Central Edmonton Community Land Trust* (CECLT) emerged as a nonprofit corporation in 1998 with a mandate of fostering community-based development through land management and affordable housing provision. CECLT received donated land and properties from the municipal government of Edmonton and received funding from philanthropic foundations and development loans from the federal government's Canada Mortgage and Housing Corporation and Edmonton's Inner-City Housing Society. Unfortunately, due to difficulties in securing mortgages in the rent-to-own arrangements, CECLT had to repay Edmonton's government for the cost of the donated properties, selling them at market rate in order to raise reimbursement funds.

The situation in Edmonton highlights some of the broader challenges that were faced by the early CLTs in Canada, including: an inability to obtain mortgages for CLT home-owners; reliance on piecemeal and unpredictable government funding; and shifting political support for CLT activities from local government.

There were major differences among the CLTs that formed during this period, both in the tenure and scale of their projects and in the extent to which organizations and their activities were led by a place-based community. Some of these efforts, such as Milton-Parc and the West Broadway CLT, were community-led at the neighbourhood level, while the majority of CLTs during this period were driven by sector-based organizations such as the Co-operative Housing Federation of Canada (in the case of Colandco) and the Calgary Homeless Foundation (in the case of the Calgary Community Land Trust). Despite the small number of CLTs that emerged prior to 2012, however, they contributed to an emerging public awareness about the model's potential for delivering affordable housing (see Canada Mortgage and Housing Corporation, 2005). They also shaped a path for the formation of a second wave of CLT organizations.

THE SECOND GENERATION OF CANADIAN CLTs
2012–PRESENT

There has been a resurgence of interest in CLT development in Canada in recent years. Out of twenty currently active CLTs in Canada, nine were established since 2014. In 2017, moreover, a new Canadian CLT Network was formed to organize a more cohesive sector. This resurgence has been driven in part by the dynamic evolution of the small group of "first-generation," sector-based land trusts, which have re-emerged as expert-led nonprofit affordable housing developers. It also includes a new and energized "second generation" of more activist-based, community-based CLTs. The activists behind these latter initiatives — neighbourhood residents, community agencies, radical planners and, in some cases, municipal staff — have organized CLTs in response to the escalating affordable housing crisis in Canadian cities, rapid gentrification, and a renewed interest in community-based responses to these problems. While contemporary Canadian CLTs from both phases of CLT development share a common objective of increasing the supply of permanently affordable housing, they differ in their respective approaches to community-led development, community ownership, and democratic governance. We explore these issues in the following sections by referring to the activities of several representative second-generation CLTs.

Community-Based CLT Development

Since 2014, nine new community-led CLTs have emerged in response to an escalating affordable housing crisis in Canadian cities and a growing sense that government and social sector responses have been inadequate. This crisis, driven by an undersupply of housing, the increasing financialization of the housing market, and the repositioning by corporate landlords and private developers of existing housing for higher-income renters and homeowners, has translated into gentrification and redevelopment pressures in particular urban neighbourhoods (August and Walks, 2018; Bunce, 2018; Walks, 2014). For low-income and vulnerable residents, gentrification is a harmful process of destabilization. It causes food insecurity, housing insecurity, eviction, and displacement. While the social costs of gentrification are well known, neither the government nor the social housing sector has cultivated an adequate response. As a result, some impacted communities have looked to the community land trust as a way to mitigate gentrification.

The CLT model is appealing because of its emphasis on removing land and housing from the speculative market and controlling the rapid rise in real estate costs, thereby securing the perpetual affordability of land and housing. As Dominique Russell of the Kensington Market Land Trust in downtown Toronto's historic and gentrifying Kensington Market neighbourhood has stated, "Gentrification is a real estate problem and we felt we needed a real estate solution" (Interview with Dominique Russell, February 2, 2019, Toronto). Similar to first-generation CLTs, the current generation of community-led CLTs is focused on securing community ownership and/or community control of the land, whether through donation, purchase, or a long-term land lease from government, and then developing housing that will be permanently affordable. While CLT organizations retain ownership of the land, ownership of the building is retained by the CLT and leased to a nonprofit organization to provide affordable housing, or the building is owned directly by the nonprofit organization. Unlike sector-based CLTs, however, which view land ownership primarily as a legal tool to ensure affordable housing provision, the community-based organizations tend to have a broader agenda where community ownership of land is seen as the means to exercise

> The CLT is not only used for land preservation and housing provision, but also for planning and preserving socially just communities.

broader community control over local development. They also engage in participatory democracy practices to fight against detrimental land uses and harmful real estate development decisions.

In urban areas like Toronto's Parkdale and Kensington Market neighbourhoods, Hamilton's Beasley neighbourhood, and the Heatherington area of Ottawa, where there is a long-standing working class, racialized, immigrant and socially progressive identity, gentrification threatens not only housing affordability, but collective social infrastructures, the local economy, and neighbourhood culture. In Vancouver's Hogan's Alley Society, the CLT acts as a way to redress the historical displacement of Vancouver's Black population. The CLT model provides a platform in such places for encouraging resident empowerment and participation and for exercising community control over neighbourhood change. In these contexts, the CLT is not only used for land preservation and housing provision, but also for planning and preserving more socially just communities.

Recent community-led CLTs have gone beyond a first-generation focus on the acquisition of land and the development of housing to engage more broadly in neighbourhood and city-wide activism, social rights advocacy, and community-led planning.

Parkdale Neighbourhood Land Trust (Toronto). The first of these second-generation, community-led CLTs to emerge was the Parkdale Neighbourhood Land Trust (PNLT). Established in 2014, the PNLT was initiated by residents and representatives from local nonprofit organizations who were concerned about the increasing gentrification of an historically working-class community. The intended role of the land trust was the acquisition and preservation of important community assets, removing them from the speculative market. A secondary goal was to enable increased democratic participation by neighbourhood residents in planning around land use. Although still in its start-up phase, PNLT has already generated strong local support. By mid 2019, it had attracted over 700 registered members and had completed two acquisitions, including an urban agricultural project and a rooming house preservation pilot project, which it intends to expand to build a portfolio of community-owned rooming houses.

Canada's charity law is more restrictive and burdensome than the 501(c)(3) designation in the United States. As a result, to accomplish its goals, Parkdale has developed a unique dual organizational model, consisting of a charity and a nonprofit that work together, but have different strategic purposes. The charitable land trust, called the Neighbourhood Land Trust (NLT), can benefit from charitable donations of land and money, but may only hold land that is used for charitable purposes and may only lease land to other charities. The charity cannot own cooperative housing or undertake community planning, both of which are not considered charitable purposes. It is also very limited in its ability to undertake political activity. The nonprofit land trust, the Parkdale Neighbourhood Land Trust (PNLT), has limited ability to fundraise, but can own and lease land more freely and has no limits on its political activity. The nonprofit land trust has a broad-based membership and community-elected board, while retaining control over the charity.

Inspired by CLTs in the United States, such as Dudley Neighbors Inc. in Boston and the Oakland CLT in the San Francisco Bay Area, PNLT has embraced the governance model of the "classic" CLT. Emphasizing community control of the organization itself, the PNLT's 15-person board of directors is elected from its resident membership. Furthermore, a tripartite board structure ensures equal representation from: "core members" who live or work on the trust's land; "organizational members" who are drawn from organizations that serve or embody the diversity of Parkdale; and "community members" who live or work within the geographic boundaries of Parkdale.

PNLT focuses its acquisition planning efforts on affordable housing and also space for community economic development, such as urban agriculture, social enterprises, and community services. With an interest in being responsive to community needs and

Fig. 7.2. PNLT members celebrating acquisition of at-risk rooming house, Toronto.

visions, the trust sets its priorities through community planning and action research. In 2016, PNLT co-led a participatory planning process, engaging 31 local organizations and over 400 residents in the creation of the *Parkdale Community Planning Study—A plan for decent work, shared wealth and equitable development in Parkdale.* The study identified an opportunity for the Neighborhood Land Trust to secure its first piece of land, a 7000 square-foot vacant property, which was acquired in 2017 through a below-market private purchase. The trust does not operate programs on the land it owns, but provides afford-able land leases to eligible operating partners. Its first acquisition, now named the Milky Way Garden, is leased to Greenest City, a local environmental charity that will redevelop this vacant lot into an urban agriculture space to enhance affordable and equitable access to healthy food for local community members.

In 2017, the PNLT undertook a Community Action Research study of rooming house loss; a neighbourhood crisis that was quickly decreasing affordable single rooms and small rental units through the rapid conversion of rooming houses into upscaled rental housing or single-family homes. In response, the PNLT recruited four community orga-nizations to implement a multi-partner Rooming House Preservation Strategy targeted to 59 at-risk rooming houses in Parkdale. Pursuing this strategy, after eight unsuccessful attempts, the Neighbourhood Land Trust has recently implemented a rooming hous-ing preservation pilot, acquiring a 15-unit at-risk rooming house with capital funding provided by the City of Toronto. It is important to note that it was necessary to undertake two years of targeted advocacy and activism in order to build political support at the City of Toronto to make capital funding available to the land trust.[7] This funding enables and requires NLT to maintain rents at or below 80% of Average Market Rent (AMR) for a 99-year affordability period. Eligible tenants can also benefit from deeper levels of affordability, however, through rental supplements. The property will be held by the charitable NLT, but leased and operated by PARC, a local supportive housing organization.

The asset bases of PNLT and NLT are not large. Nevertheless, their public advocacy and higher profile in the press have contributed greatly to the growing public awareness and interest in CLTs, both in Toronto and across Canada.

Hamilton Community Land Trust (Ontario). The Hamilton Community Land Trust (HCLT) was formed in 2014 in the Beasley neighbourhood of Hamilton, Ontario by residents and community-based organizations who saw the need for greater community control over land use and the revitalization of Central Hamilton. This historically working-class city has long suffered from economic decline, environmental contamination, and high vacancy rates, but by 2014 a new phase of real estate reinvestment and gentrification was well underway. Between 2012 and 2015, housing prices in Hamilton rose significantly. HCLT's mandate is to hold and to steward land, acquired primarily from the municipality, and to facilitate the land's use for affordable housing or other community needs. The CLT is playing a facilitative role in the development of its lands, rather than that of a developer or operator, by working with resident groups, housing developers, and other organizations to transform underutilized properties into high-quality affordable housing, gardens, and community spaces. In 2017, HCLT acquired its first parcel of land from the City of Hamilton and then partnered with Habitat for Humanity Hamilton to develop a four-bedroom home that is being leased to a lower-income family. This initial project has demonstrated the capacity of HCLT to act as a viable organizational vehicle for redeveloping vacant city land (Hamilton Community Land Trust, 2019).

Kensington Market Community Land Trust (Toronto). Kensington Market Community Land Trust (KMCLT) was initiated in 2017 by an activist-minded group of residents who had successfully mobilized to stop the development of a WalMart store near an entrance road to the neighbourhood. The group aims to utilize the CLT to protect neighbourhood affordability more generally. Dominique Russell of KMCLT states that, "The fundamental underpinning characteristic of Kensington Market is its affordability, and we want to ensure this is preserved into the future" (Russell Interview, 2019). In recent years, Kensington Market has experienced increasing condominium development around the edges of the neighbourhood, rising rents, and "renovictions" linked to a surge in residential rehabilitation and the proliferation of short-term rentals such as AirBnB in the area. For long-term tenants and small independent store owners in this historically immigrant community, there is a shared interest in finding a way to remain in the neighbourhood and to protect its unique character (Ibid.).

KMCLT is planning to utilize the CLT for community ownership of land and community control over whatever is built upon it. The organization hopes to acquire and to preserve at-risk rental housing and storefronts. Potentially it may also oversee the redevelopment of a large municipal parking lot into a new affordable housing building. While KMCLT is still in its start-up phase of CLT development, its early success has generated support from local residents and representatives of the municipal government.

Hogan's Alley Society (Vancouver). Fifty years ago, after decades of displacement pressure on the community, the construction of the Georgia and Dunsmuir viaducts displaced an area historically known as Hogan's Alley, home to the city's Black population (Hogan's Alley Society, n.d.). In recent years, the City of Vancouver has focused efforts on removing the viaducts and is planning to revitalize the area through the North East False Creek (NEFC) area plan, approved in 2018. The Hogan's Alley Society was formed as a community-led nonprofit organization in 2017 to seek redress for the displacement of the Black community by fostering social, political, cultural and economic justice for Vancouver's Black community. Through a proposal for a nonprofit community land trust, the Hogan's Alley Society seeks to steward the land and to oversee the development of affordable housing, cultural amenities, social enterprise, and small business spaces, managing these assets in perpetuity. Negotiations with the City of Vancouver are also underway for a transfer of the former Hogan's Alley site into the CLT, a commitment made in the NEFC policy by the City Council in 2018. The redevelopment and stewardship of these lands will be led by the Hogan's Alley Society, working with partners and stakeholders in applying the CLT model to support renter households (Hogan's Alley Society, n.d.).

Sector-Based Community Land Trusts

While community-led CLTs have generated new interest in the CLT as a model for bottom-up development, sector-based CLTs have continued to demonstrate that the CLT is an effective vehicle for the development and stewardship of large stocks of affordable housing. Some first-generation CLTs, such as Colandco, have halted their housing development activities and now focus purely on the stewardship of their assets. Others are forging new growth plans. The recent formation of the Vancouver Community Land Trust Foundation (VCLTF) and HomeSpace (formerly the Calgary Community Land Trust) underscore a new phase of sector-based CLT development led by organizations with expansionist business approaches. As a result, these two sector-based CLTs are building thousands of units of new affordable housing on community-owned land and, in the process, are creating broader public recognition of the CLT model in Canada.

The Community Land Trust (Vancouver). The most prolific sector-based CLT development to be undertaken in the past decade has been led by the Cooperative Housing Federation of British Columbia (CHFBC), which controls three CLTs in the wider Vancouver area, collectively branded as *The Community Land Trust.* This recent development has occurred in the context of Vancouver's expensive housing market which, in turn, has sparked a renewed interest in cooperative and nonprofit affordable housing provision. The success of the three Vancouver-area land trusts was facilitated by enabling policy and political will at both the provincial and municipal levels. In this light, the CHFBC has imagined the CLT as a development and asset management vehicle that can deliver and steward affordable housing in direct partnership with government and the broader community housing sector.

Following in the footsteps of Colandco in Toronto, CHFBC created the Community Housing Land Trust Foundation in 1993 to hold the land and buildings of multiple cooperatives. In its early years, the Foundation acquired six properties, containing 354 units, transferred from the provincial government. The Foundation retained ownership of the land and the buildings, executing leases for the land and buildings with the independent housing cooperatives.

In 2012, a unique opportunity emerged for the CHFBC to establish a second land trust, the Vancouver Community Land Trust Foundation (VCLTF), when it won a bid competition to develop four parcels of land that were owned by the City of Vancouver. That year, CHFBC re-envisioned its model and began to self-identify as a community land trust, even rebranding its multiple land trust efforts as "The Community Land Trust." This re-framing was partially political: emphasizing the nonprofit ownership and stewardship of the land and buildings in contrast to the private provision of affordable housing that was being proposed by other developers who were competing for access to public land. It also signaled that the CLT would serve the broader community housing sector, including nonprofit and Indigenous organizations, rather than serving only cooperatives.

VCLTF has since successfully developed 358 affordable housing units on these four parcels of land. While title to the land has been retained by the City of Vancouver, the CLT has a 99-year leasehold for the land and owns the buildings until the end of the lease, when all of the improvements will revert to the City. VCLTF hopes that, at the end of this lease period, the CLT and the City will work together to redevelop the property for purposes that are consistent with their respective missions (Interview with Tom Armstrong, July 21, 2019).

Three of these properties are owned by the Community Land Trust and operated as rental housing, managed through operating agreements with three different nonprofit housing organizations. The fourth property is operated by a housing cooperative. Since the housing is operated by other organizations, the VCLTF is free to focus on other

> The Vancouver CLT Foundation has become a preferred partner for doing residential development on municipally owned land.

aspects of development and stewardship. Across its entire portfolio, tenants pay rents that range from a shelter rate to 90% of Average Market Rent. Building on this successful partnership with the City of Vancouver, VCLTF won another competitive bid in 2018 to develop an additional 1000 new affordable rental units on seven parcels of City-owned land.

While CLTs in Canada have historically faced challenges in increasing their scale, VCLTF has addressed this issue by forging strong partnerships with municipalities and by maximizing the benefits of a portfolio approach to development and stewardship; that is, when planning for new developments, VCLTF utilizes revenues generated from more profitable properties to cross-subsidize less profitable properties. This has allowed VCLTF to develop properties which may not have otherwise been financially viable. VCLTF's ability to develop affordable housing on a wide range of properties has positioned it as a preferred partner by the City of Vancouver for doing residential development on municipally owned land.

Significantly, through its multiple land trusts, CHFBC has departed from the standard practice of CLTs in other countries and has occasionally chosen to encumber its landholdings with debt, thereby "unlocking" the equity to leverage the financing needed for the development of new affordable housing. As Tiffany Duzzita, VCLTF's Director, notes:

[T]he community land trust is a vehicle for keeping the affordable housing sector growing, and it comes down to benefits derived from the separation of land and buildings. The land component stays with the land trust, removing it from the speculative market and rising real estate costs. But the nonprofit land trust can actually use the land value as equity to redevelop and build new housing by borrowing against it. Since the land trust is mission based—it uses its (growing equity) to build more housing, not generate profit (Presentation by Tiffany Duzzita, 2017).

The community land trust has also proven to be a successful conduit through which to stabilize, improve, and redevelop existing cooperative housing assets. Recently, VCLTF took ownership of 94 cooperative homes in Abbotsford BC after the co-op experienced financial challenges. VCLTF worked with co-op members to design a comprehensive renovation plan that was funded through refinancing their existing mortgages. By bringing the co-op's assets into the land trust, the co-op benefited from an increased asset management capacity. Additionally, VCLTF provided a guarantee that the land would be protected for affordable housing on a long-term basis. Tiffany Duzzita estimates that in twelve years, the land trust will be able to leverage the increased value in the land to fund the development of an estimated 200 new units of affordable housing at the Abbotsford site, requiring little to no government assistance (Presentation by Duzzita, 2017).

HomeSpace (Calgary). The initial vision for Calgary's HomeSpace, in its previous incarnation as the Calgary Community Land Trust, was to focus on receiving cash and land donations for affordable housing, but not to develop or to operate the housing itself. HomeSpace now identifies as a nonprofit real estate corporation that seeks to provide development, property management, and asset management capacity to the affordable housing sector through the land trust model. As of early 2019, HomeSpace owned 27 buildings with a total of 520 rental units, and had an additional 211 units under development. Utilizing a partnership model, HomeSpace retains ownership of the buildings it develops and provides property management, while 17 agency partners provide support services to residents with the intention of serving diverse populations. Rents are offered at a "break-even" rate that is 20%–40% below market, with many tenants receiving deeper levels of affordability through housing allowances. One characteristic that sets Home-Space apart from many other CLTs is that it explicitly focuses on developing properties for supportive housing. It is also distinctive in not separating the ownership of land and buildings. HomeSpace continues to own both.

Over several years, HomeSpace has increased its capacity to become one of the largest nonprofit housing developers in Calgary. In 2018, HomeSpace won competitive bids to build affordable housing on three parcels of land that were owned by the City of Calgary. HomeSpace attributes its recent success and growth in part to the high level of coordination of affordable housing efforts in Calgary. The Calgary Homeless Foundation acts as the systems planner, working with local agencies and government to identify areas of greatest need, while HomeSpace acts as the nonprofit developer in partnership with government and specialized housing providers to develop projects and to serve as their long-term steward after they are built (HomeSpace Society, 2018).

CANADIAN NETWORK OF CLTs

There are currently twenty active CLTs in Canada, half of which were initiated since 2014. This recent surge in CLT development in Canada coalesced in July 2017 with the establishment of the Canadian Network of CLTs (CNCLT).[8] This new Network aims to unite both newer, community-led CLTs and more established CLTs into a cohesive, nation-wide movement. Initial objectives of the Canadian Network of CLTs include: (1) increasing government recognition of the CLT model through legislative advocacy; (2) increasing peer-to-peer resource sharing and capacity building; and (3) centering of social justice in CLT development.

In 2019, over 30 members of the fledgling Network met in person in Canada for the first time at a conference hosted by Communaute Milton-Parc in Montreal, entitled *From The Ground Up: Community Control of Land, Housing and the Economy.*

The Canadian CLT Network (*www.communityland.ca*) is still new and remains fairly ad hoc in its organization, but it has already increased collaboration and resource sharing among Canadian CLTs. If the Network can successfully facilitate cross-pollination and capacity building between community-led approaches and sector-based CLT approaches, the expectation is that Canadian CLTs will continue to grow as necessary structures for more socially just planning and affordable housing provision, while also having a greater impact on public policies.

$\sim$

CONCLUSION

The recent growth of CLTs in Canada builds upon several decades of organizing, from the 1980s onwards. In the context of large-scale government cutbacks in funding for social housing programs, social services, and community programs over the past several decades, Canadian CLTs have emerged as a relatively small, yet effective vehicle for meeting community needs and broader public priorities for affordable housing.

The "first generation" of CLTs that emerged in the 1980s were either large, sector-based organizations that prioritized affordable housing provision across cities and urban regions through partnerships with co-op housing societies, or neighbourhood-oriented and focused on community-based development through local affordable housing provision. This difference is evident in the organizational development of Colandco over the past several decades and its use of a land trust arrangement to include a portfolio of individual cooperative housing communities across Toronto. In contrast, the West Broadway CLT in Winnipeg chose to remain neighbourhood-focused, concentrating on the renovation of rent-to-own housing and supporting local community development efforts. Several of the CLTs in this first phase of Canadian CLT development created their own variations on the American CLT model, informed by the Canadian adoption of cooperatives, as a way to create affordable communities.

After 2012, the emergence of a "second generation" of CLTs followed a similar pattern of being either sector-based and expansionist in their approach to affordable housing provision or community-led and neighbourhood-based. The growth of CLTs during this period, especially over the last several years, has reflected the influence of local activists advocating for the particular needs of their surrounding community. This is evident in CLT initiatives that more broadly address the impact of gentrification, such as in Parkdale, Hamilton, and Hogan's Alley. Sector-led CLTs, on the other hand, such as the Vancouver Community Land Trust and HomeSpace, demonstrate innovative strategies to accrue land and to act as affordable housing developers through the formation of multi-sectoral partnerships and sophisticated management of their housing portfolios. With a city-wide service area, these sector-based CLTs are expanding affordable housing supply and, at the same time, increasing public awareness about the potential productivity and viability of the CLT model.

The recent establishment of a Canadian Network of CLTs, bringing together sector-based and community-based CLTs in a formal network for resource sharing and knowledge mobilization, points to a new phase of CLT development in Canada. CLT organizations are now actively engaged in creating links with one another and with organizations and networks in other countries. There has also been, of late, a much-needed discussion about Indigenous land rights and national reconciliation in relation to CLTs. Building on several decades of organizational development and advocacy, Canadian CLTs are now creating a new wave of innovative practices and opportunities for affordable housing provision and community-led development.

Notes

1. A National Housing Strategy for Canada, the first federal government initiative for affordable housing in several decades, was announced by the Liberal government in their 2016 budget. This Strategy is a 10-year, $40 billion plan to address homelessness and to subsidize the production of 100,000 new affordable housing units (National Housing Strategy, 2018).

2. 96% of all housing in Canada is currently built by the private sector (Cheung, 2017).

3. Throughout this chapter we use the term "sector-based" to refer to the nonprofit housing sector. This is a common colloquial term used by affordable housing advocates in Canada.

4. This $2 million seed grant was provided by the Campeau Corporation, a Canadan-based commercial and residential real estate development firm (Canada Mortgage and Housing Corporation, 2005).

5. The renovation of these buildings and other infrastructure was publicly funded at an estimated cost of $30 million (CAD), provided by the Canadian Mortgage and Housing Corporation, the City of Montreal, and the provincial government of Quebec (World Habitat, 2017).

6. In Canada, legislation for local level (municipal) governance is produced and enacted by provincial or territorial governments. There are ten provincial governments and three territorial governments.

7. Because of this project, the City of Toronto piloted a new approach to distributing capital funding through a fast-tracked approval process that enabled PNLT to act quickly to acquire the property on the open market.

8. The first meetings were held online with support from Grounded Solutions Network in the United States. They included representatives from Parkdale Neighbourhood Land Trust, Kensington Market CLT, Circle CLT, Colandco, Hamilton CLT, Vivacité (Montreal), Hogan's Alley, Communaute Milton-Parc, Vancouver's Community Land Trust, the North End Halifax CLT (Nova Scotia), and Heatherington Land Trust (Ottawa).

References

August, M. & Walks, A. (2018). "Gentrification, Suburban Decline, and the Financialization of Multi-Family Rental Housing: The Case of Toronto." *Geoforum* 89, 124–136.

Beaubien, LA. & Ring, L. (2006). *Preserving Community: Examining the West Broadway Community Land Trust.* Unpublished report.

Bunce, S. (2018). *Sustainability Policy, Planning, and Gentrification in Cities.* Routledge, Abingdon.

Bunce, S., Khimani, N., Sungu-Erylimaz, Y., and Earle, E. (2013). *Urban Community Land Trusts: Experiences from Canada, the United States, and Britain.* University of Toronto, Toronto.

Calgary Homeless Foundation (2012). *Calgary Homeless Foundation 2012 Annual Report.* Calgary Homeless Foundation, Calgary.

Canada Mortgage and Housing Corporation (2005). *Critical Success Factors for Community Land Trusts in Canada: Final Report.* Canada Mortgage and Housing Corporation, Ottawa.

Canadian Cooperative Housing Federation of Toronto (2019) <*https://co-ophousingto-ronto.coop*> Last accessed: July 1, 2019.

Communitas Inc. (1985). *Land Trusts for Non-Profit Continuing Housing Co-operatives.* Cooperative Housing Federation of Canada.

Hamilton Community Land Trust (2019). <*https://www.hamiltonclt.org*> Last accessed: July 22, 2019.

Home Space Society (2018). <*https://www.homespace.org*> Last accessed: July 22, 2019.

Hogan's Alley Society (n.d.). <*http://www.hogansalleysociety.org*> Last accessed: July 22, 2019.

Hulchanski, D. (1983). "Co-operative Land Management: The Potential of Linking a Community Land Trust to Government Housing Supply Programs," Pp. 35–50 in: D. Hulchanski (Ed.) *Managing Land for Housing: The Experience of Housing Co-operatives in British Columbia.* Centre for Human Settlements, University of British Columbia.

Hulchanski, D. (1988). "The Evolution of Property Rights and Housing Tenure in Post-War Canada: Implications for Housing Policy," *Urban Law and Policy* 9, 135–156.

Interview with Brian Finley (2013). Toronto.

Interview with Tom Clement (2019). Toronto.

Interview with Dominique Russell (2019). Toronto.

Interview with Tom Armstrong (2019). Toronto.

Kowaluk, L. & Piche-Burton, C. (eds.)(2012). *Communaute Milton-Parc: How We Did It and How It Works Now.* Communaute Milton-Parc, Montreal.

La Communaute Milton Parc (2013). *<http://www.miltonparc.org/about-us/>* Last accessed: July 22, 2019.

Presentation by Tiffany Duzzita (2017). ONPHA Conference, Niagara Falls.

Roussopoulos, Dimitrios and Hawley, Josh (eds.)(2018). *Villages in Cities: Community Land Ownership, Cooperative Housing, and the Milton Parc Story.* Montreal: Black Rose Books.

Vernon and District Community Land Trust Society (2012). *<http://www.communityland. ca/canadian-clts/>* Last accessed: July 22, 2019.

Walks, A. (2014). "From Financialization to Socio-Spatial Polarization of the City: Evidence from Canada," *Economic Geography* 90(1), 33–66.

World Habitat (2017). Milton Parc Community *<https://www.world-habitat.org/world-habitat-awards/winners-and-finalists/milton-park-community/>* Last accessed: July 22, 2019.

8.

Messy Is Good!
Origins and Evolution of the CLT Movement in England

*Stephen Hill, Catherine Harrington,
and Tom Archer*

"Housing is a messy subject." This was the insight of Professor Sir Michael Atiyah, former president of the Royal Society and arguably the United Kingdom's greatest mathematician since Isaac Newton. He made this remark in his opening speech to an international symposium of scientists in 1998, convened to propose "A Global Strategy for Housing in the Third Millennium." Hosted by the Royal Society, the symposium was intended to have a strong scientific and technological bias, but Sir Atiyah focused on morality and human rights:

> Housing is not scientific, not hard. Its themes are living, love, family, sociability and self-expression; none of which is easily quantified or measured . . . Sunshine may be more important than solar energy, and community and comfort are more important than strength and durability . . .

Another speaker, John P. Eberhard, Professor of Architecture and Planning at Carnegie Mellon University, moved swiftly from design codes and concrete testing procedures to call for a new paradigm of housing research, based on housing rights. He was scornful of "the continuing power of preferred positions" and the negligible contributions made by governments and construction industries to housing the homeless and people on modest incomes in both the developed and developing world:

> The housing industry in Western society prefers the status quo, and will not support government research programmes that might upset the "delicate balance" of the housing markets . . . I present here a case for making changes in the national housing priorities of Western societies, and argue that housing issues are interwoven with the issues of community infrastructure. . . . The barriers to effective technological solutions or design changes in housing are primarily questions of political will . . .

Barriers, industry preferring the status quo, political will (or the absence of it) — those will sound like familiar challenges to anyone working to meet the housing needs of their own community. That includes community land trusts, since producing and preserving affordable housing has been the main focus of England's CLT movement. This chapter will focus on how CLT activists in England have met the messy challenges of housing and steadily rebuilt the infrastructure in their communities, despite everything that seemed to get in the way.

This is also a story of how CLTs have reshaped political will and national policy in a country where policymaking for both housing and community development has been highly centralized; as if there were one English housing market, rather than hundreds of smaller markets. CLTs and their allies among other forms of community-led housing have helped to redesign and to redirect national policy so that local priorities, autonomy, and diversity are valued and supported—objectives that have now been substantially achieved.

The chapter covers three periods, mapping the trajectory of CLT development in England:

- Period One, 1986–2008: "Origins of CLT Thinking and Practice."

- Period Two, 2008–2018: "A Decade of Growth and Consolidation."

- Period Three, Present and Beyond: "Potential Futures for CLTs."

This chapter will celebrate the importance of "messiness" in the development of new ways of doing things in a field of activity that has historically been resistant to change and dominated by many vested political and financial interests. English CLTs are concerned both with the specific provision of genuinely and permanently affordable housing, and with what some CLTs have called "local governance," the power of self-determination on issues that are of critical importance to the wellbeing of a community.[1] Over three decades, messiness has helped to build a resilient and adaptive CLT movement, one that is now capable of generating enough possible and appropriate futures to keep that movement in good shape.

I. ORIGINS OF CLT THINKING AND PRACTICE, 1986–2008

- *Reimagining the equity structure of housing and land in villages, towns and cities.* The need for new locally based institutions to promote financial inclusion and to hold land for the common good emerged during an extended period of political change, created by financial crises and the distortion of local housing markets by the deregulation of global capital.

- *Improving the quality of life in rural Cornwall.* New ways of providing permanently affordable housing through CLTs arose in places where no other organisation could or would provide it.

- *New institutions for devolved local governance* emerged in government programmes, public housing estate regeneration, land assembly in the public interest, and urban renewal and growth area settings.

- *A statutory definition for CLTs in England and Wales* was enacted, emphasizing the "community" in CLT.

Reimagining the Equity Structure of Housing and Land in Villages, Towns and Cities[2]

The 1980s were a period of significant change in patterns of property ownership, financial services, and corporate ownership. Post-war welfare state policies were under assault on two fronts: from the privatisation of publicly funded and publicly owned assets and services, and from the deregulation of global capital markets. Before 1985, the biggest mortgage providers were mutual building societies. Trustee Savings Banks (TSB), with links to local government, provided low-cost banking services for working-class populations. Utilities were all publicly owned. Land ownership by central and local government had grown since the 1920s with the development of public housing, the building of post-WWII New Towns, and with a wide range of amenities for the "common good," including community and youth centres, swimming pools, and parks.

All this was to change. De-mutualisation led to the widespread transfer of almost all the large building societies and TSB networks to the United Kingdom's "Big Five" banks. Utilities, local buses, and train services were sold to private companies. The Conservative government's Right to Buy policy in 1980 led to the sale of council homes at generous discounts. By 2019, there were 1.25 million fewer affordable homes of all kinds than in 1980, despite all the new building that had occurred.

As banks closed branches, inner-city and rural communities were increasingly denied access to even the most basic financial services, marking a growing trend of financial exclusion for people on low and moderate incomes. Recession in the early 1990s made things worse, ushering in a time of persistently high levels of unemployment in those same inner-city and rural areas. The crisis accelerated the decline of manufacturing employment in northern England, with firms going into liquidation or relocating abroad in search of cheaper labour and more lenient regulation.

Local governments lost resources, powers, and autonomy. The central government restricted their ability to borrow and, thus, their capacity to build their own affordable housing or to assist private homeowners and landlords in improving the aging stock of terraced homes built in the 19th Century, which still formed the main source of housing in inner-city areas. With the sale of public-sector housing stock, a sharp fall across the UK in new house building, and a tidal wave of deregulated mortgage finance flooding the market, house prices rose much faster than incomes, marking the start of the process of financialisation of land and property markets. That process continues to this day, especially in London, Oxford, Cambridge and much of southern England. In many rural areas, the growth of second or holiday homeownership, and the retirement to the country of older people with accumulated housing equity from the sale of valuable urban homes, added to the upward drift in house prices.

The first pioneering CLT, the Stonesfield Trust, was set up in rural Oxfordshire in the mid-1980s. Like many other villages, rising housing prices had made Oxfordshire unaffordable for local people on a low or moderate income, but no one was building new, affordably priced homes. The Trust's founder, Tony Crofts, lived in the village and donated a small site to the Trust, an organization he had helped to set up. It was controlled by people living in the village, and aimed to provide permanently affordable rental housing for people who needed to live and work locally. The development was completed at relatively low cost, using a creative mix of investment by Crofts, loans from the local council and two social banks (Ecology Building Society and Triodos Bank) and interest-free loans and donations from the Quaker Housing Trust and ethical investors. In 1994, the equity of the first homes was used as leverage to build three more CLT homes and two affordable workspaces. This alignment of mutual interests among the community, a local landowner, the council, and funders was to be the foundation for the many rural CLTs that followed.

> They were all searching for alternative institutions that could tackle social and economic exclusion.

Crofts was a Quaker, who had been inspired by the writings of Gerard Winstanley and the Diggers, and by their ambition that land should be a "common store-house for all." Although he initiated his CLT project independently, he soon made connections with a group of activists working on new ways of addressing the impact of these wider structural changes. They were all searching for alternative institutions that could tackle social and economic exclusion, especially those that could encourage democratic and community ownership of housing, such as community land trusts.

This group of activists was greatly influenced by a 1989 book edited by Ward Morehouse, *Building Sustainable Communities*.[3] It included chapters by Shann Turnbull from Australia and Bob Swann and George Benello from the USA, highlighting the links among Community Development Finance Institutions (CDFIs), CLTs, and worker co-ops.[4]

In the late 1990s, several activists travelled to the USA from England, where they met Bob Swann, co-founder of the Institute of Community Economics, and John Davis who had helped to start the Burlington CLT (now named the Champlain Housing Trust). Their visit to the USA left them convinced that the development of CDFIs and CLTs, as new sustainable institutions to combat financial and social exclusion, would require the establishment of a nationally available support service and a treasury of retained knowledge that would make CLTs replicable and possible for any urban or rural community.

In 1999, after creating a formal action group, they developed terms of reference for a CLT action research programme and helped to establish Community Finance Solutions (CFS) at the University of Salford. CFS took the lead on policy advocacy for the growth of new CDFIs and CLTs, backed by other activists, who provided practical support for new CLT projects until the National CLT Network was formed in 2010.

The action research brief aimed to test how a CDFI and CLT strategy for rural regeneration could be aligned to win support from communities, local government, and funders. The first project was funded by the Hastoe Housing Association (a specialist rural affordable housing association), and the Housing Corporation (the government agency responsible for promoting and funding affordable housing in England). Three rural areas of England were selected for the action research. The project looked at the combined effects of the growth in second homes and a series of farming crises which had devastated rural economies across England throughout the 1990s. The most hard-hit of these areas was the southwest of England — Cornwall in particular.

Improving the Quality of Life in Rural Cornwall through Community Land Trusts[5]

That Cornwall became the first, and remains one of the most progressive and successful areas for CLTs, was the result of an ideal alignment of special circumstances that would shape the future development of CLTs. It was also due in part to the work of Dr. Bob Paterson (who lived just over the Cornish border in Devon) and by others at Community Finance Solutions.[6] Between 1999 and 2006, Community Finance Solutions began to develop practical ways of securing community ownership of land as the best way of providing permanently affordable housing.

After several years of planning, the Cornwall Community Land Trust (CCLT) began work in 2006, forming into a company in 2007. It aimed to advance CLTs by providing practical advice and support to village communities wishing to establish their own CLTs. Having an experienced housing development manager (Alan Fox) in the role of CCLT's Project Director, was instrumental.

Vital seed-corn funding was sourced from local councils and the forward-thinking Tudor Trust. A critically important relationship was forged with the project host, Cornwall Rural Housing Association (CRHA), whose chief executive at the time had previous experience in the cooperative business sector. This relationship saw back-office support and selective project finance provided by CRHA, with the Cornwall CLT providing development management services to CRHA. This cross-fertilisation of activity underpinned the financial viability of the CCLT. The success of this model of locally provided technical support was to lead, eventually, to the development of similar "Umbrella CLTs" across the country at the county, city, and sub-regional levels.

"I've lived in a caravan for all of this year, and was just really worried about what I was going to do and where I was going to live. Now, having my own home and building it myself with a garden in a place like this—it's just unreal."—new homeowner, St. Minver CLT

St. Minver, a pioneering self-build CLT. The parish of St. Minver includes a number of holiday villages on the north Cornwall coast, with some of the best surfing beaches in the UK. In 2006, average house prices were higher than in London. This caused proactive local parish councillors to begin exploring ways to overcome the difficulty experienced by local people in finding affordable housing to rent or to buy.

The St. Minver Community Land Trust Ltd emerged when a parish councillor sowed the idea of forming a CLT, when a local farmer offered land at a low price, and when a local builder and a group of residents came together. The North Cornwall District Council provided a start-up grant and an interest-free loan to underpin the development of what turned out to be the first of three phases. The self-build mortgages enabled the purchase of a serviced self-build plot from the CLT and repayment of the Council's loan. The St. Minver CLT was supported and advised by CCLT. A local allocation/sales policy was agreed with the Council, and twelve self-build applicants were selected from local people in need.

The St. Minver CLT signed a Section 106 Agreement with the local Council: a legally binding planning obligation which controls future occupancy and affordability and must be adhered to by all successive owner-occupants of a CLT home. The Section 106 Agreement is an additional protection for the principle of affordability in perpetuity. The same principle is embodied in the CLT's constitution and is incorporated into the sale of homes to income-qualified buyers.

The CLT completed its first phase of homes in Dingle's Way in December 2008, on time and on budget. They were sold on limited-equity terms. The total cost of the home represented one-third of the market value of the home on the day of completion, deemed to be affordable to local people paying no more than one-third of Area Median Income to meet their housing costs. This transformed the lives of local families who, without the CLT, would never have found secure housing. All future resales will be priced at one-third the market value of the home, with a new qualifying buyer selected by the CLT.

A partnership between the St. Minver CLT and CRHA has since seen a second phase of eight more self-build, limited-equity homes and four other rented homes completed on adjoining land in 2011. The CLT is now planning a third development in another part of the Parish.

What was the key to success for the Cornwall CLT? Three critical factors enabled Cornwall to become a rural CLT hotspot:

* Credible and sustained community leadership at the village and council level;

* Local councils offering short-term development finance through Revolving Loan Funds; and

* An alignment of interests among the council, local landowners, the CLT, and a local housing association, ensuring community support and leadership to identify appropriate sites, matched with access to locally available technical expertise.[7]

What was the key lesson from Cornwall that informed the future growth of CLTs nationwide? Individuals and organizations that had backed CLT development in Cornwall hoped to see the model spread throughout the UK. That would require, in their estimation, two building blocks. First, some sort of "national demonstration programme" was needed to refine the CLT concept, to influence public policy, and to widen acceptance of the CLT model by communities in other rural areas. Second, equity was needed to support initial experimentation and early replication of the CLT model, providing risk capital that would enable new CLTs to take on repayable debt for their first projects and to establish a track record of effective performance. Both building blocks were put in place by 2008. (The purpose and importance of the National CLT Demonstration Programme and the CLT Fund are described below, under Period II.)

New Institutions for Devolved Local Governance in Government Regeneration and Growth Area Programmes

The third strand of the early CLT story is fundamentally different. In rural areas, it had been community leaders, activists, and residents who had taken the initiative to find a solution to local problems which neither the state nor anyone else was trying to solve. In the national policy arena, the initiative for finding new ways to involve communities in housing provision and urban regeneration, thereby winning a place for CLTs, fell to a group of activist professionals: housing and public administration lawyers and specialists in housing development and finance. Their professional work was motivated by a public interest commitment to ensuring that citizens and communities woud have an effective say in major decisions that affect their lives.

These activist professionals were to play a major role in promoting and positioning CLTs to become a potential instrument of housing policy, particularly as related to:

* Methods of land assembly in government-designated Growth Areas;

* New forms of local governance to promote community wellbeing, through effective stewardship programmes for community-owned or community-controlled land; and

* The regeneration of large urban public housing estates.[8]

Although results on the ground were limited at the time, the presence of CLTs in public policy thinking were nevertheless critical to the development of the concept.

Methods of land assembly in Growth Areas.[9] The Labour Party, which led Britain's government from 1997 to 2010, backed a major expansion in housing supply, starting with its 2003 Sustainable Communities Plan, reinforced by major planning law reforms enacted in 2004. These measures aimed to empower citizens in local development of all kinds, requiring every development to have a Statement of Community Involvement.[10]

Organisations like the Joseph Rowntree Foundation believed that community ownership of land for new housing development could be a powerful way to engage communities in the future of their places, while reducing opposition to new development. That was based on its own experience with community control of development and local governance at its New Earswick development.[11] In its 2002 Centenary Year Report *Land for Housing,* the Foundation included a technical appendix explaining how CLTs could be used to secure a long-term community interest in land for new development.[12]

CLTs were also advocated by the Local Government Association (LGA) in its 2004 publication, *New Development and New Opportunities.* Although councils had very few powers, resources, or political inclination to take advantage of these "new opportunities," LGA's endorsement helped to raise the profile of CLTs and to popularize the concept.

> "A community land trust is a private non-profit corporation created to acquire and hold land for the benefit of a community and provide secure affordable access to land and housing for community residents. In particular, community land trusts attempt to meet the needs of residents least served by the prevailing market."
>
> —Local Government Association (2004)

New forms of local governance to promote community wellbeing, through the stewardship of community-owned or community-controlled assets. Alongside its planning reforms, the Labour government wanted to "modernise" local government. The New Deal for Communities (NDC), developed by the Labour government of the time, was a refinement of earlier urban regeneration programmes that had focussed on housing. It invested about £5 million annually in each of twenty deprived neighbourhoods (each containing up to 15,000 people) over a period of ten years. In 1998, councils and communities bid jointly for funding. Once selected, communities were put "in charge" of these resources. However, the central government failed to make councils cooperate with the NDC communities, thus seriously weakening the impact of this programme. Even so, a few successful NDC bodies continued after public funding ended in 2009.[13]

The NDC programme formed part of a more systemic approach to local government, integrating the use of assets, finance, town planning, and public service delivery. This approach was embedded in the Local Government Act of 2000, in which councils were given express powers to do anything they wished to promote the social, economic, and environmental wellbeing of their communities, a purpose that would later be reflected in the statutory definition of CLTs.

The regeneration of large urban public housing estates. From the late 1980s through the early 2000s, both Conservative and Labour governments funded capital programmes that enabled councils to improve aging or structurally defective public housing estates. Funding conditions often required councils to include communities in both decision making about the projects and the long-term governance of estates. Until the Financial Crash in 2007, the government's Community Housing Taskforce was investigating the potential for community-controlled CLTs to own the freehold of their estates, leasing the land to housing associations who would upgrade or redevelop this social housing.

A Statutory Definition for CLTs in England and Wales: Why There's a "C" in CLT

The activist professionals who were operating in this political environment had been inspired by the success of the Dudley Street Neighborhood Initiative (DSNI) in Boston.[14] DSNI's governance and holistic regeneration achievements were regarded as potential exemplars for both councils and communities that were being affected by plans for regeneration and new housing development.

The kind of devolved autonomy from the state, which DSNI respresented, was promoted by activist professionals in England as a model of "double devolution." This policy, adopted by the Labour government in the early 2000s, was intended to achieve a progressive devolution of powers from central to local government and from local government to communities. The Minister of Local Government considered various ideas for implementing devolution through his Local Government Sounding Board.[15] The Local Government Association, however, had no interest in the idea of transferring any powers to communities, despite its earlier endorsement of CLTs in the context of new development.

What the activists learned from this experience — and from the frustration of various CLT initiatives not quite coming off — was that CLT development could not be sustained in the face of shifting market or political conditions, unless "community" was the driving force behind the process. Even well-intentioned politicians, public servants, and professionals were no substitute for community leadership, advocacy, and organising in making CLTs happen.

Nevertheless, the activists appreciated the necessity for CLTs to obtain sufficient legal recognition that would justify a corporate existence independent of any particular government policy or programme, and any transitory political party alignment. In Cornwall, where CLTs were starting their first homes in 2007, it was especially apparent that having a national legal definition for CLTs would open up more sources of finance. Lenders were beginning to be more cautious as the Financial Crash unfolded. They needed a standardized definition of the CLT to understand what kind of organisation they were being asked to support in financing new residential development.

This Cornish justification for enacting a CLT definition was a straightforward "ask" of Members of Parliament (MPs). An amendment was added to the Housing and Regeneration Bill that was going through Parliament, specifying how a "community land trust" was to be defined in England and Wales. It was enacted into law in 2008.

Definition of a Community Land Trust in England and Wales: Section 79, Housing and Regeneration Act 2008

A corporate body which satisfies the conditions below:

1. is established for the express purpose of furthering the social, economic and environmental interests of a local community by acquiring and managing land and other assets in order:
- to provide a benefit to the local community; and
- to ensure that the assets are not sold or developed except in a manner which the trust's members think benefits the local community

2. is established under arrangements which are expressly designed to ensure that:
- any profits from its activities will be used to benefit the local community (otherwise than by being paid directly to members); and
- individuals who live or work in the specified area have the opportunity to become members of the trust (whether or not others can also become members) and the members of a trust control it.

The wording of this statutory definition was not just intended to reassure lending institutions, however. It was even more relevant for communities needing a legal form through which they could become more powerful in decision making about the future of their areas. By linking a CLT's purpose to the ownership of land for promoting the interests of residents, the definition tried to remedy the democratic deficit that had been left by the government's abandonment of "double devolution." It also addressed the absence of any obligation of landowners to serve the "common good" in English property rights and law.

Embodied in this CLT definition were three essential (and quietly subversive) concepts that would empower communities in the planning, development, and regeneration of their local areas:

- A CLT could only exist to protect and promote the economic, social and environmental interests of the existing community (directly copying the wellbeing powers given to councils in the Local Government Act 2000, and the legal purposes attributed to the planning reforms in the Planning and Compulsory Purchase Act 2004);

- Land should be owned and used for purposes of securing the "common good"; and

- Participatory, democratic control and democratic influence should be hallmarks of local development.

For most community activists, their main motivation for setting up a CLT was to restrict the price of land, curbing an out-of-control land market that was working against the wellbeing of their communities. This represented an approach to the pricing and allocation of land that elected and appointed public officials were (and still are) reluctant to adopt. The definition's overriding purpose was, therefore, to give communities status and democratic legitimacy to act in their own interests, pursuing a strategy that did not have to be decided by either the central or local government.

II. GROWTH AND CONSOLIDATION, 2008–2018

If the previous two decades sowed the seeds for a CLT movement in England, the third decade saw its rapid germination, as CLTs grew from twenty at the start of 2008 to over 300 today.[16] Crucially, this occurred during a period of further political and economic upheaval.

In 2010, after the first General Election following the 2007 Financial Crash, the new Coalition Government embarked on a radical reshaping of housing policy. This was aimed at bolstering private housebuilding and renting, whilst squeezing out affordable housing provision. Despite aspirations to tackle the "housing crisis," the government was spending 44% less public money on affordable homes by 2013, with knock-on secondary effects that limited CLT growth in some ways and stimulated it in others.

Council budgets, hit hard by austerity policies, severely limited the ability of councils to invest in housing and regeneration. In this new world of market-driven housing production and state retrenchment, civil society organisations like CLTs were expected to flourish as part of the Coalition Government's new idea: the "Big Society."

Despite being personally championed by the Prime Minister, David Cameron, the Big Society soon lost political traction. A few of his ideas survived into the Localism Act 2011, however, which introduced new community rights for civil society organisations. Neighbourhood Planning, the right to draw up a hyper-local plan, has been the most significant and widely used of these. The qualifying criteria for community organisations using this right were closely modelled on the CLT statutory definition, enacted three years earlier.

Fig. 8.1. CLT housing under construction in Dorset, England. Despite astronomical land values, unstable ground, the withdrawal of government grants, and unfavourable planning policy, the Lyme Regis CLT persisted. Nothing could stop them!

Yet the development of CLTs continued to be held back by familiar challenges: access to land, funding, and finance; local planning processes; deficits in technical knowledge and skills; and limited public acceptance of affordable housing in certain areas. With so many barriers standing in the way of CLTs, the eventual emergence of today's CLT movement is remarkable. How did this happen? What made it possible? What were the pivotal moments in its development?

We shall answer these questions by describing this stage of growth of the CLT movement through four parallel strands of activity:

- Building a support infrastructure;

- Making the voice of CLTs heard in government;

- Speaking in a united voice to government, advocating for all forms of community-led housing; and

- Improving the funding and finance system.

Building a Support Infrastructure

Despite public enthusiasm for CLTs, very few groups had actually built any homes before 2008. This was due, in part, to there being no support infrastructure to capitalise on this interest. A persuasive argument that such an infrastructure was needed was put forward by activists, academics, and professionals who had been making the case for CLTs. They convinced the Carnegie UK Trust, the Housing Corporation, and the Higher Education Funding Council for England to support an initial two-year National CLT Demonstration Programme, starting in 2008. Led by Community Finance Solutions, the goals of this programme were to promote the creation of CLTs — in both rural and urban settings — and to provide advice and support to local groups so they could get their projects off the ground.[17]

On a parallel track, the same activists successfully assembled the capital for a "CLT Fund" from a number of major charitable foundations. This Fund provided small seed-corn grants to cover the start-up stages of CLTs and offered pre-development and development loans for CLT projects.[18]

By the end of the Demonstration Programme, three CLTs were in the process of building 30 homes and another 139 homes were in the pipeline.[19] New resources and technical advice also emerged. But enabling support remained limited, political support was marginal, and the CLT movement still lacked a united voice.

Following the Demonstration Programme's final recommendations, a Community Empowerment Grant was secured from the central government in 2010, providing initial funding for two essential elements of a support infrastructure for CLTs:

- A national membership body; and

- A replicable sub-regional enabling body, called an "Umbrella CLT," using Wessex Community Assets as the pilot.

The National CLT Network was started in 2010, with a blank slate in terms of its future form and direction. The first director, who was the organisation's sole paid employee at the time, was assigned a dizzying array of initial tasks: establish governance and membership arrangements; provide support and resources for emerging groups; communicate with communities and the national and local press; and lobby central government to address barriers to CLT development. It was also vital to ensure that the first CLT members took ownership of the national mission and participated in the new organisation's governance. The Network would have credibility only if it was a genuinely representative body.

The choice of an appropriate host for the Network was important. After considering a number of civil society organisations with housing and community interests, the National Housing Federation, the representative body for housing associations in England, was selected. The Federation offered the greatest potential to increase the coverage and influence of the Network's activity, despite representing a somewhat different set of housing interests from those of the Network.

The interests of the Federation and the Network did indeed diverge between 2010 and 2014, as many housing associations became larger, more corporate, and less connected to the communities they served. Also, with the growing profile and standing of the Network, there was sufficient impetus to become legally and operationally independent; which it did in June 2014.

Umbrella CLTs —Building the Sub-regional Support Infrastructure. The Network quickly learnt that, despite the growing number of CLTs forming since 2010, the scale and pace of development would be limited if CLTs continued to rely solely on volunteers. These individuals were being asked to learn vast amounts of technical information about housing finance, company law, and development planning; in essence, becoming quasi-housing professionals, while supported by a small number of sympathetic and committed advisers willing to travel the country. Seed-corn funding from the CLT Fund, which paid for early advisory support, only took these fledgling CLTs a short way on their journey. Many could only move slowly toward reaching their goal of building homes.

Stronger support systems were required. One such system was emerging in the form of "Umbrella CLTs," including those in Cornwall, Cumbria, Lincolnshire, the East of England, and Somerset, Devon, and Dorset (Wessex). In theory, umbrella CLTs could offer end-to-end support for both organizational and project development. Each covered an entire county or several counties, supporting individual CLTs in that area, from the initial start-up stage of a CLT being a "bright idea," through incorporation, planning, and construction, to the point where people moved into new CLT homes. Some Umbrella CLTs like Wessex were based on strong partnerships with carefully chosen housing associations having shared aims and values. This enabled communities to focus on being effective participants in shaping projects, with the housing association taking on the technical and administrative burden, bringing its expertise in development and financing.

The Network actively sought funding from charitable foundations and government to support the establishment of new Umbrellas, hoping to achieve full geographic coverage of England. As these regional and sub-regional support systems grew, the Network saw that its role needed to change; it should only do what could not be adequately performed at the local, sub-regional, or regional level. This meant focusing on national advocacy campaigns, leadership, and promotion of best practices.

Making the Voice of CLTs Heard in Government— Experiments and Successes in Advocacy

Despite having secured a statutory definition for CLTs in 2008, political support for CLTs was still tentative. It became a priority of the Network to strengthen the influence of CLTs with central government and to secure capital grant funding for the development of CLT projects.

The value of CLTs could only be demonstrated when politicians could see a sufficient number of completed CLT homes. But land acquisition and housing development required some form of capitalization by government. In England, social housing was supported through the central government's Affordable Homes Programme for housing associations. In response to lobbying, £25m of that Programme was set aside for CLTs up to 2015. This supported a number of projects, particularly in areas like Wessex, where the housing association partnership model and Umbrella CLT support meant that a good number of rural schemes could progress relatively quickly.

Using public money in this way did not meet with universal support, however. Some academics and community activists saw CLTs as a critique of past housing policy failures and current forms of publicly supported housing. They argued that CLTs should draw on entirely different sources of finance and be independent of central government and its ideas about tenure and affordability. The Network had to navigate a fine line between demonstrating that CLTs were a practicable, preferable choice, therefore, creating valuable social and economic outcomes, whilst simultaneously holding onto the principle that CLTs must only develop what is locally appropriate and desired, not what is decided at a government official's desk in central London.

The 2015 General Election provided a key opportunity for the Network to mobilise its lobbying experience to influence the major parties, and any new government's policies. The Network's pre- and post-election manifestos made ambitious demands, including capital grants and funding for support and advice, and for preferential treatment of CLT projects in planning, taxation, and leasehold law.

The Network moved beyond its traditional lobbying and influencing at the national level, which had focused on government ministers, MPs, political advisors and think-tanks. It focused simultaneously on the grassroots, mobilising individual CLTs to lobby their MPs, particularly in electorally significant areas, knowing that the constituency link would prove critical in gaining MPs' support, thereby influencing national policymaking.

New urban CLTs were also showing how targeted lobbying and community organising could secure political commitments at the local and regional level. Community organisers at Citizens UK and at the London CLT extracted commitments to support CLTs from public officials. This culminated in support from London's mayors (first Ken Livingstone, and then Boris Johnson) for the first significant urban CLT project in the UK, located at the St Clements Hospital site in London's East End.

Over 80 MPs were targeted in the run-up to the General Election, many of whom pledged their support for the Network's pre-election manifesto. Once the new Government was elected, the Network, knowing that there could not be a political "ask" without a matching political "offer," set out a convincing case to government officials that CLTs could help them to achieve their own housing aspirations by:

- Gaining popular support for new housebuilding, which was often fiercely resisted by established communities directly affected by development;

- Helping diversify the house building industry after the Financial Crash, which had accelerated the demise of small- and medium-sized builders and developers;

- Innovating in an industry highly resistant to change; and

- Addressing affordability concerns for both middle-income and low-income households in electorally sensitive areas.

Despite the cross-party appeal of CLTs, one of the new government's first actions was to introduce a Housing and Planning Bill into Parliament that, amongst other measures, imposed a compulsory rent-reduction regime for social housing providers that would have left several CLTs bankrupt within 2–3 years. The government also proposed extending the existing Right to Buy to the tenants of housing associations. This would have provided tenants with a large discount to purchase their homes, including some CLT homes,[20] directly undermining the ability of CLTs to keep their homes genuinely affordable in perpetuity. The potential damage to the CLT brand, and thus the risk to the future of the CLT movement as a whole, was significant.

A twin-track national-local lobbying strategy proved critical in enabling the Network to move quickly to protect CLTs from the Bill's most damaging features. The lobbying presence in Whitehall, combined with pressure from CLTs on the ground, was highly effective in winning CLT exemptions to both rent reduction and Right to Buy proposals. Within Whitehall, the Network had gained a reputation for being an effective lobbying organisation, with Ministers repeatedly approached by MPs on behalf of CLTs within their constituencies.

A United Voice Promoting All Forms of Community-Led Housing

From the mid–2000s, attempts had been made to collaborate among the main national representative bodies of housing cooperatives, CLTs, cohousing communities, and development trusts: all forms of "community-led housing" (CLH).[21]

The aim of collaboration was to project a more powerful sector voice in national debates. Working together proved challenging for everyone. Each body started out believing they had more to gain by lobbying separately on behalf of their own memberships. They were torn between protecting their identity and promoting policies specific to their model, versus supporting a wider set of shared activities and objectives. CLTs, in particular, had a unique focus on lasting affordability, which was not universally shared among the other CLH sector bodies. Nevertheless, the CLT Network decided to take a more inclusive stance vis-à-vis other national bodies and to play a significant leadership role within this sector, because the Network's director and trustees judged that CLTs would benefit from being part of a larger landscape of community-led housing.

In 2015, World Habitat (formerly the Building and Social Housing Foundation) helpfully stepped in at this juncture. World Habitat, with its global experience of community-led housing, could act as an independent broker to forge alliances across the sector. This was fortunate timing. The first alliance between national bodies was forged between the National CLT Network and the UK Cohousing Network. The growing stature of the former and a gradual alignment of aims and values between the two Networks resulted in them sharing staff and back-office functions, and lobbying government together. The two Networks then led the efforts to bring on board the other CLH sector bodies to endorse a broader vision and to present a united front to central government. Those efforts eventually paid off. The four main national bodies now work collaboratively in a formal alliance called Community Led Homes.[22]

> The four national bodies now work collaboratively in a formal alliance.

Improving the System of Funding and Finance

Most early CLTs drew on a diverse range of funding and finance to make their projects viable, as the Stonesfield CLT had done. The CLT Fund had been designed to provide CLTs with both pre-development and development loans structured in innovative ways. Some were provided "at risk," repayable only if and when planning permission was granted. Other loans were available with lower levels of security, taking a subordinate position on the property to enable a larger lender to take the first position. By the end of 2018, the CLT Fund had supported over 44 CLTs and had helped to finance over 100 newly built affordable homes, with another 400+ in development.[23]

Whilst helpful, these funds were still no panacea, especially for groups trying to cover pre-development costs on larger projects. Other funds became available, such as the reallocation of £14m unspent Government revenue funding (from another Community Rights programme); however, the government's conditions were highly risk averse, requiring groups to have bought or secured a firm interest in their site before the government's money would be released.

Other forms of niche funding were developed, especially as interest grew in urban CLTs. A generous grant from the Oak Foundation enabled the Network to set up a dedicated Urban CLT Project, providing small grants and peer-to-peer learning for twenty pioneering urban CLTs over a period of three years. Some were in areas with very high land values; others were in areas with lower land values and a large number of empty homes. The programme also supported the first Welsh CLT in Rhyl. Recent evaluations of the Urban CLT Project highlight the critical role of seed-corn funding in leveraging wider investment for urban schemes, and showed how urban CLTs have the potential to amass large memberships which strengthen their political leverage at a local level.

The Network was also intent on trying to create a more coherent eco-system of funding

Fig. 8.2. Catherine Harrington, Co-Chief Executive of the National CLT Network and Anna Kear, Executive Director of the UK Cohousing Network, join forces to welcome Minister of State for Housing, Alok Sharma MP, to their community-led housing conference in 2017, at which he announced the next stage of the Community Housing Fund.

and finance, with a wider range of loans on sensible and appropriate terms for community groups. Social investors and ethical lenders, such as the Charity Bank, Triodos Bank, and the Ecology Building Society, stepped forward to offer new financial products. Much of this was highly bespoke, however, and still left significant gaps.

The Community Housing Fund. For the General Election in May 2015, the Network's manifesto had asked for renewed capital funding for CLTs, similar to the £25m Afford-able Housing Programme that had just ended in March 2015. When the government's first budget was unveiled in March 2016, the Network, and indeed the whole CLH sector, were delighted to hear the Chancellor announce a £60m Community Housing Fund for community housing projects in rural and coastal areas, notably where there was a high proportion of high-priced second homes. Surprisingly, civil servants then con-firmed that the fund was, in fact, £60m for each of the next five years (later reduced to four years); so £240m overall, considerably more than anything the CLH sector had seen previously.

Creation of the Community Housing Fund was a clear vindication of the Network's leadership and lobbying efforts. It provided a unique opportunity to build on the work of the preceding years, creating a stronger infrastructure and a coherent system of funding and finance for CLH groups.

The CLT and Cohousing Networks took the lead in articulating a vison and practical design for the Community Housing Fund, and led efforts to bring on board the other CLH sector bodies. The Government adopted this vision.

The Community Housing Fund is available to CLH groups across England and consists of:

- Revenue grants to set up new groups and to get them development-ready;

- Capital grants for infrastructure and the construction of affordable homes of any tenure; and

- Grants to create the national support infrastructure, building on the concept of Umbrella CLTs to create a national network of local Enabling Hubs.

General Lessons for Building and Sustaining a National CLT Movement, 2008–2018

A decade of rapid CLT growth in England and Wales offers several key lessons for movement building:

- *Lesson 1.* Lobbying efforts proved highly effective: a result of the division of tasks between the Network and communities on the ground. Individually, CLTs harnessed the power of telling their local stories to persuade those with influence and decision-making power, especially in electorally sensitive areas. The Network provided the mobilisation, information for CLTs on the key "asks" of decision makers, and the technical and policy-centred arguments in favour of CLTs. Most critically, it exerted direct influence on Ministers and significant MPs.

- *Lesson 2.* The success of the national lobbying activity flowed from a pragmatic approach, framing CLTs within the wider housing crisis and aligning CLTs with dominant ideological and political priorities. Government ministers and officials were shown how CLTs and other CLH initiatives could help them to achieve their national housing objectives.

- *Lesson 3.* Having sold the political benefits of CLTs, lobbying was directed toward influencing financial priorities, expanding access to land and finance, and enacting legal and legislative rules affecting the viability of CLT models of development.

- *Lesson 4.* The Network and local CLTs developed a clear picture of the financial requirements of CLTs over the lifetime of their projects, including: revenue for core activities, capital for land acquisition and project development, and ongoing revenue to allow CLTs to play a long-term stewardship role. CLTs need more than money. Networks of skilled professionals are required to reduce the burdens on volunteers. The argument for Enabling Hubs, which are supporting CLTs across the country, appears to have prevailed. Only time will tell, however, if that infrastucture is sustainable.

III. POTENTIAL FUTURES FOR CLTs

▪ Reinventing "left behind" rural towns, in the context of neighbourhood or other community-led plans to tackle housing, employment, heritage and landscape challenges in towns that get little if any support from public policy initiatives or public resources.

▪ Establishing "enabling hubs" and civic partnerships with city authorities, aspiring to greater devolution from the central government.

Reinventing "Left Behind" Rural Towns[24]

Cranbrook and Sissinghurst Parish lies in the glorious rolling farmland of the High Weald in Kent: a protected area of outstanding natural beauty and one of the most complete medieval landscapes in Europe. With 130 historic farmsteads, the Parish is brimming with archaeology. Architecture and place names tell of a legacy of invasion and immigration from mainland Europe.

Cranbrook town prides itself on its independent retail centre, and has more ancient buildings than many larger historic cathedral cities, many dating to the time of the medieval cloth industry, when its economy first peaked. Cranbrook also has the tallest windmill in England, a lofty medieval church, a quirky provincial museum, a theatre, and a year-round arts programme.

Even so, the town is not thriving. Outward prosperity conceals internal economic and social weaknesses. Cranbrook has lost both its rail link and its market. It does not benefit from any special programmes of government financial support. Like many other parts of the UK that voted to leave the European Union in 2016, the citizens of Cranbrook feel "left behind."

Cranbrook's modern-day economy rests on an affluent and mobile middle class, attracted by a concentration of high-performing state and private schools. The Parish's proximity to London, the prevalence of second-home ownership, the wholesale financialisation of the UK's housing markets, and the lack of new housing means the affordability gap has been stretched to the breaking point. At 19:1, the ratio of average house price to average household income makes the Parish one of the least affordable in the country. Young people who have grown up in the Parish cannot afford to stay. The majority of those working in the town or on the land are priced out and forced to commute long distances from cheaper areas.

Empowering communities to reimagine their place. The 2011 Localism Act granted new powers to communities in cities and rural villages to shape their own futures and to draw up formal Neighbourhood Development Plans (NDP). The momentum of the

CLT movement and national lobbying prompted one government minister to say "there should be a CLT in every Neighbourhood Plan." With over 1000 plans, this presented a real opportunity for growth. The implicit political message of "make your own plan, then do your own development" was just what people in Cranbrook had in mind.

In 2015, residents of Cranbrook recognized that the town needed a regeneration strategy, a body to curate it, and investment funding to make it happen. In 2017, the Council launched an NDP. A dedicated team of community volunteers also came together to initiate a CLT, so that one could support the other. The proposal to set up the Crane Valley Land Trust was backed by 500 signatures of support. Since its formation, the Land Trust has worked hand-in-hand with the NDP Steering Committee and also engaged local land owners, house builders, and potential joint-venture development partners, looking to provide the genuinely and permanently affordable housing that Cranbrook needs. A local apple grower has recently donated one acre (0.6 hectares) of land on which can be built twenty-two prototype Passivhaus homes for the community, whilst also enabling his farm manager to live on site. The homes will be affordable not only to rent or buy, but also to operate.

The challenge for Cranbrook, as with many other 'left behind' communities, is to take back control of its destiny. This is what it is doing through its NDP and the Crane Valley Land Trust, promoting sustainable housing development in policy and practical actions. The Land Trust is embodying the essential qualities and character of the town and surrounding historic rural landscape in its approach to development and as an exemplar for others to follow.

Establishing Enabling Hubs and City–CLT Partnerships[25]

The Community Housing Fund created an opportunity to build on the achievements of the first-generation Umbrella CLTs and to realise the National CLT Network's vision; that is, to develop sub-regional Enabling Hubs as support bodies for all forms of community-led housing that cover most of England with a mix of urban and rural hubs.[26] They are connected with one another in order to pool resources and to share technical expertise.

CLT East operates across the extended geography of eastern England, and is the first to have made the crossover from rural to urban political settings. One of its first successes was the project developed by the Stretham & Wilburton CLT, based on the CLT's partnership with a parish council and the East Cambridgeshire District Council. This partnership has resulted in 70 new homes, including 25 CLT homes, in a village that had previously resisted any new housing. As a result of the project, the Council developed a planning policy for enabling community-led development, and formed Palace Green Homes, a new council-owned housing development company, with part of its remit to serve as a development partner for CLTs.

A further effect of this policy innovation has been the strong support now being given to CLTs from the mayor of the recently established Cambridgeshire and Peterborough

Combined Authority, which covers an area containing those two cities as well as a range of smaller "left behind" towns, all of which may grow rapidly in the years ahead.

What is needed? The particular strength of an Enabling Hub is its understanding of the pipeline of groups and projects, and their supply chains, in a particular area. This is helpful to councils when they are attempting to get an accurate picture of the level and type of local demand, and how the council might help to meet it. Because Enabling Hubs need to operate over a wide area, and with enough volume of business to pay their way, there is an opportunity to collaborate when groups in different geographies are going through similar development processes. Collaboration is particularly valuable in urban areas where multiple groups can share in the development of a single large site or can cooperate in getting better value from local builders or off-site manufacturers.

Partnerships are key to an Enabling Hub's success. Partners may host the Hub's office functions, share staff members, and bring financial or technical support. Given that housing development can take many years, Hubs need to diversify income streams outside of project-related fees. Research may offer extra income, and help position a Hub as a thought leader in a particular area. The Oxford Hub, for example, has conducted research on the Oxford Housing Market[27] and Wessex Community Assets has conducted research

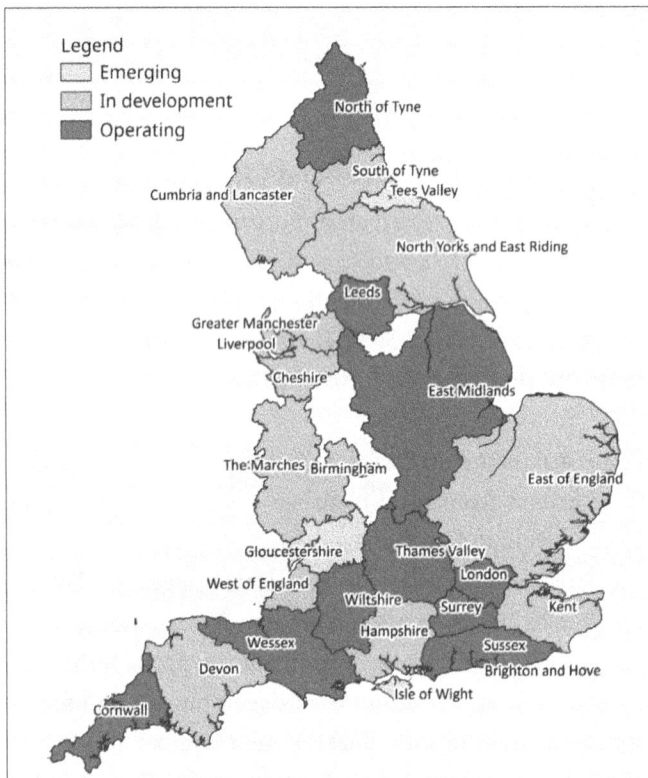

Fig. 8.3. Regions covered by the Enabling Hubs for community-led housing, as of June 2019.

on the "motivations and aspirations" of CLT volunteers in Somerset, Devon, and Dorset.[28] There are also opportunities to charge for developing and delivering training courses for prospective homebuyers, employees of local authorities and housing associations, and professionals in design, finance, and law who may have little experience working with community groups.

A new breed of civic partnerships: CLTs and City Regions. Three innovative CLTs have led the growth of city-region Enabling Hubs:

- Leeds Community Homes is a CLT created from the initiative of experienced local community-led housing organisations that had been active in the city for several decades. The CLT engages in the direct delivery of housing, funded in part through community share offers, and supports the development of other CLH organisations across the city-region.

- Bristol CLT has been a national leader in delivering innovative community-led housing projects for almost two decades. The Bristol City Council is now an integral partner of the Hub, and is offering sites to encourage the development of CLT homes and other forms of CLH.

- Oxfordshire CLT, established in 2004, had struggled to build a pipeline of projects due to the competition for sites in the highest value area in the UK, and the lack of local government support. However, the creation of the Community Housing Fund in 2016 prompted a surge of new rural and urban projects and renewed interest from the five Oxfordshire councils. In 2017, the Oxfordshire CLT forged an Enabling Hub partnership with a local philanthropic foundation and a community development charity. The CLT now focuses on holding land and partnering with smaller CLTs and other developers, rather than doing housing development on its own.

The political significance of Enabling Hubs and the wider community-led housing approach. There is no doubt that CLTs have benefited from being part of a bigger community-led housing landscape. CLTs have recognised this and have taken the lead, nationally and locally, in building community-led housing sectoral alliances — both in their own self-interest and for the survival and growth of community-led housing in general.

A handful of urban councils, moreover, have used CLTs as a response to the challenges of reduced funding from central government to maintain a supply of genuinely and permanently affordable housing. Alongside the call by CLTs for a new politics of shared control between politicians and citizens, there is now a significant potential for greater citizen involvement and community ownership of assets in urban regeneration, as a counterweight to the acceptance of regeneration as driven solely by the financial motivations of real estate developers, investors and councils.

IV. CONCLUSION: WHAT ARE CLTs REALLY ABOUT?

There are now over 300 CLTs in England and 935 CLT homes have been built. Recent research suggests there are more than 5,000 new CLT homes in the pipeline. Nationwide, the membership of CLTs has grown to over 17,000 people.

In May 2019, central government called for new information on the number of additional CLH homes that might start before 2024, to provide evidence of demand that could be met if the Community House Fund were extended beyond March 2020. Over 16,000 further CLH homes are now in prospect. Most of these are CLT homes.

The recognized impact and widespread awareness of CLTs, once distant ambitions, are increasingly visible in national and local policy making. Very few people now look puzzled when CLTs are mentioned. Familiar barriers remain, including lack of access to land, finance, and technical support, but persistent and united action by varied CLH actors is making steady progress in reducing these constraints on future development.

In June 2019, the central government reacted positively to sustained campaigns by both the CLT and Cohousing Networks to secure exemptions from potentially damaging leasehold reforms. For instance, new CLTs would have been prevented from using ground leases to protect the affordability of their homes, but they will now be "totally exempt" from any legislative changes.

The interest in CLTs as instruments for the regeneration of public housing estates, which had been proposed but abandoned in the early 2000s, is being revived. After a decade in which estate residents were excluded from decision-making by their council landlords and displaced through gentrification caused by council and developer partnerships, the political, social, and economic damage has been recognised. Councils previously hostile to community action are now working with residents on co-production for estate regeneration, with some of the new homes likely to be owned by a CLT.

The UK's main political parties are now openly endorsing CLTs. Labour's 2019 report, *Land for the Many*, argues that community land trusts should be given a greater role in alleviating the country's housing crisis.[29] A Conservative think tank has recently proposed that the estate affected by the terrible fire at Grenfell Tower should be transferred into CLT ownership.

What CLTs are really about? At the Royal Society Symposium in 1998, mentioned at the start of this chapter, housing was described as "like living, like life itself . . . messy." At the 2nd International Festival of Social Housing in Lyons, France, hosted twenty-one years later by Housing Europe, the mood was angrier and more focussed on the misuse of urban land and housing as a global speculative commodity. The potentially dire consequences for both rural and urban populations, for those at the margins, and for the now threatened middle classes, are well expressed in the catchphrase from this 2019 event: "What oil was to the industrial age, urban land is to global financial capitalism."[30]

Given the conspicuous failure of government policy and the private market to create well-ordered and fair land and housing markets that respond to needs and demand, an active citizenship is needed to refocus political attention on some fundamentals: what all citizens need; what all citizens can afford; and what all citizens should be able to afford.

> The task of citizens seeking their own housing solutions is not to become part of the mainstream, but to reshape the mainstream.

Today is a time when new institutions of local democratic control are urgently needed to bring people together around issues that matter to everyone, especially the security of their homes and the cost of shelter. The communities that have done the hard work of setting up new institutions like CLTs have done so with a passion because they represent important political ideas about the way they want to live. These ideas belong to neither "right" nor "left." They put communities in a healthier situation than before, with better quality and genuinely affordable homes, and a real sense of identity and autonomy.

In John E. Davis' wise words, CLTs are not only "problem solving," they are "problem defining." CLTs embody an approach in which citizens can take the time to explore and to understand the complexity of their villages, towns, cities, and communities, and what makes them work. CLTs do not avoid the issues that everyone else seems determined to ignore when using a meaningless political term like "affordable housing," namely the cost of land and the stewardship of public and private land to serve the common good.

The statutory language defining CLTs in England and Wales was drafted with that participatory, problem-defining, problem-solving approach to community development in mind. Implicit in that definition is a recognition of power . . . who has it and what can be done with it. The task of citizens seeking their own housing solutions is not to become part of the mainstream, but to reshape the mainstream.

The "trick" in the design of the Community Housing Fund was to create a national policy based on local support frameworks that enable different things to happen in different places. CLTs can only realistically mobilise as a credible force to counter the global financialisation of land and housing if they can develop viable and credible alternatives of many different kinds that are adapted to and appropriate to their communities and their places. Global change happens through local intelligence, innovation, and action.

Messy is both good . . . and necessary!

Postscript: Our thanks go to five people who contributed to this chapter: Pat Conaty, Kate Braithwaite, Kirsty Tait, Charlie Fisher, and Tim Kemp, all of whom have played or are still playing significant roles in the English CLT story. They each provided a distinctive and valid perspective of key events. Please excuse any minor discrepancies in joining up all the threads of that story, in the spirit of creative and productive messiness.

Notes

1. CLTs in England are concerned primarily with the provision of permanently and genuinely affordable housing that is retained in community ownership and control. Affordability is defined by reference to official Area Median Income data or local equivalents, with the traditional measure of one-third of household income being spent on housing costs. CLTs own land freehold or on very long leases, usually for 250 years or more. They either develop and own the homes directly, or they grant leases to other regulated affordable housing providers to build homes on their behalf on lease terms that maintain appropriate community controls. Council estate regeneration CLTs were also predicated on CLTs owning the freehold of the land, with other housing providers developing under leases. CLT homes may be either ownership or rental. Over the period covered by the chapter, CLTs in England became more focussed on rental housing as the economic and employment conditions for sustainable homeownership became increasingly difficult. Some CLTs have expanded from their original focus on housing to own other assets for community benefit. The Butchers Arms public house, rescued by the Lyvennet CLT in Cumbria, is one example: *http://www.thebutchersarms.pub*

2. Contributed by Pat Conaty, a Fellow at the New Economics Foundation. He was part of the Community Finance Solutions team whose research and advocacy led to the CLT Fund and the CLT National Demonstration Project.

3. See: *https://papers.ssrn.com/sol3/papers.cfm?abstract_id=1128862*

4. CDFIs are loan funds that emerged in the USA in the 1970s to support non-bankable but viable enterprises. One of the first was the Revolving Loan Fund created by the Institute for Community Economics in the USA that funded the early CLTs and was an inspiration for CDFIs in the UK.

5. Contributed by Dr. Kate Braithwaite and Kirsty Tait. Dr. Kate Braithwaite has served as CEO of Cumbria's Rural Community Council, Director of Carnegie UK Trust's Rural Programme, and Operations Director at UnLtd—the Foundation for Social Entrepreneurs. Kirsty Tait currently works for the Scottish Land Commission. She was previously on staff at the Carnegie UK Trust, where she supported English CLT pioneers and the set-up of the National CLT Network.

6. The Carnegie UK Trust was instrumental in providing financial support for this work.

7. Paterson, B and Dayson, K, *Proof of Concept: Community Land Trusts.* A Community Finance Solutions, University of Salford (2011, p. 13).

8. Further documentation relating to this aspect of CLT development is available in an archive of primary and secondary source materials compiled by Stephen Hill, Catherine Hand, and Graham Moody at: *https://independent.academia.edu/StephenHill3*

9. "Growth Areas" were designated by central government as part of its Sustainable Communities Plan to tackle the decline of urban centres in the North and Midlands, while creating new communities in response to demand in the South and East.

10. Developers mostly treated this as a box-ticking formality to secure a planning permission.

11. The Foundation's founder, Joseph Rowntree, had an interest in land and its role in the political economy of nations. He was an enthusiast for Henry George's writing on land and for Ebenezer Howard's Garden Cities. In 1902, Rowntree started building a garden village at New Earswick, in York, as "a rightly ordered and self-governing community."

12. See: *https://www.jrf.org.uk/report/land-housing-current-practice-and-future-options*

13. An NDC in Sunderland is a good example. Still controlled by the community, it owns and develops affordable housing and is continuing to improve the area and to generate income.

14. Members of the Institute of Community Economics had talked about DSNI during a visit to London in the early 2000s.

15. Included on this board was Stephen Hill, a co-author of the present chapter.

16. Aird, J. (2009). *Lessons from the first 150 Homes: Evaluation of the National Community Land Trust Demonstration Programme 2006–2008.* Salford, CFS. Nineteen CLTs are listed on page 25, incorporated as of 2008, but Stonesfield CLT was omitted.

17. Aird, J. (2009). Ibid.

18. In 2011, the National CLT Network took over the administration of the seed corn grants, thereafter called the "CLT Start Up Fund," working with the original charitable foundation donors. The Fund closed in 2020. The loans continue as the main CLT Fund, administered and funded by the Charities Aid Foundation, with Charity Bank.

19. Aird, J. (2009). Ibid.

20. 45 CLTs had adopted the Wessex housing association partnership model, and 9 CLTs had themselves become a housing association or Registered Provider, regulated by government to own and manage social rent homes. All these CLTs, and some in the process of registration, would have been affected by the 2015 Housing and Planning Bill.

21. Tenant Management Organisations (resident management of publicly owned social rent housing) and Self-Help Housing (bringing empty homes back into use and community ownership) were also engaged to create a diverse and expanding CLH sector. The definition of "Community-Led Housing" adopted by government as qualifying criteria for receiving grants or loans from the Community Housing Fund (2016–2020) draws

heavily on the CLT statutory definition. (1) Meaningful community engagement and consent occurs throughout the process. The community does not necessarily have to initiate and manage the development process, or build the homes themselves, although many may do so. (2) The local community group or organisation owns, manages, or stewards the homes in a manner of their choosing. (3) The benefits to the local area and/or specified community must be clearly defined and legally protected in perpetuity.

22. Community Led Homes is a formal alliance of the four main CLH bodies, channelling communication, advocacy and support through a single "brand:" National CLT Network leads on developing the Enabling Hub infrastructure; Confederation of Co-operative Housing leads the training and accreditation of enablers and technical advisers; UK Cohousing Network provides a single point of access, the National Advice Centre, for all types of CLH, curates the Community Led Homes website, and manages its library of technical resources; and Locality, a national membership network for community asset owning organisations, which manages a small grants programme for areas not yet covered by Enabling Hubs. The National CLT Network holds the Government contract.

23. Archer, T. Green, S. and Fisher, C. (2019). Helping Communities Build. *https://www. cafonline.org/about-us/blog-home/venturesome-blog/helping-communities-build*

24. Contributed by Timp Kemp, a co-founder of the Crane Valley Land Trust in 2017. He was Chairman of Cranbrook & Sissinghurst Parish Council Neighbourhood Development Plan steering committee 2015–2016 and Vice-Chair until May 2019.

25. Contributed by Charlie Fisher, a director of Transition by Design. He has been a trustee of the Oxfordshire CLT since 2013 and was part of the set-up team for a new Thames Valley Enabling Hub.

26. Some enabling hubs have emerged from the Action with Communities in Rural England (ACRE) Network.

27. See: *https://issuu.com/cohohub/docs/oxfordclh_finalreport_and_appendice*

28. See: *http://wessexca.co.uk/wp-content/uploads/2016/06/3016725-Wessex-Report. pdf*

29. *Land for the Many: Changing the Way Our Fundamental Asset Is Used, Owned, and Governed* (June 2019): *https://landforthemany.uk*

30. See: *http://www.housingeurope.eu/blog-1283/access-to-affordable-and-adquate-housing-is-perhaps-the-social-problem-of-our-generation#.XP-W70XcHlI.twitter*

9.

Beyond England
Origins and Evolution of
the Community Land Trust
Movement in Europe

Geert De Pauw and Joaquin de Santos

This chapter traces the context in which the European community land trust (CLT) movement was born and evolved, both from a broader European perspective and within individual countries. The scope of this chapter is to look at developments outside of England, mostly on the mainland of Europe, but recent developments in Scotland and Ireland are included as well. We take stock of the current state of the movement, highlighting similarities and differences in the ways that CLTs are structured and applied in different countries, and look ahead to the future prospects for CLT development. We also trace important connections that are being forged between CLTs in Europe and CLTs in England through a cross-national project known as "Sustainable Housing for Inclusive and Cohesive Cities."

We will first look at the broader context of housing production in Europe. As in other geographies, the production of housing in Western Europe has undergone significant changes over the last forty years. In the post-Second World War period, public authorities took the initiative in developing large numbers of housing units to accomodate those affected by the War but also to tackle the remaining pockets of inadequate housing in cities. This often led to massive housing developments that were often built at great speed and with lower-quality materials in formerly rural areas at the periphery of major cities.

In parallel, the evolution of the global economy towards more office-based jobs has created the impetus to build large office buildings in central areas (sometimes at the expense of historical neighbourhoods) or in areas with good transport links, restructuring urban space to give way to the automobile. The lucrative market in office estate has resulted in collusion between real estate developers and local politicians in many cities.

Another major development of this post-war period has been the increased earnings by a large portion of the working population as a result of the economic boom.

Lower-middle-class households could now afford to buy residential property, which was being delivered on a massive scale by real estate developers. Public policies were introduced to subsidize homeownership. As a result, these populations increasingly deserted public housing.

This post-war paradigm, often dubbed "Fordist" in relation to the logic of increasing the purchasing power of workers to enable them to acquire Ford automobiles, has given way since the 1980s to a model where the market takes on a more important role in the provision of housing. This shift has been accompanied, in many cases, by a virtual stagnation of the production of public housing (with the notable exception of France, the Netherlands, some Scandinavian countries, along with a few major cities, such as Vienna).

The evolution of the global economy during this period has created significant imbalances, with an increasing concentration of economic development in larger cities and, at times, an abrupt economic decline of former industrial areas that once had substantial manufacturing capacities. This has fostered greater competition between cities to capture capital flows that are increasingly global and volatile, caused in part by the deregulation of financial markets since the mid-1980s. One outcome is that housing in many European cities has become increasingly expensive and commodified.

These trends were accelerated by the global financial crisis starting in 2008. While housing markets in many European countries slumped as a result of the drought of real estate financing, the massive public injections of capital into failing banks quickly became a financial force of their own. Investors began looking for returns in markets that had been less financialised and profitable in the past, but were now looking like good investment opportunities. The housing market was the most important of those untapped markets, offering attractive returns that could sometimes reach double digits. As a consequence, massive amounts of capital were injected into housing, driving up prices not only in the most desirable locations, but also in neighbourhoods across entire urban areas.

In a number of areas, long-term residents were starting to get priced out of their neighbourhoods. Households had to dedicate an ever-greater share of their incomes for housing in many European countries, with even more acute situations arising in many major European cities. In other urban neighbourhoods, economic decline and a lack of investment caused an accelerated degradation of the housing stock.

With governments in many countries struggling to provide effective policy responses to these mounting problems, CLTs were envisaged and implemented as a possible solution to the affordable housing crisis. Local communities in England had begun adopting, in the early 2000s, a version of the CLT model that had been pioneered in the United States, adapting it to their own circumstances. In Brussels, local non-profits created the first continental European CLT in 2012. Municipal governments started considering the CLT model as a suitable policy response in countries such as France in 2014. Interest in the model has now spread to several other European countries.

EMERGENCE OF A CLT MOVEMENT IN MAINLAND EUROPE

In 2009, a group of community organizers and activists for the right to housing in Brussels started looking for a community-led strategy for producing permanently affordable housing. They first thought of the cooperative model. Cooperative housing organisations, often originating in the labour movement, had initiated many interesting projects in Belgium. For example, many of the garden neighbourhoods from the interwar period, inspired by Ebenezer Howard's Garden Cities, had a clear emancipatory and utopian character and were progressive in terms of urban planning and architecture. However, by the beginning of the Twenty-First Century, many of these cooperative societies had lost much of their original dynamism. Many of them, moreover, had been absorbed into a regional social housing system. Within this rigid framework, it was almost impossible to develop innovative projects; nor was it possible to create new cooperative social housing companies.

Those activists who became the initiators of the Brussels CLT (CLTB) explored the possibility of establishing a cooperative society outside the framework of social housing. That was not so easy, because this legal form was unsuitable for housing projects in Belgium. During their search for a solution, they read about an international colloquium on new forms of cooperative living in Lyon. There, they heard Professor Yves Cabannes talk about CLTs, and understood that this could be what they were looking for. Soon thereafter, in 2009, some of them had the opportunity to take part in an international study visit to the Champlain Housing Trust, which had just won the UN World Habitat Award. The trip to Burlington lit the spark. The people from Brussels met not only CLT pioneers from Vermont, but also people who were trying to get CLTs off the ground in England and Australia. The Brussels CLT was started within an international environment, therefore, and has continued to nourish that global dimension ever since.

CLTB played a major, precipitating role in helping the model to spread in Belgium and across the entire European mainland. The success of the CLT in Brussels, along with the examples of the London CLT, the Champlain Housing Trust, and the Dudley Street Neighbourhood Initiative in Boston, inspired the people who are now working in various European cities to establish their own CLTs. A number of key figures from the National CLT Network in the United States actively supported these European and English developments. They made information available, gave long-distance advice, and came to Europe several times to explain the model, talk about its origins, and testify about American CLTs. An important step was taken in 2013. The Platform CLT Ghent, CLT Brussels and the ACW, the Christian trade union movement, organized a two-day conference about CLTs in Belgium and Europe. Brenda Torpy and Tony Pickett from the United States and Dave Smith from the London CLT came to talk about their experiences, addressing an audience that consisted not only of Belgians but also of people from across Europe. In 2014, another CLT advocate from the USA, John Davis, paid visits to Flanders, Wallonia, and Brussels, giving a dozen talks over a four-day period. Here, too, there were people in attendance from outside the Belgian borders.

The American CLT Network also invited Europeans to their own conferences to report on their progress. European and global networks and organizations such as World Habitat, Housing Europe, Feantsa, and the Cohabitat Network also played a role in disseminating the model. Interest from the academic world began gradually to increase as well. In 2017, the European Union funded the SHICC project (see below), which helped to consolidate this energy and to lay the foundation for structured cooperation across European borders.

> They placed an emphasis on using rather than possessing, on common property rather than individual property.

Through all of these conferences, presentations, and meetings, it became clear that interest in this innovative model was great. CLTs seemed to be not only a way of tackling the worsening housing problems being experienced by many European cities, but also a way of responding to the economic crisis of 2008. The absence of effective responses and innovative thinking from the public sector convinced many private citizens it was time to develop alternative models themselves. The concept of "the Commons" regained interest as an alternative economic model. Everywhere in European cities, citizens began to experiment with energy cooperatives, local currencies, community gardens, food teams, tool libraries, community supported agriculture, and cooperative supermarkets, initiatives that were being developed alongside the market. They placed an emphasis on using rather than possessing, on common property rather than individual property. They attempted to deal cautiously with the limited resources that the planet offers us, rather than assuming unbridled growth. They promoted greater solidarity in place of rising inequalities. Although some of these initiatives relied on support from the state, they developed mostly in the spaces between the market and the state, attaching greater importance to civil society and self-government. Many activists and advocates for the Commons, in particular, saw in the CLT another way to apply principles of the Commons to the production and management of homes and neighbourhoods. Within this ferment of activity and experimentation, the rather unusual model of the community land trust was recognized as something compatible with their values and was seized upon by citizens in search of new alternatives.

CLT DEVELOPMENTS IN SELECTED COUNTRIES

Belgium

In Belgium, residents in Ghent were the first to show curiosity about the CLT initiative unfolding in Brussels. In April 2010, the community organisation *Samenlevingsopbouw*

Gent stirred up interest in the CLT model among a number of partners and organized a train trip to Brussels. There, they visited the housing project *L'Espoir* in Molenbeek and met with initiators of the Brussels CLT, which was still being established. In January 2012, these visitors finished a feasibility study for creating a new CLT in Ghent. A month later, they brought together a steering group composed of civil society organizations and experts, who were later joined by future residents. In March 2012, twenty-seven civil society organizations and government officials signed the *CLT Ghent Charter*. In September of that same year, they presented the results of the feasibility study at a seminar, which included lectures by Dave Smith from the London CLT and Geert De Pauw from Platform CLT Brussels. In 2013, CLT Gent and CLT Brussels, together with ACW, published *Stapstenen tussen Koop en Huur* ("Stepping Stones between Buying and Renting"). This brochure has since been used to increase the knowledge about community land trusts in Flanders, among everyone involved in the social housing field. Thanks to the CLT initiative in Ghent, political parties started to refer to CLTs in their programs, and Flemish experts and academics started to write about the model.

After a quick start, however, it took a while before CLT Ghent could put their ideas into practice. In contrast to the Brussels Region, the Flemish regional government did not give the CLT in Ghent the financial support it needed to purchase land for the development of affordable housing.

Today, CLT Ghent operates on two tracks. Through the program *Dampoort KnapT OP*, the CLT helps owner-occupiers renovate their properties via a rolling fund. Resale of renovated properties is controlled in accordance with the CLT's anti-speculative formula. In 2015, the first ten renovated homes were completed, and the project is now being continued thanks to funding from the European Union.

In the district of Meulestede, CLT Ghent now wants to develop a housing project with thirty-four homes, a 1,500-square-meter community garden, and a community space. The first plans for this development date back to 2013. As of 2020, construction is being prepared. The City of Ghent, owner of the land, has agreed upon a long-term lease on the land. A social housing company, WoninGent, will build the homes. Currently, partners are in the process of choosing an architect. If everything goes well, the first stone can be laid in 2020 and, by 2022, the first residents will move into their new CLT homes.

Ghent also took the initiative of establishing the Flemish CLT coalition, composed of some fifteen civil society organizations. This platform continued and extended CLT Ghent's efforts in propagating the model. The platform's efforts have contributed to the exploration of the CLT model in other Flemish cities.

In Leuven, a city that has faced rising house prices in recent last years, the city commissioned CLT Brussels and the research group Cosmopolis to carry out a feasibility study in 2019, with the intention of setting up a CLT in this university city in 2020. In Bruges, too, local public actors have expressed the wish to start a CLT. In Antwerp, the municipality and civil society organizations are exploring the possibility of redeveloping part of an old hospital site into CLT housing. In other Belgian cities, such as Ostend, social housing companies are examining the possibility of adopting the model.

In 2012, a CLT coalition was set up in the Walloon Region, as was previously the case in Brussels and Flanders. This coalition started lobbying for the regional government to make resources available to enable the development of CLTs. In 2014, the Walloon Minister of Housing launched the *Construire du Logement pour Tous* programme (the attentive reader will recognize the resulting acronym), which would give municipal governments and local housing organisations the opportunity to start a CLT. This attracted a great deal of attention from municipalities, but when it turned out that the funding made available by the regional government was going to be insufficient to acquire land, most municipalities lost interest.

The Walloon coalition then tried to develop a pilot project itself. They wanted to convert an empty monastery into a mixed-use project with affordable housing and a social economy project combining food production and a restaurant. They succeeded in persuading the owners to leave them the property, if they could prove the feasibility of the project. They are still raising the funds for the needed renovation, so the project is temporarily on hold. At the same time, a number of Walloon municipalities have taken a renewed interest in creating

> CLTs in Belgium are similar to what is sometimes called the "classic" CLT in the United States.

CLTs. For example, the new mayor of Ottignies/Louvain-la-Neuve has made it a policy priority, and in Comines-Warneton the municipal authorities are in the process of facilitating the establishment of CLTs.

Others in Belgium have also begun working with CLT ideas. Cohousing groups see in the legal model that the Brussels CLT has invented an alternative to the co-ownership model or the cooperative model, neither of which has fully met their expectations. Instead, by using a public interest foundation as the landowner, and by giving long-term leases to the homeowners, cohousing groups can now limit resale prices, they can control who will be the new buyers, and they have an organizational model that makes it possible to govern their projects in a democratic way. The Fondus des Petits Marais, for example, in the vicinity of Mons, has adopted features of the CLT model in its operation.

Among the many CLTs being started or planned in Belgium, there is some variation in the way they are handling the ownership of real estate and the way they are structuring the membership and governance of the CLT itself. Nevertheless, up to now, CLTs in Belgium have been organized generally along lines that are similar to what is sometimes called the "classic" CLT in the United States. Thus, the land is owned by one party and the building is owned by another. The CLT has a voting membership that elects a majority of the seats on the governing board. That board is divided into three parts, representing current and future owners, civil society, and local government. The housing that is built on the CLT's land is made permanently affordable via provisions contained in the ground lease.

Development of the Organismes de Foncier Solidaire in France
Authored by Audrey Linkenheld[1]

Activists from the academic and non-profit sectosr have been promoting the community land trust model in France for a number of years, leading to the enactment in 2014 of national legislation defining and authorizing the French version of the CLT and creating a new form of long-term ground lease. Local governments, public land organisations, and cooperative social housing organisations are currently taking the lead in implementing a national network, *Organismes de Foncier Solidaire*, throughout France. The City of Lille has played a pioneering role in laying the foundation for this fledgling—and uniquely French—CLT movement.

Lille is a prime example of a French city that was affordable until the early 2000s, but then experienced increasing pressure on its housing market as a result of high demand from students and from small households who found employment in the metropolitan area. Meanwhile, turnover in the city's social housing slowed down because poorer families were finding it increasingly difficult to move into housing in the open market as a result of the sudden rise in housing prices.

In 2008, the City of Lille adopted a comprehensive housing policy aimed at doubling the number of new housing units developed within the city, while requiring a set-aside of up to 45% of affordable housing (rental or sales) in all new residential developments of more than seventeen units. This policy supported the development of more than 3000 affordably priced units sold to households under a specific income threshold defined by the City.

The challenge that arose, however, was how to preserve this supply of affordable housing, which had been made possible by massive financial support from the municipality. The City of Lille had imposed anti-speculative clauses, but they proved insufficient in protecting the affordability of these heavily subsidized homes. This is why, as a Member of Parliament, and inspired by the example of CLTs in the USA and Belgium, I championed national legislation to enable the creation of a new type of non-profit organization, *Organismes de Foncier Solidaire (OFS)*, the French version of a CLT.[2]

After this legislation was enacted in March 2014, the next step was to create a new type of long-term ground lease, the *bail réel solidaire (BRS)*. This lease, lasting 19 to 99 years, allows land to be permanently owned by an OFS and, because it permits the ownership of land and buildings to be separated, it makes housing more affordable, since households do not have to pay for the underlying land. Clauses in the BRS also impose a limit on future prices when homes are resold. This safeguards for generations to come the public subsidies that were used to buy the land and to reduce the purchase price of the housing.

The first OFS was born in Lille in February 2017. Fifteen permanently affordable homes using a BRS lease have already been built and successfully marketed. They are part of a mixed-income, mixed-use project in an attractive neighbourhood in the city centre that will include 210 housing units (open market and social), a hotel, offices for non-profits, and an art gallery. The buyers of these fifteen homes on leased land benefited from a

> The challenge was how to preserve this affordable housing, made possible by financial support from the municipality.

very affordable price of 2110€/sqm instead of 5300€/sqm, which is what they would have had to pay without the OFS. A second OFS project with seventeen units, offered for sale at the same price, will soon be developed in the same area.[3]

Many other cities, including Rennes, Nantes, and Paris, have begun creating OFSs of their own. Meanwhile, the French Federation of Social Housing Cooperatives has encouraged the formation of OFSs by local cooperatives in places as diverse as Saint-Malo, the Basque Country, and the regions of Provence-Alpes-Côte d'Azur and Rhone-Alpes. Public landowning organisations (*Etablissements Publics Fonciers Locaux*) are also exploring the creation of OFSs in Haute Savoie, in the Basque Country, in Franche Comté, and in the overseas territories of French Guyana and la Réunion.

To date, nineteen OFSs have been established, with plans to produce 1000 permanently affordable, owner-occupied homes within the next two to three years. In 2018, following a proposal put forward by Lille, they joined together to form a new national network of OFSs, *Foncier Solidaire—France*.[4]

Netherlands[5]

Major Dutch cities such as Rotterdam and Amsterdam have been confronted with housing problems similar to those in other European cities. In Amsterdam, for example, the average sales price for housing quadrupled between 1995 and 2017. The pressure on the housing market also increased as non-profit housing corporations became less able to address the problems of pricing and supply. The Netherlands is a country with a large stock of social housing that is rented out to people with low and modest incomes. These homes have been mainly developed and managed by large housing corporations. The position of the housing corporations has been weakened, however, by decreasing governmental support, mismanagement and scandals at some of the housing corporations, and increasing pressure from the European Commission to reduce "state aid," regarded as a cause of market distortion. The housing corporations have been building less affordable housing than in the past and many of the corporations' homes have been sold to private investors on the market. Despite the Netherlands' well-deserved reputation as a country with a large stock of social housing, the waiting time for social housing in some urban neighbourhoods is now more than ten years.

It is no coincidence, therefore, that the first two initiatives to consider applying the community land trust model in the Netherlands have had a link with a social housing corporation.

In Rotterdam, the urban activists of *Stad in de Maak* (City in the Making) have concluded an agreement with the Havensteder Corporation to refurbish vacant buildings and to use them temporarily for three to ten years. These buildings are managed partly as commons: the rooms are rented, mainly to young people. On the ground floor, there is room for all kinds of social and productive activities, such as a neighbourhood canteen, a micro cinema, a launderette, and a woodcraft workshop. *City in the Making* is now reflecting on ways of getting these buildings, as well as others, off the market for good. In order to achieve this, they are exploring different strategies. They are involved in Vrijcoop, the Dutch version of the German *Mietshäuser Syndikat* model of rental housing cooperatives. This association pursues very similar goals as a community land trust, although the approach is somewhat different. Vrijcoop guarantees the continued affordability of solidarity housing projects, spread across the Netherlands, by taking shares in the projects. In parallel, members of City in the Making are also examining possibilities for the CLT model to serve as a supplement or replacement for the leasehold (*erfpacht*) model that is widely used in the Netherlands.[6]

In Amsterdam, two companies active in the social innovation sector, *And the People* and *Publieke Versnellers,* jointly took the initiative in 2018 to explore the potential of the CLT model through design thinking. As a part of their analyses, these companies looked for a suitable neighbourhood to carry out action research. They ended up in the Bijlmer, a huge modernist social high-rise district constructed in the 1960s and 1970s in Amsterdam Southeast. They soon made contact with the Maranatha Community, a religious community mainly from the African diaspora which organizes community-building and emancipatory activities in this neighbourhood.

In August 2018, these stakeholders organized a three-day design workshop in the Bijlmer where representatives from the housing corporation, the City of Amsterdam, local residents, interested social investors and all sorts of experts came together to think about the concept of possibly creating a CLT. They then organized a series of workshops in the neighbourhood. In December, a busload of Amsterdammers made the journey to Brussels to take part in a peer-to-peer exchange in the context of the European SHICC project (see below). They have now set up a steering group and have begun making contact with policymakers and interested investors. Their intention is to create dwellings and community infrastructure in the Bijlmer through new construction or the renovation of existing buildings, within the general framework of a CLT.

Germany[7]

In Germany, the Trias Foundation and the Switzerland-based Edith Maryon Foundation have been using long-term lease contracts to ensure the permanent affordability of community-led housing, productive spaces, and community facilities for decades. Both organizations own a few hundred parcels of land on which local communities have developed all kinds of projects, including Ex-Rotaprint in Berlin, a former industrial site which is now providing spaces for artists and other "makers" in the service of *Arbeit, Kunst, Soziales* (Work, Art, Community).[8] The Trias Foundation and the Edith Maryon Foundation share the same philosophy as CLTs, with regard to the long-term stewardship of land. They are not themselves CLTs, however. Their service areas cover all of Germany in the case of the Trias Foundation, and both Germany and Switzerland in the case of the Maryon Foundation. Residents who occupy the permanently affordable housing and non-residential buildings on lands that are leased from these foundations are not represented on the governing board of either foundation.

The first real CLT initiative in Germany is currently emerging in Berlin. Inspired by CLT success stories in the USA and by more recent examples of successful CLTs in Brussels and London, an informal CLT planning group was organized at the end of 2017 in the Berlin District of Friedrichshain-Kreuzberg. Housing experts, community activists, researchers, project developers, and representatives of local government have been meeting together. This CLT initiative is a response to a mounting crisis caused by exploding land values, soaring rents, and diminishing access to housing.

> The land beneath these buildings would be permanently removed from the market and managed by the new CLT-inspired organisation.

Supported by the District's Councillor for Planning and Building, who provided funding for an initial feasibility study, this CLT initiative is building on decades of activism and community-led development in the district's neighbourhoods. Strong activist traditions include squatting and many forms of self-help, self-organized and cooperative housing, as well as collective and non-profit practices for coordinating everything from small-scale industry to community gardening. The current plan is to create a new local and democratic organisation in 2020, based on the CLT model. The organisation's goal is to make a significant contribution to Berlin's housing movement by promoting private, non-speculative forms of common ownership and project development, as a complement to existing models of cooperative housing.

Initial projects are likely to involve rescuing existing older buildings in partnership with their current residents. The land beneath these buildings would be permanently removed from the market and managed by the new CLT-inspired organisation. A housing cooperative would assume ownership of the buildings and management of combinations of residential and commercial spaces, with a long-term lease for the underlying land. Provisions in the ground lease would define future uses of the land and buildings, as well as the ongoing relationship between the owner of the land (that is, the CLT organisation) and owners of the buildings. Financing and subsidies are expected to be forthcoming from public sources, as well as from private institutions and individuals. Future projects may include the provision of social spaces, commercial spaces, and community gardens, as well as the construction of new buildings.

Italy[9]

The CLT model was introduced to Italy by Homers, a non-profit organisation that is dedicated to developing community-led affordable housing. After meeting people from CLTs in Belgium and England, Homers convened a roundtable discussion of the CLT concept in Turin in 2014 to which CLT practitioners from other countries were invited.[10]

The meeting just happened to coincide with the occupation of the old royal stables, *Cavallerizza Reale*, a huge vacant historic space in Turin's city centre. CLT advocates met with the occupiers of *Cavallerizza* and discussed the possibility of applying the CLT concept to redevelopment of the royal stables. Although that particular project was never realized, the discussions around it did eventually lead to some interest in the model from the Chieri municipality, near Turin.

Starting in 2010, Chieri had joined with a few other Italian cities to develop "commons regulations," a regulatory framework outlining how local governments, citizens, and the local community can manage public and private spaces and assets together. Chieri became the first municipality to integrate the CLT model into its commons regulations as one option for common management. The City of Palermo later did the same. The idea in both cities was that the municipality would transfer empty buildings or underused plots of land to a community land trust.

In Chieri, Homers negotiated with the city government for the acquisition of two sites, *Tabasso* and *Cascina Maddalene*. Detailed legal and financial plans for the redevelopment of these derelict sites as community land trusts were made, but in the end the municipality wasn't ready to collaborate, mainly because city officials worried whether the separation of land and buildings and the restriction on resale prices were "legal," despite being assured by a registered notary that they were. Despite this setback in Chieri, which may be temporary, Homers began working to develop another CLT project on a plot of church-owned land in Turin. This project will produce forty-two family flats and two shared flats of "supportive serviced housing" for families with a physically or mentally handicapped member. The complex will include community spaces, a public garden, a day care centre, a solidarity restaurant, a shop for local food produced by social co-ops, and healthcare facilities.

Switzerland[11]

Switzerland has a strong tradition of cooperative housing. At the beginning of the Twentieth Century, a number of cooperatives were set up to produce affordable housing for the working class. In the 1990s, this movement gained new dynamism. In the wake of a squatters' movement, new community-led cooperatives emerged, especially in cities such as Zurich, Lausanne, and Geneva. Thanks to the support of the respective urban authorities, these cooperatives have been able to expand considerably in recent years and have started to develop ever larger and more ambitious projects.

In Geneva, town planning rules determine the type of housing that can be built. Some building sites are reserved for cooperatives, but only rental housing can be built there because in Switzerland the classic housing cooperative is a *tenant* cooperative. The cooperative is the owner (or leaseholder) of the land and building. Members rent their housing units from the cooperative. Until recently, cooperatives have developed and managed only rental housing, so any land that became available for the construction of owner-occupied housing was *de facto* reserved for private for-profit developers.

CODHA, a large housing cooperative in Geneva, decided in 2018 to expand its activities to include owner-occupied homes developed through long-term lease contracts on land owned by a cooperative, homes that will remain permanently affordable through resale mechanisms. As in all its other projects, the residents will participate in the development and management of the homes. In this way, CODHA wants to respond to the wish of some members to become homeowners. By doing so, CODHA can also expand its activities beyond the areas that the city has reserved for tenant cooperatives.

The first homes in Switzerland that are being owned and operated in the manner of a CLT are being created under the auspices of a cooperative housing association that was founded in 1994, one which has long shared the same commitment to community-led development of permanently affordable housing that is found among CLTs in other countries. From now on, for part of its activities, CODHA will use the CLT ownership model. The *propriété sans but lucratif* (non-profit ownership housing), as they christened this branch of their work, will start its first developments in 2020.

Spain and Portugal[12]

The CLT model has gained a growing audience among scholars and NGOs in both Portugal and Spain. Although no CLTs yet exist in the Iberian Peninsula, the CLT model has been presented and discussed over the last few years in a number of venues and contexts, thanks mainly to the tireless efforts of Yves Cabannes and Antonio Manuel Rodríguez Ramos. It has attracted particular interest among neighbourhoods with semi-formal or informal land regimes, such as Cova da Moura in the metropolitan area of Lisbon.

The grassroots platform *Morar em Lisboa* (To Live in Lisbon) has shown an interest in the CLT model as a possible strategy for addressing the negative impact of extensive touristification on the people living in downtown Lisbon. There is also growing interest in the CLT model in Cañada Real, an informal settlement in Madrid where no titling solution has yet been found.

A major development of late has been the effort to remove legal hurdles to establishing a CLT in Spain. This initiative was carried out with students from the *Laboratorio Jurídico sobre Desahucios* (Legal Lab on Evictions), as a follow-up to the first session of the International Tribunal on Forced Evictions, organized by Rodríguez Ramos and Cabannes. A new legal framework for CLTs was developed by a group of trained legal professionals and has now been presented to the Andalusian Assembly.

Some municipal governments have recently taken note of the CLT as well. The City of Barcelona has undertaken a partnership with New York City under the International Urban Cooperation Programme of the European Union to work on affordable housing—with a particular focus on CLTs. Barcelona has also witnessed the development of *La Borda,* a housing cooperative that, while not being a CLT per se, shares many of its principles, including the separate ownership of the land and buildings, community involvement, and the inclusion of anti-speculative mechanisms designed to keep the housing permanently affordable. The first housing project of *La Borda* was inaugurated in 2018 with twenty-eight apartments.

Central and Eastern Europe

The situation in Central and Eastern Europe is unique compared to the rest of Europe. In the last 30 years, ever since the fall of the Berlin Wall, housing policy in these states has gone through a series of major changes. Policy was characterized by rapid privatization of state-owned housing after 1989. The real estate market then went through intensive growth between 2000 and 2008, followed by the collapse or stagnation of housing prices after the global financial crisis in 2008.

> They are responding to the housing emergency by taking the lead in reinventing types and tenures of housing from the bottom up.

Today, housing is left almost entirely to the market. Many households have neither the necessary capital to acquire an apartment nor to qualify for a mortgage. Households struggle to cover basic housing expenses. Many people are unable to afford their own apartment. Particularly for young people, this leads to an unhealthy dependence on older generations, increasing the pressures that cause many to leave the country. Also, the communist heritage gave community housing, cooperatives, and state housing, which were the standard forms of tenure in these countries for ages, a bad reputation. Nevertheless, across the region new cooperative housing developments are now being explored by pioneering groups. They are responding to the housing emergency—unaffordability, speculation, a negligible amount of social housing—by taking the lead in reinventing types and tenures of housing from the bottom up.

The MOBA Housing network is playing a leading role in fostering this reinvention. It gathers together grassroots practitioners who are working on housing initiatives in Zagreb, Budapest, Belgrade, Prague, and Ljubljana, looking for ways to build affordably priced, community-led housing. Today, all of these groups are looking into different organisational forms and financing possibilities. Cooperative housing has received the most attention to date, but in 2018 MOBA organised a meeting in Croatia to explore whether the CLT model might also have a place in addressing the housing problems of Central and Eastern Europe.

Scotland[13]

Scotland has the most concentrated pattern of landownership in the developed world. Over 80% of Scotland is in private ownership; and half of that private land is in the hands of fewer than 500 owners. The community land movement has been one response to this unequal distribution of ownership. In the 1990s, communities in the Highlands of Scotland were experiencing depopulation and decline, partly as a result of an inability to influence the way that the land where they lived was managed and developed. In response,

> Around 230,000 hectares of Scotland are now in community ownership.

several communities raised funds to purchase land and to shape their futures by ensuring their land was managed and developed in ways that provide collective community benefits through enhanced security of housing tenure, improved employment prospects, and sustainable land management.

These early community landowners were able to turn around years of depopulation and decline through an ambitious approach to regeneration. They inspired others and provided a template for the subsequent purchase and development of land by communities, both rural and urban over the following decades. Now, around 230,000 hectares of Scotland are in community ownership. Democratically elected community trusts own the land on behalf of the communities that live there and are accountable to them for the management and development of the land. Communities have developed a huge range of assets and services on their land including renewables projects, affordable housing, business units, harbours and pontoons, and tourist facilities.

The Scottish Government established the Scottish Land Fund in 2001 to support the purchase of land by communities and, in 2003, Parliament established preemptive legal rights for communities to buy private land and buildings in certain circumstances.[14] In 2015, legislation provided a framework for the transfer of public assets to community organisations as well.[15] In 2016, the powers afforded to rural communities became applicable to urban Scotland. To exercise these Rights to Buy, communities need to have an appropriate governance structure (usually a company limited by guarantee) and must have demonstrated support for community ownership via a local ballot. The process of land reform is ongoing. In 2020, further legislation will be introduced to help communities buy land in pursuance of sustainable development.[16]

Community Land Scotland is the national network for community landowners and communities that are in the process of acquiring land. Historically, most community landowners were in rural areas, but Community Land Scotland is now also supporting a growing network of urban community landowners.

One significant example of an endeavour to apply all facets of Scottish community ownership to an urban setting is the Midsteeple Quarter project in Dumfries. This project intends to bring about mixed-use regeneration via a process of community ownership, incrementally acquiring all properties within an urban quarter and redeveloping them according to a masterplan for community facilities, business space and housing. The community organization behind this project was born out of many years of engagement, seeking to address the modern role of a market town within the context of town centre decline and absentee ownership. The group has acquired its first property within the Quarter and is taking its first steps toward delivery.

Ireland[17]

House prices in Ireland have risen enormously in recent years. Cities like Dublin have become unaffordable for many. Unlike in the UK, however, and despite the work over the past decade by people such as Emer O'Siochru and groups like the Community Land Trust Initiative, community land trusts have yet to become firmly established in Ireland.

In 2010, the *Manifesto for Rural Development* was published by the Carnegie UK Trust in association with a number of Irish actors, proposing the CLT as a vehicle for sustainable rural regeneration. Inspired by this publication, the Irish Regenerative Land Trust is currently developing a rural CLT.

The founding of the Land Development Agency (LDA) in 2018 was intended to streamline the provision of state and private land for affordable housing. The LDA and a number of local authorities have declared their intention of developing policies to enable CLTs. Limerick City, for example, is actively seeking to enable inner-city regeneration using the community land trust model.

There is limited understanding of the model in Ireland, however, and there has been neither recognition nor sanction by risk-averse state bodies. Private and religious institutions may offer a realistic alternative to the state as possible sources of land for CLTs. It is anticipated that Ireland will see the introduction of pilot CLTs in the main urban areas in the near future, and possibly in rural areas as well.

A EUROPEAN COLLABORATION TO ADVANCE CLTs: SUSTAINABLE HOUSING FOR INCLUSIVE AND COHESIVE CITIES (SHICC)

The leaders of the first urban CLTs in Europe and England turned to the European Union in search of financial resources for strengthening their fledgling movement. The European Union is not allowed to legislate with regard to housing, but social innovation is an increasingly popular policy area. Representatives of the London CLT and CLT Brussels, who had met in 2012 during a conference of the National CLT Network in the USA, partnered that year to apply for funding under an EU project call on innovation. They were not successful, but after two later attempts the European Union finally approved their proposal for a collaboration among urban CLTs in Belgium, England, and France. This project was given the name of "Sustainable Housing for Inclusive and Cohesive Cities" (SHICC). CLT Brussels took the initiative of forming the partnership, bringing together the leaders of various organizations who had met in recent years at conferences in the United States or in Europe.

Since its onset in 2017, the SHICC project has been able to achieve significant progress in four respects. First, it has played a major role as a catalyst of the European CLT movement, increasing its support base through meetings and events. The project's partners organised a major policy conference in May 2018 in Lille with speakers from a number of different countries and organisations. Around 150 participants from across

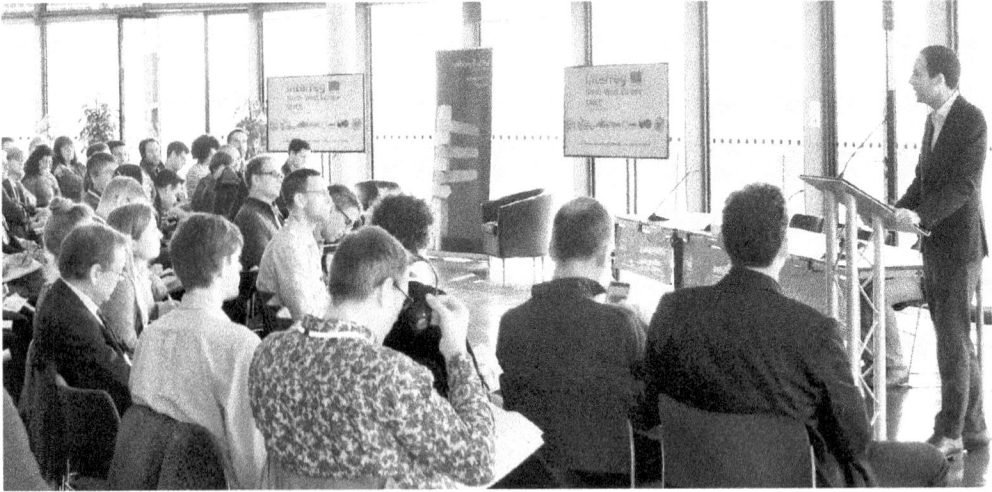

Fig 9.1. Second SHICC transnational event, London City Hall, 10 May 2019.

Europe discussed topics such as financing CLTs, how the CLT model can work for the most deprived, and how CLTs can promote resident involvement. A second major conference took place in London in May 2019. The final conference occurred in Brussels in June 2020, coinciding with a book launch for *On Common Ground* and a CLT symposium open to the general public.

Second, SHICC has provided resources to allow partners to inspire and to support other groups across the region of North-West Europe. Partners have been travelling across the region participating in reflections, presenting the CLT model, and coaching budding urban CLTs. In addition, a number of peer-to-peer exchanges have allowed established CLTs and recently formed groups to share their experiences and to learn from each other. Finally, the expansion of the National CLT Network of England and Wales' Start-Up Fund to serve the entire region is ongoing at the time of writing, with the first vouchers for technical expertise being handed out.

Third, SHICC has made new resources available for existing and future urban CLT projects. On the financial side, the first cross-regional analysis has been completed on urban CLTs' finance. This analysis provides information to interested groups on sources of funding for CLT development in France, England, Wales, Brussels, and Flanders, as well as possible funding at the European level. A measurement tool is currently being developed to evaluate the social impact of CLTs. This will be part of a broader set of tools that will help CLTs make their case to decision makers. Finally, the SHICC project will eventually produce a set of guides on how to set up a CLT, including a specific emphasis on managing the financial aspects of both the organization and its projects.

Last, but not least, the SHICC project has provided resources for four pioneering urban CLTs in London, Lille, Brussels, and Ghent to further consolidate their models, to document their progress, and to share their experience with the wider European CLT community. Papers will be delivered by the end of the project on various topics, including: community engagement, business planning, structuring deals with private and public funding, arrangements for the legal structure and governance of CLTs, and strategies for the scaling up of CLT operations.

The SHICC project may prove to have represented a watershed moment for the European CLT movement. By the project's end, it is anticipated that CLTs will have proven their value in dealing with the affordable housing crisis in Europe and will have become a true alternative for housing provision.

PATTERNS AND PROSPECTS FOR CLT DEVELOPMENT IN EUROPE

CLTs in Europe are structured and applied in many different ways and come in all shapes and sizes. Some are linked to a particular neighbourhood, while others cover an entire city, managing housing projects scattered across many areas. Some comprise only a few housing units, while others are part of larger housing developments and include dozens of units. CLTs also differ in their organization and operation, depending on whether they are initiated by municipal governments, communities, or local non-profits and depending on whether the national legislation authorizing them is more or less detailed in what a CLT is required to be.

Despite their differences, they all share a commitment to making permanently affordable housing a reality. This is why the notion of stewardship, be it through legal mechanisms or shared democratic governance, is central to the concept of a CLT. In addition, the inclusion of anti-speculative mechanisms is a key element of all CLTs, regardless of the resale formula that is used to calculate resale prices.

In the context of the SHICC project, a working definition of a CLT was put forward. SHICC's leaders believed this definition to encompass the majority of the region's urban CLTs:

> CLTs are non-profit, democratic, community-led organisations. They develop and manage homes that are affordable to low and median income households, as well as other assets that contribute to thriving local communities. They act as long-term stewards of these assets, ensuring they remain permanently affordable. This is achieved through mechanisms that ensure that any additional value generated is retained within the CLT.

Despite differences in terms of community involvement, ranging from the bottom-up approach of many English CLTs to the more top-down approach of the local authority-led French OFS model, all partners of the SHICC project have subscribed to this definition. It provides a common understanding and the common ground for all CLT initiatives in Europe.

Fig. 9.2. Informational brochure describing Sustainable Housing for Inclusive and Cohesive Cities, 2018. SHICC is a partnership of the Global Fund for Cities Development (FMDV), the National CLT Network of England and Wales, the City of Lille, CLT Ghent, London CLT, and CLT Brussels.

Prospects for Growth—and Potential Obstacles

Over the past ten years, the CLT has gained significant recognition in mainland Europe. Almost no one had heard of the model in 2008, but the CLT is now generally regarded as an attractive and effective strategy for tackling housing and urban problems.

The increasing acceptance of the CLT's approach to land stewardship and permanent affordability is primarily due to a worsening housing crisis across many countries. Living in many European cities is becoming more and more expensive; more and more people are no longer finding suitable and affordable housing. The construction of new social housing is in decline. Rising prices in market-priced housing make any subsidies available from government inadequate for low-income tenants who are trying to get into rental housing. The same is true for moderate-income households hoping to gain access to conventional forms of homeownership.

This mounting crisis in affordable housing is happening alongside problems of unsustainable urban growth, urban sprawl, and climate change, forcing governments to consider new policies and strategies for housing, land use, and urban development. At the same time, in recent years, there has been a widespread movement of citizens' initiatives, favouring a sharing economy and the Commons. There is widespread agreement on the need for new models.

All of this provided a fertile breeding ground for the new idea of European community land trusts. By focusing strongly on cooperation and cross-border exchanges from the start, the initiators of the first CLTs used this momentum to raise the CLTs' profile. Individuals in political circles, in the academic world, and in civil society, as well as activists in many citizen groups, got to know CLTs and started to see them as an interesting solution.

But setting up a community land trust is not the same as setting up a community garden. It requires a lot of money, a lot of expertise in various fields, and many adjustments to ensure that a CLT complies with a country's laws governing the ownership, leasing, and operation of real estate. For citizen activists who undertake a CLT initiative, it usually requires that they dare to take a cautious step towards cooperation with the government. Conversely, municipal governments who undertake a CLT initiative must dare to give more power to private citizens.

The flexibility of the model and the enthusiasm and perseverance of the first initiators ensured that the first hurdles to establishing a CLT and to developing CLT housing could be overcome. Hundreds of CLT homes, spread over a dozen cities, are currently in the process of being developed, mainly in England, Belgium and France. In other cities and in almost all European countries, groups are either exploring the formation of a CLT or already in the process of creating one.

Despite this great activity and attention, the CLT movement on the European mainland is still in its infancy. It remains an early and vulnerable phenomenon. The number of homes developed to date are a drop in the ocean, compared to the magnitude of the housing problem in many cities and countries. This movement will only be able to have a weighty and lasting impact if it becomes easier to set up CLTs and to develop permanently affordable homes. If every new organization and every new project is a marathon, impeded by countless hurdles, exhaustion will quickly set in.

Further growth will only be possible if European cooperation is continued and strengthened. Interesting building blocks are being developed in different cities, regions, and countries, which others will be able to use. For example, the success of CLT supporters in France, where the national government was persuaded to enact legislation authorizing *Organismes de Foncier Solidaire,* the French version of a CLT, and to create a new type of long-term ground lease, can inspire CLT activists in other countries. The fruitful cooperation that has developed in Brussels between a citizens' initiative and the government can serve as another example for citizens and cities that want to launch a CLT. The mortgage loans provided by the Brussels Housing Fund, moreover, can increase the confidence of lenders. Scholarly research, model contracts, and case studies of CLTs that are already in operation can be used to inform and to inspire new CLTs. The current European SHICC project has created a framework for lasting cross-national cooperation, which may help CLTs to gain access to more funding from the European Union, making it easier for CLTs to implement their projects.

It is too soon to say whether this young movement will succeed in playing a substantial role in addressing the housing crisis in European cities. But a foundation has been laid and a significant start has been made. In mainland Europe, the prospects look good for further growth and greater impact by CLTs in the coming years.

Notes

1. Audrey Linkenheld is Local Councillor for Innovation and Social Mix, City of Lille, and Secretary of Organisme de Foncier Solidaire of the Lille European Metropolis.

2. OFS was made a part of national housing law (ALUR law).

3. This was made possible thanks to very long-term (60-80 years) loans by Banque des Territoires, enabling OFSs to buy land.

4. Further avenues for expanding the OFS model are currently being explored. They include the resale of social housing, the fight against precarious housing, and irregular settlments.

5. Marc Neelen, Jip Nelissen, and Rense Bos contributed to this profile of CLT developments in The Netherlands.

6. Their interest in the CLT was piqued through various exchanges with CLT Brussels and by the participation of City in the Making in European CLT meetings.

7. Michael LaFond contributed to this profile of CLT developments in Germany.

8. The description of Ex-Rotaprint by one of the artists who led the campaign to acquire this former industrial site is remarkably similar to how most CLT leaseholders would describe their own form of tenure: "We have a 99-year, inheritable building rights contract with the foundations, meaning we pay them an annual lease for the ground. We then own the buildings and can work with them without having to ask for anything. The only—very important—condition is that we can't sell the compound because they [i.e., the two foundations] own the ground" (*http://www.uncubemagazine.com/blog/16598237*).

9. Matteo Robiglio contributed to this profile of CLT developments in Italy.

10. The event was part of *We-Traders,* a travelling exhibition on new forms of economy in Europe.

11. Cyril Royez contributed to this profile of CLT developments in Switzerland.

12. Yves Cabannes contributed to this profile of CLT interest in Spain and Portugal.

13. Authored by Linsay Chalmers and Mike Staples, with the assistance of Dr. Calum McLeod.

14. Land Reform Act 2003 (Scotland), followed by Land Reform Act 2016 (Scotland).

15. Community Empowerment Act 2015 (Scotland).

16. In 2017, the Scottish Government set up a Scottish Land Commission to drive forward land reform. Key aspects of the Commission's work are aimed at bringing community landownership into the mainstream and making effective use of land for the common good.

17. This profile of CLT interest in Ireland was authored by Tom O'Donnell.

PART THREE
REGIONAL SEEDBEDS

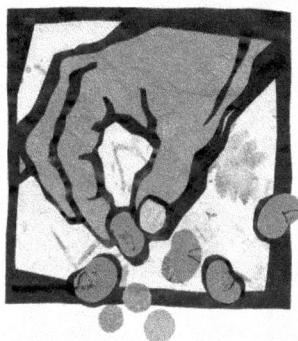

Exploring the Potential for
CLT Growth in the Global South

10.

Collective Land Tenure in Latin America and the Caribbean, Past and Present

Pierre Arnold, Jerónimo Díaz, and Line Algoed

Among the different pre-Columbian cultures, the earth—like the rivers and mountains—was considered a common good to be tilled and utilized collectively. During that period, the great metropolises were sustained by complex irrigation systems controlled by despotic political-administrative systems. There are no records, however, of private forms of land appropriation. The European invasion of the Americas in 1492 caused the destruction of entire cultures and reconfigured the territorial systems pre-established by civilizations such as the Aztec and the Inca. The new colonial order imposed, among other things, a regime of privately owned property.

With the arrival of the Nineteenth Century, the expansion of capitalism in modern nations pushed colonizing policies into supposedly "virgin" spaces, almost always inhabited by indigenous groups. The invisibility of indigenous peoples in Latin America and the Caribbean went hand-in-hand with territorial dispossession and the concentration of rural land in very few hands (Oxfam, 2016). Various forms of communal land tenure continued to exist nevertheless, especially in rural areas.[1] These lands were held collectively by indigenous peoples or by descendants of enslaved peoples, who exercised *de facto* possession. Their collective tenure was acknowledged by the State in most cases.

In the urban sphere, after decades of organizations like the World Bank promoting an ideology of "homeownership," individual private property has become entrenched as a symbol of social progress, constituting the dominant form of home occupancy, well above tenancy. Also, given the need to regularize land tenure in informal neighborhoods, the general approach in the region has been to offer individual deeds or property titles.

For middle-income sectors in most of the countries of the region, the residential horizon has been reduced to the buying of houses or flats in massive new housing complexes that proliferate along urban peripheries.[2] This housing option does not always translate into a better quality of life than tenancy, however. It may not even be better than the informal occupation of housing in well-located areas. These massive complexes are distant from centers of employment and are generally lacking in quality urban services, including access to public transportation. The time and money spent in traveling to jobs, education, health and cultural facilities increase significantly, affecting the social and economic situation of the households. Individual ownership does not guarantee security of occupancy either. This was demonstrated by the "subprime" mortgage crisis in the United States, starting in 2007, that rippled throughout Latin America and caused the eviction of millions of families who had bought their homes.

Against this backdrop, civil organizations and urban social movements have engaged in what may be defined as the "social production of habitat," meaning "all those processes that generate habitable spaces that are carried out under the control of self-producers and other social agents that operate on a nonprofit basis" (HIC–AL, 2017).

> Collective land tenure is a key factor in promoting the social production of habitat.

Collective land tenure is generally understood among these housing activists to be a key factor in promoting the social production of habitat and in consolidating urban communities over the long run. Except for the Caño Martín Peña Land Trust in Puerto Rico, the community land trust (CLT) model has not so far been a form of collective tenure that has been applied in the region by self-producers or by other social agents operating housing on a nonprofit basis. There are other interesting housing production models, however, most of which are based on the cooperative ownership of land and the cooperative management of municipally owned territorial reserves extracted from the market. These models are to be found in Uruguay, as well as in the experience of managing public land in Brazil and Venezuela.

In the special case of the Barrio Intercultural in San Martín de los Andes, Argentine Patagonia, moreover, there is an interesting link between the collective land tenure that has persisted in rural areas and the social production of habitat that has occurred in urban spaces. We shall argue, in fact, that the Barrio Intercultural provides a clear example of how the territorial rights of indigenous peoples can be restored and the housing needs of popular sectors can be addressed, without compromising the environmental quality of expanding urban areas.

I. HISTORY AND GEOGRAPHY OF COLLECTIVE LAND TENURE IN RURAL LATIN AMERICA AND THE CARIBBEAN

From Internalized Colonialism to Recognition of Indigenous Territory

Latin America and the Caribbean represent a vast and diverse region in terms of geography, environment, ethnicities and cultures. In addition to the peoples and cultures originating in Europe and those originating in Africa, there are at least 522 indigenous ethnicities who have preserved traditions, languages, and specific ways of living (UNICEF, 2009). Many of these indigenous peoples have suffered and survived five centuries of colonial domination, first under the yoke of the Spaniards, Portuguese, Dutch, English and French, and then under the domain of mixed-race Latin-Americans and Caribbeans who ended up exercising a new form of internalized colonialism.[3] Although indigenous populations participated in the independence movements that burst forth in the early Nineteenth Century (León Portilla, 2011), they were excluded from the formative processes of the new national states. Excluded too were the descendants of over 10 million enslaved Africans who were forcibly brought to Latin American and the Caribbean from Africa between the Sixteenth and Nineteenth Centuries.

In Latin America, especially in Mexico and Peru, the construction of a national identity was achieved by appropriating the symbols of pre-Hispanic antiquity in a process that paradoxically involved the destruction of the material support for the heirs to those same civilizations. With the liberal reforms of the Nineteenth Century, collective land tenure by indigenous societies was guaranteed under the so-called New Laws "for the governance of the Indies and proper treatment and preservation of the Indians." But these reforms were seen by the elites as an obstacle to modernization. The New Laws were dissolved, therefore, in order to give free rein to the integration of populations and the imposition of a property market. In the worst cases, the newly formed nations carried out their territorial unification through genocidal projects such as the "Conquest of the Desert" in the 1870s, led by the Argentine army against the Mapuche peoples of Patagonia.

Mexico. The great social uprising in Mexico, the Revolution of 1910–1917, was driven by demands for "land and freedom" for indigenous peoples, including the restitution of lands recognized since the times of the Spanish Viceroyalty. In order to pacify the country, Article 27 of the Mexican Constitution of 1917 legalized *communal property* once again, stating that: "co-owners, *rancherías* (hamlets situated on private property), settlements, congregations, tribes and other settlement organizations that in fact or by law were maintained in a communal state shall have ability to enjoy in common the lands, forests and waters that belong to them."[4]

Today, half of the land area of Mexico belongs to two types of collective entities. First of all, there are 2,392 *indigenous communities* that have managed to regain, at least partially, collective tenure over the territories recognized from the time of the Viceroyalty, totaling 17 million hectares (approximately 42 million acres). Secondly, there are about 30,000 *ejidos,* lands that were distributed to peasants and villagers through Agrarian Reform during the 1930s and 1940s. These lands are communally possessed but partly individually used. The *ejido* regime currently covers 80 million hectares (approximately 198 million acres).

Local *ejidatario* assemblies deliberate on everything concerning land use issues. All other matters are inserted into the municipal sphere and therefore do not enjoy political autonomy. It should be stressed that *indigenous communities* and the *ejidos* have common lands within those 42 and 198 million acres for activities such as hunting, fishing, grazing, maintaining forests for harvesting or gathering firewood, and for family plots. These common lands are deemed inalienable.[5]

Bolivia. The Mexican process of Agrarian Reform had an ideological impact throughout Latin America and the Caribbean. Similar reforms were implemented in other countries of the region with an objective of modernizing the countryside, while also curtailing the growth of communism among rural populations (Coque Martínez, 2002). In this context, indigenous peoples remained nearly invisible. In Bolivia, for example, the Nationalist Revolutionary Movement opted in the mid-Twentieth Century for modernization of the State, while also bolstering socio-cultural homogenization. The Agrarian Reform Act of 1953 replaced the term "indio" (Indian)—which was seen as having potential racial discriminatory implications—with "campesino" (peasant). The ethnic groups of the Bolivian Amazon became known as "selvícolas" (forest dwellers) and were placed under the authority of evangelical missions (RAISG, 2016: 46).

Recognition of multicultural realities came much later, as reflected in population censuses that began to integrate variables in the 1990s such as "self-identification" within certain ethnic groups. A key event was the 1989 adoption of "Convention 169" by the International Labor Organization, responding to demands of a nascent indigenous movement in favor of the restitution of territorial rights. This agreement stipulated that "the rights of ownership and possession of the peoples concerned over the lands which they traditionally occupy shall be recognized" (Article 14). Convention 169 was the result of a regional awareness that reached an apex in 1992, during the quin-centenary of the "discovery of America"—or, as it is known among various social movements, the "Year of Indigenous, Black and Popular Resistance."

In Bolivia, where 40% of the population is currently recognized as forming part of 36 indigenous nations, this movement has had important legal and territorial consequences. In the 1990s, after the great march "for territory and dignity," the Bolivian government ratified the Indigenous and Tribal Peoples Convention 169 and issued eight Supreme Decrees whereby the first "Indigenous Territories" were established.

This triggered a reaction among economic and political elites who insisted that the only territory recognized by the Constitution was the national one and, therefore, "states within the state" would not be tolerated (Tamburini, 2019: 10). In 1996, given the continued plundering of natural resources and the multiplication of *de facto* occupations, indigenous organizations managed to influence the Law of the National Institute of Agrarian Reform, enacted by the Bolivian government. This law established the procedure to legalize so-called "Communal Lands of Origin"—Tierra Comunitaria de Origen (TCO)—for a period not exceeding 10 years, during which time the situation of private properties within the claimed areas would be analyzed and the entitlements of landholders would be secured.

The struggle for the restitution of *ancestral lands* formed a prelude to the movement in Bolivia that led to Evo Morales becoming in 2006 the country's first president of indigenous descent (Aymara). This historic turn of events precipitated the adoption in 2009 of the Political Constitution of the Plurinational State of Bolivia, which recognized the right of all peoples to autonomy and self-determination, as well as the consolidation of their territorial entities and institutions. In 2010, the TCOs were renamed "Native Indigenous Peasants Territories"—Territorios Indígenas Originarios Campesinos (TIOC). These lands, which are collectively held, enjoy legal guarantees of indivisibility, immunity from seizure, and inalienability, and they are not subject to taxation. In order to become Autonomous Territorial Entities, these agrarian lands must undergo a legal procedure. They still remain as administrative units of the Bolivian State, together with the municipalities, provinces and departments (RAISG, 2016: 48).

According to the Rights and Resources Initiative (2015), indigenous peoples in Bolivia currently own approximately 40 million hectares of land under different *communal* modalities, the equivalent of 36% of the total area of Bolivia. Actual control over these vast territories has not been easy, however. There are pressures exerted by private agents to prevent the recognition of TIOCs and there is the constant expansion of the "agricultural frontier" of extensive agro-industries that threaten small-scale subsistence agriculture of indigenous peoples and peasants.[6] In addition, the national government has followed an extractive energy development scheme that violates the ecological integrity and autonomy of indigenous peoples, as exhibited in the Isiboro-Sécure Indigenous Territory and National Park.

Strategies for Reclaiming Indigenous Territory

There are different strategies that have been pursued by indigenous peoples to ensure that their ancestral lands are restored, from social mobilization and legal formalization of territorial claims to armed insurrection. The latter was the case with the Zapatista Army of National Liberation, formed by the indigenous Tzeltals, Tzotzils, Choles and Tojolabales of southern Mexico. Armed insurrection also characterized, to some degree, the Mapuche movement in Chile.

The most common strategy has been to articulate the territorial claims of peoples and nations within various processes of heritage and environmental conservation. In the Sierra Nevada de Santa Marta in Colombia's Caribbean region, for example, the Arhuaco people have utilized the UNESCO Biosphere Reserve Declaration to block the mining industry's incursion into its ancestral territory, estimated at approximately 600,000 hectares (approximately 1.5 million acres). Indigenous authorities have sought to extend the environmental protection perimeter to include part of the coastal mountain range within the World Heritage List.

Similar tactics have been followed by indigenous peoples in Brazil, albeit with considerable difficulty since indigenous peoples represent less than 1% of the Brazilian population. After a century of paternalistic policies conducted by the "Indian Protection Service," aimed at facilitating a "peaceful" expansion of the agricultural frontier into the Amazon region, the 1988 Constitution enshrined the principle that indigenous peoples are the "first and natural owners of the land." Thus, the Brazilian state recognizes that indigenous populations have "a permanent possession and exclusive usufruct of the wealth of the land, rivers and lakes existing in them" (RAISG, 2016: 69).

There is no space here to describe the detailed analysis that is required for the identification and demarcation of an area so that indigenous peoples can live in a traditional manner (RAISG, 2016: 55-84). It is important to understand, however, that in Brazil and in the rest of Latin America and the Caribbean the efforts to establish indigenous rights to land possession involve different types of procedures, social actors, antagonistic economic interests, and violent situations (Fernández, 2017). That said, and considering that the territories claimed by indigenous peoples almost never correspond to the "polygons" acknowledged by the State, it is possible to appreciate the scope of the indigenous and peasant territories that are maintained under various forms of collective tenure in the region.

The map presented at right (Fig. 10.1) is inspired by the global platform on *Indigenous and Community Lands.*[7] It is based on various sources of spatial data provided by public and non-governmental institutions. Some lands are omitted or under-counted due to the lack of geo-referenced information, especially significant tracts of land belonging to *Maroon* communities. These communities were formed by descendants of Africans who managed to escape slavery in the Americas, ultimately mixing with Amerindians, especially in Jamaica, Suriname, Puerto Rico, Haiti, Dominican Republic, Cuba, Saint Vincent and Brazil. Due to their generalized isolation from the colonial settlers, many of these *Maroon* communities were able to preserve African traditions relating to the shared use of land, language, music, culture, and religion.[8]

In Brazil, the Secretariat for Policies to Promote Racial Equality has recognized 2,197 *Maroon* communities, referred to as *quilombos* (Museo Afro Digital, n.d.). The 1988 Constitution grants these communities collective ownership of the lands they have occupied since the abolition of slavery in 1888. *Quilombo* residents thus have a constitutional right to a permanent and non-transferable title to the land claimed by their ancestors. It is estimated that approximately one million Afro-Brazilians have this right, although most have not yet received official recognition of their collective ownership. In 2003, the government of Lula da Silva regulated *quilombos,* but the process involved in receiving deeds has been slow.

In the Caribbean, an estimated 100,000 hectares of land are collectively owned by *Maroon* communities and by other Afro-descendant groups. Only 2% of the lands that are occupied by these communities and groups are secured through formal deeds (Rights and Resources, 2015). After the abolition of slavery in the Caribbean, many liberated laborers eventually formed part of a landless proletariat, dependent on large plantations that continued to control most of the agricultural land. In some cases, they were able to

Fig. 10.1

A Mosaic of Collective Land Tenure: Latin America and the Caribbean

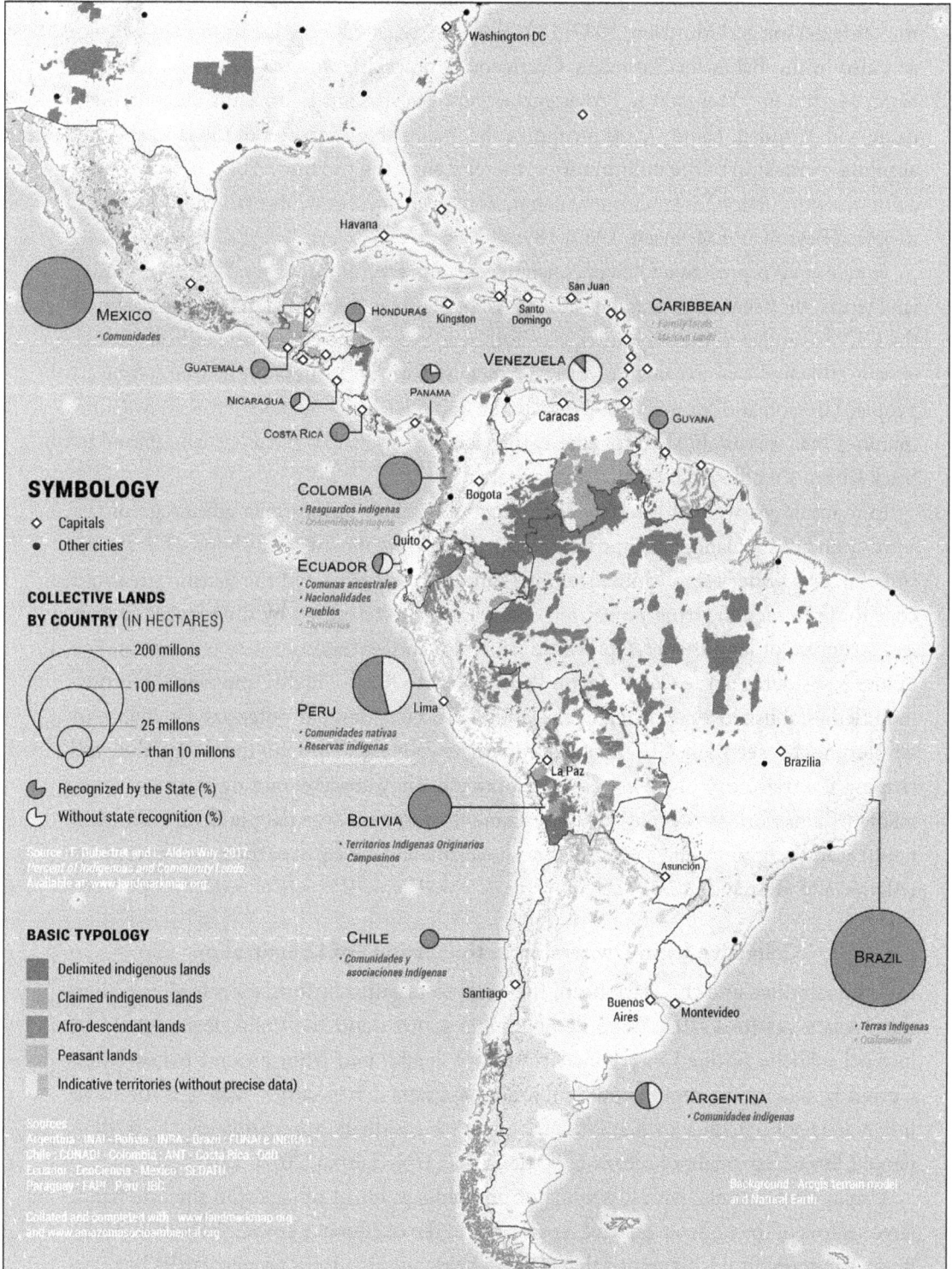

Washington DC

Havana

HONDURAS
Kingston
Santo
Domingo

San Juan

CARIBBEAN
Family lands
Mission lands

MEXICO
· *Comunidades*

GUATEMALA

NICARAGUA

COSTA RICA

PANAMA

VENEZUELA

Caracas

GUYANA

SYMBOLOGY

◇ Capitals
● Other cities

COLOMBIA
· *Resguardos indígenas*
· *Comunidades negras*

Bogotá

Quito

ECUADOR
· *Comunas ancestrales*
· *Nacionalidades*
· *Pueblos*
· *Territorios*

**COLLECTIVE LANDS
BY COUNTRY** (IN HECTARES)

— 200 millons

— 100 millons

— 25 millons

- than 10 millons

PERU
· *Comunidades nativas*
· *Reservas indígenas*
· *Comunidades campesinas*

Lima

La Paz

Brasilia

◗ Recognized by the State (%)

◖ Without state recognition (%)

BOLIVIA
· *Territorios Indígenas Originarios
Campesinos*

Asunción

BASIC TYPOLOGY

CHILE
· *Comunidades y
asociaciones indígenas*

Santiago

Buenos
Aires

Montevideo

▪ Delimited indigenous lands

▪ Claimed indigenous lands

▪ Afro-descendant lands

▪ Peasant lands

▪ Indicative territories (without precise data)

BRAZIL

· *Terras indígenas*
· *Quilombolas*

ARGENTINA
· *Comunidades indígenas*

Background : Arcgis terrain model
and Natural Earth

JERÓNIMO DÍAZ, 2019

join *Maroon* communities and consolidate so-called *family lands,* also known as "property of the children" and "generation property." *Family lands* are miniscule plots of land that are regarded as the inalienable property of all descendants of the ancestor who obtained the land (Besson and Momsen, 1987: 13). This form of land tenure is common in Jamaica and also in the Bahamas, Barbados, Carriacou, Curaçao, Dominica, Grenada, Guyana, Haiti, Martinique, Montserrat, Providencia, Saint Lucia, Saint John, Saint Vincent, Suriname and Trinidad. *Family lands* recognize the inalienable character of the land and the absolute ownership of the communities, thereby ensuring the means of production and cultural reproduction for subsequent generations of the descendants of formerly enslaved peoples (Besson and Momsen, 1987: 18).

Family lands represent a form of resistance against economic racism. Like community land trusts, they seek to guarantee land rights for future generations. In fact, the origin of the CLT is similar to the way in which Caribbean systems of collective land ownership were established—as expressions of resistance by former landless proletarian enslaved peoples (Besson and Momsen, 1987: 18). The first CLT in the United States, New Communities Inc., was established to remedy the lack of arable and buildable land suffered by black laborers employed by white landowners.

In many ways, we still see how economic and political elites take advantage of the scarcity and cost of land, harming and displacing low-income neighborhoods. Given this situation, the wider establishment of CLTs in Latin America and the Caribbean could contribute to reconfiguring power relations that are determined by the present system and structure of land ownership, where lands are concentrated in very few hands. For example, residents of the Caño Martín Peña in Puerto Rico—highly impoverished communities established on now-valuable lands with considerable potential for high-end development—see their CLT as a tool for empowerment. Through their CLT they are shaping the trajectory of their own development. They are also putting in place a permanent framework to prevent the displacement of low-income people from lands that political and economic elites would otherwise claim and develop for their own advantage (Algoed and Hernández, 2019).

Collective Land Ownership in the Context of Urbanization

In Latin America and the Caribbean, the rural-to-urban transformation took less than thirty years (1940–1970). Steep demographic growth and the rapid development of internal markets resulted in a concentration of capital and labor around major cities. Currently, 80% of the region's 588 million inhabitants live in cities, making it the most urbanized region in the world. A fifth of these urban residents, approximately 113 million people, live in informal or precarious settlements (UN-Habitat, 2013: 127).

Urbanization brings with it two major problems in terms of land. On the one hand, large sectors of the population have no security in the occupancy of their homes. In Honduras, for example, it is estimated that 80% of the population lacks property titles because of the torpidity, corruption, and weakness of the entities in charge of promoting land tenure regularization. According to recent studies, 19% of respondents in Honduras say they feel themselves to be at risk of losing their property rights, 43% say their rights are not well protected, and 32% do not trust the authorities to guarantee their property rights. These findings are similar in Colombia, Costa Rica, Ecuador, and Peru.[9]

> Urban sprawl is occurring at the expense of indigenous and peasant communities who previously occupied lands on the periphery of cities.

Urbanized areas throughout the region are expanding at a faster rate than the population is growing. The resulting urban sprawl is occurring, in many cities and countries, at the expense of indigenous and peasant communities who previously occupied lands on the periphery of cities. In Mexico City, for example, this has led to countless conflicts over the appropriation of land and water belonging to *ejidos* and peri-urban communities. Either people who cannot find alternatives in the inner city are moving into these territories or real estate developers are buying up the relatively cheap land within these territories for the massive construction of new housing.

The case of Ecuador is especially interesting. The country has had several agrarian reforms and, since 2008, its Constitution has recognized collective titles to *ancestral territories* claimed by indigenous communities. Nevertheless, the distribution of land remains uneven and there are strong conflicts linked to the development of mining and oil projects, such as the one that now threatens the Huaorani nation in the Yasuni National Park. Meanwhile, the so-called *comunas ancestrales*, ancestral communes that were established during the Spanish colonial period, have acquired public legal status and continue to survive in Quito. The 73 *communal territories* in the city and its surroundings—which are deemed by law to be unseizable, inalienable, and indivisible—face problems such as the lack of specific boundaries, poverty among the inhabitants, and the growth of informal settlements that have been occupying "available" lands without any urban planning (Andrade, 2016).

II. RECENT URBAN STRUGGLES FOR COLLECTIVE LAND TENURE IN LATIN AMERICA AND THE CARIBBEAN

National housing policies in Latin America and the Caribbean since the 1990s, guided by the so-called Washington Consensus,[10] have been geared mainly toward making it easier for the middle classes to buy low-standard housing through savings, credit, and subsidies. Initially in Chile, and later in the rest of the region, homes have been built on a massive scale in urban peripheries, in spaces often lacking any infrastructure, basic services, transportation, or security. This tsunami of construction, aimed at maximizing the profits of developers, construction companies, and the banking sector, has generated major problems of urban segregation and has led ultimately to the loss of quality of life and heritage[11] for families aspiring to "the dream of homeownership" (Arnold, 2018). At the same time, the only alternatives for access to land and housing for people who have been excluded from the formal economy and who cannot access public housing are either the illegal, informal occupation of land, often organized by social movements, or the irregular sale by "pirate" developers of parcels that do not belong to them, lands often lacking both services and authorization for residential use.

In those Latin American cities where real estate speculation is rampant, where the real estate market almost entirely excludes low-income families, and where public housing is scarce, various collective land tenure schemes have emerged to produce affordable housing for the popular sectors — some of which are described below.

Mutual Aid Housing Cooperatives

The Cooperativas de Vivienda por Ayuda Mutua (CVAM) in Uruguay are perhaps the most widely disseminated urban model of collective land tenure and cooperatively managed housing in the region. The origin of these mutual aid housing cooperatives dates back to a series of experiences in low-cost housing production for farmworkers in 1967, which served as an example for part of Uruguay's Housing Law of 1968 (N13.728). Chapter 10 of this law, "On housing cooperatives," which established the operating rules for producing, owning, and operating cooperative housing, has subsequently been embraced by several other social organizations in the region.

Uruguay's housing cooperatives are nonprofit organizations devoted to producing housing and additional services through mutual aid. This cooperative arrangement reduces construction costs, but also creates future neighborhood-based relationships in solidarity. These social organizations are also responsible for the self-management

Fig. 10.2. A cooperative neighborhood, Mesa 5: Juana de América, on the outskirts of Montevideo. JERÓNIMO DÍAZ, 2018

of funds from the Ministry of Housing, obtained through a collective loan for the purchase of land and construction of the complex. At all stages—from the formation of the group to the occupancy of the newly constructed housing and the coexistence of the residents—decision making is democratic. Each family nucleus is represented with a vote before the General Assembly of the cooperative members, where all decisions are discussed and voted on.

In Uruguay, there are owner cooperatives and user cooperatives.[12] The latter are the most common and have contributed to preventing speculation and the eviction of low-income families. Land and buildings always remain the property of the cooperative. Members acquire a "use and enjoyment" contract with the cooperative which enables them to occupy a home that can be passed down to heirs, but cannot be sub-leased or rented.[13] If members face any difficulty paying fees (due to an accident, unemployment, etc.), the cooperative can support them by providing an official subsidy or by dipping into its internal "relief fund," which is built up through monthly contributions from all members. Such protections for security of tenure do not occur in the mortgage-based market, where a bank can readily evict those who default on their mortgages.

As part of Uruguay's Housing Law of 1968, multi-disciplinary nonprofit Technical Assistance Institutes (IAT) were created and have played a key role in the success and sustainability of the country's cooperatives. These Institutes provide comprehensive technical advice (legal, financial, economic, social, operational), as well as training and support, strengthening the cooperatives' self-management and guaranteeing the proper development of each project.[14]

The first housing cooperatives in Uruguay were promoted by labor unions or rural workers and were concentrated along urban peripheries. Beginning the 1990s, with the arrival of the progressive Frente Amplio at the government of Montevideo, a municipal "land portfolio" was created, removing a significant portion of land in the inner city from the "tyranny" of market valuations. Cooperatives are offered sites at a cost that ranges between 10% and 15% of the total value of the housing project (Mendive, 2014).

Currently, some 20,000 families (approximately 90,000 people) occupy cooperative housing in one of 500 CVAM sites scattered across Uruguay. The Ministry of Housing, Land Management, and Environment allocates 40% of its yearly budget to cooperative housing, thereby subsidizing credit interest rates for households with lower incomes (Arnold and Lemarié, 2017).

The evolution and expansion of the Uruguayan cooperative model is the result of a constant political struggle by the cooperatives and by their national federation, Federación Uruguaya de Cooperativas de Vivienda por Ayuda Mutua (FUCVAM) to preserve and to expand the rights and lands they have won.[15] At the international level, moreover, FUCVAM has been sharing and disseminating its experience through regional networks of social and civil actors such as the Latin American Secretariat of Popular Housing and Habitat (SELVIHP) created in 1991 in São Paulo, together with the Brazilian union for popular housing, União Nacional de Moradia Popular (UNMP), and the Argentine movement of squatters and tenants, Movimiento de Ocupantes e Inquilinos (MOI), and other housing movements from Argentina.[16]

Recently, the Swedish Cooperative Center, known as "We Effect," has been support-ing the implementation of CVAM pilot projects in Central and South America and pro-moting public policies that support mutual housing cooperatives in Bolivia, Costa Rica, El Salvador, Guatemala, Haiti, Honduras, Nicaragua, and Paraguay (see Figure 6.3). In addition, through the Latin American Alianza Latinoamericana de Cooperativas de Vivi-enda por Ayuda Mutua (Alliance of Mutual-Aid Housing Cooperatives) and with the support of FUCVAM and We Effect, new CVAM pilot projects are being considered in Chile, Colombia, Mexico, and Peru. In 2012, FUCVAM received a World Habitat Award, recognizing the Federation's exemplary work in sharing its model of mutual aid housing cooperatives with other countries.[17]

City Centers under Dispute

Collective and anti-speculative land tenure is a strategy for reclaiming the central areas of cities where housing solutions for low-income households are usually scarce because of the absence of policies regulating land prices and because of the increase in speculation and gentrification. In central neighborhoods of Buenos Aires (Barracas, La Boca and San Telmo, for example), Montevideo (Old City) and San Salvador (Historic Center), there are now mutual housing cooperatives that ensure the perpetual availability of affordable housing for popular sectors in areas where services and sources of employment are con-centrated. Described below are cases from Argentina, Brazil and Venezuela where move-ments for affordable housing have been supported by various forms of collective land tenure.

Argentina. In the Autonomous City of Buenos Aires, the Law 341 of 2000 was an import-ant victory for social movements struggling to address the housing needs of low-income households in the face of speculation and a scarcity of affordable housing. The Law obli-gated the local government to supply urban land to housing cooperatives. The coopera-tives then construct or refurbish residential buildings through mutual aid and preserve the cooperative ownership of the land and housing in perpetuity. This regulatory frame-work, inspired by the Uruguayan CVAMs, permitted the construction of 813 homes in twenty-six cooperatives. Since the arrival of a right-wing party, however, which won con-trol of the government in 2008, no new plots of land have been added to this program by the municipality, and thirty-nine projects containing 841 homes are awaiting construc-tion (HIC–AL, 2017).

Brazil. After years of struggle in São Paulo and Rio de Janeiro, popular movements for the occupation of abandoned buildings have obtained public financing for the rehabili-tation ("retrofit") of vacant apartments. Title to these properties is transferred from the

Fig. 10.3

Exchange of Cooperative Practices and Instruments
Across Latin America and the Caribbean

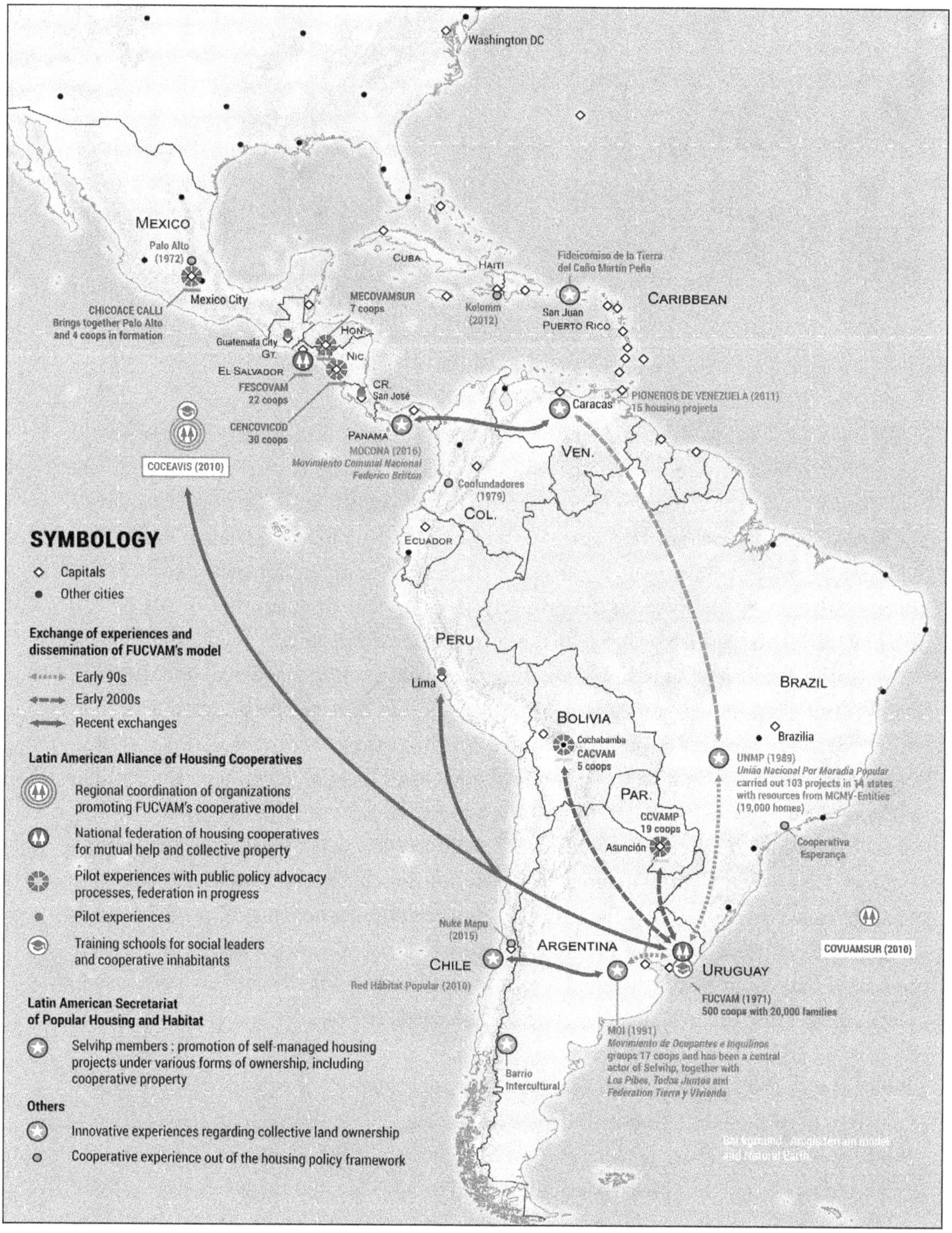

Washington DC

MEXICO

Palo Alto
(1972)

CHICOACE CALLI
Brings together Palo Alto
and 4 coops in formation

Mexico City

MECOVAMSUR
7 coops

CUBA

HAITI

Kolomm
(2012)

San Juan
PUERTO RICO

Fideicomiso de la Tierra
del Caño Martín Peña

CARIBBEAN

Guatemala City
GT.

HON.

NIC.

EL SALVADOR

FESCOVAM
22 coops

CR.
San José

CENCOVICOD
30 coops

COCEAVIS (2010)

PANAMA

MOCONA (2016)
*Movimiento Comunal Nacional
Federico Brittón*

Caracas

PIONEROS DE VENEZUELA (2011)
15 housing projects

VEN.

Cofundadores
(1979)

COL.

ECUADOR

SYMBOLOGY

◇   Capitals

●   Other cities

**Exchange of experiences and
dissemination of FUCVAM's model**

◄····►   Early 90s

◄──►   Early 2000s

◄──►   Recent exchanges

Latin American Alliance of Housing Cooperatives

Regional coordination of organizations
promoting FUCVAM's cooperative model

National federation of housing cooperatives
for mutual help and collective property

Pilot experiences with public policy advocacy
processes, federation in progress

Pilot experiences

Training schools for social leaders
and cooperative inhabitants

**Latin American Secretariat
of Popular Housing and Habitat**

Selvihp members : promotion of self-managed housing
projects under various forms of ownership, including
cooperative property

Others

Innovative experiences regarding collective land ownership

Cooperative experience out of the housing policy framework

PERU

Lima

BOLIVIA

Cochabamba
CACVAM
5 coops

PAR.

CCVAMP
19 coops

Asunción

Nuke Mapu
(2015)

ARGENTINA

CHILE

Red Hábitat Popular (2010)

Barrio
Intercultural

BRAZIL

Brasilia

UNMP (1989)
União Nacional Por Moradia Popular
carried out 103 projects in 14 states
with resources from MCMV-Entities
(19,000 homes)

Cooperativa
Esperança

COVUAMSUR (2010)

URUGUAY

FUCVAM (1971)
500 coops with 20,000 families

MOI (1991)
Movimiento de Ocupantes e Inquilinos
groups 17 coops and has been a central
actor of Selvihp, together with
Los Pibes, Todos Juntos and
Federación Tierra y Vivienda

Tile ground : Angola terrain model
and Natural Earth.

JERÓNIMO DÍAZ, 2018

Fig. 10.4. Inauguration of the CVAM in a refurbished industrial building, La Fábrica, in Buenos Aires, with members of SELVIHP and FUCVAM. JERÓNIMO DÍAZ, 2018

federal government to the municipality—after expropriation in cases where buildings are still held by a private owner. The buildings' rehabilitation is carried out by private companies under the direction of the future inhabitants, using funds from three levels of government: federal (through the Minha Casa Minha Vida-Entidades housing programme), state, and municipal (Pinho, n.d.). During the construction process, the future inhabitants take turns watching the property, so that other popular movements do not occupy it. Guards can also be hired by the construction companies.

After the construction is completed, the municipality continues to own both the land and the buildings. Inhabitants of rehabilitated buildings have secure occupancy of their apartments through a formal contract known as Concessão de Direito Real de Uso (Concession for the Real Right to Use). Under the terms of this use agreement, the families make monthly payments toward part of the cost of the retrofit. The other part is subsidized by the federal housing programme. The families cannot sub-lease their apartment, but they have a total security of tenure for their housing that permits them to better their life conditions (Ferraz, 2014). The national union for popular housing, UNMP, estimates that in the center of São Paulo there are approximately 80 unused public and private buildings that could be transformed into low-cost housing for low-income people who work within these urban centers (Arnold and Lemarié, 2017).

Venezuela. A 2002 decree by Venezuela's president, Hugo Chávez, regarding "the regularization of land tenure," gave birth to the Movimiento Pioneros de Venezuela (Pioneer Movement of Venezuela) in 2004.[18] This Movement started identifying unused plots and buildings inside the cities that could be used for well-located social housing. In 2011 the Gran Misión Vivienda (National Mission for Housing) of the government and the presidential decree of "emergency for housing and habitat" provided both the economic resources and the regulatory framework for unused sites in the inner city to be legally occupied and conveyed for the exclusive use of social housing. This housing was to be built through mutual aid organizations like Pioneros de Venezuela.

The emergency decree allowed construction to start even before the parcels were purchased by the State through a forced sale. The price paid to the private owners was based on the price they had previously paid to acquire the property, not the property's current market value. The land was then transferred to resident-controlled entities called Comprehensive Community Housing and Habitat Organizations (OCIVHa). This ensures the collective tenure of the land and any buildings constructed or rehabilitated on it. The Pioneer Movement has engineers and architects who support the OCIVHa groups from design through completion. The members of the OCIVHa who participated in planning the project can live in the housing, but they cannot sub-let their apartments to external people (HIC–AL, 2017). If they decide to leave, the Pioneer Movement decides who is entitled to replace them, on the basis of the hours of participation in the Movement's political, social, community organizing, and building activities.

Although the Venezuelan government provided the initial funds for the construction of the housing, the monthly reimbursement for the construction by the families goes into a Self-Managed Revolving Fund. This Fund facilitates the financing for the production of additional housing for families in these "socialist communities," located in central areas of the city. The materials and machinery used in construction come from the government in return for the labor contributed by the beneficiaries, who work on their own future homes and on homes in other locations (HIC–AL, 2017).

This scheme has led to the completion of approximately 1,700 homes on fifteen formerly vacant parcels in the Caracas Metropolitan Area (Torres, Pineda and Rey, 2017). Given the current international commercial blockade against Venezuela and the economic crisis within the country, certain projects of the Pioneer Movement have suffered significant delays. No new projects have been started since 2017. Nevertheless, of the 2.7 million housing units that have been financed by the national housing programme, Gran Misión Vivienda, 40% of these units have been managed and built by community-led organizations.[19]

The Barrio Intercultural Experience: Linking Cooperative Housing with Indigenous Land and World View

San Martín de los Andes, a small city in southern Argentina, offers an interesting example of how struggles for indigenous land might point the way for low-income households who are seeking access to housing in urban areas. Located on the shores of Lake Lácar among the forests and mountains of the Lanín National Park, San Martín de los Andes is an important tourist destination. Many of its 40,000 inhabitants barely subsist economically. Their housing is inadequate and precarious (HIC–AL, 2017).

The Barrio Intercultural project emerged within this particular context through an alliance between a people's organization called Vecinos Sin Techo and the indigenous Curruhuinca Mapuche community. The latter secured the restoration of its territorial rights over the Lanín National Park in 2001.[20]

More than 150 families, indigenous and non-indigenous, are involved in the Barrio Intercultural project. They have crafted a community development plan with the support of the municipality and a multi-disciplinary technical support team. A member of that team, an architect who had been working with housing cooperatives in Buenos Aires, proposed adding the mutual aid and self-management characteristics of a CVAM to the community development plan. But, informed and shaped by the world view of the Mapuche community, it was understood that the design of any neighborhood built on indigenous territory had to be based on respect for the territory's cultural and natural life in all its diversity.

> Any neighborhood built on indigenous territory had to be based on respect for the territory's cultural and natural life.

The agreement that was reached in finalizing the plan was that at least 50% of the land area (77 hectares or 190 acres) should be preserved without development, without urbanization. Where development was allowed, it should not be laid out in grid format; housing should form circles around community facilities and only be built in forest clearings. Soil waterproofing should be avoided; that is, only gravel streets would be allowed. Density should decrease as the neighborhood approached protected forest and slope areas.

After seven years of planning, participants in this project began to build the Intercultural District in 2011. The project included 100 ecological homes, constructed through mutual-aid initiatives, as well as the construction of common buildings and spaces, dry toilets, and shops at the entrance to the District, where local crafts and products could be sold. The

Fig. 10.5. Sunday morning mutual aid at Barrio Intercultural in the Argentine Andes. PIERRE ARNOLD, 2014

entire process was established within a framework of reconciliation among peoples and respect for community lands, as evidenced in this account by Vecinos Sin Techo:

> It was the lack of housing that brought us together. Hundreds of families who needed a roof over their heads assumed responsibility for their own future. Designing homes immediately posed a need for land on which to settle and this is how the idea of inter-culturality appeared. We chose to forge this path based on the act of justice that came with the historical recognition of the ancestral right of the Mapuche people to their own territory. If there are lands in this region, they are Mapuche, and therefore they are also community lands. Under this conception, land is not a speculative good for sale, it is a common good that exits the market entirely (HIC–AL, 2017: 98).

⁓

CONCLUSION

Latin America and the Caribbean present a significant diversity of collective land tenures. These include: community lands, communal lands, and indigenous reserves inherited from the region's pre-Hispanic history; colonial lands and the lands of formerly enslaved peoples (*Maroon* and *family lands* in the Caribbean, *quilombos* in Brazil and Colombia); campesino, communal, and *ejido* lands in Mexico from the region's republican and revolutionary past; the Pioneer Movement in Venezuela; mutual aid housing cooperatives in many countries: and municipal ownership of land and rehabilitated housing in Brazil.

In rural areas, collective or community property has become an instrument for the protection of ancestral lands and ecosystems, including jungles, forests, grasslands, water, and subsoil resources, preventing their loss through dispossession, extractivism (agribusiness, mining, fracking, etc.), or urbanization. The ILO Convention 169 of 1989 concerning Indigenous and Tribal Peoples in Independent Countries, together with various national laws, have led to important advances in this regard, while also providing an important precedent for current struggles.

In the most urbanized region of the world, the preservation of collective forms of land tenure and the proliferation of mutual aid housing cooperatives and similar initiatives in the social production of habitat provide a growing alternative to the hegemonic model of individual homeownership on privately owned land. These alternatives allow lower-income families, who are increasingly excluded from both the high-priced housing provided by the market and the social housing in short supply from the State, to gain access to housing for which they have secure occupancy. They no longer need to fear being evicted due to unemployment or other changes in their personal circumstances. They occupy homes that their children may inherit.

The experience of the Barrio Intercultural project in the Argentine Patagonia, moreover, provides a beautiful example of how an urban movement for the social production of housing can be united with an indigenous community, restoring and preserving indigenous rights to traditional lands through collective ownership; building wooden houses; and creating a peaceful and solidarity-based intercultural community. Barrio Intercultural demonstrates how the principles of rural collective ownership could inspire the transformation of contemporary urban spaces, as low-income groups in inner-city neighborhoods attempt to exert control over the housing and the territory they occupy.

The community land trust (CLT) may become a part of this new generation of collective and secure land tenure, a strategy for the social production of habitat; a vehicle for protection of the common good amidst the speculative and unequal spaces that define contemporary capitalist cities. Although CLTs are still largely unknown in Latin America and the Caribbean, aside from the Caño Martín Peña CLT in Puerto Rico and the CLT organizing currently underway in a few favelas in Brazil, there are connections to be drawn between the CLT and the struggles to reconquer spaces within city centers through secure and anti-speculative tenure schemes.

This chapter has tried to demonstrate that collective action that comes with collective property rights can provide a bulwark against the involuntary dispossession and displacement of low-income groups in Latin America and the Caribbean. The examples described in this chapter pose a significant alternative to the ongoing individualization of property. These forms of collective property, we predict, will only grow in importance as the urban poor struggle to secure more equitable rights in highly polarized economies.

Postscript: Our thanks go to David Auerbach for his skilled translation into English of this essay, originally written in Spanish.

Notes

1. Since the terms used in specific countries of the region for collectively used or owned land are quite diverse, we will generically use the terms "collective lands" or "collective land tenure." Local terms such as *maroon communities, communal territories, family lands, quilombos,* or *ejidos* will be italicized.

2. This massive production of housing by the private sector and promoted by the State (through subsidies and workers contributions of their incomes to public housing funds) was fostered in the region by the World Bank with publication of "Housing: enabling markets to work" (1993). Under this scheme of "Ahorro–Bono–Crédito" [Savings - Subsidy - Mortgage], more than 230,000 flats were built in Chile in the 1990s, later followed by around nine million housing units built between 2000 and 2018. In Brazil, four million units were produced under this same scheme between 2011 and 2018; and 2.7 million units were built in Venezuela (Arnold, 2018). In countries like Bolivia,

Colombia, Costa Rica, Ecuador, Panama, and Perú, the same scheme is being applied on a more modest scale.

3. Our conception of colonial domination echoes González Casanova, who understands colonialism to be "a phenomenon that is not only international but intra-national" (2009 [1969]: 130).

4. However, as Kouri (2017) suggests, the core subject and beneficiary of Article 27—which served to legitimize the two great deeds of the post-revolutionary regime, Agrarian Reform and the Nationalization of oil of 1938—were not indigenous peoples but the nation as a whole.

5. The neoliberal reforms introduced to the agrarian regime in 1993 now permit the sale of these plots, subject to the reservation that the assembly must vote as a majority for the un-incorporation of said social property. Together with the World Bank's neoliberal guidelines for the housing sector, the division of ejidos into plots with an urban land use has precipitated the massive production of housing in urban peripheries and the consequent urban sprawl of Mexican cities.

6. In the lowland areas (Amazon region), the State has recognized 58 TIOCs in the hands of 150,000 owners who occupy more than 12 million hectares, representing only 67% of the initially claimed area (RAISG, 2016: 49).

7. Available at: *http://www.landmarkmap.org*

8. Generally speaking, indigenous and peasant territories have had to resist attempts at cultural assimilation and territorial dispossession (Price, 1996). This continues to the present day. For example, Barbudans were dispossessed of the collective possession of the island of Barbuda by repeal of the Barbuda Land Act in 2018, a loss they are presently contesting in the courts.

9. See: *https://www.prindex.net*

10. The Washington Consensus defined a set of ten economic policy requirements constituting a "standard" reform package for developing countries affected by fiscal crises. It was promulgated by institutions based in Washington D.C., including the International Monetary Fund, the World Bank, and the U.S. Department of the Treasury.

11. The massive, market-oriented production of housing in the Latin American and Caribbean region caused the displacement to peri-urban areas of middle-class households who needed mortgages to access homeownership. The increase of transportation costs to get to jobs and basic urban facilities, coupled with indebtedness for 20–30 years to repay the mortgage for poor-quality housing which loses value in time, leads to the impoverishment of these households (Arnold, 2018).

12. Once the construction is completed and the mortgage has been paid, members of owner cooperatives exercise the right granted by the Horizontal Property Law over their housing unit, which regulates all non-individual real property in the country. However, with user cooperatives, which can be established with a 15% allocation of the housing value through prior-savings or mutual aid, contracts for use and enjoyment of their homes are established with each member. People living in owner cooperatives can sell their housing at market price, whereas in user cooperatives they can only sell back their social interest to the cooperative, without earning a profit.

13. Under the Housing Law, if a home is sub-leased, a member can be expelled from the cooperative. If a member voluntarily withdraws from the cooperative within ten years of living in the home, a percentage of the membership's monetary value can be retained by the cooperative.

14. By law, the cooperative chooses and hires an IAT (which must be recognized by the State) and pays it up to 5% of the total value of the project (currently being increased to between 7% and 8%).

15. Over the last few years, FUCVAM has been organizing strikes and demonstrations against the Uruguayan government. Despite being run by a left-wing coalition, the government has raised the interest rate on the public loans held by 150 of the country's cooperatives from 2% up to 5.25%, and has given private developers VAT exemptions on the cost of construction materials but not offered the same exemptions to cooperatives.

16. The SELVIHP is composed of social movements from Argentina, Brazil, Chile, Panama and Venezuela who meet at least four times a year for different activities like the Latin American Self-management School. See: Movimientos de Ocupantes e Inquilinos *http://moi.org.ar/tag/selvihp/*.

17. Outside of the region, the CVAM model is also being experimented with by FUCVAM in the Philippines and in various nations on the African continent.

18. The movement was born as a result of the nearly 7,000 Urban Land Committees (CTUs) created since 2002 across the country to encourage grassroots participation in neighborhood planning and improvement (HIC–AL, 2017).

19. According to Juan Carlos Rodríguez, head of FUNDACARACAS, the public Housing Institute of the capital, and historic member of the Venezuelan Pioneer Movement. He was interviewed by two of the authors during the Social Production of Housing Latin-American work group of Habitat International Coalition–Latin America (HIC–AL) in Tequisquiapan, Mexico, on August 20th, 2019.

20. This was enabled by and in compliance with the ILO Convention 169 and Article 72 of the Argentine Constitution, which has recognized the ethnic and cultural pre-existence of indigenous peoples since 1994.

References

Algoed, L. and Hernández, M. (2019). Vulnerabilization and Resistance in informal settlements in Puerto Rico: Lessons from the Caño Martín Peña Community Land Trust. *Radical Housing Journal*, Vol 1(1): 29–47.

Andrade, G. (2016). Las comunas ancestrales de Quito. Retos y desafíos en la planificación urbanística. Quito: Universidad Andina Simón Bolívar, Corporación Editora Nacional.

Arnold, P. (2018). Políticas de producción y gestión social del hábitat en América Latina: conquista de derechos e incidencia política frente a la vivienda de interés social orientada al mercado. En L. Salinas (coord.), Gestión Urbana y Políticas de vivienda (pp. 225-260). México City: UNAM.

Arnold, P. and Lemarié, C. (2017). Hábitat en Movimiento. Viaje al encuentro del hábitat popular en América del Sur. Mexico City: autoeditado.

Besson, J. and Momsen, J. (eds) (1987). *Land and Development in the Caribbean*. London: Macmillan Publishers.

Coque Martínez, J. (2002). Las Cooperativas En América Latina: Visión Histórica General y Comentario de Algunos Países Tipo. *CIRIEC-España, Revista de Economía Pública, Social y Cooperativa*, 145–172, núm. 43: 145–72. Available from: *http://www.redalyc.org/articulo.oa?id=17404309*.

Fernández, J.C. (2017). La propiedad comunitaria de los pueblos originarios. Su relación con el concepto de bienes colectivos, en María Cristina, G. y María Celeste, M. (coord.). Ambiente y pueblos indígenas: una mirada interdisciplinaria. Salta: Universidad Católica de Salta, EUCASA. pp. 189–212.

Ferraz, A. (2014). Minha Casa Minha Vida financia 1ª reforma no centro de SP. Autogestão e Moradía. Available from: *http://autogestao.unmp.org.br/autogestao-na-midia/minha-casa-minha-vida-financia-1a-reforma-no-centro-de-sp/*

González Casanova, P. (2017 [1969]). El colonialismo interno. *En De la sociología del poder a la sociología de la explotación: pensar América Latina en el siglo XXI*. Bogotá/Buenos Aires: CLACSO.

HIC–AL (2017). *Utopías en construcción. Experiencias de producción social del hábitat en América Latina*. Mexico City: Habitat International Coalition–América Latina.

León Portilla, M. (2011). *Independencia, reforma, revolución, ¿y los indios qué?* Universidad Nacional Autónoma de Mexico City: Instituto de Investigaciones Históricas.

Kouri, E. (2017). "La promesa agraria del artículo 27," 1 February. Available from: *https://www.nexos.com.mx/?p=31269*.

Oxfam (2016). Desterrados: Tierra, poder y desigualdad en América Latina, de Oxfam.

Mendive, C. (2014). Cartera de Inmuebles de Vivienda de Interés Social (CIVIS): Alternativas para la provisión de suelo en Uruguay. En M. Smolka y F. Furtado (Eds.), Instrumentos notables de políticas de suelo en América Latina. Cambridge: Lincoln Institute of Land Policy.

Museo Afro Digital (n.d.). Quilombos of Rio. Available from: *http://www.museuafrorio.uerj.br/?page_id=4815*

Pinho, A. (s.f.). Vazio por anos, prédio é reformado por sem-teto e agora vira exemplo em SP. Autogestão e Moradía. Available from: *http://autogestao.unmp.org.br/autogestao-na-midia/vazio-por-anos-predio-e-reformado-por-sem-teto-e-agora-vira-exemplo-em-sp/*

Price, R. (ed) (1996). *Maroon Societies: Rebel Slave Communities in the Americas*. Baltimore: The Johns Hopkins University Press.

RAISG Red Amazónica de Información Socioambiental Georreferenciada. (2016). Cartografía Histórica de Áreas Naturales Protegidas y Territorios Indígenas en la Amazonía. Available from: *www.amazoniasocioambiental.org*

Rights and Resources Initiative (2015). Who Owns the World's Land? A global baseline of formally recognized indigenous and community land rights. Washington, DC. Available from: *https://rightsandresources.org/en/publication/who-owns-the-land-in-latin-america/#.W5vMwS17GgQ*

Tamburini, L. (2019). Atlas sociopolítico sobre los territorios indígenas en las tierras bajas de Bolivia. Copenhagen: IWGIA.

Torres, A., Pineda, V. & Rey, E. (2017). Las disputas urbanas en la Caracas del siglo XXI: retos y potencialidades en la producción social del suelo. Territorios (36), 47–68. Available from: *http://dx.doi.org/10.12804/revistas.urosario.edu.co/territrios/a.4845*

UNICEF (2009). Atlas sociolingüístico de pueblos indígenas en América Latina. Cochabamba: Unicef y Funproeib Andes.

UN-Habitat (2013) State of the World's Cities 2012/2013. Available from: *https://sustainabledevelopment.un.org/content/documents/745habitat.pdf*. [Accessed 14 August 2019].

World Bank (1993). *Housing: enabling markets to work*. World Bank policy paper. Washington: World Bank. Available from: *http://documents.worldbank.org/curated/en/878771468343734154/pdf/118200PUB0SPANISH0Box71184B01PUBLIC1.pdf*

11.

Seeding the CLT in Latin America and the Caribbean

Origins, Achievements, and the
Proof-of-Concept Example of the
Caño Martín Peña Community Land Trust

María E. Hernández-Torrales, Lyvia Rodríguez Del Valle,
Line Algoed, and Karla Torres Sueiro

The Fideicomiso de la Tierra del Caño Martín Peña (Caño CLT) is a community land trust designed and controlled by the residents of seven neighborhoods along the Martín Peña Channel, a highly polluted tidal estuary that runs through the heart of San Juan, the capital of Puerto Rico. The Caño CLT was created with the aim to regularize land tenure and to prevent involuntary displacement and gentrification, precipitated by the government's planned dredging and clean-up of the channel. Creation of the Caño CLT and the channel's ecological restoration are among the main elements of the wider ENLACE Caño Martín Peña Project. This initiative has brought together community residents and partners from the private and public sectors to implement a comprehensive development plan designed to uplift a historically marginalized area, while transforming this urban area into a more habitable, just and participatory space.

Residents of seven Martín Peña neighborhoods[1] adopted the community land trust (CLT), but adapted it to meet local needs. By adding completely new elements to the model and by applying it to address the problem of land insecurity in an informal settlement, the Caño CLT has become an important reference world-wide, specifically in the Global South. Roughly 1,500 very low- to moderate-income households are now members of the Caño CLT, which currently owns and manages more than 110 hectares (272 acres) of land, most of which previously belonged to governmental agencies. The Caño CLT ensures the availability of permanently affordable housing and provides alternative housing options on its land for families who have had to relocate because of the dredging of the channel. It is also an instrument for the generation and redistribution of wealth.

The Fideicomiso de la Tierra del Caño Martín Peña is one of three institutions that resulted from a broad participatory planning-action-reflection process that took place between 2002 and 2004. During the planning process, twelve community-based organizations from the Martín Peña communities came together as a collective in the Group of the Eight Communities Adjacent to the Caño Martín Peña, Inc. (G-8). In collaboration with external partners from Puerto Rico's private and public universities and other professional and technical allies, they drafted regulatory instruments such as the Comprehensive Development and Land Use Plan for the Special Planning District of the Caño Martín Peña (the District Plan) and Law 489 of September 24, 2004 for the Comprehensive Development of the Special Planning District of the Caño Martín Peña (Law 489-2004). Through this law, not only the Caño CLT was created, but also a government corporation, the ENLACE Project Corporation, charged with responsibility for implementing the District Plan with a prominent role of the residents.

Initially conceived to regularize land tenure, to facilitate the implementation of the District Plan and to guarantee access of these consolidated communities to urban land whose value was increasing, the Caño CLT is continuing its work in the midst of a double crisis. Puerto Rico has been struggling with financial distress and an unpayable public debt since 2006. Then, two devastating hurricanes hit the island in September 2017.[2] Puerto Rico has become one of the only places in the world that is simultaneously going through the contradictory processes of both austerity and recovery, while exhibiting the designs and dangers of what is known as "disaster capitalism" (Bonilla & LeBron, 2019; Algoed & Hernández, 2019).

Puerto Rico is an unincorporated territory of the United States, a result of the Cuban-Spanish-American War when the United States installed colonial governments in the Philippines, Guam and Puerto Rico. Today, Puerto Rico and Guam continue to be under U.S. sovereignty. According to the U.S. Census Bureau, in 2018 Puerto Rico had a population of 3.2 million. Since the start of the financial crisis, however, half-a-million Puerto Ricans have left the island. Another 160,000 emigrated to the United States after Hurricane María.[3] When the Caño CLT was created, the main threats faced by the communities along the channel were involuntary displacement and gentrification, a result of an increase in the value of the area's land. Today, the main threat comes from a decrease in value which, in combination with the government's current austerity and disaster recovery policies, have created conditions favorable to speculation. Under both cycles of increasing and decreasing land value, the Caño CLT has proven to be an effective instrument to protect the community against displacement.

This chapter discusses how the Caño CLT is facilitating the regularization of land tenure in seven informal settlements, while preventing gentrification and furthering implementation of the District Plan. Inhabitants of this area transformed an infrastructure project that was initially led by the government into a participatory project of comprehensive development, one that is working to overcome historical causes of poverty, while also restructuring the government's relationship with the marginalized communities within this special planning district. Together with their external partners, the Caño residents have created a viable CLT that aims to protect their right to land, their right to adequate housing, their right to live in the city with dignity, their right to health, and their right to participate in the decisions that affect their future, including those related to the use and development of their land. The components of this project combine to counteract the way in which a lack of community participation in large-scale infrastructure projects normally leads to forced displacement and structural urban inequality.

The ability of G-8, ENLACE, and the Fideicomiso de la Tierra to unite people toward a common cause in a deeply divisive context has been recognized internationally. Since winning the United Nations World Habitat Award in 2016, the Caño CLT has become an example and an inspiration for activists around the world who are working on land tenure issues and looking for an alternative form of land regularization. One of only two community land trusts in the world that have been organized in an informal settlement,[4] the Caño CLT has become a touchstone for communities in the Global South in particular, who are looking to establish CLTs of their own to overcome the threat of displacement from lands strategically located in desirable areas.

The chapter is organized into four sections. First, we present a historical overview and political context to help the reader to understand that, although Puerto Rico is part of the United States, the multiple obstacles faced by the Martín Peña communities are both enormous and exceptional. Then, we describe how the Caño CLT was created and why the communities opted for a CLT to address their needs. After explaining how the CLT functions, we reflect on the importance of the Fideicomiso as a reference for other communities that are struggling with similar threats of displacement from their land and why they might look to the Caño CLT for inspiration.

I. LAND, DISPLACEMENT AND INFORMAL SETTLEMENTS IN PUERTO RICO

The relationship with the land has always been a subject of struggle in Puerto Rico. As in the rest of Latin America, the history of Puerto Rico is defined by colonialism and the repeated displacement of vulnerable populations. A colony of the United States since 1898, the Caribbean island lacks economic sovereignty. Decades of dependence and tax exemptions aimed at attracting and extracting wealth have put major stresses on the island's economy. With a current unaudited public debt of over $74 billion, the Commonwealth of Puerto Rico was forced to apply austerity measures, imposed by the Fiscal Oversight Board created under PROMESA (Puerto Rico Oversight, Management and Economic Stability Act). This law, adopted by the U.S. Congress in 2016 during the Obama presidency, created the Fiscal Oversight Board to guarantee payments to bondholders, most

> Little by little, control of the island's land has moved to those who do not use it for the benefit of the country.

of them speculators. Public employees and retirees have been seeing their salaries and pensions jeopardized, approximately 280 schools have been closed, and the budget of the public university has been drastically reduced. Insecurity due to the cuts, the high unemployment rate, and the high cost of living have made life on the island challenging for a large part of its population.

This economic crisis is the result of the expiration of federal tax exemptions for United States companies, which had previously turned the island into one of the more attractive places to locate for North American companies. The growth of the economy depended on these tax exemptions. When these tax exemptions expired in 2006, most of the companies abandoned Puerto Rico, leaving thousands of highly skilled Puerto Ricans unemployed. There has been virtually no economic growth since then.

Land is one of the only assets that the government can still monetize. Tax incentives that took place after 2012 have attracted investors to the island to buy land to develop luxury complexes. Little by little, control of the island's land has moved to those who do not use it for the benefit of the country, during a period when it has become increasingly difficult for Puerto Ricans to find employment, to buy land, or to pay off their mortgage loans. Disaster recovery and other policies adopted after Hurricanes Irma and María have exacerbated the situation. Puerto Rico is almost fully under the Opportunity Zones program, which provides generous U.S. federal tax exemptions to investors and is particularly attractive for the real estate sector. Meanwhile, the Action Plan[5] prepared by Puerto Rico and approved by the U.S. Department of Housing and Urban Development has a series of policies that promote the displacement of communities in high-risk areas, even when mitigation is feasible. Concurrently, the government permits privately funded reconstruction and developments in similar high-risk areas.

Investing in luxury properties in depressed sectors — which, in the case of Puerto Rico, includes most of the island — can result in increases in the land values, contributing to the displacement of low-income and moderate-income residents. The displacement of poor communities can, in turn, lead to further increases in land values (Navas, 2004: 4).

According to the government Office for Socio-Economic and Community Development, there are 742 communities across Puerto Rico that have been categorized as informal settlements. The rapid industrialization of the island in the 1930s and 1940s, which made Puerto Rico an example of "advanced capitalism," pushed impoverished peasants into the coastal cities in search of employment and health and education services for their children. As affordable housing was not available, they occupied land that was unsuitable for housing, such as mangroves, wetlands, steep mountain slopes, and areas very close to the sea. Many of these families settled in the wetlands along the Martín Peña Channel, at the outskirts of San Juan, building makeshift homes on stilts with cardboard, coconut trees, wood, and tin. They used wooden planks to create connections among the homes

Fig. 11.1. Aerial view of neighborhoods surrounding the Martín Peña Channel (top), and a house alongside the Martín Peña Channel. LINE ALGOED / J.E. DAVIS

and to have access to the dry land and roads. With time, the families and the Municipality of San Juan filled the wetlands with debris.

Today, almost 25,000 people still live in eight neighborhoods along the channel. As the city grew, their location became prime real estate next to the financial district and along the channel that, once dredged, will serve as an inland waterway connecting the main airport with tourist-oriented hubs. The once-navigable channel is clogged and heavily polluted, as most neighborhoods lack an adequate sewage system and functioning storm-water management systems.

Between the 1960s and 1980s, as development policies were aimed at eliminating "slums," several communities along the western half of the Caño were relocated to

Fig. 11.2. One of the Caño's major streets, looking toward San Juan's financial district (top) and a side street in a Caño neighborhood. DOEL VÁZQUEZ / J.E. DAVIS

public housing or evicted. There were various proposals to recover the Caño area either for conservation purposes, for highways or for high-end developments including hotels and marinas. Most of these plans called for the displacement of remaining Martín Peña communities. Relocation costs were not even considered, and neither was community participation (Algoed, Hernández and Rodríguez, 2018). With the establishment of the financial district and the advancement of individual land-titling programs, gentrification became a new threat. Speculators started buying those individually owned plots of land, particularly those closest to the main transportation corridors, knowing that the possible ecosystem restoration of the channel would drastically increase the value of the area's land. These threats, coupled with the announcement in 2002 that the government was going to pursue the dredging of the channel, would become the issues around which the residents of the Martín Peña communities organized to find a solution for their common problems.

II. CREATION OF THE CAÑO MARTÍN PEÑA CLT

Public participation in the planning process for government-sponsored projects that affect residential areas has rarely happened in Puerto Rico. That remained the pattern even after the Puerto Rico Planning Board was mandated by law to open the planning processes to comments and participation by the public. This started to change under the administration of Governor Sila M. Calderón. In March 2001, the Governor signed the first statute of her new administration, proclaiming as a public policy the empowerment of residents of low-income communities (Law 1, March 1, 2001). This public policy encouraged citizen participation, defined as a comprehensive process enabling citizens to recognize and to exercise full control of their lives, starting from their own efforts and power. According to the Law, such an initiative would be aimed at helping the residents of low-income communities to acquire the skills and levels of organization that might allow them to become authors of their own process of economic and social development. The government would act as a trainer, promoter, facilitator, and collaborator, eliminating barriers and creating the necessary conditions and mechanisms to enable communities to secure their personal and community development. Governmental agencies and instrumentalities were required to carry out well-planned actions to stimulate the participation of low-income communities in the decision-making processes related to the issues affecting their development. These communities would assume new roles as owners and producers, implementing a participatory approach to planning and improving their neighborhoods, which was radically different from the past practice of being passive beneficiaries of a paternalistic state. This public policy enabled the participatory approach that was used in the ENLACE Project.

From an Infrastructure Project
to a Sustainable Development Project

Instead of hiring engineers, the Authority hired an urban planner to lead the effort and established a Community Participation Office in a trailer located at the heart of the Caño communities, and staffed with community social workers and organizers. The Authority also pursued the establishment, by the Puerto Rico Planning Board, of the Caño Martín Peña Special Planning District, comprised by seven of the eight communities[6] remaining along the tidal channel. Residents participated in high numbers during the first round of community assemblies as they learned about the plans to dredge the channel, and strongly voiced their concern around displacement. They questioned where the families living close to the channel would be taken, as the space was needed for the dredging. Moreover, and conscious of the strategic location of their neighborhoods, they questioned who would benefit from the project, and clearly expressed their intent to oppose any attempt to gentrify. The meeting

Fig. 11.3. Election of new community council for Comunidad Las Monjas, one of the Caño's G-8 communities. LINE ALGOED

sparked one of the most successful participatory community development processes in Puerto Rico's history.

From 2002 to 2004, more than 700 participatory planning, action, and reflection activities were held in the Martín Peña communities. Concurrently, residents were envisioning the future and designing strategies, implementing projects and programs for short-term wins addressing their pressing issues, while organizing and critically thinking and learning about the process that was being implemented. The residents received the information they needed to participate intelligently in drafting the development plan, and technical consultants engaged in a dialogue that valued the knowledge of the residents rather than downplaying it. Had residents been left out of this process, the plan would have been inadequate and incomplete. The end result was the *Comprehensive Development and Land Use Plan for the Caño Martín Peña Special Planning District* (Development Plan), which was officially adopted by the Puerto Rico Planning Board and approved by the Governor of Puerto Rico in 2007. The inclusive process that produced this Plan took what had started out as a typical top-down engineering project and turned it the participatory, equitable and sustainable community development initiative called the ENLACE Caño Martín Peña Project.

Today, there are approximately 120 community leaders active within the G-8, mostly women and youth; indeed, 40% are young leaders between the ages of 11–25 years old. Another 100 residents form a network with a person per-street who is tasked with keeping their neighbors informed of the activities that are taking place, as thirty different socio-economic, housing, and urban development initiatives are underway with residents playing an active role in each.

Development Without Displacement

The Development Plan assumed that the Martín Peña communities would gain control over the publicly owned land within the Caño Martín Peña Special Planning District. This would accomplish three important goals. First, land would become available for the housing and infrastructure projects necessary to improve the quality of life of the residents and to address constant flooding with polluted water. Taking the cost of land out of the equation, moreover, would lower the implementation costs and increase the project's feasibility in the context of Puerto Rico's dire financial and economic situation. Second, having control of the land would allow residents who were living in areas where land was needed to build infrastructure projects and to dredge the channel to be relocated within one of the Caño's neighborhoods, avoiding their involuntary displacement. Third, gentrification would be prevented. Community residents were aware that once the infrastructure project took place and the channel was dredged, the cost of land and housing within the Martín Peña area would soar and existing residents would surely and steadily be pushed aside. With this in mind, having control of the land would prevent the displacement of residents who lacked land titles by regularizing their relationship with the land and allowing them to have security of tenure.

> Residents were aware that once the channel was dredged, the cost of land would soar.

Land ownership was a central piece for the community to reach its goal, so choosing the right mechanism to regularize tenure was critical. Several strategies were used to provoke discussions around land tenure. To help with the anaylsis of tenure options, a Housing Committee was created, composed of representatives from the seven Caño neighborhoods in the Special Planning District.

A workshop was held where participants were asked to identify why families wanted to have individual titles to the land — the form of tenure with which people were most familiar. The common answers included: the desire of the residents to bequeath the right to occupy a parcel of land to their legal heirs; access to public services (i.e., safe connections to the power grid required a permit); and access to mortgage credit. All participants agreed that avoiding the displacement of the community was a priority. After learning from experts about the pros and cons of individual land titles, land coops, and community land trusts, participants were able to examine how each ownership instrument might allow them to reach their objectives. The workshop opened the participants' eyes to the possibility of considering a broader range of options, beyond the one with which they were most familiar. The discussion continued in community assemblies, including one in which a Spanish-speaking member of the Dudley Street Neighborhood Initiative in Boston shared their experiences.

Deliberations of the Housing Committee were rooted in six critical rights that were deemed to be indispensable for any instrument they might choose for controlling land, including:

- the right to stay put;

- the right to land tenure;

- the right to adequate housing;

- the right to property for individual residents;

- the right to benefit from improvements to the area; and

- the right to participate in the decision-making process and implementation of the District Plan.

Residents made a conscientious and audacious decision. They concluded that some form of collective land ownership was the only way to prevent gentrification and, despite the absence of any other CLT in Puerto Rico at the time, they concluded that a CLT would be the best option for enabling the Martín Peña communities to have control of the land. A community land trust would make possible the dredging of the Martín Peña Channel, the construction of needed infrastructure, and the rehabilitation of their neighborhoods, just as residents had envisioned in the Development Plan. The land was to be collectively owned in perpetuity, while each family who formerly lacked a land title would obtain a legal document — a surface rights deed — that would secure their right to use the land beneath their home, a right they would be able to bequeath to their legal heirs. This deed would enable them to stay put and to have a livelihood in the city, while securing their right to influence what might happen in their own neighborhood. They would no longer have to fear speculators, nor gentrification and involuntary displacement. With this decision behind them, they proceeded to secure the land and to initiate a new two-year participatory process to design how the first community land trust in Puerto Rico would manage its assets.

> They would no longer have to fear speculators, nor gentrification and involuntary displacement.

III. STRUCTURE AND FUNCTION OF THE CAÑO CLT

The Fideicomiso de la Tierra del Caño Martín Peña is a community land trust, constituted as a private, nonprofit organization created in perpetuity with an independent juridical identity. The Caño CLT is authorized to acquire land within and outside the Special Planning District, to develop and to sell housing (and other buildings), and to re-acquire these structural improvements, exercising a right of first refusal whenever owners desire to sell. The Caño CLT is entitled to create strategies and to design resale formulas which ensure the affordability of housing in perpetuity.

The CLT is a membership organization with an eleven-member Board of Trustees that is composed of community, private and government representatives, as follows: four

Trustees are Caño CLT members, whose homes are located on the lands owned by the Caño CLT; two Trustees are residents of the Martín Peña communities, designated to serve on the CLT's Board by the G-8; two Trustees are non-residents of the District, selected by the Board's members, based on skills and knowledge they can contribute to the CLT. The three remaining spaces are occupied by representatives of governmental entities, one from the Corporación del Proyecto ENLACE Board of Directors, one from the San Juan Municipality designated by the city's mayor, and one selected by the Governor of Puerto Rico.[7]

Caño CLT General Regulations

The legal grounds for the *Reglamento General para el Funcionamiento del Fideicomiso de la Tierra del Caño Martín Peña*, Rule 7587 (hereafter Caño CLT General Regulations), are the Puerto Rico Law No. 489, September 24, 2004, known as *"Ley para el Desarrollo Integral del Distrito de Planificación Especial del Caño Martín Peña"* (Law 489-2004), and the Puerto Rico Administrative Procedures Law. Through a democratic and participative process, a community committee was organized during 2006–2008. This committee gathered representatives from all seven communities who participated in several activities and workshops in order to establish the basis for the Caño CLT's General Regulations in accordance to the needs and concerns of Martín Peña communities' residents. The Caño CLT General Regulations were adopted on October 8, 2008, setting the regulations for the governance and operation of the Caño CLT and the rules and procedures for guaranteeing the administration of the land in favor of the communities' residents.

Law 489-2004 entrusted the Proyecto ENLACE Corporation with the constitution and promulgation of the Caño CLT's regulations. Law 489-2004 also defined the basic processes through which land would be identified and entitled to become part of the Caño CLT and established the framework for the Caño CLT to assign members to its Board of Trustees (23 L.P.R.A. section 5048).

The Caño CLT's General Regulations consist of fourteen articles which regulate the administrative aspects and the operational processes of the Caño CLT.[8] They define the organization's mission, vision, goals and objectives; the land trust's assets; the criteria to qualify as a member of the CLT; the rights of membership; the collaborative arrangements with ENLACE Corporation and the G-8; and other obligations and powers of the Caño CLT. Also, the Caño CLT's General Regulations carefully ensure community participation in all governing bodies within the project and decision-making processes. In order to ensure such participation, a Registry of Members is used to notify and summon Caño CLT members for activities such as assemblies, elections, and other deliberations, all convened after timely notification. The General Regulations also set standards and procedures for convening assemblies, establishing a quorum, and making announcements.

The Proyecto ENLACE Corporation, which was also created by Law 489-2004, is a governmental corporation created with a sunset provision. It is charged with the responsibility to advance the implementation of the Development Plan. The ENLACE Corporation and the Caño CLT converge in a multidisciplinary and multifaceted project called Proyecto ENLACE. These entities play complementary roles in achieving the goals of Proyecto ENLACE. The relations and interactions between them are established in the General Regulations, including how they work together to identify plots of land in the District, to plan new developments, and to allocate economic and human resources to achieve common goals essential to advance Proyecto ENLACE. Standards and procedures to address and review short- and long-term strategic plans and priorities for housing allocation are also delimited.

Aims and Objectives of the Caño CLT

The Fideicomiso de la Tierra del Caño Martín Peña was created to safeguard the land tenure and residential permanence of residents living in the seven neighborhoods along the Martín Peña Channel, while allowing and promoting development within the District. Among others, the aims and objectives of the Caño CLT were specified in Law 489-2004 as follows:

- Contribute toward the solution of lack of ownership rights of many Special Planning District's residents through collective title landholding;

- Address with equity the physical or economic displacement of low-income residents arising from gentrification, avoiding displacement and eradication of the communities;

- Guarantee affordable housing within the Special Planning District;

- Acquire and administer lands on behalf of and in the best interest of the community, increasing local control over the land, and avoiding absentee owner decision-making; and

- Enable the reconstruction and valuation of urban spaces.

Law 489-2004, and other regulations adopted in accordance to this Law, vested the Caño CLT with the authority and powers to accomplish these objectives.

Transferring Public Land to the Caño CLT

Following its participatory planning-action-reflection process, the community decided to adopt the community land trust ownership structure for addressing the lack of legal title among hundreds of families living on both sides of the Martín Peña Channel, families whose homes were located on public lands. This publicly owned land was to be transferred to the Caño CLT, all of which would be permanently owned and managed by the Caño CLT. Rights to individual parcels within the Caño CLT's landholdings would be conveyed to the families who were already living there through a durable surface rights deed for each parcel. These transfers and tenures united elements of Puerto Rico Civil Law and United States Common Law. This arrangement also incorporated the definition of the community land trust model found in amendments to the National Affordable Housing Act, passed by the U.S. Congress in 1992.

Elements taken from a civil trust model were the basis for transferring the public land to an entity controlled by the residents of the communities along the Martín Peña Channel through the Caño CLT. This transfer was constituted by the following components:

- The *settlor* who transfers the land, which in this particular case was the government of Puerto Rico;

- The *trustee* who receives ownership of the land with responsibility for possessing and administering it for the benefit of the communities, which in this particular case was the Caño CLT; and

- The *beneficiaries* who benefit from the administration of the land, which in this particular case were the residents who owned a structure on a portion of the land that was transferred to the Caño CLT.

Law 489-2004, Article 22, establishes that the corpus of the Caño Martín Peña CLT is comprised of all the lands transferred to the ENLACE Corporation for the purpose of creating the Caño CLT, as well as those acquired in the future in accordance with Law 489-2004. In addition, the Caño CLT was required to be governed according to the CLT General Regulations referenced above. Creation of such regulations were entrusted to the ENLACE Corporation.

The Caño CLT has an express limitation under Law 489-2004, forbidding the CLT from selling the public lands that were transferred to it. The Caño CLT is required by law to retain permanent ownership of the land. The Caño CLT is able to sell or to transfer rights over the edifices that are built on the land, however, and is also authorized to grant surface rights deeds and long-term leases, subject to hereditary rights. Homeowners who live on the once-public lands that were conveyed to the Caño CLT individually own their buildings, but they do not own the underlying land. The land is owned and managed by the Caño CLT for the common benefit of the Martín Peña communities, present and future.

Surface Rights Deeds

The transfer of public lands to the Caño CLT was mandated by Law 489-2004.[9] A majority of the government agencies that owned and controlled these lands at the time could not provide official documentation identifying the land registrar information, however; nor was there an official record of boundaries and value, making it difficult to proceed with transferring these public lands. This situation slowed down the work plan of the ENLACE Corporation.[10] To get a jump-start, volunteers for the Caño CLT made good efforts and identified registry information for some of the biggest parcels of land. Accordingly, a deed was authorized, specifying registry data for such properties.

The process of identifying and acquiring land is continuous, as the Caño CLT is constantly undergoing title investigations to identify parcels of land that may be transferred into its ownership. Currently, the Caño CLT owns and administers just over 110 hectares (272 acres) of land. Most of it (200 acres) was part of the original transfer of publicly owned land under Law 489-2004; another part of the CLT's landholdings (72 acres) was added gradually over the years as ENLACE acquired privately owned houses (with title to the land) to relocate homeowners directly impacted by the canal's dredging and then conveyed those parcels to the CLT.[11] All of this land, which is scattered throughout the seven neighborhoods of the Caño Martín Peña Special Planning District, is administered in the best interests of the Caño's residents, consistent with Law 489-2004, the District Plan, and the General Regulations.

One of the responsibilities of the Caño CLT is to identify those households who can benefit from a surface rights deed and to grant them such a deed in accordance with Law 489-2004. There are approximately 1,500 households living on the CLT's lands. To date, 110 surface rights deeds have been executed.[12] It is a slow and laborious process, since prior to executing the deed all documentation must be in place and the person or persons who appear on the deed must be the ones who have the legal right to do so.[13]

Through these surface rights deeds, the Caño CLT conveys individual property rights to those residents who own a housing structure on the Caño CLT's land. Homeowners possess the right to occupy and use the surface of the land beneath their homes, but they do not own the land itself. Generally, surface rights are granted in perpetuity or for a specific term. For its validity, surface rights are secured through public deeds that are then registered in the Puerto Rico Property Registry. After being officially registered, this legal instrument allows for two owners to co-exist in possessing separate portions of the same space: the Caño CLT owns the land and the resident owns the structure. The latter enjoys all the benefits of using, improving, and even mortgaging the surface right, as delimited by the Caño CLT in the surface rights deed.[14]

Fig. 11.4. Sixta Gladys Peña-Martínez, Caño CLT member and G-8 community leader, signing the surface rights deed for the land beneath her home, May 20, 2016. MARÍA E. HERNÁNDEZ-TORRALES

Publicly registered surface rights deeds specify the footprint under a resident's home, delineating the portion of land for which the right is granted. These deeds also identify the rights and obligations of the person to whom the surface right was conferred. Contained in the public deed, there is also a description of the housing structure. This is a legal requirement that allows the registration of the housing structure as a unit separate from the land. Other contents included in the surface rights deed are designed to protect houses on the CLT's land from non-mortgage or non-governmental debt claims under Puerto Rico's Safe Home Act.

The surface right's value amounts to 25% of the value of the plot of land on which a resident's home is located, becoming straightaway an asset for a family and increasing their wealth.[15] Surface rights can be inherited and mortgaged. Families can sell their surface rights, but not the underlying land. The Caño CLT retains a first right of refusal to purchase both the house and the surface rights whenever a homeowner decides to sell. By these means, the Caño CLT permanently holds title to the land and permanently controls the future disposition of the buildings located thereon, managing these assets for the benefit of the Martín Peña communities and future generations.

To the best of our knowledge, the Caño CLT is the first community land trust that has been used for the relocation of families, allowing for the construction of public infrastructure and following the parameters of the federal Uniform Relocation Act. Using a transfer of rights mechanism, the relocation process cost is reduced. Families can trade the houses in which they have been living — which, in most cases, are deteriorated and likely located on plots of land to which the families do not have a right — in exchange for a new house in better conditions, joining the Caño CLT and enjoying surface rights. The Proyecto ENLACE Corporation is in charge of the process of acquiring and building homes and relocating families.

IV. THE POTENTIAL FOR WIDER USE OF CLTs IN INFORMAL SETTLEMENTS

As of 2016, it was estimated that approximately 54.5% of the world's population lives in urban settlements; 828 million of these urban dwellers live in densely populated informal settlements, characterized by the lack of land tenure, inadequate and unsafe infrastructure, and insufficient sanitary installations (UN-Habitat, 2013: 112). In Latin America and the Caribbean, approximately 113 million people live in informal settlements (UN-Habitat, 2013: 127).

After almost a century of marginalization, the residents of the neighborhoods along the Martín Peña Channel, who had lived and struggled for decades with the collateral damage of living in an informal settlement, organized to create the Fideicomiso de la Tierra del Caño Martín Peña that is now working to overcome infrastructural, residential, environmental, and socio-economic deprivations and inequalities that accumulated over many decades.

The Caño CLT is an innovative, effective, and empowering organization that may serve as an example for other informal settlements around the world. Its potential for inspiring and informing land rights struggles in other countries was the reason for the

Caño CLT being internationally recognized by World Habitat in 2016. Since receiving a World Habitat Award, members of the Caño CLT have been widely sharing their experiences and instruments with community leaders in informal settlements in Latin American, the Caribbean, and South Asia, encouraging them to adapt the practices pioneered in San Juan to their own needs and contexts, possibly using a CLT to enable residents to gain secure use of land, to stop displacements, and to take control of local development.

Communities that are the most similar to the Martín Peña communities — and that have the greatest potential for adopting and adapting a Fideicomiso de la Tierra — are those that exhibit the following characteristics:

- A significant number of residents live on lands to which they do not have a valid or legal title for lands that may be owned by the government, by private individuals, or by a corporation. Alternatively, these lands may be occupied and used under some form of communal landholding system that has yet to be recognized and registered by the state.

- There are mechanisms available to acquire the land, including donation, adverse possession, purchase, or intervention by the state;

- A significant percentage of the population has a high sense of community cohesion and belonging; and

- The informal settlement is located within an area — or proximate to one — where land values are rising or where lands are coveted by speculative investors, threatening the present population with displacement.

The following ingredients have been essential to the success of the Fideicomiso de la Tierra del Caño Martín Peña. They should be considered by other communities when contemplating, planning, or attempting to create a CLT of their own.

Holistic Approach

The Caño CLT is part of a broader plan that was designed using a participatory process. This plan presumed that community organizations and inter-sectoral alliances would both be involved in its implementation. The plan itself included a multi-faceted focus on environmental justice, personal health, violence prevention, food sovereignty, young leadership, a solidarity economy, educational transformation, adult literacy, equitable relocation, quality public spaces, a right to the city, and securing land tenure and affordable housing in perpetuity.

Community Organization and Democracy

A CLT should be designed and developed through democratic processes promoting citizen participation, where citizens are the ones who identify their needs and priorities and who make decisions about the best ways to address these needs. For a CLT to be effective, communities must take part in the planning process and adapt the CLT to their context, needs, and expectations. Organizing and participation must continue even after a CLT has been created. Residents who live on a CLT's land and around that land must have a sense of solidarity and tranquility that comes from being part of an organization that protects their homes and interests. When asked to describe in one word what the Caño CLT means to her, Margarita Cruz, a resident of the Las Monjas community, said "Us. We are the Fideicomiso". A goal of every CLT should be to foster such a sentiment.

Capacity Building, Leadership and Skills Development

Popular education is a significant tool to achieve effective participation of communities. Community leaders should facilitate and promote the participation of residents in the activities of the community and in the design of participative strategies, ensuring that the needs and concerns of residents are heard and considered. Participatory processes are continuous and require capacity building and spaces for constant reflection.

Alliances

Professional support is fundamental. A multidisciplinary team of social workers, planners, urbanists, lawyers, architects, engineers, artists, and many more must work together with communities to advance and to execute a holistic plan. This kind of multidisciplinary team must value community knowledge, must promote critical thought, organization, and the exchange of knowledge between residents and professionals, and must stimulate alternate visions to understand local realities. By observing attentively and listening respectfully, outside professionals can respond to the community's agenda.

Multi-sectoral Associations

Community projects need the support of private and public sectors and academics in order to succeed. These associations expand the exposure of a community's struggles, giving more visibility, while also contributing technical knowledge and resources.

Legal Framework

It is necessary to pay close attention to the legal framework for the ownership and management of land, even if it means a community must create new instruments. Residents of the communities along the Martín Peña Channel examined different forms of land tenure, evaluating individual and collective options for owning the land. They decided on a community land trust, an innovative form of tenure never before used in Puerto Rico. Thereafter, new legislation was promoted in order to establish the Fideicomiso de la Tierra del Caño Martín Peña. The creation of Law 489 in 2004 was the result of an extensive dialogue among many knowledgeable people, but it was also the consequence of an intense political process.

Solidarity with Communities in
Other Countries Facing Similar Challenges

With the aim of sharing the strategies and instruments developed by residents of the Caño Martín Peña with other communities around the world, the Caño CLT is working on a new initiative called the "Espacio de Encuentro Internacional del Fideicomiso de la Tierra." This initiative will facilitate dialogue among community leaders, activists, academics, and politicians from countries and cities in the Caribbean, Latin America, Asia, Africa, North America, and Europe on collective, cooperative, and community-controlled forms of land tenure in informal settlements. It will also serve as an educational center and monitoring network, aimed at producing new knowledge about the creation of community land trusts and the effective participation of community residents in the equitable development and inclusive improvement of informal settlements. Through this initiative, the Caño CLT is now developing the logistics to spread the tools and instruments of the Fideicomiso throughout Puerto Rico and globally.

The Caño CLT convened an international peer exchange on April 29–May 4, 2019 in San Juan. With the title "Community Development and Collective Land Ownership," the Caño CLT gathered community members and residents from informal settlements around the world who are threatened with displacement or who anticipate such a threat in the near future. Community leaders from Argentina, Barbuda, Brazil, Belize, Bolivia, Chile, Ecuador, Jamaica, Mexico, Bangladesh and South Africa traveled to Puerto Rico. In every case, there was a representative from a community-based organization and/or from other allies who could support the development and organization of a CLT in their communities once they returned to their countries of origin.[16]

Participants shared experiences from their own communities and organizations. Many of their stories mirrored the experience of the Martín Peña communities, as participants reflected on the relevance of the Caño's struggle and trajectory for their own realities, identifying common factors in the struggles they face and finding similarities in their own journeys. They saw they have many things in common, even when they are from different countries. Strong bonds were established, based on similarity and solidarity. During the peer exchange and in feedback provided at the end, participants expressed how important it was to gather together and to realize that people are struggling with similar issues all around the world. They are not alone. They are stronger together.[17] It became clear that community organizing that provokes critical thinking and participation is central to addressing land tenure issues, particularly under a collective ownership regime.

CONCLUSION

A majority of CLTs in other countries have been established on lands that were vacant when acquired, allowing the construction of new homes; or CLTs have acquired vacant buildings and rehabilitated them. In both cases, these newly developed homes have been made available to a new group of low-income renters or homeowners. The Fideicomiso de la Tierra del Caño Martín Peña is different. It was created on lands where the homes of hundreds of families were already in existence and already occupied prior to creation of the CLT. "This CLT was born big," as residents often say.

The CLT developed by residents living in the seven Martín Peña communities provides a "proof of concept," demonstrating that CLTs can be an effective tool for regularizing land tenure in informal settlements threatened by displacement. A CLT can also provide for the redistribution of wealth and allow its members to gain control over a settlement's land, increasing their collective power.

The Caño CLT was developed by communities that experienced displacement firsthand, either by direct state action or by gentrification processes. It was designed to ensure that the much-needed environmental rehabilitation of the Caño did not result in the disappearance of the communities through increases in the value of the area's land. It was also born out of an aspiration for justice and equity, so that long-neglected communities and their residents would be the ones to benefit from a large-scale project they had long dreamed of, a project with the potential to transform both their neighborhood and the city.

Fig. 11.5. Mural in one of the Caño's neighborhoods, which reads: ". . . and for the first time we residents are creators of our own future." LINE ALGOED

As one of the late community leaders of the G-8, Mrs. Juanita Otero Barbosa, has said: "The Fideicomiso is the only salvation we have of continuing to exist and living in this community, so that they do not take us out of here" (Carrasquillo et al., 2009). In the current context, as the value of real estate in Puerto Rico is decreasing and as opportunities are soaring for speculation by outside investors who are buying up prime real estate all across the island, the Caño CLT has become increasingly relevant for the Martín Peña communities. Lands that used to belong to the government now belong collectively to the residents through the Caño CLT. These lands have been permanently removed from the market. There is no longer a risk of the government someday selling the land underneath the Martín Peña communities in order to monetize its value. As residents from the Martín Peña communities can often be heard to say, with pride and tenacity: "This land is ours, and nobody can take it away from us."

Notes

1. The Caño communities are: Barrio Obrero, Barrio Obrero Marina, Buena Vista Santurce, Israel-Bitumul, Buena Vista Hato Rey, Las Monjas, and Parada 27.

2. Puerto Rico is an archipelago in the Caribbean Sea. Besides the main island of Puerto Rico, there are two other important islands, Vieques and Culebra, as well as other keys and islets. For the purpose of this essay, we will refer to all of Puerto Rico as an "island."

3. This emigration estimate comes from the Center for Puerto Rican Studies at Hunter, City University of New York.

4. The other is the Voi-Tanzania CLT in Kenya, the subject of Chapter 14 in the present volume.

5. The Action Plan guides the use of the Community Development Block Grant for Disaster Recovery (CDBG-DR) allocated to Puerto Rico to cover the unmet needs remaining after emergency assistance and to mitigate risks.

6. The Cantera Peninsula community was a pioneer in elaborating its own comprehensive development and land use plan, adopted by the Puerto Rico Planning Board in 1995. Badly hit by hurricane Hugo on September 18, 1989, the first major hurricane that struck Puerto Rico since 1932, and as the reconstruction process was underway, residents realized their neighborhood was to be displaced for high end development projects. After partnering with others and organizing, in 1992 the Puerto Rico Legislature enacted Law 20 to create a government corporation that would work along with the community residents to rehabilitate the impoverished sector. The Cantera Community is not part of the Caño CLT, but the community leaders are part of the G-8.

7. Reglamento General para el Funcionamiento del Fideicomiso de la Tierra 2008, Art. V, sec. 2 (Caño CLT General Regulations).

8. These "general regulations" function much like the articles and bylaws that legally constitute most nonprofit organizations in the United States.

9. There are about 188 hectares (466 acres) of land within the Caño Martín Peña Special Planning District, but only the publicly owned land would be transferred to the Caño CLT, on which about 1,500 households were already living.

10. It is important to note that almost half of the residents at the Martín Peña communities have individual land titles as a result of clientelist practices of politicians, both at the state and municipal level. This means there are many instances where, comparing two neighbors on the same street, one might have had a land title conveyed by the government at a $1.00 cost to acquire the land underneath his or her home, while the other neighbor would remain without a land title. This practice endured for more than 30 years.

11. Most of the households who needed to be relocated to make space for the dredging have chosen to become members of the CLT have been provided with a new house and a surface rights deed.

12. This means that, as of October 2019, another 1390 households who are members of the CLT and who are living on lands owned by the CLT, were still waiting to receive their surface rights deed.

13. During the five years since 2014, the Caño CLT has received pro bono assistance from civil law notaries for the execution of these surface rights deeds.

14. 30 L.P.R.A. sec 6261-6276.

15. For persons who already owned and occupied houses on publicly owned land at the time it was transferred to the CLT, the CLT's board of trustees decided to award them a 25% share of the market value of the land underlying their houses. Should they later want to sell, the CLT will pay them that 25% of the land value. In the future, if the CLT develops new houses on land that it owns, a different policy may be put in place for these homes.

16. The peer exchange was divided into two sessions: one for Spanish and Portuguese speakers, gathering together fifteen international participants and participants from two communities in Puerto Rico; the other was for English speakers, gathering together thirty-one community leaders and representatives of community-based organizations.

17. During the peer exchange, an international conference was also held that was open to the general public, entitled "Recovery, Land Tenure, and Displacement: Perspectives from Grassroots and Community development." The conference discussed recovery initiatives after Hurricane María, land tenure issues in a global and local context, and the effects of gentrification that lead to displacement. Approximately 136 people heard about the Fideicomiso de la Tierra, followed by a dialogue with grassroots leaders from South Africa, Barbuda, and Argentina who talked about informality and threats to their homes and neighborhoods.

References

Algoed, L. and M.E. Hernández (2019). "Vulnerabilization and Resistance in Informal Settlements in Puerto Rico: Lessons from the Caño Martín Peña Community Land Trust." *Radical Housing Journal,* Vol 1(1): 29-47.

Algoed, L., M.E. Hernández Torrales, and L. Rodríguez Del Valle (2018). "El Fideicomiso de la Tierra del Caño Martín Peña: Instrumento Notable de Regularización de Suelo en Asentamientos Informales," Working Paper. Cambridge: Lincoln Institute of Land Policy.

Bonilla, Y. and M. LeBron (2019). *Aftershocks of Disaster: Puerto Rico Before and After the Storm.* (Chicago: Haymarket Books).

Carrasquillo, J., A. Cotté, V. Carrasquillo, and M. S. Pagán (2008). *Fideicomiso de la Tierra: Experiencias en el Proceso de Creación.* Escuela Graduada de Trabajo Social Beatriz Lasalle, Universidad de Puerto Rico.

Navas Dávila, G. (2004). "Fideicomiso social de la Tierra." Trabajo preparado para el Dr. Fernando Fagundo, Secretario de Transportación y Obras Públicas del Estado Libre Asociado de Puerto Rico.

UN-Habitat (2013). *State of the World's Cities 2012/2013.* Available from: *https://sustainabledevelopment.un.org/content/documents/745habitat.pdf* [Accessed 14 August 2019.]

UN-Habitat (2012). *Estado de las ciudades en América Latina y el Caribe, Brasil.* See also *Urban Development and Energy Access in Informal Settlements. A Review for Latin America and Africa,* ResearchGate. Available from: *https://www.researchgate.net/publication/309273730_Urban_Development_and_Energy_Access_in_Informal_Settlements_A_Review_for_Latin_America_and_Africa* [Accessed 25 Jul, 2019.]

12.

Community Land Trusts in Informal Settlements

Adapting Features of Puerto Rico's
Caño Martín Peña CLT to Address Land Insecurity
in the Favelas of Rio de Janeiro, Brazil

Tarcyla Fidalgo Ribeiro, Line Algoed,
María E. Hernández-Torrales, Lyvia Rodríguez Del Valle,
Alejandro Cotté Morales, and Theresa Williamson

This chapter is the result of a collaborative research project between a nongovernmental organization based in Rio de Janeiro, Catalytic Communities, and Latin America's first community land trust — one of the world's only CLTs in an informal settlement—the Fideicomiso de la Tierra del Caño Martín Peña in San Juan, Puerto Rico. The aim of the research project was to study the potential of CLT instruments and strategies developed by the communities along the Martín Peña channel as a way to tackle insecure tenure in Rio's favela communities.[1]

Based on this research, we present recommendations on essential lessons when considering the creation of a community land trust in informal settlements, such as those that exist in Puerto Rico, Brazil, and most countries in the Global South. For the purpose of this essay, we have defined "informal settlements" as those where settlers have self-built homes in communal areas, on land to which they lack legal ownership, and on which they continue to live.[2] Many of these settlements have existed for several generations. Over time, therefore, they may become *consolidated*, whereby the building stock, access to some services, community ties, and a way of life have become firmly established, even as the residents' tenure has remained precarious; that is, their legal right to occupy the land beneath their homes has remained "informal." Regularization becomes a primary objective in these cases, the process to legally secure the occupancy and use of the lands underlying an informal settlement.

In this chapter, we identify a set of conditions that we have concluded must be in place in an informal settlement before considering the creation of a CLT as a primary land tenure and regularization strategy. We also present an analysis of legal strategies that we deem necessary to implement CLTs, specifically in the favelas (the informal settlements) of Rio de Janeiro. Our hope is that this chapter can serve other communities, organizers, and professionals who are interested in understanding the process of establishing a community land trust in an informal settlement.

There are very special elements to take into account in the creation of CLTs in the Global South, specifically in the context of informal settlements. The challenges of establishing a CLT in an informal settlement are quite different from those that are faced by CLTs in North American, British, and European cities. In those cities, new homes are usually being developed by a CLT at great financial cost, either through construction or rehabilitation, and then marketed to prospective homebuyers or renters who choose whether they want to come and live in this newly created housing. Before moving in, they can weigh whether living on land that is owned by a CLT and whether purchasing homes with limits on equity at resale will be acceptable to them. In informal settlements, by contrast, residents may in effect already own their homes, which were built by themselves or by previous generations. They often feel a sense of ownership of the underlying land, even when lacking legal documentation of their right to that land. Residents may be reluctant to share control over the land with a new organizational entity under a form of tenure that is foreign to them.

The type of organization we will discuss and propose here is designed, in part, to address such reluctance. A CLT in Brazil, therefore, like the one in Puerto Rico, would have to be organized and directed by community residents themselves in order to be successful.

In informal settlements across Latin America, especially in Brazil, there is an urgency to finding new strategies for securing land tenure. About half of Brazil's territory is estimated to lack full property rights (Ministério das Cidades, 2019). The legal precariousness of land tenure in the favelas has allowed arbitrary evictions by governments, like the many evictions that preceded two international sports events in Rio: the 2014 World Cup and the 2016 Olympic Games. The precariousness of tenure has also served as an excuse for governments to neglect the development of local infrastructure and the provision of adequate public services. Security of tenure and the regularization of land rights in the favelas thus become essential for realization of the right to secure, fully serviced neighborhoods and the right to the city (Soares Gonçalves, 2009).

Land regularization programs that have emphasized individual titling, where deeds to lands that were once occupied informally are conveyed to individual occupants, have often increased the risk of involuntary displacements, a result of market pressures that intensify in the wake of the legalization of land tenure. Even where forced evictions are not being implemented or where governments have invested public resources in on-site

Fig. 12.1. Fogueteiro favela, Central Rio de Janeiro. CATALYTIC COMMUNITIES

rehabilitation and upgrading programs, centrally located favelas face gentrification. In Rio, during the pre-Olympic period, gentrification, locally called *remoção branca*, or "white eviction," was widely reported in the local and international press, and debated during community events.

It is thus time to expand the conversation around land tenure beyond the legal aspects of land titling, and move away from the emphasis on individual ownership as the strategy for land regularization in informal settlements. Individual ownership has not protected informal communities from involuntary displacement and gentrification. The strategy to regularize land tenure must not be framed solely on "legalizing" how each individual relates to the parcel of land they occupy. Rather, it should be chosen by the residents themselves as part of a participatory process that helps them to move towards their vision for the future of their community. Land titling should not be an end in itself, but rather an instrument to achieve both collective and individual objectives. Such a process implies that there are options beyond individual titles, and that such options should be evaluated by the residents in accordance with their own priorities. A participatory approach of planning – action – reflection becomes the key to addressing land tenure.

This chapter starts with an overview of the situation in Rio de Janeiro's favelas today, where land insecurity has led to threats of eviction and gentrification. We describe past and present policies of land regularization in Brazil, arguing that these policies have not been able to put an end to involuntary displacements, which is why looking at mechanisms and policies that favor community ownership of land is a matter of great urgency. We then focus on the Fideicomiso de la Tierra del Caño Martín Peña, describing how residents of the Caño communities came to the conclusion that a community land trust was the best strategy to protect lands they and their families have inhabited for almost a century.

Finally, drawing upon lessons and insights we have gained from peer-to-peer exchanges between community leaders and staff of the Caño CLT in Puerto Rico and community leaders and technical supporters in Brazil, we present the legal implications for the establishment of a CLT in Rio de Janeiro's favelas. We then provide an analysis of conditions that must be present to make organizing a CLT both possible and feasible and we offer recommendations for community leaders, organizers, and supportive professionals to consider when taking the first steps toward creation of a CLT in an informal settlement.

I. RIO'S FAVELAS: INSECURE HOMES ON INSECURE LAND

Rio de Janeiro today has over 1000 favela communities, ranging in size from a handful to over 200,000 residents. Over 24% of the city's population lives in favelas, which constitute the city's primary affordable housing stock. The first community to be called a "favela" is today known as Morro da Providência (Providence Hill). The community's founders were formerly enslaved Africans who were recruited to fight in the bloody war of Canudos in Brazil's arid Northeast. They had been promised land in Rio de Janeiro, the nation's capital at the time, as payment for their military service. When they arrived in Rio in late 1897, however, no land was made available, so they settled on a hillside between the city center and the port. They named the hill "Morro da Favela" (Favela Hill) after the robust, spiny and resilient *favela* bush that dotted the hillsides of Canudos. Eventually, all of Rio's informal settlements — including ones settled long before, such as the community of Horto (settled in the early 1800s, still standing and fighting eviction today) — became known as favelas.

There are a number of facts essential to understanding why, over 122 years after the first favela was settled, the potential for Favela CLTs is currently galvanizing local organizers. First is the *scale* of the challenge. Rio's 1000 favelas today house over 1.4 million people, the vast majority of whom have no legal title for the land they occupy.

Second is the role of *race.* Rio was the largest slave port in world history and received five times the number of enslaved Africans as the entire USA. Slavery also lasted in Brazil 60% longer. Free men, who had previously been enslaved, had served in the bloody Canudos battle on behalf of their adopted nation. Denied their promised compensation, they squatted on land, starting a favela next to Rio's Port. Across the city, hundreds of thousands of other descendants of enslaved people and rural migrants joined them over

Fig. 12.2. Morro da Providência today, Rio's first favela. CATALYTIC COMMUNITIES

the following generations. As a result, today's racial maps of Rio show that black and mixed-race Brazilians tend to live in favelas, particularly in distant ones, while white Brazilians live mostly in upscale and centrally located regions.

Third is the historical *longevity* of these informal settlements. Rio's favelas, on average, are not the precarious "shanties" or exodus-desiring "slums" they are depicted as being in the mainstream media. Rather, they are well-established communities with a long history and a strong local cultural production and community investment.[3]

Finally, it is necessary to understand the intentional *neglect* inflicted on these communities. After 120 years, favela neighborhoods continue to be underserviced, over-policed, and insecure in their tenure. Rio is not a city that is only now beginning to urbanize. This happened decades ago, providing ample time for quality upgrades which never materialized.

Favelas Today: Products of a Cycle of Legitimized Neglect

One might argue that, at the outset, the founding of an informal settlement constitutes a failure of government, especially the failure to produce affordable, livable housing and a supportive neighborhood environment. Once consolidated, however, the real failure is to deny communities recognition, preservation, and improvement on their historic investment. When residents value their community and identify their *permanence* in the territory as a primary goal, however — not to mention when they have established a solid stock of self-built housing and other community amenities — this is a clear sign of a consolidated community or one that is on the path to consolidation. At this point, public policy should focus on identifying such communities and working with residents to detect needs and provide the services they lack, along with preserving community-built assets. In self-built communities, only residents are capable of accurately identifying their assets and needs and how best to preserve them and to address them. Thus, the need for community control over development becomes increasingly critical and just.

This realization has been recent. It came over the past decade, after Rio de Janeiro was selected the host city for the 2014 World Cup and the 2016 Olympics. Prior to 2008, the city had experienced economic stagnation for thirty years, and it was often assumed that underinvestment was due to a lack of public funds. During the Olympic build-up, however, the government spent over US$20 billion on infrastructure and other public improvements in Rio. Promises that were made to the favelas fizzled — including the Morar Carioca program which was supposed to upgrade all favelas by 2020 (Osborne, 2013). Instead, 77,000 favela residents lost their homes to forced evictions (Children Win, 2016).

In a handful of other favelas, the government gave out land titles and invested in policing to bring down crime rates. It also invested in formalizing public services (water, electricity) and community businesses. Community moto-taxi stands and other informally operated businesses now had to be registered, with associated fees and taxes paid up. That was also the case of access to critical utilities. Not coincidentally, this happened in favelas located in the city's touristy South Zone where land values are highest, and where eviction is the most politically difficult. These communities consequently experienced the beginning processes of gentrification, with the cost of living increasing, property values

Fig. 12.3. Vidigal favela, Rio's most notably gentrifying favela. FELIPE PAIVA

skyrocketing, renters leaving, hotels and bar chains opening up, and some homeowners selling, unaware that the value of their homes was monetarily (and emotionally) much greater than what they ended up accepting (Timerman, 2013).

It was at this point, and with the added support of community and international media (which replaced previous dependence on local media monopolies), that the government's policy of neglect and exploitation became explicit. A public official, unaware of the implications of his own comments, noted in 2013 that, "Favelas in the South Zone were fine when they provided cheap labor nearby. Not anymore." Residents of favelas are meant to serve, in other words, not to be served, or so it seems. When they are no longer useful, they need to move. When their land becomes valuable, they need to move. Such is the logic that permeates public policy and social relations across Rio's territory.

Favela organizers today are much more aware that what they are now experiencing and have always known is a vicious cycle of legitimized neglect. This has been the default policy of municipal and state governments toward favelas over generations. Lack of investment in the triad of services most-needed by communities (health, education, and sanitation) produces lack of opportunity and marginalization by the wider society, which in turn propels some residents toward criminal activity. This also makes favelas easy targets for criminal activity. When neighborhoods become known for crime, officials further justify their repressive actions, neglect, and evictions. And the cycle continues.

Despite this cycle, however, residents have built many resilient and culturally vibrant communities with immense potential. In Rio, favelas are also generally well-located across the urban fabric, most having been founded due to nearby employment and services. It is this patrimony they seek to defend and to build upon when residents insist that they want to remain in their neighborhoods. And this is why a tension surfaced during the pre-Olympic period: at the same time as communities facing eviction were being denied the titles they desired, communities facing gentrification spoke against individual titling. How could this be? Because titles, long thought to be a panacea, clearly didn't offer the type of protection that communities desired (Williamson, 2015).

Looking at land tenure alternatives is thus particularly urgent in the context of Rio de Janeiro. Instead of adopting mechanisms that offer the "right to speculate," favela organizers are searching for mechanisms that ensure the right to stay, along with greater access to public services, recognition of self-built community assets, and community control.

The Failure of Regularization Policies in Solving the Problem of Land Insecurity in Brazil's Favelas

More than fifty percent of Brazil's national territory is occupied in an informal or irregular way; that is, without formal title to the land. This started during Portuguese colonialism in the 16th Century. The change of this situation was only pursued in the 19th Century with enactment in 1850 of the Law of Lands.[4] Despite this legislative change, the scenario of uncontrolled land occupation continued, aggravated by a strong urbanization process that began in the 20th Century. Decades passed following passage of the Law of Lands, with no progress being made toward regularizing tenure in informal settlements. Nor were any new legislative or practical measures undertaken to solve the problem.

This scenario of neglect finally began to change in the urban context with the enactment of the Federal Constitution of 1988. It included a chapter dedicated to urban policy, the result of pressure applied by various social and technical movements in a struggle for urban reforms. This chapter of the Constitution would later be regulated by Federal Law 10.257 (2001), known as the City Statute, which introduced an important set of instruments for land regularization, providing a general guideline for national urban policy.

Despite growing attention to the problem of land insecurity in the form of legislation, land regularization as a public policy with wide-ranging pretensions was only instituted as a result of Law 11.977 (2009). This Law provided a basis for regularization of tenure that was focused on guaranteeing rights to the inhabitants of informal settlements and increasing the accountability of developers and real estate agents who contributed to the situation of land informality. The Law created a framework for land regularization, including provisions for the legal title and land registry for the lands occupied by residents of informal settlements. The Law also provided for territorial improvements and increased construction safety, and included measures aimed at improving social and economic conditions for residents of the country's favelas.

> Where land is most valuable, individual titling strengthens speculative investment.

Law 11.977 (2009) had little impact, however, because of its short duration. Its chapter on land regularization was revoked by Law 13.465 (2017), enacted after President Dilma Roussef was ousted from power. The new legislation altered the previous land regularization model, reducing it to a focus solely on the registration aspect; that is, the granting of title deeds to residents living in informal settlements. This Law emphasized individual titling through full private ownership, prioritizing registry regulation to the detriment of other dimensions of land regularization, especially those related to infrastructure improvements in the favelas and social assistance to residents, which had been essential components of the previous legislative framework, Law No. 11.977 (2009).

The most direct threat to the security of tenure came from the option given to the Brazilian legislature under this new law to distribute property titles to residents of informal settlements. In areas of the city where land is most valuable, individual titling strengthens speculative investment in real estate and increases the cost of living for the poorest residents. The increase in the cost of living is due to the introduction of (often exorbitant) fees for basic services such as water and electricity, the collection of property taxes, the forced formalization of local businesses, and the growth in new local businesses targeting a higher-income clientele. Meanwhile, the introduction of speculative development stimulates property sales by residents, which typically take place at values below the formal market rate, but above the values practiced in the informal market where properties were previously traded.

Nevertheless, like every policy intervention before it, this latest piece of legislation for land regularization has been marked by disputes and contradictions. Because it will fuel speculation, this new law directly threatens the security of tenure. It also denies the guarantee of low-income residents' right to services. On the other hand, this legal framework also makes it possible to mold a CLT, should full land rights be yielded to communities who want to create one. Careful monitoring of the implementation of this law is thus in order to ensure the security of the possession of the poorest.

II. ADAPTING INSTRUMENTS AND STRATEGIES OF THE CAÑO MARTÍN PEÑA CLT FOR POSSIBLE APPLICATION IN RIO'S FAVELAS

After ten years of work supporting hundreds of favela community organizers and then helping their communities to fight both government-sponsored evictions and market-led gentrification — one due to the absence of land titles and the other to their presence — Catalytic Communities (CatComm), a Rio de Janeiro-based nonprofit organization, began studying the potential of CLTs for Rio de Janeiro's favelas. In the early 2010s, the organization engaged with a number of academic and business partners who were familiar with the CLT model in the United States, theorizing and imagining its possible application to favelas. CLTs seemed to offer a solution that would support the residents of consolidated favelas in achieving their primary land security objective: *permanence*, the ability to stay put in neighborhoods where they are financially and emotionally invested, places where they feel a sense of belonging.

Fig. 12.4. Asa Branca favela street life. CATALYTIC COMMUNITIES

CLTs seemed to CatComm like they might be a good fit for formalizing Rio's favelas because a CLT is organized and operated along the same lines as a favela: homes are built, bought, inherited, and sold on a parallel, affordable housing market, while the underlying land is seen as a common good. Meanwhile, residents work collectively to build and to maintain their community and to fight for improvements. Favelas are often on land that is publicly owned. These informal settlements are regarded as providing for the "social function" of land, as required by Brazil's Constitution. CLTs can guarantee the security of land tenure of vulnerable populations, while also retaining the non-monetary values that residents have often built in their communities. This is done through a flexible arrangement that is easily adapted to different local realities. But it is also an emancipatory arrangement, since all planning and management of the territory arises from the residents, who are now in a position to officially define development within their own territory.

Despite suspecting that CLTs might have potential for formalizing Rio's favelas, however, Catalytic Communities did not feel capable of introducing something so unfamiliar and theoretical into the public debate. The mental leap required to take a North American model in which CLTs are built from scratch, and applying it to decades-old informal settlements in Brazil, building demand (and power) in the favelas for adopting this model, seemed an impossibility.

It was in this context that CatComm learned of the Caño Martín Peña CLT in Puerto Rico. Not only did seven San Juan communities successfully make this mental leap, they also *realized* a vision of what informal settlements could achieve when building upon the basics of the North American CLT model and creating a CLT to fit their own circumstances. The Caño CLT had successfully demonstrated that establishing CLTs in Rio's favelas might be an effective strategy to halt forced evictions, while also addressing the challenges that typically come with individual land titles. These challenges include: higher costs of living, real estate speculation, and gentrification; individualistic thinking and the atomization of community; and a change in local culture due to the growth of *lógica mercadológica* (market-oriented logic), circumventing the traditional collective and demonetized exchanges on which favelas have historically been based. Community organizers in Rio's favelas typically spend so many years seeking individual titles as the primary solution to land insecurity that they rarely think about the brand-new set of challenges that await residents once those titles are issued. It is then too late to tackle these new challenges, since the mechanisms that might support resistance have by then been blunted through the introduction of the individualized logic of conventional titling.

> The CLT could function as an instrument of emancipation and empowerment.

The CLT, by contrast, seemed to offer a solution to *both* the first challenge (land security) *and* these secondary challenges. The CLT was not simply an arrangement for owning and managing land. As the Caño CLT had shown, it could also function as an instrument of emancipation and empowerment. The Caño CLT had demonstrated a growth in *unity* among seven neighborhoods as they participated in the community planning process that led to the establishment of their CLT, resulting in an incredibly rare level of *power* in their relationships with public authorities.

Caño Martín Peña CLT: Latin America's First CLT

For approximately 80 years, nearly 25,000 residents of the communities along the Caño Martín Peña (Martín Peña Channel) were invisible to government officials, at both the local and state levels. These communities, located in the heart of San Juan, Puerto Rico's capital city, were the result of rural migration during the economic crisis of the 1920s through the 1950s. Impoverished peasants moved with their families to the San Juan area looking for jobs and better living conditions. Most self-built their own housing. A number of families occupied dry land, but many built their homes on the wetlands along the Martín Peña Channel using cardboard, tin, and wood. A great number of them built their houses literally on the water. Over time the families and the municipal government filled the wetlands with all kinds of debris, creating dry land to sustain their makeshift homes. The city continued to grow, and soon the Caño communities found themselves in the heart of San Juan, next to its financial district. A place that no government administration wanted to look at or to care for became strategically located on valuable land that presented manifold development opportunities for the city and the country.

Government disinvestment and neglect, along with poor watershed management, led to a clogged channel. This was coupled with lack of adequate infrastructure, exposing residents of the Caño communities to an unhealthy environment. In 2002, however, after decades of studies and a lack of concrete action, the government announced its intention to dredge and to restore the Martín Peña Channel, reconnecting the lagoons, canals, wetlands, and beaches that are part of the San Juan Bay Estuary.

Having faced evictions and displacement in the past, residents of the Caño's communities inserted themselves into the planning process of what became the Caño Martín Peña Special Planning District in order to protect the permanence of their communities. They created the ENLACE Caño Martín Peña Project to spearhead the effort, completed with a strong community organizing and participation component.

Their participation turned an engineering project (unaware of its negative externalities) into a comprehensive development project (taking action to prevent such externalities) and led to the creation of public policy and institutions to make it feasible. Not only would the channel be cleaned and dredged, but improvements in stormwater and sewerage infrastructure were also planned in order to avoid further contamination, along with needed upgrades to the potable water and power infrastructure. It was recognized, too, that interventions would be needed to improve the quality of public spaces and inadequate housing, along with a sensible relocation strategy and socio-economic development initiatives.

The Comprehensive Development and Land Use Plan for the Caño Martín Peña Special Planning District (Development Plan), created with the active and informed participation of the residents, made it clear that for its implementation to be possible the community had to have control of the land. Of the approximately 188 hectares (466 acres) that comprise the Planning District, 78 hectares (194 acres), were scattered throughout and were owned by five different governmental entities. Although there were some vacant lots and public buildings, most of this acreage was occupied by residents lacking any kind of land title. The planned eco-restoration of the channel and rehabilitation of the District's infrastructure would have made these residents vulnerable to involuntary displacement and gentrification. That is why the Caño's communities held a long and thorough deliberation process to assess what kind of land ownership strategy might be available that would ensure the permanence of their communities (Algoed, Hernández-Torrales, Rodríguez Del Valle, 2018).

Within the Caño Martín Peña Special Planning District there had previously been different strategies and experiences regarding land ownership. At the beginning of this informal settlement, the peasants who occupied government-owned and publicly owned land without legal title became owners of the improvements on the land, but the land continued to be public or under the government's ownership.[5] During the 1960s and early 1970s, some of the Caño communities, with the government's assistance, formed land cooperatives that allowed many residents to acquire the land they occupied and to develop basic infrastructure for their communities. On July 1, 1975, the Puerto Rico Legislature enacted a law that made it possible for low-income families or individuals without land title, like residents of the communities along the Caño, to be able to acquire the title to public land at a very low cost, mostly for just one dollar (US$1.00). This measure was used by politicians as a clientelist strategy, however, to gain electoral votes and not all community residents benefited from the law.

By the year 2002, there were homeowners in the Caño communities who had individual title to their land, but almost fifty percent of the Caño's residents were still living on land over which they had neither ownership nor control. Residents realized that, because of the strategic location of their neighborhoods, restoring the Caño would further encourage the sale of plots of land with titles to speculators at higher prices than their market value, but significantly below their market potential, and continue to fragment the communities. Those who sold their plots would not be able to find alternative housing within the city for the money they had received for their land.

As part of the participatory planning, action, and reflection process that led to the eventual adoption of the Development Plan, residents evaluated various options to address insecurity of tenure against a set of priorities that included: avoiding displacement and gentrification as an unintended consequence of restoring the Caño; getting access to credit; and ensuring their heirs could inherit the right to occupy and use the land, supported by a valid title. Residents considered those forms of land ownership they already were familiar with, such as individual land titles and land cooperatives, and also explored ways of owning and managing land that were new to Puerto Rico, including the community land trust.

After thorough consideration, they found the CLT to be an instrument that is flexible enough to fulfill their needs and more. Three basic characteristics distinguished the CLT from other forms of ownership, namely community-led development on community-owned land for the provision of affordable housing for low-income families. Within that general framework, the CLT could be adapted and applied in any way a community might prefer. In the Caño's case, the residents concluded that a CLT would allow them to have collective control over the land and would ensure implementation of the Development Plan, including providing housing for families in need of relocation. The Caño's residents designed a CLT that would enable them to achieve security of tenure and to regularize their relationship with the land beneath their houses. Through the *Fideicomiso de la Tierra del Caño Martín Peña*, their right to use the land would be validated through a legal document (a deed) that recognized their right to use the surface of the land; that right would be inheritable under Puerto Rico's laws; the improvements (the house) would be registered at the Puerto Rico Registry of Real Estate Property, together with the surface rights deed; residents would be able to develop new housing; and they would have access to mortgage credit, among other important benefits they had not previously enjoyed.[6]

> The Caño's residents designed a CLT that would enable them to achieve security of tenure.

The Legal Framework of the Caño Martín Peña CLT

The CLT is a variable tool, allowing wide possibilities of adaptation according to the conditions of the legal system of each country. Puerto Rico was a Spanish colony until it was invaded by the United States in 1898. This caused a change of jurisdiction in legal terms. In the areas of private law (e.g., persons, property ownership and its modifications, different ways of acquiring ownership, obligations and contracts), Puerto Rico still applies fundamentals of the Spanish Civil Code, as do most Latin American countries. However, in areas such as corporate law, administrative law, and constitutional law, Puerto Rico uses the Anglo-Saxon common law as a primary reference.

Securing community control of the Caño's publicly owned land was critical for the implementation of the Development Plan and to provide housing for those residents who needed to be relocated to provide the physical space for the infrastructure projects. The costs of all the work planned for the dredging of the channel and rehabilitation of the Caño communities was initially estimated at $700 million, but Puerto Rico soon started to suffer from a severe economic and fiscal crisis that has now extended for more than fifteen years. Hence, in order to ensure the implementation of the Development Plan and to alleviate costs, it was essential not only that all public land within the Special Planning District would be put under the control of the organized communities, but that the cost to the communities of acquiring the land would be negligible. Otherwise, the cost of completing the Caño infrastructure projects would be rendered unbearable.

These considerations led the organized communities of the Caño to decide not to create the Caño CLT as a nonprofit corporation under the Puerto Rico General Corporations Law. Instead, the Caño communities decided to draft a bill that would create their CLT as a trusteeship, along with all the other instruments needed for implementation of the Development Plan. Among the other purposes of this innovative strategy, enactment of this special law by the government of Puerto Rico would enable the free transfer of public land to the Caño CLT.

Law 489-2004, as amended, gave life to the *Proyecto ENLACE del Caño Martín Peña* as an independent project. It also created the tools needed for its implementation. The legislation created a government corporation, the ENLACE Project Corporation (ENLACE). This new corporation was charged with responsibility for coordinating the dredging of the Martín Peña Channel. It would also be responsible for coordinating the rehabilitation and new construction of infrastructure (stormwater and sanitary sewers, potable water systems), the relocation of power lines, streets, and public spaces, and the relocation of families and housing. These interventions were deemed crucial not only for the ecological restoration of the channel, but also to reduce the risk of flooding with polluted water that recurrently affected the communities. The ENLACE Corporation was charged with creating the conditions for the economic and social development of the Caño communities as well.[7]

The Fideicomiso de la Tierra del Caño Martín Peña (Caño Martín Peña CLT) was also created by means of Law 489-2004 as a private legal entity, separate from ENLACE or from any other governmental agency or instrumentality, and was invested with the legal authority to fulfill its responsibilities. All the public land within the Special District was transferred by this Law to ENLACE, which then transferred the land to the CLT by means of public deeds.

The Caño Martín Peña CLT is governed by regulations and by a board of trustees designed by the residents as a result of a two-year participatory planning process. The composition of this board differs somewhat from the three-part model used by most CLTs in the United States. Residents of the Caño communities decided that they would retain a majority of the seats on the governing board, while still providing for representation by the government and by other parties who are not residents of the Caño. The CLT's eleven-member board of trustees is constituted as follows: four are individuals residing on CLT land, elected by their peers; two are community residents, delegated by G-8, a coalition of community-based organizations representing all of the Caño's neighborhoods; two are experts, selected by the board, according to the organization's needs; two are representatives of governmental agencies;[8] and one is a representative of the municipality of San Juan.

A Proposed Legal Framework for Brazilian CLTs

The Caño Martín Peña CLT provided the comparative starting point for Catalytic Communities' own research into how a CLT might be established in Brazil. As CLT practitioners around the world have discovered, the model and instruments developed in one country must be modified to conform to laws and politics in another country. That is true in the Brazilian case as well.

The trusteeship (*fideicomiso*) used by the Caño Martín Peña CLT, for example, which was established through an act of the legislature in Puerto Rico, cannot be used for the purpose of establishing a CLT in Brazil, unless a specific law were to be adopted. Any attempt to enact such a law would run into political and bureaucratic difficulties. Even so, CatComm and organizers in favela communities may eventually pursue the presentation of a CLT bill as a political strategy to foster debate on the issue. They would propose a model that is able not only to guarantee security of tenure, but also to integrate the community and to increase its capacity for self-management and political negotiation.

But, for now, an arrangement was sought using instruments already existing in the Brazilian legal system which are capable of providing the basis for the present-day implementation of a Brazilian model of the community land trust, tailored to local specifications and needs. A legal framework was developed and proposed by CatComm that unites several instruments for the construction of a community land trust that could be specifically applied to addressing the problem of land insecurity in the favelas of Rio de Janeiro. This legal framework for a Brazilian CLT has three components, which may be assembled sequentially in different stages or pursued on parallel tracks. They are as follows:

- Acquisition of land and regularization of title by community residents;

- Constitution of the legal entity to receive the land and to be responsible for the continuing ownership and management of the land; and

- Separation of ownership of buildings from the ownership of land, transferring surface rights back to community members who manage the legal entity that owns the land.

Land acquisition and regularization. The legal reality in Rio's informal settlements, as well as in favelas throughout Brazil, is of people occupying land for which they have neither ownership nor control. Sometimes this land has not even been registered. Considering that the community land trust relies on gaining possession of land, where the ownership of lands and buildings will then be separated, the regularization and registration of title and the transfer of ownership are indispensable for the implementation of a CLT. There are many instruments for the regularization and conveyance of land in Brazil. The most significant in terms of dealing with land insecurity in informal settlements are adverse possession, concession of use, donation, purchase and sale, and land legitimization.

* *Adverse possession (usucapião)* is used for the acquisition of titles of property by populations residing on privately owned land. The basic argument is that the registered owners have failed to fulfill the social function of the property for a certain period of time, stipulated by law, during which the residents occupied the property and, as a result of continuous occupation over many years, they now have a legal claim to that land.

* *Concession of use* is an instrument that usually applies to publicly owned land, where it is not possible to apply adverse possession. This is an administrative contract that grants the use of a property for a certain period of time. Generally, in order to provide the instrument with more security, concessions have a 99-year term that can be extended for an equal period.

* *Donation* is an instrument through which public or private owners donate, free of charge, the land inhabited by low-income residents to said residents.

* *Purchase and sale* demands a financial contribution from the residents.

* *Land legitimization* is a new instrument provided by Law 13.465 (2017), which was intended to become the main land regularization instrument in Brazil. Applicable in public or private areas, it seeks to ensure private property for residents of informal occupations, be they low-income or otherwise.

Constitution of a legal entity. With the use of one of these instruments, once title is regularized and the ownership of land is poised to be conveyed to a community land trust, there must be a legal entity in place to constitute the CLT, receiving title and becoming responsible for the ownership and management of the land for years to come. This legal entity may take various forms (e.g. association, condominium, etc.) in accordance with the Brazilian legal system. A case-by-case analysis will be required to decide the best format in a specific situation. CatComm's analysis has recommended that each CLT be established as a nonprofit legal entity with a dual objective of holding and managing land on behalf of a particular favela and preserving its affordability for low-income residents.

Separating land ownership and building ownership. Once these other stages have been achieved, the ownership of any buildings already existing on the land when it was acquired by the CLT, and, typically, the ownership of future buildings constructed on the land, must be separated from ownership of the underlying land. (The legal entity that owns the land — i.e., the CLT — must, in turn, be collectively controlled by residents who live on the land.) When it comes to the separation of ownership, there are several instruments available in the Brazilian legal system. The most appropriate of them, as concluded by CatComm's analysis, will be the surface rights deed, similar to what is being used by the Caño CLT in Puerto Rico.

With the separation of ownership, the three components of the legal constitution of a Brazilian CLT would be put in place. The crafting of each component will then depend upon the objectives and needs of the communities that are building the model. What is presented here is only a basic legal framework, which offers several options suitable to serve the diverse needs that will present themselves in practice.

Coming to the end of this legal sequence, the CLT will be able to exert its full potential in the territory it has chosen to serve. Especially based on a collective management model designed by the community according to its own needs and specificities, the CLT will be able to recognize local realities and to strengthen community assets as it seeks territorial improvements.

This methodology releases any CLT implementation from the need to wait or to depend on the approval of enabling legislation, which could take years considering the unstable Brazilian political scene. That said, the fight for specific CLT enabling legislation should be pursued in parallel to the application of existing instruments described above, since legislative support could significantly facilitate, support, and boost efforts to establish favela CLTs.[9]

The CLT is seen by a growing number of favela leaders, NGOs, legal experts, practitioners, academics, and public servants in the urban planning and land titling fields in Rio, as a *ferramenta de costura*, a "seaming tool" that integrates and addresses diverse conclusions reached separately over the years by residents and supporters working on supportively addressing the problem of informality. CLTs provide a foundation for:

- securing the social function of land;

- realizing the need for land regularization;

- respecting the typology and self-management already inherent in favelas;

- promoting and preserving the affordability of housing;

- respecting people's sense of belonging and deeper concern for permanence (rather than seeing homes as a "speculative investment");

- recognizing the importance of community-controlled, participatory planning processes;

- guaranteeing a re-ordering of the community, so that services can be provided, consistent with a "do no harm" approach; and

▪ engaging technical expertise in support of community planning, rather than through top-down models.

III. GUIDELINES WHEN CONSIDERING A CLT AS A POSSIBLE STRATEGY FOR REGULARIZING LAND TENURE AND PROTECTING HOMES IN INFORMAL SETTLEMENTS

The collaborative research project that was conducted by CatComm and the Caño Martín Peña CLT involved peer-to-peer exchanges between community leaders and staff of the Caño Martín Peña CLT and interested favela communities and professionals during five days in Rio de Janeiro in August 2018. From that collaboration, we tentatively offer guidelines and recommendations for other communities that might be interested in implementing a similar strategy in their own territory.

It should be noted that every community is different and, therefore, every CLT will also be different. There is no universal recipe as to how to create one. Community residents design the bylaws, policies, priorities, and internal procedures, which will define the CLT and will be different for every new CLT in accordance with the community's particularities, circumstances, and needs. It is worth repeating, as well, that a CLT that is designed to address the challenges of regularizing land tenure in informal settlements will be organized and operated differently from a CLT freshly created to provide new housing in neighborhoods where ownership of the land is already formal(ized). Our recommendations are aimed, in fact, at neighborhoods like Brazil's favelas where people have

Fig. 12.5. Delegation from the Caño Martín Peña visiting the Barrinha favela, August 2018.
CATALYTIC COMMUNITIES

occupied land for years which they neither own nor control. In such settlements, activists who are interested in creating a CLT must consider two questions: What are the *conditions* that must be present to make a CLT feasible in an informal settlement; and what is the *process* that organizers must follow to make a CLT a reality?

Conditions: Where Might It Be Feasible to Establish a CLT in an Informal Settlement?

Community leaders and activists, public officials or others interested in developing CLTs should take into account that CLTs may not work in every community. For a CLT to be considered in the first place, as a possible strategy for addressing the need for regularization and upgrading in Rio de Janeiro's favelas — and, for that matter, in the informal settlements of many other countries — the following conditions need to be present:

- Consolidated communities are located on lands where residents perceive a threat — or experience the reality — of gentrification, forced eviction, or other human-induced involuntary displacement;

- A large percentage of families lack legal titles and want to address the problem of insecure land tenure;

- There is a possible path to acquiring title(s) to the land;

- Residents feel a strong sense of belonging and a desire to remain in their community; and

- There is a solid process of community organization in place, supported by organizations that are ready to accompany the community and that are able to provide technical assistance.

The experience of Puerto Rico and discussions to date in Brazil reveal that there are additional conditions that may be essential to the process of establishing a CLT in informal settlements. Amongst them are:

1. An organized community and mature leadership that fosters horizontal participation, new leadership and decision-making among all sectors, and that is willing to assume new responsibilities and to make a commitment that will last the life of the community.

2. Supportive organizations and technical allies that are prepared to: (a) accompany the community in strengthening an organizing process and, if necessary, to facilitate and to provoke difficult conversations that will ensure that the participatory planning, action, and continuous reflection process needed to choose and implement a CLT will be controlled by the community and have widespread participation; (b) engage

in dialogues with residents to help inform their decision-making process, where the technical allies are willing to both listen and to learn from the residents and to share their knowledge; and (c) help to strengthen and to complement the community and economic resources that are required to fulfill the community's development plan.

3. Community planning that comes first. CLTs that are designed to regularize land tenure must emerge and develop from existing resident desires and demands. Residents must come together to evaluate their options and make an active choice to adopt a CLT, and that CLT must provide a path to addressing their very real needs. Residents must also reach a broad understanding that some form of collective or community ownership of the land will best serve their needs and will allow them to accomplish their development objectives, both social and economic.

4. Communities that have a strong sense of belonging. The Caño's leaders made it clear that residents with this strong sense of belonging are those that are the most supportive of their own CLT, and that the pride in one's community and a strong sense of history can be strengthened and stimulated in the process or creating a CLT.

5. A legal entity that is controlled by the community, which can receive land rights as a means of collective or community ownership, along with the mechanisms to make the transfer a reality.

These five conditions are key to a successful CLT, but not all of them need to be present at the first moment of considering whether or not to form a CLT. In fact, several get put in place during the process of mobilization and reflection leading up to the decision to move forward in establishing this instrument. What should be emphasized and observed in every case of creating and applying a CLT in an informal settlement is community initiative and broad participation, both in the design of the CLT and in the definition of the goals to be achieved.

Process: How Might Residents Get Started in Establishing a CLT in an Informal Settlement?

As a result of the peer-to-peer exchanges between community leaders and staff of the Caño Martín Peña CLT and interested favela communities and professionals, a number of recommendations were made on essential steps to be taken when considering the formation of a new CLT in an informal settlement.

Start a process of community planning-action-reflection. Before anything else, residents have to decide whether a CLT is the right mechanism for land regularization in their community. A thorough process of planning with active and continuous resident participation is crucial to make informed decisions about the type of land tenure that will best serve their needs and, if it is decided that a CLT is the right mechanism, how the CLT will be established and governed and how the land will be managed as a collective asset to realize the community's vision. A *CLT is not an end in itself, but rather an instrument to achieve the goals of the community.*

In the Caño, residents engaged in a participatory planning–action–reflection process, where through concrete actions they could obtain short-term wins to keep the community engaged, and continuously reflect on their actions so as to learn from them and inform their planning process. Such a process can be started by residents, community leaders, community-based organizations, government agencies or NGOs. In every case, however, supportive technical allies must recognize their role as being one of helping to create the conditions that will enable residents to strengthen their organizations, to take control of the process, and to participate effectively.

Further recommendations for this participatory process include:

- Start small. Think from less to more. Sports or cultural events can help as a mobilizing method.

- Get residents involved who are influential in the community and who are trusted by a wide range of residents.

- Organize events where residents can think of their ideal community and define what they want their neighborhood to become.

- Develop and use popular education techniques such as street theater, comic books, videos, and others, and engage youth in their design and as communicators.

- Remember that it always seems impossible until it is done.

Create CLT structures, policies, and procedures. If it is decided that the CLT is the right mechanism to meet the needs of the community, residents need to decide how the CLT will function. The bylaws, policies, and activities of every CLT will be somewhat different. Residents must formulate what the shape and function of their CLT should be, which may change over time when conditions or contexts change. The organizational structures and operational priorities of other CLTs can be consulted as inspiration. (See, for example, the rules and regulations of the Caño CLT in "Reglamento General para el Funcionamiento del Fideicomiso de la Tierra del Caño Martín Peña," 2008.)

Technical assistance from professionals. NGOs, universities, or government will be necessary to support residents in achieving their goals. Professionals — social workers, urban planners, architects, engineers, lawyers — should support the process, not lead it. They are not the ones to provide answers to questions, as the knowledge lies within the community. Rather, they can help to expand possibilities. Social workers and community organizers that accompany the community can help facilitate discussions, find alternative ways to engage residents, promote critical thinking, and ensure that participation is productive and inclusive. Planners can help the community to keep a comprehensive perspective throughout the process. Engage experts after residents have defined what they need and what they want. If experts come too early or without proper orientation to promote a balanced dialogue, they may downplay the community, co-opt the process, or impose their own standards on communities.

Define the legal possibilities. After the community has defined what it wants, lawyers can get involved to guide the community through which legal instruments already exist that make the transformations legally possible. If certain legal instruments do not yet exist, they can be created to meet the needs of the community, or elements can be borrowed from other legal instruments. Also here, residents themselves must design these new legal instruments, with the help of lawyers (not the other way around). If elements are taken from existing legal instruments, it is essential to focus on the final goal and to make adjustments in the process in order to ensure the community's goal is reached. If members of a community have decided they want to hold their land collectively, for example, but their only legal option is to pass through individual titles first (as is currently the case in Brazil for publicly-owned lands), it will be necessary for residents to have reached a decisive conclusion to combine their titles under a CLT well prior to receiving those titles, and execute that decision immediately. Otherwise, speculation can curtail the process. Ideally, in this case, the CLT organization should be established in advance and be ready to receive those titles as soon as they are issued.

Strategize. The process to establish and to maintain a CLT requires continuous organizing and strategizing on how to choose partners and on how to communicate and to engage with third parties in order to achieve such objectives as securing the land, dealing with conflicts, and attracting resources, among others. Taking the time to stop and to reflect on the challenges and opportunities within and beyond the community is key to developing a successful path forward.

⸺

Community land trusts are always unique. The Caño CLT borrowed some elements from other CLTs, but residents and their allies also created many new elements completely from scratch in order to address the needs of their community and to find ways to make their CLT function properly within their own context. CLTs in Brazil will undoubtedly take on a whole new shape, and will differ from community to community, depending on the goals of residents and the circumstances of each community.

It is essential to remember, however, that there should never be discussions about the community—including discussions about forming a CLT—without the community being present. As organizers in informal settlements, from Johannesburg to Rio, often say: "Nothing for us, without us."

At the time this essay is being written, a working group comprised of 154 community leaders and technical allies has formed in Rio de Janeiro and is supporting the development of pilot CLTs in two communities that meet the conditions described above: the Trapicheiros and Esperança communities. This working group is also developing enabling legislative proposals and outreach materials to share the CLT model with other communities. Trapicheiros and Esperança have each embarked on the process of establishing their own CLT and are currently holding regular community social events and workshops, engaging residents in a participatory planning process towards forming a CLT.

The working group formed after the August 2018 visit by a delegation of five Caño Martín Peña CLT organizers, who came to Rio to share their story. This city-wide, multi-partner working group includes leaders from over twenty communities, land rights agents from the state, planners and lawyers from Rio's universities, public defenders, NGOs and others. Some of them traveled to Puerto Rico in May 2019 to participate in a peer-to-peer exchange hosted by the Caño Martín Peña communities. Community leaders and their support organizations from Argentina, Bangladesh, Barbuda, Belize, Bolivia, Brazil, Chile, Ecuador, Jamaica, Lebanon, Mexico, Peru, South Africa, and the United States came to San Juan learn more about the Caño CLT.

Seeds are being sown for new CLTs across the world. To be continued!

Notes

1. The study was financed by the Latin America program of the Lincoln Institute of Land Policy.

2. We are focusing here on the informal occupancy of land as an *urban* phenomenon. Throughout the world, however, there are also millions of acres of *rural* land that are occupied and used for housing, farming, grazing, and woodcutting by people who have no formal title to these lands.

3. In recent years, twelve favelas have opened museums documenting their histories. The social museology movement is growing.

4. The land law of 1850 established purchase-and-sale as a form of land acquisition in Brazil, breaking with the previous model that had recognized effective occupation of a territory as a criterion of acquisition. In addition, it provided for a system of land registration aimed at the formal regularization of the national territory, which was not applied in practice, however.

5. Original inhabitants built their homes themselves. Over time, as people moved on, houses were sold using informal documents or private contracts that clearly established that the buyer was only acquiring the house, not the land. Almost all of those documents stated that the land was public land. None of the documents were registered, however, which precluded buyers from accessing mortgage credit.

6. From a procedural perspective, the Caño Martín Peña opted for a surface rights deed, instead of a ground lease, for regularizing use of the land and for securing and registering a family's ownership of the house. A ground lease agreement may be used for other owners, however, like businesses or organizations established on the CLT's land.

7. This government corporation was set up with a sunset provision. It is scheduled to go out of business after twenty-five years.

8. One of these should be a board member of the ENLACE Project Corporation.

9. In effect, there are two possible legal ways to enable the formation of a CLT in informal settlements: (1) the approval of a specific law, detailing a CLT's application and creating legal instruments to put the CLT into effect; or (2) the use of instruments already existing in the legal system, combining several of them for the CLT's formation and operation.

References

Algoed, L., A. Cotté Morales, T. Fidalgo Ribeiro, M.E. Hernández Torrales, L. Rodriguez Del Valle and T. Williamson (forthcoming). Community Land Trusts and Informal Settlements: Assessing the feasibility of CLT instruments developed by the Caño Martin Peña communities in Puerto Rico for Favelas in Rio de Janeiro, Brazil. Working Paper. Cambridge: Lincoln Institute of Land Policy.

Algoed, L., M.E. Hernández Torrales and L. Rodríguez Del Valle (2018). El Fideicomiso de la Tierra del Caño Martín Peña: Instrumento Notable de Regularización de Suelo en Asentamientos Informales, Working Paper. Cambridge: Lincoln Institute of Land Policy.

Corporación del Proyecto ENLACE del Caño Martín Peña (2008). Reglamento general para el funcionamiento del Fideicomiso de la Tierra, Núm. 7587. San Juan: Departamento de Estado.

Children Win (2016). *Rio 2016 Olympics: The Exclusion Games. https://www.childrenwin. org/wp-content/uploads/2015/12/DossieComiteRio2015_ENG_web_ok_low.pdf*

Ministério das Cidades. Regularização Fundiária Urbana—Lei 13.465/17. Accessed March 12, 2019. *http://www.cohab.mg.gov.br/wp-content/uploads/2017/11/Reurb-out..pdf*

Osborne, C (2013). "A History of Favela Upgrades Part III: Morar Carioca in Visio and Practice (2008–2013)." *RioOnWatch,* April 2. *https://www.rioonwatch.org/?p=8136*

Robertson, D. and T. Williamson (2017). "The Favela as a Community Land Trust: A Solution to Eviction and Gentrification?" *Progressive City,* May 2. *https://catcomm.org/law-clt/*

Soares, G. R. (2009). "Repensar a regularização fundiária como política de integração socioespacial." *Estudos Avançados* Vol. 23 No. 66. http://www.scielo.br/scielo.php?script=sci_arttext&pid=S0103-40142009000200017

Timerman, J. (2013). "Is a Favela Still a Favela Once It Starts Gentrifying?" *CityLab,* December 2. *https://www.citylab.com/equity/2013/12/favela-still-favela-once-it-starts-gentrifying/7726/*

Williamson, T. D. (2015). "A new threat to favelas: gentrification." *Architectural Review,* May 30. *https://www.architectural-review.com/opinion/a-new-threat-to-favelas-gentrification/8682967.article*

Williamson, T. D. (2018). "Community Land Trusts in Rio's Favelas: Could Community Land Trusts in Informal Settlements Help Solve the World's Affordable Housing Crisis?" *Land Lines,* July 31. *https://www.lincolninst.edu/sites/default/files/pubfiles/land-lines-july-2018-full_2.pdf*

Williamson, T. D. (2020). "Favela vs. Asphalt: Suggesting a New Lens on Rio de Janeiro's Favelas and Formal City," *Comparative Approaches To Informal Housing Around The Globe,* edited by Udo Grashoff. London: UCL Press.

Williamson, T. D. (forthcoming). "Proporcionar seguridad de tenencia para los actuales habitantes del barrio," *Barrio 31,* los inicios de una operación transformadora, edited by Agustina Gonzalez Cid. Washington, DC: Inter-American Development Bank.

Williamson, T. D. (2017). "Rio's Favelas: The Power of Informal Urbanism." *Perspecta 50: Urban Divides,* M. McAllister and M. Sabbagh (editors). Cambridge: MIT Press, September.

Williamson, T. D. (2019). "The Favela Community Land Trust: A Sustainable Housing Model for the Global South," *Critical Care: Architecture and Urbanism for a Broken Planet,* Angelika Fitz and Elke Krasny (editors). Cambridge: MIT Press.

13.

A Watershed Land Trust in Honduras
Profile of Foundation Eco Verde Sostenible

Kirby White and Nola White

The Honduran nonprofit organization known as FECOVESO (*Fundación Eco Verde Sostenible*) serves rural communities in northwest Honduras. Financial support for these services is provided by a charitable nonprofit in the United States, the Honduras Community Support Corporation. FECOVESO is a specialized community land trust that acquires and holds parcels of land surrounding the water sources for gravity-feed systems serving small mountain communities. FECOVESO also functions as a funding vehicle for a variety of community development projects in these and other small communities in the region.

BACKGROUND

The origins of FECOVESO can be traced to the early 1990s, when a Peace Corps volunteer named Nola White was sent to Honduras to assist with the development of gravity-feed water systems in mountain communities in the northwest. Until then, water for local households had been carried from nearby streams, usually in large jars borne on the heads of women. The Peace Corps and the Honduran Government provided materials and technical assistance to build these systems. The physical labor was provided by residents of the communities themselves. Nola's role involved initiating, organizing, and supporting these projects in one community after another. It was a role for which she was exceptionally well-qualified through her social skills and her previous experience as a community organizer in the USA.

Three years with the Peace Corps left her with many friends in Honduras. She returned a number of times in the next few years to visit the communities where she had worked, as well as neighboring ones. These were not only social visits, however; she also became increasingly involved in supporting a variety of community development projects in the places she visited, acquiring watersheds, improving water systems, and constructing schools. She was known locally as "the *gringa* who came back."

It quickly became apparent that these projects needed funding that was going to be impossible to find in Honduras, so she recruited friends and family to establish a non-profit organization in the United States to serve as a vehicle for raising funds in the USA that could be directed to projects in Honduras. The Honduras Community Support Corporation (HCSC) was founded in 2002. She then worked with community leaders and others in Honduras to establish a second nonprofit, *Fundacion Eco Verde Sostenible* (FECOVESO). The dual mission of this Honduran organization was to manage and to allocate funds received from HCSC and to function as a regional land trust, perma-nently protecting the water sources and watersheds on which community water systems depended.

THE REGION AND ITS COMMUNITIES

The mountainous region served by FECOVESO measures roughly 60 kilometers from north to south and 60 kilometers from east to west. It is bounded on the north by the Caribbean Sea, on the west by the Guatemala border, on the east by the highway between the port city of Puerto Cortez and the inland industrial city of San Pedro Sula, and on the south (roughly) by the height of land between the north and south slopes of the moun-tain range. Except for the fringes along the coastal highway and the Puerto Cortez-San Pedro Highway, the entire region is off the national electric grid. It is also roadless, except for a few *caminos* that are more or less passable for four-wheel-drive vehicles, but are used mostly by people on foot or on horse-or-mule-back.

By modern standards of countries in the Global North, the people living in the small communities scattered throughout this rural region in Honduras would be seen as deeply "deprived" and extremely "poor." They live very much as people have lived in these moun-tains for countless generations — without motor vehicles, without electricity and, for the most part, without money. Yet, in some important ways, they are much better off than the majority of Honduran city-dwellers, who are beset by varying degrees of physical insecu-rity, violence, displacement, and potential starvation.

The mountain people live in circumstances that may not appear to offer many ben-efits — the homes in each community are widely scattered, with no recognizable street grid, no stores (the nearest store may be a day's walk away), and no regular medical ser-vices (the nearest clinic may also be a day's walk away). What these people do have is the security, connections, and comfort of living in genuine communities. They know who all of their neighbors are, who all of their neighbors' relatives are, and how the various extended families within the community are interrelated. (One of the communities with which FECOVESO has worked is called *Los Mejias* — *Mejia* being the last name of most of the people in the community.) As a resident of such a community you may or may

Fig. 13.1. Honduras mountains. SUSAN ALANCRAIG

not like all your neighbors and relatives, but you are unlikely to fear them. And if you need help, it is likely they will do what they can for you. There is real security in such a community.

There is also security in the kind of homeownership such people have, even though very few of them hold what others would recognize as secure legal title to their homes. In some cases, their ownership rights are based on no more than their neighbors' acknowledgement that "the family has always lived there." In other cases, they may have a written record of the property having been sold to them — the equivalent of a quitclaim deed in what is likely to be a long chain of unrecorded quitclaim deeds. If some wealthier person were to have a financial motive for legally dislodging them, it would be quite easy to do, but this rarely happens.

The dwellings that the mountain people have on such properties are, by most standards, primitive. Some of them are traditional "bajareque" (mud and stick) structures with thatched roofs. Others are built with planks slabbed from local timber with a chainsaw, and roofed with (typically recycled) metal sheeting. Most homes have hard-packed dirt floors. Cooking is done on wood-fired stoves, which also provide some comfort during chilly days in the rainy season — though the climate is relatively mild year-round.

The diet of the mountain people, like their shelter, is simple and sufficient. Corn and beans are the core of their diet. A household's corn is typically grown in small patches of approximately an acre in size (sometimes some distance from the household's dwelling); beans are more often grown in dooryard gardens. All crops are cultivated with a hoe. When corn is harvested, the ears are usually stored, still in their dried husks, on overhead racks in the stove-dried kitchen area — to be shucked and shelled as they are needed. The shelling is likely to be done by a woman sitting in the kitchen door with a pan in her lap, and typically with the dooryard chickens gathered around to chase after any kernels that escape the pan. The shelled corn is then ground in a hand-cranked grinder — the cranking of which is one of the many tasks that typically fall to the children of the house. Meat is rarely a part of the diet. But there are many kinds of fruit — including citrus, bananas, avocados, mangos, papayas, coconuts, and more — that can be grown in the dooryard or gathered from where they grow wild, and there are always kids who know where things grow and are ready to climb the trees and pick what's ripe.

This way of life remains mostly as it has been for many generations. The one thing that is new, for the more fortunate of these remote communities, is that water is now piped directly to each family's home. This benefit is provided by gravity-feed water systems that typically collect water from small streams, which have been dammed to create retention pools as high in the watershed as possible.

FECOVESO AS A LAND TRUST

A majority of the funding that FECOVESO receives from HCSC has been used to purchase watershed lands that surround the sources of water for these mountain communities. Control of such lands is crucial, because larger parcels tend to be owned by non-residents whose interest in the land is likely to include commercial cattle grazing and logging, uses that are not in the best interest of the people who live nearby. Honduran law does give local communities a collective right to draw water from springs or streams on private land. It is virtually impossible, however, for these communities to protect the quality of this water against the polluting effects of grazing and logging if they do not have control over the surrounding watershed, including not only the immediate pool from which the water is piped, but the more distant areas from which the water drains. To exert such control, the land in question must be held — in legally enforceable terms — either directly by the communities served or by a reliable stewardship institution, holding the property and protecting the water on a community's behalf.

There are practical reasons for vesting ownership of watershed lands in a regional stewardship institution.

Direct, collective ownership by the communities themselves is not practical in most cases. The communities are very small and are typically not incorporated, so they cannot hold recorded title to real property. Even if a community has been incorporated — as a few have been with FECOVESO's assistance — there are practical reasons for vesting ownership of watershed lands in a more extensive regional stewardship institution, rather than having these lands owned and managed by a very small community and governed by a board of supervisors (*patronado*) that is subject to all the complications of local politics.

Fig. 13.2. Water source for a mountain village, Honduras. SUSAN ALANCRAIG

FECOVESO's founders did consider the possibility of direct community ownership, but quickly decided in favor of ownership by a regional organization. The founders also considered the possibility of allowing certain other land uses on FECOVESO's watershed lands if such uses did not interfere with watershed protection. Here again, however, they chose not to involve the organization in the complicated process of deciding what did or what did not interfere with watershed protection in a particular locale. As a land trust, therefore, FECOVESO has a single, very specific purpose — to protect the watersheds on which households within the communities depend for their domestic water supply.

As of this writing, FECOVESO has acquired and presently holds 17 parcels of land, totaling about 376 acres, in watersheds supplying 15 water systems. (Some systems serve multiple communities.) The organization has also purchased fencing materials to protect otherwise unenclosed parcels, and has supported reforestation in some of the watersheds. Fencing and reforestation work is done by members of the communities being served by the water supply, although a substantial amount of reforestation work was done in one watershed by personnel from a nearby Honduran naval base.

FECOVESO AS A COMMUNITY DEVELOPMENT ORGANIZATION

Community development projects carried out by FECOVESO include the construction of new water systems and the expansion and repair of existing systems. (The U.S. Peace Corps is no longer doing such work in Honduras.) Other significant community development projects have included the construction, expansion, and repair of schools. These buildings are important to the communities not only in providing for elementary education, but also as community meeting places. FECOVESO has provided materials for constructing or expanding twelve schools, and for repairing nineteen others. It has provided desks, or the materials to make desks, for six schools. FECOVESO has also helped some communities to build or to improve basic medical facilities, to build footbridges over mountain streams and, in a few cases, to improve mountain roads so that four-wheel-drive vehicles can deliver materials to remote communities.

The nature of FECOVESO's role in such projects is defined by three important principles. First, the needs to be addressed by a project must be identified by community members themselves. Secondly, there must be evidence of community-wide support for the project. Lastly, the work required by the project must be carried out by community residents. (Exceptions are work that requires operating special equipment such as a bulldozer or work that requires special expertise, such as the masonry entailed in constructing a water tank.) FECOVESO's role is limited to covering the cost of necessary materials and to providing expertise that the community itself does not possess and cannot possibly pay for.

> The needs to be addressed by a project must be identified by community members themselves.

FECOVESO GOVERNANCE AND OPERATIONS

The Board of Directors for FECOVESO includes representatives of the communities where FECOVESO owns watershed land, plus other individuals with legal, financial, or technical expertise. (HCSC is not formally represented on the FECOVESO board, although Nola White serves on the boards of both organizations.) The governing board of FECOVESO meets monthly in an office facility located on a parcel of land that is owned by FECOVESO.

The organization's staff currently consists of two part-time employees, native Hondurans who are paid modest salaries. Nestor Lainez does the record-keeping for the organization and has extensive experience with water systems, building construction, and other practical matters. Marivel Reyes Ayalla is an attorney who deals with legal and financial matters for FECOVESO, functioning as the de facto executive director. She lives in a house immediately adjacent to the office.

Communities seeking assistance for either watershed protection or a community development project must submit a written proposal (*solicitud*) to FECOVESO's board, specifying the need to be addressed by the project and detailing the cost of meeting that need. The *solicitudes* are reviewed by a board committee that includes Nestor Lainez, who visits proposed sites and evaluates construction plans and budgets. Based on Nestor's analysis, the committee may recommend modifications of the proposed project to increase its effectiveness and/or to reduce its cost. Once satisfied that a proposed project meets FECOVESO's criteria, the committee presents the project to the full board of directors for consideration at its next monthly meeting. In reviewing a proposed project, the board takes into account not only the committee's recommendation but also the availability of funds at that point in the current fiscal year. In FECOVESO's early years, final approval for both watershed acquisitions and community development projects was given by the

HCSC board; however, the current practice provides annual "block grants" from HCSC to FECOVESO. All decisions determining how to allocate funds *within* Honduras are made by FECOVESO's board.

In supporting more expensive projects — such as those involving the purchase of larger parcels of land — FECOVESO has sometimes been able to partner with other institutions to put together the necessary funding. Most notably, it has been possible to leverage support for several projects from the *Municipalidad de Omoa*, which is the equivalent of a county government in the USA in its geographical extent and political function. Included within the jurisdiction of the *Municipalidad de Omoa* are most of the communities served by FECOVESO.

THE FUTURE OF FECOVESO

FECOVESO has come of age as an accomplished and sustainable organization. It has a strong track record and the respect of other institutions in Honduras. It is staffed, administered, and governed by Hondurans, who run the organization without the on-site presence of Nola White, who is now 82 years old and has begun cutting back on the three-to-four months of every year that she used to spend in Honduras.

Financially, however, FECOVESO still relies on HCSC, its organizational partner in the United States, for most of the funding that is needed to continue the current level of activity in Honduras. HCSC is staffed entirely with volunteers and has almost no administrative overhead, so nearly every dollar that is raised goes directly to support the projects and operations of FECOVESO (*http://www.hcsc-honduras.org*).

Fig. 13.3. FECOVESO board of directors, Honduras, 2019.

14.

Seeding the CLT in Africa
Lessons from the Early Efforts to Establish
Community Land Trusts in Kenya

Claire Simonneau and Ellen Bassett,
with Emmanuel Midheme

Informal settlements remain one of the biggest challenges in urban Africa. These are under-serviced settlements that have developed through the unauthorized occupation of land (Huchzermeyer and Karam, 2006: 3).[1] Kenyan cities are no exception in this regard, since more than 50% of the urban population lives in such settlements (Syagga, 2011). Nairobi's informal settlements are renowned worldwide for their scale, density, and extremely poor living conditions relative to housing quality and access to water, electricity, sewerage, and solid waste disposal.[2]

Like most former colonies, Kenya inherited its land and planning laws from Europe — Great Britain in this case. It is a centralized system, initially serving the colonial project to conquer territories at the expense of indigenous people, which has enabled a deep-rooted patron-client relationship among the land administration and widespread corruption in the distribution of land to elites (Bassett, 2017). Such a legal framework has revealed itself to be incapable of dealing with the rapid urban growth that has been happening in Kenya since the 1960s. Public and private mechanisms for land and housing delivery have offered very limited supply and/or were inaccessible to the majority of urban dwellers.

As a result, informal settlements have become the only viable means for accessing land for housing for the urban majority (Durand-Lasserve, 1988; Gulyani and Bassett, 2007; Midheme, 2015). Diverse policies have been implemented to deal with this form of urbanization since the 1950s, with the substantial — although uneven — support of international development agencies.[3]

The Tanzania-Bondeni Community Land Trust emerged in 1994 as a reaction to these policy responses — and their failures. This experiment was deemed successful during its first decade.[4] The CLT still exists, but is far less renowned today. No other CLTs have been established in Kenya, nor in any other country on the African continent. One of the questions we will attempt to answer in this chapter, therefore, is what can be learned from the Tanzania-Bondeni experiment that might shed light on why CLT development has stalled in Kenya and in Africa in general.

We will examine the Tanzania-Bondeni Community Land Trust from several perspectives.[5] This chapter starts with a historical overview of governmental policy regarding the country's informal settlements. We will then describe the Tanzania-Bondeni CLT today, exploring its achievements and current challenges. In the final section, we will discuss the notion of community and its sustainability over time.

I. POLICY RESPONSES TO INFORMAL SETTLEMENTS IN KENYA

A brief historical overview of policy responses since the country's independence from Great Britain in 1963 provides a useful context for comprehending the emergence of the Tanzania-Bondeni Community Land Trust in Voi. These governmental responses fall into four periods, which reflect both national and international thinking regarding informal settlements, slum upgrading, and land and housing policies (Gulyani and Bassett, 2007; Jenkins, Smith, and Wang, 2007; Kamunyori, 2016; Midheme, 2018).

During the decades of the 1950s and 1960s, informal settlements were mostly ignored by national and municipal officials who put their money and remedial efforts into building public housing. This line of action was supported by the belief that informal settlements would gradually disappear with economic growth and public housing policies. However, the delivery of public housing was never able to keep pace with continuing growth of the urban population.

Through the 1970s and early 1980s, it became evident that informal settlements were not an ephemeral phenomenon. The central government engaged in slum clearance (demolition), with the paradoxical effect that informal settlements got rebuilt in other parts of the city, just relocating the problem, not actually solving it. Following the World Bank strategy of that time, relocation programs were then implemented through site and services schemes[6] or through low-cost building. Nevertheless, these programs failed to reach their objectives. Land-market pressure, coupled with political patronage and corruption in plot allocation, resulted in "filtering up"; that is, initial beneficiaries of such programs were replaced by better-off households and original slum dwellers moved into newly created informal settlements — again.

Thus ensued the third policy response, based on the idea that informal settlements should be upgraded rather than eliminated. This intervention gradually gained momentum both in international thinking and within the Kenyan government. Upgrading programs took different forms and addressed diverse issues, including provision of basic services, land tenure regularization, and infrastructure improvement. These upgrading programs were better adapted to local realities, but a number of criticisms were leveled at them, highlighting three main inadequacies. First, Kenyan informal settlements are

> Restrictions on resale in upgrad-
> ing programs were revealed to
> be both costly to implement
> and easy to circumvent.

characterized by a high proportion of tenants, a population that has rarely been taken
into consideration in upgrading programs.
Here is highlighted a particular feature of the
Kenyan land system: upon independence in
1963, Kenya embraced both capitalism and
private property and enacted policies to change customary tenures to leasehold or freehold, particularly in peri-urban areas. By contrast, in many other African countries land
access continued to be determined by customary systems of land tenure.[7] In Kenya, however, land has a market value. This is especially true in Nairobi where the land and buildings in informal settlements are characterized by a very high commercial value and there
exists a vibrant rental market (Kamunyori, 2016).

A second criticism of upgrading programs was the turnover in beneficiaries, who resold
lands and homes to which they had been granted title, either due to market pressures (voluntary or distress sales) or to reap a speculative windfall. This remained a conundrum.
Restrictions on resale that were imposed in upgrading programs were revealed to be both
costly to implement and easy to circumvent. Consequently, informal sales continued to
take place, creating a growing gap between official registration and actual landowners as
recognized on the ground. Third, there was poor involvement of targeted communities in
the design and implementation of upgrading programs, ignoring a potential resource that
might have enhanced the programs' efficiency.

The idea of a community land trust (CLT) was introduced in Kenya in the early
1990s, representing a fourth policy response to the problem of informal settlements. The
CLT was touted as a credible answer to the recurrent problems encountered in upgrading programs. The CLT model, as developed and applied in the USA, had two advantages over the way that upgrading had previously been done. First, the CLT had been
designed as an anti-speculation tool for reducing gentrification. Ownership of land and
ownership of structural improvements are separated. Land is held in trust in perpetuity
and not subject to speculation. Land-value appreciation is "locked" in the community,
while long-term land use rights are provided to individuals or households on a leasehold
basis. Second, the CLT model was considered a powerful vehicle for community empowerment, through community control of the land and community-based management of
the neighborhood. In this regard, it offered an interesting way to better involve dwellers
in upgrading programs, thus ensuring short-term upgrading achievement and long-term
community development.

These advantages attracted the attention of Kenya's Ministry for Local Government.
They also attracted interest and support from the German governmental organization for
technical cooperation (GTZ),[8] municipal officials of Voi town, and residents of an informal settlement in Voi named "Tanzania-Bondeni." This led eventually to the creation of
Africa's first and only CLT in the 1990s.

II. EARLY HISTORY OF THE TANZANIA-BONDENI CLT

Tanzania-Bondeni is an informal settlement located in Voi, a secondary town in Taita-Taveta County. The town had a population 13,000 inhabitants in 1989. Tanzania-Bondeni is located approximately 1.5 km from the city center and covers approximately 22 hectares (see Figure 14.1 below).

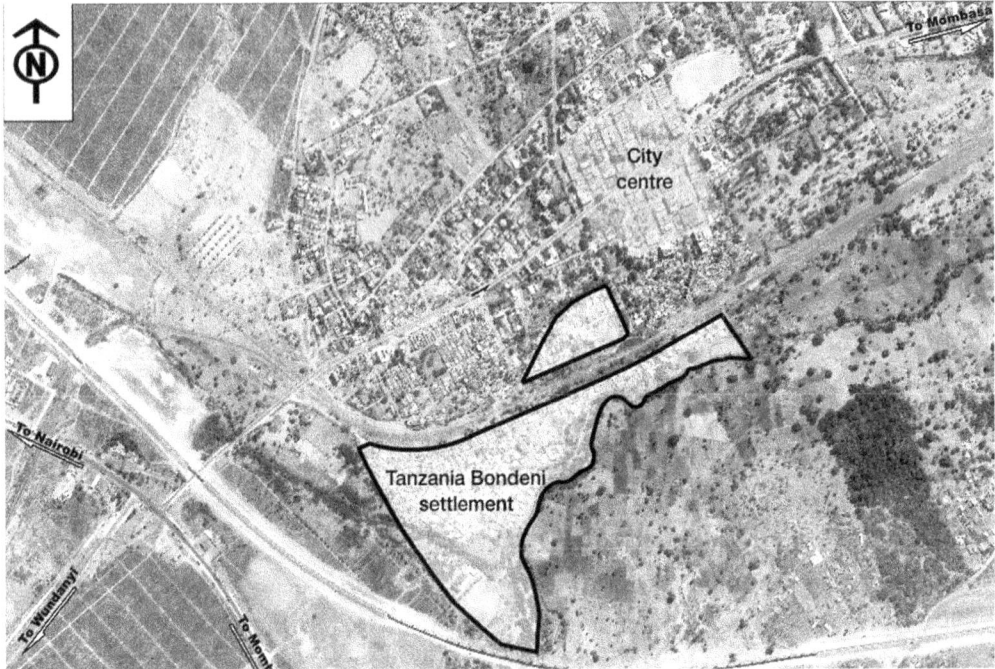

Fig. 14.1. Location of the informal settlement of Tanzania-Bondeni. Map scale: 1:10,000.
© SEVERIANO ODHIAMBO, MODIFIED BY CLAIRE SIMONNEAU

Nearly 3000 inhabitants were living in this informal settlement in 1990. Income levels were very low, with 70% of the inhabitants unemployed or earning less than $8 US a month. The community was quite heterogeneous in terms of ethnic background. The settlement had resulted from unauthorized occupation of public land — more precisely, land owned by Kenya Railways and Voi Sisal Estates, a large plantation growing sisal for industrial production (Bassett, 2001; Midheme and Moulaert, 2013). The condition of the settlement's housing was precarious. More than 60% of the houses were built with temporary materials like mud walls and thatch roofs. The settlement's other houses were made of semi-temporary materials — namely *but mabati* (corrugated iron) roofs and concrete floors.

Against this background, the Tanzania-Bondeni settlement was selected as a beneficiary of the Small Towns Development Project (STDP), an urban development program funded by the German government through GTZ. In its work in Voi, STDP had a tripartite steering committee composed of representatives from the Ministry for Local Government, the local authority of Voi town, and GTZ.

STDP clearly intended to innovate in the field of slum upgrading. After taking stock of the limits of previous approaches to squatter settlement, the project's managers gave careful attention to questions of land security and protections against eviction, including eviction by market forces. The project also benefited from reflections on innovative strategies for upgrading informal settlements that were conducted in the early 1990s by local, national, and international stakeholders. Several initiatives are worth mentioning.

In 1991, a national forum on alternative land tenure models in Kenya took place in Nairobi. It was held at the initiative of the Mazingira Institute, in conjunction with the Ford Foundation. The experience of CLTs in the United States was then presented. At the same time, a study was commissioned by the Ford Foundation to examine the potential for transferring the American CLT model to Kenya. Two American consultants, Chuck Matthei and Russell Hahn, were hired by Ford to conduct this study. They concluded, in light of the high housing demand and the prevalence of absentee ownership in low-income communities, that CLTs seemed relevant to Africa on the social and cultural level and could help in providing affordable housing in informal settlements (Matthei and Hahn, 1991). Over the next two years, an NGO called Kitua Cha Sheria (Legal Advice Center) engaged in the process of creating a CLT in a squatter settlement in Nairobi, based on the strategy of purchasing land on the market. The project was eventually abandoned, due to the excessive cost of acquiring land (Jaffer, 2000). In 1992, however, inspired by these previous events, STDP's program managers and the Project's national steering committee began considering the possibility of establishing a CLT in two other settlements that had been selected for upgrading: Mtaani-Kisumu Ndogo in Kilifi town and Tanzania-Bondeni in Voi town.

The upgrading sponsored by the Small Towns Development Project was meant to be participatory. It operated within a series of guidelines aimed at ensuring durable results and local ownership of the project. These guidelines called for gradual and systematic improvement of the neighborhood and full involvement of local communities in the planning and execution of the project. External actions and actors were meant to support local efforts, not replace them (Jaffer, 2000).

The land tenure option, in particular, was to be chosen by the community itself. A series of activities with the residents prepared for this vote, including preliminary community mobilization and the election of residents committees. In November 1992, a last discussion was held among planners of the Ministry and the STDP, the Voi municipal council, and members of the residents committees around three options for holding land in the informal settlements in Kilifi town and in Voi town: individual leasehold titles; individual titles coupled with housing cooperatives; or a group leasehold coupled with a community land trust. The resident committees in both towns held six community meetings dedicated to choosing among the three options. Attention was paid to helping residents fully understand all three options. STDP observers attended the meetings in order to ensure that only *bona fide* structure owners were allowed to vote and that both advantages and drawbacks of each option were thoroughly explained.[9]

The residents of Kilifi voted for individual titles. In Voi, however, over 90% of the structure owners finally opted for the CLT option. Jaffer (1996) documented the "push from below" in favor of the CLT option, which he observed in Voi. From the outset of the project, the Voi community demonstrated a great capacity for mobilization. The Voi resident committee, led by older long-term residents (*wazee* — elders), was fully informed of slum upgrading issues, including land issues. Local interest in the CLT also reflected a serious threat felt by the residents: land grabbing by outsiders — a phenomenon that had begun to occur in the neighborhood at the beginning of the upgrading project.[10] Residents were also attracted to the CLT option by: (1) the social security offered by community tenure and its protection against eviction by the market; (2) the possibility of keeping individual land rights within a community land tenure framework; and (3) the promise of having facilitated access to collective loans.

The decision was definitely related to the socio-economic situation of the Tanzania-Bondeni community. From interviews later conducted by Bassett (2001) and Midheme and Moulaert (2013), it can be seen that residents feared they would be unable to retain their land individually due to economic poverty and their lack of political power and patronage networks.[11] In other words, they felt they were too poor to pay for the costs associated with individual leaseholds (notably property taxes), and would be powerless to prevent "cashing out" behaviors within the community or by their own family. The Tanzania-Bondeni community also included numerous female-headed households. These women were attracted to the community control offered by CLT, since they considered it to be a way of protecting them from pressures within the family to sell the land (Bassett and Jacobs, 1997: 225).

GTZ and other institutional stakeholders such as the central and communal governments had their own reasons for promoting the CLT model: the avoidance of the "windfall effect" of upgrading projects; the prospect of community organization for other development partnerships; the prospect of extending financial sources, including property taxes; the upgrading of the slum; and the prevention of further squatting (Bassett and Jacobs, 1997). The decision of the Voi community was somewhat surprising for the central government and for STDP's project managers, however, given the overall preference for individual property in Kenya (Bassett, 2001: 164).

A. Complex Process of CLT Formalization

Once the CLT model had been chosen, its translation into Kenyan terms faced serious challenges. Four main legal issues emerged. To begin with, at that time Kenyan land law favored individual landholding. Communal landholding such as Group Ranches were reserved for specific regions in the country. Moreover, the legal form of the land trust was problematic, since incorporation in Kenya provided only for profit-making entities.

Lastly, the "rule against perpetuities" that exists in Kenyan law prevented anyone from holding the land outside of the market permanently, whereas this is one key objective of the CLT.

Lawyers had to find an innovative arrangement to overcome these obstacles. Two legal bodies were created in 1994: (1) a Settlement Society, registered under the Societies Act, representing the residents; and (2) a trust, registered under the Trustees (Perpetual Succession) Act, holding the land head-lease and administrating the land in conjunction with the Society, including decisions on land uses, alienation, and purchase of land. Through this latter body, the community applied for a head-lease; the CLT in turn was supposed to issue subleases to households (Bassett and Jacobs, 1997; Midheme and Moulaert, 2013).

The governance of the Tanzania-Bondeni Community Land Trust was structured around two main bodies: a Board of Trustees (9 members) that was to hold the head-lease and to grant subleases; and a Residents Committee (30 members) that was to run the daily affairs of the Settlement Society. An annual general meeting was the supreme body that approved audited accounts. Members were to pay annual fees to finance the recurrent spending of the Trust. In addition, four housing cooperatives were created at that time.

The Tanzania-Bondeni CLT in Voi also adopted conventional rules that were common in American CLTs such as preemptive rights of purchase by the CLT when a member leaves, and a restriction on absentee landlordism. Efforts were also made to accommodate the low-income situation of the residents: payments for collective services could be staggered; a local development fund was put in place to conduct local development projects; and, most importantly, the local government was persuaded to recognize existing dwellings within the settlement, even if they did not conform to existing building standards.[12]

B. Short-term Positive Impacts on the Whole Settlement

The creation of the CLT, along with additional interventions funded by STDP, had significant positive impacts in the short run. To begin with, the settlement benefited from physical planning that provided space for residential and commercial development, and also for community facilities.[13] This plan was developed with extensive input from the community and was rapidly implemented on the ground: houses were relocated, roads built, and infrastructure installed. Bassett and Jacobs (1997) also noticed that residents soon started to build with more durable materials or to plant long-term crops such as fruit trees even before the head-lease had been issued, revealing their confidence and their newfound feeling of land tenure security.

Besides, the CLT has facilitated the residents' systematic access to housing finance, notably through the four housing cooperatives that allowed access to funds from the National Cooperative Housing Union.

Community participation, a basis of the STDP project and the CLT's governance, should also be considered a positive impact on the community. An interesting feature of the Voi CLT lies in the fact that both landlords and tenants are involved as full members of the CLT — whereas tenants are often left out or pushed aside in upgrading projects.

Last but not least, the CLT has fostered the growth of what Midheme (2013: 80) has described as "a vibrant community premised on the principles of democracy, inclusiveness and horizontality." He went on to say that the Tanzania-Bondeni CLT has been successful in promoting:

> Solidarity — those symbiotic relations of trust, reciprocity and mutual obligation among neighbours that are so essential for community life — as a basic ingredient of the CLT. … In Voi, communal landholding under the CLT has offered more than just a model of land tenure; the CLT has provided the basis for residents to unite under a one-for-all, all-for-one philosophy designed to prop up each other in times of adversity.

III. THE TANZANIA–BONDENI CLT TODAY

More than twenty-five years have passed since the creation of the Tanzania-Bondeni CLT. What is the current state of the community land trust, as a neighborhood and as a community organisation?[14]

Today, the Tanzania-Bondeni settlement is a well-planned neighborhood, one that has greatly benefited from the Small Towns Development Project. The planning provisions made at the beginning of the project have been largely maintained. The physical planning undertaken in the 1990s is still visible today: the overall layout is respected and plots reserved for public utilities are respected. Although some of the plots are not yet developed and limited encroachments can be observed on areas set aside for public circulation or public utilities, a great majority of the allocated plots have been developed and the houses that were built on them are inhabited.[15]

The neighborhood still benefits from infrastructure facilities installed in the 1990s, including water, roads, and electricity. These improvements have been maintained, even upgraded. For example, the nursery school that was installed at the time of the STDP has been converted to a primary school. On the other hand, one can identify some shortcomings regarding the physical planning and regulations. The sanitation plan that was prepared at the time of the original project has not yet been implemented.

The CLT and the surrounding project have also facilitated the gradual improvement of the settlement's housing through several means. First, the local municipal government was persuaded to recognize existing dwellings on an "as-is" basis; at the same time, dwellers were required to improve their houses over a period of time to meet official building standards. Second, the CLT was accompanied by the formation of housing cooperatives, an organizational scheme that was necessary to draw public funds — especially from the National Cooperative Housing Union. As a result, the settlement has today mainly permanent structures, whereas 62% of the houses were classified as temporary structures in

Fig. 14.2. Tanzania-Bondeni. Improvement of dwellings (left) and elementary school (right).
CLAIRE SIMONNEAU

1991. A small percentage of the buildings are even multi-level dwellings.[16] However, one can still discover mud houses dispersed throughout the neighborhood, estimated at 20% of the total structures in Tanzania-Bondeni (Midheme, 2013).

A. Secured Tenure for Low-income Residents

The population in Tanzania-Bondeni is still primarily low-income. Residents use their plots and houses as their main residence and often as a place of livelihood and production as well. Importantly, absentee ownership—a threat even in a secondary town—has been avoided. As such, one can suggest that the CLT has succeeded in providing land tenure security to low-income residents over the long term.

Data from the field gathered by Midheme (2018) indicate that the average income of the majority of the population ranges from $3 to $5 per day. Additionally, 72% of the households reported that they do not own any other property outside of the settlement. The respondents who do own a property outside of the settlement are actually renters and come from outside of Voi, in other parts of the country. The survey also found out that more than 46% of the households have lived in the settlement for over 10 years.

However, the CLT has never received the head-lease for the land (only a letter of allotment) and only beacon certificates have been delivered to individual households. As a result, a lower level of legal tenure security has been ensured than would have been provided by the subleases that were initially planned.[17]

Despite that, the CLT has been effective in improving and securing land tenure for a low-income urban settlement and has restrained gentrification and mass displacement, which have happened so often in other informal settlements during the course of upgrading programmes or upon their completion.

B. Faltering Governance Structures and Unenforced Rules

The picture is less encouraging when it comes to the CLT's governance. The CLT governance mainly rests on two bodies: (1) the Tanzania-Bondeni Settlement Society, which includes all residents (tenants and structure owners) and is supposed to meet every year through an annual general meeting (AGM), and (2) a residents committee in charge of the daily affairs of the CLT, elected every two years during the AGM. Yet there has been a radical disconnection between the two bodies during the last decades, and poor implementation of the CLT's key principles.

Many key rules of the CLT are not followed anymore. In this regard, fieldwork conducted by Emmanuel Midheme, Severiano Odhiambo, Sharlet Mkabili, and Claire Simonneau in 2018 confirmed several trends that had been identified by Bassett (2005) nine years before. For example, absentee ownership is supposed to be banned within the settlement, responding to a key concern of the settlement's residents at the creation of the CLT. However, many multi-storey buildings containing rental apartments are owned by persons who are not living in Tanzania-Bondeni.

Another core commitment of the CLT model is also not being respected, namely the ban on selling land to people outside of the community. This rule is instrumental for preventing gentrification as it ensures that land is locked within the community. Residents report many land sales, however. They are called land "transfers,"[18] but a survey of residents revealed that substantial amounts of money have changed hands for these "transfers."

These violations of the CLT's founding purposes and rules are directly linked to the governance environment. First, since no sublease contractually spells out these rules, the committee has no hook to enforce them. Second, and maybe more alarming, the democratic system of the CLT seems to have collapsed.

The annual general meeting has not been held for more than 15 years. The last AGM was held in 2002, an election that had to be forced by the municipal administration. This gives a idea of the poor democratic dynamics that have characterized the community for quite a long time now. Furthermore, leaders of the residents committee (RC) are

Fig. 14.3. Tanzania-Bondeni. Multi-storey residential building. CLAIRE SIMONNEAU

perceived by the residents to be corrupt and to run the affairs of the community in their own private interest. Residents seem extremely suspicious towards their leaders, as suggested in this quotation from a resident: "Leaders are selling our lands. Leaders are selfish. Leaders are corrupt." Beacon certificates of questionable legality, signed by the RC's leaders, have been observed in the field. Also, the Tanzania-Bondeni settlement office that lies in the middle of the settlement has been deserted by the community leaders, so that there is absolutely no contact between the residents and their (so-called) representatives.

C. Community Involvement Needs to be Revived

The failure of the CLT's governance structures has contributed to a dismantling of the whole community. There are no meetings, no financial contribution to the local saving groups, a weak mobilization, and a general feeling of distrust within the community. "The CLT is good, but we have corrupt management and docile membership," says a resident. Many residents talk about the "death of the community." More than half of the residents of Tanzania-Bondeni are not members of the CLT (53%), and are not even aware of the CLT's existence.[19] They are mostly renters who settled in the neighborhood quite recently, since many owners of structures circumvent the ban on renting their houses. Thus, the CLT seems trapped in a vicious circle of land "sales" and an informal market for rental housing that fosters distrust towards leaders and fellow members of the neighborhood, even as new residents are coming into the settlement who are not aware of the CLT.

Nevertheless, there is currently a youth group that is trying to bring new life and direction to the community. This group is tracking evidence of corruption and is endeavoring to bring legal action and is pressuring to organize new elections. A local WhatsApp group has been created to foster community mobilization and to disseminate information on the mismanagement of the settlement and to discuss possible alternatives. In February 2016, the CLT office was covered with graffiti demanding elections. More recently, the youth group sent a letter to the county council and anti-corruption agency to inform them about the situation in Tanzania-Bondeni.

In sum, the Tanzania-Bondeni community and its structure of governance have been weakening over the last decade, but some recent initiatives might break the vicious circle of mismanagement and the lessening of internal cohesion and community spirit.

IV. HOW TO SUSTAIN A COMMUNITY?
LESSONS OF THE VOI CASE

The fundamental issues in Voi with regard to the current state of the Tanzania-Bondeni CLT seem to involve a lack of community spirit and a flawed structure of governance. These are challenging issues that should not be overlooked in creating a CLT.

The discussion of community organizing in Sub-Saharan Africa often revolves around the notions of ethnicity and customs — especially when it comes to land. Natural or traditional communities are based on ethnic groups and often a religious notion of the territory (such as animist or Islamic). This notion is opposed to contractual or intentional communities, which derive from discrete decisions to cooperate and to manage common resources via intentionally created institutions.

On the one hand, traditional communities based on ethnicity are still a frame of reference in politics and social relationships in Kenya and generally in Sub-Saharan Africa. Traditional landholding is based on the following principles: land is considered a sacred good, and thus is strictly unalienable and off-limits to the market logic; it is managed at a community level and people have use rights on it, not property rights. Such African traditional communal landholdings still exist, albeit with some evolution, in rural areas, and were even one source of inspiration for the first CLTs (Davis, 2010; Simonneau, 2018). Nevertheless, this framework has little relevance within the Tanzania-Bondeni community.

On the other hand, experiments with other forms of collective land holding in Kenya offer a different perspective on community building. Several legal provisions allow for collective landholding in urban Kenyan: housing cooperatives, land-buying companies, and savings-and-credit cooperatives. They are used for the sole purpose of accessing land for housing. What often happens is that the group is very active during the process of accessing the land (gathering money for buying the land jointly in the case of land buying companies for example), but as soon as the land is obtained and divided among the members, the group disbands. In other words, the organization is not an end in itself, but a means to access land in a cheaper and easier way than through formal individual landholding, which is a very long and expensive process.

Is this what happened in Voi? Probably not. The history of the Tanzania-Bondeni shows a more complex process. First, it was not based on customs or ethnicity. The Tanzania-Bondeni community was born quite naturally: people often settled there because they knew someone in the settlement. Besides, they were assigned a piece of land by a local chief. In this sense, there were *de facto* community land rules. It was a community in the full sense of the term: the settlement had been built largely through self-help; people knew each other, were aware of each other's activities and families, and had concern for each other (Bassett, 2001). The group was quite homogenous in terms of their socioeconomic situation, and there was not much ethnic heterogeneity.

Second, land insecurity made the settlement unify and become intentional at the beginning of the upgrading project. Residents realized that if they wanted to preserve the assets they already had (especially their access to land) the best method was to stay together.[20]

Third, the upgrading project fostered a modicum of community organisation and catalyzed energy in the intervening years. The project was also able to generate a large amount of positive political attention from the local to the national level and even at the international level.[21]

Nevertheless, support for the CLT was temporary. By the end of the 1990s, internal problems at the CLT had reached the ear of the local administration and had started to weaken political support for the CLT. Up until 2016, moreover, the legal and political environment in Kenya for communal landholding was clearly hostile. The recent Community Land Act theoretically offers new opportunities, but with no certainty regarding real change on the ground (Alden Wily, 2018; Bassett, 2019). This context of legal and political hostility towards communal landholding, combined with mismanagement problems, have made the CLT model less attractive for newcomers to the Tanzania-Bondeni community today.

⁓

V. CONCLUSION:
PROSPECTS FOR CLT DEVELOPMENT IN KENYA AND IN AFRICA

Having access to land is extremely important, since ownership builds pride and is directly connected to the sense of belonging. In Kenya and in Africa in general, the dismantling of traditional and customary institutions in the contemporary era has not eradicated the social signification of land possession. Africans still speak of being "sons of the soil."

Given the legal and political context in Kenyan, it would seem that this fundamental aspiration to participate in ownership of a piece of land is destined to be fulfilled by means of the formal or informal land market and by individual ownership. The CLT experiment in Voi has not been able to create a successful counter-example, which might serve as a compelling alternative to that of individual ownership.

From this perspective, it seems that further CLT development in Kenya and Africa would require a genuine *movement*. What is needed for a CLT movement, according to DeFilippis, Stromberg, and Williams (2018), is a strong process of community organization and empowerment. It cannot emerge if a CLT is considered solely a strategy for land access. Second, what is needed is political support that can be translated into favorable legal protections. Lastly, what has been missing in Africa is continued and targeted technical support for CLT development, which is often underestimated in upgrading projects.[22] Such support must be able to deal with the complexities of national juridical systems and also to organize national and cross-national exchanges of experience and knowledge. A substantial CLT movement might then arise in Africa and be able to influence the political economy regarding land and housing. It might then be able to exert weight in the power relations between actors of land and housing sectors, tipping the scales in a more equitable direction (DeFilippis et al., 2018).

Notes

1. We follow the definition of informal settlements elaborated by Huchzermeyer and Karam (2006: 3): "settlements of the urban poor that have developed through unauthorised occupation of land. Tenure insecurity is the central characteristic of informal settlements, with varying attributes of unhealthy and hazardous living conditions to which overcrowding, and lack of basic services may contribute."

2. Nairobi is also characterized by absentee landlords and a level of tenancy exceeding 90% (Amis, 1984; Gulyani, Bassett, and Talukdar, 2018). In other cities of the country, land squatting and a family's ownership of the building it occupies are very common.

3. An international influence that is reinforced by the presence of the headquarters of UN-Habitat (the United Nations Human Settlements Programme) in Nairobi.

4. For instance, it was selected as one of the Kenyan "Best Practices" for the 1996 UN-Habitat conference in Istanbul.

5. This essay is based on in-depth research of the Voi CLT conducted successively by Ellen Bassett and Emmanuel Midheme for their respective doctoral dissertations and by further research. Recent fieldwork was also conducted in 2018 by Emmanuel Midheme, assisted by Severiano Odhiambo and Sharlet Mkabili (Maseno University), with the participation of Claire Simonneau. For this fieldwork, we recognize and thank the financial support of the French Development Agency, which supports a research program in land-based urban commons for housing in the Global South (*https://cfuhabitat. hypotheses.org*). This work has also benefited from a fruitful exchange with the editors of the present volume.

6. Households were allocated a plot in a serviced area and were responsible for building their dwelling.

7. Even if not officially provided by the law. In Kenya in the 1990s, customary occupancy of land was quite secure since access to land was determined by the group, not necessarily by the government. Customary tenures are mostly large rural tenures. In contrast, informal settlement tenures are urban, in areas of active land markets. Customary tenure has been protected in Kenya's new constitution (2010).

8. GTZ means *Gesellschaft für Technische Zusammenarbeit,* the Agency for Technical Cooperation. GTZ is now GIZ *(Gesellschaft für Internationale Zusammenarbeit),* the Agency for International Cooperation.

9. The steps that were taken before the final vote on the land tenure option were documented by Bassett (2001: 164).

10. This was happening despite the fact that land in the Tanzania-Bondeni settlement had little market value compared to land in bigger cities.

11. Residents used two aphorisms in Swahili to express this idea: *Umoja ni nguvu* (unity is strengthen) and *Kidole kimoja hakifanyi kitu chochote* (one finger can't do anything).

12. The owners were required, however, to gradually improve their houses to conform to municipal building standards.

13. There were 818 plots, far beyond the number claimed by original structure owners.

14. This section is largely based on fieldwork conducted by Emmanuel Midheme in June 2018, and a conference given in September 2018 in Paris. Both are part of the research program on land-based commons for housing.

15. 93% according to fieldwork done in 2018.

16. 1.6% of the whole settlement; up to 8% in some specific areas (2018 fieldwork).

17. A beacon certificate is an indicator for a parcel's holder that s/he has a right to build and to stay on the parcel within the CLT. Head-leases are issued by the Ministry of Land.

18. Land transfers to relatives are allowed according to the CLT's rules.

19. Bassett (2005) previously documented this ignorance of the CLT, based on interviews dating from 1999.

20. An additional dimension relative to Voi was the age of the leadership in the RC. The Voi RC was led by older long-term residents of the community. A few of them had actually been freedom fighters. They remembered the fight for independence as a fight for land. The concept of Harambee really resonated with them; there was something of an age split on the decision, with the younger people wanting individual leaseholds. There was a high level of respect for the *wazee* (old people) in Voi.

21. The Voi Settlement Upgrading Project was selected as one of Kenya's "Best Practices" for the 1997 Istanbul Habitat II Conference. At Habitat II, the project was designated as one of the 100 best practices globally.

22. Technical support in the USA, during the early years of the American CLT movement, was provided by the Institute for Community Economics, an organization led by Chuck Matthei in 1991 when he and Russ Hahn were asked by the Ford Foundation to study whether the CLT model might be applied in Kenya.

References

Alden Wily, L. The Community Land Act in Kenya Opportunities and Challenges for Communities. *Land,* 7 (12) (2018).

Amis, P. Squatters or Tenants: The Commercialization of Unauthorized Housing in Nairobi. *World Development,* 12 (1), 87–96 (1984).

Bassett, E. M. *Institutions and Informal Settlements: The Planning Implications of the Community Land Trust Experiment in Kenya.* (Department of Urban and Regional Planning), University of Wisconsin–Madison (2001).

Bassett, E. M. Tinkering with tenure: the community land trust experiment in Voi, Kenya. *Habitat International,* 29 (3), 375–398 (2005).

Bassett, E. M. The challenge of reforming land governance in Kenya under the 2010 Constitution, *Journal of Modern African Studies,* 55 (4), 537–566 (2017).

Bassett, E. M. Reform and resistance: The political economy of land and planning reform in Kenya. *Urban Studies,* 1–20 (2019).

Bassett, E. M., and Jacobs, H. M. Community-based tenure reform in urban Africa: the community land trust experiment in Voi, Kenya. *Land Use Policy,* 14 (3), 215–229 (1997).

Davis, J. E. Origins and evolution of the community land trust in the United States. In J. E. Davis (Ed.), *The Comunity Land Trust Reader.* (Cambridge: Lincoln Institute of Land Policy, 2010).

DeFilippis, J., Stromberg, B., and Williams, O. R. W(h)ither the community in community land trusts? *Journal of urban affairs,* 40 (6), 755–769 (2018).

Durand-Lasserve, A. Le logement des pauvres dans les villes du Tiers Monde. Crise actuelle et réponses. *Revue Tiers Monde,* 29 (116), 1195–1214 (1988).

Gulyani, S., and Bassett, E. M. Retrieving the baby from the bathwater: slum upgrading in Sub-Saharan Africa. *Environment and Planning C: Government and Policy,* 25, 486–515 (2007).

Gulyani, S., Talukdar, D., and Kack, D. *Poverty, living conditions, and infrastructure access: a comparison of slums in Dakar, Johannesburg, and Nairobi.* (Washington DC: World Bank, 2010).

Huchzermeyer, M., and Karam, A. The continuing challenge of informal settlements: an introduction. In M. Huchzermeyer & A. Karam (Eds.), *Informal Settlements: a Perpetual Challenge?* (Cape Town: UCT Press, 2006).

Jaffer, M. The Tanzania-Bondeni Community Land Trust, Voi, Kenya (1996). Retrieved from *http://www.hic-gs.org/document.php?pid=2548*

Jaffer, M. Expanding equity by limiting equity. In *Property and Values: Alternatives to Public and Private Ownership* (pp. 175–188). (Washington D.C.: Island Press, 2000).

Jenkins, P., Smith, H., and Wang, Y. P. (Eds.). *Planning and Housing in a Rapidly Urbanising World* (New York: Routledge, 2007).

Kamunyori, S. W. *The Politics of Space: Negotiating Tenure Security in a Nairobi Slum.* London School of Economics (2016).

Matthei, C., and Hahn, R. *Community Land Trusts and the Delivery of Affordable Shelter to the Urban Poor in Kenya* (1991).

Midheme, E. *Modalities of Space Production within Kenya's Rapidly Transforming Cities: Cases from Voi and Kisumu.* (PhD Dissertation), KU Leuven (2015).

Midheme, E. *Do urban land commons foster urban inclusion? Kenya case study. Report on the methodological framework* (2018).

Midheme, E., and Moulaert, F. Pushing back the frontiers of property: Community land trusts and low-income housing in urban Kenya. *Land Use Policy,* 35, 73–84 (2013).

Simonneau, C. Le Community Land Trust aux États-Unis, au Kenya et en Belgique. Canaux de circulation d'un modèle alternatif et jeu d'intertextualité. *RIURBA Revue internationale d'urbanisme,* 6, (2018).

Syagga, P. Land tenure in slum upgrading projects. *Les cahiers d'Afrique de l'Est, IFRA Nairobi,* 103–113 (2011).

15.

The Origins and Evolution of the CLT Model in South Asia

Hannah Sholder and Arif Hasan

The South Asian subcontinent has a long history of community-based landholding and community-led housing development.[1] The subcontinent also has a direct link with the evolution of the "modern" community land trust (CLT) model in the United States, given that one of its pioneers, Ralph Borsodi, was inspired by the land ownership restructuring work of India's Vinoba Bhave.[2] Bhave, who was one of Mohandas (Mahatma) Gandhi's devoted followers, spearheaded the *Bhoodan Yajna* and *Gramdan Yajna*, or land gift and village gift, movements after India gained independence from Britain in 1947.

In this chapter, the *Bhoodan* and *Gramdan* movements will be reviewed, given their historical significance for the CLT model, and their relevance as a regional precedent to current land reallocation efforts in the subcontinent. This will be followed by an overview of one of the most prominent contemporary examples of community-led development in the region, which is facilitated by the Orangi Pilot Project (OPP) in Pakistan. In the case of the OPP, while the land ownership system in which they operate does not fit the classic CLT model, their programs reflect the CLT's governance and development aspirations—led by and for the people. The OPP's programs also adapt the CLT model's housing development component, both financially and structurally, to the context of informal settlements, which is critical if the model is to flourish across the Global South.

Drawing on lessons from both the *Gramdan* movement and OPP's programs, the chapter will conclude with a look at one of the most recent efforts in the subcontinent to adapt the CLT model for tenure regularization and housing upgradation in Bangladesh's "Bihari Camps."[3] The long-term residents of these camps are seeking a permanent solution to their tenure insecurity and inhumane living conditions. They are also coming to recognize, after nearly 50 years of inaction in terms of comprehensive redevelopment by the local government and foreign donors, that no one will do this work for their benefit but themselves. Given the value of the camp lands, particularly in the increasingly overcrowded capital city of Dhaka, the residents are now facing the risk of displacement, and are thus primed to consider options such as the CLT that have the potential to protect and keep their community together.

COMMUNITY-OWNED LAND: THE EARLY INFLUENCE OF *BHOODAN YAJNA* AND *GRAMDAN YAJNA* ON THE CLT MOVEMENT

The modern CLT has its roots in the Indian *Bhoodan* and *Gramdan* movements, due in part to Ralph Borsodi's exposure to the *Gramdan* movement in India during its height in the 1960s. Starting back in the 1920s and 1930s, though, both Borsodi and Gandhi (Vinoba Bhave's predecessor) both began to experiment with alternative, community-centered lifestyles.

Borsodi and his family had left Depression-era New York City and moved to rural New York. The main impetus for their shift in lifestyle was their dislike of the increasing dependence, in urban areas, on big industry to meet one's daily needs, including shelter, clothing, and food. They opted to become "homesteaders"—building their own house and learning how to grow their own food and to make their own clothing (Borsodi, 1933; 2012). As a way to encourage others to follow suit, Ralph Borsodi founded The School of Living in 1934.

Around the same time, Mohandas Gandhi was beginning to think of such experiments as well, inspired in part by John Ruskin's *Unto This Last*, which he read while working as an attorney in South Africa. Upon his return to India in 1915, Gandhi began to carry out his visions of *Sarvodaya*, welfare of all, and *Gram Swaraj*, village self-rule, in which people would no longer be obligated to be "cogs in the machine" of industrialization. They would, instead, work together as part of self-sufficient communities. A bottleneck in the realization of *Sarvodaya* and *Gram Swaraj*, however, was that most land was owned by wealthy landowners, or *zamindars*.

In order to obtain and redistribute land for the actualization of *Sarvodaya* and *Gram Swaraj*, one of Gandhi's disciples, Vinoba Bhave, launched the land gift movement, *Bhoodan Yajna,* in 1951.[4] Coinciding with the launch of *Bhoodan Yajna,* Indian states had begun to abolish the *zamindar* land ownership system, in which wealthy individuals held large swaths of land and had many poorer individuals working their land. *Bhoodan Yajna* became one way that land was redistributed, along with new tenancy laws, registration drives, and landholding ceiling laws (Deininger, 2007).

As part of *Bhoodan Yajna,* Bhave began to travel around the Indian countryside, seeking voluntary donations of land, which were then redistributed to the landless, including former tenants of *zamindars*. However, many of these former tenant-farmers had a hard time maintaining their newly acquired land due to lack of access to credit and tools, compounded in some cases by discrimination resulting from the persistent social stigma associated with their often-times lower caste. Without larger support systems, these new small-scale farmers were vulnerable to eviction, either by physical force or by the forces of land speculation (Shepard, 2010).

Community leaders sought to address these problems through the formation of agricultural cooperatives for financial assistance, as well as through the reconfiguration of *Bhoodan Yajna* into the *Gramdan Yajna*, the village gift movement (Bhave, 1961; Shepard, 2010). The main difference between the two was that, in the village gift movement, land titles were collectively held by the Village Assembly, which was made up by all adult men and women of the village and governed by consensus. Among all the acreage contributed to the Assembly, 5% from each contributor was made available for occupancy and use by the landless; the remainder would continue to be cultivated by the original owner; but in both scenarios the actual land title would be vested in the Village Assembly. The land that was retained in use-right by the original owner was inheritable and transferable, but only within the village and only with permission of the Assembly (Dhadda, 2014).

> By 1970, over 160,000 "Trusteeships" had been established.

By 1970, over 160,000 "Trusteeships," as these communal land holdings were known in the Western world, had been established; over 4 million acres had been redistributed (Shepard, 2010). However, the movement lost traction by the mid-1970s, due to shifts in national economic policy and difficulties maintaining the Trusteeships because of a lack of funds. According to the Indian government, in 2004 only 0.7 million hectares (1.7 million acres) were still held by Village Assemblies and were largely relegated to the states of Bihar, Orissa, and Uttar Pradesh (Deininger, 2007).

Despite its decline in popularity, the *Gramdan Yajna* made a lasting impact worldwide through the growth of the CLT movement in the United States, which has now been adopted and adapted in many other regions globally. Ralph Borsodi had spent time in India tracking the land crusade of Vinoba Bhave, while on a teaching fellowship from 1961–1965. Before going to India, Borsodi had already begun to experiment with a self-sufficient lifestyle, similar to the style that Gandhi and his followers were promoting in India around the same time. But the village gift movement that Borsodi had observed in India got him thinking that what he had experimented with in rural New York could be replicated on a larger scale. In particular, he saw that land could be held in trust by the residents themselves, for the benefit of the entire community.

Inspired by *Gramdan Yajna*, Borsodi established the International Independence Institute (III) in 1967 in order to spread these new ideas of land ownership across the United States and in other parts of the world. Eventually, this organization morphed into the Institute for Community Economics and, later still, to the present-day Grounded Solutions Network, which supports CLTs across the United States. The first field director for III, Bob Swann, was directly involved in supporting the first CLT prototype, New Communities Inc., which arose in rural Georgia out of the civil rights struggle of the 1960s. In the context of the American South, civil rights leaders understood the positive impact that owning land could have on the lives of African-Americans, but they realized that:

1. Land ownership was oftentimes outside the economic reach of individuals;

2. Holding land in trust could potentially protect individuals better than private title (as experienced in the land loss that occurred in the post-Reconstruction South—similar to what happened initially with the *Bhoodan* land redistribution scheme); and

3. New landholding organizations would need the support of the wider community in order to ensure their success.

These realizations eventually gave shape to the modern CLT with its tripartite board governance system. While New Communities Inc. experienced tumultuous times as a landholding organization due to persistent discrimination, it helped give birth to a movement that continues to grow across the United States and elsewhere. Over time, as the movement spread to urban areas, the focus of many CLTs turned to the production of permanently affordable housing in addition to underpinning the ownership and stewardship of land for the common good.

COMMUNITY-LED HOUSING:
THE ORANGI PILOT PROJECT IN PAKISTAN

Back in South Asia, experiments with the production of affordable housing during the 1970s and 1980s were also taking place. One of the most prominent examples of community-led housing development emerged in Pakistan during the early 1980s. While not happening on community-owned land, the work supported by the Orangi Pilot Project (OPP) builds on the "modern" CLT's model of governance and development led by the community, with support from professionals with relevant technical expertise. It also adapts the CLT's model of housing development to the context of informal settlements, which is critical if the CLT model is to be a constructive tool for low-income households across the Global South. To this end, lessons can be taken from OPP's pragmatic model of community-financed and community-managed infrastructure upgrades, the standardization of housing repairs, and the mapping of existing tenure systems.

Background: Origins of Orangi
Township and the Orangi Pilot Project

Before the the large-scale urbanization of Karachi (with a present a population of approximately 17 million), Orangi Township, which lies in the northeastern sector of the city, was a cluster of villages inhabited by Baloch clans.[5] The area was also pasture land for their cattle and goats. Given the mass migration to Karachi following the partition of British India beginning in 1947, and other economic forces causing rural-urban migration, Karachi's population began to expand rapidly during the 1950s. In response, during the early 1960's the Karachi Resettlement Plan was put into effect, with the vision of creating two fully serviced satellite towns, including government-built housing, on Karachi's periphery for resettling migrants from India. However, the plan wasn't fully implementable due to a lack of financial and institutional capacity within the provincial government.

Given the burgeoning population's housing needs, which persisted despite the provincial government's lack of capacity, the government opted to subdivide land in peripheral townships, but not to build the housing, and only to provide the most basic services. To this end, 590 hectares (1,458 acres) of land were subdivided into small lots of 120 square meters (approximately 400 square feet), which became the core of Orangi Township. Migrant families were relocated here from inner-city informal settlements for their permanent re-settlement. The families subsequently built their own homes with the help of informal developers and contractors, while the provincial government provided them with water through truck tankers, as well as built an access road and provided transportation to the major commercial districts in Karachi.

Following Pakistan's civil war in 1971, which led to the creation of Bangladesh (formerly East Pakistan), a second immigration wave hit Karachi. Emigrants from Bangladesh, known as the "Stranded Pakistanis," resettled themselves in informal settlements which they built around the townships, including Orangi.[6] These settlements were developed by informal developers, who negotiated with officials from government land-owning agencies. A plot of land was then "sold" to the new residents, with the proceeds of the sale being divided among the land-owning department officials, the police, and the developer (Hasan, 2010).

In response to this ad-hoc development, the provincial government passed the Sindh Katchi Abadi Act in 1978 in order to regularize land tenure in these informal settlements (known locally as *katchi abadis*). While the idea of community-based collective ownership was discussed in the lead-up to the Act, what finally prevailed was a system where the provincial government maintains the ownership rights, but gives the residents of *katchi abadis* the ability to apply for a 99-year, renewable, and transferable ground lease. As this is the common practice across Karachi, residents with such a lease are able to obtain loans and can sell their houses.

With the question of urban land tenure essentially being resolved through the Sindh Katchi Abadi Act, attention became focused on improving the quality of housing and upgrading basic services and infrastructure in what had previously been informal settlements. It is with these needed improvements in mind that Dr. Akhtar Hameed Khan, a prominent South Asian social scientist, established the Orangi Pilot Project (OPP) as a nonprofit organization in 1980. Dr. Khan believed that the collapse of community-based governance systems, which had once supported community life, was causing great social and physical dislocation. In order to establish a healthy relationship between people and their government, he concluded that communities must organize once again and become directly involved in development activities. Understanding the limits of the local and provincial governments, which were under the strain of providing services to a burgeoning population with a limited tax base, Dr. Khan suggested establishing a pragmatic partnership for things like sewage system upgrades. Residents would finance and manage the sewers serving individual homes; the government would finance and manage the main trunk sewers.

This unique, pragmatic partnership took hold in Orangi Township, among other localities, increasing the political engagement of residents and improving their living conditions. In the section below the model of governance for these infrastructure upgrades will be explored, along with other innovations of OPP, including the standardization of housing upgrades, the mapping of customary tenure systems, and advocacy for the recognition of customary tenure rights in rural areas that continued to be swallowed up by urban sprawl.

Community-Financed-and-Managed Infrastructure Upgrades

When OPP began its investigation into living and social conditions in Orangi in 1980, Dr. Khan found that poor sanitation was the issue cited by residents as being the most serious problem. According to Dr. Khan, the residents knew that above-ground sewers, soak pits, and bucket latrines were causing problems not only for their health, with a significant percentage of their income being spent on medications to treat diseases spawned by unhygienic sewage systems, but also that poor sanitation reduced the value of their houses and leaseholds. Therefore, OPP conducted a survey to figure out why nothing was being done by the residents to improve their conditions if they recognized the many problems that emerged from having an inadequate sanitation system. OPP found that the major barriers to resident-led action included (Khan, 1996):

1. The belief that infrastructure development was the duty of official agencies; a charity and patronage model was also being encouraged by politicians, which led many residents to believe that an improved system would be constructed as a "free gift" before election time.

2. The conventional cost for sanitary latrines and underground sewage lines was beyond their paying capacity.

3. The residents and local masons lacked technical skills for constructing underground sewage lines.

4. Social organization for collective action was lacking in Orangi, before OPP intervened.

To address these problems, OPP initiated a Low-Cost Sanitation Program in 1981. Within three years of the program's inception, a community-government partnership had emerged, whereby the government built the external infrastructure and residents agreed to build the internal infrastructure.[7] For the management and financing of internal infra-structure, OPP staff worked with the residents to form a community organization—with a "lane," usually consisting of 20–30 households, being the primary unit of organization.

Meetings were held for each lane, during which OPP staff explained the health and economic benefits of constructing an underground sewage system and why a self-fi-nanced approach was appropriate. A lane's residents were informed that, if they elected, selected, or nominated a lane manager, then OPP would provide them with technical assistance and managerial guidance to construct and to finance a neighborhood under-ground sanitation system. Once OPP received a request, its technical team surveyed the lane and drew up a plan for the underground sewage system, along with estimates for the materials involved.

The plans and cost estimates were given to the lane manager, whose job it was to col-lect the necessary funds from each household, arrange for materials, and assist in the monitoring of the construction process. Supervision of the work was provided by the OPP technical team.[8] Sometimes two lane managers were selected by the community, with one focusing on accounting, and the other on acquiring materials and monitoring the construction process. In addition, lane managers participated in a larger federation, to handle issues such as building the intermediate sewers, which served multiple lanes (Hasan, 2010).

In addition to helping organize the lane residents for collective action, OPP offered a package of technical research, and support for replication throughout the community. As part of the research process, OPP appointed a Karachi-based architect as the principal consultant for the project. He provided advice on how to reduce costs, while increas-ing the quality of the products. As part of the process of implementing this advice, local masons were then trained by OPP in these new construction techniques.

For replication throughout the community, OPP gave the contact information for these newly trained masons to the lane managers so that they could be employed in the construction of the lane sewage systems. In order to facilitate the work of the lane orga-nizations, OPP created a technical team including a professionally trained engineer and architect, and an Orangi-based plumber, draftsman and surveyor. Surveying and leveling instruments were provided to the team with financial support from a local charity and other donors. In consultation with the lane managers, the technical team surveyed the land, drafted construction documents, and drew up a list of estimated fees for labor and materials. It was then the lane manager's responsibility to call a meeting and to collect the money from each household to implement the plans in collaboration with the OPP-trained masons.

Since the program's inception, the residents have invested Rs. 138.2 million (almost $1 million USD) for internal development in 7,356 lanes (96% of households have participated). The government has invested Rs. 111.8 million in external development (OPP, 2018). Since its first iteration, the program has expanded beyond Orangi Town to 641 other urban locations in Pakistan. The 77,895 households that have participated in those locations have invested Rs. 206.2 million in internal development, and the government has invested Rs. 813.7 million.

> Lessons from OPP might refine the CLT model to be applied in informal settlements across the Global South.

Due to the success of the program, in 2005 OPP's component-sharing model was made a part of the sanitation policy of the Pakistani federal government and is taught at the National Institute of Public Administration, where government officials are trained. Lessons from OPP's experience also have the potential to refine the CLT model into something that could be applied in informal settlements across the Global South. In particular, lane-based community governance and pragmatic partnership with local government could be key features to help CLTs emerge in the context of existing densely settled areas, where residents can build (or learn to build) better and cheaper for themselves, but still seek to hold the government accountable for some level of basic service provision.

Standardization of Housing Upgrades

Building on the success of OPP's sanitation program, a housing improvement program was launched in 1986. The housing program followed a similar process of research, extension, and replication. In this case, research was done to better understand the major housing issues faced by residents, with the goal of being able to offer them a package of assistance which would make construction cheaper, while improving the quality of their houses.

Research results on the major housing defects included (Khan, 1996):

1. Concrete blocks that were made manually at the *thallas* (construction yards) were substandard, brittle, and not properly compacted or cured.[9]

2. Cracked walls, on account of the weak blocks and poor masonry work, that led to excessive dampness and consequently respiratory health problems.

3. Poor ventilation, due to improper orientation of windows or mere lack of them.

4. Use of asbestos roofing materials, causing respiratory health problems and cancer, and making it difficult to build a second story (residents would have to destroy the whole structure in order to build multiple stories, since the original walls were only created to support an asbestos or tin roof).

It was also discovered that 97% of households turned to their local building component manufacturing yard (locally known as *thalla*; and the entrepreneur who operates it known as the *thallewala*) for everything from supplies and credit to design and construction services. Given the key role these *thallas* played in the housing production process, OPP's technical advisory team determined that their initial intervention to support housing upgrades should target the *thallas*. Thus, they started the extension process by working with one *thalla* to upgrade its materials and production processes, endeavoring to create better quality and cheaper materials, and to train its workers in new building techniques. In terms of replication, OPP documented the process and invited other *thallas* to demonstrations using these newly developed materials and techniques. Within two years, 75 *thallas* adopted OPP's recommended processes and design of materials. Today, *thallas* in Orangi Township are a major exporter of quality cement blocks to the rest of Karachi.

In 1990, OPP's technical advisory team also began to train community members to serve as para-architects, in order to extend their package of construction advice and to bring more community members into the housing improvement process.[10] Topics that the *thallewallas* and the resident para-architects were trained in included (Khan, 1996):

1. How to design and build appropriate *in-situ* concrete foundations for a minimum ground floor plus one additional floor.

2. How to manufacture machine-made blocks, and build 6-inch-thick load-bearing walls.

3. Design advice for proper housing orientation and ventilation.

4. Molds for pre-cast concrete batten and tile roofing, as well as pre-cast staircases which reduced the cost by one-third.

Furthermore, in order to improve communications and to help set expectations among the para-architects, *thallewallas* and the residents, OPP created a series of informational posters and flyers. The para-architects were also deployed, when necessary, to monitor the work of the *thallewallas* so as to guarantee the quality of their products. This monitoring work was done by mobile teams that visited the *thallas* as well as the houses under construction.

Mapping and Regularization of Customary Land Tenure Systems

As Karachi's population continued to expand and to encroach on rural village lands, known as *goths*, OPP realized that it must also work with the original inhabitants of these *goths* (who were mainly Sindhi and Baloch pastoralists) to ensure that their customary land tenure arrangements would be recognized and honored by the government and by private developers. During the early 2000s, many different development players were confronting these original *goth* inhabitants and claiming that, if they couldn't show any legal documentation of their land rights, then their occupancy and use of the land would no longer be recognized. Through a mix of threats, violence and pay-offs, many of the original inhabitants were evicted. OPP's campaign to halt these evictions and to restore the rights of the *goth* residents took the form of three phases:

1. mapping the *goths* and documenting their tenure arrangements;

2. forming a network of support actors, including media personnel; and

3. facilitating advocacy by the residents, including meetings with political leaders, government bureaucrats and the media.

In particular, the mapping process played a key role in the eventual recognition of the land rights of the original *goth* inhabitants, and could be a replicable and functional starting point for emerging CLTs working in informal settlements or in situations of customary landholding. In this case, OPP, through its network of support actors, was granted access to the government's existing inventory of *goth* maps, and was able to verify and to further document long-established landholding patterns. OPP then shared these augmented maps with *goth* elders, activists, government departments, and developers so that information on land ownership would be transparent.

Using these maps, *goth* leaders were empowered to take up their land tenure issues with their elected representatives, and ultimately negotiate in a more equitable manner with officials and developers. This advocacy led to the extension of the Sindh Katchi Abadi Act to the *goths,* including an extended cut-off date of December 31, 2000. This extension helped to formalize the land holding of the original *goth* inhabitants. By 2012, 1,131 *goths* were recognized through the Sindh Katchi Abadi Act (OPP, 2018).[11]

TENURE SECURITY AND UPGRADING: COMBINING FEATURES FROM CLTs AND OPP'S PROGRAMS IN BANGLADESH'S "BIHARI CAMPS"

In Bangladesh, there is a community that may be primed for the next phase of experimentation, with a potential for fruitfully combining the CLT model of land ownership with OPP's model of community-led development, in order to increase tenure security and allow for comprehensive slum upgrading in the country's "Bihari Camps." The origins of this community's tenure insecurity and current displacement risks will be discussed, followed by an analysis of their options for "rehabilitation;" that is, ways to permanently resolve tenure insecurity and improve housing conditions. Recommendations for action will also be made based on key lessons from the CLT model and OPP's programs.

Background: The Housing and Land Rights Situation
of the Camp-Dwelling Urdu-Speaking Community

After Pakistan's civil war in 1971, which led to the formation of an independent Bangladesh, hundreds of thousands of people belonging to the Urdu-speaking ethno-linguistic minority were categorically denied citizenship (in the newly formed Bangladesh) and removed from their homes. This was largely the result of the allegiance by some members

Fig.15.1. Bangladesh: roof-top view of Geneva Camp, population 25,000.

of the Urdu-speaking community to the Pakistani army during the war, who were fighting to keep the country united. Members of this linguistic minority, who also became known as "Stranded Pakistanis" or "Biharis," were to await repatriation to Pakistan in temporary internal displacement camps. However, the repatriation efforts fell short and the camps became semi-permanent.[12] At present, over 160,000 members of this linguistic-minority continue to reside in 116 camps across Bangladesh.

In 2008, after 37 years of internal displacement, a handful of the community's youth, who were born in the camps, petitioned the Bangladeshi government to reinstate their citizenship as a matter of their birthright. In an unprecedented ruling, the High Court in Dhaka affirmed their citizenship rights, which has enabled them to vote, to obtain a passport, to register for school, and to apply for jobs—albeit with persistent discrimination due to their camp address. The ruling has also impacted living conditions in the camps, although not in a positive way. It has, in fact, made the residents more vulnerable to eviction. The reason they have been allowed to stay all these years on the camp lands has been due to their status as internally displaced people. Now that they have been declared to be citizens, both the government and private owners are vying to get their land back, given that many of the camps, especially those in the capital city of Dhaka, are situated on land that has increased in value as the city's population has risen (Sholder, 2011).[13]

Options for "Rehabilitation"

In some parts of Dhaka, camp evictions have already begun, and the residents are fighting for "stay orders" from the courts until a final rehabilitation solution is determined. The camp residents are coming to realize, however, that a solution imposed from the outside may not be in their best interest, and that they must act now themselves to address their tenure insecurity. There are, conceivably, five options available to them:

1. *Return to their pre-1971 houses.* One option could be to recover the ownership and occupation rights for their pre-war housing from which they were removed. While this is the least likely option in terms of its political and logistical feasibility, it could be brought into the debate, if only as a point of leverage for the other options.

2. *Demolition and on-site redevelopment.* In 2010, the local government in Dhaka made a proposal to demolish the largest and most politically central of the camps (Geneva Camp, a population of approximately 25,000) and to house the camp's residents in 40 newly constructed, multi-storied buildings within the borders of the existing camp. Through a financial feasibility study, it was discovered that these units would be completely unaffordable for the camp's residents. In order for the project to be affordable, it would need to be heavily subsidized; given the unlikelihood of such subsidies, this plan may in reality be an instrument for the community's removal from a parcel of prime real estate (Sholder, 2014).

3. ***Demolition and off-site development.*** Another option, proposed by the local government, would be the demolition of the camps and construction of multi-storied buildings on the outskirts of Dhaka or in other localities where land is less costly. Even if the cost of land was less than in central Dhaka, the cost of construction would still need to be covered and might still result in the project not being affordable for the camp residents. In addition, removal to the hinterlands could threaten the socio-economic fabric that holds this community together—specifically living in proximity to one another and to the main commercial districts.

4. ***On-site upgrading with private title.*** Working within the existing structure of incrementally built housing, this option has enabled residents to maintain the flexibility of building as their family expands and/or as their income increases, but private titling would likely rob the camp residents of their land and improvements over the long run. The improved value, resulting from titling and upgrading, and the pull of the private market could eventually lead to gentrification. The community would likely disperse over time, as individuals "sell out."

5. ***On-site upgrading with CLT land stewardship.*** The model of community land ownership offered by a CLT may be a good option, if a camp's residents have as their primary goals to keep the community united, to secure the camp's lands for those who wish to continue to live there, and to pass on the value of their improvements to the next generation. To this end, a camp's land could be held in trust by a CLT, with its Board of Directors primarily comprised of the camp's residents. The housing on the trust land could still be privately owned and inheritable, but the CLT would have the option to set resale restrictions to ensure permanent affordability.

Recommendations and Lessons
from CLTs and OPP's Programs

There are 116 camps scattered across Bangladesh. Different camps may require—and their residents may adopt—different options for a camp's rehabilitation. Not all will choose Option #5, described above, but the experiences of OPP in Pakistan and CLTs across the globe provide guidance on how residents can proceed in developing a plan of action that is right for them.

1. ***Research and consultation.*** A camp's leaders should begin by learning about the intricacies of all five options for rehabilitation. This has already begun with hundreds of camp youth attending a "community development leadership training program" from 2011–2018. Several of the trainees also attended a CLT peer exchange in Puerto Rico in 2019. A camp's leaders should then bring these options before the wider community of camp residents in order to build consensus about a way forward. The results

of these meetings would inform the organizational structure for designing and implementing an action plan.

2. ***Settlement mapping.*** Based on the experience of OPP, community-based mapping should be carried out to document not only who lives on a camp's lands, but also the pattern of ownership within the camp. Both pieces of information are fundamental, as they would inform any action planning to address the twin problems of tenure insecurity and the inadequacy of housing and infrastructure.

3. ***Organizational governance.*** Learning from the experiences of OPP, as well as from CLTs in the United States that emerged from the Civil Rights Movement, a fundamental step in moving forward would be to form an organization that not only represents and is controlled by a camp's residents, but also includes key allies. These key allies may include individuals from the majority-Bengali population, as well as experts in land law, housing development, and infrastructure upgrading. If the organization spans more than one camp, a governance structure that reflects this geography should be considered. For example, drawing on OPP's lane governance model, each camp might have its own sub-committee consisting of democratically elected managers for that camp. One or more of these managers from each camp might also serve on the larger Board of Directors of the overarching organization.

4. ***Land ownership.*** Once an organization is created that can speak on behalf of a camp's residents (or at least its membership) as to their united vision for rehabilitation, the organization could begin legal proceedings and/or negotiations to acquire land for the camp residents' rehabilitation. Before and after lands are acquired, a camp's residents, as represented through a newly formed CLT or some other organization, must decide how land ownership is to be structured—whether owned and stewarded by a CLT, distributed through individual land titles, or held and managed by some other arrangement.

5. ***Housing and infrastructure upgrading.*** If the plan for rehabilitation includes upgrading on the camp's lands, the organization should draw on financing and management lessons from OPP. In terms of finance, the Bangladeshi government may be unwilling or unable to finance upgrades in their entirety, and yet the camp residents, as newly-reinstated citizens of Bangladesh, deserve support for and access to basic services. With this in mind, OPP's pragmatic partnership with local government, splitting the cost of infrastructure upgrades, may be a reasonable approach to adopt in the context of the camps.

    In terms of management, training residents in the process of housing and infrastructure upgrades (as per OPP's experience with lane managers and para-architects) could provide key oversight. Likewise, training local construction workers in new low-cost and high-quality techniques would not only augment the local economy, but also ensure that upgrades are affordable for the camp residents, while increasing the safety and health of their homes and their neighborhoods.

———

CONCLUSION

The CLT model, adapted to the context of informal settlements, has the potential to be a useful tool for tenure regularization and upgrading across the South Asian subcontinent. The model's biggest advantages are that a CLT can keep the residents of these settlements safe from pressures and predations of the private market, and can keep the upgrading process affordable and within the community's control.

Land acquisition would be a key hurdle for CLT development in South Asia, as it is in every country. One of the main tools for acquiring rights to lands upon which informal settlements are built, especially in South Asia, could be "adverse possession" laws. While the amount of time one has to occupy the land before qualifying varies across and within countries, it may be the most financially feasible way to secure tenure by the residents of informal settlements.[14]

Despite the possibilities, one must take extreme care and caution when dealing with the issue of land rights in South Asia, and in many other parts of the world. Given that real estate is one of the most lucrative resources and industries worldwide, the process of claiming rights on land upon which there are multiple claims—whether legitimate or not—is a tricky and sometimes risky business.

> "We are the solution, not the problem!"

As a heartbreaking example of this harsh reality, it is believed that the land rights and mapping work of the late Executive Director of the Orangi Pilot Project, Perween Rahman, led to her assassination in 2013 (Ali and Zaman, 2018).

With abundant caution to the real risks of this work, we must proceed forward on the path of justice and equity. With this in mind, our Bangladeshi colleagues are launching their campaign to address the long-outstanding issue of the "rehabilitation" of the camp-dwelling Urdu-speaking community in Bangladesh. They are also investigating the possibility of utilizing the CLT model of land ownership and governance along with Bangladesh's adverse possession law to claim rights to lands within the "Bihari Camps." They are holding meetings to build support and consensus on a path forward, and will then propose their plan to the government. As leaders from several of these camps discovered, when attending a peer exchange with leaders of the Caño Martín Peña CLT in Puerto Rico, "We are the solution, not the problem!"

Notes

1. Prior to the Mughal period of rule in the South Asian subcontinent (1526–1857), during which the *Zamindar* system of private land ownership grew, most land was considered the aggregate wealth of a community and collectively managed (Bandyopadhyay, 1993).

2. The modern CLT is based on the ownership of land for the common good, instead of "ownership in common." The land is held by a nonprofit organization that is typically governed by a tripartite board, with two-thirds of the members being from the identified service area (one-third residing on the CLT's land and one-third living in the surrounding neighborhood); the remaining third is made up of technical experts, representatives of other NGOs, and (sometimes) representatives of government.

3. The "Bihari Camps" are internal displacement camps in Bangladesh that have been in existence since Pakistan's 1971 civil war, which led to the formation of an independent Bangladesh (formerly East Pakistan). To this day, 160,000 people still reside in 116 camps.

4. An acute land conflict in the South Indian village of Pochampalli is what instigated the *Bhoodan* movement. In this village, two-thirds of the residents were landless and had been seeking support from the government, but to no avail. The landless residents sought guidance from Bhave while he was passing through on his quest to implement *Sarvodaya* and *Gram Swaraj*. Bhave called a meeting to see if this conflict could be resolved without intervention from outside forces. Perhaps being influenced by Bhave's vision for the future, one of the village's wealthy landlords offered 100 acres of his own land to be redistributed among the landless residents (Mehta, 2001).

5. The Baloch are an ethnic group living predominantly in the Sindh and Balochistan provinces of Pakistan.

6. Approximately 25% of Orangi's inhabitants today are "Stranded Pakistanis," now also referred to as "Biharis," who came from the internal displacement camps in Bangladesh following Pakistan's 1971 civil war.

7. The external infrastructure consists of trunk sewers, long intermediate sewers, and treatment plants. The internal infrastructure consists of a latrine in the house, a one-chamber septic tank connecting the latrine to the lane sewer (to prevent solids from entering the sewers), the sewer in the lane, and the intermediate sewer, when not too long.

8. At no point did OPP touch the money of the lane organizations or determine how it was to be spent, or interfere in the election of the lane managers.

9. Manual block-bearing load = 100 pounds per square inch (psi) versus a mechanized block-bearing load = 800–1000 psi.

10. In 1999, two community members who were trained as para-architects also founded the Technical Training Resource Center, providing design advice, complete with drawings and estimates, to Orangi residents. The Center also helps to build social infrastructure such as schools and clinics (Hasan, 2010).

11. Building off the success of OPP's mapping program, its sanitation and housing programs along with a savings and loan program were extended to the *goths*. Although, shortly after these programs were initiated in the *goths*, they were scaled back due to the assassination of OPP's Executive Director, Perween Rahman (which is discussed in this chapter's conclusion).

12. Some of those who were interned in the Bihari Camps eventually made it to Pakistan and resettled on the outskirts of Orangi Town in Karachi. Of those who settled in Orangi Town, some have become the beneficiaries of OPP's outreach; thus, providing a direct connection between these now geographically-distinct communities, which could ultimately facilitate the extension of advice.

13. Some of the Bihari Camps were built on vacant parcels of privately and publically owned land. Other camps take the form of former schools and market halls, as well as abandoned houses, which were used as temporary housing following the 1971 war. However, these lands and buildings were never returned to their original uses. Plans by the government, international donors or community members themselves were never made for their "rehabilitation."

14. Adverse possession may apply in Bangladesh after 12 years of occupation if the rightful owner does not bring eviction proceedings within this period (Red Cross, 2017). In India, the timeframe is separated for private and public lands, with 12 years and 30 years being the respective occupation thresholds (Law Commission of India).

References

Ali, N.S. and Zaman, F. (2018). "Perween Rahman's murder: the great cover up." *Dawn.* *https://www.dawn.com/news/1319812/perween-rahmans-murder-the-great-cover-up*

Bandyopadhyay, R. (1993). "Land Systems in India: A Historical Review." *Economic and Political Weekly* 28 (52):149–155.

Borsodi, R. (2012). *Homesteading: Flight from the City. An Experiment in Creative Living on the Land.* Reprint of 1933 edition. Middletown: CreateSpace Independent Publishing Platform.

Bhave, V. (1961). "The Path of Love." Pp. 186–205 in M. Brown (ed.), *The Nationalist Movement: Indian Political Thought from Ranade to Bhave.* Berkeley: University of California Press.

Deininger, K., Jin, S., Nagarajan, H. (2007). "Land Reforms, Poverty Reduction, and Economic Growth: Evidence from India." Washington DC: The World Bank.

Dhadda, S. (2014). "Vinoba Bhave's Gramdan Movement." Satyagraha Foundation for Nonviolent Studies. *http://www.satyagrahafoundtion.org/vinoba-bhaves-gramdan-movement/*

Hasan, A. (2010). *Participatory Development.* Karachi: Oxford University Press.

Khan, A.H. (1996). *Orangi Pilot Project: Reminiscences and Reflections.* Karachi: Oxford University Press.

Law Commission of India. (n.d.). "Consultation Paper-cum-Questionnaire on Adverse Possession of Land/Immovable Property." *http://lawcommissionofindia.nic.in/reports/Adverse%20Possession.pdf*

Mehta, S. (2001). "Bhoodan-Gramdan Movement—50 Years: A Review". Mumbai: Gandhi Book Center. *http://www.mkgandhi-sarvodaya.org/bhoodan.htm*

Orangi Pilot Project. (2018). Quarterly Report. *http://www.opp.org.pk/opp-rti/*

Red Cross (2017—draft). "Housing, Land and Property Law in Bangladesh." *ShelterCluster.* *https://www.sheltercluster.org/sites/default/files/docs/bangladesh_hlp.pdf*

Shepard, M. (2010). "Gandhi Today: A Report on Mahatma Gandhi's Successors." Pp. 108–112 in J.E. Davis (ed.), *The Community Land Trust Reader.* Cambridge: The Lincoln Institute for Land Policy.

Sholder, H. (2011). "Housing and Land Rights: The Camp-Dwelling Urdu-Speaking Community in Bangladesh." Dhaka: Refugee and Migratory Movements Research Unit.

Sholder, H. (2014). "Physical Rehabilitation and Social Integration: The Camp-Dwelling Urdu-Speaking Community in Bangladesh." Berkeley: UC Berkeley Department of City and Regional Planning.

PART FOUR
URBAN APPLICATIONS

Measuring the Progress of
High-Performing CLTs
in Selected Cities

16.

Take a Stand, Own the Land

Dudley Neighbors Inc., a Community Land Trust in Boston, Massachusetts

Harry Smith and Tony Hernandez

Dudley Neighbors Inc. (DNI) is the community land trust formed in 1988 to serve the Roxbury-North Dorchester area of Boston, Massachusetts. DNI was an outgrowth of years of grassroots organizing and participatory planning by the Dudley Street Neighborhood Initiative (DSNI). These two organizations remain tightly intertwined, sharing staff, resources, and a corporate umbrella. More importantly, they share a mission and vision of comprehensive neighborhood revitalization in which community ownership of land and community empowerment of the area's residents go hand-in-hand.

This chapter details the conditions in the Dudley neighborhood that led to the creation of DSNI and the launch of the "Don't Dump on Us" campaign to address blighted vacant lots in the area. The success of those early anti-dumping campaigns led to a new campaign, "Take a Stand, Own the Land," and formation of the DNI community land trust. The chapter will describe how the community came together to create a comprehensive revitalization plan and to win eminent domain power from the City of Boston for vacant, blighted land in the Dudley Triangle. The authors will describe the strategies DSNI/DNI used to deeply engage residents in and around DNI's housing and will explain how the community-owned land in the DNI portfolio leverages the neighborhood's influence over public and private development throughout the neighborhood.

The chapter will conclude by detailing current efforts to acquire land outside of the original target area, partnering with the City of Boston and others to acquire private land and buildings to turn into mixed-use, affordable developments. DSNI is also playing a key role in supporting the formation of new CLTs in the Boston area and in helping to create a new city-wide organization to promote cooperation and coordination among all of Boston's CLTs, young and old: the Greater Boston CLT Network.

By sharing the lessons learned from thirty-five years of community organizing, planning, and development, the authors hope to contribute to the growth of the global CLT movement by highlighting the benefits of community control over land.

BACKGROUND

"Affordable housing in perpetuity through Dudley Neighbors Inc. is the gift that keeps on giving for families in our community. The land trust is a powerful tool guided by the voices of residents in low-income communities to ensure that housing is forever affordable and that land is used for the public good."—Sister Margaret Leonard, long-time DSNI board member

Located less than two miles from downtown Boston, the Dudley area of Roxbury-North Dorchester is a tri-lingual neighborhood of more than 25,000 African-American, Latin American, Cape Verdean, and White residents where English, Spanish and Cape Verdean Creole is spoken.

Dudley's population is among the poorest and youngest in Boston. Approximately 27% of the area's population falls below the poverty line, as defined by the federal government. More than 40% of the neighborhood's households earn less than $25,000 annually and the neighborhood's high unemployment rate of 15% is more than twice the city-wide average. A few other statistics set the stage for our story: 18% of Dudley's residents are 14–24 years of age; 40% of the neighborhood's households contain children who are younger than 18 years; 26% of adults in the neighborhood do not have a high school degree; and 62% of Dudley's households are considered "cost burdened" by virtue of spending more than 30% of their household's income for the housing they occupy.

THE BIRTH OF DSNI: "DON'T DUMP ON US!"

By the 1980s, Dudley contained a staggering amount of vacant land—a total of 1300 parcels—representing nearly a third of the acreage of the entire neighborhood. This was a consequence of three decades of disinvestment, redlining, abandonment, poorly planned urban renewal, and arson-for-profit. The neighborhood had also become an illegal dumping ground for trash from around the city and state. In the dead of night and in broad daylight, trucks would roll into the neighborhood and deposit on the neighborhood's vacant lots old cars, old refrigerators, rotten meat, toxic chemicals, and debris from construction sites.

"When I first came here, all I remember is trash and vacant lots and house fires," says Evelyn Correa, a current DSNI board member. "All of a sudden you would see a home go up in flames and we would say, 'That must have been for the insurance.'"

In 1984, the Riley Foundation, one of the larger charitable foundations in Massachusetts, decided to focus on the revitalization of Dudley after touring the neighborhood's most blighted sections with leaders of local nonprofit organizations. The Dudley Advisory Group was created, made up mostly of community development corporations and social services organizations doing work in the area. On October 15, 1984, with 22 people in attendance, the group voted unanimously to establish a new organization. Three months later, it was given the name of the "Dudley Street Neighborhood Initiative."

When the grand plans envisioned by this new initiative were first presented to the neighborhood, however, "all hell broke loose," as one of the participants in that roll-out meeting later described it. Neighborhood residents challenged the Advisory Group's assertion that this was to be an initiative of, by, and for the community. Local resident Che Madyun asked the Advisory Group, "How many of you people up there live in this neighborhood?" When only one hand was raised, there was an angry demand from the floor for resident control of the planning process — and of the organization itself.

This triggered a fundamental reconsideration of the assumptions behind DSNI, forcing the Dudley Advisory Group to go back to the drawing board. The Riley Foundation and the nonprofit organizations that had backed the original approach were quick to accept the demand for resident control. They immediately began weaving this principle into the bylaws being drafted for the new organization. A governing board with thirty-one members (later expanded to thirty-five) would have a resident majority. Minimum representation would be guaranteed for each of the neighborhood's four major cultures: African-American, Cape Verdean, Latino, and White.

The election of the inaugural board of directors occurred on April 27, 1985. More than 100 people were in attendance, filling the front pews of St. Patrick's Church. Local resident leaders were elected as the co-chairs. The following year, the board unanimously approved a new slate of officers, with Che Madyun being named DSNI's president.

In 1986, DSNI hired Peter Medoff, a veteran community organizer, as its first executive director. He won the job at DSNI because he emphasized the need for community organizing and community empowerment to remain at the center of the new organization's plans for the neighborhood's physical, social, and economic revitalization.

As the organization completed its initial process of extensive door knocking and surveying of local residents and merchants, it became clear that the issue of illegal dumping and blight was the issue where DSNI would need to start. The "Don't Dump on Us" campaign was created to clean up vacant lots, to stop illegal dumping, and to force government oversight of the large number of poorly regulated trash-transfer stations in the neighborhood. Residents organized their own clean-up efforts, while pushing the City of Boston to take greater responsibility for removing garbage, construction debris, and abandoned cars from City-owned and privately owned vacant lots.

TAKE A STAND, OWN THE LAND:
THE CREATION OF DUDLEY NEIGHBORS INC.

"DNI was created to carry out the neighborhood's redevelopment strategy. Instead of simply responding to plans created by private developers or the City, we created the community land trust as the vehicle to exercise community control over our land. The land trust helps us sustain our vision and make it a reality."—Bob Haas, long-time DSNI leader

By 1987, DSNI had successfully pressured the City to close three illegal trash-transfer stations and had made progress in cleaning up vacant lots. Leaders came to understand that in order to realize the dream of community revitalization, DSNI would need to move from organizing against harmful practices such as dumping to planning proactively for future development of the neighborhood. Only in this way would the community be able to break out of the deadly cycle of real estate speculation followed by disinvestment that had plagued the area for decades. After an intensive process of bottom-up participatory planning, DSNI completed The Dudley Street Neighborhood Comprehensive Revitalization Plan, which laid out a blueprint for rebuilding the neighborhood. At its center was an overall commitment to development without displacement. DSNI then wielded the community power it had built over the course of earlier organizing campaigns to convince the City of Boston to abandon the master plan that had been drafted by city officials and to adopt DSNI's community-generated plan as its own.

Two years later, DSNI made history by becoming the first and only community-based organization in the United States to win the power of eminent domain. DSNI had begun assembling the funds to implement its Comprehensive Revitalization Plan, including the promise of a $2 million Program Related Investment from the Ford Foundation. But absentee owners of the neighborhood's vacant parcels were reluctant to sell their land to DSNI. They had caught the scent of potential profits in the air. The City of Boston was in the process of rebuilding the subway line on the neighborhood's western edge, a massive investment in public infrastructure. Private speculators had taken note and begun to buy up lands and buildings in the neighborhood.

In 1988 when the DNI community land trust was formed, approximately thirty of the sixty-four acres of land in the Dudley Triangle consisted of blighted, vacant lots, with fifteen acres owned by the City of Boston and fifteen acres owned by private individuals or corporations. Because of the organizing and advocacy of DSNI, city officials were willing to transfer the fifteen acres of City-owned land to DNI. However, because the City-owned land was scattered among the privately-owned lots, DSNI's leaders realized that it would be a nearly impossible task to assemble enough contiguous land to carry out the community's development vision. The majority of the private holdings were tax delinquent, but given the length of the tax foreclosure process, it would take years to acquire these parcels. In order to more quickly achieve a critical mass of land for development, the organization decided that acquiring the privately-owned land by eminent domain was the only way to accomplish their ambitious urban village plan.

DSNI's leaders began a new campaign of grassroots organizing in 1989, as they lobbied Mayor Flynn and the Boston Redevelopment Authority (BRA) to grant DSNI the power to assemble contiguous sites that were large enough for building the affordable housing contemplated in the Comprehensive Revitalization Plan. "Take a Stand, Own the Land" was the campaign button that was distributed throughout the neighborhood. Residents were asking for the legal right to compel the absentee owners of vacant land in the central part of the neighborhood, the 64-acre Dudley Triangle, to sell their land for a fair price to DSNI. On November 10, 1989, the BRA board voted unanimously to grant the power of eminent domain to DSNI.

On the advice of DSNI's attorney, David Abromowitz, who was made available on a *pro bono* basis by one of Boston's most prestigious law firms, DSNI established a subsidiary corporation in 1988, Dudley Neighbors Inc. Structured and operated as a community land trust, DNI was set up not only to exercise the power of eminent domain in acquiring land within the Dudley Triangle; it was also established to retain ownership of land forever, holding it in trust for present and future generations.

> How do you avoid displacing the very people you are trying to help?

By holding onto the land — and by employing long-lasting ground leases to control the use and resale of whatever was built on its land — DNI positioned itself to be the permanent steward of affordable housing, commercial space, and other buildings that, in time, were to be constructed on its parcels. The goal, in every case, was to maintain the affordability of these buildings forever, while also preventing foreclosures during downturns in the local economy.

Community-owned land was to be an antidote to the ultimate dilemma of community development: How do you avoid displacing the very people you are trying to help? In the words of Paul Yelder, the first director of Dudley Neighbors Inc., "How do you improve a neighborhood, but still make it accessible, make it affordable?"

Placing the community land trust within a subsidiary corporation allowed DSNI to maintain its focus on community organizing and participatory planning, while ensuring that the community's vision and plans were carried out. In 1990, as a new decade began, DSNI adopted a new slogan, "Building Houses and People Too," highlighting its commitment to a holistic approach to Dudley's revitalization. The construction of affordable housing, parks, and playgrounds was a priority; but community organizing was deemed to be just as important.

BUILDING AN URBAN VILLAGE IN
THE DUDLEY TRIANGLE AND BEYOND

"I'm a city girl. I appreciate having a house in Boston that I can afford. And especially with the prices of houses now, I don't know how people could afford it. The fact that I got my house is a blessing."—Diane Dujon, DNI homeowner

Through the use of eminent domain and a deep partnership with the City of Boston, DNI had managed to acquire nearly all of the public and private vacant lots in the Dudley Triangle by 2019, giving the land trust control of more than thirty of the sixty-four acres in the Triangle. These vacant lots have been transformed into 227 high-quality, permanently affordable homes — including owner-occupied houses, cooperatives, and nonprofit rentals. The land trust's holdings also include two acres of community farms, a greenhouse, and neighborhood parks, playgrounds, gardens, commercial space, and other amenities of the urban village that Dudley residents had envisioned as they were organizing to clean up vacant lots.

The creation of hundreds of new, permanently affordable homes over the last 25 years on the sites of formerly abandoned, blighted lots has had an incredible impact on the Dudley community. The homes include ninety-seven homeownership units, seventy-seven limited-equity cooperative units, and fifty-three rental units, reflecting the desire to provide housing opportunities to families with a broad range of incomes. In accordance with the neighborhood plan, the majority of rental, cooperative, and ownership units have three bedrooms and are targeted to families earning between 30%–60% of Area Median Income, approximately $30,000–$60,000 for a family of four. In fact, recent surveys of families living in DNI homeownership units show that more than half of the families earn less than $40,000/year, and yet are able to enjoy the benefits of owning their own homes.

The resale formula employed by DNI on homeownership units places an emphasis on stability and long-term ownership, with an owner's equity increasing each year that the owner stays in the home.

The positive impact of the revitalization of the Dudley Triangle can be measured in many ways: improved public safety; higher rates of homeownership, compared with the surrounding community; and a high level of resident satisfaction, as reported in the regular quality-of-life surveys that DSNI conducts.

"My dream was always to own my own home, but with the housing situation in Boston, everything was always so expensive," says Evelyn Correa, who was able to buy a home on the land trust in 2010 and has served as president of the Dudley Neighbors Inc. board for the past five years. "Now I just love having my little house. I hope to hand it down to my kids."

Figs. 16.1. Neighborhood revitalization, Dennis Street to Winthrop Street, before and after.

Diane Dujon, another homeowner in the land trust who has lived in Roxbury and Dorchester her whole life, says that one of the most important things to her about the land trust is that "it stabilizes the neighborhood. Once people move into their home, they don't leave, so I know my neighbors. We watch out for each other and help each other out."

Stabilization is a consequence of stewardship. DNI is able to preserve the affordability of any homes that are built on its land, no matter how hot Boston's real estate market may become. But there is also stability that comes from DNI's ongoing support for its homeowners and renters, helping them to stay in their homes, even when the economy goes bad. DNI staff build trusting relationships with residents and lenders. When necessary, DNI will invoke its power of "Consent to Mortgage" to prevent predatory lenders from marketing a destabilizing mortgage product in the Dudley neighborhood. The impact of this level of engagement and oversight is dramatic: while the larger neighborhood suffered more than two hundred foreclosures during the Great Recession, 2008–2013, there were no foreclosures of DNI homes over the same span of time. The entire portfolio has had only four foreclosures in 25 years, making the land trust an island of stability in a volatile real estate market. This is consistent with the performance of CLT homes across the nation. From 2008–2010, during the height of the foreclosure crisis, fewer than 1% of CLT homes across the country were foreclosed on, compared to 5% of total mortgage loans.

In keeping with the community's vision of an urban village, DNI has also stepped up efforts to develop retail and commercial spaces on land that it owns. DNI is currently partnering with a local community development corporation to build a commercial building on one of the last vacant lots in the Triangle. This project will fill a large gap in the business district and provide opportunities for new retail spaces to meet the needs of local residents.

As the final vacant lots in the Dudley Triangle have been developed and as the red-hot Boston real estate market has brought new threats to the stability of the Dudley neighborhood, DNI leaders have developed new strategies to add housing and commercial spaces to the land trust's portfolio. The most dramatic step was taken in 2017 when DNI acquired a former bank building in nearby Upham's Corner, with acquisition funds and technical support provided by the City of Boston. It was an historic move for the land trust, as it marked the first significant purchase of a property by DNI in many years and the first major acquisition of property outside of the Dudley Triangle. The goal of the project is to develop a mixed-use building that will include affordable housing, some of which will be reserved for artists, commercial space, and cultural spaces. This project will further the community's vision to transform Upham's Corner into an "Arts Innovation District" that will include the revitalization of the Strand Theater and the creation of a new public library. Because of DNI's successful track record, residents are hopeful that it will be possible to improve neighborhood arts amenities without raising rents and without displacing local families, businesses, and artists who have built the culture of Upham's Corner for generations.

In addition to pursuing new housing and commercial development opportunities, DNI is also utilizing the land trust model to promote community development through urban agriculture. Urban farms and gardens have always been a part of the vision and plan for revitalizing the Dudley neighborhood, a strategy to increase access to local food and to create open spaces that benefit the community. In 2004, DNI built a 10,000 square-foot community greenhouse on the site of a former auto body shop. DNI owns the underlying land and leases out the greenhouse to a local nonprofit partner, The Food Project, along with nearly two acres of urban farmland. The Food Project trains young people to operate farms and to organize farmers' markets serving neighborhood residents. DNI has also partnered with the Urban Farming Institute (UFI) to develop new neighborhood farms that will be managed by local residents who have graduated from UFI's farmer training program. The land trust model provides long-term stability to groups leading the urban farming movement in Boston and helps to fulfill the community's desire for open space and access to healthier food.

Fig. 16.2. Greenhouses operated by The Food Project on land leased from Dudley Neighbors Inc.

PUTTING THE "C" IN COMMUNITY LAND TRUST

"Many scholars and housing activists view market forces and housing affordability as mutually antagonistic: either a community remains affordable for its low-income residents, or it attracts capital investment, development and growth. If there is a way out of this fundamental contradiction, Boston's Dudley Street Neighborhood Initiative (DSNI) has found it. . . . The strong organizing base of the DSNI has created a unique resident-driven model of planning. This is in stark contrast to the conventional path by which city government develops a master plan before seeking community input."

—Fannie Mae Foundation, "Just-Right Neighborhoods" (2000)

From the founding of the organization, DSNI leaders realized that cleaning up lots and stopping illegal dumping were not enough. Without community control over planning and land use decisions, the neighborhood's residents would just continue to react to the next threat that came down the road. During that time, the City of Boston had in fact developed a master plan for the Dudley neighborhood, but they had neglected to involve community residents in their planning process. DSNI's "Take a Stand, Own the Land" campaign and the planning that accompanied it resulted in the City tearing up its plan and endorsing the DSNI vision. For the first time in Boston, residents, merchants, and youth — most of whom had never been engaged in urban planning — were able to come together to develop a plan that incorporated the principle of "development without displacement" into a City-approved master plan.

> Intensive focus on community engagement and leadership development is the key to DSNI's long-term success.

Thirty-five years later, DSNI and its community land trust are still organizing and involving both the people who live in DNI's housing and the people who live in the surrounding neighborhood. This intensive focus on community engagement and leadership development is the key to DSNI's long-term success and highlights one of the biggest impacts of successful CLTs. Rather than focusing only on the success and maintenance of CLT properties, DSNI integrates CLT residents into its organizing and planning initiatives to build community power and to improve the quality of life for the whole neighborhood.

DSNI's leaders view the CLT model as one of a number of tools they use to ensure strong resident engagement in land use decisions over the long-term. Through its Sustainable Development Committee, which reviews all private development projects to assess their adherence to the neighborhood's development vision, DSNI has been able to organize residents to shape private development in the neighborhood, ensuring that projects meet the standards established in DSNI's community plans, including affordable housing and access to local jobs.

"In addition to getting involved in CLT activities, land trust residents also serve on the board and committees of DSNI and play leadership roles on issues across the neighborhood," according to Tony Hernandez, Director of Dudley Neighbors Inc. "In this way, the CLT is able to be an effective steward of the land, while remaining in service to DSNI's larger vision of development without displacement and community control of the land."

Although winning eminent domain authority by the City has been rightly viewed as one of the major accomplishments of DSNI, there have been other lesser-known mechanisms that have sustained DSNI's power over private development in Dudley. For example, in 1999, DSNI and the City's Department of Neighborhood Development signed a Memorandum of Understanding that stipulated that DSNI would conduct the community planning process for City-owned land in the Dudley neighborhood. In the Dudley neighborhood, DSNI and the City continue to jointly convene community land use and housing design meetings, issue requests for proposals, and designate developers.

The combination of DSNI's role as community planner and DNI's stewardship of land means that residents are fully engaged in land use decisions in a large portion of the neighborhood. In the words of a long-time DSNI board member, "Developing a shared vision is absolutely crucial. By developing a shared vision, people come to sense that anything is possible. People really come to believe that." The results of this deep engagement are clear: in addition to the 227 homes that have been built on DNI's land, nearly 1,000 affordable homes have been produced or preserved elsewhere in the neighborhood by other nonprofit and for-profit developers because of DSNI's organizing and advocacy, an effort led by the organization's Sustainable Development Committee. This is a reflection of DSNI's power to affect land uses throughout the neighborhood.

SUPPORTING THE CITY-WIDE GROWTH AND SUSTAINABILITY OF CLTs

Despite the successes of the community in creating and preserving affordable housing through the land trust and larger advocacy efforts, the Dudley neighborhood is dealing with new threats as the development boom in Boston intensifies. Resident-led improvements have led to the neighborhood facing outside investors seeking opportunities for development and new, wealthier residents moving in. The opportunity for DNI to acquire vacant parcels of land at little or no cost is a thing of the past, as private developers move into sections of the neighborhood they would not have touched a decade ago. These circumstances are not unique to Dudley; similar patterns are apparent across Boston and neighboring towns. In response, DSNI and ten neighborhood groups from across the city launched the Greater Boston Community Land Trust Network in 2015. The goal of this regional effort is to expand the CLT model and to work with allies to make a city-wide push for the kind of community control over land disposition, ownership, and development that has been won in the Dudley neighborhood.

"This launch is coming at a critical moment in Boston history," said Harry Smith, DSNI's former Director of Sustainable Economic Development, speaking at the press conference announcing the Network's creation. "As one of the fastest-gentrifying cities in the United States, we're here to either claim the future of our neighborhoods . . . or risk losing them to gentrification and displacement."

With the formation of the Greater Boston Community Land Trust Network, DSNI is working towards its goal of building the capacity of partners in other neighborhoods to develop resident-led plans, to control land-use decisions, and to take ownership of land in their own communities. Over the past year, several new CLTs have formed in the Boston area with the Network's support and assistance, including the Chinatown CLT, Somerville CLT, Boston Neighborhood CLT, and the Urban Farming CLT, creating a sense of momentum and solidarity across multiple neighborhoods. With a growing membership, the Network is also serving as a vehicle to advocate for municipal policies and public resources that will promote development without displacement across the entire city.

CONCLUSION

In the documentary film, *Arc of Justice,* Charles Sherrod, one of the founders of New Communities Inc., the nation's first CLT, says, "All power comes from the land." This is undoubtedly true. At the same time, the experience of DSNI and the DNI bears witness to the political reality that the reverse is true as well: "All land comes from community power." The leaders of DSNI and DNI have come to believe that the only way to realize the community's vision over the long-term is to meld the community ownership and governance features of the CLT with sustained organizing and planning in order to get land and to use it wisely for the benefit of the entire community.

As DNI's Director, Tony Hernandez says, "Without a clear vision and development plan that has been created by neighborhood residents and without structures in place to monitor and to oversee the development of that vision, the CLT will not be effective in the long run." Or, in the words of a long-time community leader, "Usually we, the community, are fighting to have a seat at the table to fight for affordability and avoid displacement. But because of the land trust, I'm proud to say that we not only have a seat at the table, we *own* the table."

17.

Lands in Trust for Urban Farming
Toward a Scalable Model

Nate Ela and Greg Rosenberg

In cities around the world, people are looking to urban agriculture for a wide range of benefits, from providing fresh food and supporting healthy eating habits to teaching job skills and offering access to nature. Urban farms are increasingly seen as a possible engine for economic development, whether as the main source of income for full-time farmers, growing the raw materials for value-added products, or supplementary income for growers who hold other jobs. Community supported agriculture[1] (CSA) farms can be a good fit for urban settings, bringing the farm into close proximity to the membership. And finally, community gardens are a particularly compelling application of urban agriculture, making land available to residents of neighborhoods where access to fresh, healthy food is limited — or nonexistent.

None of this can happen, however, without land on which to grow crops.[2] A wide range of people — from individual growers to mentors, foundation officials, university researchers, urban planners, and policy makers who would like to see urban farms succeed — have been grappling with questions related to land. Which models of tenure are best suited to securing access to land for urban farming? Which models are most effective in preserving access and affordability over time? Which models are most efficient in allocating scarce resources, while also promoting equity and engagement with community residents who will be an urban farm's neighbors and customers?

The high cost of urban land relative to rural land poses a major problem for would-be urban farmers. Unlike rural farmers, they are competing for land with many other potential uses, which creates inflationary pressures on land prices. In Wisconsin, for example, rents for rural cropland averaged $140 per acre in 2018 (USDA, 2018). This is a small fraction of the price an urban farmer would pay for an acre of tillable land at market rates in Chicago or other cities. Yet, food grown in cities must remain price-competitive with food grown in rural areas. Few if any crops can be sold at prices that would cover the higher land costs, and urban growers cannot simply add a premium to reflect the value of the contributions they make to their neighborhoods.

If affordable land is key to commercially viable, community-engaged urban farming, the question becomes how to protect affordability over the long term. This means ensuring that urban farms — and community gardens — are not displaced by rapidly rising prices in a speculative real estate market, while ensuring that land is not allocated haphazardly in neighborhoods where values may be stagnant or declining. In both cases, the struggle is how to ensure space is available for agricultural projects that are rooted in and beneficial to surrounding communities.

> People are looking to land trusts to hold land for urban farms and community gardens.

Over the last several decades, housing and environmental advocates have developed land trust models to ensure that community priorities for the use of land are not displaced by speculative market forces. Open space and conservation land trusts have focused on protecting ecologically valuable land at the urban fringe. Community land trusts have sought to preserve housing affordability and security of tenure in cities and suburbs. These models are increasingly being brought to bear on the challenge of providing and protecting land for urban agriculture.

PROGRAM DESIGN — EIGHT STRATEGIC QUESTIONS REGARDING LANDHOLDING FOR URBAN FARMS

1. Who Should Be the Landholding Entity?

Different types of entities could hold land for urban agriculture, including government agencies, land banks, agriculture cooperatives, or even private firms. Cities have large amounts of unused acreage owned by churches, corporate headquarters, educational institutions, and public agencies that may be appropriate for urban agriculture. Cities such as Oakland, California; Portland, Oregon; Madison, Wisconsin; and Philadelphia, Pennsylvania have conducted inventories to determine where such opportunities exist.

However, increasingly around the United States, people are looking to land trusts as an entity that is well-suited to holding land for urban farms and community gardens. When considering whether a land trust should hold title to land or, instead, should manage lands held by public entities, property tax issues are an important consideration. Market-value property tax assessments can make land unaffordable, even for a nonprofit land trust. (For this reason, the Athens Land Trust in Athens, Georgia opted not to own urban farmland; unfavorable property tax treatment would have yielded a full market-value assessment for the land, despite the long-term restrictions placed on it.)

2. How Will the Landholder Relate to Community Members?

Whether land is held by a nonprofit land trust, a government agency, or some other entity, the relationship between the landholder and community members will be a key question. Are community members included as board members of a land trust and, if so, how? Are they consulted by public officials, if the land is held by a city agency or county land bank, and if so, how?

3. How Will Land Be Made Affordable?

If urban farmers are to have any hope of sustained success, their cost to access land should be roughly on par with that of rural farmers. Thus, one reasonable target for affordability would be for urban farmers to devote the same percentage of the cost of access to land as rural farmers do. For rural farmers, this proportion will depend on the main crop that is being grown, whereas urban farmers will be more likely to have a more intensive and diversified growing strategy.

4. How Will Land Be Used?

What type of land is appropriate depends on how growers plan to use it. Will they grow in greenhouses, hoop houses, or outdoors? Will they be growing flowers, herbs, or vegetables? Will they set up composting facilities? Land use will also depend not only on growers' desires, but on zoning and other regulations.

5. Who Will Be the Growers?

Again, a land tenure model must be responsive to different types of growers. These types include job trainees working on nonprofit urban farms, new commercial growers testing their business models on incubator farms, independent commercial growers with just a few years or decades of experience, and noncommercial community gardeners who are growing food for their own consumption. A tenure model can also help encourage community-engaged urban agriculture by minority-run firms, and by prioritizing access to land for farmers who will grow in their own neighborhood.

6. How Will Land Be Conveyed to Growers?

Although this is the central question to be answered by a land tenure model, we do not expect there to be a single answer. Land may be secured differently for growers with different purposes and with different levels of experience. Before securing land for particular farmers, however, there is the question of how to protect land for agricultural use. This could mean transferring publicly or privately owned land into a land trust, which then provides leases to individual farmers or to an urban farming organization.

It makes sense to have different terms for different types of farmers. Nonprofit urban farms could be eligible for long-term leases—perhaps 99-year renewable leases for the most well-established organizations. Such leases would ensure long-term agricultural use and provide security to urban farms committed to being an ongoing resource for a neighborhood. For individual farmers, a renewable short-term lease could have performance measures negotiated by the farmer and the leasing entity, with input from community members. Farmers could thus work their way into long-term security of tenure by demonstrating their ability to pay the (below-market) rent and provide community benefits.

7. What Type of Support Will Growers Need to Be Successful?

Support will vary widely based on the experience of the farmers, issues relating to the land, and challenges in accessing the local market for their produce. For land-related issues, farmers may need support for soil remediation, installation of infrastructure (water and electricity), construction of agricultural buildings, negotiating favorable property tax assessments if they are the landowners, and zoning changes in some cases. Again, the support of a team of people and organizations is usually required to address all these issues.

8. How is Success Defined? What Expectations Are Realistic?

In defining a system for land tenure, people must grapple with what a successful urban farming sector looks like. Although nonprofit urban farms have been demonstrably effective, most cities have not seen many small, for-profit urban farms that have created well-paying jobs. If communities or government officials expect urban farms to be a major vehicle for near-term job creation, those expectations may be unrealistic.

A successful land tenure model should support land remaining in agricultural use over a long period of time, so that urban farmers can test out for-profit and nonprofit business models. It will take time for farmers to learn which business models provide an acceptable mix of economic return and community benefits. Along the way, some farms will fail. This is normal with small businesses; the Small Business Association (2012) has found that only about half of small businesses survive the first five years. Rather than taking such failures as a sign that land should not be preserved for agricultural use, a successful land tenure model would quickly provide access to a new grower.

THE ROLE OF LAND TRUSTS IN PROVIDING AND PROTECTING AFFORDABLE LAND FOR URBAN FARMING

As in other areas of community development, the nonprofit sector has a special role to play in kick-starting urban farming.[3] Urban agriculture is a relatively low-cost approach to job creation and neighborhood revitalization, compared to other forms of revitalization. An urban farm can be built more quickly and cheaply than housing or mixed-use development. In practice, of course, the fact that business models for urban farming are

Urban agriculture is a relatively low-cost approach to job creation and neighborhood revitalization.

still being tested means delays are often encountered in raising capital and satisfying regulatory requirements.

Over the past thirty years, the land trust has emerged in the United States as a preferred model for holding land for community gardens and urban farms. This reflects the convergence of two trends: the creation of specialized open space land trusts to conserve land for community gardens, and the moves that some community land trusts (CLTs) have made to promote urban agriculture.

There is a distinction between open space land trusts and community land trusts. Open space land trusts — which may also be called conservation land trusts – focus on the protection and preservation of lands on which are built few (if any) residential structures and which are not being productively used to grow food or fiber. Open space land trusts, moreover, do not generally have an organizational structure that fosters community-based governance.[4] Community land trusts, by contrast, acquire and hold land for the benefit of a place-based community to which the organization is accountable. They generally have a tripartite board structure that includes seats dedicated to beneficiaries of the trust (usually people who live in housing held by the trust), residents from neighboring communities, and people with needed expertise or organizational connections.

Under both types of land trust, a nonprofit organization owns or holds rights to use parcels of land, but leases out parcels of land for productive use. The size of the lease fees will depend on what is needed to cover the lessor's costs of holding the land and paying for its own administrative overhead, some of which may be subsidized through public or private philanthropy.

Open Space Land Trusts:
New York Community Garden Land Trusts

In 1999, the administration of New York City Mayor Rudolph Giuliani announced a plan to auction off over one hundred pieces of city-owned land that were home to community gardens. Gardeners and their allies mobilized in resistance to the plan, organizing demonstrations and filing lawsuits (Brooklyn Queens Land Trust, n.d.). In 2002, after a negotiated settlement of the lawsuits with Mayor Michael Bloomberg's administration, sixty-nine gardens were purchased by the Trust for Public Lands (TPL). The New York Restoration Project (NYRP), a nonprofit founded and funded by the singer Bette Midler, took ownership of dozens more gardens.

In the years since, TPL has established three local land trusts to hold and manage the gardens: the Manhattan Land Trust, the Brooklyn Queens Land Trust, and the Bronx Land Trust. The board of each land trust is a mix of community garden leaders and staff from New York City nonprofit organizations. NYRP has now taken on a broader mission to provide green space to underserved areas of the city, and is being led by a range of New

York philanthropists, businesspeople, and civic leaders. At some of its sites, the amount of space available for community-managed gardens has been reduced in favor of tidy pocket parks (New York Restoration Project, n.d.).

Community Land Trusts

Since the 1980s, community land trusts in the United States have had a primary focus on permanently affordable housing, but there has also been a parallel, albeit less common, focus on agricultural practices, both in rural and urban settings. Especially in the last decade, CLTs have played three roles in support of urban agriculture. First, some CLTs formed to provide affordable housing have begun to hold land for community gardens and urban farms. Second, some housing-focused CLTs have provided programmatic support for urban agriculture, rather than taking on ownership of agricultural land themselves. Also, a few organizations focused exclusively on urban agriculture have been founded and structured as community land trusts, adapting some of the organizational and operational features of CLTs that develop housing.

Fig. 17.1. Troy Gardens in Madison, Wisconsin, an award-wining project combining affordable housing and urban agriculture, developed by the Madison Area Community Land Trust.[5]

Here we focus on several applications of the CLT model to urban agriculture, starting with the Southside Community Land Trust, which remains the only CLT in the USA with a sole focus on preserving land for community gardens and urban farms.

Southside Community Land Trust

Southside Community Land Trust (Southside CLT, n.d.) holds title to sixteen community gardens in Providence, Rhode Island. Southside CLT provides programmatic support (such as arranging for bulk purchases of organic fertilizers) for these gardens, as well as for the twenty-five gardens in its network that are owned by other organizations. Southside differs from other community land trusts in that it only holds land for gardens and farms rather than for affordable housing. However, like traditional CLTs, it has built community representation and engagement into its governance structure. Fifty-one percent of its board members must be elected directly from the gardeners (Yuen, 2012: 36–37).

In addition to protecting land for community gardens, Southside CLT manages two commercial farms. City Farm is a three-quarter-acre commercial urban farm in south Providence that began in 1986. Urban Edge Farm is a fifty-acre farm in nearby Cranston, Rhode Island; its mission is to support seven new farmers who collaboratively manage the land (Southside CLT). The land for Urban Edge was purchased by the state in 2002, pursuant to the state's Open Space Preservation Act (Rhode Island Department of Environmental Management, n.d.). The site, which was formerly a dairy farm, is now owned

Fig. 17.2. Southside Community Land Trust, Providence, Rhode Island.

and protected by the Rhode Island Department of Environmental Management, which leases it to Southside CLT for one dollar per year (ibid.; Ewert, 2012: 97). About twenty of the fifty acres are cultivable.

Southside CLT initially operated its own CSA farm at Urban Edge Farm, but within a few years it became clear that production would not cover the significant staffing costs (Ewert, 2012: 91). Through Urban Edge Farm, Southside CLT now teaches farming practices to new farmers, rents them farm equipment, provides compost and fertilizer, and plows the land once a year (Snowden, 2006). After going through training, these beginning farmers can rent up to two acres of land at below-market rates. These farming businesses are owned and operated by people who have experience in farming, but weren't able to buy or rent land on their own at market rates. They sell through CSAs, directly to institutions, and through growers' cooperatives.

Athens Land Trust

As an adjunct to its affordable housing and land conservation efforts, the Athens Land Trust (ALT) in Athens, Georgia has made a deep commitment to community agriculture programming as a strategy for community engagement and neighborhood revitalization. The three-fold mission of their Community Agriculture Program is (a) to promote sustainable agriculture, (b) to increase access to healthy food, and (c) to support economic and entrepreneurial opportunities for underserved youth and adults. This Program has five components:

Fig. 17.3. Athens Land Trust, West Broad farmers market, Athens, Georgia.

1. *Community Garden Network:* The CGN is a partnership among organizations that grow and promote school and community garden projects.

2. *Farm to School:* ALT is working with the local school system to expand school gardens and to incorporate fresh food grown on school grounds into cafeteria meals.

3. *Vendor Development:* The West Broad Farmers Market provides retail space for underserved farmers and small business owners.

4. *Young Urban Farmers:* In partnership with the Clarke County School District, ALT established the Young Urban Farmers program in order to provide underserved high school students with sustainable agriculture education, hands-on work experience, and leadership development.

5. *Farmer Outreach:* This program is a collaborative effort with the Natural Resources Conservation Service to conduct outreach and educational activities for underserved groups in northeast Georgia.

Oakland Community Land Trust

The programming of the Oakland Community Land Trust in Oakland, California is focused on three core initiatives: residential anti-displacement; career pathways/construction training; and land access for food production. In their Urban Agriculture and Community Gardens program, they are building an administrative and legal capacity to acquire and to steward land in perpetuity for a variety of open space, agricultural, and gardening uses that directly serve low-income families and neighborhoods. They are collaborating with community partners to reuse blighted, tax-defaulted parcels in ways that engage existing neighborhood residents in the production of healthy food.

The Oakland Community Land Trust is currently in the process of acquiring a number of tax-defaulted and lien-burdened parcels from Alameda County. Once taking ownership, the land will be prepared for community use, with long-term ground leases provided to partner organizations for urban agriculture initiatives.

THE CENTRAL SERVER MODEL —
A SCALABLE APPROACH TO URBAN FARMING?

The "central server" is a model developed within the community land trust movement to facilitate the scaling and stewardship of permanently affordable housing on a regional or city-wide basis, while striking a balance between local control and centralized services. The model was introduced in 2009 in Atlanta, and proposed soon thereafter in New Orleans.[6] Supporters hoped to spur the growth of neighborhood-based community land trusts

> A central server could do the "heavy lifting" that is beyond the ability of small, neighborhood-based organizations.

by creating a central entity that would provide a variety of technical services, including: accounting, development, and real estate transactions; negotiating with funders and lenders; and managing resales — all of which require more expertise than a neighborhood-based organization can easily muster.

From the experiences in Atlanta and New Orleans, affordable housing advocates soon learned that the burdens placed on a central server can be difficult to bear from a legal, political, financial, and community relations perspective. There is not the space in this chapter to evaluate the effectiveness of the central server model for affordable housing,[7] but it is worth noting that affordable-housing CLTs in a number of cities in the United States are continuing to explore the best ways to design and to fund a regional operation serving multiple CLTs in multiple neighborhoods.[8]

In the context of urban farming, where transactions are more straightforward because they do not involve housing or residents, we believe that a central server model may hold significant promise. Successfully implementing such a model in the urban farming context, as it does in the housing context, would depend on striking a balance between local control and centralized economies of scale. An appropriate architecture would involve a web of neighborhood-based "satellite" organizations served by a citywide organization, the "central server." The central server would provide a suite of services for the satellites and for the farmers to whom the satellites provide land.

Possible Roles of a Central Server in an Urban Farming Context

A central server could do the "heavy lifting" that is beyond the ability of small, neighborhood-based organizations that are necessarily focused on starting up urban farming projects. With expertise in land use and real estate transactions, a central server could negotiate with local government to secure publicly owned land for agriculture, obtain favorable tax treatment, and gain access to city services to provide needed infrastructure to gardens and farms. In addition, a central server could help to provide training and technical support to satellite organizations. Providing such services in group settings would be less costly, and would create opportunities to build connections between satellite organizations.

A central server could also provide a single point of connection to funders. This would increase the collective leverage of neighborhood organizations beyond what they could accomplish individually, and reduce overhead for funders by packaging what might otherwise be numerous similar grant applications. (Of course, satellite organizations may also seek funding for their own operations.) A central server would also have access to officials and decision-making in city government that is beyond the reach of smaller organizations.

The term *server* is key to understanding the model. A central server would exist to serve satellite entities in each of the neighborhoods encompassed by the central server. The staff for a central server would have to be skilled at "playing well with others" and studiously avoid engaging in turf battles or picking favorites. This would not be easy, especially in cities where local elected officials have a strong say in how projects are developed in their districts.

Roles of Neighborhood-Based Satellites in a Central Server for Urban Farming

Satellite organizations would serve as the voice of their community. They may be existing nonprofits (community development corporations, community land trusts, etc.), new start-ups, or more informal entities. No matter what form they take, they should be able to speak credibly on behalf of their neighborhoods and ensure that land use decisions are in the best interest of residents.

A central server would free neighborhood-based satellite organizations from the heavy lifting of real estate transactions, infrastructure installation, and negotiating favorable property tax treatment. Satellites would then be able to focus on the critical work of managing productive land with the oversight and engagement of neighborhood residents, through participatory planning and recruiting growers who are committed to integrating farming into the fabric of their community.

Satellite entities would have to play some governance role in the central server. This would help to ensure that the central server's staff would keep their eyes on the prize of supporting neighborhood organizations.

Who Should Own the Land in a Central Server Model?

In an urban agriculture context, it would likely make more sense for the central server to be the landholding entity. As described below, this is the approach that NeighborSpace has used to great success in Chicago. It takes advantage of economies of scale and real estate expertise, and provides a single point of contact for public agencies that provide land for farms and gardens.

On the other hand, satellite organizations may want to own the land themselves to secure better local control over neighborhood development. A "hybrid" approach might also work, where the land was initially owned by the central server, but satellite organizations would have the option to purchase lands in their neighborhood once they had built a management and stewardship capacity locally. Such a hybrid approach might also provide that, in the event a satellite organization failed, lands would revert to the central server.

NeighborSpace: A Central Server Case Study

NeighborSpace is the closest existing organization to what might be considered a central-server land trust model for urban agriculture. Founded to help conserve Chicago's community gardens, the land trust has recently begun to hold land for commercially oriented urban farms as well. Its history and structure point toward how a central server model might be further developed in other cities.[9]

NeighborSpace was founded in 1996 as a response to a city planning report that found Chicago lagging behind other major cities in terms of open space per capita (City of Chicago et al.,1998). The report noted that some of the city's 55,000 vacant lots had been converted or appropriated for neighborhood uses, including community gardens. Yet even as development threatened many of these gardens, no public agency was tasked with conserving community-managed open space.

The report recommended creating a citywide land trust to hold urban gardens. In response, the City of Chicago, the Cook County Forest Preserve, and the Chicago Park District joined to found and to fund NeighborSpace, which would officially be an independent nonprofit (Chicago City Council, 1996). NeighborSpace has continued to operate with support and oversight from these three governmental entities, each of which provides $100,000 in annual funding, with each appointing two representatives to serve on the land trust's board of directors. The remaining three seats are reserved for non-governmental representatives.

As of mid-2019, NeighborSpace owned or leased 115 sites. Although accounting for only a fraction of the hundreds of community gardens in Chicago (Taylor and Lovell, 2012), NeighborSpace nevertheless protects a sizable amount of land: 26.4 acres of green space, the equivalent of fifteen football pitches.

NeighborSpace takes on many of the roles of a central server while leaving certain other roles to community organizations. Community gardens are managed by groups of gardeners, while NeighborSpace takes on vital and often costly tasks that would prove burdensome for individual groups of gardeners, including:

- Acquiring land;

- Securing title;

- Completing environmental testing and remediation;

- Securing liability insurance;

- Applying for property tax exemptions;

- Arranging for water access; and

- Responding to stewardship emergencies like fallen trees.

Fig. 17.4. Drake Garden, built by residents on an empty lot in the Albany Park neighborhood, Chicago, Illinois.

> NeighborSpace's ownership also ensures that public investments will continue to benefit the public.

NeighborSpace is careful, however, to leave community organizing to community organizations. Before it will consider securing title to a community garden, the land trust requires a community partner to take responsibility, along with at least three garden leaders and at least ten community stakeholders (Helphand, 2015: 2). NeighborSpace also leaves the governance and management of gardens to community partners, so long as they meet minimum insurance requirements.

Around 2010, NeighborSpace began holding land for urban farms (Ela, 2016). This happened after Growing Home, a successful nonprofit urban farm, saw an opportunity to expand onto a nearby city-owned parcel. Rather than seeking to have the city transfer ownership directly, the farm sought to have the city transfer the land to NeighborSpace, which would then lease the land to Growing Home.

For NeighborSpace, holding land for commercial farming was a new proposition. After considering the issue, the land trust's directors agreed that supporting urban farms fit with the mission of preserving community-managed open space. In addition to requiring that farms be operated by not-for-profit entities, NeighborSpace disallows any permanent structures (hoop-houses are permissible), and ensures that a farm's size is suited to the neighborhood context.

From the city's perspective, NeighborSpace's ownership of land being used for urban agriculture solves several problems. The land trust can help coordinate and raise funds for environmental testing and remediation, expenses that can run to several hundred thousand dollars. NeighborSpace's ownership also ensures that, if a particular gardening group dissolves or if an urban farming organization ceases operations, public investments will continue to benefit the public.

This new model has expanded. In the West Side neighborhood of East Garfield Park, NeighborSpace now leases 2.6 acres to Chicago FarmWorks, a nonprofit farm that sells its produce at wholesale prices to the Greater Chicago Food Depository (Heartland Alliance, 2012). Beyond these two sites, officials from city agencies and local foundations have come to see NeighborSpace as a useful tool for expanding Chicago's commercial agriculture sector.

NeighborSpace is the organization closest to what a central server might look like. But the point is not that its model should simply be adopted in other cities. The conditions surrounding the founding and funding of NeighborSpace are unique to Chicago. Elsewhere, urban farming organizations might need to spearhead a process to create a new land tenure model and might need support from local foundations, rather than government partners. That could produce a more formalized network of community-controlled, neighborhood-level satellite organizations than exists in Chicago. NeighborSpace provides a helpful example, but the structure of new urban farming land trusts will surely vary, depending on the contexts and resources available in different cities.

Best Practices for Designing a Central Server

- *Encourage government buy-in.* The vast majority of land for urban farming will likely come from the public sector. In addition, public subsidies for remediation and operations will often be needed. As a *quid pro quo*, government may seek to control the central server's functions. A central server will work best, however, when government has a voice, but not a veto.

- *Engage with communities.* Community engagement in the guidance and governance of the central server will be important for growers, consumers, and neighbors to support the central server and to work cooperatively with the central server in managing land for urban agriculture.

- *Establish a clear division of roles and responsibilities.* There should be a clear division of roles and responsibilities between the central server and neighborhood-based satellites, as well as between the central server and government, community organizations, and farmers.

■ *Land should be owned by the central server.* Land ownership by the central server will generally work best, but there may be an option for local entities to eventually purchase lands in their own neighborhoods (with reversion to the central server if the satellite goes under).

■ *Central server should do the technical work.* The central server should attend to legal and financial issues that require technical expertise beyond that of growers. Such expertise includes title, insurance, land preparation, construction of infrastructure, and property taxation.

■ *Central server should foster communication and education.* The central server should be transparent in its own policies, operations and finances, while encouraging communication among growers, sharing information about best farming practices.

■ *Central server should seek favorable property tax treatment.* To protect the ongoing affordability of urban farmland, the central server should look for opportunities to reduce or to stabilize property taxes on its holdings.[10]

CONCLUSION

Farms and gardens are hardly a new feature of America's urban landscapes, having repeatedly cropped up and withered away since the late 1800s (Lawson, 2005). This coming and going frames a puzzle: how might urban agriculture become, and remain, a permanent part of our cities? How might we reimagine and restructure land tenure to help urban farmers contribute on a long-term basis to the health (and perhaps the wealth) of the cities and communities in which they grow?

Answers to these questions are emerging in fits and starts, as people tinker with ways that urban farmers can gain access to land on a long-term basis. In all likelihood, no single dominant model will emerge; instead, we will see the development of a diverse mix of strategies, including the increasing use of land trusts.

We have proposed, in this chapter, a way in which current strategies — the central server model, in particular — might be extended and expanded to help urban farmers and community gardeners to become more securely rooted in their communities. Community ownership of land, combined with long-term ground leases, offers a tried and true approach that provides security of tenure for urban growers, while preserving the community's voice in land use decisions. We hope this approach will prove fruitful, grafting onto, hybridizing with, and fertilizing ongoing efforts to expand urban agriculture in the United States and in other countries as well.

Notes

1. Community-supported agriculture (CSA model) is a system that connects producers and consumers within the food system more closely by allowing consumers to subscribe to the harvest of a certain farm or group of farms. It is an alternative socioeconomic model of agriculture and food distribution that allows the producer and consumer to share the risks of farming.

2. Although urban agriculture takes a wide range of forms, we focus here on land tenure models that can best support ground-based, outdoor growing of commercial crops. Such growing practices, compared to growing on rooftops or indoors, are more likely to yield the full range of community benefits mentioned above. Also, because community non-profit organizations or individual growers may have less access to capital than rooftop or indoor growers, the cost and availability of land is an even more pressing constraint.

3. It is certainly possible for entities other than nonprofits to serve as landholding entities. Here we focus on the role of nonprofits both for reasons of space and because the non-profit form is often adopted in situations where there is "at least one class of patrons for whom both the costs of contracting and the costs of ownership are quite high" (Hansmann, 1996: 228), meaning that vesting ownership in a single group can result in severe inefficiencies. Here, government entities and potential donors would face significant contracting costs if they were to retain ownership of land and to contract with individual growers.

4. There is movement in this direction, however. Openlands, the regional open space land trust in Chicago and its environs, is focused on the ecological potential of farmland when used as a buffer for conservation lands. Also, the Trust for Public Lands has recently developed a "working lands" initiative (Trust for Public Lands, n.d.). Meanwhile, a move is under way in the open space land trust community to promote "community conservation" initiatives (Aldrich and Levy, 2015).

5. Community gardens and an urban farm were incorporated into the Troy Gardens project of the Madison Area Community Land Trust, alongside affordable housing. A case study of the project is available at *http://www.troygardens.net*

6. For more on the Atlanta model, see the web page of the Atlanta Land Trust (*https://atlantalandtrust.org*). It is also described in PD&R Edge (2012) and Schneggenburger (2011). The Crescent City Community Land Trust in New Orleans adopted a central server model on its founding in 2011 (Khanmalek, 2013).

7. For more information on how the CLT central server model has played out in Essex County, New Jersey, see DeFillipis (2012). A detailed examination of central server initiatives across the United States can be found in Baldwin (2016).

8. In 2015, a group of CLTs in Boston formed the Metro Boston Community Land Trust Network, exploring the possibility of Dudley Neighbors Inc. functioning as a central server. (See the DNI profile in the present volume.) Other "central server" initiatives are currently under development in Denver and New York City.

9. This case study draws upon an article by the executive director of NeighborSpace (Helphand, 2015).

10. In some cases, this may require the central server to agree to a long-term ground lease when accepting land from a public entity, instead of receiving title, trading a bit of control in exchange for lower taxes.

References

Aldrich, Rob, and Melissa Levy (2015). Assessing, Planning and Measuring Comunity Conservation Impact: A Tool for Land Trusts. Land Trust Alliance. Accessed November 24, 2015, at *http://www.landtrustalliance.org/publication/community-conservation-tool*.

Atlanta Land Trust (n.d.). Accessed November 24, 2015, at *https://atlantalandtrust.org*.

Baldwin, Ben (2016). Networked Community Land Trusts: An Analysis of Existing Models and Needs Assessment for the Greater Boston Community Land Trust Network. Unpublished Master's Thesis. Tufts University.

Brooklyn Queens Land Trust (n.d.). About BQLT. Accessed November 24, 2015, at *http://www.bqlt.org/About/*.

Chicago City Council (1996). Committee on Finance, Authorization for Execution of Intergovernmental Agreement with Chicago Park District and Forest Preserve District of Cook County for Establishment of "NeighborSpace." Accessed October 31, 2015, at *http://www.eatbettermovemore.org/sa/policies/pdftext/ChicagoNeighborSpace.pdf*.

City of Chicago, Chicago Park District and Forest Preserve District of Cook County (1998). CitySpace: An Open Space Plan for Chicago.

DeFillipis, James (2012). "New Research on the Fundamental Issues of Central Server CLTs," Available at: *https://impact.adobeconnect.com/_a1162566415/p69u9e9xyjg/?launcher=false&fcsContent=true&pbMode=normal*.

Ela, Nate (2016). "Urban Commons as Property Experiment: Mapping Chicago's Farms and Gardens." *Fordham Urban Law Journal* 43(2): 247–294.

Ewert, Brianna (2012). Incubating New Farmers. Master's Thesis, University of Montana. Accessed November 24, 2015, at *https://scholarworks.umt.edu/cgi/viewcontent.cgi?article=2165&context=etd*.

Growing Power (2013). Farmers for Chicago. Accessed October 29, 2015, at *https://www.chicago.gov/city/en/depts/mayor/press_room/press_releases/2013/march_2013/mayor_emanuel_launchesnewfarmersforchicagonetworkforchicagourban.html.*

Hansmann, Henry (1996). *The Ownership of Enterprise.* Cambridge, MA: Harvard University Press.

Heartland Alliance (2012). Heartland Human Care Services Breaks Ground on West Side Urban Farm. Accessed October 29, 2015, at *https://www.heartlandalliance.org/press_release/urban-farm/.*

Helphand, Ben (2015). Permanently Grassroots with NeighborSpace. *Cities and the Environment (CATE)* 8(2): Art.19. Accessed November 24, 2015, at *http://digitalcommons.lmu.edu/cate/vol8/iss2/19.*

Khanmalek, Azeen (2013). CCLT Investment Strategy. American Planning Association Louisiana Chapter, October 2013 Monthly Bulletin. Accessed November 24, 2015, at *https://sites.google.com/a/louisianaplanning.com/homebusiness/2010newsletter/2013-october.*

Lawson, Laura (2005). *City Bountiful: A Century of Community Gardening in America.* Berkeley: University of California Press.

New York Restoration Project (N.D.). Target East Harlem Community Garden. Accessed November 24, 2015, at *http://www.nyrp.org/green-spaces/garden-details/target-east-harlem-community-garden.*

PD&R Edge (2012). Community Land Trusts in Atlanta, Georgia: A Central Server Model. Accessed November 24, 2015, at *http://www.huduser.gov/portal/pdredge/pdr_edge_inpractice_112312.html.*

Rhode Island Department of Environmental Management (N.D.). Forest Stewardship: Rhode Island Landowners Discover New Strategies in Forest Conservation. Accessed November 24, 2015, at *http://www.dem.ri.gov/programs/bnatres/forest/pdf/forstew.pdf.*

Schneggenburger, Andy (2011). Bringing CLTs to Scale in Atlanta. *Shelterforce,* Feb. 7, 2011. Accessed November 24, 2015, at *http://www.shelterforce.org/article bringing_clts_to_scale_in_atlanta/.*

Small Business Association (2012). Frequently Asked Questions About Small Business. Accessed November 24, 2015, at *http://www.sba.gov/sites/default/files/FAQ_Sept_2012.pdf.*

Snowden, Mary (2006). Farm Profile: Pak Express Farm. Accessed November 24, 2015, at *http://www.farmfresh.org/food/farm.php?farm=766#profile.*

Southside Community Land Trust (N.D.). Urban Edge Farm. Accessed November 24, 2015, at *https://www.southsideclt.org/category/urban-edge-farm/.*

Taylor, John R., and Sarah Taylor Lovell (2012). Mapping public and private spaces of urban agriculture in Chicago through the analysis of high-resolution aerial images in Google Earth. *Landscape and Urban Planning* 108: 57–70.

Trust for Public Lands (n.d.). Working Lands. Accessed November 24, 2015, at *https://www. tpl.org/our-work/our-land-and-water/working-lands.*

USDA National Agricultural Statistics Service (2015). Quick Stats: Average Cropland Cash Rent by State. Accessed November 24, 2015, at *https://bit.ly/3clo1ei*

Yuen, Jeffrey (2012). Hybrid Vigor: An Analysis of Land Tenure Arrangements in Addressing Land Security for Urban Community Gardens. Master's Thesis, Columbia University.

18.

The Best Things in Life
Are Perpetually Affordable
Profile of the Champlain Housing Trust,
Burlington, Vermont

Brenda M. Torpy

The Champlain Housing Trust (CHT) was born in a small city with a big idea: by creating a stock of permanently affordable housing, everyone could have access to a decent, affordable home, regardless of income. This was the grand vision of a newly elected progressive government led by Mayor Bernie Sanders who came into office in 1981, the same year as Ronald Reagan became President of the United States.

The so-called Reagan Revolution resulted in massive reductions in federal funding for affordable housing and forced the Sanders administration to develop innovative solutions to address Burlington's housing problems. Equally challenging were double-digit mortgage rates that prevailed during the 1980s, the threatened gentrification of Burlington's traditional working class neighborhoods, and the long-standing neglect of housing quality and affordability by previous mayors. They had favored downtown commercial development and had allowed low-income neighborhoods to be bulldozed in the name of Urban Renewal.

A cornerstone of the progressive agenda was to open up City Hall to all citizens — especially those who had been previously excluded — involving them in decisions about city planning and public funding. One of Bernie's earliest allies on the City Council, Terry Bouricius, had heard about community land trusts and suggested it might be a good fit for Burlington. The model's democratic structure and its commitment to permanent affordability made a lot of sense in a city where housing costs were on the rise, where a lack of code enforcement and the absence of landlord-tenant law made low-income tenants nearly powerless in the overheated housing market, and where proposed waterfront development adjacent to the city's lowest-income area, the Old North End, threatened further gentrification.

When Mayor Sanders created the Community and Economic Development Office (CEDO) in 1983 to help implement his progressive agenda, work on establishing a community land trust soon got underway. CEDO sent several employees to the first national CLT gathering in Voluntown Connecticut, hosted by the Institute for Community Economics (ICE). Included in this CEDO delegation were Michael Monte, the City's community development director, and Brenda Torpy, the City's housing director. At the Voluntown conference, they met John Davis who was a technical assistance provider on ICE's staff. A few months later, CEDO contracted with ICE to bring Davis to Burlington to introduce the CLT idea to Burlington's citizens and to see if it would take root.

> The Burlington Community Land Trust was the first municipally initiated and municipally supported CLT in the United States.

It did. The Burlington Community Land Trust (BCLT) was incorporated in 1984 after thousands of hours of volunteer work. Recruited and coordinated by CEDO staff, these volunteers wrote bylaws for the new organization, developed its policies, and fashioned strategies for finding the funds that would be needed to support the organization's operations and to produce affordable housing. Among the BCLT's incorporators were Howard Dean, the state's future Governor, and Sarah Carpenter, future director of the Vermont Housing Finance Agency. The Old North End was chosen as the BCLT's area of priority, although the BCLT's bylaws allowed the organization to look for housing development opportunities in any of Burlington's neighborhoods.

The City government seeded the fledgling CLT effort with a $200,000 grant for operations and provided a pair of million-dollar loans from the Burlington Employees' Retirement System. The BCLT later received regular municipal funding for its operations and its projects through federal funds that passed through the City's hands, including monies provided by the federal Community Development Block Grant and HOME programs, and from local funds disbursed by Burlington's Housing Trust Fund. Beyond financial support, the BCLT also had the benefit of continued assistance from CEDO staff and from Davis, the ICE staffer assigned to Burlington under a CEDO contract.

The Burlington Community Land Trust was the first municipally initiated and municipally supported CLT in the United States, a direct result of the City's embrace of permanent affordability, a policy deemed by Progressives in City Hall to be the only socially equitable and fiscally prudent way for the public to create and to sustain affordable housing. Mayor Bernie Sanders and his immediate successor, Peter Clavelle, were outspoken champions of "decommodifying" publicly assisted, privately owned housing. Their administrations acted to embed this principle into municipal policy and multiple ordinances. Their goal was to ensure that public investments in affordable housing would go primarily — even exclusively — into housing that would be kept *permanently* affordable. This was viewed as a revolutionary idea at the time, an outgrowth of Bernie's socialist agenda. But over the years, and for very practical reasons, this commitment to permanent affordability became accepted wisdom throughout Vermont. It also slowly gained acceptance among city officials in many other states.

SEEDING INNOVATION OUTSIDE OF CITY HALL

It came as a surprise to many of Bernie's political opponents — and to some of his sup-porters — that a majority of the most progressive measures enacted by this self-described socialist were delegated to *non*governmental organizations, either to private, nonprofit organizations that had been around for many years or to nonprofits that were newly cre-ated. These progressive measures may have been initiated by City Hall, but they were nei-ther administered nor controlled by city government. That was true for the BCLT as well.

What was the thinking of the Sanders Administration in choosing to establish the Burlington Community Land Trust as an autonomous entity *outside* of city government, one that was guided and governed by private citizens? The reasons behind this deci-sion were both practical and political, a multi-faceted rationale that unfolded as follows.

First, nonprofit, non-governmental organizations (NGOs) in the United States have access to sources of project funding and operational support that governmental organizations do not. NGOs like the Burlington Commu-nity Land Trust can receive an exemp-tion from federal income taxes, a status known as a 501(c)(3) designation. This status helps nonprofit organizations to raise donations from private citizens, since donors may deduct such gifts from their own federal taxes. Today, the

Fig. 18.1. Bernie Sanders, speaking at the National CLT Conference, Burlington, Vermont, 1990.

Champlain Housing Trust raises $200,000 a year in this way, and has also built to date a capital endowment of $2,000,000 from private donations. CHT uses a portion of the annual earnings from this endowment to help fund its operations, keeping the princi-ple intact while collecting about $100,000 a year in revenue. This "rainy day fund" has enabled CHT to be a bolder and more innovative developer. CLT's 501(c)(3) status also allows the organization to apply for funding from corporate and private philanthropic foundations, as well as from government programs that often require applicants to have a tax exemption as a condition of eligibility.

Second, the BCLT was established outside of the municipal government because city administrations come and go. Policies, programs, and priorities can change dramatically with every change in government. In Burlington, the Progressives never dreamed they would control City Hall throughout the 1980s and for much of the 1990s. They hoped to perpetuate progressive policies like permanent affordability, therefore, by institutionaliz-ing them outside of city government.

The BCLT adopted the "classic" CLT model of a broad-based membership and a representative board because it met the Sanders administration's commitment to a more democratic approach to community development. From the outset, the BCLT's leadership consciously used this structure to expand the constituency for its mission by recruiting leadership from beyond the Progressive circle and found that, when separated from the heat of Burlington's partisan politics, the BCLT's mission found wide support. Even some conservative politicians came to embrace permanent affordability, recognizing it to be a more efficient use of public funds.[1] The BCLT's leadership was also well aware that the whole idea of a community land trust was pushing against the conventions of the private real estate market and the powerful interests that undergird it. A community-based NGO that embraced advocacy and education as part of its core mission could mobilize its members to support and defend progressive projects and policies as needed.

For example, in 1993 the citizens of Burlington elected a Republican mayor, Peter Brownell, after a decade of Progressive rule. The new mayor soon proposed to redirect community development funding away from affordable housing in order to support economic development and public works instead. The BCLT led the resistance to his efforts. When City Councilors met to take the vote on the mayor's proposal, they found themselves surrounded by seventeen quilted banners hanging from the upper balcony of the council chamber. Each colorful banner, three feet wide and eight feet in length, was made up of dozens of hand-sewn squares. These quilt squares, 500 in all, had been crafted by residents of affordable housing and homeless shelters throughout Burlington, who had been asked to depict the meaning of home in images and words of their own choosing. One square, in particular, captured the BCLT's unique approach to housing: "The Best Things in Life Are Perpetually Affordable." As the City Council's meeting got underway, volunteers stepped to the microphone during the public forum, reading statements that spoke of the importance of affordable housing in their own lives. In the end, the Council voted to restore the housing funds, rejecting Mayor Brownell's proposal. The Mayor himself lasted for only a single, two-year term. He lost the next election and Progressives returned to power.

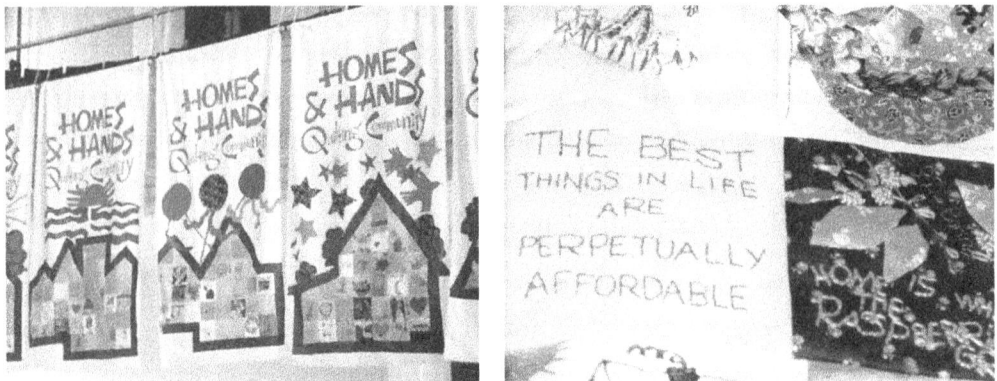

Fig 18.2. Quilted banners hanging in Burlington City Hall, 1993 (left). Detail of quilt squares (right).

Another reason for establishing the BCLT outside of city government was the sheer unfamiliarity of the whole idea of developing and selling resale-restricted, owner-occupied homes on leased land. It was easier to market such homes if the landowner was a charitable, nonprofit organization rather than a governmental entity. It was easier for the public to accept the overall concept as well. If the Sanders administration had attempted to institute *government* ownership of land, it would have fed into the Red-baiting narrative of Bernie's opponents. Vermont was and still is a very liberal part of the United States, but property rights are jealously guarded and government interference in these rights through any type of property restriction has always created a strong backlash.

There was a final, practical reason for creating a community land trust outside of city government, one that became increasingly clear in subsequent years. The BCLT was going to be a better steward for a growing portfolio of permanently affordable, owner-occupied homes than city officials could ever be. Long-term stewardship required a specialized staff who were fully committed to watching over the housing entrusted into their care, acting to protect the housing's affordability and intervening, when necessary, to prevent foreclosures among any homeowners who might get behind in their mortgage payments.[2] Stewardship, in order to work easily and effectively, would require a cooperative relationship between the land trust and its homeowners, who are also members of the CLT. This is not the kind of relationship that can be easily created or maintained with a government agency.

CULTIVATING A FAVORABLE POLICY ENVIRONMENT

As Burlington's Progressives worked to create new resources for the development of affordable housing, they also worked to enact new laws that would protect vulnerable renters and produce permanently affordable homes through funding and policy initiatives. This dual commitment to expanding the supply of housing and to preserving the affordability of that housing was woven into guidelines for the Housing Trust Fund, capitalized through a penny increase on the property tax rate; ordinances that regulated the conversion of rental housing to condominiums and retarded the loss of existing housing from demolition or conversion to commercial uses; and an Inclusionary Zoning (IZ) ordinance, where the affordability of all IZ units had to be preserved for 99 years.[3]

Creating these laws required the active participation of many of the same neighborhood activists and housing advocates who had come together to create the BCLT in 1984. The board and staff of the BCLT were actively involved in all of these legislative efforts to expand funding for affordable housing, as well as several unsuccessful campaigns to enact ordinances to protect the rights of vulnerable renters, including an anti-speculation tax and just-cause eviction.

There continued to be considerable overlap among city government, the emerging Progressive Party created by activists who had helped to elect Bernie Sanders, and the BCLT. The BCLT's first executive director was Tim McKenzie, a neighborhood activist

> Conservationists and housing advocates united in their opposition to the threat of unfettered land speculation.

who had helped to mobilize voter support for Bernie's first successful campaigns for mayor. Gretchen Bailey, an Assistant City Attorney who had been one of Bernie's first hires, conducted much of the legal research that enabled the BCLT to craft a ground lease compatible with Vermont law. The first board president of the BCLT was Brenda Torpy, who served as the City's housing director until moving to a job at the Vermont Housing Finance Agency. Torpy was followed in the housing director's job by John Davis, the former employee from ICE who had assisted CEDO in establishing the BCLT. When Tim McKenzie stepped down as the BCLT's executive director in 1991, Torpy was hired as his successor, assuming leadership of the organization she had helped to establish seven years before.

Burlington was the fulcrum and the leader of the effort in Vermont to make permanent affordability the cornerstone of all housing policy. In the 1980s, when affordability restrictions began expiring on federally subsidized, privately owned rental housing that had been built twenty years earlier, Vermont was one of the states hit the hardest by the threatened loss of this affordable housing. At the same time, an overheated real estate market was causing a steep rise in the price of for-sale, owner-occupied housing throughout Vermont. These twin crises allowed advocates to bring the CLT model and other progressive housing solutions to the attention of the Vermont legislature. With the support of both the legislature and Governor Madeline Kunin, advocates were successful in incorporating a priority for permanent affordability into an increasing number of state laws and plans.

During this same period, Vermont began experiencing a wave of speculative development in the countryside that threatened its traditional agricultural landscape. Conservationists and housing advocates found themselves united in their opposition to the threat of unfettered land speculation, luxury development, and gentrification. An outcome of this convergence of interests and concerns was a powerful coalition of affordable housing providers, conservationists, and preservationists who convinced the state legislature and the Kunin Administration in 1987 to create and to fund the Vermont Housing and Conservation Board (VHCB).[4] This quasi-public entity was funded by a portion of Vermont's property-transfer tax, money that was then used by VHCB to preserve open space, working farms, historic landmarks, and affordable housing. The priority recipients of the grants disbursed by VHCB were a network of nonprofits doing land conservation or affordable housing that were obligated to steward these land-based resources permanently. Funding from VHCB helped to create and to sustain the operations and the projects of community land trusts in Burlington and throughout the state. Indeed, this new crop of CLTs became the principal means by which VHCB sought to accomplish its affordable housing mission.

The Burlington Community Land Trust was able to grow and to thrive in this favorable policy environment. With the government of its city and the government of its state both embracing the principle of permanent affordability—and both directing public capital toward projects and organizations that would make this principle a reality—the BCLT was able to turn a forward-thinking policy into the sticks and bricks of new housing.

BUILDING A DIVERSE PORTFOLIO OF PERMANENTLY AFFORDABLE HOUSING

The BCLT's original strategy was twofold: to expand homeownership by creating a resale-restricted, leased-land homeownership product/program that would be accepted by public funders, private lenders, and prospective homebuyers; and to improve the Old North End, a neighborhood with an aging housing stock that was in poor condition but losing its affordability because of the neighborhood's proximity to the downtown, the waterfront, and the University of Vermont.

On the homeownership side, the first challenge was to gain acceptance for the CLT model and, in particular, its separation of land and buildings. This dual-ownership model frightened lenders and daunted appraisers. There were few other CLTs to point to in the early 1980's. Thus there was no track record to reassure skeptical lenders and public leaders that, first, there would be a market for limited-equity homes on leased land, and second, that the benefits would outweigh the risks to either buyers or lenders. Even Bernie Sanders worried, at first, that this might be "second class homeownership for working people."

The BCLT also faced the wrath of private realtors and for-profit developers who objected strenuously to the removal of land and housing from the speculative market. A few years after the organization was established, some of them organized Homeowners Against the Land Trust (HALT) to oppose a proposed BCLT development in which single-family detached houses were to be built on donated land. They picketed City Hall, singing "Oh give me a home with land that I own," to the tune of *Home, Home on the Range*.

This was a stark reminder that what the BCLT was committed to doing was a scary departure from business as usual. Burlington's progressive government may have embraced permanent affordability as a necessary response to the inequities of a profit-oriented housing market and as a way to retain the value of the public investment in housing, but that didn't mean that the private sector—or the NIMBYs living near BCLT housing—were ready to do so.[5]

The BCLT appealed for help to the Vermont Housing Finance Agency (VHFA), a state agency that had been established to provide mortgages for first-time homebuyers. After much hemming and hawing, VHFA accepted the CLT model, but only half-way. VHFA's solution for persuading their participating banks to chance this new thing was to create a rider to the ground lease, which gave banks the option of taking the entire property (land and home) if the BCLT did not cure a mortgage default in a specified time. The BCLT's leadership was confident of prevailing and never letting a property go to foreclosure, so

> Local bankers became ardent supporters when they saw there were virtually no foreclosures.

they reluctantly agreed to this bargain, at least until the model was proven. Later, a more favorable arrangement was negotiated that protected BCLT's interest in the entire property. No longer was BCLT required to pledge its land as collateral when a homeowner obtained a mortgage through VHFA. Once VHFA was on board, the BCLT was able to engage with local bankers who eventually became ardent supporters — especially when they saw there were virtually no foreclosures among the low-income homeowners being served by the land trust.

The first home purchased by the BCLT was a vacant, single-family house. It had been spotted by a single mother, an assistant librarian named Kathy Neilson who happened to attend a public forum at the library introducing the BCLT. She wanted a decent, secure home in which to raise her two daughters, so Kathy volunteered to be the "guinea pig" for the new model of tenure that the land trust was trying to establish.

As the BCLT's founders continued to worry their way through all the policies and structures for the new CLT and continued to negotiate with VHFA to create a mortgage product for resale-restricted homes on leased land, Kathy and her daughters cleaned up the site of what she hoped would be her new home. By autumn, she told the new BCLT board: "I mowed the grass all summer, and I'm raking the leaves now, but I will *not* plow the snow unless I am living there." Goaded by this passionate, prospective homebuyer who was growing a bit impatient with how long it was taking to put a roof over her head, the BCLT's leaders speeded up their efforts. All the pieces were pulled together and BCLT had its first closing in 1985. Kathy Neilson got her home at last — before the winter.

Since then, over 234 single-family houses have been placed under the CLT's stewardship, along with 372 condominiums and 5 duplexes. All of these owner-occupied homes are encumbered with permanent contractual restrictions that ensure they will be resold in the future to income-eligible households for an affordable price. The BCLT's ongoing stewardship of this owner-occupied housing — a portfolio currently totaling over 600 homes — also prevents absentee ownership, deferred maintenance, and predatory lending, while allowing the CLT to intervene (if necessary) to prevent foreclosures.

From its earliest days, the BCLT strategically purchased small, multi-family rental properties containing two to six housing units in the Old North End to avert tenant displacement. The initial plan was to work with existing tenants to convert these properties into limited-equity cooperatives, but over time the BCLT came to realize that larger multi-unit buildings were more likely to succeed as cooperatives. *Converting* existing rental housing into a cooperative was much harder to do (and less likely to succeed) than *constructing* a new building and organizing a new group of residents to create a cooperative association from scratch. There are now six limited-equity and zero-equity housing cooperatives in the organization's portfolio, containing a total of 121 co-op apartments.

On the neighborhood development side of its mission, the BCLT quickly evolved beyond its initial anti-gentrification commitment to the Old North End. By the 1990s,

Fig. 18.3. Celebration of CHT's 500th owner-occupied home, 2011. Featured in photo: CHT executive director, Brenda Torpy (l), former Mayor, Bob Kiss (c), and Vermont Housing and Conservation Board executive director, Gus Seelig (r).

the BCLT possessed a growing portfolio of rental housing and had already started to build its internal capacity to be a good social landlord. At first, it managed a relatively small number of scattered-site, rehabilitated rental properties, primarily in the Old North End. Over time, it expanded its service area beyond the Old North End and also began developing affordable rental housing, making use of Low Income Housing Tax Credits, a new federal program that provided equity for the construction or rehabilitation of housing served tenant households below 60% of Area Median Income. By the end of 2019, the community land trust owned and managed 2,431 rental apartments.

A LARGER GEOGRAPHY AND A BROADER MISSION

The BCLT had been founded with a city-wide focus, confining its activities during its first years to housing development within Burlington's boundaries. The BCLT expanded its service area in 1987 to include all of Chittenden County. In 2001, it expanded even further to cover the three northwest counties of Vermont, bordering Lake Champlain on the west and Canada to the north. This three-county service area encompasses 1,506 square miles, with a total population of 217,042 people. At the request of town governments within that area, the BCLT began to construct new rental housing and to operate a regional housing rehabilitation loan program for low-income homeowners.

The BCLT's greatest change and biggest leap came in 2005, when the leaders of the Lake Champlain Housing Development Corporation (LCHDC) invited the staff and board of the BCLT to explore a formal alliance and, possibly, a merger. By that time, decades of HUD cutbacks and a draconian shredding of the social safety net by a succession of federal administrations were putting both nonprofits at risk. A Republican Governor in Montpelier posed a threat to housing development funds coming from the state as well.[6] It no longer seemed feasible for LCHDC and the BCLT to share a relatively small service area and to compete for a scarce supply of dollars, sites, and political support. LCHDC possessed about 1,200 rental apartments. The BCLT's holdings included about 700 homes, divided equally between homeownership and rentals. Neither portfolio was large enough to be truly sustainable.

After a year of conversation, negotiation, and planning, the two organizations decided to merge into one. The BCLT was chosen to be the surviving corporation due to its strong membership base, broad donor support, and the diversity of its programs and funding sources. The name chosen for the newly merged corporation was the Champlain Housing Trust (CHT).

The model of membership and governance of a "classic" CLT was embraced by both boards during the negotiations leading up to the merger. Champlain Housing Trust continued to be structured as a membership organization with a tri-partite board, although that structure was modified slightly to incorporate LCHDC's strong link to the municipal governments that had created LCHDC back in 1984. Five seats on the governing board were reserved for homeowners, renters, or co-op members living in one of the homes in CHT's portfolio. Five seats were reserved for representatives of CHT's general membership: people who live within CHT's service area and support CHT's mission, but who do not live in a CHT home. Five seats were reserved for officials from the public sector, drawn from various municipal governments and regional bodies within CHT's three-county service area.

In the financial crisis of 2008, Vermont did not experience a crash in real estate values, but the state was hit hard by the subsequent economic downturn, producing a startling, multi-year rise in homelessness. Shelters and homeless assistance programs sponsored by the state government were overwhelmed and sought CHT's assistance. This was not an entirely new activity for CHT, but the scope of its role grew substantially in response to this crisis. CHT's ability to rapidly finance and develop properties enabled CHT to promptly create a new homeless facility, a converted motel where individuals and families could be temporarily housed and have access to services provided on-site. The success of this project led to CHT's most recent contribution to the region's housing needs: a partnership with the University of Vermont Medical Center Hospital to house people who are chronically ill and homeless. The Hospital has contributed three million dollars in capital, along with operating subsidies for on-site health services at two housing sites, enabling CHT to work towards its goal of eliminating chronic homelessness.

Over the years, the land trust has gradually added a number of non-residential projects to its portfolio as well. Beginning in the 1990s, the BCLT assumed a broader community development role in the Old North End: redeveloping polluted sites and returning abandoned and blighted properties to community use. BCLT not only built housing. It also developed a pocket park, a food shelf, a multi-generational community center, and buildings for nonprofit offices delivering everything from affordable health care to legal services. A former bus barn was converted into commercial spaces for a neighborhood restaurant, a laundromat, a garage for repairing and recycling cars, and a shop for repairing and selling bicycles. Since the 2006 merger, CHT has developed downtown office spaces, including a multi-story, mixed-use building in which CHT is headquartered. At present, organization's real estate portfolio contains over 160,000 square feet of nonresidential space.

Fig. 18.4. Vermont Transit bus barn, rehabilitated and re-purposed for neighborhood retail.

CHT's most recent non-housing venture is the acquisition and rehabilitation of a former Catholic elementary school in the Old North End, which had been mostly vacant for many years. CHT converted the building into a thriving community center. An anchor tenant is the City's Parks and Recreation Department, which is making full use of the building's gym for year-around recreation and sports, and also hosting arts and cultural activities and a daily senior center. Sharing the building with Parks and Recreation are a family center, a cooperative child development center, an amateur theatre, and a non-profit organization providing refugees and New Americans with legal, health and social services, job training, youth services, translation, and English language classes. A large community room and a commercial kitchen accommodate neighborhood meetings and provide an affordable space for family gatherings like weddings and memorials, as well as for cultural celebrations and festivals.

CHT's ever-expanding array of projects and services requires a large staff. A hundred employees oversee a diverse real estate portfolio that, in addition to several nonresidential buildings, currently contains over 3000 homes. CHT's residential holdings include shelters for the homeless, community homes with built-in services, rental apartments, limited-equity cooperatives, limited-equity condominiums, co-housing, and resale-restricted houses on leased land, providing a continuum of housing options for low-income and moderate-income households. CHT's staff provides a rich mix of services

Fig. 18.5. Participants in the international study visit sponsored by World Habitat, 2009.

> A hundred employees oversee a diverse real estate portfolio of over 3000 homes.

for homeowners and renters alike, helping them to succeed in the housing that is theirs and enabling them to move along this continuum to achieve the type and tenure of housing that is best for them. These services include financial education and counselling for applicants seeking to rent, purchase, or retain housing, as well as case management for those with special needs. Staff support is also provided for community-building activities like gardens and youth programs.

In 2008, CHT received the United Nations World Habitat Award for the Global North, recognizing the fiscal, environmental, and social sustainability of the community land trust model. This brought international attention and acclaim for CHT's distinctive approach to the decommodification of housing. As a component of that award, CHT hosted an "international study visit" in June 2009 with participants from thirteen counties. The peer-to-peer relationships formed during this visit helped to hasten the spread of the CLT model to other countries, including Australia, Belgium, and the United Kingdom. More recently CHT has established connections with fledgling CLTs in Canada and France.

Meanwhile, back in the USA, the Champlain Housing Trust has continued to be a leader in state-wide housing coalitions in Vermont and is also heavily invested at the national level in supporting the Grounded Solutions Network. GSN provides training, technical assistance, and advocacy for CLTs and other organizations that are dedicated to creating housing with affordability that lasts. This is precisely the principle that CHT has championed for over thirty-five years, believing that the best things in life truly *are* perpetually affordable.

Notes

1. At one point, CHT's board president was a registered Republican who was proud to advocate for CHT's model because of its adherence to the "republican" virtue of thrifty public spending.

2. The BCLT— and, later, CHT— was the first community land trust in the USA to conduct longitudinal studies evaluating the model's performance, providing quantitative evidence that stewardship works. See: Davis and Demetrowitz, 2003; Davis and Stokes, 2008.

3. Burlington's inclusionary zoning (IZ) ordinance, enacted in 1990, requires developers to earmark a specified percentage of the units in a newly constructed or substantially rehabilitated housing project, units that must be offered for rent or sale at a below-market price. This percentage ranges from 15% to 25%, depending on the zoning district in which the project is located. The City has the first option to purchase all IZ units, an option that is often assigned to BCLT/CHT, bringing new units into the land trust's portfolio of permanently affordable housing.

4. More about VHCB — and its legislatively mandated commitment to permanent affordability— can be found in an essay by Jim Libby (2010).

5. Opposition from homeowners who live near a proposed housing project is a common
   occurrence in cities and suburbs in the United States, especially when a project is slated
   to be occupied by persons whose income is lower or whose skin is darker than most of
   the neighborhood's current residents. Among city planners and affordable housing advocates, these opponents are often characterized as "NIMBYs," an acronym for "Not in My
   Back Yard."

6. Vermont elected a Republican Governor in 2002, Jim Douglas, who served until 2010.
   During this period, funding for VHCB continued, but advocates for affordable housing
   and land conservation were called upon again and again to defend VHCB in the legislature against proposals from the Governor to reduce VHCB funds or to redirect funds
   toward for-profit developers. BCLT played a key role in these legislative fights, stepping
   forward as one of VHCB's most vocal and persuasive defenders. The success of BCLT's
   projects, programs, and published evaluations helped to demonstrate the effectiveness of
   VHCB's priority for investing in projects with permanent affordability.

References

Champlain Housing Trust website: *http://www.getahome.org/*

John Emmeus Davis, "Building the Progressive City." Pp. 165–200 in J.E. Davis (ed.), *The Affordable City* (Philadelphia PA: Temple University Press, 1994). Available at: *https://ecommons.cornell.edu/handle/1813/40513*

John Emmeus Davis and Amy Demetrowitz, *Permanently Affordable Homeownership: Does the Community Land Trust Deliver on Its Promises?* (Burlington VT: Burlington Community Land Trust, 2003).

John Emmeus Davis and Alice Stokes, *Lands in Trust, Homes That Last.* (Burlington VT: Champlain Housing Trust, 2008). Available at: *http:/www.burlingtonassociates.com/#!/resources*

Jim Libby, "The Challenge of Perpetuity." Pp. 552–561 in J.E. Davis (ed.), *The Community Land Trust Reader* (Cambridge MA: The Lincoln Institute of Land Policy, 2010).

Kenneth Tempkin, Brett Theodos, and David Price. *Shared Equity Homeownership Evaluation: Case Study of Champlain Housing Trust.* (Washington, DC: The Urban Institute, 2010). Available at: *http://www.urban.org/uploadedpdf/412243-CHT.pdf*

Brenda Torpy, "The Community Land Trust Solution: The Case of the Champlain Housing Trust." Pp. 64–66 in Christopher Niedt and Mark Silver (eds.), *Forging a New Housing Policy: Opportunity in the Wake of Crisis* (National Center for Suburban Studies, Hofstra University, 2010).

19.

Stewardship of Urban Real Estate for Long-Term Community Benefit
Profile of the Urban Land Conservancy in Denver, Colorado

Alan Gottlieb and Aaron Miripol

The Urban Land Conservancy (ULC) was established in 2003 as a nonprofit corporation with a service area encompassing the Denver metropolitan area. Since then, ULC has grown and evolved to the point that it is now a major player in Denver's real estate scene. Its influence extends beyond the number of acres it owns and the number of developments it has sponsored. An integral part of both its internal success and its wider influence also comes from the organization's early adoption of key features of the community land trust (CLT).

ULC is not a traditional CLT. It actively involves community residents in planning its developments, but ULC does not have a community-based membership that elects a majority of its governing board. Unlike most CLTs in the United States, moreover, ULC's development of affordable housing has not included homeownership. Nevertheless, by any other measure, ULC has exemplified and championed the CLT model to a degree that few organizations have matched. ULC owns land in perpetuity. It strategically uses 99-year ground leases to preserve prime pieces of land in multiple neighborhoods facing the pressures of gentrification, ensuring the availability of those lands for the lasting benefit of low-income people in a booming real estate market. Its ground leases provide ULC with a legal mechanism for ensuring the permanent affordability of its place-based investments in multi-family rental housing and nonprofit facilities.

ULC is a unique organization with a singular history. We will review the organization's origins and describe the major projects that ULC has developed using the CLT model. We will also examine how ULC emphasizes and involves community, even though ULC's organizational structure differs significantly from that of a traditional CLT. Finally, we will consider what the future holds for CLT development in Metro Denver, as ULC incubates the Elevation CLT, a new organization that will be structured and operated along lines of the "classic" community land trust.

FROM IDEA TO EXECUTION

It was 2003 when the pieces of a puzzle snapped into place for Denver oilman Sam Gary. A philanthropist who had founded the Piton Foundation as well the Gary-Williams Energy Corporation, Gary had long admired how nonprofits like the Trust for Public Land and Colorado Open Lands acquired land in beautiful places to ensure the parcels would always provide a public benefit.

Why, he wondered, couldn't something similar be done with land in cities where real estate costs are rapidly escalating? Shouldn't there be a way to acquire urban land to ensure that any investment in the preservation of existing buildings or the development of new buildings would accrue as a lasting benefit to the public? In Gary's words:

> I developed my understanding of the value of land conservation early on, in the open lands conservation movement. I broadened my focus from open lands to urban lands. That sensibility converged with my desire to strengthen our urban communities where our most underserved children and families live.

As the funder of a philanthropic foundation, Gary had also grown frustrated with the struggles of nonprofits to buy buildings for the purpose of housing their own operations, only to see those properties occasionally lost to bank foreclosure when a nonprofit organization hit financial difficulties down the road.

After Sam Gary's epiphany, the leadership of his charitable foundation and his energy company began working together to flesh out his idea of creating a structure for acquiring and holding urban land for public benefit. Initially, Gary favored creating a land bank inside the Piton Foundation. But over time, he was persuaded that something more robust was needed. He realized, according to his nephew, Tim Howard, that "starting an organization that had a good mission and a sustainable operating model was a better way to go than creating a new program area within a small private foundation."

Tim Howard, despite his employment on the oil exploration side of the Gary-Williams Energy Corporation, had an abiding interest in helping Gary to create a land bank inside the Piton Foundation. He was given the assignment of putting together a plan for the nascent ULC and running the organization while a board was being put together and as ULC was getting off the ground.

"You can imagine a line of army recruits standing there," wryly commented Howard years later. "The drill sergeant says, 'all volunteers take one step forward,' and everyone takes one steps back except one guy who didn't quite hear the instructions. I was that guy."

Howard was a quick study, but he had no background in community development. Thanks to the deep connections within Denver's real estate community that Gary and his staff had formed over decades of philanthropic endeavors, however, ULC was able to assemble a powerhouse board of real estate developers, finance experts, and local philanthropists to oversee its operations, even before the organization officially existed.

The board's first chair was Tom Gougeon, who in the 1980s had served as a senior aide to Denver Mayor Federico Peña. He went on to head the Stapleton Redevelopment Foundation, leading the planning for what would be built on the massive site of Denver's old airport. He later became a private real estate developer, which was his role when he took the helm of the ULC board. He currently serves as president of the Gates Family Foundation in Denver. He recalls:

> We starting thinking about whether there was room for a land trust equivalent focused on the urban marketplace. It was a broader and different idea than the CLT model. It was more than housing. It was really this all-purpose real estate agent that could go out and intervene in the marketplace on behalf of the community. We were interested in schools and nonprofit space, health, and parks.

Conversations ensued with the Denver Foundation, a local community foundation, which adopted ULC as a "supporting organization" and provided ULC with administrative and accounting services during its first decade, while managing ULC's cash as a donor-advised fund. The Foundation also appointed half the members of ULC's board, a practice that has continued to the present. Otherwise the Foundation does not intervene in ULC's development decisions or in its day-to-day operations.

ULC GROWS UP

In its early years, with no staff, ULC operated in an opportunistic fashion, pursuing attractive real estate deals as they became available. Susan Powers, a Denver-based developer and former head of the Denver Urban Renewal Authority who served on the inaugural ULC board, recalled developing with Tom Gougeon and with other members of the board a list of projects they'd like to pursue.

The new organization got a major boost in 2007, when the Gary-Williams Energy Corporation donated three properties to ULC, together valued at more than $7 million. This included the Tramway Building, occupying a square block in the low-income Cole neighborhood, and a former Budget Motel in northeast Denver, leased to the Colorado Coalition for the Homeless serving families coming out of homelessness. The Corporation also endowed ULC with a donation of cash to leverage other real estate purchases. There were no written restrictions placed on how the money could be used. Susan Powers later recalled the feeling of amazement that came over them in that moment:

> Then one day Sam Gary said he wanted to have a phone call with me and Tom, and on that call he told us he wanted to give us $10 million. Obviously, it was extremely generous, and it meant that we weren't going to be a land conservancy starting from scratch. But it did make us wonder how we were going to do this as a group of volunteers.

Gary's largess prompted ULC's board to decide that the time had come to hire a full-time president & chief executive officer. The board launched a national search. Several board members were already familiar with Aaron Miripol or knew him by reputation. Miripol had been running Thistle Community Housing in Boulder County since 1998. Thistle was a community development corporation that had established, developed, and administered a successful CLT as an internal program, one of only two CLTs in Colorado at the time.

Miripol, a CLT expert and an evangelist for the model, had impressed Sam Gary, Tim Howard and others from Gary-Williams and the Piton Foundation during an earlier trip they had taken to Boulder to learn about Thistle's CLT. "Aaron gets a lot of credit for really pushing forward the CLT concept. So when it came time to hire a leader for ULC, he was the first person I thought of," Howard said.

The rest of the board agreed. Miripol took the helm of the ULC in mid-2007. In Howard's estimation, time has proven the wisdom of the board's choice:

> ULC would be another one of those nonprofits that the foundation community tried to start and get off the ground but somehow wasn't sustainable if Aaron hadn't taken that job. The key is the overlap between his belief in and understanding of permanent stewardship through the CLT and all the different manifestations it has to take to adapt to different community needs. That and the fact that he is like an energizer bunny. His go-go ability to get stuff done and motivate people, whether partners or his staff, is a unique thing that has allowed ULC to succeed.

COMMUNITY LAND TRUST PROJECTS, 2007–2019

After being hired by ULC, Miripol's first task was to build the organization's internal capacity to manage the properties donated by Sam Gary and to begin planning and developing large-scale projects. In the ensuing years, ULC has gone from a staff of one to a staff of 17 full-time employees.

One of Miripol's enduring contributions to ULC has been his ability to attract and hire high-quality staff, with both knowledge of the development field and passion for the work. It's the strength of the staff from top to bottom that provides ULC with sufficient capacity to do such a high volume of excellent work. The extraordinarily strong, committed staff makes ULC a true, mission-driven organization.

By 2019, the organization had overseen the development of eight major projects using the CLT model, representing a total investment of $37 million in equity. Five of these CLT projects are described below. They provide insight into the diversity of ULC's activities and the versatility of doing equitable and sustainable development on community-owned land.

Jody Apartments, Housing Preservation Near Public Transit

ULC's first CLT investment was the $725,000 purchase in 2007 of two acres of land under Jody Apartments, an existing 62-unit rental housing complex serving lower-income households located on Denver's western border. These apartments are next to a stop on the light rail line of the Regional Transportation District (RTD), connecting downtown Denver to the western suburb of Golden.

NEWSED, a community development corporation that has operated in Denver since 1973, had wanted to buy the property with the intention of rehabilitating the four buildings and preserving them as affordable housing. NEWSED initially approached ULC to ask about receiving a construction loan. ULC declined. Instead, hewing to its mission, ULC used its investment to buy the land underneath Jody Apartments, while NEWSED continued to own and to manage these buildings as rental housing.

NEWSED leases the land from ULC through a 99-year ground lease. Under the terms of the ground lease, 52 of the 62 apartments must remain permanently affordable. Twelve of the 52 are reserved for extremely low-income households (families earning $20,000 or less per year).

More recently, ULC acquired four additional acres adjacent to both Jody Apartments and the light rail station, thereby maximizing the opportunity to provide permanently affordable housing and nonprofit facilities at the site. Development is underway on the first phase. ULC is partnering with two for-profit affordable housing developers, Brinshore Development and Mile High, in building Sheridan Station Residences, 133 permanently affordable apartments atop a 99-year ground lease with ULC. Ultimately, the balance of the four-acre site will provide 250 additional affordable homes, along with up to 50,000 feet of commercial space.

Holly Square Shopping Center

ULC's highest-profile and most impactful CLT investment to date has been the redevelopment of the Holly Square shopping center in the historically African-American neighborhood of Northeast Park Hill.[1] The Holly, as it is widely known, was formerly a center of Denver's African-American community, and a source of pride for many. In its heyday, from the mid-1950s to mid-1970s, the shopping center was anchored by a Safeway supermarket, and also featured a barber shop, a hardware store, a dentistry office, a general apparel store, a dry cleaner, a variety store and a candy store, among other small businesses. Many of these enterprises were owned by African-Americans.

When the supermarket closed in the mid 1970s, The Holly began to deteriorate. Its anchor space remained vacant for several years until the Hope Center, a local nonprofit, purchased the supermarket for its home in 1979. Then, in the late 1980s, on the heels of the crack cocaine epidemic that swept the nation, local affiliates of Los Angeles street gangs arrived on the scene. A newspaper article described The Holly of the late 1980s as "home base for the Park Hill Bloods."

The center hit its nadir in May 2008, when a rival gang firebombed The Holly in retaliation for the fatal shooting of one of its leaders. The burned-out center could have become a blighted eyesore, casting a pall over the surrounding area. Instead, community leaders vowed to replace it with something better.

After city officials initiated conversations about The Holly's future with Aaron Miripol, ULC bought the 2.6-acre property for $625,000, part of which was covered by a $200,000 forgivable loan from the City of Denver. Working together, community residents, city officials, the Denver Foundation, and ULC created a participatory community-planning process known as the Holly Area Redevelopment Project (HARP).

Members of the HARP steering committee gathered input from neighborhood residents about the kinds of services, programs, and businesses that should occupy the space.[2] What ultimately resulted was a plan for the complete transformation of Holly Square, anchored by a new Boys & Girls Club and a public elementary school, housed within new buildings that sit atop land that is owned by ULC.

The Boys & Girls Club has a 99-year land lease with ULC, which will automatically renew for another 99 years. The Boys & Girls Club paid ULC for development rights that were 75 percent below market-rate with annual land-lease payments to ULC of less than $5,000 per year. The development fee paid off ULC's debt on the land and a portion of its holding costs.

Fig. 19.1. The new Boys & Girls Club at Holly Square.

Unfortunately, the Roots Elementary School closed in 2019 due to low enrollment, caused in part by poor educational performance. However, because ULC still owns the land under the Roots building, ULC is leading the negotiations with interested nonprofits who want to call the Holly their home.

The shopping center also has an adjacent public library and city recreation center, making it a true hub of the community. The former head of Roots Elementary called The Holly a "mini Harlem Children's Zone." Thanks to the land leases, both the Boys & Girls

Club and the former school facilities will remain community assets far into the future. This is a lasting community benefit, described by Miripol as follows:

> We want to be good stewards of the Holly property, and one way of doing that is protecting the future use through our CLT 99-year ground leases. When you combine what HARP has done with all of the positive changes taking place at Dahlia (another recently redeveloped shopping center in the neighborhood), you have a number of impactful assets, all of them important pieces of a vibrant community.

Curtis Park Community Center

ULC purchased the vacant Curtis Park Community Center in 2012 for $600,000 from the American Baptist Church of the Rocky Mountain Region. The purchase price was partially offset by a $350,000 forgivable loan from the City of Denver. The center is located in the heart of the Curtis Park neighborhood, a rapidly gentrifying area filled with stately Victorian homes.

Fig. 19.2. Playground, Family Star Montessori.

ULC entered into an agreement to revitalize the site with a venerable early childhood program, Family Star Montessori, which serves children from low-income families. ULC partnered with Family Star in completing $1.2 million in renovations that were needed to open the school. In 2017, Family Star bought the renovated building from ULC for $885,000, with a 99-year ground lease for the underlying land. Family Star makes annual lease payments of $7,000 to help compensate ULC for the roughly $750,000 that ULC "left in the land." These lease payments provide ULC with a one percent return on its investment in the land. ULC plays a unique role in not only ensuring the nonprofit's beneficial use of the property, but also providing opportunities for mission-driven organizations to become anchors in their communities.

New Legacy Charter School

The New Legacy Charter School Project provides another example of how land ownership has allowed ULC to preserve and, in this case, to create important community assets. New Legacy is a small charter high school designed to serve teen parents and their children. The school is home to a fully licensed infant-through-early-childhood center, so that teen parents can attend classes knowing their children are close at hand and safe in an enriching environment.

Before the school existed, its founder approached ULC for help in finding a facility in NW Aurora, a low-income section of Denver's largest inner-ring suburb. After a few failed attempts to secure a facility, ULC purchased a vacant bowling alley in 2014 for $675,000 with plans to convert it to a school. Ultimately, ULC and New Legacy decided that a better solution would be to demolish the building and to start fresh. The result was a new, gleaming 23,000 square-foot school building that opened in the fall of 2015. It was made possible by the creative financing assembled by ULC.

After protracted negotiations, the school and ULC agreed on a formula for determining rent payments for the building. Under the terms of the lease, New Legacy has an option to purchase the building from ULC upon expiration of the original five-year agreement (in 2020). Should the school eventually buy the building, ULC will retain ownership of the land, conveying the site to the school through a renewable 99-year ground lease.

The Site at 38th and Blake Streets

In 2011, ULC purchased two abandoned buildings out of foreclosure at 38th Street and Blake Street for $1.7 million ($26/square foot), just ahead of a real estate boom in the Cole neighborhood that has seen the land's value appreciate by 500 percent. This 1.5-acre site, adjacent to the Blake Street Station on RTD's light rail line, was purchased using Denver's Transit Oriented Development (TOD) Fund. The site is located on the edge of Cole, a working-class community caught in a vise between the booming, gentrified River North neighborhood and a massive reconstruction of Interstate 70 running through central Denver.

ULC had originally envisioned developing a five-story residential building on the site, providing 114 income-restricted units. However, ULC's partner, Medici Consulting Group (MCG), was denied twice by the Colorado Housing and Finance Authority (CHFA) when it applied for tax credits for the project, due to fierce statewide competition for the credits. Following the second rejection, ULC opted to split its holdings into two parcels: 3789 Walnut Street and 3750 Blake Street. MCG then applied successfully for tax credits for the Walnut Street Lofts and ULC began working to sell the Blake Street site to another developer.

In March 2019, MCG broke ground on 66 units of permanently affordable housing at the corner of 38th and Walnut on the southeast side of the property, providing one-, two- and three-bedroom units for households earning 30%-60% of the Area Median Income. In addition, the property will join ULC's growing community land trust through the implementation of a 99-year renewable ground lease agreement to ensure the property remains affordable in perpetuity.

In selling the other parcel, ULC negotiated with a developer to include at least 30 income-restricted units, 11 more than was required by the City's zoning overlay. In addition, ULC negotiated a First Right of Refusal (at a below-market price) to purchase the

Fig. 19.3. Before and after: the site at 38th and Blake Streets when first acquired by ULC in 2011 (top); a rendering of the rental housing built on the site (bottom).

30 units if the owner were to decide in the future to convert the rental building into for-sale condos.

Together, the 3789 Walnut Street and 3750 Blake Street parcels will provide 96 permanently affordable, income-restricted apartments. The proceeds from the sale of the Blake Street lot to the developer also allowed ULC to plan for additional affordable housing four blocks away at Cole Train, next to the Tramway Nonprofit Center.

The Site at 48th Avenue and Race Street

ULC purchased a six-acre site at East 48th Avenue and Race Street in April 2015 for $5.5 million with loans from the City of Denver and the Calvert Impact Fund. The Colorado Health Foundation provided additional funding to support healthy design and development. The site is located near a new, soon-to-be-opened commuter rail station in Elyria-Swansea, a neighborhood that was cut in two in the early 1960s by the construction of Interstate 70. The area is home to a number of industrial sites and adjacent to the National Western Stock Show. The latter is being redeveloped into a year-round tourist destination. It will also provide new and improved multi-modal pathways to reconnect Elyria and Swansea, bringing life back into these communities.

In 2018, after conducting a year-long community engagement process to create designs for future development, ULC announced that Columbia Ventures LLC would be its development partner for the $150 million project on ULC's six-acre site. Plans include both permanently affordable housing and market-rate housing, as well as the construction of 50,000 square feet of community commercial space.

This development project will also provide a new home for Clinica Tepayac, a 25-year-old nonprofit health clinic providing culturally competent health services for the medically underserved. Clinica Tepayac's 25,000 square-foot facility will become part of ULC's community land trust to ensure long-term community benefit. With the recent award of federal and state tax credits,[3] 150 permanently affordable apartments will be built above Clinica's new health clinic. The eventual completion of all parts of this transit-oriented development at 48th and Race will more than quadruple the supply of permanently affordable housing in the neighborhood.

HOW ULC PUTS THE "C" IN CLT

The Urban Land Conservancy is not a typical community land trust. Many CLTs across the country are formed to work in a single neighborhood, with a sole focus on homeownership. That is not the case with the ULC, which has acquired and developed multiple properties across the Denver metropolitan area and does no homeownership. All of the housing on its lands are multi-unit rentals. As Tom Gougeon has noted:

> ULC never was going to be built on the classic homeownership land trust model: community grass-rootsy, advocacy-based organizations. This is partly because of the small geography of those organizations, compared to the ULC's geographical scope.

It is also the case that most CLTs across the country are overseen by a board with significant representation from the people who live in the CLT's properties. Because ULC has not done homeownership, it does not have the same representation. Instead, board members are chosen from the community for their expertise in development, law, finance and/or government. The complexity of the organization and the variety of its projects makes an expertise-based board a necessity. Again, according to Tom Gougeon:

> If you think about what ULC has been doing, it is a much more sophisticated operation with a broader set of skills required than even a good-sized CLT. ULC projects include housing, yes, but also office buildings and retail space and schools. They all have different financing structures and regulatory structures, and are spread across many municipalities. That is why you need a board with the attributes of ULC's board. You may not

need all of that in a traditional CLT, which leaves more room for resident representation. ULC is a kindred enterprise to a CLT, but an outlier because of those factors.

Still, ULC puts significant effort into community involvement. The clearest example is the Holly Square redevelopment, where the Holly Area Redevelopment Project committee included significant community representation. HARP members chose the partners that ultimately occupied the property.

In the summer of 2018, ULC hired two "managers of neighborhood partnerships" to oversee the organization's work in communities where it owns properties. Both individuals have deep roots in Metro Denver neighborhoods, and extensive experience in community organizing.

"Hiring them was critical to building stronger relationships with community stakeholders," Miripol said. "That was an area where we hadn't had the capacity we needed." In 2018, ULC added a CLT committee to its organization. The committee consists of representatives from organizations that "own the improvements" on lands owned by ULC.

Why has it taken so long for ULC to create a CLT committee? According to Miripol, it takes a certain economy of scale to form such a committee. ULC currently has five CLT entities, with a sixth and seventh coming in the next year. In previous years, it wouldn't have made sense to form a CLT committee because there would have been few members, representing a small number of properties. But recent and upcoming growth in ULC's CLT properties made this the right time to put together a committee.

SUCCESSES AND CHALLENGES IN THE CLT REALM

From Aaron Miripol's perspective, ULC's most notable successes in the CLT realm have come when partners have understood the value to both parties of community-owned land and long-term ground leases. Conversely, the biggest challenges have arisen when there was a lack of understanding of the model used by ULC to preserve affordability and to protect community assets.

The Holly Shopping Center redevelopment is the jewel in ULC's community land trust crown. "It's a quintessential use of the CLT because stakeholders have confidence that the land will never go to market, regardless of what happens to the programs currently operating there," Miripol said. Indeed, the site will remain a hub of the community for 198 years, thanks to automatically renewing 99-year ground leases on the land under the Boys & Girls Club and the former Roots Elementary School.

In a similar vein, the Curtis Park Community Center purchase ensures long-term community benefit for a property in the heart of a neighborhood undergoing an inexorable transformation caused by gentrification. And the Jody Apartments will remain affordable in perpetuity, thanks to a long-term ground lease.

In all three cases, initial reluctance on the part of ULC's partners about entering into a ground lease rather than buying the land was overcome by the cost savings realized by not having to purchase the land.

Conversely, ULC's most challenging projects have been those where long-term ground leasing would have made sense but the projects' partners couldn't be persuaded that this approach would serve them better than owning the land. As Miripol explains:

> Even with our successes, there continues to be a lack of commitment to the use of CLTs. We have folks that struggle with the idea of ULC owning the land, as if it limits their ability to get full market rate in the future. Owning the land is a value we bring by taking the up-front risk of purchasing a property. We don't want to ever sell the land because we believe that regardless of whether you're the greatest nonprofit or for-profit developer, we don't know what a neighborhood is going to look like 20–30 years from now and what its changing needs will be.

Another challenge to expanding ULC's portfolio of community-owned land is Denver's real estate boom. Land is overpriced at the moment, making it difficult to do any kind of real estate deal, be it a CLT or something more traditional.

But it is at precisely such moments that an organization like ULC becomes so vital to maintaining the essential fabric of the community. According to Susan Powers, a private developer who served on ULC's board for a decade, "Timing is everything. ULC has to be the organization that looks well into the future and finds ways to keep projects alive when no one else can."

WHAT THE FUTURE HOLDS FOR ULC AND CLT DEVELOPMENT IN COLORADO

The Urban Land Conservancy currently owns several parcels of land where it plans to employ CLT ground leases in future developments. One is the site of a former Thrift-way supermarket in a low-income neighborhood in southwest Denver that is beginning to experience gentrification. ULC bought the property in 2014, demolished the building, and contracted with a local community organizing group to solicit deep community involvement in determining how the site should be redeveloped.

In 2016, following an intensive community engagement process, ULC completed construction of an interim pocket park and futsal court on the property. Long-term plans for the site are to do beneficial development that addresses the needs of the community. Through a future community engagement process, ULC will create a catalytic neighborhood asset for Westwood residents. One thing is certain: Whatever permanent facilities are built on the site will sit on land that ULC continues to own.

In the summer of 2018, ULC received its largest donation to date with the former Excelsior Youth Campus in Aurora, a 31-acre site that includes seventeen buildings. Now called Oxford Vista, the campus is headquarters for the Southwest Division of Americorps' National Community Conservation Corps. Another nonprofit, Family Tree, is leasing four buildings on the site to provide housing, early childhood education, and other services for families coming out of homelessness. ULC's long-term expectation is that the entire campus will be in a community land trust

Finally, ULC has played a leading role in starting the Elevation Community Land Trust (ECLT). In this case, ULC is developing an organization, rather than developing or redeveloping a parcel of land. Elevation CLT is a regional CLT that focuses on affordable homeownership. It is being incubated by ULC until the program can be spun off to become its own independent, tax-exempt, not-for-profit corporation.

"Elevation will provide all of the stewardship components related to homeownership like homebuyer counseling, which are services ULC doesn't provide," said Dave Younggren, President and CEO of Gary Community Investments and the Piton Foundation, the successor organization to Gary-Williams Energy Corporation.

Rather than being concentrated in a single neighborhood—or in a single city—Elevation CLT will use a scattered-site approach and have the flexibility to go to scale in any community at risk of gentrification and displacement. Its service area will eventually

Fig. 19.4. Aerial view of the 31-acre Oxford Vista site in Aurora, Colorado.

Elevation CLT will have the flexibility to go to scale in any community at risk of gentrification and displacement.

expand beyond Denver Metro to support CLT homeownership across Colorado. To further support low-income families in the communities it serves, the Elevation CLT aims to align itself with comprehensive supportive services programs that provide residents with increased access to health care and healthy food, early childhood education, workforce training and placement, and wealth-building opportunities.

Elevation is being launched with a $24 million investment from a consortium of local philanthropic foundations, led by Gary Community Investments. Sam Gary's original vision for land ownership has now come full circle. It has ended up right back where it started — preserving urban land for community benefit.

Since its founding in 2003, ULC has made 37 real estate investments totaling over $120 million. Through its developments, ULC has leveraged an additional $700 million for the development of affordable housing (over 1,000 homes) and nonprofit facilities (700,000 square feet). Its projects have created more than 2,000 jobs. Its impact on the Denver metro area is undeniable. As Dave Younggren has observed:

> The community land trust as implemented by ULC has worked extremely well. The organization has done a remarkable job working in our community and is widely viewed as a real community resource and asset.

Controlling the land means controlling the impact and affordability of real estate, not only in the immediate future, but for multiple generations. It is important to think about how urban real estate fits into the fabric of community. ULC has proven how a CLT can ensure a positive impact in perpetuity.

Notes

1. A full history of the project can be found here: *https://www.urbanlandc.org/wp-content/uploads/2018/06/Holly-Final-reduced.pdf*

2. Staff from the Denver Foundation's Strengthening Neighborhoods initiative did much of the legwork of recruiting members for the HARP steering committee and ensuring that it represented the community's varied voices and interests.

3. Much of the equity raised by ULC for the recent development of three multi-family CLT projects — Sheridan Station, Walnut Lofts, and 48th & Race — has come from the Low Income Housing Tax Credit (LIHTC) program. This program was created in 1986 under Section 42 of the IRS Tax Code. It is currently the largest source of federal funding for the production of affordable rental housing. More than 900 units of housing have been built on ULC's sites using this program, roughly 80% of ULC's total affordable housing production.

20.

London Community Land Trust
A Story of People, Power, and Perseverance

Dave Smith

Ponti's isn't there anymore. It was a little Italian café which hung from the rafters of Liverpool Street train station — one of London's considerably more perfunctory termini, which sits on the boundary of where the historic City of London meets what is commonly known as the East End.

Ponti's was never particularly famous for very much, although reportedly its full English breakfast and coffee wasn't all that bad. But in 1996 it did star — albeit very briefly — as the setting for a conversation between two of the leading protagonists in a new Hollywood film that was to be called *Mission: Impossible*. So it is rather apt, perhaps, that it was also here, in the late autumn of 2008, that the initial conversation about a potential site for London's first-ever community land trust project took place.

This is the story of that site — St Clements Hospital — and of the people and organisations who, over the next ten years, fought so long and so hard to turn that initial conversation at Ponti's into the permanently affordable CLT homes that stand there today. But whilst it is a good story in many ways, it lacks what is perhaps the key ingredient of any great story: namely, a definitive and happy ending. Not because there haven't been some real highs and lasting achievements within the organisation's first decade — there have been many. But because what has also emerged during this time is the sheer scale and deepening extent of the housing problem, and how desperately the CLT's work is needed. And so it is unlikely that this is a story that will come to an end any time soon.

Today, the London CLT has active campaigns relating to twelve potential further sites across the capital. Based upon its most conservative projections, the organization is now on track to deliver some 110 new permanently affordable homes by 2022. This will see upwards of 300 people living in CLT homes in parts of the city as far apart as Croydon and Redbridge; in places of such historical and cultural significance as Cable Street and Brixton; and maybe even on the Olympic Park. But with over 8,500 people sleeping rough last year, with 365,000 children under the age of 16 still living in accommodations that are legally deemed "overcrowded," and with over 240,000 households still on government waiting lists for affordable housing in one of the wealthiest cities in the world — St Clements was only ever going to be able to be considered a success if it was merely the beginning of a much longer story, laying the foundation for a CLT that could do even more in the future.

AN UNAFFORDABLE CITY — A BRIEF HISTORY

The housing crisis in London (and especially in the city's East End, where the London CLT got its start) is nothing new. Charles Booth — the great Victorian social researcher and reformer — in his famed "Poverty Maps" of 1891, described some of the neighbouring streets around what is now the St Clements site as being typified by the "Very poor, casual. Chronic want."

Where Victorian slums had dominated, post-war governments of all political colours took the opportunity afforded to them by the Luftwaffe to remake vast swathes of the East End following the annihilation of its Docklands between 1939–45. In their place were built large-scale social housing estates — concrete monoliths promising "streets in the sky." Local politicians looked to outbid each other in regards to the number of new homes they promised to build during each election cycle. This interventionist consensus, broadly speaking, remained the case until the end of the 1970s, when Horace Cutler (the Chairman of Housing and, later, Leader of the Conservative party within the Greater London Council), and then Margaret Thatcher, actively sought to curb the ability of local councils to build subsidized public housing in an attempt to reduce their political opponents' power base. The effect was that the overall number of new homes being built in London — and particularly the number of *affordable* homes being built — fell off a cliff edge: down from about 35,000 a year in total in 1969 to fewer than 14,000 a year in 1985. The private sector (thoroughly aware of the impact that a decrease in supply would have on its profitability) never picked up the slack. So prices began to rise in relation to earnings — albeit at a relatively moderate rate at first, as the great legacy of the welfare state clung on and the economic volatility of the 1980s gave way to recession in the early 1990s.

The picture changed, however, in the closing years of the Twentieth Century. With an economic recovery, coupled with the election of a New Labour government in 1997 and a belief in all things "third way," the British housing market embarked upon a record run of unbroken economic growth that would last for fifteen years. These were boom times. One of the nation's largest mortgage lenders, Northern Rock, demutualized to become a bank in the same year. It infamously offered "120% loan-to-value interest-only" mortgages to first-time homebuyers, a sign that both the bank and homebuyers were convinced that the property market would rise indefinitely. As such, borrowers were encouraged to take out a loan for more than a house's value, spend the extra capital on moving and furnishing costs, and plan to never repay the capital sum, believing all the while that they could still make money out of the property's appreciation.

House prices in London rose from an average of £96,000 in 1997 to over £300,000 just ten years later. The global economic crash of 2008 took its toll briefly, but by the summer of 2012 house prices were back to where they had previously been and quickly rose again. As of 2019, the average house price (the geometric mean) across the whole city of eight million people stood at £478,853 ($631,998). This was approximately fourteen times the average Londoner's salary of £34,000 ($44,873) and nearly twice that of the national average house price of £243,583 ($321,485) in a country that is known to have a nationwide housing crisis.

COMMUNITY ORGANIZING AROUND LONDON'S BID TO HOST THE 2012 OLYMPICS

The impact of these macro-economic trends was plain for all to see at street level. In East London, at meetings of The East London Communities Organisation (TELCO) — the country's first and now largest community organising federation, known today as Citizens UK — stories poured forth about the crippling costs of rent and a homeownership market out of reach. Following its earlier transformative success with the Living Wage Campaign, Neil Jameson — TELCO's founding Executive Director, who had trained at the Industrial Areas Foundation in the late 1980s and exported Saul Alinksy's organising model to the UK — decided that housing needed to form a central plank of the organisation's new agenda. And a prime organising opportunity soon appeared in the summer of 2005, thanks to a meeting taking place some six thousand miles away in Singapore.

London had recently declared its intention to bid for host city status for the 2012 Summer Olympic Games. Sensing their chance to leverage influence within a formative political debate — and especially given the desire of the authorities to secure local support for a bid that was premised on a promise of a "legacy" of

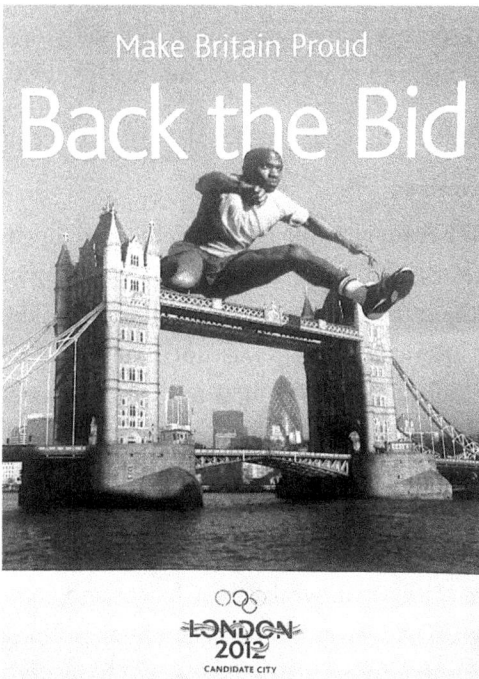

Fig. 20.1. Poster urging London's citizens to support the city's bid to host the 2012 Olympics.

regeneration for East London, amidst an anticipated total spend of £8.7 billion — TELCO forced itself into a relationship with the London 2012 Bid Team and invited the Team to one of TELCO's public assemblies. Built on a foundation of thousands of one-to-one conversations within trades unions, churches, mosques, schools, and other civic institutions across East London, the result of the organizing effort was the preparation and public signing of an "Ethical Charter for The Games." This agreement guaranteed a defined set of community benefits in exchange for TELCO's support for the Olympic bid. Amongst them was a commitment to new jobs and the payment of a Living Wage for all staff at the Olympics. There was also a commitment to build, once the Games were over, "2012 permanently affordable homes for local people through a Community Land Trust and mutual home ownership."

The announcement by the International Olympic Committee in Singapore on July 6, 2005 that London was to be awarded the right to host the Games of the XXX Olympiad was largely unexpected and met with mixed emotions across the British capital. Paris had been widely expected to win, and many Londoners greeted the news with a combination of stereotypical British disdain and reserve, as well as newfound fears about the implications for where they would be able to park. But for those in TELCO, the mood could not have been happier. The Ethical Charter for The Games had been signed by none other than Lord Sebastien Coe, head of the Bid Team and now the Chairman of the London Organising Committee of the Olympic and Paralympic Games (LOCOG), and by the Mayor of London, Ken Livingstone. That agreement looked set to ensure that London's first CLT was a done deal and headed for rapid success in the years ahead. But sadly, and perhaps inevitably, as so often happens when land and power and money are involved, this was not to be the case.

Broken Promises

Little communication was received from the Bid Team after the announcement in Singapore. The newly formed Olympic Delivery Authority (ODA) then ignored the agreement with TELCO, refused to meet with TELCO's representatives, and even claimed that the Ethical Charter was not their concern, since the ODA had not been in existence when the agreement was signed. Some mild and well-mannered agitation from TELCO followed — including gatherings outside ODA meetings. The Authority responded with a letter in 2006 that stated that, whilst the Charter and commitment to a CLT was still an aspiration, the ODA viewed that agreement as nothing more than a memorandum of general understanding "in principle," subject to "considerations of delivery." As such, after the Games, any highly-prized land at the Olympic Park would be considered for the development of CLT homes only if a "working pilot" could

> Land at Olympic Park would be considered for the development of CLT homes only if a "working pilot" could be established.

be established elsewhere in the city beforehand, as a functioning proof of concept for this unfamiliar model.

What was becoming increasingly clear was that waiting on the Olympic authorities and city officials to deliver London's first CLT was unlikely ever to work, so East London's communities decided to take matters into their own hands. On a bright sunny morning in July 2007, TELCO descended on the land immediately opposite London's City Hall, pitched fifty tents, and refused to move until Mayor Ken Livingstone came out and promised to make some land available for a CLT pilot. After much to-ing and fro-ing — first with his staff and then with the Mayor himself — Livingstone appeared, and pledged that a site would be made available. After snapping some smiling pictures, everyone left, convinced once more that progress towards London's first CLT was being made.

The land that Livingstone eventually proposed, however, was a disused industrial path called Bow Lock on the very eastern edge of the borough of Tower Hamlets: a forgotten space between a main arterial road and the River Lea. The chief problem, however, as TELCO later discovered, was that the land promised by the Mayor was not actually his to gift. Rather than belonging to his office, the land belonged to the local council, which was far less keen on the idea of their land being given away. And so, despite four years of campaigning, come the beginning of 2008, the campaign was back at square one. A new site needed to be found.

The Meeting at Ponti's

It was around this time that the campaign decided it needed to professionalize in terms of its housing expertise, and employ a different organisational structure beyond just the broad-based community organising tactics it had previously utilized. In response to the cry of "Give Us Some Land!," the repost from those in power at the Authority and at City Hall had become clear: "What land? And to Whom? (You expect us to give land to that rabble waving placards?!)."

The East London Citizens Community Land Trust Ltd had been formed in 2007, but up until now it had been just a campaign. Neil Jameson, TELCO's Executive Director, along with Matthew Bolton, the Lead Community Organizer for East London, had long been on the lookout for allies who could help them put a firmer structure in place. Amongst those they discovered was Stephen Hill — a long-established and well-respected housing expert, who after years of working for a number of social housing organisations and public bodies, had taken to doing what he described as "only the interesting and worthwhile work" as a freelance contractor. By chance, he had briefly been employed by the Olympics planners, helping them to run some public workshops around potential uses of the Olympic Park after the Games. It was at one of these meetings — when TELCO had arrived yet again to make a nuisance of themselves — that Stephen quietly mentioned to Neil and Matthew that he was very much "on their side." He offered to meet up afterwards to see if he might help to move things forward.

Around the same time, TELCO appointed its first dedicated Housing Organizer — a twenty-two-year-old named Dave Smith. He had recently returned from a stay in Massachusetts, volunteering on the Obama primary campaign, and was eager to become involved in community organising like that he had read about that was going on in the US. In Neil Jameson's words, he "simply wouldn't leave us alone." This was — by all accounts — Smith's chief, and perhaps only, qualification for being offered the job. Nevertheless, he set about starting to formalize the campaign and to search for a new site. However, given TELCO's limited resources, he could only be paid for one day a week. So the rest of his time was spent keeping bar at a local pub called The Little Driver, at the end of the road where he was living in Bow.

Each Monday, he would walk the mile or so to TELCO's offices in Whitechapel to meet with the formative campaign membership that TELCO had begun to put together, heading along Mile End Road past a disused hospital site called St Clements. His induction to the new job was short — a two-day seminar on Alinsky and organising, and a list of three names of people to meet with. Top of this list was Stephen Hill — who suggested that they meet for coffee at Ponti's Café in the Liverpool Street train station.

THE CAMPAIGN TO ACQUIRE ST CLEMENTS

At that very first meeting, Stephen and Dave discussed the prospect of acquiring the boarded-up St Clement's hospital site as the potential home for London's first CLT. Designed by a renowned architect Richard Tress and constructed in 1849 for £55,000 (a princely sum for that time!), the building had had a succession of occupants and uses over the years. It had originally operated as a workhouse for the poor, with accommodations for 800 inmates. It boasted Siberian marble pillars, a chapel with stained glass, and an elegant Board of Guardians Room for those who oversaw its operations.

As workhouses were phased-out throughout the country, it became the Bow Infirmary in 1874, and was then renamed the Bow Institution in 1912, caring for the long-term sick. The building became a psychiatric unit in 1936 under the new name of St Clement's Hospital. Despite being bombed heavily during the Second World War, it remained a sight to behold, until eventually closing its doors in 2005. Ownership of the land and buildings then reverted from the National Health Service (NHS) to the office of the Mayor of London. The site then sat vacant for years, awaiting its planned sale for private housing development.

Walking along the Mile End Road in 2009, Dave Smith had noticed that the vacant buildings, despite being weathered and derelict, remained architecturally impressive. But from a community organizer's point of view the site was even more special. It straddled almost the exact midpoint of the road running from the center of London to the proposed site for the Olympic Stadium. As he later recalled:

CITY OF LONDON UNION WORKHOUSE.——Mr. R. Tress, Architect.

Fig. 20.2. Original design and purpose of the St Clements site, 1849.

It was in the heart of our power base . . . surrounded by our member institutions. And above all else, it had the capacity to take the campaign out of the abstract — away from theory and policy — and root it in a sense of place for families who needed somewhere to call home. They could actually see themselves potentially living there. And from the moment we first set our sights on it, the campaign truly took off.

The newly revitalized campaign group met for the first time on a cold winter's Saturday in November, in a flat overlooking the muddy expanse that was set to become the Olympic Park. The group had identified four potential sites. A vote on which of these to pursue was taken a few weeks later in a second meeting at Bryant Street Methodist Church. But there was never any question of which site was going to win. Unanimously, the campaign group chose St Clements as its target for developing London's first CLT homes.

Soon after, the campaign took another early giant step forward with the arrival on the scene of Chris Brown, Chief Executive of an ethical property developer named "igloo Regeneration." East London CLT had no track record, little direct development expertise, and only just enough money to pay its one-person staff for one day a week. This fledgling organization needed quickly to transform itself to be able to competitively tender for prime real estate worth tens of millions of pounds in one of the UK's hottest housing markets. The newly elected Board — drawn mostly from the community organising base — met with Chris Brown and entered into a partnership with igloo Regeneration.

Over the next year, this highly progressive developer and the CLT's board collaborated in developing both a competitive housing proposal and a high-profile political campaign to win the tender. As soon as Brown's team were on board, architects were appointed, plans were drawn up, financial modelling was commissioned, and the bid to build London's first CLT homes was at last in full motion. The CLT's founding Chairman, Paul Regan, later said: "Few did more in those early days than Chris Brown — and Stephen Hill throughout — to drag our pipe-dream of acquiring St Clements from a well-meaning longshot to a viable proposition."

> The CLT was given a classic lesson in the trials and tribulations of community-led development.

It was also around this time that a talented young architect named Calum Green — who would go on to lead the organisation in the years ahead — joined the staff team. Pioneering the CLT's community-led design work, he and Dave worked together over the three years that followed, as the tender process was drawn out and the East London CLT was given a classic lesson in the trials and tribulations of community-led development. Reluctant bureaucrats at City Hall sought to temper the public commitments made in front of Citizens Assemblies by Mayor Ken Livingstone and, subsequently, by Mayor Boris Johnson. The tender documents were reissued approximately fifteen times. The multinational private developers who were also bidding for the contract set up a pseudo, one-person "CLT" in order to try and win the competition.

Fig. 20.3. St Clements action, circa 2009.

But the East London CLT persisted, continually building their organisation and their political campaign. The CLT worked closely with local civic institutions in Tower Hamlets, including Darul Ummah and the East London Mosque. Students at Queen Mary, University of London, under the tutelage of Professor Jane Wills, studied the site and assembled data that could be used in planning its redevelopment for lower-income families. And the CLT's Vice-Chair, Colin Glen, and his black-majority New Testament Church of God in Mile End, hosted boisterous Annual General Meetings which kept CLT members and the general public both informed and enthused about the campaign.

Compromise on Everything
Except Your Principles and Winning

The eventual outcome of the tender was a political compromise. It was decided by Mayor Boris Johnson that ownership of the St Clements site should go in part to the East London CLT. This was undoubtedly a win for the organization and set it on the path to becoming the largest CLT in the United Kingdom. But, sadly, he also ruled that the East London CLT/igloo Regeneration bid would not win the contract to redevelop the site. Instead, the City awarded the contract to a private developer, Linden Homes. Because of the political stir the CLT had caused, however, including coverage on the front page of the *London Evening Standard*, the selection of Linden Homes was conditional on the developer being able to strike a deal with the East London CLT to integrate a specified number of resale-restricted CLT homes into the new development.

The pressure from City Hall to build a new relationship and to make it work quickly was now on, but so too was the pressure from the local community to strike a deal that stayed true to the CLT's promises and original purpose. An all-member Open Meeting of the East London CLT was thus called in the Methodist Church opposite the St Clement's site to discuss the forthcoming negotiation with the private developer. The CLT would get 23 homes, slightly fewer than it had sought in its original bid. It would also be forced to abandon the relationship with igloo Regeneration and to team up with a developer with whom the East London CLT had no prior relationship in order to deliver a scheme that differed drastically from the CLT's community-led designs. On the other hand, the option on the table was still significant. Andy Schofield, a founding Board Member and later the CLT's Project Director, led the Open Meeting. A hundred people participated in a formal discussion of what they felt "a CLT must be," "a CLT could be," and "a CLT could not be."

Inspired by their community organising training — which draws upon the lessons of Thucydides and the debate between the Athenians and the islanders of Melos — East London CLT members collectively crafted a negotiating position that reflected their priorities:

- The CLT must deliver permanent affordability;

- The St Clement's project should be based-upon principles of community-led design, so the site plans proposed by the developer should be revisited and redrawn; and

- The CLT's homes must not be controlled, managed, or owned by other parties.

With the battle lines drawn, the Board Chair and the Director for the East London CLT headed into their first meeting with executives from Linden Homes in a hotel just opposite Buckingham Palace. The CLT's representatives had a magnificent platform from which to press their case, due to the power of ordinary citizens organizing. Three hours later, with all of the CLT's conditions met, the deal for London's first community land trust project was signed. It was April 2012.

THREE LESSONS FOR CLTs EVERYWHERE

The story goes on from there — through a series of community-led design charrettes and a total redesign of the site plan; through the planning application process; through the financial and contractual negotiations; to the ground-breaking in March 2014, which featured Mayor Boris Johnson happily driving a bulldozer around the site. There were ups and downs along the way, too numerous to tell. But for those of us who went through the whole process — many of whom are still actively involved today, in what has since expanded and so been renamed the London CLT — there have been three lessons within our experience that we believe to be relevant to the CLT movement worldwide.

1. A "Classically" English CLT?

The first is a reflection upon an incredibly important debate: namely, to what extent should the "classic" CLT model — with its history, its proven track record, but also its chiefly American practice and legal construct — be open to interpretation and change in other countries? And how should a new organisation find the appropriate balance between adapting the model to meet local conditions, whilst maintaining a common understanding of the model's features and purpose, among all organisations that wish to call themselves a CLT?

Definitions and explanations of the CLT model in the UK are inherently ambiguous, and intentionally so. When the community land trust was first written into law as part of the Housing and Regeneration Act of 2008, the CLT pioneers who drafted that legislation did so in a manner they believed would allow CLTs to be expansive and innovative. Their proposal was adopted with minimal alteration. As a result, there were no statutory requirements for a CLT to follow the "classic" model, as it had evolved in the United States, nor was there any mention in the law of the necessity of ensuring the permanent affordability. The law said only that a CLT was *"to ensure that the assets are not sold or developed except in a manner which the trust's members think benefits the local community."*

A case could be made that such organizational ambiguity, where a CLT may be organized and operated in many ways, has been essential to the growth and success of CLTs in the UK. The London CLT chose very consciously, however, to adopt many of the traits of the "classic" model. Outward looking, it drew a clear line of distinction between CLTs and established housing associations and co-ops in the UK, which had long provided affordable housing of various types, but which didn't involve the community in the same way.

The result was an organization that is structured as closely to the "classic" CLT as possible within the legal confines of the UK system. In fact, the London CLT follows the American tradition more closely than any other CLT currently established in the UK. This was not without its problems. In many ways, there are tasks that would probably have been more quickly and readily achieved had the organization entirely anglicized its structures. But the organizers, leaders, and members of the London CLT felt that a too drastic departure from the "classic" model would excessively distance themselves from a growing international CLT movement. They felt strongly aligned to that movement, so they wanted to promote a structure and purpose that were consistent with most other CLTs in the world.

The resulting arrangements, at least on paper, can look somewhat messy. The tripartite composition of the London CLT's board does not always resonate immediately with members and needs constant explaining. And leaseholder laws in the UK mean that "owning the land" outright is both far less common and less simple than elsewhere. (London CLT does not own the "freehold" at St Clements in the same way as CLTs elsewhere, but in terms of local property laws this is a technicality rather than a meaningful distinction.)

Fig. 20.4. Board of directors, London Community Land Trust, 2019.

As such, we have come to conclude, much like John Davis said on one of several visits to the London CLT, that CLT organizers must confront the difficult challenge of finding the right balance between adopting the "classic" model and adapting that model to their own peculiar local and national circumstances, for the sake of balancing practical challenges and maintaining a movement worldwide. Davis went on to say:

> It was absolutely essential for us [in the United States] to develop a common language, a common understanding of what a CLT is. Without that, it was hard to distinguish the CLT from competing models, competing traditions; it was hard to draw people together under the banner of CLTs until there was a common vocabulary. Conversely, once you have agreement as to what a CLT is, it gives you the freedom to innovate within that structure and to improve the "classic" model . . . . But if you modify too much, you risk severing the connection to our roots, to our values, to the sense of purpose and struggle that comes from them. . . . So a common understanding of the model creates a yardstick of values and performance against which you can assess whether a proposed innovation will help or hinder.

2. Linking House Prices to Local Wages to Create True Affordability

The second lesson we learned is the importance of a locally-determined definition of the term "affordable housing." In the UK, following changes made by the national government in 2010, the term "affordable housing" became a source of derision, having been adjudicated in law to mean anything "up to 80% of the open-market rate," which in London is now rarely affordable to anyone. As such, the term has lost all meaning. Yet, in the first instance, the London CLT had planned to devise its sales values in a similar way. The original plan had been to sell fixed, capped-equity shares at approximately 60% of the open-market value. That changed in October 2011, when board members and staff from the London CLT attended the National CLT Conference in the United States.

As part of that conference, after a long boat journey from Seattle to OPAL Community Land Trust in the San Juan Islands, the visitors from London had an in-depth conversation with Lisa Byers, OPAL's Executive Director. Thoughtful and eloquent in her exposition, she extolled the virtues of linking the cost of homes not to any percentage of the open market value — "which we all accept is an inherently broken and an unrelated assessment of what people on local wages can afford"— and tying it instead to a multiplier of average local incomes. This was a transformative moment for the London CLT, for it not only provided a clear mechanism for its stated aim of delivering "truly affordable homes," but also provided the CLT with a unique and compelling narrative for what it was about —"homes that local people on local wages can afford."

Back home, those on the trip crunched the numbers and — after a lot of work with local groups to gut-check the impact of this new resale formula — established their own wholly unique but quite brilliant mechanism by which the homes were to be sold. Prices were to be determined by: (a) taking the median average wage in the area in which the homes were to be built; (b) applying the principle that no family should be forced to spend more than one third of their income on housing; and then (c) multiplying this figure out by a standard set of mortgage assumptions (e.g., 25-years at an average rate of interest and with a 10% downpayment). This calculation yielded a price that local people could genuinely afford to pay — a price that was created by working backward from their own circumstances, rather than being derived from market conditions. If residents ever chose to move, they would be bound to apply the same formula in calculating the resale price of their homes. CLT house prices would always rise in line with wage inflation, therefore, rather than rising in relation to market-driven house and land prices that are increasingly beholden to the whim of foreign investors or buy-to-leave landlords.

> London CLT strives to be not only a social justice campaign, but also the best consumer choice.

The London CLT — which strives to be not only a social justice campaign, but also the best consumer choice available to any median-income household — had found its niche. With three-bedroom houses (including a garden) at St Clements going on sale for £235,000 ($295,000) through the CLT, compared to costs starting at £600,000 ($755,000) for market-rate homes offered next door by the private developer, the London CLT had created a defining, replicable, and sustainable proposition for permanently affordable housing across the city.

3. Keeping Community in the CLT

The third and most important reflection on this journey is that, above all else, community land trusts must "keep the C in CLT." It is this, ultimately, that lies at the heart of the St Clement's story. Community is what gives the London CLT its greatest potential for having lasting success, whilst at the same helping the CLT to stay rooted to its original purpose and promise. In the UK — where the provision of affordable housing has long been established through state-run council housing — it is the CLT's *relational* rather than *bureaucratic* culture, its focus on people as individuals rather than as numbers, that sets it apart.

One of the clearest examples of this relational aspect in the St Clement's process came when one of our first residents (a family who had been with the campaign throughout and had passed through the CLT's allocations process and affordability assessment) was refused a mortgage at the last minute by their lender. This was due to a technicality, based on previous debts which were not wholly theirs. In such circumstances, the easiest thing to do from a risk management perspective, and what most other traditional affordable housing providers would have done, would have been to rescind the offer and to go to the next family on the waiting list. But the governing board of the London CLT took a conscious decision not to do this. Instead, the board spent a lot of time and political capital

Fig. 20.5. London CLT Annual General Meeting, 10-year anniversary, September 2017.

negotiating with the local housing authority so as to achieve a planning amendment, which allowed the family to rent the property until they could qualify for a mortgage. That way, they could move into their new home and wouldn't have their hopes dashed yet again. The London CLT stands by our people — our mission starts and ends with them rather than rigidly following any bureaucratic or abstract quasi-utilitarian definition of "housing need."

But this family's story also illustrates a further obstacle that the London CLT has had to overcome. One of the hallmarks of doing housing development in the UK (and in much of Europe as well) is that it takes a very long time to plan, design, finance, and complete every project. This poses an enormous challenge for CLT practitioners: How do you keep prospective homebuyers interested? How do you keep the larger community of members and allies actively engaged throughout? How do you keep your power from bleeding away while waiting for something to get built?

In this regard, we would contend that building the organisation is as important as building the homes themselves. London CLT has always put a strong emphasis on its non-housing activities as a way of ensuring that our wider social justice mission is supported and sustained. One of the best examples of this — when trying in the early days to get the local community involved with the redesign of St Clements — was the work of then board members Kate MacTiernan and Lizzy Daish who, in collaboration with film director and East End resident, Danny Boyle, put on the Shuffle Film Festival for the CLT. Held over the course of a week, it opened up the St Clements site to the local community and helped them to re-engage with it, to reimagine what had been a rather sad place, and to reconceive of it as a new, accessible and exciting opportunity.

THE END OF THE BEGINNING

The London CLT at St Clements has never been just about delivering permanently affordable homes. More than that, it is about community, social justice and, quite simply, contributing to happiness in life and emotional well-being.

When our very first residents, Humayra and Ruman and their young baby Yunus, whose parents had immigrated to the East End from Bangladesh in late 1960s, moved into their new CLT home, you could see how much it meant to their whole family. In Ruman's own words:

> Before we moved into St Clement's, we were living with my parents, brother, and sister. There were six of us all in one flat. My wife (Humayra) and I shared a room whilst we had a baby on the way. It was not easy to live as a family within a family — it meant my wife felt like a stranger in her own home. I remember the day we moved in well — my whole extended family turned up. It was pouring with rain but I was beaming inside. There is so much space! I feel really lucky we get to own our own home — it has changed my family's life. There was a moment the other day when Humayra, Yunus and I were in the flat, and my Dad came over. He sat on the sofa with his arms spread out and he burst out into singing some sort of oldy goldy traditional Bengali song. My Dad only sings when he is feeling the happiest he's felt in years. That's how you know when Dad's happy; he doesn't smile, he sings. When you have that sense of space, it opens up your mind. He felt that, and he had to let it out.

Since then, Humayra has given birth to a little girl, making her the first baby born in a London CLT home! There will, we hope, be many more to come. Because the CLT movement, above all else, starts and ends with people and their lives — not housing, or resale formulas, or anything else.

To that end, many more people should be mentioned and thanked. And whilst to write an exhaustive list is impossible, and the injustice of omission is great, it would be wrong not to mention at least the incredible work along the way of Pablo Absalud, Sister Una McCreish, Fr. Sean Connolly, Fr. Tom O'Brien, David Rodgers, Peter Ambrose, Suzanne Gormann, Miranda Housden, Professor Tim Oliver, Fr. Angus Ritchie, Bethan Lant, Ruhana Ali, Nick Durie, Colin Ivermee, Tim Carey, Joe Ball, Jenny Lumley, Neil Hunt, Lina Jamoul, Emmanuel Gatora, Sebastien Chapleau, Alison Gelder, Ruby Mahera, Nano McCaughan, Hannah Emery-Wright, Ben Cole, Grace Boyle, Charles Campion, the Butler Family Fund, and the Oak Foundation. This is as much their story as it is the story of our residents and of the homes we have built.

Whilst the first 23 homes at St Clements may not be everything we set out to achieve, and whilst they most definitely have not solved the housing crisis in our city, they have proved one thing beyond doubt: when local communities get together and organize, and when the universal principles of the CLT are carefully applied, it does not matter what city you are in, or how challenging the market may be, because what we do works. There is no mission impossible.

Fig. 20.6. Future residents of St Clements, looking out the window of their home-to-be, January 2018.

21.

From Pressure Group to Government Partner
The Story of the Brussels Community Land Trust

Geert De Pauw and Nele Aernouts

A housing crisis has been raging in the Brussels Capital Region for decades. The failure of government to address this problem prompted neighborhood associations and housing rights activists in Brussels to join forces in 2008 and to look for solutions of their own. In their search, they stumbled upon an Anglo-Saxon model that had remained largely unnoticed in the European mainland: the community land trust. It seemed to comprise everything they were looking for.

In 2013, the Community Land Trust Brussels (CLTB) was established and received support from the regional government. The first newly constructed CLT homes were inhabited in 2015, and new housing projects are now being built at various locations in Brussels. Meanwhile, CLTB has been playing an important role in disseminating the CLT model in Europe.

In this chapter, we will provide an overview of the housing crisis in Brussels. We will then discuss the origins of the Brussels CLT. Starting the CLT was relatively quick and easy, but the road to putting the organization on a firm footing has not been without challenges. From the beginning, CLTB has had to cope with a number of legal, organisational, and institutional barriers. We will discuss some of these struggles and the agreements put in place to resolve them, before concluding with a look at future prospects for CLT growth in Brussels.

I. WELCOME TO BRUSSELS, CAPITAL OF EUROPE!

The implementation of a CLT in the Brussels Capital Region can only be understood within the context of the region's chronic housing problems. For several decades, a substantial fraction of the housing stock has been unaffordable for a considerable share of the population. A severe mismatch between average household incomes and average housing prices is at the core of the problem: for half of households living in Brussels, the share of their household budget going to pay for housing exceeds 40% (Romainville, 2009). This problem, which academics and housing activists have come to term a "housing crisis," is based on several dichotomies and inadequate policy responses.

A Socio-Economic Dichotomy

Since the restructuring of the labor market in the 1980s, the Brussels Capital Region has been marked by considerable economic growth. This growth has been driven by the service sector, which is dominated by European, federal, and regional administrations and has attracted international and multi-national corporations (Loopmans & Kesteloot, 2009).

This economic growth is not entirely to the benefit of the population residing within Brussels, nor are the benefits of growth shared evenly among them. Here are a few indications. Half of the jobs in the Brussels Capital Region (BCR) are held by inhabitants of Belgium's two other regions, Wallonia and Flanders, who commute into Brussels on a daily basis. Among all of the regions in Europe, the BCR is ranked 4th in Gross Domestic Product (GDP),[1] but it is ranked 145th when it comes to the disposable household income of BCR's population (Englert et al., 2018). The BCR also exhibits a pattern of high levels of poverty and large numbers of people on welfare. The percentage of BCR's population who are at risk of poverty is significantly higher than in Belgium's other regions: 39% of the Brussels population is at risk of poverty, compared to 27% in Wallonia and 14% in Flanders.[2] At least 23% of the children in Brussels are growing up in households in which no income is earned through the job market (Englert et al., 2018).

An External and Internal Migration Dichotomy

Another dichotomy can be identified when looking at external and internal migration patterns, fueled by different streams of migration following World War II. Among all inhabitants of the Brussels Capital Region, 35% of them have a non-Belgian nationality, while 72% have non-Belgian origins.[3] On the one side of the spectrum, every expansion of the EU brings highly skilled EU migrants and an increased attractiveness for foreign corporations and new highly skilled migrants (Englert et al., 2018). On the other side, the migration waves of the 1960s and 1970s brought mainly Moroccan and Italian guest workers, few of whom were able to climb the social ladder due to the economic crises of the mid-1970s and 1980s. Later on, these immigrants were joined by family members and a more diverse group of new immigrants. They have often ended up in informal or low-paid economic circuits, such as the building, cleaning, transport and catering sectors (Loopmans & Kesteloot, 2008).

Spatially, the high-skilled native and foreign populations have settled in peripheral municipalities, while lower-income groups have found housing in the more central, post-industrial neighborhoods of Brussels along the Canal, an area known as the "poor crescent" (Kesteloot, 2000).[4] For decades, this area has been dealing with severe problems of housing quality that range from moisture problems to a lack of heating systems, and to phenomena such as overcrowding and subletting (Englert et al., 2018). In more recent years, problems of affordability have also emerged.

Inadequate Policy Responses

Public policy has historically given an inadequate answer to these dichotomies. From its very inception, Belgian housing policy has been marked by an anti-urban attitude, represented by a persistent priority for stimulating homeownership outside of the cities. Spatial planning policies, meanwhile, have been nearly absent (Dedecker, 2008).

Belgian housing policy has had its greatest impact on the residential movements of upwardly mobile families, supporting homeownership outside of cities through fiscal grants and cheap railway tickets. From the 1950s onward, families in search of a green, less-dense environment were helped to buy houses in the peripheries outside the Brussels Capital Region. This focus on homeownership didn't change fundamentally after the regionalization of the nation's housing policy.[5] Today, half of the region's housing budget goes to supporting homeownership, a policy intended to keep middle-class households within the BCR and, simultaneously, to increase tax revenues. This public support for homeownership takes the form of tax deductions,[6] soft mortgages,[7] and direct grants for the development of housing serving homeowners with modest incomes.[8] Such development has often been concentrated in the "poor crescent," in order to increase the area's "social mix" and to create a domino effect of attracting further private investment.[9]

> The amount of social housing is stuck at 7.5%, even though half of the population qualifies for social housing.

Despite taking such a large share of the housing policy budget, the homeownership rate has declined during the last decades, due primarily to a steep rise in housing prices.[10] Furthermore, among the beneficiaries of this homeownership policy, middle-income households are overrepresented. These households enjoy the benefit of this "extra encouragement," but are not necessarily in need of additional funding to become homeowners (Dessouroux et al., 2016, p.24).

The persistent focus on conventional, market-priced homeownership has impeded the growth of community-based housing and creation of a decent social rental market (Geurts and Goossens, 2004). Today, the amount of social housing is stuck at 7.5%, even though half of the BCR's population qualifies for social housing (Englert et al., 2018). Due to the small amount of social housing, there is excessive demand in the private rental market, which allows landlords to impose strict requirements for the selection of tenants. Not surprisingly, these requirements are characterized by discrimination and racism, especially targeting prospective tenants with a social assistance benefit or a disability benefit and/or those having a particular ethnic background (Heylen & Van den Broeck, 2015).

The BCR launched several programs to build additional social housing, but very few homes have been constructed and the impact on the housing crisis has been close to zero.

Urban policies and programs aimed at the redevelopment of inner-city neighborhoods have been inadequate at best and harmful at worst, with regard to affordable housing. (Dessouroux et al., 2016). For decades after putting into effect the 1953 slum-clearing law (*Wet op de Krotopruiming*) and high-rise replacements of the 1960s and 1970s, no decent urban renewal program was developed to address the deterioration of under-privileged areas. Deindustrialization in the Belgian economy left these neighborhoods with a deteriorating housing stock, poor-quality public spaces and an impoverished, transient and aging population. Not until 1993, with the introduction of "neighbor-hood contracts" by the Brussels government, did public policy begin to tackle these problems. These "contracts" enhanced local regeneration through investment in pub-lic spaces and services, programs to promote social-economic integration, renovations of buildings, and the construction of housing on residual parcels (Vermeulen, 2009).

Two additional policies for territorial development, the Regional Zoning Plan (2012) and the International Development Plan (2018), focused on revitalization of the area and the development of housing along the Canal.

The urban policies of the past twenty-five years have been widely praised for tak-ing a more integrated and inclusionary approach to neighborhood development and for explicitly addressing the social-spatial fragmentation of Brussels. But there has also been a darker, less praiseworthy side to these policies. The reservation of large lands for redevelopment by private investors and the repeated mantra in government policies and plans of needing a better "social mix" in inner-city neighborhoods have had an implicit aim: attracting higher-income groups to these areas. As public and private investment increases, however, land values and housing prices rise, making it harder for lower-in-come people to gain access to affordable housing.

In sum, the benefits of economic growth in the Brussels Capital Region have been inequitably shared across geographic areas and across social classes. Patterns of gentrifica-tion have been supported by a housing and urban policy promoting the revitalization of inner-city neighborhoods. These economic and social realities, combined with a housing system fraught with problems of deterioration, discrimination, unaffordability, and the meagre production of social housing, eventually pushed concerned activists and com-munity organizations into the housing domain, seeking alternatives to forms of housing provided by either the state or the market.

II. CREATION OF THE BRUSSELS COMMUNITY LAND TRUST

In 2007, the "Ministry of Housing Crisis," a grassroots initiative launched by squatters, homeless people, community organizations, and housing activists, occupied the empty Gesu Monastery in Sint Joost to call attention to the housing problem. In addition to initiatives asking the government to take responsibility for the housing crisis, there were also experiments with new solutions. For instance, the community center, Bonnevie, initiated l'Espoir in the municipality of Molenbeek with the support of CIRE, an association that mainly works with refugees and newcomers. CIRE had previously developed solidarity savings groups, where low-income families collectively save money to finance the purchase of individual homes. The l'Espoir housing project produced fourteen affordable, energy-efficient, owner-occupied homes. The low-income families who purchased these homes were closely involved in the project's development, right from the start. Through design workshops, they influenced the building plans, they started a savings group to prepare for the purchase of the homes, and they became an important partner in discussions during the building process, alongside Fonds du Logement (the developer), the architect, and the municipality (De Pauw, 2011).

The l'Espoir housing project successfully linked a dimension of collective endeavor and solidarity to individual homeownership. However, the sponsors realized that the classic homeownership formula used in this project did not provide a structural solution for the housing crisis. The project required substantial subsidies from government to make it work, which would be lost whenever the homes were subsequently resold. Nor were there guarantees against future speculation. The project's sponsors started looking for an alternative strategy that would make the homes permanently affordable and would structurally integrate resident participation into the design and operation of the housing.

In the United States they discovered the CLT model, which was largely unknown on the European mainland until then. In September 2009, the British Building and Social Housing Foundation (named World Habitat today) invited four community developers from Brussels to take part in an international study visit to the Champlain Housing Trust in Burlington, Vermont.[11] After a week, the group returned to Brussels convinced that the CLT model was what they were looking for. During a conference on cooperative housing in Brussels, they publicly launched the plan to start campaigning for the creation of a CLT in Brussels, which was received with great interest.

This eventually led to a charter for the establishment of the Community Land Trust Brussels. The charter was signed on May 25, 2010 by fifteen associations. During three public meetings, the concept was explained and discussed with the participants: families in need of housing, community organizers, housing rights activists, and academics interested in the model. Hundreds of people participated in these events, while a small core group met regularly to set out a strategy and to seek further support for the plan. Out of this dynamic, the Platform Community Land Trust Brussels, the precursor of the Brussels CLT, eventually grew.[12] The Platform, a group of supportive organisations, set itself the aim of promoting the CLT model in Brussels. The organization's leaders wrote a few articles about their ideas, talked to the press, and arranged a series of trainings, lectures, film performances, and public assemblies to explain the model. They started to develop scenarios for the establishment of a CLT in Brussels and to search for subsidies to make this happen. In 2011, the Green Minister for Housing of the Brussels Capital Region commissioned a feasibility study. The recommendations of the study were put into practice in 2012 and led to establishment of the actual community land trust.

In Brussels, the CLT is composed of two bodies, a nonprofit association and a Foundation. Both were officially founded in 2012. The Region granted a subsidy covering the costs of development for CLTB's first housing project. Financial support from the Brussels Capital Region enabled CLTB to start constructing dwellings that could be made affordable for the lowest income groups soon after its formation. Monies from the government also financed the creation of a team of four people who started working for CLTB in September 2012.

In 2013, community land trusts were included in the Brussels' Housing Code.[13] The Code mentioned CLTs alongside existing tools such as social rental housing and social mortgages. It defined what CLTs are and stated that the government could define, in an implementing law, the rules according to which CLTs could get recognized by the Region. To date, this law hasn't been drafted, but the fact that CLTs were quoted in the Code had an important symbolical function.

In 2014, the government secured the financing of CLT operations by including CLTB as a participant in the Housing Alliance. This investment program for new affordable housing in the Brussels region ensured that 2 million euros could be invested each year between 2014 and 2018 for the development of new CLT projects. CLTB could use this money for the acquisition of land and for covering a part of the construction costs.

Early Projects

Together with local partner associations, CLTB has created a development pipeline of twelve projects to date. Most of them are located in neighborhoods of the "poor crescent," adding to an "in situ" regeneration of these areas. These projects include a total of more than 180 dwellings and six spaces for community infrastructure. Almost all of the projects are multi-family homes. The first CLTB project, *l'Ecluse* (9 homes), has been inhabited since 2015. Five new projects are in construction; five others are being prepared.

The *Arc-en-Ciel* project in Molenbeek, the largest project until now, is one of CLTB's flagships. The vacant land that used to include a house and workshop was bought in 2013. However, due to several delays within the construction process, notably for obtaining the building permit, it took more than six years to build *Arc-en-Ciel*. Together with the Housing Fund,[14] a social housing agency, and several partner associations, CLTB developed 32 dwellings, a community garden, and a women's community center on this land. Since the very beginning, the future residents have been intensively involved in the project's development, participating in architecture workshops, assemblies, and general meetings. Construction was completed at the end of 2019 and the homeowners began moving into their new homes.

Fig 21.1. l'Ecluse, CLTB's first homes. MARC DETIFFE

A kilometer away, in the municipality of Anderlecht, an old Parish Centre is being transformed into seven owner-occupied homes, a community garden, and a building for a neighborhood association. This project was also launched in 2013. The group of future residents was composed that same year. They called their project *Le Nid*, which means "the Nest." Like *Arc-en-Ciel*, construction was completed in the summer of 2019.

The *Liedts* project, which includes four senior dwellings above a service center in Schaerbeek, focuses on intergenerational living.

The most emblematic project in preparation is called CALICO. This project, constructed by a private developer, is funded by the European Union through an Urban Innovative Actions grant.[15] To obtain this funding, CLTB partnered with two cohousing groups. One of them focuses on women and gender issues, while the other aims to develop a "home for birth and end-of-life" where women can give birth and the elderly can spend their last days in a warm, homelike environment. The project consists of 34 dwellings, the home for birth and end-of-life, and a community center. It focuses on solidarity and community care and is scheduled for completion in 2021.

Finally, one single-family home deserves special mention. In a city as dense and expensive as Brussels, CLTB didn't consider single-family dwellings a possibility. It took two devoted families to convince CLTB of the contrary. An elderly couple who lived near the *l'Ecluse* CLT project was looking for a smaller, single-story dwelling that might better fit their age and family size. Their house with a garden had become too big for them to handle after their children left home. They met one of the families living in *l'Ecluse*, who was looking for a bigger home after their family had expanded. The families decided to swap homes. Doing so, the first family offered the land under the house to CLTB, in order to make it affordable for the family from *l'Ecluse* and to preserve its affordability for generations to come. CLTB hopes this example can inspire others, thus creating affordable homes without any subsidies.

III. CREATIVITY AND REFLEXIVITY

In the beginning, the idea to develop a CLT in the Brussels Capital Region was met with a lot of skepticism from housing experts and politicians. It was said that such a "North American model" could not be applied in Europe. The legal systems were too different; the gap between common law and civil law too great. Other criticisms were aimed at the residents of CLT housing. The community-led process inherent in the CLT model was said to be intertwined with an Anglo-Saxon tradition that was foreign to Belgium. The low-income groups inhabiting CLT projects would not properly take care of their homes, leading to a decrease in property values. The collectively led model would need too much public funding.

Although the Brussels CLT was established relatively quickly, the initiators had to face all of these criticisms and challenges. They were forced to apply a strong dose of creativity and reflexivity throughout their praxis in developing strategies to cope with them, beginning with the problem of legally separating ownership of the dwellings from ownership of the land.

A Bundle of Property Rights

Similar to CLTs in other countries, CLTB includes resale conditions in its land lease contracts in order to keep its homes permanently affordable. This is a renewable, fifty-year right in which CLTB gives the residents permission to own a dwelling on land that is not theirs. An owner may resell his/her property whenever he or she wants, but the resale price is limited and the CLTB will indicate to whom the property must be sold. In this way, the dwellings remain affordable without the government having to invest a second time. Owners are also not allowed to rent out their dwellings, except under certain conditions and for a social rent specified in the land lease. Otherwise, CLTB homeowners have the same rights and obligations as any other homeowner.

CLTB largely modelled its own land lease contracts, resale formulas, bylaws and regulations on those of CLTs in the United States. Integrating the North American community land trust model into the Belgian legal system was not a simple matter, however. Especially challenging was to find a legal solution to separating the ownership of land and dwellings, but this proved to be easier for CLT organizers to accomplish in Belgium than for CLT organizers in the United Kingdom, another common law country.

Belgian law includes two rights that enable the separation of land from the buildings on it: the surface right (*droit de superficie*) and the long-term lease (*bail emphytéotique*). The biggest difference between these two rights is the maximum duration, 50 years for the first and 99 years for the second. Neither can be automatically renewed and extended beyond the maximum period, presenting a potential obstacle to a CLT's commitment to preserve the permanent affordability of land and housing. That is one of the reasons these rights haven't been commonly used for housing.

There is a significant exception, though. In the early 1970s, a new university town was built in Belgium, inspired by contemporary innovations in urban planning. The city of Louvain-la-Neuve was constructed entirely on a concrete slab, separating underground car traffic and parking from overground pedestrian traffic. The land on which the university town is built is owned by the university, which leases out parcels under the principle of *bail emphytéotique*. The houses on these leaseholds are mainly owned by residents or private landlords. The leasehold contracts contain a clause that ensures that, each time a house changes hands, a new duration of 99 years begins to run. By "re-starting the clock" for each new homeowner, a leasehold comes very close to being permanent.

In Louvain-la-Neuve, however, no anti-speculative conditions were attached to the land leases.[16] The university remains the owner of the land, but it does not have the right to restrict price increases on resale of the dwellings. It is doubtful the university wanted to do so, but it is also true that it is difficult to regulate resale prices under *bail emphytéotique* due to the strong protection of property rights within Belgian law. Even if a buyer and seller were to agree to accept a number of contractual resale conditions, there would always be the risk of a court overturning them, deciding such restrictions to be in conflict with property rights.

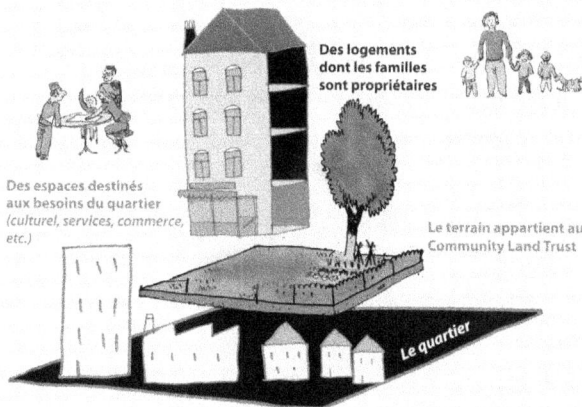

Fig 21.2. Detail of poster created by the Brussels CLT, illustrating the separate ownership of land and buildings.

It is easier to impose restrictions on the resale price, as well as other conditions concerning the use of the home, through the shorter 50-year duration of the *droit de superficie*. Therefore CLTB finally opted for the *droit de superficie*, combining clauses similar to those used in Louvain-la-Neuve with clauses, such as restricting the resale price, thereby creating a lease that is close to everlasting. This leads to fairly complex contracts. Since almost all CLTB dwellings are part of condominiums, even more conditions and variations get added to the ground lease depending on the building developer and on whether the building is renovated or newly constructed.

Undoubtedly, the government could play an important role in the future by facilitating the development of specific legislation oriented towards this variety of property regimes, specifying conditions on the use of the dwelling, the condominium, and the land on which the project is built. Such legislation could simplify the contracts and enhance the legal enforceability of the conditions.

Supporting and Strengthening the CLT Community

CLTB is composed of two closely affiliated legal entities: a nonprofit association[17] responsible for the day-to-day operations; and a public utility foundation[18] that owns the land. They are connected to each other through their bylaws. Both are run by a board of directors whose members include three groups of stakeholders: residents living in dwellings on CLTB land or waiting for a CLT home; representatives of civil society, including members of partner organizations and neighbors of CLT homes; and representatives of the Brussels government. Each stakeholder group gets one-third of the seats.[19]

In contrast to the practice of most CLTs in the United States, once people are interested in buying a house from the CLT, they must become a member of CLTB. As a member of the association, they are automatically registered on a waiting list, and are entitled to vote in electing their representatives to the managing board. Each year some hundred members gather in the general assembly to elect their representatives. These meetings are always one of the highlights of CLTB's community life.

In order to purchase a property from CLTB, households must meet the same income qualifications as required for renting in social housing. While this is a maximum income limit, CLTB is also committed to serving people whose income is even lower. To make this possible, it sets different selling prices depending on the income of the buyers. To this end, the target group is divided into four different income categories. Depending on the income category in which a homebuyer falls, he or she will pay a higher or lower price for the same type of dwelling. Homes for each of these four categories will be realized in each new project. Members on top of the waiting list get priority, according to their income category and their family size.

When launching a new housing project, future residents are selected from the waiting list and brought together in a "project group."[20] These future residents are involved in the design and preparation of the housing project and will be in charge of its management, once the dwellings are built and occupied.

It is stating the obvious that the participation of such a mixed community in the collective management of both CLTB and its projects, a community that includes professionals from ministerial cabinets, social workers, and low-income groups, can be complicated.

Fig 21.3. Project group for a future CLTB project, Luminiere du Nord.

But CLTB is convinced such a mix of interests and perspectives is essential. Through the participation of public officials and civil society, CLTB tries to ensure a long-term integration of public concerns and common interests, such as the integration of the dwelling within the neighborhood, the importance of affordable housing for low-income groups, and the necessity of developing a certain amount of dwellings. Similarly, the active participation of future residents, even when many of them are low-skilled and some have only a basic level of French,[21] is deemed by CLTB to be indispensable, since all decisions that are made will concern their future well-being. Once installed in their homes, they become responsible for keeping the condominium going. As condominium owners, they will have to ensure that the common charges are paid, that costs are correctly distributed, that necessary repairs are made, that a reserve fund is created, and so on. Training and guidance are key, therefore, to preparing and supporting residents in the management of their own housing.

The preparation period, which can sometimes take more than five years, is used to train residents about their legal rights and obligations; the architecture, use, and maintenance of their dwelling; and the management of a multi-unit project. To do this, CLTB collaborates with local partner organizations, who organize training sessions and individually supervise the members of the group. This leads to the establishment of important agreements and initiatives. Future residents draw up a set of rules and divide the dwellings in joint consultation; they write a charter on how they want to live together; and they take

Fig. 21.4. Annual General Meeting, Brussels CLT, 2015.

the initiative in introducing the project to people who already live in the neighborhood.

In Molenbeek, for instance, every month the *Arc-en-Ciel* group organizes the Bazar Festival on the pavement in front of the construction site of their housing project. The Bazar Festival is a festive flea market for the neighborhood. Members of the project groups have indicated how all of this helps them to acquire new skills, to cultivate self-confidence, and to strengthen the cohesion in the group (Aernouts & Ryckewaert, 2017).

Another strategy to strengthen the (future) residents and to help them in taking up their role in these different levels of management is to actively bring together the somewhat artificial CLTB community. This community is made up of approximately two hundred sympathizers and nearly four hundred families who would like someday to obtain a home through CLTB. They live in different places in the Brussels Region and usually do not know each other when they sign on as a member. They meet each other, at best, only at the annual general meeting. CLTB has now started a membership program that wants to overcome this separation and unfamiliarity among this large constituency. The program aims to strengthen both the connections among individual members and solidarity across the entire community by developing collective projects outside of the housing domain. Thanks to this program, CLTB's members have set up a group that organizes cycling lessons, they have organized the temporary use of buildings that are awaiting demolition or renovation, and they have participated in fundraising activities for CLTB.

Institutionalisation without Bureaucratization?

CLTB has grown from an informal citizens' initiative into a professional organization in just a few years. The number of dwellings produced is still limited, mainly due to the long duration of the development of real estate projects in Brussels. The plan, from now on, is to deliver twenty to thirty new homes annually. But CLTB has the ambition to increase production even further, with a goal of having a thousand dwellings on its land by 2030.

Whether this is possible will largely depend on political support and the willingness of governmental bodies to continue making funds and lands available. The growth of the organization's portfolio and CLTB's strong dependence on governmental resources for such growth pose a number of challenges.

First, as a consequence of this dependence, CLTB is obliged to follow strict policies and procedures required by governmental entities for certain aspects of CLTB's daily operation. Aspirations and value systems of CLTB and public institutions are not always similar, and strict governmental frameworks have an impact on CLTB's autonomy. For instance, when using public subsidies, CLTB is obliged to adopt public tendering procedures, complicating the participative nature of the development process.

Second, CLTB is particularly vulnerable to political changes (Aernouts, 2017); that is, every change in the regional government can lead to a new positioning of acceptance and support for the community land trust model. Every four years, CLTB has to win the trust of the political party in charge and enter into a new relationship. Strategic battles and power games between political parties add to the difficulty. In the beginning of 2017, for instance, a regime change within the regional government led to the party in power giving serious consideration to forcing the CLT Brussels to transfer ownership of its lands to other housing providers in Brussels. Fortunately, thanks to the efforts of a strong network of supporters, this proposal, which would have undermined the entire rationale and operation of CLTB, was not adopted. But it demonstrates CLTB's vulnerability to changes in the political wind.

Meanwhile, political support for the CLT model is growing. After the regional elections in May 2019, the new government, composed of social democrats, greens, and regionalists, presented its coalition agreement. It stated that all public housing operators should make greater use of long-term lease contracts and that the government should "increase its support for the projects developed by Community Land Trust Brussels" and recognize CLTB as a "regional land alliance," accompanied by a management agreement so that CLTB can become "a partner in urban renewal programs."

Thirdly, the increase in scale and professionalization adds a dose of bureaucratization to CLTB's operations, even as the organization strives to remain a community-led movement that is guided and governed by its members. Also, as the number of inhabited homes steadily increases, CLTB will have to find ways to help residents to be fully in charge of managing their housing projects, while keeping them involved in the wider CLT movement.

In order to cope with these challenges, CLTB has entered into several agreements and has developed measures to increase its autonomy. Until recently, for example, CLTB has mainly worked with large, publicly-sponsored housing organizations such as the Housing

Fund in managing its construction projects, but CLTB has decided to be in charge of its own construction management in the future. Naturally, this will create a whole new set of financial and organizational issues. CLTB will now have to finance and to staff building operations itself. Within its organization, a building division will have to be organised. Also, the double position of simultaneously being a builder and a community organizer can be challenging, especially when problems occur during the building process.

Next, CLTB has recently made efforts to attract private donors and investors to finance its operations. In 2017, for the first time, the organization started a fundraising campaign. This led to a few important gifts by private charity foundations a year later. CLTB wants to expand this practice in the near future by creating a land cooperative. Such a cooperative would enable civil investors to invest their money in the acquisition of community land for affordable housing and spaces for social, cultural, and economic activities. Alongside the Public Utility Foundation, which purchases land through grants and donations, CLTB's cooperative would purchase land with its shareholders' investments. Such a cooperative would not only increase CLTB's capacity and autonomy; it would also enable CLTB to diversify its production — for instance, by integrating rental units into its projects and by helping social and cultural projects to gain access to affordable land.

Furthermore, CLTB has worked hard to expand and to strengthen the larger CLT movement within Brussels, across Belgium, and in neighboring countries. By disseminating the model more widely, CLTB hopes more individuals and organizations will become active defenders of the community land trust. Since the very beginning of CLTB, its initiators have been making the case for CLTs in the rest of Belgium and Europe. Several conferences have been organized in Brussels, where invited guests from the UK and the USA have presented their work. At these gatherings, the foundation for an informal network among European activists, practitioners, and academics interested in the CLT model was laid. Later on, CLTB staff and board members have been regularly presenting their work. They helped the CLT in Ghent to take its first steps toward becoming established. After visiting CLTB, a busload of city officials, politicians, and legal experts from Lille (France) were convinced to adopt the model as well. This precipitated the enactment in France of national legislation enabling the establishment of CLTs (*Organismes de Foncier Solidaire*, OFS) and led to the creation of the country's first CLT, initiated by the municipal government in Lille. CLTB has also taken the initiative in bringing together urban CLTs from the northwest of Europe by starting Sustainable Housing for Inclusive and Cohesive Cities (SHICC), a project aimed at promoting further dissemination of the CLT model throughout Europe.[22]

> CLTB has taken the initiative in promoting further dissemination of the CLT model throughout Europe.

IV. (IN) CONCLUSION

CLTB has succeeded in building a solid operation in a relatively short period of time. Several precipitating or sustaining factors allowed this to happen: the CLTB network, composed of community organizations, neighborhood groups and housing activists; a housing policy traditionally paying great attention to homeownership, providing a favorable regime for developing owner-occupied CLT homes; new public budgets for affordable housing; the lagging construction of social housing; and the regional government's willingness to invest in socially innovative alternatives in the housing market. Another prerequisite for CLTB's success was the basic mentality of CLTB's initiators, members, and leaders, which has hovered between lobbying for their core values while implementing them with a level of pragmatism.

First, expanding and maintaining a broad network of both associations and public bodies has been essential. The close collaboration with a professional social housing organization such as the Brussels Housing Fund and with local community organizations, for example, was very important for developing the first real estate operations and for shaping the CLT community. CLTB's commitment to disseminate the model and to support start-up groups elsewhere also contributed to its own success, when CLTs in other cities and countries began referring to Brussels as an example worth emulating.

Second, CLTB's initiators have negotiated firmly to ensure the autonomy of the organization and to have residents and civil society represented on the board of directors.

Third, the organization has been relying on step-by-step problem-solving. The feasibility study that formed the basis for founding the CLTB more or less described the organization that is starting to take shape today. To get there, numerous obstacles had to be overcome, while almost all CLT components had to be (re)invented and adapted to the Brussels legal and political context. Today, for instance, now that more and more homes are becoming occupied, much thought is being given to how CLTB can help residents to manage their condominiums.

Although CLTB has succeeded in operationalizing the CLT model in the Brussels Capital Region and in developing several successful housing projects, the organization is today facing significant challenges in going to scale. In the years ahead, CLTB will have to diversify its resources, attracting private investors and donors. It will have to strengthen its regional legislative framework to ensure continued regional support. It will have to create the internal capacity and expertise to fiscally optimize the construction of new projects. New competences within the organization, such as project development and condominium management support, will have to be developed. CLTB must also be diligent in protecting its autonomy despite its dependency on governmental funding, while preserving the predominant role of residents and civil society in governing the organization. The staff, board, and membership of CLTB will have to be steadfast in continuing to advocate for the central position of *community* within a community land trust.

> Such advocacy does not aim
> to replace the social housing
> policy that already exists, but
> to supplement it.

Beyond dealing with these many issues, CLTB hopes to work with its allies inside and outside of government to structurally embed some key CLT principles into the government's regular housing policy and spatial policy, including: non-speculative land use; permanent affordability of publicly subsidized homeownership; and community participation in the development of affordable housing and in the governance of the organizations doing development. Such advocacy does not aim to *replace* the social housing policy that already exists, but to *supplement* it, making the general housing policy in Brussels and in Belgium more equitable, inclusive, and sustainable. Ultimately, CLTB aims to dissiminate the principle that lies at the heart of a community land trust, the principle that elevates the use value of real estate over its exchange value.

Ten years ago, a community land trust in Brussels was still an utopian idea, a distant dream of a small number of activists and community workers. Today, Community Land Trust Brussels is firmly established. The organisation has removed from the Brussels real estate market the first small pieces of land, colouring in the first pieces of a map where other rules apply. There is still a lot of work to be done before this unique approach to integrating resident participation into the design and operation of permanently affordable housing on land that is community-owned becomes mainstream. But CLTB is ready and eager to accept the challenge.

Fig. 21.5. CLTB staff, 2018. ANTOINE MEYER

Notes

1. After West London, Luxembourg, and Hamburg.

2. The so-called "At Risk of Poverty or Social Exclusion" (AROPE), an indicator developed in the framework of the Europe 2020 strategy, measures the share of people that meets at least one of the following conditions: 1) the household's disposable income is below the national poverty risk limit; 2) is between 0 and 59 years old and lives in a family with a very Low Work Intensity (LWI); 3) is in Severe Material Deprivation (SMD).

3. This means they have a foreign nationality, they are born with a foreign nationality, or one of their parents has a foreign nationality.

4. The term "poor crescent" refers to the crescent-shaped sequence of neighbourhoods marked by a concentration of poverty indicators.

5. In 1989, the federal government of Belgium delegated housing policy to the regions of Brussels, Flanders, and Wallonia. This has been part of a larger federalization process, in which different former federal state domains were transferred to the regions.

6. The Brussels Capital Region has only recently abolished the housing bonus, a tax reduction for homeowners. It has replaced this measure by registration fee reduction, whereby all registration fees are waived on the first 175,000 EUR of a real estate purchase (Art. 46bis of Brussels-Capital Region's Registration, Mortgage, and Clerk's Office Fees Code).

7. Cheap loans are offered by the Brussels Housing Fund, a subsidized organization that also develops rental and owner-occupied housing for households with a low and modest income.

8. Thanks to regional support, Citydev.brussels, a "regional development company," develops homes and sells them to middle-income households for only two-thirds of their market value. In addition, the buyer can buy the property with a reduced VAT rate of 6%.

9. This information is explicitly mentioned on the Citydev-website: *https://www.citydev.brussels/nl/onze-filosofie.*

10. Between 2001 and 2011, the proportion of homeowners in the BCR fell from 42.7% to 38.81% (CENSUS 2011).

11. The Belgians who participated in this study visit were Michel Renard, from the Municipality of Molenbeek, Loïc Géronnez from Periferia, Geert De Pauw from Community Centre Bonnevie, and Thomas Dawance, researcher. Geert and Thomas later became part of CLTB's first staff.

12. For more on this dynamic, see: *http://www.periferia.be/Bibliomedia/PUB/EP2011/ periferia_2011_construire_politique_publique.pdf.*

13. The Brussels Housing Code includes all instruments and measures of the housing policy in the Brussels Capital Region.

14. For several CLTB projects, the Brussels Housing Fund, a subsidized organization that also develops rental and owner-occupied housing for households with a low and modest income, has acted as the building's developer.

15. Each year, the European Union launches "Urban Innovative Actions," supporting the development of innovative and participative projects around Europe that address urban challenges. Urban authorities, together with key stakeholders such as agencies, associations, private sector organisations, research institutions and NGOs are eligible to submit proposals.

16. Interestingly, Louvain-la-Neuve will be one of the first Belgian cities, after Brussels and Ghent, to start a community land trust. After being elected in 2018, the new mayor launched a plan for building 140 CLT homes, as part of a bigger new sustainable neighbourhood.

17. In French, Association Sans But Lucratif (ASBL).

18. In French, Fondation d'Utilité Public, a non-profit entity different from an ASBL, mainly used for the management of assets. One of the important differences between them is that a Foundation doesn't have members, making it very difficult to implement the CLT governance principles. CLTB resolved this issue by determining that board members of the Foundation would be designated by the members of the ASBL.

19. The representatives of the first two groups are elected by the NGO's general assembly. The government representatives are designated by the government, and approved by the assembly. Members of the Foundation's board are designated by the members of the ASBL, thus guaranteeing a strong link between both entities.

20. For the first projects, these groups were composed at the moment CLTB purchased land, thus enabling the future residents to have a say in the content of the public tender for an architectural project. Because of the long process in building any project, this meant that groups were composed 5 to 6 years before the residents could move into their homes. Today, groups are composed later on in the process, once the building permit is obtained, reducing the preparation period for homeowners to 2 or 3 years, if all goes well.

21. The vast majority of potential buyers have a migrant background, with a predominance of people with roots in Guinea, Morocco, and Congo. Furthermore, most of the families have a very modest income or benefit from a replacement income.

22. SHICC is a three-year initiative funded by the European Union. CLT Brussels, CLT Ghent, the London CLT, and the Lille CLT are SHICC's founding members.

References

Aernouts, N. and Ryckewaert, M. (2017). "Beyond housing: On the role of commoning in the establishment of a Community Land Trust project," *International Journal of Housing Policy* 18 (4), 503–521.

Aernouts, N., Ryckewaert, M. van Heur, B., and Moritz, B. (2017). *Housing the social. Investigating the role of commoning in the development of social housing initiatives.* Unpublished doctoral thesis.

De Pauw, G. (2011). *Passieve woningen, actieve bewoners* (Brussels: Opbouwwerk).

Dessouroux, C., Bensliman, R., Bernard, N., De Laet, S., Demonty, F., Marissal, P. and Surkyn, J. (2016). "Huisvesting in Brussel: diagnose en uitdagingen," *Brussels Studies* 99, 1–32.

Englert, M., Luyten, S., Fele, D., Mazina, D., Mendes Da Costa, E. and Missinne, S. for Commission Communautaire Commune (2018). *Welzijnsbarometer 2018.* Brussels: Observatoire de la santé et du social.

Geurts, V. and Goossens, L. (2004). "Home ownership and social inequality in Belgium." (In K. Kurz and H.P. Blossfeld. *Home Ownership and Social Inequality in Comparative Perspective,* Stanford, California: Stanford University Press, 79–113.

Loopmans, M. and Kesteloot, C. (2009). "Social inequalities." *Brussels Studies* 16, 1–12.

Romainville, A. (2010). "Who benefits from home ownership support?" *Brussels Studies* 34, 1–20.

Vermeulen, S. (2009). *Needed: an intelligent and integrated vision for Brussels' urban planning.* Paper presented at the 4th International Conference of the International Forum on Urbanism (IFoU), Amsterdam/Delft.

PART FIVE
CRITICAL PERSPECTIVES

Meeting the Challenges
of a Changing Environment

22.

The Burden of Patience in a Long March Toward Racial Justice

Tony Pickett

The modern community land trust (CLT), by purpose and design, was always intended to be one part of a broader strategy for systemic social and economic change. It was to be a platform for increasing opportunity and economic prosperity for American families of color who were historically excluded from land ownership, one exclusion among many that reinforced widespread racial segregation. CLTs, in this regard, attempt to provide both a corrective action and a challenge to many current American socio-economic systems that are the result of flawed public policies often aligned with racist goals. Richard Rothstein's highly acclaimed book, for example, *The Color of Law: A Forgotten History of How Our Government Segregated America,* presents incontrovertible evidence of this racist intent in shaping public policy and institutionalizing discrimination across housing, education, and employment.

As CLT leaders contemplate our goals for the next 50 years of progress, we must question whether we too are inadvertently supporting the same systems that limit power and success for people of color. It is fine for us to challenge our peers and the larger society to make a commitment to embrace diversity and inclusion, but we cannot avoid examining the many ways that we fall short ourselves. A limited number of CLT leaders of color is merely one indicator of our collective shortfall. If, in Gandhi's words, we are to "be the change that you wish to see in the world," there must be honest self-examination and an intentional shift in our priorities. Within our own sector, that should include an acknowledgement that we have not done nearly enough to nurture and provide leadership opportunities for diverse candidates. The first CLT was implemented by African-American organizers and leaders, but the harsh reality is there hasn't been a substantial increase in their numbers, visibility, influence, and power over the past 50 years of CLT expansion and evolution.

We must never forget that the modern CLT was created out of necessity. It was a practical strategy to provide collective ownership of precious land to support African-Americans in realizing and exercising their constitutional right to vote, as well as to lessen and eventually eliminate the daily suffering and often violent oppression faced by descendants of African slaves who were living in the rural American South. It was born out of the American Civil Rights Movement. The notable milestones of that nonviolent struggle for racial justice included:

- The 1955 bus boycott sparked by the refusal of Rosa Parks to surrender her seat on a city bus to a white man in Montgomery, Alabama;

- The 1957 desegregation of Central High School in Little Rock, Arkansas by nine African-American students;

- Year-long mass protests to end all forms of segregation and discrimination in Albany, Georgia, 1961–1962; and

- Passage of the Voting Rights Act of 1965 and the Civil Rights Act of 1968, the latter of which is commonly called the Fair Housing Act.

Despite the sweeping changes caused by these events, the actual realization of equality, economic security, and the freedom to enjoy the many privileges of our nation remain elusive for far too many African-Americans, as well as for many other people of color in the United States. Governmental policies, legal systems, and societal norms are still deeply flawed, a result of both the passive legacy and the still-active tolerance of racism.

SELF-EXAMINATION IS REQUIRED

A simple statement by Civil Rights activist and CLT pioneer, Mrs. Shirley Sherrod, summarizes the longing of so many of us who remain committed to achieving a nation of equals: *"I wish that somehow, some way we could learn to live together in this country."* That desire is inherently expressed when using the term *community*. As the CLT model continues to evolve and expand to achieve an increasing number of goals and a widening variety of land uses, defining exactly whose interests are being served by our work remains an essential requirement for measuring CLT progress. CLT residents, leaders, partners and investors routinely seek to balance the role of *community* in our work, but often overlook the multiple, nuanced interpretations captured by the word *community*.

Varying understandings of the word tend to fall within the range of two distinct classifications derived from highly personal perceptions: (1) a group of individuals with common interests, based largely on their shared proximity within a defined physical space, geography, or neighborhood; or (2) a group of individuals who acknowledge and value their social cohesion with some implied level of trust, due to a shared racial or cultural experience or heritage. Tensions often arise in conversations when *community* is used without acknowledging these distinctions and without first reaching a common understanding of which classification of *community* is being discussed.

It is important, therefore, for CLT practitioners to clarify what they mean when they talk about *community* representation, *community*-led planning, or *community* benefits. Such clarity is especially needed in a time of continuing growth and evolution of the CLT model, along with the emergence of nonprofit entities administering affordable housing programs that are large-scale and regional in scope. Active expansion of their real estate holdings and their service areas will require a reassessment among CLT leaders of our cherished ideals regarding *community*-based decision making, a place-based membership, and a tripartite board as core elements of the "classic" CLT model.

All CLT leaders, particularly those advancing the model across the United States, must also personally explore and come to terms with today's socio-political context for achieving CLT progress, while striving to maintain alignment with the values and vision of the CLT model's origins in the Civil Rights Movement. Part of that context must include consideration of progressive national policy proposals, which are intended to redistribute wealth for the benefit of all American working families. These proposals are routinely decried as "socialist" in conservative-led attempts to taint and to discredit their potential effectiveness. This is not a new tactic, since it closely parallels the debate and circumstances of the 1966 Freedom Budget that resulted from the collective work of Martin Luther King Jr., A. Phillip Randolph, and Bayard Rustin. They had wisely proposed leveraging a period of strong U.S. economic growth to provide a guarantee of federal jobs, universal health care, and a basic income for all U.S. citizens, linking the goal of racial justice to that of economic justice.

Similarly, the CLT model was first envisioned by leaders who had conceived and pioneered the model as being a complement to other political and economic strategies for advancing the broader goals of the Civil Rights Movement. I would argue, based on the original intent of our founders and out of respect for their courage and personal sacrifices, that modern CLT leaders should perhaps cease making references to CLTs as a self-contained "*movement.*" Instead, we should highlight, embrace, and acknowledge with conviction our direct connection to the *original* Civil Rights Movement as the source of the model. We should position our own collective work as being a component and continuation of a broader struggle for new national policies and programs, aimed at achieving progressive social, political, and economic changes that directly address the ongoing impact of racism.

Our next 50 years of progress must also include creating a system with clear goals for training the next generation of CLT technical experts and leaders, who embody the values of the CLT model's founders. Our next generation of leaders must be collectively diverse and intentionally representative of the *communities* we serve. Our most experienced and seasoned practitioners must be prepared to "pass the baton" in the march toward equity. We must be prepared to mentor and to support a new cadre of leaders who are waiting in the wings, preparing to play a larger role in bringing CLTs and other forms of shared equity homeownership to scale.[1] These leaders must have a variety of skills, including: executive management, real estate finance, fund development, communications, and technical assistance. They must also have personal familiarity with the history of our collective struggle and a deep appreciation for the core values in which the CLT model is rooted.

New CLT formation is rapidly occurring in core urban neighborhoods of color such as the Fruit Belt in Buffalo, NY and Anacostia in Washington, DC. New organizations with local leaders of color are exercising power, as in the Houston CLT in Texas and in the City Roots CLT in Rochester, NY. At the national level, the Grounded Solutions Network is leading CLT support and training that has reached more than 5,500 people through its virtual CLT start-up hub aimed at educating and inspiring potential CLT model adopters. The Network has also formed a multi-racial and multi-cultural group of thirty-two "Resident Ambassadors" who have volunteered their time to promote the benefit and impact of CLTs by sharing their unique experiences as homeowners.

> Our most experienced and seasoned practitioners must be prepared to "pass the baton" in the march toward equity.

At the same time, a new cohort of larger-scale CLT entities are arising, guided by multi-year growth plans for rapid expansion of their residential portfolios, operating expenses, and revenues. The role of *community* within this new generation of large-scale CLTs remains a work in progress. Their formation provides a working laboratory and the chance to evolve the model toward new best practices which balance continued accountability to a CLT's local constituency with expanded productivity of both rental housing and homeownership, maximizing a CLT's scale and impact to meet a broader continuum of housing needs.

This approach recognizes that the trend of declining resources for affordable housing from our federal government is likely to continue. It is not reasonable to assume that increased support from state and local governments will make up the shortfall. We are going to need to embrace and to expand new partnerships with well-capitalized private-sector financial institutions such as the largest U.S. affordable housing lender for each of the last nine years, Citi Community Capital. Citi resources provided over $6 billion of lending to finance the production of 36,000 affordable rental housing units in 2018 alone.

In light of the recent 2019 study by Habitat for Humanity, which reported that 1 in 6 American families — 19 million households — are spending at least *half* their income for a place to live, we CLT leaders must push ourselves to address such key questions as: How big can a single CLT become? How can we advance our often-discussed collective goal for increasing CLT housing production at a reasonable pace? Can we achieve greater scale and leverage partnerships with private financial institutions and development partners without sacrificing our commitment to community-led values?

EXTERNAL CRITICISM CAN BE ADDRESSED

During 2019–2020, CLTs in the United States are celebrating the 50th Anniversary of the founding of the first CLT, New Communities Inc. In that 50-year span, the model has been extended and adapted from its original focus on agrarian working-land ownership to mitigate the effects of sharecropping and discrimination for rural farmers. Fifty years later, with some 260 CLTs in existence across the USA, the model is focused largely on *community* ownership of land and the creation of housing with permanent affordability.

> Families only earn wealth from homeownership if they are able to hang onto their homes over time, despite the ups and downs of a fluctuating economy.

Ironically, a model that emerged from African-American innovation and leadership has attracted its fair share of African-American critics, who object to the standard CLT practice of imposing resale controls on owner-occupied homes. They argue that families of color deserve the same full wealth-building opportunity offered by real estate ownership that white families have historically enjoyed.

Such criticism ignores two practical realities. Families only earn wealth from homeownership if they are able to gain access to homeownership. Once they do, families only earn wealth from homeownership if they are able to hang onto their homes over time, despite the ups and downs of a fluctuating economy. Research conducted by the Grounded Solutions Network and the Lincoln Institute of Land Policy, some of which is summarized below, has shown that CLTs are increasingly helping families of color to purchase homes. The majority of these first-time homeowners are building wealth. And, as previous studies have shown, the owners of CLT resale-restricted homes rarely lose their homes to foreclosure.

Beyond these practical rebuttals to CLT critics, I believe we must also directly challenge our critics to address the broader question of whether the main performance metric of racial equity should be based primarily on comparison to a benefit resulting from a racist system of land ownership and wealth creation. That system was created by white American culture, another undeniable expression of white privilege, dominance, and assumed superiority.

A baseline for the next 50 years of CLT progress has been established by a recent research paper commissioned by the Grounded Solutions Network entitled, *Tracking Growth and Evaluating Performance of Shared Equity Homeownership Programs During*

> Resale-restricted, owner-occupied homes are increasingly benefiting lower-income families of color.

Housing Market Fluctuations.[2] Published by the Lincoln Institute of Land Policy in 2019, it is the largest study of the performance of shared equity housing programs to date. It evaluates the impact of 58 shared equity homeownership programs in the USA, documenting homeowner characteristics and performance outcomes for 4,108 homes over a 33-year span, 1985 to 2018. Thirty-two (32) of these programs are administered by CLTs; 73% of the properties included in the study are CLT homes. Key findings highlighted by the report, based on quantitative data include:

- The shared equity sector is increasingly serving people of color. Homeowners of color have steadily increased from 13% in the pre-2001 period to 43% today.

- Wealth building in these shared equity homes is benefitting homeowners. The median shared equity household accumulates approximately $14,000 through their participation in shared equity programs, while the median equity investment that was originally made by homeowners at purchase was $1,875.

- A majority of shared equity homeowners are eventually choosing to transition to traditional homeownership. When the owners of shared equity housing resold their homes, a majority (58%) purchased another home, instead of reverting to renting.

- The majority of shared equity home purchasers are first-time homebuyers from households headed by women in their late 30s, earning 51%–80% of Area Median Income, and employed predominantly in office, retail, or service jobs.

The shared equity housing sector, of which CLTs make up a major part, now boasts a track record of *equitable* performance, whereby resale-restricted, owner-occupied homes are increasingly benefiting lower-income families of color. This represents indisputable proof that the CLT model can be effective in addressing our nation's documented racial wealth gap for African-American households.[3] These benefits will remain limited to a small fraction of the population, however, unless our programs are expanded in capacity and unless our portfolios are increased. We need to focus on such practical aspects as standardization of shared equity mortgages, consistent governmental guidelines for resale formulas, a uniform appraisal methodology, access to greater amounts of dedicated public funding, greater access to private commercial financing, and increased attention to the sustainability of our organizations. Unless we rise to the challenge of shared equity expansion, a majority of Americans still suffering the impact of discrimination — and those who are most in need of quality housing — will remain untouched by our efforts.

AN EXCITING PATH FORWARD

Among several ambitious large-scale shared equity housing initiatives currently unfolding is a new CLT in Washington, DC. Its origin story is noteworthy as an example of the interplay of land ownership, public policy, and community control as we attempt to shape a vision for the next cycle of CLT growth. The Washington neighborhoods of Wards 7 and 8, located east of the Anacostia River, have a combined population of approximately 154,000 people, 93% of whom are African-American. Ward 8 contains the historic Anacostia neighborhood, one of Washington's first African-American suburbs. Here, in September 1877, the celebrated African-American abolitionist and social reformer, Frederick Douglass, paid $6,700 to purchase a home on 9¾ acres of land.[4]

Today, the residents of both Wards 7 and 8 face a mounting threat of massive displacement, a consequence of Washington's robust real estate market, which has gentrified one low-income neighborhood after another.[5] This process has been encouraged by bad public policy through which thousands of federally subsidized rental housing units were created with short-term affordability protections designed to lapse in the near future.[6] Area residents and small business owners fear that displacement pressures will also be heightened by the planned construction of the 11th Street Bridge Park, a new elevated public park, the first of its kind in Washington, DC, that will span the Anacostia River.

Fig. 22.1. Bridge Park rendering, aerial view. IMAGE COURTESY OF OMA+OLIN

Fig. 22.2. Cultural Equity Open House, Anacostia Arts Center. Ward 7 resident, Dennis Chestnut. COURTESY OF SCOTT KRATZ, 11TH STREET BRIDGE PARK

These concerns spurred organizing and outreach within the Anacostia neighborhood where the threat of gentrification loomed the largest, especially those areas adjacent to the proposed 11th Street Bridge Park. Residents were mobilized to inform the Bridge Park Equitable Development Plan, completed in 2015. The Plan acknowledged that *"construction of signature public parks can significantly change land values and uses in surrounding areas."* It recommended, as an antidote to displacement, the creation of a new CLT to secure and to re-position existing residential properties located east of the Anacostia River as new permanently affordable housing.

The area's resident leaders and Bridge Park advocates agreed on shared priorities for the new park and acted decisively. They found a partner in a local nonprofit developer of shared equity housing, City First Homes, secured dedicated philanthropic funding, and retained expert technical assistance from the Denver-based Urban Land Conservancy. In August 2017, they invited me to deliver a public presentation on the CLT model's origins in the Civil Rights Movement. This "Power to the People" presentation occurred at the Anacostia Arts Center. It was filled to capacity and helped to fuel efforts by various community leaders, nonprofits, and funders to establish the appropriately named "Douglass Community Land Trust."

Today, the Douglass CLT (*http://douglassclt.org*) boasts a 12-person board that is predominately African-American. Neighborhood residents make up a majority of the board. The new CLT has already secured funding and partnerships to preserve an existing 65-unit multifamily rental project in Ward 8, as the first step toward creating a total portfolio of 750 permanently affordable homes over the next ten years, balanced equally between rental and homeownership.

Some may take issue with this ten-year timespan as being too little or too slow, but we must all exercise patience, recognizing that one decade is a brief moment in the cycle of neighborhood change and community development, as well as a fraction of the full lifespan of a single generation. Although still a work in progress, the Douglass CLT shows promise as a new approach for using the CLT model to mitigate displacement and to manage equitable growth.

Resident concerns about the potential for market-driven investments and publicly funded infrastructure improvements leading to displacement and gentrification in communities of color are certainly not limited to Washington, DC. The federal government's national Opportunity Zone Program, for example, is the newest attempt to direct private capital investment toward low-income communities, providing tax incentives for investors to re-invest unrealized capital gains in eligible low-income census tracts. There is no provision in the program's guidelines, however, for including community decision making in directing this private investment, nor are there any specifics as to the types of community benefits or outcomes that will be used in evaluating the program's success.

> We hope to achieve a "new normal" of community-owned land, community-led decision making, and access to opportunity for current residents.

We cannot continue to allow federal policy to remain silent on the challenges of including community decision making and achieving equitable outcomes. We must demand, in particular, that our elected leaders and policymakers fully integrate a racial equity lens across a range of federal policies, new and old, spanning housing, economic development, and environmental justice. Such a lens might include targeted reparations for African-Americans, stemming from the historic injustice of slavery, and could be combined with the investment of billions of dollars required to improve the aging public infrastructure of our nation.

One potential example of this transformational infrastructure investment is suggested in the current work of the High Line Network, a national alliance of 19 transformative public open space infrastructure project leaders. The Network's website states:

> As cities become denser and land for traditional parks becomes scarce, citizens are finding creative ways to bring greenspace to their neighborhoods. Projects in the High Line Network transform underutilized infrastructure into new urban landscapes. Redefining what a park can be, these hybrid spaces are also public squares, open-air museums, botanical gardens, social service organizations, walkways, transit corridors, and more.[7]

The 11th Street Bridge Park in Washington, DC is included among the High Line Network's partners. It will serve as an early proof-of-concept, validating the critical need for equitable development strategies which use the CLT model. Working together, we hope to achieve a "new normal" of community-owned land, community-led decision making, and access to opportunity for current residents, prioritizing existing neighborhood cultures and traditions instead of focusing only on the highest market-based returns.

PERSONAL COMMITMENTS ARE REQUIRED

The CLT model must continue to adapt and to expand over the next 50 years to remain relevant, especially if we hope to adequately address the needs of communities in the face of profit-focused economic interests. In place of the current status quo and repeated public policy and systemic failures, CLT leaders must foster a new vision, evolving toward a more responsive system of proactive economic development with a racial equity lens. Our work must be intentionally targeted to promote *community* values, while preserving social and cultural cohesion, leading to an expanded exercise of democracy with broader civic engagement and inclusion.

CLT leaders must also be thoughtful regarding the individuals we collectively support and train for the next generation of expert practitioners. I challenge us all to expand our personal relationship circles and to provide more opportunities for leaders of color to champion and to expand the impact of our work. Future CLT leaders will be required to do a better job of educating the general public, real estate developers, financial investors, and policy makers to prioritize *development without displacement* as a goal. We all must advocate and implement progressive land use and zoning policies that balance community-driven priorities with a reasonable financial upside for those assuming the significant risk of investment in future development.

I have come to accept that I personally may not see the full flowering of the CLT model's acceptance, adoption, and growth during the span of my working years. No doubt this conclusion has been reached by many other CLT pioneers and practitioners who have come before me, some of whom have been serving as my own trusted mentors for over a decade. Like many of them, I now see myself as making a place and holding the space for future leaders, who will hopefully inherit from our efforts better tools, dedicated resources, and new policies with which to expand the scale and impact of our CLT model. Progress in growing our model, I have come to understand, like our nation's prolonged and grudging progress toward racial justice, will neither come rapidly nor easily. Each of us is required to commit to continuing the long march toward a better collective future, based on the social justice ideals that were clearly envisioned and effectively stated by inspirational leaders of the American Civil Rights Movement.

While the bold opportunities and enormous challenges ahead may appear intimidating and burdensome to many, I draw strong motivation from my exchanges with CLT leaders across the world and directly from the words of Mrs. Shirley Sherrod, who repeatedly has known both tragedy and triumph during her 50-year journey with the model that she and her partners were the first to call a "community land trust." In November 2018, I visited Albany, Georgia. As I stood beside her at *Resora*, the community-controlled farm and retreat center that represents the latest incarnation of New Communities Inc., she gestured to the 1,600 acres that surrounded us and shared these words: *"Don't give up! If we had given up, we would never have achieved all this."*

Notes

1. "Shared equity homeownership," as defined by the Grounded Solutions Network, is "a self-sustaining model that takes a one-time public investment to make a home affordable for a lower-income family and then restricts the home's sale price each time it is sold to keep it affordable for subsequent low-income families who purchase the home." This sector includes CLTs, limited-equity cooperatives, deed-restricted homes, and other forms of permanently affordable housing. See: John Emmeus Davis, *Shared Equity Homeownership*, National Housing Institute, 2006 (*https://shelterforce.org/wp-content/uploads/2008/04/SharedEquityHome.pdf*); and Emily Thaden, "The State of Shared Equity Homeownership," *Shelterforce*, May 7, 2018 (*https://shelterforce.org/2018/05/07/shared-equity/*).

2. Ruoniu Wang, Claire Cahen, Arthur Acolin, and Rebecca J. Walter, *Tracking Growth and Evaluating Performance of Shared Equity Homeownership Programs During Housing Market Fluctuations* (Cambridge, MA: Lincoln Institute of Land Policy, 2019).

3. Brian Thompson, *Forbes Magazine*, February 18, 2018, "The Racial Wealth Gap: Addressing America's Most Pressing Epidemic" (*https://www.forbes.com/sites/brian-thompson1/2018/02/18/the-racial-wealth-gap-addressing-americas-most-pressing-epidemic/#10d3ab317a48*).

4. Frederick Douglass National Historic Site (*https://www.nps.gov/frdo/index.htm*).

5. The experience of Washington's U Street Corridor provides a cautionary tale, where a once-thriving community of working-class and middle-class families, 90% of them African-Americans, was rapidly transformed through cycles of economic decline and gentrification. By 2001, the Corridor's African-American population had plummeted, composing just 30% of the area's families (Daniela Deane, "Going Upscale on U Street," *Washington Post*, March 24, 2001).

6. In Ward 8 alone, there are estimated to be 10,925 units of publicly subsidized, privately owned housing with affordability restrictions that are due to expire.

7. High Line Network (*https://network.thehighline.org/about/*).

23.

A Reflection on the Bioethics
of Community Land Trusts

María E. Hernández-Torrales

> That the house of every one is to him as his
> castle and fortress as well for defense against
> injury and violence, as for his repose . . .
> —*Sir Edward Coke (1552–1634), English judge and jurist*

Housing is a topic that invites us and summons us. It invites us to reflect on the meaning of housing with regard to the development of human beings. It also summons us to act, moving from passive reflection to active intervention in order to secure the well-being of those who lack the means to satisfy the fundamental right to housing. We shall focus here on the community land trust (CLT), a nonprofit organization that is built around the strategy of acquiring and holding land for the purpose of satisfying the common needs of a place-based community such as the provision of land for affordable housing or for farming and food security. The CLT can be analyzed from two basic perspectives. The first perspective is organizational, examining the structure that ensures that a CLT's objectives are met. The second perspective is moral, pertaining to the values that move human beings to work for other human beings who lack fundamental rights such as the right to housing and food.

Our attention will be directed mostly toward this last perspective, demonstrating that the CLT is an ethical model to pursue. We will analyze the moral values that inspire community-based nonprofit organizations to embrace this practice, motivating them to establish a CLT. We will use a bioethical analysis, a comprehensive perspective that takes into consideration not only the needs and development of human beings, but also our relationship with everything that surrounds us as inhabitants of a planet where resources are finite. By examining the CLT model from a bioethical standpoint, we focus predominantly on the balance between the personal interests of individuals and the collective interests through which a community is formed. From this standpoint, we conclude and affirm that the CLT is an ethical model, one imbued with a particular set of values pertaining to satisfaction of a right to housing and a right to a decent life. In this regard, a CLT walks a path and reaches a destination that is distinct and separate from the path typically followed by a fragmented and individualist society.

BIOETHICS AS A TOOL FOR ANALYSIS AND REFLECTION

In the essay "The Land Ethic" of his classic book, *A Sand County Almanac*, Aldo Leopold (1949) reflected on how human beings are part of a bigger ecological system and how, together, characteristics of the Earth and of the people who inhabit it determine the course of historical events. Additionally, all ethics are sustained by the belief that every individual is a member of a community composed of interdependent parts; accordingly, an individual's ethics, guiding personal action in complicated or new situations, move him or her toward collaboration with other community members.

> Bioethics advocates a concept of progress that places an equal emphasis on the individual and the collective.

The term "bioethics" was coined in 1971 by Van Rensselaer Potter in his monograph *Bioethics: Bridge to the Future*. The publication's lofty purpose was to contribute to the future of humanity by uniting two cultures, science and humanities, through the formation of a new discipline which he named *bioethics* (Potter, 1971). Potter stated that all ethics imply action aligned with moral standards. He specified that it is necessary to remember that ethics have to be accompanied by a realistic understanding of the relationships amongst all living creatures and the environment in which they live in — ecology, in its broadest sense. Ethical values cannot be separated from biological facts.

Potter also argued that "[w]e are in great need for a Land Ethic, a Wildlife Ethic, a Population Ethic, a Consumption Ethic, an Urban Ethic, an International Ethic, a Geriatric Ethic, and so on . . . All of them involve Bioethics." There are many problematic situations that we encounter as a society, including limited resources like water and energy, the pressures of population growth and an aging population, the lack of adequate and decent housing, our disrespect and damage of nature, global warming and climate change. In the face of these many problems, scientific knowledge and philosophical values have to be combined and transcribed into practical wisdom, so that knowledge can be used to address holistic human needs. Knowledge has to strengthen the individual, while simultaneously strengthening society. Bioethics advocates a concept of progress that places an equal emphasis on the individual and the collective. Individual progress and societal progress are interdependent and, ideally, they are pursued in such a way as to be equitably and sustainably in balance (Potter, 1971).

Over the course of its forty-eight years of existence, bioethics has become one of the most highly developed fields in the study of applied ethics. A major contribution was made to bioethics by Tom Beauchamp and James Childress (1979), according to Professor Jorge José Ferrer (2016, 97), when they proposed four general principles as the basic pillars on which a bioethical analysis could be built: (1) respect for the autonomy of our choices; (2) non-maleficence; (3) beneficence; and (4) distributive justice.[1] As discussed by Professor Ferrer, these principles do not establish specific standards for all the situations we face daily, but by using the principles as a basic framework for deliberation, we can generate the precise details that will guide our actions in a situation at hand (Ibid., 71). Within this framework, according to Diego Garcia, the deliberation process should take into consideration facts, conflicted values, the course of action or duty, and finally, the best solution that is also in accordance with norms established by the law (Seoane, 2016, 493).

Respect for the *autonomy* of our choices assumes that our actions are taken freely and with informed consent. To determine if any given action is autonomous, it has to be intentional, understood, and free from external controls or influences. *Non-maleficence* entails an intentional abstention from causing harm. *Beneficence* requires us to contribute to the well-being of others and to act positively on their behalf. *Distributive justice* is based on the fair distribution of scarce resources. A material principle of distributive justice is based on the fair distribution of scarce resources, providing everyone with the material means to develop essential capabilities for a productive life (Ferrer, 2006).

THE RIGHT TO HOUSING

Housing that is decent, affordable, and secure is one of the key factors in the life of every human being. It is a social determinant of health (Hernández, 2016). In the words of the Supreme Court of the United States (*Block v. Hirsch*, 256 US 135, 156 [1921]): "Housing is a necessary of life." Without housing, it is not possible to exercise any other right. Mathew Desmond (2016, 293) has argued that housing is the center of life: it is the shelter where we rest from all external pressures, the place where we can be ourselves. He adds that housing creates psychological stability, which permits people to invest in their homes and in their social relationships (Ibid, 296). It is also a crucial element for young people to achieve academic excellence and to complete their studies. The stability that housing provides to individuals and to families is the basis for a supportive community where residents are in control. The opposite is also true. When families or individuals lack decent, affordable and secure housing, they tend also to lack stability in their homes, family life, neighborhood, school, job, and possessions.

Housing is such an important matter that it is included in the International Declaration of Human Rights,[2] adopted by the United Nations in 1948. Article 25 declared housing to be one of the necessary components for a decent and adequate life (UN, 1948, Art. 25). Within the framework of human rights, housing is related to solidarity in the sense that people live in homes, but they are also part of a neighborhood and part of a community, with an established social fabric and their own web of relations. We can infer, therefore, that housing is an overarching concept that surpasses the physical aspects of a living space (Madden, 2017). Safe, decent, affordable housing gives people the stability and ability to build durable social networks and to live in vibrant communities.

In October 2016, the Third UN World Conference on Housing and Sustainable Urban Development (Habitat III), held in Quito, Ecuador, endorsed the *New Urban Agenda* (ONU, 2017). Basing itself on the estimate that by 2030, six out of 10 people will live in cities, the *New Urban Agenda* highlights the relationship between urbanization and equitable development, where the politics and strategies of urban renovation are intertwined with the creation of jobs, expanded opportunities for generating a livelihood, and the improvement of quality of life (ONU, 2017, iv). Housing is at the center of the *New Urban Agenda*, as it is in another UN document, the *2030 Agenda for Sustainable Development and the Objectives for Sustainable Goals (SDGs)*. Sustainable Development Goal 11, §11.1. seeks to ensure that by 2030 all people will have access to adequate, safe and affordable housing, access to basic services, and all slums will have been improved (ONU, 2015).

Despite international acknowledgement of the importance of housing, however, recognized by sovereign countries and the United Nations alike, the reality experienced by millions of people around the world contradicts this acknowledgement. According to Clerc (2016), forty years after the first Habitat Conference (Habitat I), which became the foundation for the UN's Habitat Program, close to 100 million people now reside in substandard settlements or live on the streets. Stigmatized and negatively stereotyped, these people are deprived of essential services and basic infrastructure. Millions of others have been displaced, stripped of their homes due to inadequate planning or disasters associated with climate change (UN High Commissioner for Refugees, 2019); or they have been forced to live in refugee camps as a result of war or discriminatory public policies (Newey, 2019). Numerous people who *do* have a roof over their heads are forced to live in a disgraceful and inadequate manner as a result of poverty, inequity, discrimination, and environmental injustice (Clerc, 2016).

> When land and housing are viewed as commodities, they are far from being treated as a human right.

There are also many communities of low-income people who live in constant fear of being displaced because of market pressures. This is especially true in informal settlements where hundreds, sometimes thousands, of people are living on land to which they have neither a secure right of ownership nor a secure right of use.[3] Similarly, extreme natural events like hurricanes, floods, wildfires, rising seas, or droughts can cause the involuntary displacement of low-income people, who are then prevented from returning and rebuilding by a combination of public policy and private speculation by "disaster capitalists" who have snatched up newly cleared land.

Many developed and underdeveloped countries treat land and housing as luxuries for those who can pay the price. They become objects of speculation, unlimited accumulation, and wealth generation. When land and housing are viewed in such a way — i.e., as private commodities rather than common necessities — they are far from being treated as a human right (Farha, 2018).

HOUSING AS A CAUSE OF SEGREGATION AND DISCRIMINATION

There is a crisis in housing that affects people all over the world. The bioethical analysis presented in this essay is valid wherever the inadequacy of housing exists, affecting individuals and families in many countries. For the purposes of the current analysis, we will focus on the housing situation and its trajectory in the United States.

Discriminatory practices in the USA have been manifested in all spheres, public and private, but especially in the production, financing, and regulation of housing. In his important book, *The Color of Law: A Forgotten History of How Our Government Segregated America*, Richard Rothstein (2017) describes how the federal government developed housing during World War I for individuals working in defense-related industries; that is, for those who worked in shipyards and ammunition plants. The 83 housing projects that were developed by the government across 26 different states were occupied by 170,000 white workers and their families. Black workers were excluded from these housing projects, even from those developed close to industrial sites where black people represented a significant percentage of the workforce. During the same period, policies established by the federal government and by state governments imposed segregationist practices, forcing black people to live in overcrowded slums, far from city centers and employment opportunities (Rothstein, 2017). Urban planners designed neighborhoods that were reserved for white people. The black population was intentionally excluded or removed from those areas.

During World War II, the housing shortage became acute for both low-income and moderate-income families in the United States. As a response, the New Deal policies implemented by Franklin Delano Roosevelt led to the creation of the first public housing projects for civilians who were not part of a defense program. Race determined the program's design. Separate housing projects were built for black people, who were completely excluded from projects designated for white people. In the rare cases where both races occupied the same project, buildings were segregated by race.

The first project of the Public Works Administration, Techwood Homes in Atlanta, inaugurated in 1935, is a prime example of the application and impact of this discriminatory policy (Rothstein, 2017). Techwood Homes was built on land where a racially diverse community of 1,600 families had long existed, composed of both black and white

> Government policy caused the creation of new slums as the only housing option for black and economically poor people.

families. In order to build the new housing complex, the federal government demolished the structures where those families lived and replaced them with 604 housing units — all of which were reserved exclusively for white people. This government action not only created a segregated community where there had once been an integrated community; it forced displaced families to look for housing in places were black Americans already lived in overcrowded conditions, intensifying racial segregation in Atlanta.

Government policy also caused the creation of new slums as the only housing option for black and economically poor people. The *Housing Handbook*, written by the U.S. Housing Authority as a guide for states, established that the racial nature of communities had to be preserved. This justified segregation in places where it already existed and implemented segregation in places where it did not exist (Rothstein, 2017). The *Handbook* also reinforced the prevalent belief that any movement of black people into communities made up of white people could threaten property values.

Much of the housing produced using funds provided by the Housing Law of 1949 and its subsequent amendments promoted even more segregation. In 1984, according to Rothstein, investigative reporters from the *Dallas Morning News* visited federally funded public housing projects in 47 metropolitan areas of the United States. The reporters found that close to 10 million residents were living in projects that were segregated by race. They also found that in projects where residents were predominantly white, the facilities, amenities, services, and maintenance were superior, compared to those projects where black people lived.

Nowadays, segregationist policies and practices might not be manifested in such an obvious manner. Many are disguised, but they combine and conspire to make it practically impossible for low-income people of color to have access to decent housing. Included among these discriminatory policies and practices are exclusionary zoning, exorbitant pricing of land and housing, the development of gated neighborhoods, and the lack of public investment and private lending in poverty-stricken areas, especially in areas where people of color reside. Likewise, the quality of public infrastructure and government services offered in poverty-stricken areas is usually inferior to that offered in areas where people with greater economic power reside.

Every day, fewer people have access to adequate housing. According to the renowned architect and urban planner Jaime Lerner (2014), the lack of access to housing is one of the main causes of poverty in the United States and one of the country's most pressing issues. In the same vein, Mathew Desmond (2016) from Harvard University, in an ethnographic study conducted in Milwaukee, Wisconsin, found that families had seen their wages come to a standstill and even lowered, while the cost of housing had increased dramatically. Families that were part of this study became more impoverished with each eviction. Desmond stated that, to this day, the majority of low-income families who rent their housing are forced to spend more than half of their household income on rent and utilities and at least one of every four low-income renters must spend more than 70 percent of their household income for housing.

Millions of people in the United States are evicted every year because they cannot pay their rent. They are displaced through eviction notices rendered by the court, or informal evictions occurring on the fringes of the law. In 2013, one of eight tenant families in the United States could not pay their rent; a similar number were sure that they would eventually be evicted (Desmond, 2016).

Renters are not alone in facing the possibility of losing their homes. This can happen to low-income homeowners too. According to Gottesdeiner (2013), between 2007 and 2013 ten million North Americans lost their homes due to foreclosures. The Great Recession harmed people of color far more than it hurt white people. African-Americans, Hispanic-Americans, and Asian-Americans experienced, in the words of James Carr and Katrin Anacker (2012, 3), "a catastrophic loss of wealth as a result of the burst of the national house price bubble in 2006 and the ensuing foreclosure crisis that started in early 2007, both of which have had a disproportionate impact on families and communities of color."[4] In Puerto Rico, according to government statistics, 40,136 mortgages were foreclosed in the decade between 2008 and 2018, which likely means that the same number of families lost their homes.

Discriminatory policies, practices, and patterns must be tackled, whether by governmental intervention or by private action, putting an end to them. It is also the responsibility of individuals who believe in racial and economic justice to denounce discrimination and to search for solutions that alleviate the disparity in the provision of adequate and decent housing for people whose income does not enable them to have access to it.

THE BIOETHICS OF COMMUNITY LAND TRUSTS

The policies that affect housing are tied to policies on land use (Clerc, 2016). The different approaches and regulations on real estate determine who benefits (or not) from the use of land, from the opportunities provided by land, and from the wealth that land produces. It is also important to highlight that land-related decisions are influenced by the values and ethical perspectives of those who are making use of the land. If land is considered a common good, an inheritance received from past generations and entrusted into our care for future generations, our actions in using land will be shaped and constrained in accordance with that perspective. Conversely, if we consider land — and whatever is built upon it — to be a marketable good, subject to price speculation and social exclusion, we will act accordingly.

This latter perspective is prevalent throughout the world, despite consequences that have proven detrimental and hurtful for millions of people who lack secure access to land and housing. This is a social problem on a global scale, requiring solutions that take into account both the personal needs of individuals, for whom adequate housing is essential, and the collective needs of the larger community. Such measures must be sensitive to finding this balance, while also having an ethical, axiological focus on creating the conditions for a decent life.

The CLT model, in this regard, is an ethical model that satisfies an individual's need for safe, decent, and affordable housing, even as it takes into consideration the surrounding community. Individual interests are secured through personal ownership of the housing structure. Collective interests are secured through the community's ownership, control, and care of the land on which the homes are built. Ownership and management of the land in a CLT are carried out by a nonprofit organization with a structure of democratic governance that is sensitive to the community's needs. Both the housing structure and the land are placed beyond the reach of market speculation, which ensures that families of moderate-income or low-income, no matter their race or origin, can exercise a right to decent housing. Since the housing continues to be affordable in perpetuity, that right is protected and extended far into the future.

> Finding and sustaining an equitable balance between the individual and the community is at the heart of the CLT.

It is important to mention, for the purpose of this essay, the values that constitute the roots of the CLT model. Davis (2010) has documented the origins and development of the CLT in the United States, a model that emerged in the 1970s from the Civil Rights Movement in the American South and from an earlier seedbed of theoretical ideas, political movements, and social experiments that had accumulated over many decades. Everything began with a different perspective on how land should be owned and used: recognizing the intrinsic value of land as a shared inheritance; rejecting the speculative buying and selling of land; and using land to capture wealth for the common benefit of all residents, not for the exclusive benefit of a few landowners. Homes could rightfully belong to individuals, but land rightfully belonged to the community, which had a shared responsibility to nurture and preserve it for future generations.

This principle of finding and sustaining an equitable balance between the individual and the community is at the heart of bioethics. It is at the heart of the CLT as well. As far back as 1982, in one of the first books written about this new model of tenure, the authors described why a CLT was needed and how it worked in the following way:

> Our present property arrangements are not working well enough. It makes sense to look for alternative approaches that are based on respect for the legitimate interests of both individuals and communities and that provide an effective means of balancing these interests. The community land trust is one such approach (Institute for Community Economics, 1982, 8).

It is also worth emphasizing the democratic and inclusive character of the governance of most CLTs. The model strengthens and empowers community members, allowing them to exert a degree of control over the lands held by the CLT, the structures that are built on these lands, and the stewardship services that are provided for the long-term care of the buildings and the people who occupy them. The organization has a constant presence, since its corporate membership and governance structure are composed of residents from the community it serves. This relationship is also nurtured by engaging a body of informed people in the organization's development decisions and policy making processes.

The CLT model has three intrinsic elements, namely: sustainable community development that is led by an organization accountable to its community; development that is carried out mainly for the purpose of providing housing that will remain affordable in perpetuity for people who are low-income; and development that occurs on community-owned land that the market cannot reach. This mixture of elements enables a place-based community to maintain its physical integrity, to preserve its cultural inheritance, and to protect the land's natural attributes for future generations.

According to Davis (2010), behind and beyond this basic structure — what is sometimes known as the "classic" CLT — there lies great adaptability, allowing organizations to adjust the model according to the needs and preferences of their own community. Notwithstanding such versatility, however, the model is imbued with similar values each time a CLT is established. These values arise from a sense of responsibility to prevent the displacement of vulnerable populations and to fulfill the basic needs of people who have been excluded from the political and economic mainstream. This is not welfare, but personal improvement and collective empowerment, a program that is focused on the development of humans as citizens exercising their rights and their duties.

The CLT that arose on the mainland of the United States has been an inspiration for community organizations in other countries. This includes two very different CLTs that are geographically distant, but rather similar in terms of their purposes. One of these CLTs was organized in San Juan, Puerto Rico and the other in Voi, Kenya.[5] The purpose of both was to formalize and standardize the relationship with land for residents who were living in informal settlements without land titles. Their CLTs gave them security of tenure as individuals, but it also allowed them to take collective control of their own development and the environment surrounding them, preventing the involuntary displacement of low-income people.

The ownership and use of land in the CLT are far from the dominant tradition of treating land as a commodity, subject to market pricing and speculative hoarding. CLT's live and practice a land ethic that is closer to what Aldo Leopold had urged in *A Sand County Almanac* (1949), treating land as an inheritance that is entrusted to our stewardship for

> The common ground of the CLT is put to use for the common good.

future generations. The common ground of the CLT is put to use for the common good. Furthermore, when land is placed under the control of an organization that is accountable to a particular community, it can be managed and developed with a sense of permanent care and shared responsibility by people who are caring for something that does not personally belong to them.

This land ethic is combined with the attention that is also owed to the person who will make use of the structure or improvements on the land. According to data provided by the Grounded Solutions Network, covering 2,844 families or individuals living in home-ownership units in 32 CLTs across the United States of America, 63% are occupied by female-headed households (Grounded Solutions Network, 2019).

Two legal entitlements coexist harmoniously within the same form of tenure: the collective entitlement of land under community governance and the individual entitlement of the structural improvements, owned and occupied by the person who acquires or builds it. Both contribute to the empowerment of the community that surrounds this property, strengthening the social fabric and creating a foundation for personal well-being and collaboration.

At the same time, this mixed-ownership model of tenure contributes to the creation of environmentally conscious communities that have the ability to manage change and are committed to the sustainable development of their surroundings. This has been the experience of many CLTs, especially the one created by the Caño Martín Peña communities in San Juan, Puerto Rico. The Caño Martín Peña CLT is making possible the Martín Peña Canal Ecosystem Restoration Project, an environmental justice project that will benefit not only the Caño Martín Peña communities, but also the capital city of San Juan. For many years, highly contaminated water from this canal has flooded the impoverished houses of the residents of the adjacent Caño Martín Peña communities. In order to control flooding, the canal had to be dredged. As a consequence, many households needed to be relocated and new infrastructure needed to be built. As the owner and steward of lands along the canal that were formerly owned by the government, the CLT has made them available for the relocation of residents and for the construction of the appropriate infrastructure that will keep the canal's water clean after dredging.

Making land available for such purposes was a conscious and conscientious decision of the CLT and of the residents who live on the CLT's land. It is worth noting that market-oriented, individual land ownership would have prevented the Caño Martín Peña communities from realizing these benefits: clean water, a dredged canal, and the permanence of the communities in an area that people have been calling home for a century (Algoed, Hernández and Rodríguez, 2018).

As important as the contribution of CLTs in terms of the conservation of the environment, we should also pay attention to what CLT organizations do for the people who benefit from a CLT's sensible management and stewardship of land and other assets.

Applying the four general principles that constitute the framework for bioethics that were introduced at the beginning of this essay — respect for the autonomy of our choices, non-maleficence, beneficence, and distributive justice — we may put in perspective the ethics of the CLT model.

Thus, CLT organizations provide community assets for low-income families and marginalized communities who would otherwise not have had access to such resources and to the benefits they entail. When a low-income family or individual acquires a home from a CLT, their decision is taken voluntarily after a well-informed process about the structure of the CLT model, its purpose of providing lasting affordability and benefits for the community, and the implications of this arrangement for the buyer. The CLT educates and alerts the family or individual about resale restrictions in order to keep homes affordable for future generations of low-income buyers; the governance structure of the CLT that requires community engagement; and the fact that the CLT retains ownership of the land, while the family or individual purchases only the improvement built on the land.

CLT organizations make it possible for low-income families to buy and to enjoy a home without jeopardizing other important necessities. In this sense, the CLT is complying with the principle of non-maleficence. The principle of beneficence is also widely met by the CLT model since it provides an effective way to meet one of the most important and urgent needs of every human being; that is, to attain a home. But CLT organizations go farther, for they are also creating jobs, promoting quality of life, creating energy-efficient homes, and revitalizing neighborhoods (Thaden and Lowe, 2014).

Market-oriented practices have proven to be a failure in meeting the housing needs of low-income and moderate-income families and individuals. In a market environment, there is neither fairness nor equality when a buyer lacks the resources to acquire or sustain a home. Mortgage banks and other financial institutions have a single priority; that is, to make money for their investors. CLT organizations, on their part, have made it possible for poor people to attain and keep decent and quality homes that are within their economic means; and at the same time, the CLT model has helped these families or individuals to build wealth and to enhance their future.

The question that guides a bioethical analysis is the same question that drives us to ask ourselves and to determine, "What is right?" When deliberating over the negative consequences of treating land as a commodity — whether in the provision of housing or in the preservation of farmland — there is no doubt that a CLT, in its ethical management of land, is more likely to produce results that ensure both a right to housing and an opportunity to promote food security. We should give serious consideration to the CLT model. Said reasoning is supported by the fact that, at the moment, the CLT model is helping to alleviate inequity in the provision of adequate and decent housing for thousands of people whose income does not allow them to have access to these resources. This is confirmed by the growing number of CLTs being organized throughout the world, of which the preceding chapters of this book provide testimony and bear witness.

Notes

1. Beauchamp and Childress introduced the four principles of respect for autonomy, non-maleficence, beneficence, and justice in *The Principles of Biomedical Ethics* (1979). Currently in its 7th edition, their book heavily influenced the newly emerging fields of biomedical ethics and bioethics.

2. *The International Bill of Human Rights* consists of the *Universal Declaration of Human Rights, the International Covenant on Civil and Political Rights with the two Optional Protocols, and the International Covenant on Economic, Social, and Cultural Rights.*

3. The Caño Martín Peña communities in San Juan, Puerto Rico and the favelas of Brazil, described in previous chapters of this book, are prime examples.

4. See: James H. Carr and Katrin B. Anacker, *Long-Term Social Impacts and Financial Costs of Foreclosure on Families and Communities of Color: A Review of the Literature* (Washington DC: Annie E. Casey Foundation, National Community Reinvestment Coalition, 2012: 3).

5. The CLT in San Juan, Puerto Rico is discussed in Chapter 11 in the present volume; the CLT initiative in Voi, Kenya is discussed in Chapter 14.

References

Algoed, L., Hernández, M., and Rodríguez, L. (2018). El fideicomiso de la tierra del Caño Martín Peña Instrumento notable de regularización de suelo en asentamientos informales. *https://www.lincolninst.edu/publications/working-papers/el-fideicomiso-la-tierra-del-cano-martin-pena*

Beauchamp, T.L. and Childress, J.F. (1979). *The Principles of Biomedical Ethics.* New York: Oxford University Press.

Block v. Hirsch (1921). 256 Supreme Court of the United States, 135, 156.

Clerc, V. (2016). "An outcry against informality. The impact of land on the treatment of precarious settlements, as spaces of political competition." Pp. 105–118 in *Rethinking Precarious Neighborhoods.* Paris: AFD.

Constitución de la Nación Argentina (1994, 22 de agosto).

Constitución Española (1948, 29 de diciembre).

Constitución de la República de Ecuador (2008, 20 de octubre).

Davis, J.E. (2006). "Development without displacement: Organizational and operational choices in starting a community land trust." Reprinted in *The Community Land Trust Reader*, J.E. Davis (ed.). Cambridge, Massachusetts: Lincoln Institute of Land Policy (2010: 259–268).

Davis, J.E. (2010). "Origins and evolution of the community land trust in the United States." Pp. 3–47 in *The Community Land Trust Reader*. Cambridge, Massachusetts: Lincoln Institute of Land Policy.

Desmond, M. (2016). *Evicted: Poverty and Profit in the American City*. New York: Crown Publishers.

Farha, L. (2018). *Report of the Special Rapporteur on Adequate Housing as a Component of the Right to an Adequate Standard of Living, and on the Right to Non-discrimination in this Context*. *https://www.undocs.org/A/73/310/rev.1*

Ferrer, J. J. (2013). "Teoría ética y deliberación bioética." Pp. 41–85 in *Ensayos en Bioética: Una Perspectiva Puertorriqueña*. San Juan, Puerto Rico: Universidad de Puerto Rico.

Ferrer, J. J. (2016). "Bioéticas principalistas." Pp. 91–116 in *Bioética: El Pluralismo de la Fundamentación*. Madrid: R.B. Servicios Editoriales, S.L.

Gottesdeiner, L. (2013). "10 million americans have had their homes taken away by the banks — often at the point of gun." *https://www.alternet.org/2013/08/10-million-americans-foreclosed-neighborhoods-devastated/*

Grounded Solutions Network (2018). HomeKeeper National Data Hub Administrative Data. Obtained through information request on 4/30/2019.

Hernández, D. and Suglia, S. (2016). "Housing as a social determinant of health." *https://healthequity.globalpolicysolutions.org/wp-content/uploads/2016/12/Housing2.pdf*

Housing Act of 1949, Public Law 81–171, 1949.

Institute for Community Economics (1982). *The Community Land Trust Handbook*. Emmaus, Pennsylvania: Rodale Press.

Leopold, A. (1949). "The land ethic." Pp. 237–264 in *A Sand County Almanac*. New York: Oxford University Press, Inc.

Lerner, J. (2014). *Urban Acupuncture*. Washington: Island Press.

Madden, D. and Marcuse, P. (2017). "The residential is political." Pp. 26–30 in *The Right to the City: A Verso Report*. Brooklyn, New York: Verso.

McNaughton, C. (2010). "Housing, homelessness and capabilities." *Housing, Theory and Society*. doi: 10.1080/14036090902764588

Midheme, E., Moulaert, F. (2013). "Pushing back the frontiers of property: Community land trusts and low-income housing in urban Kenya." *Land Use Policy*, 35, 73–84.

Millones de personas viven sin techo o en casas inadecuadas, un asalto a la dignidad y la vida. (2018). *https://news.un.org/es/story/2018/07/1437721*

Newey, S. (2019). "More than 70 million people forced to flee their homes because of war and persecution." *The Telegraph*. *https://www.telegraph.co.uk/global-health/climate-and-people/70-million-people-forced-flee-homes-war-persecution/*

Oficina del Comisionado de Instituciones Financieras (2019, marzo). Foreclosure Unit Residential by Institution. *http://www.ocif.pr.gov/DatosEstadisticos/Pages/default.aspx*

Organización de las Naciones Unidas (1948). Declaración universal de derechos humanos. *https://www.un.org/es/documents/udhr/UDHR_booklet_SP_web.pdf*

Organización de las Naciones Unidas (2015). Objetivos de desarrollo sostenible. Nueva agenda urbana. *https://www.un.org/sustainabledevelopment/es/cities/*

Organización de las Naciones Unidas (2017). Nueva agenda urbana. Conferencia de las Naciones Unidas sobre la Vivienda y el Desarrollo Urbano Sostenible (Hábitat III). *http://habitat3.org/wp-content/uploads/NUA-Spanish.pdf*

Potter, V. (1971). *Bioethics: Bridge to the Future*. New Jersey: Prentice-Hall, Inc.

Rothstein, R. (2017). *The Color of Law: A Forgotten History of How our Government Segregated America*. New York: Liveright Publishing Corporation.

Seoane, J. A. (2016). Argumentación jurídica y bioética. Examen teórico del modelo deliberativo de Diego Gracia. Anuario de Filosofía del Derecho, XXXII, 489–510.

Swann, Robert, Shimon Gottschalk, Erick Hansch, and Edward Webster (1972). *The Community Land Trust: A Guide to a New Model for Land Tenure in America*. Cambridge, Massachusetts: Center for Community Economic Development.

Thaden, E., and Lowe, J. (2014), "Resident and community engagement in community land trusts." *https://www.lincolninst.edu/sites/default/files/pubfiles/2429_1774_thaden_wp14et1.pdf*

United Nations High Commissioner for Refugees (2019), *Climate Change and Disaster Displacement*, accessed August 27, 2019 from *https://www.unhcr.org/climate-change-and-disasters.html*

24.

Community Control of Land
Thinking Beyond the Generic Community Land Trust

Olivia R. Williams

No progressive housing pitch today is complete without a mention of community land trusts. CLTs have become a hot topic — especially in today's affordable housing crisis — because they decommodify land, taking it out of the speculative market so that no one can flip a house or build luxury condominiums on it.

The first CLT, New Communities, Inc., was designed by organizers from the Civil Rights Movement in the late 1960s as a mechanism for community control of land — especially for African-Americans in the rural South — in response to devastating rates of Black land loss.[1] The original CLT involved agricultural land, cooperative businesses, and plans for constructing four villages with new educational, recreational, and industrial systems to meet the needs of residents.

In the 1980s and 1990s, CLTs emerged in cities too, where they proved useful in reducing blight and providing stability in disinvested neighborhoods while providing affordable housing. Now, the model is often touted by many organizers as a "radical" way to secure community control of land and housing for the working class as prices go up, especially in the urban core of many American cities.

But when talking with hundreds of people in the CLT field across the United States while doing research on CLTs, it became clear to me that the CLT model is increasingly being perceived and promoted by housing advocates and practitioners as primarily an economically efficient affordable housing strategy, rather than an organizational approach that empowers poor, working-class, and marginalized people to take control of the land they occupy.

The creators of the CLT model intended for collective decision-making around site planning and development to be controlled by the users of the land, with a board of CLT trustees (some living outside of the CLT's land) acting to ensure that the land stayed affordable for generations. But as the model grew and proliferated, highly professionalized boards and staff started running the show in more and more CLTs without significant input from low-income residents and neighbors on what they needed in their neighborhoods.

One executive director from a CLT in Minnesota told me and my research team their thoughts about some of the old-time radicals at the early national CLT conferences:

> This is a business. This is about economic sense. I'm not drinking the Kool-Aid. You can't make me. I think you're all nuts that you're taking the commune kind of approach to life. That's not what we're about. We're about getting people into homeownership.

A staff person from another CLT, who responded to a question about community engagement initiatives in their CLT, said:

> It's about offering these opportunities [affordable homeownership] to more and more families who desperately need it. So we'll do whatever we can do to expand those opportunities. If it comes through some form of homeowner engagement, that's great, but we aren't reliant on that and we see it as a secondary issue.

These sentiments are not unusual among CLT practitioners in the United States. Even Grounded Solutions Network, the national organization for CLTs (which now promotes other housing strategies as well), has come to define its primary purpose as providing "permanently affordable housing." Most mainstream CLTs have become so narrowly focused on bricks-and-mortar housing production and the long-term stewardship of affordable housing that other uses and aspects of the model are often overlooked. As the ideal of community control has been erased from practitioners' internal dialogue and organizational mission statements, it has all but faded from practice.[2]

HOW DID THIS HAPPEN?

This has happened, in part, because CLTs face a common financial problem: the monthly lease fees (for the land) that are paid by CLT residents to a CLT organization are so modest — typically $25 to $50 per month — that they cannot sustain the organization. Theoretically, there's a point at which the number of housing units would be large enough to cover the basic costs of staffing and operating the CLT from lease fees alone. But the number of houses required to reach that break-even point — the "magic number," as some have called it — may be well into the thousands. Few CLTs have reached it. Most never will.

So, if an organization wants to sustain itself as a CLT, it has to bring in external grant money by actively pursuing new development projects on a rolling basis. In the United

> Dependence on external institutional sources of funding can make the goals of community control and non-housing development difficult to achieve.

States, the most readily available sources of grant funding for the development of affordable housing come from city governments, the housing trust funds administered by municipal and state governments, the federal government's Department of Housing and Urban Development (HUD), or private foundations. Most CLTs only stay alive by continually imploring these agencies and institutions for funds and by continually acquiring land and adding housing to their portfolios.

The increasingly competitive nature of most grants and the high price of land and housing development means that CLTs sometimes struggle to make ends meet. Often, CLTs find they are better off supplementing their affordable housing projects with a more profitable side-venture, so they also become a developer, lender, real estate agency, or the provider of other services to help pay for the operational costs of the CLT. This process of revenue diversification helps to ease the burden of the constant search for outside grants to operate the CLT, but it can also divert attention away from the needs of the most marginalized people in a community.

CLTs do important work in the context of rapidly rising land and housing values. They take property off the speculative market and hold it in perpetuity for low-income people. No developer can snatch up a plot of land once it is part of a CLT's portfolio. No real estate giant can develop that corner lot into luxury condos. The neighborhood around a CLT's holdings may become desirable, pricy, and gentrified, but CLT-held land will remain more affordable and accessible. This function of the CLT is what gets organizers and activists excited about the model, and for good reason.

But the dependence of CLTs on external institutional sources of funding can make the goals of community control and non-housing development difficult to achieve, since foundation and government funders tend to be most interested in encouraging CLTs to develop housing as quickly as possible. Financing the development of affordable commercial space, for example, can be more logistically challenging and financially risky than developing housing, so most CLTs stick to housing. Similarly, keeping CLT land undeveloped for the use of community gardens is not a lucrative use of valuable property, so that option is often rejected by CLT boards in favor of more housing.

Building affordable housing as prices rapidly rise is not *bad*, to be clear. But neighborhoods are so much more than housing. To radically change the way decisions are made about what we want our neighborhoods to be—and to create and maintain community-owned institutions and common amenities that are accessible—community land movements must look beyond the most common, generic ways that the CLT model is being operated, funded, and applied, seeking more independence from external funders.

FUNDER REQUIREMENTS:
A CASE IN POINT

In 2018, I was appointed to the Citizen Advisory Committee (CAC) in my city to oversee the distribution of Community Development Block Grants (CDBG), a federally funded program that allows cities and states to decide which local community development projects serving low-income people might be worthy of support. I saw the absurdity of a funder's requirements first-hand.

Every local government body that allocates CDBG funds is required to have a CAC, nominally to give localities more control over the administration of federal grants. In practice, sitting on the CAC felt like being a cog in the federal bureaucracy, a volunteer administrator checking boxes and adding up points, making sure all the prospective recipients of the grants we were distributing would fulfill their end of the agreement.

The resulting requirements are nearly impossible for small nonprofits to meet. For example, for an organization simply to purchase program supplies using CDBG funds, they must:

- Request a withdrawal of CDBG funds from the municipality;

- Buy the supplies within three days, write a justification for why the purchase took longer than three days, or return the funds;

- Produce and keep a purchase order or requisition form from an authorized representative of the organization;

- Keep an invoice from the vendor with a signature from the organization's representative, verifying the goods were received;

- Document where the supplies are stored;

- Document which objective(s) were fulfilled by the purchase of the supplies;

- Document which budget line item the supplies fall under; and

- Ensure that three separate individuals in the organization (1) authorize the transaction, (2) record the transaction, and (3) maintain custody of the goods purchased.

All of these requirements come after an organization has already written a detailed grant application meeting the objectives and checking the boxes required by HUD, including documentation of highly regimented accounting practices in their organization.

The regulations around CDBG allocations represent just one example of how the dominant paradigm of grant funding inhibits the autonomy of nonprofits. Private foundations can be just as cumbersome and biased in their grant stipulations. And, of course, only specific activities fall under the funders' goals. Federal money, for example, cannot be used for any "political activities." Private foundations, too, shy away from funding advocacy and organizing that are aimed at changing public policy and making governments more responsive to the needs of low-income and working-class communities, activities that are deemed "political."

THE RESULT:
PROFESSIONALIZATION AND THE
ABANDONMENT OF COMMUNITY ORGANIZING

> In the old days, we had many conversations using the language of movement, about land reform, the importance of community control, and the fight for social justice. Community land trusts are, after all, children of the U.S. civil rights movement. But that language doesn't seem to surface much anymore, and the words we adopted to appease lenders, funders, and lawyers has become the internal language we use as well.
>
> —Greg Rosenberg[3]

Funder requirements and restrictions like those I encountered in my own city are what earlier led the authors of *The Revolution Will Not be Funded* to argue for the abandonment of grant funding for nonprofit work.[4] Just the administrative burden of meeting the conditions of funders requires paid staff, office equipment, budgeting software, and professional skillsets beyond the capacity of many grassroots organizations. Once they grow to the capacity to handle grant applications and administrative tasks, many organizations find their original mission and goals getting gradually eroded or swiftly diverted to meet the requirements and priorities of their funders. The energy they once had for grassroots organizing gets channeled into bureaucratic work.

This argument is not new. Frances Fox Piven and Richard Cloward in their 1979 book, *Poor People's Movements: Why They Succeed, How They Fail,* made the case that "organizations endure, in short, by abandoning their oppositional politics."[5]

Many CLTs in the United States have followed suit, paring down their initial commitment to engaging, involving, and empowering the communities they serve in order to chase grant opportunities. There are exceptions of course, but CLTs with more radical ideals of community empowerment, community ownership of land, and anti-gentrification organizing tend to have a harder time finding the funds to fulfill their expansive, transformative missions.

Most public and private funders of CLTs are concerned primarily with the number of affordable homes that are being produced and preserved for lower-income people, not the ways that residents are engaged *after* they become the occupants of those homes, nor the needs that residents may have for non-housing development in their neighborhoods. CLTs that are serious about resident engagement often struggle to find the funds to support community organizing and any other kinds of non-housing activity.

The effect of funders' externally-imposed goals is particularly insidious considering how routinely and systematically low-income and marginalized communities are cut off from opportunities to assert their voice and agency in urban development. When improvements come to a low-income neighborhood, land values go up and can ultimately displace the population. Therefore, if you're poor, you're stuck between a rock and a hard place: live in blight or welcome new development and get kicked out of your neighborhood. For these reasons, CLTs can be important tools to bring improvements to neighborhoods, while insulating them from market speculation. Improvements *can* mean housing, but also so much more. When the market so inexorably limits marginalized communities' choices, it should be up to low-income residents to decide what they need in their neighborhood. Ultimately, CLTs can and should be vehicles of empowerment for people who are systematically disempowered. Indeed, this was the intention of the model's founders. Without this piece, CLTs lose a vital part of their legacy and marginalized communities remain voiceless in decisions about their neighborhoods.[6]

Paul Kivel's chapter in *The Revolution Will Not be Funded* encourages organizations to think about to whom they are accountable: their funders or a grassroots constituency in the communities they serve? He writes:

> In the nonprofit industrial complex, accountability is directed toward the ruling class and its managers — toward foundations, donors, government officials, larger non-profits, research institutes, universities, and the media. These are all forms of top-down accountability. I am suggesting a bottom-up accountability guided by those on the frontlines of grassroots struggles for justice. In which direction does your accountability lie?[7]

Most CLTs in the United States have become beholden to the goals of their funders, letting their missions drift away from some of the most radical pieces of the model's potential for impact. As a result, CLTs' accountability comes "down" from the stipulations of its funders instead of coming "up" from the preferences and needs of its community.

BEYOND GRANT FUNDING:
POSSIBLE DIRECTIONS FORWARD

So how might a movement for community control of land and housing, which is where the CLT movement began, become more accountable to "those on the frontlines of grassroots struggles"? The challenges faced by CLTs today are primarily the result of two specific problems: the model's dependence on external funding, and the stipulations for receiving that funding.

Collective ownership of land *without* grant funding has long been proven possible, most notably in the cooperative housing field. Housing cooperatives have, for many generations, relied upon the capital of their founding members to acquire buildings *without* using external grant funding. But for low-income residents, finding the capital for a

Maintaining participation must be an ongoing goal and practice of any community-owned land initiative.

downpayment on a building can be nearly impossible, and getting a group of people to commit to buying a building together can feel like a pipe dream.

Even when efforts to collectively buy property are successful at first, they are at high risk of failure if there isn't a backstop. Among housing cooperatives in the United States, close to half of all limited-equity cooperatives (LECs) eventually demutualize their assets; that is, their owners decide to sell either the entire building or their individual shares at market prices so that the co-op's units are no longer affordable.[8] For their part, group-equity cooperatives (independent group-owned houses) often run into legal and financial hurdles that undermine organizational sustainability, economic independence, and the development of additional housing.

Recognizing these challenges faced by housing cooperatives and the shortcomings inherent in the reliance of CLTs on grants from governments and foundations, there are new visionaries who are exploring community-funded models for the acquisition and ownership of land. Two examples: the East Bay Permanent Real Estate Cooperative[9] in Oakland, California and the Ecovillagers Alliance,[10] which already owns land and is starting a project in Lancaster, Pennsylvania. These are prototypes of collective ownership where non-resident members can invest in property that will still prioritize resident control of development and stay affordable for generations. The details of these models-in-development differ, but both of them involve different membership categories, including (residential and commercial) tenant members and investor members — and even individuals who choose to be *both* tenants and investors. With equity sourced from the community outside of the tenant pool, these organizations can grow without appeasing institutional funders for grant money to buy property, and they will be able to rely less on banks to finance property development.

Importantly, these two initiatives act as investment vehicles for people who want to pull their money out of ethically questionable markets and invest in affordable, sustainable, democratic land stewardship. Even tenants can build wealth this way by investing in cooperative land ownership and receiving dividends from the pool of rents collected on the land. They become tenants and landlords simultaneously, making decisions about their neighborhood's development collectively. Each tenant member gets only one vote in local decisions, no matter how much equity they invest. In terms of governance, tenant control is prioritized, with community investors having appropriately limited voting power.

CLTs can also experiment with and benefit from new strategies of community land investment. Homeownership-based CLTs by themselves tend not to generate enough revenue to repay a loan (even one sourced from the community). But in the right conditions, CLTs can find community financing strategies to be helpful in securing capital for site acquisition with revenue-generating community partners. The Oakland CLT, for example, has begun partnering with other community groups and cooperatives to purchase properties using community financing to keep commercial rent affordable for important community-based institutions in a rapidly-gentrifying city.[11] The Oakland CLT's vision for acquiring multiple community-financed sites in partnership with a set of mission-aligned local organizations may indeed light the way for other CLTs struggling with the tensions between grant funding and community control.

Because acquiring real estate requires considerable capital input as well as legal and financial knowledge, some degree of professionalism is necessary in all collective land-ownership strategies. The key is to combine that professional knowledge-base with an organizational infrastructure that fulfills the needs of marginalized communities, seeking as much of their leadership and input as possible. Maintaining a culture of participation and collective support must be an ongoing goal and practice of any community-owned land initiative, through social organizing, inclusive leadership, community-building activities, and partnerships with strong grassroots initiatives. While many CLTs find it difficult to be productive developers *and* sincere community organizers simultaneously,[12] some CLTs have managed to maintain organizers as full-time staff. And other CLTs partner with already-organized community groups to help them to attain the overall development and empowerment goals for their neighborhoods.[13]

THE SOCIAL JUSTICE CLT:
BACK TO BEING A MOVEMENT

This is a critical time in the movement for affordable land and housing. As real estate prices soar and wages stagnate, activists are seeking a way forward and often latch onto CLTs. But as Oksana Miranova has argued,[14] to address the housing crisis head-on, CLTs must be part of a comprehensive strategy involving rent control, public housing, and a network of other community ownership strategies. Organizers looking to keep land democratically controlled should be aware of the structural limitations of the CLT model and the limited funding environment we currently find ourselves in. Even if more funding sources are dedicated to CLT expansion, more CLTs will not necessarily mean more community-controlled development or grassroots planning efforts.

Without a continued focus on community control in CLTs, we lose opportunities to build and to cultivate multi-faceted CLTs with neighborhood amenities *beyond* housing. Admittedly, there are not as many clear funding sources or technical assistance providers for CLT applications and uses beyond housing. CLTs therefore find themselves pulled in the direction of housing development by their peer networks and grant providers, and the housing-focused CLT field perpetuates itself as a self-fulfilling prophecy. Those CLTs that have managed to develop community centers, playgrounds, commercial spaces, and urban farms — which they saw as important for their local communities — have done so by getting more creative with their budgets and funding sources. But nearly all of these CLTs have had to build their non-housing projects from scratch, without a guide to follow.[15] The result is that CLTs continue to be seen and funded primarily as an affordable homeownership tool.

For these reasons, I have highlighted a few new strategies for community-financed development focused on local needs and tenant control. Those of us who are passionate about democratic control of development must be willing to find creative ways to fund and to use CLTs, thinking beyond the usual applications that pull CLTs away from the communities they serve and away from the original intentions of the visionaries who brought the CLT into being.

Acquiring and administering property should not be the only goals of a movement for affordable housing and land. To confront the inequalities perpetuated by private property ownership — including deepening wealth disparities and the domination of urban development decisions by the elite — affordability must be coupled with bottom-up control of neighborhood development by residents. Somewhere along the road, the CLT movement largely abandoned this vital piece of its legacy. It is not too late, however, to reignite a passion and possibilities for community control.

Notes

1. New Communities, Inc., was subject to repeated discrimination by the State of Georgia, lenders, and insurance companies that put them in a difficult financial situation. They eventually lost their land in 1985 and won a settlement in 2009 that allowed them to purchase new property. See *https://www.newcommunitiesinc.com/about.html.*

2. There is ample evidence for this claim. See: J. DeFilippis, B. Stromberg, and O. R. Williams (2018). "W[h]ither the community in community land trusts?" *Journal of Urban Affairs* 40 (6): 755–69. Available at: *https://doi.org/10.1080/07352166.2017.1361302.* Also see: B. Stromberg (2016). "Radical roots and pragmatic politics: The performance of land tenure reform in community land trusts." Doctoral dissertation, Rutgers University. Available at: *https://rucore.libraries.rutgers.edu/rutgers-lib/50192/.*

3. Greg Rosenberg was the long-time executive director of the Madison Area Community Land Trust and a founder and director of the National CLT Academy. He currently serves as co-director of the Center for CLT Innovation. For this reference, see Rosenberg, G. (2013). "Sell the CLT movement for what it is: radical and superior." *Rooflines: The Shelterforce Blog.* Available at: *http://www.rooflines.org/3389/sell_the_clt_movement_for_what_it_is_radical_and_superior/*

4. INCITE! Women of Color Against Violence, ed. (2007). *The Revolution Will Not Be Funded: Beyond the Non-Profit Industrial Complex.* Cambridge, Mass: South End Press.

5. F. F. Piven and R. Cloward (1978). *Poor People's Movements: Why They Succeed, How They Fail.* Unknown edition. New York: Vintage. *https://www.penguinrandomhouse. com/books/131609poor-peoples-movements-by-frances-fox-piven-and-richard-cloward/9780394726977/.*

6. This argument is drawn in part from an earlier academic journal article: DeFilippis, B. Stromberg, and O. R. Williams (2018). "W(h)Ither the community in community land trusts?" *Journal of Urban Affairs* 40 (6): 755–69. Available at: *https://www.tandfonline. com/doi/abs/10.1080/07352166.2017.1361302?journalCode=ujua20.*

7. P. Kivel (2007). "Social service or social change?" In = INCITE! Women of Color Against Violence, ed. (2007). *The Revolution Will Not Be Funded: Beyond the Non-Profit Industrial Complex.* Cambridge, Mass: South End Press. pp. 129–150.

8. See UHAB (2016). "Counting Limited-Equity Co-Ops, Research Update." Available at: *https://www.uhab.org/sites/default/files/feb_update_for_website.pdf*

9. East Bay Permanent Real Estate Cooperative is organizing residents of the East Bay in California to cooperatively invest in, own, and develop mixed-use projects especially for marginalized communities of color. See *https://ebprec.org*

10. Ecovillagers Alliance is developing a replicable community land cooperative model that can be used to create affordable, mixed-use, urban retrofitted communities funded by community investors and linked to one another through regional or national networks through which equity can be transferred and shared. See *https://www.ecovillagers.org*

11. See O. P. Abello (2019). "A Worker Cooperative and a Community Land Trust Bought a Building Together." *Next City,* June 18, 2019. Available at: *https://nextcity.org/daily/ entry/a-worker-cooperative-and-a-community-land-trust-bought-a-building-together*

12. The tensions and challenges that arise for CLT organizations doing development at the same time as community organizing have been detailed here: M. Axel-Lute and D. Hawkins-Simons. (2015). "Organizing and the Community Land Trust Model." *Shelterforce,* October 15, 2015. Available at: *http://www.shelterforce.org/article/4279/ organizing_and_the_community_land_trust_model/*

13. For details, see: M. Axel-Lute and D. Hawkins-Simons (2015). "Community Land Trusts Grown from Grassroots: Neighborhood Organizers Become Housing Developers." *Land Lines,* July 2015.

14. See O. Mironova (2019). "How Community Land Trusts Can Help Address the Affordable Housing Crisis" *Jacobin,* July 6, 2019. Available at: *https://jacobinmag. com/2019/07/community-land-trusts-affordable-housing.*

15. See, for example, this thesis on the known US-based CLTs with commercial space, which summarizes the many different strategies and funding models the CLTs have used to secure commercial space in their portfolios: A. Curtis (2018). "Extending Community Control over Commercial Development: Community Land Trusts and Community Finance Models." Masters Thesis, Tufts University.

Acknowledgments

This article is a revised amalgamation of three previously-published pieces, listed below:

1. O. R. Williams (2019). "Community land without grants and debt." *Communities Magazine*, #182 Spring 2019. Fellowship for Intentional Community. Available at: *https://www.ic.org/community-bookstore/product/communities-magazine-community-land/*.

2. O. R. Williams (2019). "The problem with community land trusts". *Jacobin*, July 7, 2019. Available at: *https://www.jacobinmag.com/2019/07community-land-trusts-clts-problems*

3. O. R. Williams (2019). "Are we diluting the mission of community land trusts?" *Shelterforce*, August 30, 2019. Available at: *https://shelterforce.org/2019/08/30/are-we-diluting-the-mission-of-community-land-trusts/*

The CLT research and practitioners' quotes referenced in this essay came out of a collaborative research project that took place between 2014 and 2016 based on 124 interviews of stakeholders involved in eight CLTs in Minnesota. I want to acknowledge my CLT research team for the many hours of work they put into this project with me: Deborah G. Martin, Joseph Pierce, James DeFilippis, Richard Kruger, and Azadeh Hadizadeh Esfahani. This research was funded by the National Science Foundation BCS-GSS, grant #1359826.

25.

Preserving Urban Generativity
The Role of Porous Spaces
in CLT Projects

Verena Lenna

In the last thirty years—at the very least—the urban condition has been described as increasingly segregated and enclaved (Blakely and Snyder, 1997; Soja, 2000; Low, 2001). Cities are the places where the war among corporations happens in the form of the enforcement of existing regulations and the construction of perimeters of consumption. The loss of urbanity is the result of processes of privatisation, dispossession, and expulsion (Sassen, 2014; 2015). Privatisation, by appropriating urban land, takes away from most citizens the right of access and use, resulting in a loss of urbanity. Privatisation of land also takes away the right to *decide* its use, since the property is in private hands. This is often the case with privately owned public spaces as well.[1] Despite conditions imposed by a municipality when approving new developments, requiring ongoing public access to a plaza or courtyard, these spaces can perform in rather exclusive terms because of poor design choices and the scarce involvement of the local community (Schmidt, Nemeth, and Botsford, 2011). This is also true for many buildings acquired by foreign corporations and wealthy investors that are removed from any use by a local community. They stand vacant, occupied only part of the year or waiting for some form of renovation.[2]

On the other hand, spontaneous occupations and the establishment of temporary uses by local communities have frequently shown the variety of needs that abandoned buildings and spaces could respond to, both at an individual and at a collective level. The claim of the right to the city in recent years has produced a city of rights. The multiplication of citizens' initiatives demonstrates the unexhausted creativity of local communities when taking care and making use of available resources, inventing new ways of governing them, while mobilising a wide range of resources and capabilities often unknown to public officials or incompatible with their policies (Ferguson and Urban Drift Projects, 2014). In many cases, practices that have informally emerged around the need to share

Community land trusts can be considered laboratories where urban generativity is fostered.

and to manage a common pool of resources have been so successful as to trigger the interest and the support of municipal governments.[3]

Because of an exclusive approach to the use of resources, what is being lost is not only urban land and the right of concerned communities to decide about its development and use. Also lost is the possibility of spontaneous encounters among actors and communities, interacting with one another and sharing their needs and capabilities. Such encounters enable actors and communities to develop reciprocities, to react to oppressive conditions where necessary, and to generate innovative approaches and answers to emerging needs.

This capability of cities to continuously produce new resources, as a result of the diversity and complexity of the urban milieu, can be called *urban generativity*. As this chapter will try to show, community land trusts can prevent the loss of this capability. They can be considered laboratories where urban generativity is fostered.

URBAN GENERATIVITY AS THE COMMON WEALTH OF CITIES

The concept of generativity was first suggested by Edmund Husserl, mostly in the 1930s, to describe the transformational nature of the process of becoming, generation after generation, based on pre-existing elements and materials, rather than happening as an unconditioned creation started from scratch.[4] Applied to cities, generativity could effectively explain their resourcefulness and resiliency. As their histories show, cities are adaptive organisations. They have an inherent ability to continuously generate the resources they need in order to transform and to tackle the socio-spatial challenges that emerge over time, expected or unexpected. This is made possible by the accumulation of material and immaterial resources and by forms of knowledge and expertise that are constantly attracted by a city: what Hardt and Negri have called the "common wealth" (Hardt and Negri, 2009).

Such resourcefulness is also currently being theorised by the rising discourse on the "commons." While some scholars regard the city as a whole as being a commons (Salzano, 2009; Marella, 2012; Stavrides, 2016), others prefer to refer to the "urban commons," pointing at the specificity of some forms of commons generated in an urban context. In both cases, what is implied is a generative process of commoning. Among countless definitions and conceptualisations of the commons, the one elaborated by Massimo De Angelis and Stavros Stavrides (AnArchitektur, 2010) highlights precisely such a process:

Commons are not simply resources we share—conceptualizing the commons involves three things at the same time. First, all commons involve some sort of common pool of resources, understood as non-commodified means of fulfilling people's needs. Second, the commons are necessarily created and sustained by communities. . . . Communities are sets of commoners who share these resources and who define for themselves the rules according to which they are accessed and used. . . . In addition to these two elements—the pool of resources and the set of communities—the third and most important element in terms of conceptualizing the commons is the verb "to common"—the social process that creates and reproduces the commons.

The common wealth of cities is their latent ability to generate innovations and solutions by recycling and reinventing existing resources, both material and immaterial. Intuitively, the more that individuals and collectives, citizens and actors are able to interact and to interweave, the larger becomes the field of possibilities, capabilities, and expertise from which new resources and innovative approaches can emerge, meeting a variety of needs. Urban generativity is about the abundance that derives from the opportunity for

> A common wealth is fuelled by creating the conditions for the interaction of different actors and their expertise.

continuous cooperation and exchange, compensating for the scarcity of many resources, real or artificial; resisting, thereby, the narrow vision of the world that scarcity brings, along with the related risks of both individualism and *désaffiliation*, as Castel has pointed out (Castel and Haroche, 2001). This capability is of the utmost importance to counterbalance the growing privatisation of resources and the shrinking capacities of welfare states, for it operates by disrupting the enclaving, exclusionary trends in the management of resources.

Urban generativity depends on conditions that allow existing resources and expertise to circulate, combine, disassemble, recombine, and transform according to the contexts and the specific needs of the concerned communities. Urban generativity is impeded by policies and forms of appropriation that define exclusive and homogeneous realms of interactions and governance; and by the imposition of externally conceived, a priori forms of governance that are incapable of being site-responsive. By contrast, a common wealth is fuelled and valorized by creating the conditions for the interaction of different actors and their expertise. The model of the CLT suggests a viable approach in that direction.

SPACE MATTERS

The model of the CLT is founded on the recognition of a *bundle of rights*.[5] The rights are those possessed by specific groups of users, inhabitants, owners, and managers of land and buildings who co-create the rules and share the responsibilities concerning a given CLT's project. Their equitable and sustainable allocation should enable a CLT to fulfil its main purpose: the preservation of the land and its development for the common good.

Rights, rules and responsibilities are necessarily defined by the context and the conditions under which a given project is supposed to be established. There is no recipe, however, for ensuring the coexistence and compatibility of those rights in the framework of a given project, including the right of the community to have access to the land and to the built assets in the long run, the right to homeownership of individual households, the right of local actors to have a voice concerning the potential transformations of their neighbourhood, and the right of public agencies to decide about assets that could benefit the city as a whole. Which form should the allocation of these rights take? How many square meters of space should be occupied by each household? How should access to the shared spaces be organised? How should the inhabitants get involved in the maintenance of the building? It is through the concrete uses made possible by a specific project that those rights will be expressed and substantiated. On the one hand, the recognition of those rights is the *sine qua non* for establishing a CLT project; on the other hand, the bundle of uses is what allows the residents of a CLT project to practice them and to verify their compatibility and related responsibilities.

Above all, coming to terms with the *space* in a particular project is what allows a given bundle of rights to exist. The morphologic qualities of a site and a building provide the

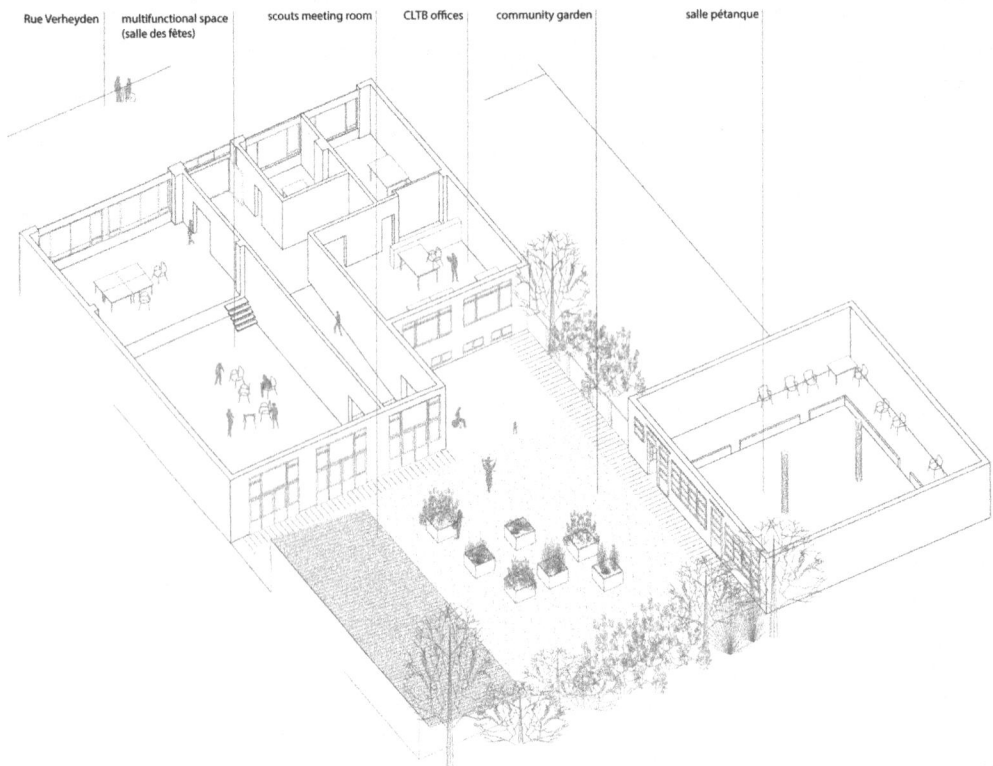

Fig. 25.1. Diagram depicting the spaces and activities interweaving at the ground floor of 121 Rue Verheyden, during the initial occupation of the site. VERENA LENNA

form and envelope for specific uses, pushing the concerned actors and users to work together not only so they can coexist, but also —and most importantly — so the project's resources can be preserved (Lenna, 2019). The CLT projects being realised in Brussels are good examples. They show how space can contribute to the interweaving of individuals and collectives, and the related rights and uses, thus increasing their sustainability.

Le Nid ("the nest") is one of the first projects developed by the Brussels CLT (CLTB). The property once belonged to the Catholic Parish. This helps to explain the spatial characteristics of the main building and of the site as a whole (see Fig. 25.1). Before renovation, a green metallic door and a generous entrance gave access to a large ramp into the ground-floor corridor, sloping directly into the *interieur d'îlot*. On the right of the entrance, there was a huge *salle des fêtes*. This hall was used by CLTB, during the long period between acquiring the building and beginning its rehabilitation and conversion to permanent housing, to organise meetings, assemblies and other activities, including those of other local associations. On the left side of the entrance, a cafeteria served as office space for the small CLTB team. At the second and third floor, each room was occupied by tenants whose rents were set to cover only basic expenses.

The ramp from the front door provided a direct connection from the public dimension of the street to the semi-hidden, collective space of the courtyard. Located in the courtyard, there was a small white construction normally used by local groups of scouts and a *salle pétanque*. A few chairs and a small table allowed the building's occupants to enjoy the sun during lunch breaks or any other occasions. The courtyard was occupied by plant containers and by a small, makeshift greenhouse for gardening activities involving neighbours and other users of the building. Outside of working hours for CLTB's staff,

Fig. 25.2. Interior courtyard at 121 Rue Verheyden. VERENA LENNA

the courtyard was used mostly for convivial activities, allowing future inhabitants and present users to gather, to meet their neighbours, and to expand their network of social relations.

Such a variety of activities was orchestrated by CLTB's staff and board as part of giving life to a new organisation and for creating some relational premises for Le Nid to be established on sustainable terms. They were possible because of the peculiar morphology of the plot and of the building, a factor that subsequently would play a crucial role in realising Le Nid. Mainly conceived as a residential project for seven households, Le Nid was also planned from the very beginning to host a community garden, to offer shared spaces for the inhabitants, and to provide a multi-functional building for both the inhabitants and the neighbourhood, once the *salle pétanque* was renovated.

The interweaving of different uses is a characteristic not only of Le Nid, but of most of CLTB's projects. It implies the pragmatic involvement of other local actors — beyond the households who will occupy the housing — in planning, designing, and utilizing the space in a given project. Such involvement is both a product and pre-condition of CLTB's tripartite structure of governance and CLTB's commitment to participatory decision making. At the same time, the combination of functions and the ensuing convergence of actors are intended to promote the integration of both the project and its inhabitants in the neighbourhood. The result thus is twofold. In a virtuous circle, not only would the neighbourhood's liveliness be improved, but also the CLTB project would be better maintained, a result of the interest and involvement of different users, contributing according to their specific forms of expertise and availability.[6]

Therefore, in the specific case of Le Nid, accessibility to a common pool of resources — the courtyard, the former *salle pétanque*, the shared spaces — was planned not only to fulfill the needs and rights of different communities of users. It was also intended to enable these communities to take care of their common resources and to assume their responsibilities, so that those uses could be maintained in the long run for the common good of present and future generations. For this to happen, as noted already, a project's spatial conditions are crucial to fostering exchange and encounter among the newly arrived households, users of the site, and the pre-existing urban fabric. It is also for this reason that the CLTB has implemented an intensive participatory process, mostly focusing on spatial issues.

By designing the articulation of space at Le Nid and in its other projects, CLTB has the purpose of creating the conditions for a sustainable coexistence of the different activities and of the needs of the inhabitants and other users. As a result, a good living environment can be maintained, both on a relational level and in terms of preservation of the built assets. Motivated by individual needs and pushed by the challenge to collectively manage what will become their shared resources, households and local actors are called to imagine, through a series of *ateliers* and other meetings, what their future homes will look like and how their life together might be. They are asked to envision and to plan the activities they would like to organise and might be able to maintain according to their concrete possibility to engage. This exercise not only leads to the elaboration of a number of suggestions concerning the design of the space, a *cahier des recommandations* for those architects interested in proposing a project; it also encourages examination of the distribution of responsibilities. What should the function of the common spaces be? Which activities could be imagined in the former *salle pétanque,* compatible with the everyday lives of the households? Who will take care of the community garden? What access to the courtyard should be allowed during the weekend?

> Space determines the possibilities for interacting and collaborating to preserve a common pool of resources.

Space matters. The morphological characteristics of a building or of an urban block play a crucial role, either impeding or facilitating the encounter and the collaboration of the concerned communities. It is by coming to terms with the specific spatial potentials and limitations of a given site or building that inhabitants and users become aware of their actual possibilities, necessarily reconsidering their own plans and needs so that those of others can also be realised. In that way, individual rights and needs are fulfilled as part of a larger collective endeavour, overcoming individualism in the name of the common good. It is by confronting the actual characteristics of space that inhabitants and users can learn about their actual capacities to manage their living environment, to engage, and to assume responsibilities.[7] Shaped by design preferences, space determines the conditions under which different users will practice their rights; space determines the possibilities for interacting and collaborating around the shared responsibility to preserve a common pool of resources.

CLT PROJECTS AS LABORATORIES
OF URBAN GENERATIVITY

What can be learned from the Brussels CLT is that an inclusive approach to expanding and protecting land-based resources, founded on the collaboration of different concerned actors and inhabitants — a hallmark of the CLT model — seems to be made easier and more consistent when a project creates the spatial conditions for cooperation to happen. Like a sponge allowing water to leak in and to enter every available cavity, the morphology of the building and the site at Le Nid allows different users to access the internal courtyard, the *salle pétanque,* and the housing units. Such a spatial configuration, which could be described as "porous," can be found in many of CLTB's projects, though with variations determined by the characteristics of a given site and by the specific choices made by the future users during the design process. Delimitations and openings, corridors and

> The porous perimeters of a CLT's projects provide the physical and relational conditions to revive the existing urban fabric.

thresholds, shared spaces: they allow the rights of different concerned communities to be fulfilled and their resources to be protected. Inappropriate uses are impeded, while the inclusive attitude of CLT model is maintained. Accessibility is regulated by collectively conceived design choices and rules. They make possible the interweaving of private, collective and semi-public activities, thus realising the bundle of rights that CLTs recognise and allocate.

The concept of porosity has been used by urbanists Bernardo Secchi and Paola Viganò to depict urban spaces that are designed to pay attention "to practices, changes, fractures in space, urban materials and availability, possibilities for new flows" (Viganò, 2009). A porous spatial configuration, such as that found at Le Nid, reinforces an inclusive, collaborative approach to the management of property and spatial resources, based on the CLT's unique allocation of rights. By making room for different users and their needs, a porous space, almost by definition, has a potential for triggering socio-spatial experimentation. It is a space of encounter and reciprocal adjustment, where the coexistence of different activities and communities can be tested, so that their different rights can be practiced. It is a space where different forms of expertise and the capabilities of the concerned actors, challenged by the need to oversee and to care for a common pool of resources, can combine and complement each other, leading eventually to required solutions and innovations.

Additionally, a porous space is a space where site-responsivity can be built. All CLT projects have in common the same basic approach to property rights and governance, but each project is quite site-specific: that is, each has a unique combination of inhabitants and local users with different needs and expectations, along with different socio-spatial conditions within a given context and moment in time. Each project, therefore, to be realised and maintained in the long run will have to conceive and to implement *ad hoc* solutions and forms of collaboration, creating occasions of exchange with the pre-existing urban fabric and taking into account the potentials and limitations of the specific piece of urban ecology that will support it. The porous perimeters of a CLT's projects provide the physical and relational conditions for future inhabitants, users, local actors and administrators to encounter and to create a new piece of the city or to revive the existing urban fabric, based on their capacity to contribute, realising what Castel and Haroche would call their *stratégies de vie* (Castel and Haroche, 2001).

By embedding themselves in a given section of the city, these projects necessarily have the capacity to transform it. This means that by being inclusive and porous, CLT projects not only have an *introverted* dimension, concerning the adjacent, directly interested inhabitants and users; they have an *extroverted* dimension as well, involving the neighbours and other local actors. They allow not only specific solutions and spontaneous forms of reciprocity to emerge, but also to become the starting point for further innovations. Other contexts and other actors are benefited beyond the boundaries of the specific projects that engendered them and beyond the immediate concerns of developing and maintaining a newly constructed or rehabilitated residential building or urban block.

What the CLT model seems to suggest is that inclusion is not only about a passive coexistence of uses and users; that is, who will have gained access to a space or resource. It is not only about simply accepting or integrating the newly arrived. Inclusion is, first and foremost, about the possibility of contributing. It is about the incommensurable, generative potential of diversity, combining and recombining different perspectives, expertise and approaches; completing each other's availability and capabilities. Out of these assemblages comes the hybridisation of forms of knowledge and innovative strategies, resources, and answers to the emerging needs of cities. These forms are sustainable because they are being proposed by a range and variety of concerned communities. From a design perspective, spatial porosity is an element that can promote urban generativity: because after having absorbed, a sponge necessarily releases its liquids.

———

CONCLUSION

Community land trusts are known for holding land and developing it for the common good. However, another major capability of CLTs—less recognized or emphasised—is that of fuelling urban generativity. A form of property and of governance that entails the convergence of a variety of actors and communities, with the purpose of co-creating the rules and sharing the responsibilities for site-specific projects, can trigger urban generativity, thus engendering a common pool of new resources and innovative approaches for meeting the emerging needs of cities. The projects developed by the CLT in Brussels show that such a capability is fuelled not only by an inclusive system of decision-making. The spontaneous interweaving and cooperation of individuals and collectives are also fostered by porous spatial configurations, especially when resources are collectively used and governed.

CLTs interject inclusive forms of governance and rights of property into an urban social-spatial grid that is otherwise becoming more and more exclusive. Functioning as urban laboratories, through their porous delimitations, a CLT's projects pour out experiments in governance, new forms of reciprocities and collaboration, and institutional innovations and arrangements that can potentially address a variety of issues, benefiting the city as a whole. Through their *modus operandi*, what these projects suggest is that urban generativity, as a vital common wealth of cities, can only exist through inclusion.

Notes

1. "Privately owned public spaces, also known by the acronym POPS, are spaces dedicated to public use and enjoyment and which are owned and maintained by private property owners, in exchange for bonus floor area or waivers." Source: *https://www1.nyc.gov/ site/planning/plans/pops/pops.page*

2. This was reported by some of the local actors I interviewed, concerning the situation in the Brussels Capital Region. The same is happening in many other cities in Europe, Great Britain, and North America, where residential (and commercial) buildings are being used by foreign investors for "wealth storage," instead of being renovated and made available for use by residents of local communities. See, for example: *https://inequality. org/wp-content/uploads/2018/09/Towering-Excess-Report-Final.pdf*

3. Examples can be found in cities such as Barcelona, Ghent, Lille and in many others in Italy, where a sort of protocol has been established to help local governments to develop commons-oriented policies for the management of shared resources (*https://www. labsus.org/*). Some scholars, however, have questioned the actual contribution an urban landscape that is fragmented by one thousand alternatives could bring to the making of a democratic scenario, with the risk of losing sight of the need for more structural efforts (Armony, 2004; Bianchetti, 2016).

4. According to Steinbock (1995), "For Husserl, generativity is both the process of becoming, hence the process of 'generation,' and a process that occurs over the 'generations,' hence specifically the process of historical and social movement."

5. The "bundle of rights" is a metaphor to explain the coexistence of different rights and responsibilities concerning the use, access, and temporary or permanent possession of real estate. Especially in Common Law countries, it is employed to describe property ownership as a collection of different rights.

6. At the start of a project, the CLTB has the main responsibility for guiding the inhabitants and future users in how to maintain the project. Over time, however, the inhabitants should assume increasing responsibility for their own project, converging around the need to govern and to manage their common living environment. The stewardship role that is played by the CLTB is about teaching and guidance as much as it is about direct responsibility for overseeing a specific project.

7. The whole participatory process, even when not focusing on spatial matters, provides the occasion for the inhabitants and future users of the project to voice their needs and desires concerning their future living environment. Spatial issues and choices however have the power of guiding imagination towards plausible everyday-life scenarios.

References

AnArchitektur. 2010. "On the Commons: A Public Interview with Massimo De Angelis and Stavros Stavrides." *E-Flux Journal*, no. 17.

Armony, Ariel. 2004. *The Dubious Link. Civic Engagement and Democratisation.* Stanford: Stanford University Press.

Bianchetti, Cristina. 2016. *Spazi Che Contano. Il Progetto Urbanistico in Epoca Neo-Liberale.* Roma: Donzelli.

Blakely, Edward J. and Mary Gail Snyder. 1997. *Fortress America: Gated Communities in the United States.* Cambridge, Massachusetts: Lincoln Institute of Land Policy.

Castel, Robert and Claudine Haroche. 2001. *Propriété Privée, Propriété Sociale, Propriété de Soi: Entretiens Sur La Construction de l'individu Moderne.* Paris: Fayard.

Ferguson, Francesca, and Urban Drift Projects. 2014. *Make Shift City. Renegotiating the Urban Commons.* Berlin: Jovis.

Hardt, Michael and Antonio Negri. 2009. *Common Wealth.* Cambridge, Massachusetts: The Belknap Press of Harvard University Press.

Lenna, Verena. 2019. "The Project of Property as Emancipation: A Community Land Trust in Brussels." Ph.D. Dissertation. Università IUAV di Venezia and Katholieke Universiteit Leuven.

Low, Setha. 2001. "The Edge and the Center: Gated Communities and the Discourse of Urban Fear." *American Anthropologist* 103 (1).

Marella, Maria Rosaria, ed. 2012. *Oltre Il Pubblico e Il Privato. Per Un Diritto Dei Beni Comuni.* Verona: Ombre Corte.

Salzano, Edoardo. 2009. *La Città Come Bene Comune.* Bologna: Ogni Uomo è Tutti Gli Uomini.

Sassen, Saskia. 2014. *Expulsions. Brutality and Complexity in the Global Economy.* Cambridge, Massachusetts: The Belknap Press of Harvard University Press.

———. 2015. "Who Owns Our Cities — and Why This Urban Takeover Should Concern Us All." *The Guardian*, 2015. *https://www.theguardian.com/cities/2015/nov/24/who-owns-our-cities-and-why-this-urban-takeover-should-concern-us-all.*

Schmidt, Stephan, Jeremy Nemeth and Erik Botsford. 2011. "The Evolution of Privately Owned Public Spaces in New York City." *Urban Design International*, 270–84.

Soja, Edward W. 2000. *Postmetropolis: Critical Studies of Cities and Regions*. New York: Wiley.

Stavrides, Stavros. 2016. *The City as a Commons*. London: Zed Books.

Steinbock, Anthony J. 1995. *Home and Beyond: Generative Phenomenology after Husserl*. Evanston, Illinois: Northwestern University Press.

Viganò, Paola. 2009. "The Metropolis of the Twenty-First Century: The Project of a Porous City." *Oase* 80 (On territories).

26.

Better Together

The Challenging, Transformative Complexity of Community, Land, and Trust

John Emmeus Davis

There is nothing simple about the community land trust. It is a complicated construct with many moving parts, all of which must work in concert for the CLT's unique approach to community-led development of permanently affordable housing on community-owned land to be done well. Its complexity is compounded by the fact that not every CLT is the same. The model's design is being continuously reinvented, giving rise to numerous organizational and operational variations.[1] These refinements have been crucial to the CLT's proliferation, helping it to adapt to a wide range of local conditions in a dozen different countries and to find acceptance among populations with diverse social, political, and economic interests.

The CLT's organizational and operational complexity is not merely a matter of the multiplicity and mutability of its constituent elements, however. The biggest challenge in mastering the model and making it sing lies in understanding that the whole is greater than the sum of its parts. It is the combination of community, land, and trust that contributes the most to a CLT's performance. The dynamic interaction of its three main components is what enables an organization to be a CLT and to behave like one.

Describing this complexity to people who are hearing about the CLT for the first time has never been easy. The most common technique employed by instructors like me has been to picture the CLT as a Venn diagram, where the model's principal components and essential concerns are depicted as three intersecting circles. "Community" is described in terms of a CLT's distinctive approach to involving residents of its chosen service area in guiding and governing the organization. "Land" is described in terms of the organization's distinctive approach to holding land forever, acreage that is scattered throughout a CLT's service area and conveyed via long-term ground leases to the owners of residential or commercial buildings. "Trust" is described in terms of a CLT's distinctive approach to the long-term stewardship of lands and buildings entrusted into its care, an operational

COMMUNITY
(Organization)

LAND
(Ownership)

TRUST
(Operation)

Fig. 26.1. Venn diagram depicting the "classic" community land trust.

priority that plays out in the programs of most CLTs through policies and procedures designed to preserve the affordability, quality, and security of heavily subsidized, privately owned housing.

This three-ring schematic has the advantage of simplicity. It allows a complicated model to be readily grasped in its entirety and then directs attention toward each component, inviting a closer examination of the key features and common variations that constitute the CLT's unusual treatment of organization, ownership, and operation. But simplicity can also have negative, unintended consequences. Indeed, I have come to suspect that our go-to image for illustrating and discussing what is widely known in the United States as the "classic" CLT may be inadequate at best and harmful at worst. It obscures too many of the complex interactions that invigorate the model. It overlooks too often the transformative potential of such complexity, as a CLT goes about its virtuous business of rebuilding a place of residence by restructuring the twin pillars of property and power.

Simplification is not only a problem for pedagogy but for practice as well. How a CLT is depicted has an effect on how it is implemented. Our attempt to cope with the model's messiness by stuffing it into three tidy circles on a static diagram means that we spend most of our time investigating the contents of each circle, while frequently failing to relate one circle to another. When that happens, when the interactions among the model's components are overlooked, we accidentally suggest that any one of them may be safely removed without damaging the whole. After all, if organization, ownership, and operation can be separately examined, they can be separately implemented — perhaps even discarded. Or so it would seem.

This occurs with distressing frequency in everyday practice. For example, a city government or non-governmental organization (NGO) may endorse a CLT's operational commitment to the lasting affordability of publicly subsidized, privately owned housing, while also embracing ground leasing as the most effective strategy for implementing and administering a stewardship regime. But the prospect of including a neighborhood's residents in planning a CLT's projects, in shaping its policies, and participating in its governance is considered an arduous, time-consuming annoyance. So this troublesome component is deleted from the start — or diluted along the way.

Another frequent occurrence: an NGO may behave like a CLT organizationally and operationally, engaging local residents in the guidance and governance of its activities while also providing a full complement of stewardship services, but the organization's leaders or funders decide to dispense with community ownership of the underlying land. Developing and financing affordable housing on leased land is deemed too difficult to do, so the CLT's bedrock commitment to owning land on behalf of a place-based community — and never reselling it — is set aside.[2]

This propensity for pruning cannot be attributed solely to the imagery that is commonly used in introducing the CLT. But when practitioners or funders who profess to support community land trusts do not hesitate in removing one or two of the model's main components for the sake of convenience, sawing off branches that have historically defined the CLT, it is fair to ask whether some of the blame for bestowing a license to lop should be assigned to the manner in which the model is described.

Perhaps the moment has come to find a different image to illustrate the CLT. If so, one option might be to substitute the dynamic mobile of Mr. Calder for the static diagram of Mr. Venn. I've been wondering of late whether it might be helpful, in other words, to portray the CLT as something akin to one of Alexander Calder's kinetic creations: a suspended apparatus that is finely balanced to turn freely in the breeze while remaining stably in place. *Community* would constitute one of the cross-pieces from which a variety of organizational configurations were hung. *Land* would be the second, balancing various interests of ownership. *Trust* would be the third, an operational strut to which were attached the multi-colored duties of stewardship, each festooned with weights and counter-weights all their own.

The best thing about this whimsical image of the CLT-as-mobile is that it cautions against the reckless removal of any component, lest the whole construct collapses. It also accepts as ordinary the real-world tensions that are intrinsic to community development. The artistry inherent in the construction of a mobile, like the artistry inherent in designing, constructing, and managing a CLT, lies in making a virtue out of necessity. Rather than pretending that interests are not in competition (and sometimes in conflict), the tensions that exist among various groups who share the same territory become the raw material for a creative endeavor that has as its greatest challenge and highest accomplishment a mastery of balance.[3]

A friend of Alexander Calder's, Saul Steinberg, once said of Calder that he was "a particular American type: the dogged tinker. We saw in him the face of a man who is always working on a perpetual motion machine, which he then sends to the patent office."[4] Mirrored in the image of the CLT-as-mobile, we find the faces of inventive practitioners engaged in a similar project. They are dogged tinkerers all, even if many of them are not American, as the model spreads to other countries. They are artistic realists who accept the challenge of finding the practical fulcrum at every point in a CLT's design. By their hands, the weighty concerns of "community," "land," and "trust" are adapted to the windy conditions within their own communities and kept stably, durably in balance.

Such a balancing act doesn't happen by itself. The CLT is a rather elegant model of community development, displaying a remarkable degree of adaptability and resiliency across a range of conditions, but it depends upon talented people to put it in place and to keep it aloft. Agency is as important as structure in fashioning and maintaining this perpetual motion machine. There are artists behind the art.

Much as I like this metaphor for describing how a CLT is built and behaves, however, I'm not quite ready to abandon the three-ring diagram that has long been used in trainings to depict the "classic" CLT. Yes, that familiar schematic has made it harder to appreciate the carefully balanced complexity of the model as a whole. Yes, it has made it easier to prune the model beyond recognition. But the fault lies less in Mr. Venn than in ourselves. Instead of substituting one metaphor for another, a more reasonable course of action would be for us to make better use of the imagery already in hand.

> More than the model's reinvention of each component, it is their combination that gives vitality, resilience, and power to a CLT.

We are not mistaken in picturing the CLT as a trio of interlocking circles; nor are we misguided in taking the time to understand, separately and thoroughly, the internal workings of the model's main components. Where we go wrong, I believe, is devoting too little attention to the spaces where the circles overlap. As a result, we tend to overlook the dynamic interaction of organization, ownership, and operation — and the delicate balance that must exist among them for a CLT to prosper.

These interactions are seldom discussed, rarely studied, and poorly understood. Such neglect is a major blunder, because the synergies produced by these interactions are what enable a CLT to perform to its highest potential. Organization and operation are made more effective by the innovative way in which a CLT's property is owned. The ownership and operation of a CLT's property are made more effective by the innovative way in which a CLT is organized. Ownership and organization are made more effective by the innovative way in which a CLT's lands and buildings are operated. More than the model's reinvention of each component, it is their combination that gives vitality, resilience, and power to a CLT.

Why go to all the trouble of identifying these interactions? What advantages would advocates and practitioners derive from a deeper understanding of the mutually reinforcing relationships among a CLT's main components? To my mind, they would possess a new set of tools for making their case. They would have at their fingertips a more compelling rationale for upholding the integrity of the CLT, which might stiffen their resolve in resisting the model's dismemberment. They would also have in hand a more robust measure for evaluating the model's performance, gauging when a CLT is working well and when it is not; providing them, too, with a finely calibrated scale for weighing whether a proposed adjustment to one of the model's main components is likely to preserve — or disrupt — the balance on which a CLT depends.

A few additional remarks about this balancing act. The particular genius of practitioners who are charged with implementing this unusual model of tenure, as suggested earlier, is their artistry in managing property-based interests that often compete — and sometimes conflict. CLT practitioners neither wish away these pesky tensions, nor regard their persistence as a sign of failure. They fashion them into something equitably in synch and sustainably in balance. Within the CLT's two-party structure of ownership, the ground lease is designed to balance the competing interests of the nonprofit landowner and those of the owners of any buildings located on the nonprofit's lands. Within the CLT's organizational structure, the two-part membership and three-part board are designed to balance the competing interests of the people who live on the nonprofit's lands and the neighbors who live around them. Within the model's operational structure, a CLT's stewardship regime is designed to balance competing priorities of enabling low-income households to gain access to homeownership and to build wealth in the present versus preserving that same homeownership opportunity for lower-income households in the future.

These difficult and daunting acts of balance are on daily display within the three-ring circus of a CLT. They capture our attention and win our applause. But we often fail to notice the other high-wire acts of derring-do that are being performed with quiet aplomb where the rings overlap. Here, too, CLT practitioners must skillfully balance competing interests and concerns.

There is an inherent tension, for instance, between the roles of CLT-as-developer and CLT-as-organizer. A CLT that tilts too heavily toward the former, giving too little weight to building a base of support within its service area, is unlikely to have the political clout to compete for land and money from its local government. It is unlikely to possess the legitimacy and loyalty that enables an organization like a CLT to surmount not-in-my-backyard opposition to its projects and to build local support for its unfamiliar form of tenure. Conversely, a CLT that tilts too heavily the other way, giving too much weight to every objection that might be raised by a vocal minority within its own service area or within its own membership, is likely to stumble in striving to acquire land, to assemble capital, and to develop affordable housing. Every CLT is forced to find a point of equilibrium, in other words, between building a substantial portfolio and cultivating an engaged constituency, maintaining a delicate balance between ownership and organization.

Another example. A community land trust that becomes too heavy-handed in carrying out its operational duties of stewardship can steadily undermine the "marriage of convenience" that must be maintained with the individuals and organizations that use its land. An imbalance in this pivotal relationship can increase the organization's costs, requiring constant intervention by the CLT to ensure that homes on its land are kept affordable, that buildings are kept in good repair, and that mortgages are paid. Conversely, a CLT that operates with too little oversight runs the risk of failing to fulfill its operational commitment to preserving the affordability, condition, and security of housing and other buildings entrusted into its care. There is a delicate balance between operation and organization.

Performing these feats of balance will always be a challenge. But the odds of success are greatly improved when practitioners appreciate on a deeper level the many interactions among a CLT's main components. There is a certain irony here. At the same time that practitioners are handed a stronger rationale for upholding the integrity of the "classic" CLT, they are allowed a wider latitude in modifying that model as needed. They are able to weigh with greater precision any proposed adjustments, watching closely to make sure their well-intentioned tinkering with the internal workings of organization, ownership, or operation does not throw their carefully designed construct completely out of whack. Practitioners who come to appreciate the model's interactive complexity discover that their license to lop has been revoked, but their freedom to improvise has been expanded.

> The transformative potential of a CLT is greatest when every part of this complex composition is present and performed in harmony with the others.

A deeper appreciation for the power of complexity also puts practitioners in the best position to bend the trajectory of local development toward justice. That is not to say that programs or policies that embrace less than the full package of the "classic" CLT are without merit. By itself, a community's ownership of land provides a platform for protecting access to goods, services, and homes for lower-income residents who might otherwise be extruded or excluded from a neighborhood. By itself, an organization's commitment to giving residents a voice in guiding development in their own locale and a role in governing the organization doing that development are marked improvements over top-down approaches to neighborhood revitalization. By itself, an operational commitment to the lasting affordability of housing, secured through a watchful stewardship regime, is a vast improvement over policies and programs that allow affordably priced homes produced through public dollars or private donations to leak away. Each reinvention of organization, ownership, and operation has value; each helps to make place-based development more equitable in the short run and more sustainable over time. But two components are better than one, and three are best. The transformative potential of a CLT is greatest when every part of this complex composition is present and performed in harmony with the others.[5]

At the risk of trotting out one metaphor too many, let me end with a story that predates my personal involvement with community land trusts. Nearly fifty years ago, I spent summers in the mountains of southern Appalachia, doing community organizing as a member of a project called the Student Health Coalition.[6] One of my fellow organizers, who was eager to immerse himself in Appalachian culture, managed to persuade a retired coal miner to give him weekly lessons in playing the country fiddle. My friend was a quick study in mastering the instrument's fingering because he already played the guitar. He had a harder time making the fiddle sing, however, as he sawed clumsily across the strings. Exasperated by his pupil's lack of progress, the gray-haired fiddler would interrupt their sessions again and again with the same admonishment: "Charles, any damn fool can figure out where to put his fingers. The music is in the bow, boy; the music is in the bow."

Faced with the challenge of teaching people to play an instrument as demanding as the CLT, I am frequently reminded of the old fiddler's advice. Whether introducing the model to a new audience or bringing the model to a new venue, the first lessons must always be focused on getting the fingering right within the separate spheres of ownership, organization, and operation. A novice must have a basic command of each component before tackling more difficult exercises. But that will never be enough to coax a compelling tune from a CLT. Any damn fool can figure out where to put his or her fingers, sliding along the taut strings of organization, ownership, and operation. Mastery of the model only comes when they are played in combination. It is here, among the complex harmonies of *community, land* and *trust*, that a song of transformation is most likely to be heard in the places people call home. The music is in the spaces, boys and girls; the music is in the spaces.

Notes

1. These variations extend to the manner in which the CLT itself is characterized. Many practitioners employ terms like "strategy," "mechanism," "vehicle," or "platform" when describing the CLT. I have done the same, sometimes using these terms interchangeably with "model." My use of the last is not meant to champion model as the best of these terms. It is merely to follow the custom that began in 1972 with the first book about the CLT, which called it "a new model for land tenure in America."

2. This is hardly the first time I've bemoaned (and ridiculed) the readiness to discard this component of the "classic" CLT whenever funders, bankers, or practitioners consider community landholding and long-term ground leasing to be "too difficult." See, for example: "Ground Leasing Without Tears," *Shelterforce Weekly,* January 29, 2014. Available at: *https://shelterforce.org/2014/01/29/ground_leasing_without_tears/*

3. An early attempt to develop a theory of the formation and interaction of these "property interest groups" can be found in J.E. Davis, *Contested Ground: Collective Action and the Urban Neighborhood* (Ithaca, NY: Cornell University Press, 1991).

4. Adam Gopnik, "Wired: What Alexander Calder Set in Motion." *The New Yorker* (December 4, 2017: 73–77).

5. A more detailed argument for the transformative potential of the "classic" CLT can be found in J.E. Davis, "Common Ground: Community-Owned Land as a Platform for Equitable and Sustainable Development." *University of San Francisco Law Review* 51 (1), 2017. Thoughtful critiques of this argument, addressing the question of whether nonmarket models of ownership are, in fact, "politically transformative," appear in James DeFilippis, *Unmaking Goliath: Community Control in the Face of Global Capital* (Routledge, 2004) and his more recent essay, "On the Transformative Potential of Community Land Trusts in the United States," co-authored with Olivia R. Williams, Joseph Pierce, Deborah G. Martin, Rich Kruger, and Azadeh Hadizadeh Esfahani. *Antipode* (February 12, 2019).

6. An online archive of materials about the Appalachian Student Health Coalition is part of the Southern Historical Collection at the University of North Carolina (*www.coalition. web.unc.edu*).

ABOUT THE CONTRIBUTORS

NELE AERNOUTS is an architect, urban designer, and researcher. She is a postdoctoral researcher at Cosmopolis and teaches in the MSc in Urban Design and Spatial Planning (SteR*) at the Vrije Universiteit Brussel. Her research interests include collective housing, social housing, and participatory planning, with a specific focus on underprivileged groups. During her PhD, she studied diverse forms of housing commons and land tenures in the Brussels Capital Region, such as community land trusts and housing cooperatives, focusing on spatial and participatory dimensions. Currently she coordinates a LivingLab project tackling the regeneration of large-scale social estates.

LIZ ALDEN WILY, PhD (Political Science), is a specialist in land tenure, working as a researcher, technical adviser, and practitioner on community landholding. She has worked on this issue in approximately twenty countries. Liz has been instrumental in helping to launch regional and global initiatives in support of community land rights such as LandMark, an online facility which collates maps and information about community lands. She is a Fellow at the Leiden Law School's Van Vollenhoven Institute, a Fellow at Katiba Institute, a constitutional advocacy body in Africa, and a Fellow of the Rights and Resources Initiative, a global coalition.

LINE ALGOED is a PhD researcher at Cosmopolis, Center for Urban Research at the Vrije Universiteit in Brussels and a Research Fellow at the International Institute of Social Studies in The Hague. She works with the Caño Martín Peña CLT in Puerto Rico on international exchanges among communities involved in land struggles. She is also an Associate at the Center for CLT Innovation. Previously, Line was a World Habitat Awards Program Manager at BSHF (now World Habitat). She holds an MA in Cultural Anthropology from the University of Leiden and an MA in Sociology from the London School of Economics.

TOM ARCHER, PhD, is a Research Fellow at Sheffield Hallam University, specialising in housing and community development. Between 2010–2016, he was one of the National CLT Network's Technical Advisors, providing support to urban CLTs in England. Tom's doctoral research focused on the factors affecting housing collectivism in England and Canada, and its costs and benefits. Tom has led major evaluations of community-led housing programmes, alongside other large housing market studies. He has co-authored influential reports on the private housebuilding industry in the UK, and the growth of community-owned assets.

PIERRE ARNOLD is a Franco-German civil engineer and urbanist who specializes in analysis and advice on housing policies and the social production of habitat. He has done urban research and consulting in Mexico (IRD and UN-Habitat), Colombia (French Embassy), the public sector in Argentina and France, and for a Mexican NGO. He is co-director of a documentary and a co-author of several articles and the self-published book, *Habitat in Motion. A Journey to Meet the Popular Habitat in South America*, published in French (2016) and Spanish (2017). He is an active member of UrbaMonde France, HIC-Latin America, and Global Land Alliance.

JOSHUA BARNDT is Executive Director of The Parkdale Neighbourhood Land Trust, a nonprofit, community-based organization that acquires land for affordable housing, supportive housing, and community economic development in Toronto's Parkdale neighborhood. He is a co-founder of the Canadian Network of Community Land Trusts. He previously worked as Community Liaison Officer coordinating a community benefits agreement as part of the Lawrence Heights Revitalization. Earlier, he served as Communications and Campaign Consultant for the "Right to the City Alliance" in New York City. He holds an MS in Design and Urban Ecologies from the Parsons School of Design, The New School.

ELLEN M. BASSETT is a Professor in Urban and Environmental Planning at the University of Virginia and Chair of the department. She worked from 1989 to 2001 as a technical advisor with bilateral aid agencies and international NGOs in Kenya and Uganda. Her current research is focused on land rights and planning law reform in Kenya. Among other publications, she is the author of *Institutions and Informal Settlements: The Planning Implications of the Community Land Trust Experiment in Kenya* (2001). She holds a PhD, MS, and MA from the University of Wisconsin-Madison.

SUSANNAH BUNCE is an Associate Professor in the Department of Human Geography at the University of Toronto Scarborough, Toronto, Canada. She has researched community land trusts in cities since 2009 and was the principal investigator on a three-year research project that examined urban community land trusts in Canada, the United States, and the United Kingdom, funded by the Social Sciences and Humanities Research Council of Canada. Her research on CLTs has been published in international academic journals and in a recent monograph published by Routledge. She holds a MES Planning and PhD in Environmental Studies from York University, Toronto.

YVES CABANNES (y.cabannes@ucl.ac.uk) is an urban specialist, activist and scholar. Over the past forty years he has been involved in research and development on urban issues, people-led initiatives, and local democracy with NGOs and local governments in Asia, Latin America, Africa and the Middle East. Since the early 1990s, he has supported, researched, taught, and advocated for participatory budgeting and planning, urban agriculture, community land trusts, and housing rights in different regions of the world and has published widely on these topics. He became Emeritus Professor of Development Planning at the University College London/Development Planning Unit in 2015.

ALEJANDRO COTTÉ MORALES holds a PhD in Social Policy from the Graduate School of Social Work of the University of Puerto Rico, Río Piedras Campus, where he is an Adjunct Professor. He has 25 years of experience as a community social worker. From 1994 to 2002, he directed the Community Development Area of the Península de Cantera Project. In 2002, he became Director of Citizen Participation and Social Development for ENLACE and the Caño Martín Peña CLT. He was instrumental in guiding grassroots organizing and participation processes around those initiatives, as well as advising on comprehensive development.

JOHN EMMEUS DAVIS is a founding partner of Burlington Associates in Community Development, a national consulting cooperative. He was housing director in Burlington, Vermont under Mayors Bernie Sanders and Peter Clavelle. Community land trusts have been a prominent part of his professional practice and scholarly writing for nearly 40 years. His publications include *Contested Ground* (1991), *The Affordable City* (1994), *The City-CLT Partnership* (2008), *The Community Land Trust Reader* (2010), and *Manuel d'antispéculation immobilière* (2014). He co-produced the film, *Arc of Justice,* and is co-director of the Center for CLT Innovation (*https://cltweb.org*). He holds an MS and PhD from Cornell University.

GEERT DE PAUW has been active for more than 20 years championing the right to housing in Brussels as an activist and community worker. In 2008, following a study visit to the Champlain Housing Trust, he began advocating for the establishment of a CLT in Brussels. He coordinated the CLT feasibility study that was commissioned by the Brussels Capital Region. He has been a coordinator of the CLT Brussels since 2012. He was also a co-founder of SHICC (Sustainable Housing for Inclusive and Cohesive Cities), a European partnership whose goal is to create a thriving CLT movement in Europe.

JOAQUÍN DE SANTOS studied political science and European politics in Switzerland, the UK, France and Belgium. After working in European affairs and on industrial heritage projects for seven years, he joined the staff of the CLT Brussels in early 2018 to coordinate the European project, Sustainable Housing for Inclusive and Cohesive Cities (SHICC). He has had a long-standing interest in urban struggles for the right to the city and industrial and social heritage. In his spare time, he is pursuing a PhD in urban policy at the University of Antwerp, Belgium.

JERÓNIMO DÍAZ is a geographer and graduate of the University of Toulouse II. In 2008, he joined the Interdisciplinary Center for Urban Studies (Lisst-Cieu), also in Toulouse, for a doctoral thesis on gentrification of the Historic Center of Mexico City. Between 2015 and 2018, he worked in the Latin America Office of the Habitat International Coalition (HIC-AL), where he coordinated a working group on the social production of habitat. Currently, he is a visiting research professor of urban sociology at the Azcapotzalco Unit of the Autonomous Metropolitan University in Mexico City.

NATE ELA is a visiting researcher at the American Bar Foundation. He recently received his PhD in sociology from the University of Wisconsin-Madison. He also holds a JD from the Harvard Law School. He is currently working on a book explaining why urban reformers have repeatedly turned to farms and gardens as a means of redistributing resources and supporting people in need. His writing on property, social policy, and human rights has appeared in *Law & Social Inquiry, Social Science History,* and the *Fordham Urban Law Journal.*

TARCYLA FIDALGO RIBEIRO is Co-coordinator of the Favela CLT program at Catalytic Communities in Rio de Janeiro and a researcher for the Metropolis Observatory, a project led by Rio de Janeiro's Federal University which encourages reflection about cities and urban planning in Brazil. She holds a Bachelor's Degree in Law and a Master's Degree in Urban Law from the State University of Rio de Janeiro. She has done post-graduate work in urban sociology and in urban planning and policy at the Federal University of Rio de Janeiro, where she is presently enrolled as a doctoral candidate.

ALAN GOTTLIEB is a Colorado-based writer, editor, journalist, and nonprofit entrepreneur with more than 20 years of experience in education policy and education journalism. Currently, Alan is owner of Write.Edit.Think.LLC, an independent communications consulting firm. Alan co-founded Chalkbeat, a growing and increasingly prominent national news nonprofit focused on PreK-12 education policy, policy implementation and practice. From 1988-97, he was a reporter and editor with *The Denver Post.* From 1997 until June 2007, he served as education program officer at The Piton Foundation in Denver. He is the author of two books, one fiction, one non-fiction.

CATHERINE HARRINGTON is co-Chief Executive of the National CLT Network (*http://www.communitylandtrusts.org.uk*) in England and Wales, having founded the organisation in September 2010. Catherine joined the Network from the Ministry for Housing, Communities and Local Government. Previously she worked at the Notting Hill Housing

Trust and the Institute for Public Policy Research. In 2017, she received the Swann-Matthei Award from Grounded Solutions in the USA, recognizing her many contributions to the CLT movement. Catherine has an MSc in City Design and Social Science from the London School of Economics and holds a BA Hons in Social Anthropology from the University of Cambridge.

ARIF HASAN is a Pakistani architect, planner, activist, teacher, and researcher who has taught at universities in Pakistan and Europe and served on several UN committees dealing with urban issues. He is the author of numerous books, research papers, and monographs on poverty, planning, and development. He was the Principal Consultant and, later, the Chairperson of the Orangi Pilot Project-Research and Training Institute (1981–2017). He is the founding Chairperson of the Urban Resource Centre Karachi, a founding member of the Asian Coalition for Housing Rights, and a member of the boards of multiple international academic journals and research organisations.

MARÍA E. HERNÁNDEZ-TORRALES holds an LLM in environmental law from the Vermont Law School and an MA in Business Education from New York University. She studied for her undergraduate and Juris Doctor degrees at the University of Puerto Rico. Since 2005 she has been doing pro bono legal work for the Proyecto ENLACE and for the Fideicomiso de la Tierra del Caño Martín Peña. Since 2008, Hernández-Torrales has worked as an attorney and clinical professor at the University of Puerto Rico School of Law where she teaches the Community Economic Development Clinic.

TONY HERNANDEZ is the Director of Dudley Neighbors Inc., a community land trust established by the Dudley Street Neighborhood Initiative in 1988. DNI has combined community ownership of land, community control of development, and permanent affordability of housing to revitalize a large section of Roxbury that had long been scarred by vacant lots, abandoned buildings, and arson-for-profit. DNI's high-profile success in achieving "development without displacement" has inspired other communities to create CLTs of their own in Boston and elsewhere. Tony has been a CLT homeowner for the past 18 years. He has a Master's degree in architecture.

STEPHEN HILL (smdhill@gmail.com) is an independent public interest practitioner in planning and housing development, advising central and local governments, developers, housing associations, and community housing groups. In 2014, he visited the USA and Canada as a Churchill Fellow, reporting on approaches to the co-production of housing and neighbourhood development by the "state" and citizens through community organising. He recently retired as trustee of the National CLT Nework (for England and Wales) and Chair of the UK Cohousing Network. In 2017, he received the "John Emmeus Davis Award for Scholarship" from Grounded Solutions, and has a lovely wizard's hat to prove it.

DAVID IRELAND is Chief Executive of World Habitat, a UK-based international housing charity that helps to scale up solutions to the world's housing problems, from slum upgrading to post-disaster housing and homelessness. His organization also operates the World Habitat Awards in partnership with UN-Habitat, and runs programmes aimed at ending homelessness and scaling up community-led housing. David is trustee of Action Homeless and was previously CEO of the Empty Homes Agency where he persuaded successive UK governments to introduce legislation and to fund programmes to get empty homes into use. He was awarded OBE in 2013 for services to housing.

STEVE KING is Executive Director of the Oakland Community Land Trust in Oakland, California (*https://oakclt.org*). He has spent the past 15 years working for community-based organizations in the areas of equitable development, affordable housing, and applied social research. Steve previously served as the Housing and Economic Development Coordinator at the Urban Strategies Council, also based in Oakland. He holds a MS in Urban Planning from Columbia University, and a BA in Environmental Science from Boston University.

VERENA LENNA is an architect and urbanist (PhD at IUAV and KU Leuven). Through her work and research, she explores the relationship between emancipation and the living environment. Whether design-based or not, her projects and collaborations are mainly action-oriented and community-based. She has focused on themes such as labour conditions, arts, and culture. More recently, she has worked on property, looking at the role of the design process in the realisation of Brussels Community Land Trust projects. She is a co-founder and member of Commons Josaphat, a collective created to transform a 24-hectare site in Brussels for the common good.

JERRY MALDONADO is Director of the Cities and States Program at the Ford Foundation. He joined Ford in the aftermath of Hurricanes Katrina and Rita, overseeing the Foundation's Gulf Coast Transformation Initiative. Over the past decade he has developed and managed several of the Foundation's national, regional, and state grant-making initiatives, working at the intersection of equitable development and civic engagement. Prior to Ford, Jerry worked with the Rockefeller Brothers Fund, Carnegie Council on Ethics and International Affairs, and the United Nations Non-Governmental Liaison Service. He has a master's degree from Columbia University and a bachelor's degree from Brown University.

EMMANUEL MIDHEME teaches at the School of Planning and Architecture, Maseno University, Kenya. He earned his PhD in Spatial Planning and Urban Development from the University of Leuven, Belgium in 2015. Emmanuel's current research focuses on the role of land tenure and property in the production of equitable and inclusive spaces in rapidly transforming cities of sub-Saharan Africa. He is interested in how marginalized urban groups employ everyday practices of commoning and social innovation to meet needs unsatisfied by conventional market and state mechanisms. Emmanuel has previously researched and published on the Tanzania-Bondeni Community Land Trust, Africa's first CLT.

Aaron Miripol is a leader in nonprofit real estate development with a focus on growing CLTs for the benefit of local communities. Since 2007, as President of the Urban Land Conservancy, he has overseen 38 investments in Metro Denver, including multi-family affordable housing, schools, and commercial space. Prior to ULC, Aaron led Thistle Community Housing, increasing its portfolio from 100 to 1,000 permanently affordable homes, including 250 for-sale homes. In his career, Aaron has overseen $800M in affordable housing and community development. He gained an early appreciation for CLTs while working at Moshav Kerem Maharal, a cooperative farm in Israel.

Tony Pickett is Chief Executive Officer of the Grounded Solutions Network, advancing a racial equity agenda to increase the scale and impact of shared equity housing with lasting affordability. His career spans over 35 years, including LEED Accredited Professional work as a commercial architect and affordable housing developer. His expertise includes CLT financial business planning/modeling. He is a member of the Center for CLT Innovation's advisory committee and a co-author of "Community Land Trusts: Combining Scale and Community Control to Advance Mixed-Income Neighborhoods," an essay published by Case Western Reserve University in 2019. Tony holds a BA in architecture from Cornell University.

Lyvia Rodríguez Del Valle is the former Executive Director of the Caño Martín Peña CLT and Corporación Proyecto ENLACE del Caño Martín Peña. For over 15 years, she worked with an interdisciplinary team and community organizations on implementation of the ENLACE Project. Lyvia previously worked on urban revitalization in San Juan and risk management and decentralization in Quito and Asunción. She holds a master's degree in Urban and Regional Planning and a graduate certificate in Latin American Studies from the University of Florida, Gainesville, and a bachelor's degree in Environmental Design from the School of Architecture, University of Puerto Rico.

Greg Rosenberg is Co-Director of the Center for Community Land Trust Innovation (*https://cltweb.org*) and a principal of Rosenberg and Associates, a consultancy focused on affordable and sustainable housing, cohousing, community land trusts, and urban agriculture. He was a founder of the CLT Network and the CLT Academy in the USA and served as the Academy's first director. He previously led the Madison Area CLT, where he developed Troy Gardens, an urban ecovillage featuring a working farm, community gardens, a restored prairie, and a 30-unit mixed-income cohousing project. Greg is licensed to practice law in Wisconsin and is a LEED Accredited Professional.

PHILIP ROSS (rosspe97@gmail.com) is the former Mayor of Letchworth Garden City and is the current Chairman of the New Garden Cities Alliance, an organization that champions the social goals of the Garden City Movement. He is an international speaker on Garden Cities and, together with Yves Cabannes, wrote the book *21st Century Garden Cities of To-Morrow — A Manifesto*. He still lives in Letchworth and is married with three children. He works as a freelance business analyst.

HANNAH SHOLDER is a housing, community, and economic development specialist who has worked with a formerly displaced community in Bangladesh since 2009, supporting efforts to improve their housing and land rights situation. Also in Bangladesh, she co-founded a minority youth leadership summit in 2011 and a women's handicraft cooperative in 2014. In the Washington D.C. area, where she currently resides, Ms. Sholder serves as Director of Land Stewardship for a nonprofit that creates, preserves, and manages urban farms for the purpose of hands-on agricultural education. She is a Fulbright Scholar with two MAs from the University of California, Berkeley.

CLAIRE SIMONNEAU is a geographer and an urban planner. She is currently a researcher at CNRS, the national scientific research center in France, coordinating a research program on land-based commons for housing in the Global South. She holds a PhD in urban planning from the University of Montreal, Canada. Her research interests relate to land issues, urban management and governance in the Global South, and the field of "urban commons." She has also had substantial professional experience working with development aid organizations in West Africa.

DAVE SMITH is a community organizer, affordable housing practitioner and writer, based in London, England. From 2008–2014, he served as the founding Executive Director of the London Community Land Trust, which is now the largest CLT in the UK. Prior to this, Dave worked for the British Council and on Barack Obama's 2008 primary and presidential election campaigns. More recently, he has worked at the National Housing Federation and is currently a freelance consultant and author. He holds degrees from King's College, the University of Cambridge, and The Bartlett School of Planning, University College London.

HARRY SMITH is a Community Development and Organizing consultant with 25 years of experience in the field. He most recently served as Director of Sustainable Economic Development for the Dudley Street Neighborhood Initiative, including managing the activities of Dudley Neighbors Inc., one of the nation's largest urban community land trusts. He currently works with a number of community-based organizations on projects related to community organizing, land use, strategic planning, and support for emerging CLTs. He earned a BA from Brown University and an MS in Community Economic Development from Southern New Hampshire University.

BRENDA M. TORPY helped to create the Burlington CLT, now the Champlain Housing Trust, in 1984, while serving as Burlington's Housing Director under Mayor Bernie Sanders. She has been executive director since 1991. CHT is currently the largest CLT in the USA, with 3,000 homes, and won a United Nations World Habitat Award in 2008. Brenda was a Ford Foundation Leader for a Changing World in 2002. She is on the board of Grounded Solutions and on the advisory board of the Center for CLT Innovation. She was a past member of the Boston Home Loan and Federal Reserve Banks' advisory committees.

KARLA TORRES SUEIRO (ktorressueiro@gmail.com) is a lawyer specializing in socio-economic and citizenship rights. She is a Staff Attorney at the ABA Pro Bono Asylum Representation Project, providing legal representation for unaccompanied children in immigration detention at the south Texas border. Karla previously assisted with appeal cases from EU citizens in the UK who were exercising their rights of citizenship and residency. She joined the Caño CLT in 2016, where she helped to manage the worldwide exchange of knowledge about forms of collective land tenure. She holds an LLM in International Criminal Justice and Human Rights from the University of Kent.

KIRBY WHITE worked for the Institute for Community Economics in the 1980s and 1990s, writing and editing technical materials for CLTs, including *The Community Land Trust Handbook* and the first two editions of the *Community Land Trust Legal Manual*. He was a co-editor of ICE's journal *Community Economics* (1983–1996) and provided direct technical assistance to CLTs in urban and rural communities throughout the United States. Later, he was employed by Equity Trust, Inc., developing technical materials for agricultural land trusts, including the 2009 publication, *Preserving Farms for Farmers*. He has also written several novels dealing with environmental and community development subjects.

NOLA WHITE is a founder and the current president of the Honduras Community Support Corporation (*http://www.hcsc-honduras.org*). She also helped to organize FECOVESO (*Fundación Eco Verde Sostenible*), a regional land trust and community development organization based in Honduras. Previously, Nola supervised Bennington College's "Field Work Term" program; worked as a tenant organizer, fighting to save an "expiring use" rental housing project; coordinated a local food cooperative; and provided transportation and support for immigrant farmworkers. In the 1980s, she served on the board of the Institute for Community Economics and was a member of ICE's loan committee, evaluating loan applications from CLTs.

OLIVIA R. WILLIAMS is an independent scholar and organizer living in Madison, Wisconsin. She received a PhD in Geography in 2017 from Florida State University with research on community land trusts. She currently serves on the staff of the Madison Area CLT and the Madison Community Cooperative. Olivia also works to sustain and promote group-equity housing cooperatives through her board service at North American Students of Cooperation Development Services and is actively developing a new model of community land investment and ownership called the community land cooperative (CLC) with the Ecovillagers Alliance.

THERESA WILLIAMSON, PhD, is a city planner and founding executive director of Catalytic Communities, an NGO working to support Rio de Janeiro's favelas through asset-based community development. CatComm produces *RioOnWatch*, an award-winning local-to-global favela news platform, and recently launched Rio's Sustainable Favela Network and a Favela Community Land Trust program. Theresa is an advocate for the recognition of the favelas' heritage status and their residents' right to be treated as equal citizens. She received the 2018 American Society of Rio prize for her contributions to the city and the 2012 NAHRO Award for her contributions to the international housing debate.

INDEX

www.ingramcontent.com/pod-product-compliance
Lightning Source LLC
Chambersburg PA
CBHW080555030426
42336CB00019B/3196